D0350859

ALSO BY GREG MITCHELL

Truth and Consequences: Seven Who Would Not Be Silenced

Acceptable Risks (*with Pascal Imperato*)

THE CAMPAIGN OF THE CENTURY

RANDOM HOUSE
NEW YORK

THE CAMPAIGN OF THE CENTURY

UPTON SINCLAIR'S RACE FOR GOVERNOR OF CALIFORNIA AND THE BIRTH OF MEDIA POLITICS

Greg Mitchell

 Published in the United States by Random House, Inc., New York, and simultaneously in Canada by Random House of Canada Limited, Toronto.

All acknowledgments of permission to use previously published material may be found following the index.

Library of Congress Cataloging-in-Publication Data
Mitchell, Greg.
The campaign of the century: Upton Sinclair's race for governor of California and the birth of media politics/Greg Mitchell.—1st ed.
p. cm.
Includes bibliographical references and index.
ISBN 0-679-41168-2
1. Governors—California—Election—History—20th century.
2. Sinclair, Upton, 1878–1968. 3. Mass media—Political aspects—California—History—20th century. 4. California—Politics and government—1850–1950. I. Title.
F866.M65 1992 979.4'05—dc20 91-29758

Manufactured in the United States of America
The text of this book is set in Times Roman
Book design by J. K. Lambert
98765432
First Edition

FOR

Andy, Jeni, and John B.

Half the truth is often a great lie.

—Benjamin Franklin

PREFACE

Pretty Boy Floyd ran wild in the Midwest. Father Coughlin ruled the airwaves, and Huey Long seized control of Louisiana. More than a year into the New Deal, ten million Americans were still without work, and even Shirley Temple could not lift their spirits for long. Out in California, a general strike shut down San Francisco, vigilantes attacked union organizers in the Central Valley, and the Red Squad hunted suspected Communists in Los Angeles.

From his Santa Monica ranch, Will Rogers revealed that a famous author, a socialist no less, was running for governor of California—"a darn nice fellow, and just plum smart, and if he could deliver even some of the things he promises, should not only be governor of one state, but president of all of 'em." Six weeks later, on August 28, 1934, socialist writer, Upton Sinclair, swept the Democratic primary for governor of California, and all hell broke loose from San Diego to Sacramento. The *Los Angeles Times* denounced Sinclair's "maggot-like horde" of supporters. Former president Herbert Hoover called the coming campaign the most crucial in California history. Earl Warren, the Alameda County district attorney, warned that the state was about to be overcome by communism, and the movie studios threatened to move back East if Sinclair took office.

Upton Sinclair, author of *The Jungle* and dozens of other muckraking books, had created a crisis not just for his home state but the entire nation. No politician since William Jennings Bryan had so offended the vested interests, *Time* declared. "Upton Sinclair has been swallowing quack cures for all the sorrows of mankind since the turn of the century," H. L. Mencken explained, "is at it again in California, and on such a scale that the whole country is attracted by the spectacle." Political pundits, financial columnists, and White House aides for once agreed: Sinclair's victory represented the high tide of radicalism in the United States. The country stood at a crossroads, and some predicted that a Sinclair win in November would set America squarely on the path to destruction.

The prospect of a socialist governing the nation's most volatile state sparked nothing less than a revolution in American politics. With an assist from Hollywood, Sinclair's opponents virtually invented the modern media campaign. It marked a stunning advance in the art of public relations, "in which advertising men now believed they could sell or destroy political candidates as they sold one brand of soap and defamed its competitor," Arthur M. Schlesinger, Jr., has observed. In another twenty years, these techniques "would spread east," Schlesinger added, "achieve a new refinement, and begin to dominate the politics of the nation."

The 1934 governor's race in California showed candidates the way from the smoke-filled room to Madison Avenue. Media experts, making unprecedented use of film, radio, direct mail, opinion polls, and national fund-raising, devised the most astonishing (and visually clever) smear campaign ever directed against a major candidate. "Many American campaigns have been distinguished by dirty tactics," Heywood Broun commented in October 1934, "but I can think of none in which willful fraud has been so brazenly practiced."

The political innovation that produced the strongest impact, both in the 1934 race and long afterward, was the manipulation of moving pictures. Alarmed by the Sinclair threat, MGM's Irving Thalberg produced outrageously partisan film shorts. For the first time, the screen was used to demolish a candidate—a precursor of political advertising on television.

Today, political consultants package candidates for the media and advertising has an overwhelming impact on public opinion. For most voters, an election campaign does not exist apart from television. The electronic media, not the political party, mediate between the candidate and the voter, and there is evidence that they are failing in this role. As the Bush-Dukakis race in 1988 neared its conclusion, *Newsweek* asked: "Couldn't we just call the whole thing off and start over?" The 1990 midterm elections featured some of the most distasteful "attack" advertising yet; and the bare-knuckled 1991 Senate battle in Pennsylvania only confirmed this trend. *The New York Times* previewed the 1992 race for president under this heading: TELEVISION IS THE CAMPAIGN.

It was the riotous 1934 race for governor of California that pointed political campaigns down this path.

Political techniques introduced in 1934 transformed the electoral process, but the California campaign was significant for other reasons as well.

For the first time, Hollywood plunged full tilt into politics. Led by Louis B. Mayer, studio executives raised enormous funds, intimidated their employees, and produced sophisticated propaganda films for the public. Leftists like James Cagney and Dorothy Parker opposed the studios' tactics and vowed never to take a backseat politically again. Dozens of Hollywood personalities became embroiled in the '34 campaign, sometimes unwillingly, including Charlie Chaplin, Katharine Hepburn, and Billy Wilder.

Sinclair's candidacy challenged, perplexed, and ultimately embarrassed Franklin Roosevelt. The muckraker emerged as a political messiah at a tender hour for the White House. After an auspicious start, the New Deal was foundering. Progressives implored FDR to move to the left, businessmen and bankers exerted pressure on the right. Sinclair put the profoundly ambivalent President on the spot: if he endorsed his party's candidate in California, FDR's critics would accuse him of supporting socialism; if he didn't, some of his friends might call him a coward. A *Washington Post* columnist captured FDR's dilemma in verse:

> This is the question that's
> Thinning my hair;
> What'll I do about
> Upton Sinclair?

Win or lose, Sinclair's End Poverty in California—or EPIC—movement was, in the words of Theodore Dreiser, "the most impressive political phenomenon that America has yet produced." *The New York Times* called it "the first serious movement against the profit system in the United States." EPIC radicalized a generation of activists in California. Roosevelt may have revived the Democratic party in the state in 1932, but it was EPIC that established it as a progressive force. A number of men who would become legends in California politics, on both sides of the ideological fence, virtually cut their teeth on the '34 campaign, including Asa Call, Edmund G. "Pat" Brown, Jerry Voorhis, Augustus F. Hawkins, Murray Chotiner, Ralph Dills, William F. Knowland, and John Anson Ford. Clem Whitaker and Leone Baxter, pioneers in the field of political consultancy, managed their first statewide candidate in 1934.

On top of that, the '34 race was perhaps the most entertaining political contest of our time. It featured dirty tricks and hilarious stunts, and some of America's most influential figures—William Randolph Hearst, Cecil B. DeMille, evangelist Aimee Semple McPherson, advertising genius Albert Lasker, and movie czar Will Hays—helped stir the controversy. Earl Warren chaired the GOP effort and Louis B. Mayer ran the show in Hollywood. Even Ty Cobb, Melvin Belli, and Ezra Pound played a part.

Despite its significance and its appealing cast of characters, the 1934 governor's race in California has not been widely studied. For that reason, among others, *The Campaign of the Century* is based largely on primary source material, contemporary newspaper accounts, and interviews. It includes excerpts from hundreds of letters, telegrams, diaries, and newspaper columns, drawn from dozens of archives.

Among those who contributed compelling firsthand observations were Alistair Cooke, Melvin Belli, Leone Baxter, Sam Yorty, Pat Brown, Augustus Hawkins, Clark Kerr, and Dean McHenry. I gained considerable insight by talking to several sons of famous fathers: David Sinclair, Will Hays, Jr., Will Rogers, Jr., Edward Lasker, Clem Whitaker, Jr., Raymond Haight, Jr., and Don Belding, Jr. I also spoke with writers who observed Hollywood's anti-Sinclair activities at close range, including Budd Schulberg, Billy Wilder, Joseph L. Mankiewicz, Sam Marx, John Bright, Philip Dunne, Allen Rivkin, and Maurice Rapf.

Although I interviewed more than a dozen EPIC activists, including the late Jerry Voorhis, I decided to focus my research on the campaign *against* Sinclair, for this reason: After the election, EPIC was quickly consumed by the Democratic party; the campaign techniques introduced in 1934 had a life of their own.

Because *The Campaign of the Century* concentrates on the chaotic response to Sinclair's emergence as the Democratic nominee—not the remarkable grass-roots movement that propelled him to victory—the book begins a bit belatedly. Upton Sinclair started running for governor in the autumn of 1933, but no one in Hollywood, in the Republican party, in the national press, or in the White House took him seriously until he won the Democratic primary on August 28, 1934. *The Campaign of the Century* opens the following morning, and unfolds chronologically (occasionally skipping over an uneventful day), concluding on November 7, 1934, the day after the election.

Events and conversations actually took place on the precise day they appear in this book. (In other words, I resisted shuffling the note cards.) A few incidents which could not be traced to an exact day are described in a less specific way. None of the dialogue is "re-created"; it appears exactly as transcribed in the diaries, correspondence, and memoirs of the participants.

Although this book covers a campaign in California, little more than half the narrative is set on the West Coast. This reflects the national, even global, interest in the contest. During any day of the campaign, we may follow events from Europe to Washington, D.C., to Chicago (or Louisiana), and then finally to Los Angeles and San Francisco.

Although many famous figures parade across these pages, the three major characters in *The Campaign of the Century* are Franklin Roosevelt, Upton Sinclair, and "Hollywood" (as a collective entity). Of the three, Sinclair is certainly the least well known.

One of the original muckrakers, Sinclair is remembered for just a single book, *The Jungle,* the classic exposé of Chicago meat-packing, of which the author said: "I aimed at the public's heart, and by accident I hit it in the stomach." More often than not he is confused, as he was during his lifetime, with another writer, Sinclair Lewis, often to comical effect. *The Jungle* was published in 1906 when Uppie, as he was known to friends, was still in his twenties, and he wrote dozens of popular and influential books thereafter, winning a Pulitzer Prize in 1943. Sinclair may not have been a literary stylist, but in his day he was a prominent figure indeed. For most of his career, he was one of this country's foremost socialists and, according to H. L. Mencken, by far the most widely translated American author abroad. "When people ask me what has happened in my lifetime," George Bernard Shaw told Sinclair in 1941, "I do not refer them to the newspaper files or to the authorities, but to your novels."

Few public figures jumped from so many frying pans into so many fires, and "none has ever managed to keep so sunny and buoyant while the flames were leaping around him," Robert Cantwell commented. No American writer converted more young people to socialism. "Upton Sinclair first got to me when I was fourteen or so," Kurt Vonnegut, Jr., has confessed, in explaining how he became a lifelong socialist. Saul Bellow told Sinclair's biographer, Leon Harris, that the muckraker's books made a strong impression on him as a youth, even though he understood right from the start that the author was "something of a crank—one of the grand American cranks who enriched our lives."

Like Norman Mailer circa 1968, Upton Sinclair was often in the news for reasons that had little to do with writing: getting arrested (on several occasions), running for office (numerous times), or financing films (just one, but what a fiasco). His engine was forever racing. Ezra Pound called him a "polymaniac." Accused of having a Jesus complex, Sinclair cheerfully pointed out that the world needed a Jesus more than it needed anything else. Practically alone among the writers of his generation, Upton Sinclair "put to the American public the fundamental questions raised by capitalism in such a way that they could not escape them," Edmund Wilson observed. In this regard, Sinclair's career reached its climax with his EPIC crusade in 1934, and Hollywood, Democrats in California, and the American political campaign would never be the same.

ACKNOWLEDGMENTS

I would like to thank Sarah Lazin, who made it happen; Ann Godoff and Barbara Bedway, who made it better; John Ahouse, who helped make it right; and Andy Mitchell, for sleeping through the night.

Also, Patricia Vigderman, for assigning the article that started it all in 1982; Jean Sinclair, for generously allowing me to quote from her father-in-law's writings; Gina Lobaco and Bill Blum, for putting up with my presence; and Charles B. Strozier and Robert Jay Lifton, for accepting my absence.

I would also like to acknowledge the assistance of the following: Edward Allatt, Gary Bailey, Janet Bedway, Marcia Bedway, Fay Blake, Kaye Briegel, Ruth Cashman, Everett Clary, Ed Cray, Carla Fried, Enrica Gadler, Ronald Gottesman, Ray Haight, Jr., Will Hays, Jr., Robert Hahn, Marlys Harris, Matthew Kapsner, Bertha Klausner, Leonard Leader, Stanley Mitchell, Don Muchmore, Mort Newman, Kitty Parker, Beth Pearson, and James B. Welles, Jr.

Since so much of this book is based on archival material, I am obviously indebted to the dozens of research librarians, curators, and archivists who assisted me, usually in person but sometimes from afar. Special thanks to Blaine Bartell, Nicole Bouché, and Saundra Taylor. Also, Marybelle Burch, Ann Caigers, Ned Comstock, John Ferris, William Frank, Sam Gill, Bonnie Hardwick, Kristine Krueger, Patricia Lowe, Paul McLaughlin, Andrew Murdoch, Cora Pedersen, Carolyn Strickler, Craig St. Clair, Mike Sutherland, Dace Taube, and Nancy Zimmelman.

UPTON SINCLAIR

1878 Born on September 20 in a boardinghouse in Baltimore.
1888 Moves with family to New York City.
1892 Enters City College of New York.
1895 *Argosy* accepts his first story, about a pet bird.
1897 Graduates from City College, enrolls in Columbia University.
1900 Marries Meta Fuller.
1901 First novel, *Springtime and Harvest,* published. Son, David, born.
1904 Starts research on meat-packing conditions in Chicago.
1905 Founds Intercollegiate Socialist Society with Jack London.
1906 Landmark muckraking novel, *The Jungle,* published. Runs for Congress in New Jersey as a Socialist. Establishes Helicon Hall Colony.
1911 Sues wife for divorce after she has a public affair with one of his friends. Joins single-tax colony in Delaware. Arrested for playing tennis on a Sunday.
1913 Marries Mary Craig Kimbrough.
1914 Arrested in New York and spends three days in the Tombs for picketing John D. Rockefeller's office following Ludlow massacre.
1915 Compiles influential anthology of socialist writing, *The Cry for Justice.*
1916 Moves to California, eventually settling in Pasadena.

1917 Expelled from the Socialist party for supporting U.S. involvement in European war. Writes *King Coal.*

1918 Founds *Upton Sinclair's Magazine.* Writes *The Profits of Religion.*

1920 Runs again for Congress as Socialist. Writes *The Brass Check,* an exposé of big-city journalism.

1923 Cofounds ACLU in southern California. Arrested for reading First Amendment aloud before an "unlawful assembly" in San Pedro. Publishes exposé of colleges and universities, *The Goose-Step.*

1926 As Socialist candidate for governor of California, draws roughly fifty thousand votes.

1927 Writes a popular novel, *Oil!,* which is banned in Boston. Produces what he calls the "fig-leaf" edition and sells it himself on the streets of the city.

1928 Writes a novel based on Sacco-Vanzetti case, *Boston.*

1930 Writes a book based on telepathy experiments, *Mental Radio.* Runs for governor again as Socialist, again gets about fifty thousand votes.

1931 Writes a Prohibition novel, *The Wet Parade.*

1932 Writes autobiography, *American Outpost.* Bankrolls Sergei Eisenstein film project in Mexico. Irving Thalberg makes a movie of *The Wet Parade.*

1933 Writes a book about movie mogul William Fox. Changes party registration from Socialist to Democrat, writes *I, Governor of California, and How I Ended Poverty,* reveals EPIC plan, and announces candidacy for governor.

1934 Wins Democratic primary on August 28, in a landslide.

PART I

THE MUCKRAKER AND THE PRESIDENT

AUGUST 29

WEDNESDAY

While America slept, Will Rogers and Louis B. Mayer heard the news in Europe. When morning came, the startling dispatch from California topped the front page of *The New York Times* and *The Washington Post.* "I don't know where the country is going," a White House aide commented, "but it is certainly on its way." Up at Hyde Park, the President read the newspapers and knew he would be questioned about California at his morning press conference. The report swept west with the sun: to Father Coughlin in Detroit and Huey Long in Louisiana, to Albert Lasker in Chicago, and finally to California. "The State faces an emergency," the *San Francisco Chronicle* announced, "which only resolutely united action can meet." Last night's radio broadcasts had only hinted at the outcome of the Democratic primary for governor; now there it was in the *Los Angeles Times,* a landslide in cold type. Up and down the state, terrified Republicans and outraged Democrats faced a nightmare of their own making. Earl Warren in Oakland, A. P. Giannini in San Francisco, Herbert Hoover in Palo Alto, Harry Chandler in Los Angeles, Irving Thalberg in Hollywood—they all knew they could no longer sit back and let California be captured by the muckraking author, militant vegetarian, erstwhile Socialist, scourge of the ruling class, and now Democratic nominee for governor, Upton Sinclair.

William Randolph Hearst happened to be in Munich, one of his favorite cities, when he learned that Upton Sinclair had swept the Democratic primary in California. W.R. had been abroad since the end of May, but his aides kept him abreast of the calamitous events in California. Hearst wanted his newspapers to encourage "patriotic conservatism" and oppose "radical schemes." He had come to believe that the New Deal was itself socialistic, so that made Upton Sinclair's End Poverty in California plan—EPIC for short—so far left it was laughable.

Still, Hearst was having such a fine time overseas it was hard to get agitated about anything back home, even the prospect of communism coming to California. W.R. had assembled a sultanesque entourage, with his three sons and their wives joining his mistress, Marion Davies, a dozen other high-spirited junketeers, and Miss Davies's dachshund, Gandhi. He hoped to collect the usual bounty of rare antiquities and observe two of Europe's fascist leaders at close hand.

After a few weeks in Spain, Great Britain, and Africa, Hearst had watched Mussolini harangue a huge rally in Italy, and was disappointed when il Duce expressed little interest in seeing him. Louis B. Mayer, head of Metro-Goldwyn-Mayer, suggested that W.R. seek an audience with Hitler and use the opportunity to put in a good word for the Jews. Hearst's longtime support for Germany weighed in his favor, and the publisher had a friend in Berlin: Hitler's foreign press officer, Dr. Ernst Hanfstaengl, a Harvard-educated con artist widely known by his nickname, Putzi.

When Hitler won a smashing victory in the August 19 plebiscite, gaining the title of president (in addition to that of chancellor) of Germany, Hearst told Hanfstaengl, in a published interview, that "anything benefiting Germany will eventually benefit the entire world . . . The struggle of Germany for liberation from the iniquities of the Versailles Treaty, and for freedom from the malignant oppression and compression of nations which are selfishly but shortsightedly hostile to her progress, is a struggle which should be watched with sympathetic interest by all liberty-loving people everywhere." He hoped that Putzi could arrange a conference with Hitler sometime in September. The fact that Hitler had just expelled journalist Dorothy Thompson from his country did not deter W.R. in the least.

Preoccupied with courting Hitler and hunting antiques, Hearst nevertheless maintained his usual vigilance over his publishing empire back in the States. Hearst owned twenty-eight newspapers in eighteen cities around the country, but his influence in California was particularly intense: the paid circulation of his five daily papers equaled that of all of the others in the state combined. Traveling abroad, he kept in constant telegraph contact with his editors, who called him Chief. Two weeks ago, the Chief had wired home an editorial he called "The Creed of a Progressive," which revealed his latest slant on the New Deal. "I prefer a good dependable domestic dog," Hearst wrote, "to any unbalanced, speculative political theorist, and I wish our good President would get rid of his revolutionary Communist advisers."

From Munich, Hearst planned to travel to Bad Nauheim for a prolonged spell at the famous spa. This afternoon, while preparing for that trip, W.R. received a cable from his most trusted adviser, attorney John Francis Neylan. From his office in the Crocker Building in San Francisco, Neylan wired:

> SINCLAIR BEATS CREEL OVERWHELMINGLY. SINCLAIR SUPPORT NOT ULTRA RADICAL BUT IN LARGE PART PEOPLE DISGUSTED WITH ENDLESS EXPERIMENTATION AND LACK OF JOBS. . . . AT MOMENT SITUATION MUCH CONFUSED. TENS OF THOUSANDS DEMOCRATS WILL NOT SUPPORT SINCLAIR. . . .

The cable closed with the request, "Advise further," but Hearst put it aside. Whatever advice he offered might change the course of California history, but it could wait, at least for another day.

Upton Sinclair's victory in California wasn't the only chill from the west to reach Washington, D.C., this morning. A cold front gripped the normally sultry nation's capital, dropping temperatures into the low fifties, as two prominent Irishmen, James A. Farley and J.F.T. O'Connor, compared political notes over breakfast at the Mayflower Hotel. Each had predicted a Sinclair win; neither expected a rout.

Within the Roosevelt administration, James Aloysius Farley played two complementary roles: patronage boss (as postmaster general) and election strategist (as chairman of the Democratic National Committee). This was especially true when it came to California. FDR wanted no part of that state. His secretary, Louis Howe, once confessed that whenever a party leader from California approached the President, "I crawl out and tell them that James A. Farley is handling all political matters today." California "is certainly one H—— of a State," Howe argued, and who could dispute it?

Farley had visited California back in July. Most of Big Jim's barnstorming tours mixed politics and postal business in equal measure, although it was often impossible to tell them apart: Farley liked to dedicate new post office buildings in states where local Democrats needed a boost. The California trip got off to a rousing start in Los Angeles. A distinguished audience of fifteen hundred witnessed Farley's initiation into the Breakfast Club, and what a sight it was: the stocky Irishman, his bald head shining, dressed in his usual double-breasted suit, sitting on a hobbyhorse, swearing the oath with his right hand resting in a pan of scrambled eggs and bacon.

A luncheon in Farley's honor at the Warner Bros. studio in Burbank attracted two hundred guests, including James Cagney, Edward G. Robinson, and Bette Davis. Farley met MGM's Irving Thalberg, earned the praise of movie czar Will Hays, and shook hands with all seven of the Democratic candidates for governor, including Upton Sinclair.

"I have heard a lot about you," Farley said, his eyes twinkling.

Sinclair bowed slightly, and replied: "I think it would be nice for us to have a talk."

"Yes, can't you come over to my hotel?" Farley inquired. Sinclair said he'd try, but kept a date at a rally instead.

Then Farley left for San Francisco to address the Commonwealth Club and cavort at Bohemian Grove. Everywhere he went, Democrats begged Farley to do "something" about the governor's race. The Democrats needed to close ranks if they wanted to stop Upton Sinclair, the former Socialist, in the primary. More than 425,000 Californians were out of work, meaning 1.5 million people required private charity or public relief. (This was one-fourth of the state's population.) Sinclair promised an end to all this. A pen his only weapon, Sinclair led an army of crazed utopians, unemployed laborers, and all-purpose leftists flying the flag of his End Poverty in California crusade. Hundreds of End Poverty League chapters had popped up like mushrooms all over the state. The *EPIC News,* an eight-page tabloid, reached over a half million readers every week. Back in the spring, Farley had advised California Democrats to let Senator William G. McAdoo select an anti-Sinclair compromise candidate, but none of the hopefuls accepted the idea; now they all faced defeat.

When Farley returned from the West in July, he informed FDR that "everyone out there wants you to come out against Sinclair." Roosevelt instructed Big Jim to keep hands off, calling this the "best course to follow to avoid difficulties." Although he went along with the President's wishes, Farley confided to Louis Howe that he was "not so sure that our attitude in the matter is the right one."

Yesterday's balloting in California seemed to confirm this. Sinclair received more votes than his six opponents put together. George Creel, Woodrow Wilson's wartime propaganda chief, beat him in San Francisco, but Sinclair carried Los Angeles and adjacent Long Beach by margins of three to one. Nearly fifty EPIC-backed candidates, including impressive newcomers Jerry Voorhis, Augustus Hawkins, and Culbert Olson, won primary races for seats in the state legislature. The so-called EPICs virtually swept L.A. County.

Now, with Sinclair the party's overwhelming choice in California, what would Roosevelt do? With pressure mounting from his right flank, led by the recently formed American Liberty League, FDR doubted the political wisdom of embracing a former Socialist. On the other hand, progressives were his strongest allies in Congress, and repudiating Sinclair would send the wrong message to the La Follettes and Borahs just as the New Deal approached a legislative showdown.

Sitting across a table at the Mayflower, reviewing the election returns in California, Jim Farley and Jefty O'Connor couldn't have looked more different. The top of Farley's bald head gleamed—it was almost preternatural. O'Connor, a Democratic leader in California now serving as FDR's comptroller of the currency, had a headful of dark hair. Yet they had much in common: They were amiable, politically ambitious sons of Ireland devoted to Franklin Roosevelt and the Democratic party, not necessarily in that order, and neither gave a damn about Upton Sinclair. Yet they disagreed sharply over whether a Sinclair victory in November might be good or bad for the party, the President, and themselves.

Farley told O'Connor that the party should get behind Sinclair now that the Democratic voters in California had spoken; after all, Sinclair's elderly GOP opponent, Governor Frank F. Merriam, was an anti-Roosevelt reactionary. O'Connor argued for caution. "I hope no statement will be made," he advised, "until Sinclair comes here and we all know just what he intends to do." Several days ago, Sinclair requested a meeting with the President, but the White House had not yet responded. O'Connor wanted to find out whether Sinclair planned to campaign as a New Dealer or as leader of the radical social movement known as EPIC. Would he support FDR when the chips were down? Secretly, O'Connor favored the third-party candidate in the race, Raymond L. Haight, a political moderate.

When breakfast ended, Farley headed to the White House to find out what FDR, vacationing at Hyde Park, thought about California. The President had a penchant for postponement, a genius for evasion; he hated firm commitments and loved to manipulate insecurity. Before the day was out, however, Roosevelt would have to make two decisions: Should the White House congratulate the victorious Democrat in California? And could FDR afford to put out the welcome mat at Hyde Park for America's most prominent socialist?

When the sun finally came to California, another warm, clear day dawned in Los Angeles. The temperature lingered in the sixties as Webb Waldron drove across the curving Arroyo Seco bridge into Pasadena for Upton Sinclair's first interview as Democratic nominee for governor. Waldron, on assignment for *Today* magazine in New York, was anxious to find out whether the EPIC leader lived up to his billing as a crank, a zealot, and a Red.

A few days ago, a friend of Waldron's, an astronomer at Cal Tech (also located in Pasadena), was sitting in the living room of his home discussing with an associate the problem of how to grind the mirror of a telescope. The technical term *surface of revolution* came up in conversation and evidently drifted out through an open window into the night. Suddenly an angry voice from next door rang through the window: "Shut up that talk about revolution or I'll call the police!" This and other incidents had convinced Waldron that California had Red phantoms on the brain, perhaps the product of too much exposure to an intoxicating sun. Ironically, the Communists seemed to despise Sinclair. But who could know for sure? Waldron had found Reds everywhere in the pages of the newspapers, but he had trouble locating an actual Communist on the streets.

When he reached the home of Upton Sinclair on North Sunset in Pasadena, not far from the Rose Bowl, Waldron discovered a rather shabby, jerry-built structure in a modest workingman's neighborhood. Set back slightly from the street, it was painted pink and looked as if several small clapboard houses had been shoved together to create one long, rancho-style structure. Eucalyptus trees, a fruit orchard, and rosebushes filled the yard. Rocking chairs dotted the sprawling front porch. Around back, Waldron spotted a tennis court and a small in-ground pool. Inside the topsy-turvy dwelling, he found a battered piano and numerous pieces of junk-shop furniture.

Sinclair, a spry fellow about five feet seven inches tall, greeted his visitor in pajamas and bathrobe. He had white hair, piercing blue-gray eyes, a prominent nose, and a thin, inquisitive face. Despite weeks of campaigning and a long night studying election returns, his face showed only faint lines of fatigue, and he answered one question after another, sharply, concisely, and soothingly. His words rang with urgency—he had heavy artillery in his heart—but his voice was soft, his manner boyish, charming, bemused, almost Old South. There was something elflike about him, although he was not unusually short. He seemed to Waldron not quite of this earth.

How does he do it? Waldron thought to himself. *What a dynamo!* Interview over, Waldron went away wondering whether this gentle soul, stamped with noblesse oblige, really was the bogeyman who was throwing such a scare into California.

At 704 Cathedral Street, the sage of Baltimore searched for the proper adjectives to describe Upton Sinclair's smashing success in California. Finding the right words was rarely a problem for the author of *The American Language.* At the moment, however, he was exhausted from investigating the King's English and how it was faring on this side of the Atlantic. Material for a new edition of *The American Language* was crammed into anything that would hold it in his office. Hundreds of samples of Americanisms contributed by far-flung correspondents blanketed a Victorian sofa. Piles of newspaper clippings, stacks of books, and fifty pounds of notes added to the congestion.

Henry Louis Mencken vowed never to undertake such an atrocious task again. After hours of sorting, cutting, and pasting, an overpowering thirst would send him dashing to the nearest gin mill. On top of everything, his beloved wife, Sara, had picked up a mysterious illness during a Mediterranean cruise and was still bedridden. Fortunately, Mencken wouldn't have to dig too deep into his reserve of words to poke fun at Upton Sinclair.

In a typical critique, Mencken had once called Sinclair an "incurable romantic, wholesale believer in the obviously not so. The man delights me constantly. His faith in the wisdom of the incurably imbecile, the virtue of the congenitally dishonest, the lofty idealism of the incorrigibly sordid, is genuinely affecting. I know of no one in all this vast paradise of credulity who gives a steadier and more heroic credit to the intrinsically preposterous." Sensitive to the sorrows of the world, yet susceptible to quacks, Sinclair was, in Henry Mencken's view, the embodiment of what William James called "the tender-minded." There was nothing to be done about people like Sinclair. "He must suffer vicariously for the carnal ease of the rest of us," Mencken observed many years ago. "He must die daily that we may live in peace, corrupt and contented."

Although they were both merciless critics of American society, two men more different in temperament and intellect could hardly be found. Sinclair was a puritan and an idealist, Mencken a cynic and a free spirit. Sinclair championed (from a distance) the common people, whom Mencken considered, in his famous phrase, "the booboisie." Mencken argued that literature should never serve a moral purpose, and lamented that the artist in Sinclair was frequently undermined by the "tin-pot evangelist." When they were together, their personal habits clashed, particularly over the issue of alcohol.

They were irreconcilable, yet the two writers liked and respected each other enormously, were congenial when they met, and had conducted a rigorous correspondence covering more than sixteen years and 150 letters. "I am against you and against the Liberals because I believe you chase butterflies," Mencken told Sinclair, "but I am even more against your enemies." They both hailed from Baltimore. They were ardent civil libertarians. They appreciated each other's energy, courage, and dedication to the craft of writing. Mencken, Sinclair believed, was "better" than his opinions; Sinclair at least was consistent in his wrongheadedness, Mencken admitted.

His sting may have been lethal, but Henry Mencken was hardly an imposing figure. He had virtually no neck, and his legs were so short he seemed taller when he was sitting down. He was a hypochondriac and a compulsive hand washer. Now fifty-four years of age, he still parted his brown hair in the middle, and the twin cowlicks brushed his forehead. Sinclair considered him a "solidly made gentleman with bright china-blue eyes and the round rosy face of a cherub."

Now, on the morning after his friend's great triumph in California, Mencken happily put aside his labors on *The American Language* to gently put the skewer to Sinclair. Which was not to say that Mencken necessarily wanted him to lose the election. Sinclair was no more ridiculous than any other politician, and government in any event was irrelevant, "the common enemy of every decent man." For now, Mencken would merely lampoon the candidate instead of composing a scathing attack.

Sinclair's victory was "of a kind unparalleled in human history," Mencken wrote, tapping on the typewriter keys with his two index fingers, a parody of the unreconstructed newspaper reporter. "He not only beat George Creel, Wall Street and the booze trust. He also beat Thomas Jefferson, Alexander Hamilton, George Washington, Benjamin Franklin and the whole Adams family, not to mention St. Thomas Aquinas, Duns Scotus, Plato, Aristotle, Socrates and Solomon." But the real losers in California, Mencken commented, all kidding aside, were "the taxpayers."

When Steve Early arrived at his press office in the White House he found Jim Farley waiting for him. Farley thought they ought to remind the President that the administration had failed to acknowledge Sinclair's triumph. Farley had congratulated all previous Democratic victors, and making Sinclair the single exception would draw attention to a dilemma the White House wanted to diminish.

Last night, when asked about Sinclair at a press conference, Farley had stammered weakly, "The party has never failed to support its nominees." Now he wanted to give that statement some spine. If nothing else, the old muckraker had revitalized the party in California, pushing Democratic registration in the state past the Republicans' for the first time. Sinclair had also promised to support the President and his programs. In his victory speech last night he called his triumph "a victory not for me [but] for the New Deal." He also predicted that his election would "end the absurd situation under which the funds of the New Deal are given to the State of California and used by a reactionary administration in an effort to wreck the New Deal." Perhaps most important, Sinclair vowed to put California in the Roosevelt column in 1936. That was more important than ideology, and Farley didn't care about policy matters anyway. Sinclair might be radical and hard to control, Farley reasoned, but the alternative—a Republican controlling the California statehouse during the President's reelection bid—was even worse. And besides, it looked as though Sinclair was going to win with or without the President's help and become the state's first Democratic governor in more than three decades.

It was left to Steve Early to pass Farley's suggestion along to the

President. Earlier this year in his pungent book *The New Dealers,* John Franklin Carter had placed Early squarely in the center of what he called the Praetorian Guard, along with FDR's wife, Eleanor, stenographer Missy LeHand, secretary Louis Howe, and appointments secretary Marvin H. McIntyre. All five had been with FDR since his 1920 campaign for vice president. Now entrenched at the White House, Early was probably the most efficient press representative a president had ever had.

At ten minutes to eleven—twenty-five minutes before the President's press conference was set to begin—Early wired Marvin McIntyre at Hyde Park. "If no message is sent Sinclair more stress will be put on the failure to congratulate than will be given if the usual procedure is followed," Early declared. Farley, he observed, wanted to offer Sinclair his "heartiest congratulations" and let it go at that, but Big Jim wanted McIntyre to check with "the Boss" to find out whether even that noncommittal message was acceptable.

That still left problem number two: Sinclair's proposed trek to Hyde Park for an audience with the President. Ten days ago, Sinclair had informed FDR that he wanted to see him "at once" following the primary, to "consult you and ask your advice . . . also, of course, to assure you of our loyalty and regard." Upon receipt of this letter at the White House, one member of the Praetorian Guard had taken a pencil and scrawled a three-inch question mark in the upper right-hand corner. Sinclair followed up with a note to Eleanor Roosevelt, asking her to call her husband's attention to the importance of his visit. Eager to please, vain but by no means self-conscious, he even enclosed postage stamps so Eleanor could reply via airmail. Now there was probably nothing for the President to do but invite Sinclair to Hyde Park—on FDR's terms, of course.

A Roosevelt press conference was hardly a novelty. The one scheduled for the President's study at 11:15 A.M. would be the 140th since FDR took office, an average of one session every fourth day. He enjoyed these intimate meetings nearly as much as the reporters did. Much good-natured joshing passed between them. FDR called many of the reporters by their first name. He solicited their ideas and entertained them with anecdotes. A master of the harmless half-truth, FDR's first instinct was to lie, *New York Times* correspondent Turner Catledge believed; halfway through an answer the President would realize he could tell the truth and get away with it, so he would shift gears and something true would trickle out. Performing at a press conference, Roosevelt once confided, was "a special art all by itself."

Three mornings ago, the special train from Washington had arrived at Hyde Park carrying the President, a skeleton staff, and a clutch of newspaper correspondents. While the President settled in for a prolonged stay at the family estate, which rambled along the eastern heights of the Hudson River, Marvin McIntyre established temporary offices on the second floor of the Nelson House in nearby Poughkeepsie. Through these offices and direct telephone lines to Washington, the President would keep in close contact with the White House. FDR planned to relax for a few days before convening meetings over Labor Day weekend aimed at reshaping hit-and-miss New Deal emergency measures into a cohesive social program.

The press conference this morning might touch on almost anything; after all, four whole days had passed since the last one. A national textile strike involving half a million workers would begin no later than September 1. The National Recovery Administration was under fire, and even some of FDR's closest aides demanded the ouster of its director, General Hugh ("Ironpants") Johnson. Eight cities had just reported on unemployment, and the picture, eighteen months into the New Deal, was not pretty: nearly one in six residents of Philadelphia, Pittsburgh, and Cleveland was on relief, one in five in Denver, and nearly one in four in New York—about 1.6 million people in that city alone. The news from Europe was ominous. Mussolini talked about an "eventual" war, and Germany was arming to the teeth. "Chancellor Hitler is no longer a man," Dorothy Thompson had said earlier this week in Paris following her expulsion from Germany, "he is a religion." The strain of executing twelve Nazis and nine Socialists in six months had sent Austria's hangman, Johan Lang—who invariably wore a silk hat and evening clothes to work—into an asylum.

Clearly there was much to discuss, minimize, or parry. Nevertheless, when the reporters finished crowding around the President, who was sitting in a wheelchair in his study looking healthy and tan from his summer travels, the first thing he said was: "I do not think I could even invent news—and that is saying a lot." He waved at a mound of papers sitting on the desk in front of him. "Somebody wrote a new song," he explained, "somebody had a golden wedding, somebody was a hundred and two years old. That is all." The correspondents chuckled.

"We can't use any of it," one reporter grumbled.

"Several towns had hundredth anniversaries," the President said helpfully.

The questions started to fly. Roosevelt declined to speculate on "the textile situation" and the possible resignation of the NRA's Hugh Johnson.

"Have you any comment to make on the outcome of the California primary?" a reporter asked.

"No," FDR replied. Then, as if fearing a simple *no* would resound with multiple and profound meanings, he added, "No more than on any other primary—that should be added to it."

The press conference started winding down. A reporter asked whether FDR would attend the Dutchess County Fair the following day, as advertised. The President wasn't sure and wondered if any of the assembled had seen the shell game played on the midway there. Marvin McIntyre remarked that some people complained they often saw the same game played "without shells, in some of these press conferences." The President threw back his head and roared. The reporters joined in. Like a shell game, the Roosevelt flimflam was insultingly transparent, but there was nothing anyone could do, or wanted to do, about it.

———

It was five days after the wedding, and Alistair Cooke still didn't know where his best man was or why he hadn't shown up at the ceremony. It was the second time Charlie Chaplin had snubbed the young Englishman in recent weeks. All summer Cooke and Chaplin had worked on a script for a movie about Napoléon. A few days before the wedding, Cooke was up at Chaplin's house in Benedict Canyon. The two men were playing piano duets, when suddenly Chaplin said, "By the way, the Napoléon thing, it's a beautiful idea—for somebody else." And that was that.

So Cooke was touched when Charlie agreed to be best man at his wedding. Chaplin ribbed his young colleague about the misfires sure to befall the ceremony. As it turned out, Chaplin himself was the disaster waiting to happen. Instead of standing up for his friend, he took his girlfriend Paulette Goddard out to Lake Arrowhead and worked on the script for his next film, about a factory worker and a waif. Shooting was set to begin soon, and Chaplin, an outspoken critic of talkies, was still undecided about whether to include spoken dialogue in the film. He hadn't made a film in three years, since *City Lights,* and some Hollywood columnists suggested that he was an artist in decline. So there was plenty of reason for Chaplin to prove unreliable when Alistair Cooke's wedding rolled around on August 24.

Five days later Charlie was still hard at work on his as yet untitled film. For the past year, he had elaborated on an early list of simple ideas for gags: "Dock working . . . Strikes . . . Police raid . . . Bread line . . . Stomach rumbling. . . ." Now that process was nearly complete, or as finished as it could be for an improvisatory artist, and so Chaplin, his assistants Carter DeHaven and Henry Bergman, and a secretary had gathered at Lake Arrowhead, a favored retreat for the wealthy of Los Angeles, to hammer out a semblance of a script. Along the forested southern rim of the lake, clusters of cafés, dance halls, theaters, shops, and hotels had erupted. Here Chaplin learned of Upton Sinclair's startlingly easy victory in the Democratic primary.

That was OK with Charlie, virtually the only major figure in all of Hollywood who supported the old muckraker. (His apolitical friend Alistair Cooke felt EPIC was brave but foolish.) Chaplin considered Sinclair his mentor in the study of socialism. This relationship began one day when he was driving to Sinclair's home in Pasadena for lunch, and Upton asked him, in his soft-spoken way, whether he believed in the "profit system." Chaplin, the richest man in Hollywood, answered facetiously that he would have to consult his accountant, but privately he felt disarmed. Sinclair had exposed a true paradox—want in the midst of plenty—and from that moment on Chaplin looked at politics through the prism of economics, not history. Like Sinclair, he repeatedly referred to capitalism as a dying system.

Chaplin would meet other socialists, like George Bernard Shaw and H. G. Wells, but Sinclair had a special place in his political heart. Sometimes he entertained friends by imitating Sinclair's manner of discourse, which Charlie referred to as speaking-through-a-smile. Once Chaplin's conversion to what he called "true socialism" was complete, he and Upton rarely discussed politics. Instead, Chaplin would talk about his work; inevitably he became so excited he would start acting out the scene he was presently working on at the studio. Sinclair once sent Chaplin a scenario for a farce called *The Hypnotist,* but nothing came of it. After that, he concentrated on enlisting Charlie in left-wing causes, such as sponsoring screenings of Russian movies and benefits for pro-Soviet groups.

The most controversial Soviet cause of the early 1930s in Hollywood was the great Russian film director Sergei Eisenstein. When his attempt to make a studio-backed film in California sputtered, Eisenstein informed Chaplin that he wanted to create an epic in Mexico. Chaplin had all the money and know-how in the world, but inexplicably he turned Eisenstein over to the relatively impoverished and naïve Upton Sinclair, who subsequently lost nearly all his money managing the artistic and political scandal that was *Qué Viva México!*

Despite the Eisenstein flap, Upton and Charlie remained friends; so when Sinclair launched his candidacy for governor in the fall of 1933, he appealed to Chaplin for an endorsement. Chaplin informed Sinclair that he felt it would be a "mistake" for him to enter politics; he wished to remain "nonpartisan."

By the summer of 1934, however, Chaplin had weakened. Perhaps he believed that endorsing a long-shot candidate was meaningless; now Sinclair was the people's choice. So when Upton asked him to deliver a speech at an EPIC fund-raising affair at the Shrine Auditorium in Los Angeles, Chaplin accepted. The event was dubbed a double world premiere—the first showing of a truncated version of the Eisenstein film, called *Death Day,* and a performance of a new one-act satire, *Depression Island,* penned by Sinclair. Chaplin addressed the rally, the first time he had ever made a partisan speech to a large crowd (so far as Sinclair knew).

Now another two months had passed, and so much had changed: Upton was now the Democratic nominee for governor, and Charlie was deeply absorbed in his factory film. Chaplin would return from Lake Arrowhead in a few days. He had just stood up Alistair Cooke. Now he was expected to be Upton Sinclair's best man.

Upton Sinclair sat in his study sifting his mail. Dozens of letters addressed to him arrived nearly every day at Station A, Pasadena, California. They contained heartfelt thanks and crackpot economic schemes, small contributions to the EPIC campaign and desperate pleas for his photograph. Some of his fans offered to work as his personal servant or bodyguard. Many were old Socialists; a few were ardent New Dealers. They hailed from all sections of the country. Nearly everyone wanted Sinclair to be governor, and some openly predicted the presidency in 1936.

Every imaginable hope and dream crossed Sinclair's large, carved wooden desk, which was pushed against a row of windows overlooking his sunny backyard. The desktop supported a tiny lamp, some paper, utensils for writing, and not much else. It was here, a little less than a year ago, that Sinclair wrote his campaign manifesto, an immodest little book called *I, Governor of California, and How I Ended Poverty: A True Story of the Future.*

Like the rest of the rambling house, the study looked lived in, worked in. It was, in fact, a former tailor shop. Sinclair's wife, Craig, had bought up cheap offices, shacks, and bungalows, moved them to North Sunset, and attached them together in a more or less even row. With a uniform coat of pinkish paint, the disjointed structure almost looked Southern Colonial from the outside. Inside, no two ceilings, floors, or windows seemed to match. Craig knocked out the ceiling of the tailor shop, giving the study an airy effect, which did little, however, to levitate her husband's earthbound prose. A worn Oriental rug rested on the floor; a comfortable old couch (where Sinclair sometimes dozed) and an easy chair sat just to the left of his desk.

Sinclair rarely wrote letters in longhand, choosing instead to dictate to one of his secretaries. He was a fanatical dictator. At a single sitting, he might compose as many as fifty letters. Many of his correspondents were sorry to interrupt him, they didn't expect a reply, yet each promptly received some sort of personalized response, even if it was little more than an apology for not being able to answer a specific question because Upton had to go out and win an election first. It was this "fundamental earnestness and sweetness," Edmund Wilson once commented, that took the curse off Sinclair's "attitude of moral superiority."

The candidate had a few other things to do today—polish a nationwide radio address and prepare to leave for a trip across the country—but as usual his mail came first. Congratulatory telegrams accumulated on his desk. Cornelius Vanderbilt, Jr., a well-known journalist and a close friend, exclaimed from New York, "Always knew you would do it . . ." George Creel, beaten by Sinclair in the primary by roughly 150,000 votes, wired: "Congratulations on your remarkable victory." This was significant not for what it said (Sinclair's triumph was nothing if not remarkable), but for what it didn't say: that Creel would actually support him.

As noon approached, Sinclair still had not heard from the White House. He had promised the press he would leave for the East Coast to confer with FDR immediately following the primary. Overlooked was one small detail: receiving an actual invitation. "It is important,"

Sinclair intoned, dictating a telegram to Franklin Roosevelt, "that we should win next November not merely for California but to keep California in line two years later. I would like very much to consult you. The interview may be strictly confidential on my side, all statements being issued by you. I will come on receipt of wire."

President Roosevelt addressed a series of microphones, a characteristic smile on his face. His right hand held a fishing line, from which dangled a large fish. Eleanor Roosevelt, in an evening dress, stood to his left; like the President, she wore a small crown. Secretary of the Treasury Morgenthau sat in front of the Roosevelts, clad in a clown suit, juggling coins and bills and rubber checks. Hands reached up, beggingly, from the surface of a pool of water. Demons assembled on either side of FDR and his wife; those on the right dribbled money into a trough from which pigs wearing tall hats were eating. Jim Farley happily dispensed mail and money. Uncle Sam dangled from a cross, as vultures hovered overhead. . . .

While FDR decided whether to lend a hand to Upton Sinclair, the good folks of Tarrytown, New York, a solidly Republican enclave forty-seven miles down the Hudson River from Hyde Park, were paying twenty-five cents apiece to view a four-by-eight-foot mural entitled *The Nightmare of 1934* at the Westchester Institute of Fine Arts. An article about the exhibition appeared this morning on the front page of *The New York Times.* Thanks to the publicity, several hundred people invaded the gallery, one day after the official opening.

Charles A. Birch-Field, president of the institute, described the mystery artist, known only as Jere Miah II, as "a Voltaire with the brush." Apparently the artist worked for FDR's own Public Works Administration. In the explanation framed beside the oil painting, Jere Miah II called FDR "a most charming person, adept at fishing and the art of microphony, [who] made a world's record catch of suckers at the last election." Eleanor Roosevelt was "his helpmeet to help meet the microphonies." The demons were "the strange beings called the Brain Trust." And so on. A local Democratic leader had announced that his party "might do something about" the painting, and so when six men described as tough-looking visited the gallery today, Birch-Field posted two armed guards as a precaution.

Up in Dutchess County, the President declined to comment on the controversy. Marvin McIntyre called a midafternoon press conference, however, to talk about Upton Sinclair, who threatened to become FDR's own nightmare of 1934. How would FDR escape? Telegrams from leading California Democrats carrying wildly conflicting messages arrived at Hyde Park almost hourly. Sinclair was either Mussolini or the messiah. Depending on where the Democrat sat, Roosevelt was sunk if he supported him, discredited if he didn't. John B. Elliott, vice-chairman of the Democratic party in California, had already come out against Sinclair, stating that "party lines now mean nothing."

With press secretary Steve Early manning the fort in Washington, it was up to McIntyre to spar with the reporters in Poughkeepsie. The Nelson House served as a newsroom, hotel, and watering hole for the visiting correspondents. McIntyre, a wraithlike figure three years older than the President, known as Mac to one and all, had the soul of a lobbyist, but reporters appreciated his warmth, his humor, and his enjoyment of wine, women, and song.

When the reporters gathered, Mac told them he had just informed Sinclair that he would be glad to arrange a visit with the President, but the two men could not talk about the California campaign or any other political subject. He would confirm the meeting only if Sinclair had a "distinct understanding" of these terms. This was to be a social visit, nothing more.

The newsmen were naturally skeptical that two voluble politicians could sit in the President's study for more than two minutes without talking politics. What else, really, was there to talk about? What the reporters found most intriguing was McIntyre's assertion that the President would maintain a hands-off policy in regard to *all* state campaigns, no matter how worthy the Democratic candidate. He called this a "fixed rule." FDR had always stayed out of primary contests between competing Democrats, or when a conservative Democrat was opposed by a progressive Republican friendly to the New Deal. That made political sense. Why, now, withhold support from liberal Democrats running against reactionary Republicans? It seemed painfully clear to many of the reporters that Sinclair had forced Roosevelt into a self-defeating position. FDR might avoid a mishap in California, but sabotage key supporters elsewhere who needed his electoral help—imperiling the New Deal itself.

McIntyre tried to put a practical spin on the President's predicament, asserting that if Roosevelt met with Sinclair to offer his support he would have to extend this courtesy to every Democratic candidate. The Boss didn't want a parade of office seekers tramping to Hyde Park. FDR was not singling out Upton Sinclair and, McIntyre stressed, the terms the President had set for their meeting should not be interpreted as a rebuff. While the newsmen scattered, eager to attach their own interpretations, Steve Early wired McIntyre, declaring that in light of Sinclair's visit, "I think we had better lay low on congratulatory message from Farley. Farley agrees to delay message for several days."

———

Four days ago, former president Herbert Hoover informed Henry P. Fletcher, the Republican national chairman, that Upton Sinclair, "the Socialist who is also running on the Democratic ticket," would win the Democratic primary, but he predicted his defeat in November at the hands of Governor Frank F. Merriam. This was by no means assured, however, so Hoover, at his home in Palo Alto, picked up a pen to offer his assistance in bringing it to pass. It would be a note important and personal enough to write in longhand, not dictate to a secretary. "My dear Governor," Hoover announced, "I want you to know that I am at your service. It is the most momentous election which California has faced."

———

It was 10:45 P.M. in Washington and New York, 9:45 in the Midwest, and 7:45 in California when Upton Sinclair, who was already packing his bags for the trip east, delivered his first nationwide radio address, originating from KHJ in Los Angeles.

Until the past few days, the Sinclair campaign had received little notice nationally. Sinclair himself was a famous author, but what was he known for? Exposing the meat-packers, defending Sacco and Vanzetti, producing an Eisenstein film. What did that have to do with running for office and leading a social movement called EPIC? The author of *The Jungle* was portrayed by many in the press as a dangerous, demagogic champion of the underdog. Was he another Huey Long or Father Coughlin? And if he was, was that good or bad? With the New Deal faltering, anyone promising to end poverty, even in one notoriously eccentric state out West, deserved a listen, and so millions of Americans—bankers, breadliners, and Brain Trusters alike—gathered around their radio sets to find out whether Upton Sinclair embodied their fondest hopes or their deepest fears, or perhaps a little of both.

"I have been asked to explain to you the political movement which has just achieved such an extraordinary victory in the state of California," Sinclair began. "I did not make this victory, it has been made by the people of our state. It is a spontaneous movement which has spread all over the state by the unpaid labor of tens of thousands of devoted workers. They were called amateurs but they have put all the professional politicians on the shelf. In less than a year they have built a movement which has carried a state of more than six million population. It has been called a political miracle and the rest of the states will wish to know what it means.

"We confront today the collapse of an institution which is worldwide and age-old," Sinclair exclaimed in his pinched, nasal tenor, with just the suggestion of a lisp, sounding a bit like a patrician Jimmy Cagney. "Capitalism has served its time and is passing from the earth. A new system must be found to take its place, and that event is the same thing to our society as childbirth is to the individual: The child may be born, but both child and mother may perish in agony.

"Consider what has happened in Germany. An obscene demagogue has seized power; a great civilized nation has fallen into the hands of gangsters. Liberty is at an end and the most scientifically advanced of modern states is sliding back into the dark ages. Do not think that was an accident! Do not attribute it to the magic of a demagogue's tongue. Those events in Germany were planned, they were bought and paid for. It is the steel kings of Germany who have seized the country and prevented a new birth of freedom for the people.

"And now we have the same breakdown in the United States. The same poverty and insecurity. The same unemployment and suffering, the same Wall Street kind of bond slavery. Can we free ourselves or will Wall Street give us a dictator and fasten the chains about our ankles for a generation, and perhaps forever? Can democracy work? Can the people use its instruments in their own interest or can they be fooled and lied to and frightened away from their goal?

"We have put a plan before the people," Sinclair said, his voice insistent but rarely wavering in pitch or volume. Whatever his words, he was no fire-and-brimstone preacher, no Mussolini, no Huey Long. "We have shown them the way out of the depression. We have made it as simple as possible. We have made it gradual so as to be painless. We are not proposing to replace the whole collapsing system by a new one all at once. We are proposing the first step, a trial stage.

"We say to the voters: There are half a million persons in our state out of work. They cannot be permitted to starve. These persons can never again find work while the present system endures. They are being supported by public charities, and the burden of that is driving the state to bankruptcy and the taxpayers to ruin. There is no solution to this problem except to put these unemployed at productive labor, to make them self-sustaining, to let them produce what they are going to consume and so take them off the backs of the taxpayers.

"That is the simple proposition. There can be no valid objection to it. But the whole power of vested privilege rises up against it. Why is this? The answer is because they are afraid of the precedent. They are afraid the plan will succeed, and show the unemployed how to produce *for use* instead of *for profit.* It will put into the minds of the unemployed the idea of getting access to land and machinery by the political method, by the use of their ballots. And once they get access to good land and modern machinery they will produce so much, they will make such comfort and plenty for themselves, that they will never again be content to support the parasites of Wall Street."

Sinclair explained the foundations of the so-called EPIC plan. "There are a couple of thousand factories in our state standing entirely idle and the rest are working less than half time," he asserted matter-of-factly. "Many of these concerns are running into debt, and to them the state of California will say, 'We offer to rent your factories. Keep your organization going, call in your workers, and run your machinery under the supervision of the state.' The workers will turn out goods and they will own what they have produced.

"The farmers of California, meanwhile, are producing huge quantities of foodstuffs for which they cannot find a market. The farmers are losing their land because they cannot pay their taxes. To these farmers the state will say, 'Bring your foodstuffs to our warehouses and you will receive in return receipts which will be good for your taxes.' The farmers will eagerly comply and the food will be shipped to the cities and made available to the factory workers in exchange for the products of *their* labor. These products will go out to the stores in the farmers' communities and be exchanged for more of the farmers' goods. So we will get going, by the credit power of the state, a new system of production in which Wall Street will have no share."

The EPIC plan also called for the establishment of what Sinclair referred to as land colonies. "All around our cities and towns are tracts of land which speculators have been holding out of use," he insisted. "They also cannot pay their taxes and will be glad to rent the land to the state. The state can furnish machinery, and the unemployed can go to work and grow their own food, making gardens where now are patches of weeds.

"The possibilities of this system once started are beyond any man's imagining. We are going to have to tax the great corporations of our state to make up the present deficit. If we make these taxes payable in services and goods, we shall have lumber, cement, and other building materials out of which our people can make homes. We shall have heat, light, and gas for our offices and stores, and power for our factories.

"Our opponents have told you that all of this is socialism and communism. We are not the least worried, because we note that Mr. Hearst has been cabling from Europe that President Roosevelt's policies are also communism," Sinclair said, playing his FDR card at last. "Our enemies' efforts to crush this movement by lies and intimidation are not merely an attack upon me in California, they are a preparation for the scrapping of the New Deal at the presidential election of 1936. Make no mistake about the meaning of the decision which you are going to make in November. The news has gone out to the whole country, and if the Democratic party of California adopts the EPIC plan, it will mean hope, courage, and guidance to the unemployed of all our forty-eight states.

"All my life I have believed in the people. All my life I have insisted that democracy could be made to work. The years since the world war have been years of cynicism and heartsickness. But all through these years I have stood by my faith, in spite of all ridicule. I have believed in the people, and the one thing the people of California have done for me is to vindicate that faith, out of which my life and books have been made.

"Our opponents have told you that we cannot put this plan through," Sinclair confessed, his maiden speech as a national political figure drawing to a close. "Let me answer just this: If you should give me a chance to end poverty in California, and if I should fail to do it, life would mean nothing to me thereafter. All that I have taught all through the years would be without meaning. Believe me, and stick by me, and we together shall not fail!"

AUGUST 30

THURSDAY

The Depression was deepening in New York, so a morning of record cold carried the reminder that conditions would only worsen as winter approached. Local officials minimized reports that New York supported more families on relief than any other city. Mayor La Guardia asserted that the numbers were skewed by the fact that families in melting-pot New York tended to be larger than those anywhere else.

The Giants and the Yankees vied for a pennant, while the Brooklyn Dodgers stumbled twenty-five games out of first place. Milton Berle opened on Broadway in a musical called *Saluta,* his performance running the gamut "from vulgarity to grossness," according to critic Brooks Atkinson. Hearn's department store on Fourteenth Street canceled $176,000 in customers' debts to help speed the Roosevelt recovery. California evangelist Aimee Semple McPherson arrived at the Commodore Hotel en route to Canada, where she would lecture on the evils of teaching evolution in classrooms.

All in all, just another day in New York.

Far from typical, however, was the amount of attention New York newspapers lavished on an election contest nearly three thousand miles away. The *Times* carried no fewer than five articles about the California campaign. It portrayed Roosevelt's refusal to talk politics with Sinclair as a clear snub, despite Marvin McIntyre's insistence to the contrary. FDR did this, the *Times* reported, to avoid "possible reaction against the New Deal in conservative quarters." At first regarded as a joke, Sinclair's bid for high office had turned into a grim portent, a *Times* editorial declared. "If the government sets out to try daring experiments," the editors scolded, "it is certain to raise up experimenters even more daring." Other New York papers reacted similarly.

Like H. L. Mencken, Arthur Brisbane chose to mock Sinclair, in his column for the *New York American,* rather than attack him, and for the same reason: he and the candidate were old friends. Once they worked the same side of the street, Sinclair as muckraker, Brisbane as an early master of yellow journalism. Now Brisbane was the star Hearst columnist, whose views reached roughly thirty million readers every day. Thirty million was also the reputed size of Brisbane's fortune, mostly in New York real estate: he and Hearst co-owned the Ziegfeld Theatre, among other properties. His $250,000-a-year salary easily made him America's best-paid newspaperman.

Brisbane once thought so much of Upton Sinclair that he tried to hire him to cover prizefights for Hearst. Later he succeeded where Mencken, Jack London, Edmund Wilson, and many other disciples of alcohol failed: he got the temperate Sinclair to take a drink. The year was 1914. Georg Brandes, a noted literary critic visiting from Europe, informed Brisbane that the American he most wanted to meet was Upton Sinclair, who had just been jailed for picketing John D. Rockefeller's office following the Ludlow massacre in Colorado. Brisbane took Sinclair and Brandes to lunch at Delmonico's. The two men playfully insisted that Upton try some champagne. Sinclair hadn't imbibed since he last took Communion as an Episcopalian youth, but he accepted the invitation. Unfortunately, he found the taste of champagne disagreeable, and he hadn't touched a drop since.

In this morning's syndicated column, Brisbane observed that his old friend Uppie ("an always was, always will be radical") wasn't really much of a menace. A political candidate is like a mule galloping around the pasture, threatening to kick everything to pieces, Brisbane wrote, but "when he is between the shafts, in harness, he goes along quietly like any other mule! So it is sometimes with candidates before and after elections."

Something more disturbing than Sinclair's primary win bothered Brisbane today. The gallery in Tarrytown showing Jere Miah II's satiric mural on the New Deal should be ashamed, he wrote, for allowing the artist to include in the painting a caricature of the President's wife. The portrayal of FDR as a despot, the secretary of the treasury as a clown, and Uncle Sam on the cross didn't bother Brisbane; he just didn't like bringing Eleanor Roosevelt into the picture. Caricaturing a First Lady, Brisbane complained, "had not been done hitherto in America."

Huey P. Long, senator from Louisiana and head of the Share Our Wealth movement, which claimed several thousand chapters across the country, quietly celebrated his forty-first birthday in Baton Rouge with a plate of cowpeas and corn bread. Sharing the feast was his boyhood chum, O. K. Allen, the aptly named Louisiana governor. Upton Sinclair's win in California gave Senator Long another reason to whoop it up. Long hoped to run for president in 1936 and the Sinclair landslide, Huey crowed, "shows the mind of the country."

Unlike the work-oriented EPIC plan, Long's Share Our Wealth proposal was basically an income-distribution scheme. "Every Man a King," it promised. The government would seize all inheritances over one million dollars and tax income at a devastating rate. Bursting with new revenue, the state would guarantee every family a minimum income of two thousand to five thousand dollars a year, as well as a basic "household estate" (a radio, a washing machine, an automobile), and provide pensions for the aged and free college education for the young.

"He advocates limiting the size of fortunes far more than I ever mentioned," Huey said today, referring to Sinclair. "He may be nearer right on the limits than I have been. Fortunes must be limited to save the country. The powers that be," Huey hollered, "can take warning or send themselves to hell!"

Birthday celebration over, Governor Allen declared martial law and called out the militia to make sure nothing stood in the way of Senator Long's investigation of vice and corruption in New Orleans. The probe just happened to coincide with local elections. "We'll be quizzing witnesses in New Orleans within forty-eight hours," Huey promised.

To no one's surprise, Upton Sinclair accepted the President's half-hearted invitation to visit him at Hyde Park. "Thanks for your very clear telegram," Sinclair wired the White House, indicating that he understood the stringent conditions. If this was to be pantomime, Sinclair for once would play along, if he could.

The administration was in public disarray over Sinclair. By the time the President's gag order came down from Hyde Park, two of the left-leaning New Dealers, Harry Hopkins and Henry Wallace, had already voiced approval of the EPIC candidate. Hopkins, administrator of federal relief programs, called Sinclair's nomination "great business" and said parts of the EPIC plan were "very good." Asked by newsmen in Washington whether it bothered him that Sinclair was a Socialist, Hopkins replied, "Naw—he's a good Democrat. He's on our side." What side is that? a reporter wondered. "I mean *our* side," Hopkins affirmed, "and we're at bat. I like to see everybody on our side win." Secretary of Agriculture Wallace pointed out that Sinclair's EPIC plan "simply proposed our present plan of subsistence homesteading," which he believed would be regarded one day as the New Deal's outstanding achievement.

Jefty O'Connor, for his part, was having none of that. He had political aspirations of his own back in his home state, where he had observed Sinclair's often bizarre behavior from close range. Sinclair could not keep a secret; he was honest to a fault and often indiscreet. Since he was doing God's work and the facts were usually on his side, Sinclair might justify a betrayal of confidence if it was for the public good. Someone had to warn the President not to be seduced by Sinclair. O'Connor, the comptroller of the currency, dashed off a telegram to Hyde Park advocating that a third party monitor the meeting, just to be safe.

Telegrams from California continued to arrive at the White House, asking (and in some cases begging) the President to repudiate Sinclair before it was too late. A leader of the National Roosevelt Association in Long Beach warned that Sinclair was nothing but a Communist. A top executive with Travelers Insurance in San Francisco reported that the citizens of California were "terror-stricken" and that prominent Democrats believed a Sinclair victory would lead to disintegration of the party and Socialist control throughout the United States. Even Democrats in other states expressed alarm. A Tucson man observed sadly that if the invitation to Hyde Park and the Hopkins endorsement represented a trend, the Democrats of Arizona "will rapidly lose confidence in the New Deal."

The most influential newspaper in the nation's capital, *The Washing-*

ton Post, seemed to take delight in what *Post* commentator Elliott Thurston called "the spectacular emergence of an avowed Marxian in the cloak of a New Dealer." Thurston waxed apocalyptic. Democrats around the country would revolt, he warned, and business leaders lose confidence unless FDR disavowed Sinclairism. "It may prove to be the event that forces an already overdue showdown on the New Deal's meaning and purpose," Thurston declared.

Perhaps attempting to lighten the mood, *Post* columnist H. I. Phillips referred to Dorothy Thompson, just banished from Germany, as Mrs. Upton Sinclair when she was really Mrs. Sinclair Lewis. This continued the popular tradition of confusing the two famous Sinclairs. Just this past Tuesday in California, Sinclair Lewis received four write-in votes for governor in the GOP primary. Herbert Hoover earned only two.

Five days after the wedding, Louis B. Mayer was still reeling from the marriage of his paramour, Jean Howard, to Charles K. Feldman. Mayer's wife was confined to a hospital outside Paris, delaying his return to Hollywood. And now, Mayer learned from his aides at MGM, Upton Sinclair seemed certain to sweep into office in November, unless L.B. took action.

The Mayers had been abroad for weeks, but the trip hadn't worked out quite the way L.B. had planned. Jean Howard, a glamorous young actress, meant to visit him on the sly. Mayer was infatuated with Howard, the twenty-four-year-old former Ziegfeld girl from Texas. Some of Mayer's associates considered it the silliest romance in Hollywood. The movie titan was like a bashful boy around her; his idea of courtship was finding her a good dentist.

Head of the largest Hollywood studio and the highest-salaried executive in the country, Mayer could have had women by the score, whatever his unattractive qualities (and he had many). He had an eye for beauty—after all, he was the man who discovered Greta Garbo—and, after years of playing the family man, he had lately become a social lion, dancing the rumba at the Trocadero and attending stag parties with United Artists boss Joe Schenck. Mayer was pudgy and crude and pushing fifty, but he was full of vigor and he could talk anyone into anything. The Talmud, he insisted, "says a man is not responsible for a sin committed by any part of his body below the waist." Sex was not often on his agenda, however. L.B. was a prude at heart, perhaps the most straitlaced man in town.

As Jean Howard sailed for France, Mayer thought about divorcing his ailing wife, right there in Paris. But the same ship that brought Jean Howard to Le Havre also carried a report from a Los Angeles detective agency. Howard, the memo revealed, had taken up with agent Charlie Feldman, who was known as the Jewish Clark Gable (he was darkly handsome and had a mustache). Charlie and Jean had even set a wedding date. When L.B. confronted the actress in his room at the Hôtel George V and she confirmed the account, Mayer went wild, thrashing on the floor and weeping. It took three people to keep him from throwing himself out a window. Then he gathered himself together and vowed to blackball Feldman from the movie industry.

Howard returned to America, where she married Feldman on August 25. Mayer, meanwhile, did everything possible, in penitence, to cure his wife, stricken with double pneumonia. But L.B. was getting itchy to return to California. Like a caged animal, he prowled the suite at the George V, barking orders across the room at MGM publicity chief Howard Strickling and talking into two or three telephones at once.

L.B.'s formidable secretary, Ida Koverman, kept him posted on the California governor's race. It was she who had introduced Mayer to power politics in the first place. Koverman met Mayer while working for the Coolidge campaign in Los Angeles in 1924, and enlisted L.B. as a volunteer. It wasn't hard: Los Angeles was rock-ribbed Republican, no group more so than the immigrant Jewish movie moguls. Mayer later hired Koverman, a capable but rather humorless widow, as his personal secretary; and through her friendship with Herbert Hoover (and his own relationship with W. R. Hearst), he quickly rose in the ranks of the Republican party. At the 1928 GOP national convention, he helped swing Hearst's crucial support from Andrew Mellon to Hoover. Mayer contributed heavily to the campaign, and as a reward he and his wife had the honor of being the Hoovers' first dinner guests in the White House. It was the thrill of Louie B's life: imagine a Russian immigrant, son of a junkman, sleeping in the White House.

Privately, Koverman referred to Mayer as a "small boy—new at the game and used to a great deal of attention." In 1932, L.B. campaigned tirelessly for the Republican ticket. He declared the Depression over and predicted a smashing GOP victory. This nearly destroyed his friendship with Hearst, who had endorsed FDR. Later, when Mayer visited the White House to meet the new president, he dropped his watch on FDR's desk and said, "Mr. President, I'm told that when anyone spends eighteen minutes with you, you have them in your pocket." Seventeen minutes later he walked out.

In politics, Mayer had no peers, not even a serious challenger, in Hollywood. As vice-chairman of the state Republican party, he liked nothing better than showing visiting politicians around the MGM lot, hosting luncheons in their honor, inviting them to his Santa Monica home (which was practically off-limits to mere movie people), and introducing them to Mae West. Consequently, Mayer had clout, and he intended to wield it mightily against Upton Sinclair.

Cables and telephone calls from Hollywood had shot across the Atlantic ever since primary day. Sinclair threatened to impose new taxes on the studios. . . . Sinclair felt film workers had the right to organize. . . . Sinclair, furthermore, was a Red. . . . Back in 1932, when Irving Thalberg, over L.B.'s objections, bought the movie rights to Sinclair's *The Wet Parade,* Mayer told his top producer he didn't want to see that Bolshevik "bum" around his studio. Three years later Mayer sure as hell didn't want Sinclair running his *state.* It was time to forget about losing Jean Howard and concentrate on destroying Upton Sinclair.

Jack Neylan, at his office in the Crocker Building in San Francisco, felt a bit annoyed. W. R. Hearst didn't seem to be taking the crisis in California all that seriously, judging by the latest directive from Munich. If Sinclair won, it would not be the end of the world, Hearst maintained. "Let's try get conservative Congress anyway," W.R. advised. It was not like Hearst to be so passive. Just that summer the Chief had mobilized opposition to the San Francisco general strike all the way from Europe; Neylan merely executed his orders.

Attempting once again to capture the Chief's attention, Neylan fired off an alarmist cable to Munich:

> NATIONAL ADMINISTRATION EMBARRASSED BY SINCLAIR NOMINATION, REFUSING TO SUPPORT HIM. IN VIEW OF HIS IDIOTIC PROGRAM THINK IT ESSENTIAL TO TAKE POSITIVE STAND AGAINST HIM. DANGER LIES IN FACT MERRIAM WEAK CANDIDATE AND HAIGHT STRONG AND ABLE CAMPAIGNER. STATE BECOMING AROUSED RAPIDLY . . . [SINCLAIR] ELECTION WOULD BE DISASTER AND STAMP CALIFORNIA AS NUT STATE. THINK SANE FORCES IN CALIFORNIA SHOULD ENDEAVOR TO CONCENTRATE ON ONE CANDIDATE. DO YOU WISH ME TO SEE WHAT CAN BE DONE ALONG THIS LINE?

While they were strong in number and influence, the anti-Sinclair forces in California faced several enormous hurdles. Some of their leaders, like Hearst and Mayer, were far from home. The political momentum in the state raced in the direction of the Democrats, following Roosevelt's surprising victory in the state in 1932 and the success of Sinclair's voter-registration drive. Just four years ago, Republicans outnumbered Democrats by nearly four to one; now the two parties were dead even. On Tuesday, Sinclair had polled 436,220 votes, outdistancing Governor Merriam's tally by almost 90,000. Nearly 10,000 Republicans took the trouble to write Sinclair's name on their ballots.

Many Democrats wished to flee their nominee, but that only pointed to the Republicans' biggest obstacle of all: Frank Finley Merriam. The Republican incumbent, who had taken office in June following the death of James ("Sunny Jim") Rolph, was an old war-horse as out of step with trend-happy California as a silent movie. A native of Iowa, he had served as speaker of the California assembly and as a campaign director for Coolidge and Hoover before his election as lieutenant governor in 1930. He was sixty-eight years old and looked every day of it. Behind his back, many of Merriam's associates called him Old Baldy.

Two days after the EPIC earthquake, signs of recovery nevertheless appeared. The board of directors of the California Real Estate Association resolved that "no man who boasts that he never has owned any real estate and does not believe in owning real estate as a matter of principle, should ever be elected to the office of governor of this state or any other state." The first Democrats-for-Merriam Club formed in Fresno. "Sinclair is no more a Democrat than a Hottentot," declared Henry Monroe, a leader of the San Francisco Democratic Club.

With the anti-Sinclair forces still in flux, it was up to the overwhelmingly Republican press to clarify the issues and sound the alarm. Although demographics and political alignments in California shifted rapidly, the editorial policies of most of the state's newspapers still reflected the reactionary views of their longtime owners. The *San Diego Union* called Sinclair "another bitter lesson the people must learn while groping their way back to the road they lost." In a front-page editorial, the *San Francisco Chronicle* labeled Sinclair a fanatic; his EPIC plan, "revolution by bankruptcy," would turn California into an "experimental cauldron." The constructive forces of California, regardless of faction or party, must rally behind Merriam in a holy crusade "worthy of nothing less than the best there is in all of us." But it was Harry Chandler's *Los Angeles Times* that led the press attack.

Sinclair and the *Times* had been feuding almost from the day the muckraker arrived in California in 1916. He had barely set foot in the state when a *Times* editorial identified him as an "effeminate young man with a fatuous smile" who made "no secret of his sympathy with dynamiters and murderers." Sinclair had responded by labeling the *Times* "the propaganda organ of the forces of repression," adding that he had "never heard anybody in Los Angeles maintain that the *Times* is an honest newspaper, or a newspaper which serves the public interest."

Now it was up to the *Times,* as defender of the status quo in southern California—Hearst's papers were far too erratic for that—to set the tone for the anti-Sinclair campaign, and it rose to the challenge in a few hundred sensationally well-chosen words. Under the headline IS THIS STILL AMERICA? the editors of the *Times* declared that the nomination of Upton Sinclair had created a crisis not only for California, but for America. It was up to the California voter to decide whether the ideals on which the nation was founded were to be perpetuated or shattered:

> What is eating at the heart of America are [*sic*] a maggot-like horde of Reds who have scuttled to [Sinclair's] support. . . . They are termites secretly and darkly eating into the foundations and the roof beams of everything that the American heart has held dear and sacred. . . . To this end they rally uncleanly to every sore spot. They drop poison in every bruise. . . .

Unfortunately, the editorial continued, "the foe is camouflaged. The Reds are not lined up in solid ranks. Their menace is secret and subtle. Their agent may be your cook or your trusted friend or the movie star whom you admire on the screen. . . ." Even if Upton Sinclair was only a harmless visionary himself, he was "opening the gate of our defenses to a vicious horde" who had every intention of fostering a violent revolution.

Readers of the *Times* had heard this kind of rhetoric before, just recently during the tumult over the San Francisco longshoremen's strike and the wave of vigilante attacks against farm workers in the Central Valley. So the *Times* had to raise the stakes, dramatize the danger, and clearly explain the crucial difference between labor agitation and a Communist assault on the statehouse. "We are standing at a fatal crossing of the roads," the editorial sang. "There can be no turning back. Either we take the Red path, or we close that gate right now—forever. This year and the next few years to come will tell the story and settle the fate of our children and our children's great-grandchildren. A revolution has been predicted for the United States—to come somewhere around the years 1940 to 1945.

"It can easily be made to happen by the seeds that are sowed this year. Or the weed sprouts can be cut down.

"By a twist of fate it is for the people of California to decide for America."

———

Earl Warren took a break from his duties as Alameda County district attorney to accompany Robert Gordon Sproul, president of the University of California, to the American Legion's noontime anti-Communist rally at Oakland's Municipal Auditorium. He could have skipped the event; Warren had only token opposition in his race for a third term in office. But the forty-three-year-old D.A. was a rising star in the Republican party, and a new state chairman would be named within a month. According to party rules it was time for a Republican from northern California to get the nod.

It shaped up as an important autumn for tall, strapping Earl Warren. With his reelection assured, he campaigned to put on the ballot an amendment to the state constitution extending the civil service system. For Republicans, whose one-party rule in the state was drawing to a close, this was more of a necessity than an exercise in good government. Patronage was wonderful so long as the GOP held power, but no one wanted to give Upton Sinclair a chance to play God.

Back in his law-school days at Berkeley, Warren had considered Sinclair one of his favorite authors. He used to go down to the First and Last Chance Saloon, the hangout for sailors on the Oakland estuary frequented by Sinclair's friend and fellow socialist Jack London. Earl would buy a glass of beer, sit down at a rickety card table, and listen to London talk about his experiences in the far north and the South Seas. Warren, still known to his old school friends as Pink or Pinky—because of his complexion, not his politics—had no use for radicals now. Last week, in fact, he had sent a form letter to some of his constituents thanking them for joining with other citizens "in protecting life and property from the activities of Communists during the recent general strike."

Public speaking was not one of Warren's strengths, so he was happy to let Bob Sproul, another young man in a hurry, step front and center at the rally. Sproul, a gifted orator, had considerably more experience dealing with Communists than Warren. The University of California, by some accounts, was infested with Reds. Whether this was true was beside the point: it was the public perception, the newspapers exploited it, and so Sproul had to confront it daily.

For the past month, Sproul had been summoning professors to his office and gently telling them that he had received information that they were members of pro-Communist groups or were taking part in the activities of the Social Problems Club, which he had banned from campus. Sproul notified the president of the Alumni Association that he had been identified as a Red sympathizer and suggested that he "vigorously combat" that perception. The intimidation tactics worked. Most of the suspects promised to sever their links to leftist groups, and some even offered to act as informers. Others felt so threatened they confessed they favored Upton Sinclair—apparently wishing to come clean before an informer fingered *them.*

The university-wide crackdown did not remain secret for long, although no one suspected Bob Sproul of taking part in it. In mid-August, *The Nation* reported that "liberal professors are terrorized with threats of expulsion" as part of the current witch-hunt in California. This meant trouble for Sproul, who in just four years as head of the university had established himself, along with the University of Chicago's Robert M. Hutchins, at the forefront of the enlightened new generation of college leaders.

Sproul had managed to steer clear of the California governor's race so far, but Upton Sinclair alarmed him. Years ago, Sinclair had referred to Sproul's domain as the University of the Black Hand, dominated by "sycophants" and "sluggards"—where immorality "is more common than scholarship." Just yesterday, Sproul informed an adviser to the *Daily Californian* that it would be "unfortunate" if the student newspaper ran an interview with Sinclair, which would provide a "sounding board" for the EPIC candidate on campus.

The Oakland Municipal Auditorium was hopping this afternoon. The American Legion had lately earned notoriety for supporting (and in some cases leading) vigilante bands that beat up hundreds of labor organizers in California. According to this week's *Nation,* "thousands" of workers had "been gassed, had their skulls cracked, been trampled upon and shot. . . . The class-conscious workers of California are living in terror today. Except in Los Angeles, their movement has been driven underground." Just this morning two farm workers were shot and scores more injured in clashes with police and self-styled security personnel in Salinas. A Legion official recently insisted that his group did not intend to "go out and string up anybody, but it wouldn't affect my eyesight if it did."

For Robert G. Sproul, the Legion's anti-Communist rally represented a splendid opportunity to reason with his university's harshest critics. It might be indiscreet to boast about intimidating radical professors, so Sproul took the high road of principle instead. On campus, no one is punished for his beliefs, Sproul told the crowd, and every *ism* is taught: from socialism to nudism. Freedom of thought, speech, and assembly is revered, and despite all of this freedom only a tiny number of faculty members and students chose to be Communists. "The University," Sproul said, "respects personal belief as the private concern of the individual."

In case this sounded a little too liberal, Sproul eagerly assured the audience of his own patriotism. "I am no flag-waving Jingo," Sproul insisted, "but I have grown infinitely weary of the deprecation of America and American institutions during the past few years. We are not even approaching political, economic or social bankruptcy." The path out of the Depression did not veer to the left but "lies straight ahead," Sproul declared. That seemed to make clear where this "sluggard" stood on Upton Sinclair, and it surely satisfied his friend Earl Warren, whose future as a statewide candidate might hinge on how ruthlessly this sentiment could be exploited over the next nine weeks, perhaps even by Warren himself.

It should have been a tough day for the President. Negotiations to stem the first nationwide textile strike, scheduled to start Saturday night, had broken down, sending shock waves through mill towns from New England to Alabama. But at least the cotton workers had jobs. William Green, president of the American Federation of Labor, charged in Washington that unemployment had risen steadily since May and demanded that the President do something about it. To make matters worse, FDR received from Jim Farley the confidential results of an ongoing *Literary Digest* poll suggesting for the first time a downturn in the President's popularity.

Newspaper editors across the country, like their counterparts in New

York and Washington, savored FDR's "Sinclair problem." In light of Sinclair's triumph, asked the *Dallas Weekly,* "how could anyone say that the launching of the American Liberty League came a moment too soon?" Calling Sinclair the apotheosis of the New Deal, the *Boston Transcript* observed that California had offered itself as "the proving ground for the greatest experiment in socialism ever attempted in this country." One of the most telling charges against the New Deal was that it was socialist at heart, and Sinclair's proclamation that he was a New Dealer lent color to this charge. There was no way for FDR to treat Sinclair as anything less than a blood brother, *Baltimore Sun* political columnist Frank Kent observed. He had jumped into the New Deal bed with Roosevelt and could not be tossed out, even though "the sudden emergence of the most prominent socialist in the United States as a New Deal Democrat" would drive conservatives out of the party and boost the pro-business Liberty League, Kent predicted.

If the President was concerned about any of this he didn't show it as he sat in his car for two hours at the Dutchess County Fair watching the horse show and chatting with old friends. Returning to Hyde Park, the President's motorcade stopped at a farm where a thousand supporters had gathered to hear Roosevelt's annual welcome-home speech. From the front porch of a rambling farmhouse, Roosevelt disputed a columnist's claim that he had put on twelve pounds. OK, he had gained weight, but it was only two pounds, and now he resolved to take off five.

The off-the-cuff remarks continued in this vein. FDR fretted about spending two more years in Washington away from Hyde Park, but no one took this as a pledge not to run for reelection. Quips aside, he eased into what he allowed was a sermon. His recent trip out West had profoundly affected him, he confessed. Although great public-works projects were underway, millions of farmers suffered in areas stricken by harsh weather and overcultivation. Congress had appropriated half a billion dollars in farm relief, but drought continued to spread, and these funds would prove inadequate. The President plunged ahead, apparently speaking from the heart. When this happened, his words usually pulled him to the ideological left, undoing all of a previous day's caution. He was an emotional radical, a political middle-of-the-roader. Today he seemed to favor experimental local recovery programs, not unlike EPIC. He even cited Lord Bryce's admiration for America's "trying-out system" in different states.

Then, speaking for himself, Roosevelt said he was certain that "the good people of our town will be willing to go along and cooperate in a big program that has nothing to do with party and nothing to do with section, which is merely trying to be square to all Republicans and Democrats and Socialists and everybody else, no matter what they call themselves, no matter to which party or church they belong." It was hard to tell whether the words just tumbled out or if the combative Roosevelt wanted to show cynical journalists and jittery party bosses that being in bed with socialist experimenters who supported his "big program" was nothing to be ashamed of.

Returning home, Roosevelt took tea with Lewis W. Douglas, his embattled budget director, whose efforts to cut spending on public works and other New Deal programs irritated the President. Douglas dropped a bombshell, informing FDR that he planned to resign. Whatever their differences, the President was not ready for that.

Despite, or perhaps because of, the Douglas resignation, FDR was in a jolly mood when he arrived at Henry Morgenthau's nearby farm in Hopewell Junction for a big clambake. He laughed, he joked, he joined in the singing of many songs. It was as if some great burden had been lifted from his shoulders. Morgenthau hadn't seen his boss in such good spirits since FDR took office. Roosevelt was finding out who the real friends of the New Deal were. Maybe it was true what they were saying in California, that party labels now meant nothing. Democrats like Lew Douglas and Al Smith opposed FDR, Republicans such as Hiram Johnson and Bob La Follette supported him—and then there was Upton Sinclair. Perhaps it was time to take off the kid gloves and go to war with the reactionaries.

While Franklin Roosevelt tried to make the best of a dark day, Upton Sinclair basked in the sunshine of sudden celebrityhood. His quirky Pasadena residence was in an uproar. An unlisted telephone wouldn't stop ringing, and one visitor after another appeared at the front door. The living room served as a political clubhouse, a newspaper office, a portrait studio. Sinclair posed at his typewriter, gathered figs from a tree, and shook his fist for the benefit of photographers. White suit buttoned to the chest, he stood in his backyard and, squinting into the sun, peered in the direction of a Paramount newsreel camera and said, "We are behind President Roosevelt in his effort to give the New Deal to the whole nation. We are resting upon the consent of the entire people—and we expect to get it." Sinclair hadn't merely embraced the New Deal; in California he had engulfed it.

It was almost one year to the day since Upton Sinclair set a remarkable social movement in motion, simply by changing his registration from Socialist to Democrat. A group of Democrats in Santa Monica led by Gilbert Stevenson, former owner of the landmark Miramar Hotel, had insisted that Sinclair run for governor. On four previous occasions in two states he had failed to tally more than sixty thousand votes running for office on the Socialist line, but now California seethed with discontent and Stevenson argued that Sinclair might be able to win as a Democrat. Sinclair, a constant crusader, could not resist the siren call. "I seem to have lost interest in novels," he wrote to a friend, Fulton Oursler, back East. "That Hitler thing has made me realize the seriousness of our danger." He had written enough; what the world needed now, he said, was a deed.

So, on September 1, 1933, Sinclair quietly switched his party affiliation from Socialist to Democrat, and started constructing a platform to run on, drawing on the writings of Edward Bellamy and some of his own books, from *The Industrial Republic* (1907) to *The Way Out* (1933). A few days later he completed a fable entitled *I, Governor of California, and How I Ended Poverty.* It pictured a certain well-known California writer rallying a mass movement behind a twelve-point EPIC plan, which spurs him to victory in the 1934 governor's race. Putting his platform into practice, Governor Sinclair eradicates poverty without much fuss (the only poor person left is a religious hermit who lives in a cave) and retires after one term in office to resume his career as a novelist.

By the time Sinclair had finished the manuscript, the story was becoming more and more real to him, so he self-published ten thousand copies of *I, Governor* and officially announced his candidacy. This marked "the first time an historian has set out to make his history true," Sinclair boasted. Within weeks, *I, Governor* had become the hottest-selling book in California—it was sixty-four pages long and sold for twenty cents—and eager Sinclairites had organized several dozen End Poverty League chapters across the state. A few months after that, sales of the book topped ninety thousand and EPIC clubs exceeded a thousand.

Now, *I, Governor* read more like prophecy than fantasy. Congratulatory telegrams arrived at the Sinclair household in Pasadena from Oswald Garrison Villard, editor of *The Nation,* and Edward M. House, former adviser to Woodrow Wilson. One of the great American attorneys, Samuel Untermyer, wired from New York that he had analyzed Sinclair's platform and found his policies "sound and workable."

Even more significant was a wire from Dr. Michael Shadid, a member of the executive committee of the national Socialist party. For nearly a year, the SP had been in an uproar over Sinclair's change in allegiance. (Among those denouncing Sinclair's switch: his own son, David.) Even after Tuesday's landslide, Socialist leader Norman Thomas termed the Sinclair campaign a "tragedy to himself and to the cause of radicalism." Upton was getting it from all sides. Democrats accused him of being a Socialist, and the Socialists disowned him for running as a Democrat. Politicians said he should stick to writing, and writers charged that he was selling out his art to politics.

From Dr. Shadid, however, came this profound expression of forgiveness: "You have justified your 'defection,' " he wrote. Perhaps other SP leaders would jump on the bandwagon, recognizing that the Sinclair heresy might just be the greatest thing to happen to the Socialist cause since the days of Eugene V. Debs.

The most fervent testimonial, however, came from Mr. and Mrs. Clyde C. Marshaw, a Los Angeles couple on relief who on primary day became parents of a baby boy and named him Upton Sinclair Marshaw.

Night fell. Dressed in a gray three-piece suit and topcoat, Sinclair gathered up his battered suitcases and bid fond farewell to his wife, Craig, who was so self-conscious about her appearance—she was no longer a Southern belle—she would neither pose for photographers nor see her husband off at the station. When Sinclair, accompanied by two young assistants, met the train at midnight, he found a mob waiting to wish him well. Reporters cried out questions. Did he think Merriam would put up much of a fight? Yes, because Wall Street would send ten million dollars to California to destroy EPIC. Did he still consider himself a Socialist? "I'm through theorizing; I'm a Democrat now. I consider the President my boss." Sinclair pointed to Roosevelt's speech that afternoon as proof that Socialists were being invited into the party to push FDR's "big program."

Then, with a wave to the crowd, Upton Sinclair disappeared into a Pullman car, and at twelve-fifteen the *Santa Fe Chief* rumbled off into the black of night, New York bound.

AUGUST 31

FRIDAY

Aimee Semple McPherson told her troubles to Guido Orlando in a room at the Commodore Hotel in New York. The messy dissolution of her marriage to nightclub singer David Hutton had stained an image already soiled by an implausible kidnapping in 1926 and Sinclair Lewis's portrait of the Aimee-like Sharon Falconer in *Elmer Gantry.* Sister Aimee's financial control of the Angelus Temple back in Los Angeles was under siege. Two days ago, the publicist Paul Block, just back from Germany, took her name in vain, calling Adolf Hitler "a male Aimee McPherson." What could she do, Aimee asked Orlando, a show-business impresario, to pull herself out of the doldrums?

By most standards, Sister Aimee wasn't doing badly at all. Thousands of the faithful continued to pack her magnificent Echo Park temple, one of the largest church buildings in the country, donating enough money to keep her Foursquare Gospel ministry growing. Newly slender, her thick hair dyed blond, Aimee McPherson was the Sarah Bernhardt of revivalism, her elaborate pageants a mixture of Pentecostalism and Holy Rollerism by way of Broadway. A poet once imagined himself onstage at Angelus Temple standing in Aimee's shoes:

Bearer of Gospel-glory I
With singing angels in my sky,
And earthly chorus at command,
The trumpets of my silver band!
The cripples to my temple crowd,
I heal them, and they shout aloud.

(The poet was Upton Sinclair.)

Aimee lived in a mansion, had a shiny new car, and spared no expense when it came to clothes. Radio station KFSG, emanating from the temple, was one of the most powerful in Los Angeles. Her "native angels" guarded the radio tower "love-wand," Edmund Wilson observed, to make sure that "not a tittle or vibration of their mistress's kind warm voice goes astray as it speeds to you in your sitting-room and tells you how sweet Jesus has been to her." The soup kitchens Aimee sponsored in downtown Los Angeles fed thousands, and the Angelus Temple commissary operated one of the most sophisticated relief operations in the city. The poor adored her. On the whole, she was "a very remarkable woman," as Will Rogers put it, who did "much good."

But Aimee wanted it all; and she knew that although her name was nationally known, her impact outside California was slight. She constantly battled lawsuits. Angelus Temple, she complained, was forty thousand dollars in debt, and she wanted to do something dramatic to make people forget the sex scandal that surrounded her disappearance in 1926. Who better to consult than Guido Orlando—an evangelist of shtick?

The pair had met briefly in 1933 while Aimee was in New York seeking financial backers for a traveling tent show, *The Rich Man and Lazarus.* The script was even worse than its title, Guido decided. At the age of forty-four, Aimee was a desperately unhappy woman, he believed, but he kind of liked her. While not blessed with spectacular natural beauty, she projected an aura that could outshine a roomful of Marlene Dietrichs.

When Aimee returned to New York later in 1933, she again asked Guido for help. Major Bowes was threatening to terminate her engagement at the Capitol Theatre—her first crack at legit show biz—due to sparse attendance. The cancellation would cast a pall over her entire barnstorming tour, and was doubly embarrassing because just down Broadway her estranged husband was appearing at the Palace, billed as

"Big Boy, the Baritone of the Angelus Temple." Guido begged Bowes for more time, calling Sister Aimee the "greatest draw in America." Then he hired a bunch of actors, dressed them in rented police uniforms, and instructed them to mill around outside the theater. Naturally, a crowd formed, and the real cops who arrived only added to the hubbub. Guido called in reporters and cameramen and urged his actors to start a couple of fights. Onlookers lined up at the ticket office to find out what sparked all this excitement.

Aimee took Guido on the road with her after that. It was a battle to break even in every city. In Philadelphia, dressed as an angel, Aimee knocked out a professional boxer in a red devil's costume. Heading for Virginia Beach, Guido learned that the advance sale in that city was practically nil, so he had Sister Aimee taken off the train and rushed to a hospital by ambulance. That night she appeared on stage wearing thick white makeup, as if risen from the dead. By the end of the tour, Aimee had logged fifteen thousand miles and preached 336 sermons, reaching an audience of millions over the radio.

Now, as the autumn of 1934 approached, Aimee Semple McPherson was back at the Commodore after another national tour. Yesterday, *Variety* hinted that she was about to forsake the Angelus Temple for "the more lucrative and less troublesome vocation of one-night stand revivals." Aimee again asked Guido Orlando to consider flacking a revised version of *The Rich Man and Lazarus* for which she had written over sixty new songs. The pageant, Guido responded, would only make her a laughingstock. OK, what do *you* suggest? Sister Aimee asked. Well, he replied, anticommunism appears to be a rising sentiment, particularly in Los Angeles, and especially among the press and the financial elite Aimee wished to impress.

This would set Sister Aimee's healing ministry in a new direction, perhaps a dangerous one. Until now she had steered clear of politics, confining her anticommunism pretty much to its militantly godless character. Many of her followers were among the dispossessed, who had the most sympathy for the ideals, if not the practice, of communism. Most of them probably favored the radical candidate Upton Sinclair. Aimee had sided with Sinclair in various moral crusades over the years. He had even moderated the celebrated debate at Angelus Temple between McPherson and film star Walter Huston—and did everything possible to make sure Aimee's Prohibitionist argument won. Sinclair's puritan values were exemplary, and if he really ended poverty in California, Aimee's collection plates would overflow.

Still, when it came to theater, what greater satanic opponent could Aimee conjure than atheistic communism? She might play a modern-day Joan of Arc wielding God's terrible swift sword against the Reds.

———

Rash acts were occurring everywhere, as if all of the despair, anger, and lunacy kept largely in check by the hopeful early months of the New Deal had suddenly been set loose. Armed troops swept into New Orleans in support of Senator Huey Long's corruption probe, seizing and beating reporters. In drought-stricken Waxahachie, Texas, a rainmaker was killed when a "cloud-blasting" bomb he was about to release from an airplane exploded prematurely. In Tarrytown, New York, a house painter from the Bronx, John Smiukese, strolled into the gallery displaying Jere Miah II's *The Nightmare of 1934,* flung the contents of a bottle of varnish remover across the surface of the painting, and touched a match to it. Then, as the canvas burst into flames, he ripped the painting from the wall and started to demolish it.

Seized by gallery attendants, he was taken to the office of Charles Birch-Field, president of the Westchester Institute of Fine Arts, where Smiukese, a Russian émigré, explained, "I had the day off and decided that something should be done about this picture, which is disgraceful to the whole nation. This art business up here is the meanest racket in the whole country." Asked what he disliked about the painting, he replied, "It was all right, except for including Mrs. Roosevelt. I thought it was a disgrace to bring a woman into a political thing of this kind. Anyway, it wasn't good art. It wasn't worth five cents. It should have been destroyed a long time ago. There is still some chivalry in this country."

Placed under arrest, Smiukese faced a judge within hours, pleaded guilty to malicious mischief, and was sentenced to six months in jail. "I guess," Birch-Field observed, "that this means art should keep its nose out of politics." Jere Miah II added, "I can understand where an inarticulate person would use fire instead of a brush to express his feelings."

A few miles north, Franklin Roosevelt vented his own pent-up emotions while taking a bath at Hyde Park. When Henry Morgenthau entered the room, having been summoned from Hopewell Junction to hear the news about the Lew Douglas resignation, FDR sat straight up in the tub, looked him in the eye, and declared, "Henry, in the words of John Paul Jones, we have just begun to fight." (A navy man like the President, John Paul Jones was the subject of a screen treatment Roosevelt wrote for Paramount in 1923.) Morgenthau wasn't sure what this statement encompassed, but it sounded promising and terrifying at the same time.

Some of Morgenthau's fellow New Dealers would soon arrive to take part in the economic summit conference planned for the holiday weekend. The day after Labor Day, Upton Sinclair would materialize at Hyde Park. Marvin McIntyre had just wired Sinclair care of the rail depot at Gallup, New Mexico: See you at five o'clock Tuesday. Teatime at Hyde Park.

Artie Samish, the self-proclaimed secret boss of California, was in a jam. John B. Pelletier, the bum he'd plucked off skid row to run for the state assembly in Los Angeles, had won the Democratic primary on Tuesday, as an EPIC candidate no less. Now the joke had to stop, or did it? The Pelletier saga was a scriptwriter's dream, Artie decided, and it would be a shame if it didn't have a happy ending.

The state's leading lobbyist, Arthur H. Samish was a larger-than-life character in every way. Tall and portly, wearing a straw hat and an innocent grin, he was part Falstaff, part carnival barker. Instantly recognizable around the capitol, Samish was not well known to newsmen back home in San Francisco. That was all right with Artie: the less the public knew, the more influence he could wield, and the more money he could make (he'd already made his first million). Samish was so powerful that many of the other lobbyists in Sacramento lobbied *him.* Once, when Cecil B. DeMille proposed legislation that would curb union organizing, a lawyer for the famous director made the mistake of informing Artie that C.B. would hold him accountable if the bill failed to pass. "No one gives ultimatums to Art Samish!" the lobbyist thundered. "*Now* just try and get that lovin' bill through!"

Samish was a trailblazer, a new type of political chieftain. With the decline of the political parties, there was a vacuum that he was only too willing to fill. If the governor and the party bosses no longer could control the legislature, the special interests would, and Samish was their man in Sacramento, the Guy Who Got Things Done for the bus companies and the bankers, the racetracks and the railroads. Samish boasted that when he did business, he could quickly tell whether a legislator wanted "a baked potato, a girl, or money." He joked that he could start a riot in the rotunda of the state capitol any time he wanted by simply scattering a few dollar bills on the floor.

Purchasing votes was unnecessary, however, if the legislator could be bought, or brought into line, at election time. And so, in the spring of 1934, Samish had acceded to a request from a client in the beer industry who wanted to throw a scare into Clair Woolwine, a state assemblyman whose independent manner aggravated the brewers. Artie not only bought and sold legislators, he elected and unelected them, but this time he was stumped. Where could he find someone willing to run against Woolwine, who was accustomed to winning the nominations of both major parties in his slum-ridden district? With a two-thousand-dollar donation from the beer magnate in hand, Samish's assistant, Bill Jasper, volunteered to visit EPIC headquarters in search of a potential patsy. At the EPIC office, an old storefront, Jasper discovered forty campaign workers, disheveled and unshaven, who had been recruited from soup kitchens and flophouses. They were tying up bundles of campaign literature for four bits a day.

"Any of you fellows from the Forty-fourth District?" Jasper inquired.

"I am," replied one fellow with bad teeth and a protruding chin. He said his name was John Pelletier. Although he had a degree from Bates College in Maine, Pelletier was presently on relief and sharing a ramshackle house on top of Bunker Hill with ten other men.

"How'd you like to run for the state legislature?" Jasper asked. Pelletier looked askance. "Come with me," Jasper instructed, and Pelletier followed.

After feeding his candidate and buying him a new suit, Jasper rang Samish at his Flood Building office in San Francisco and asked whether he could proceed with the campaign. Spruced up, Pelletier didn't look half-bad. "Sure, go ahead," Artie said, "we can have a lot of laughs with this one."

Jasper printed up a hundred thousand cards sporting a photograph of the candidate taken when he was in college. Pelletier stumped the district, passing out the cards, gaining the support of the EPIC organization and his old buddies on the Hill. On primary day, he defeated Woolwine by a thousand votes out of nine thousand cast, becoming one of more than fifty EPIC candidates running for the legislature as Democrats this fall.

Still, Pelletier's prospects weren't good, for Woolwine had the GOP nomination. "The fun's over," the beer magnate informed Samish. But Pelletier had twelve hundred dollars left over from the primary, and Bill Jasper had taken a liking to "the little guy."

"And you'd like to lay that twelve hundred on his campaign?" Artie Samish inquired. This was too rich.

"Well—yes," Jasper stuttered.

Samish pondered the proposal. At election time, Artie's motto was "Select and elect": select the candidate most favorable to his clients' interests, and then make sure that he was elected, sparing no expense. A new breed of political boss, Artie didn't care whether the candidate was Republican or Democrat, rich man or poor man, progressive or reactionary. A party machine could be challenged in elections; the Samish machine was protected by anonymity.

But where did Pelletier fit in, now that he had served his function? It didn't make sense to try to elect the bum, because Pelletier was so naïve he didn't know that Artie owned him. That made him potentially dangerous. He was an EPIC candidate, to boot. This morning the *Los Angeles Times* called the EPIC sweep of assembly races in the south "one of the startling features" of the election. Still, an opportunity like this didn't come along very often, and Artie, the eternal child, loved to light firecrackers under the seats of stiff-necked incumbents.

Besides, he had other things to worry about right now, such as making sure that Frank Merriam remained in office. Merriam had just asked Artie to set up his campaign headquarters and raise money to keep it operating. To Samish, Merriam was nothing more than a necessary evil. Old Baldy, at least, would respect Samish's fiefdom; Sinclair might try to appropriate it.

Distracted by the governor's contest, Samish told Jasper to go all out for Pelletier. "It's no skin off my ass," Artie confessed. "Go ahead and have your fun."

Ray Haight spent the day trying to turn the Merriam-Sinclair showdown into a three-sided donnybrook. Haight must have done something right: the Republicans reportedly offered him an appointment to the U.S. Senate if he'd quit the race.

For someone never elected to office, Haight was having a riotous impact as a third-party candidate. Sinclair supporters charged that the young Los Angeles attorney, a former state corporation commissioner, was not in the race to win but simply to draw votes from Uppie, while the GOP declared he was out to destroy Merriam. No wonder everyone questioned Haight's motives. He was a Republican supporter of the New Deal who had voted for Norman Thomas for president in 1932. A clean-cut man of principle, Haight's political patron was Fighting Bob Shuler, the bigoted, fundamentalist preacher. A foe of big business, Haight accepted financial backing from, among others, Leonard Firestone of the wealthy tire family. As a descendant of a former governor, Haight explained, he felt a special duty to lead the state to better days, and he could only do that by improvising his way into office.

His hopes rested on the fact that Sinclair and Merriam together received only 40 percent of the total vote in the primary. Haight had managed to secure two ballot lines, as candidate of both the Progressive party (led by Hiram Johnson) and the Commonwealth party (controlled by Bob Shuler). If Haight renounced Shuler and ran solely as a Progressive, W.R. Hearst might support him. Hearst was sentimental about the Progressives—he still backed Hiram Johnson in every election. It was not out of the question that Senator Johnson himself would support Haight, and if he did, Sinclair was dead. A. P. Giannini, founder of Transamerica and the Bank of America, already favored him, and Haight had at least one friend at the White House: J.F.T. O'Connor.

Everyone wanted Haight's ear. Today he lunched with John B. Elliott, the Democratic leader in southern California who had just denounced Sinclair. Wallace Beery and Robert Montgomery, the actors, endorsed Haight, as did Judge Robert Kenny, Francis J. Heney (one of the great Progressives), and football star Ernie Nevers. The *Stockton Record* called Haight a "young, vote-getting Lochinvar out of the south, who must be reckoned with in the finals." A columnist for the Los Angeles *Daily News* went so far as to suggest that Merriam was a non-factor in the race. If liberals in both major parties united behind Haight, the *San Francisco News* suggested, he just might win.

Ray Haight tried to make clear that he was not doing Merriam's bidding in an effort to draw liberal votes from Sinclair. Referring to "Merriamites and their ilk," Haight predicted that if "these political chiselers and racketeers are permitted to dominate California for another four years, instead of 400,000 it will be 1,400,000 votes for radicalism." Already he'd heard all sorts of proposals and deals, "intimated to get me out of the campaign," Haight cheerfully reported. "But I went into this fight on a principle. It's a fight to the finish, and if anybody gets out, it's going to be Frank Merriam."

Haight was off to a good start, running down the middle, but supporters feared that soon he would smash headlong into the perception that in the caldron of extremes that was America in 1934, moderation was no virtue. Among the leading proponents of this view were Mark Sullivan and David Lawrence, two of the founding members of that new breed of syndicated opinionmonger known as the political columnist.

Calling the Sinclair victory "unprecedented," Mark Sullivan announced that the terms *Republican* and *Democrat* had almost ceased to have any meaning, overshadowed as they were by the split of the entire country into two camps, socialist and "traditionalist." With the formation of the Liberty League and now Sinclair's miracle, "the division of the country between conservatives and radicals," Sullivan observed from his perch in New York, "is greatly accelerated."

In Washington, David Lawrence had been agitating for party upheaval for months. Lawrence wanted to liquidate the Republican party, with GOP stalwarts joining Democrats like Al Smith to form a Constitution party, the new home for all "liberal conservatives." The other national grouping would be the Socialistic Democrats—no longer just an epithet, but a full-fledged political party—led by such radicals as George Norris and Franklin Roosevelt. Now, in the wake of Sinclair's victory, David Lawrence believed his dream of a ghettoized New Deal was coming true. "California's decision to award the Democratic nomination for governor to a socialist is a milestone in the development of the American party system," Lawrence gushed. "It means the eventual realignment of parties in the United States."

Over lunch with Frank Merriam in San Francisco, Herbert Hoover offered to help shore up the governor's GOP base. Hoover did not believe in reaching out to fickle Democrats. He was one person who did not buy the David Lawrence–Mark Sullivan notion of a coalition of conservative Republicans and moderate Democrats, even though he stood to gain from such an alignment more than anyone.

The former president, just now emerging from political hibernation, still harbored a grudge against the Democrats for misrepresenting his record in 1932. The Liberty Leaguers had repented too late, and he doubted the purity of their motives. Hoover believed that any attempt to forge a bipartisan alliance of anti-Roosevelt elements would lead to disaster for the Republican party. The Liberty League had no grassroots Democratic support and GOP agitation on its behalf would only incite true Democrats to a fever pitch.

Hoover applied the same reasoning to California. Plenty of Democrats would split away from Sinclair without any special pleading from the Republicans. Since the two parties were nearly evenly matched in terms of voter registration, all Merriam had to do to win was hold his GOP support, and that's where Hoover might play a role. He would concentrate on preventing thousands of Republican progressives from shifting comfortably to Haight or taking a flier on Sinclair. Hoover also offered to raise campaign funds and, with Chester Rowell, editor of the *San Francisco Chronicle,* draft a moderate party platform for Merriam to run on.

Just yesterday, Hoover had labeled Merriam an "ultra-conservative" in a letter to Frank Knox, publisher of the *Chicago Daily News.* Now, over lunch in San Francisco, the former president, whose own political comeback was about to follow a rightward course, pointed Merriam down the only path to victory in California in November, and that road ran left.

Portentousness reigned, and there was in the national press a solid strain of incredulity as well, a determination not to take Upton Sinclair seriously because it was, well, only California. Calling the state "incalculable" and Los Angeles, where EPIC was strongest, "most puzzling of all, with an inordinate bent for freak religions and an insatiable curiosity in genealogy," the *Boston Herald* denied that the Sinclair victory had any implications whatsoever. *The Boston Globe* muttered, "What is the matter with California? That is the farthest shift to the left ever made by voters of a major party in this country."

Showing the stylistic influence of its sage, H. L. Mencken, the *Baltimore Sun* confessed to an irresistible temptation to congratulate Sinclair, a Baltimore boy who made good, and to feel that "if ever a community deserved a radical Socialist governor, with an EPIC plan, that community is California." The state's outrageous antilabor laws, its hounding of radicals like Tom Mooney into prison, "plus the climate, contribute to the feeling that Upton Sinclair as governor would be an appropriate hair shirt for California to wear in penitence," the *Sun* insisted.

For the past year the press had portrayed southern California—in particular, "Louse Angeles"—as the home of flapdoodle, hokum, and boob-bait. It was, at any rate, a hothouse of offbeat economic theories. Utopian ideas circulated so freely that Santa Monica's favorite citizen, Will Rogers, had to amend his most famous quip, "All I know is what

I read in the papers," adding, ". . . or what I gather from pamphlets that people send me solving the world situation."

The four major California movements—technocracy, the Utopian Society, EPIC, and Dr. Francis E. Townsend's Old-Age Revolving Pension scheme—each emerged in the L.A. area, where a million refugees from the Midwest had recently settled. Some had crossed the Rockies to retire or improve their health; others simply wanted to work in a sunnier clime. At first they made Los Angeles even more reactionary than it was before. Finding food abundant and living expenses low, they cared little about such abstract issues as free speech and the rights of laborers. Suddenly, in 1930, hard times hit, and they became acquainted with want. The Depression scuttled their investments, seized their bungalows, and stripped them bare; they had lost everything but hope. Now many looked to a messiah to set things right.

Technocracy caught on first. Its founder, Howard Scott, proposed that technicians run the economy using the full efficiency of automation. One of Scott's famous friends, author Theodore Dreiser, felt that if an Engineer Dictator took control of raw materials, machinery, and labor, he would smother Americans under an avalanche of goods and services.

Scott's theories, publicized by Manchester Boddy's *Daily News,* gained a wide audience in Los Angeles, but were too technical to spark a mass movement. Three technocrats therefore decided to form a secret order, the Utopian Society, to mystify the scientific jargon. Strange rituals and stage presentations depicted a culture of abundance made possible by producing "for use" instead of for profit. Utopians were known by their numbers, not by their names. (The emcee at one gathering was introduced as "1 × 1809 × 56.") The Society grew so popular during the summer of '34, it claimed a paid membership of half a million.

Meanwhile, down in Long Beach, a gaunt, white-haired physician named Townsend, outraged by the sight of old people rummaging through garbage cans for scraps to eat, challenged the federal government to pay everyone past the age of sixty $200 a month. Money for the fund would be raised by a special sales tax. The payments would spur the economy in two ways: aging workers could retire, providing jobs for younger people, and small businesses would thrive, since those receiving pensions would be required to spend every penny of their stipend each month. By August 1934, a thousand Townsend clubs had formed across the country, attracting several hundred thousand members and pressuring President Roosevelt to accelerate plans for proposing his own social security program.

Upton Sinclair enjoyed the support of a vast legion of Utopians, a far fewer number of the conservative Townsendites. By primary day in California, the Utopian Society, wracked by internal disputes, was on the wane, while the Townsend movement remained on the rise. This spelled trouble for Sinclair. Dr. Townsend, like Frank Merriam, was an elderly expatriate from the Midwest presently living in Long Beach. If Townsend directed his forces to support Merriam, EPIC might be sunk.

———

While recognizing that Upton Sinclair's victory in the primary had given the state's reputation for wackiness an unwanted boost, the press in California enjoyed the opportunity to bask in the national limelight. Sinclair had the whole country wondering whether California represented an exception or a tendency. "The eyes of the world are on California," Chester Rowell happily observed in his *San Francisco Chronicle* column. "From the end of the earth, we have become almost its center."

At the moment, however, the center of attention was rushing away from California at a rapid clip, crossing the Southwest en route to New York. California could do little more than mark time in unconscious rhythm with the clickety-clack of the *Santa Fe Chief* speeding eastward across Arizona and New Mexico.

On board, Upton Sinclair barely wasted a minute. This was no time to relax: there were letters to compose, telegrams to respond to, radio addresses to write, a campaign pamphlet to put into final form. With him were two handsome young assistants, Bob Brownell and Crane Gartz. Sinclair did not rely on seasoned political advisers. The name of his campaign manager, he often explained, was Grim Necessity.

At every station, local reporters interviewed the candidate while his two aides dashed to the telegraph office to send or retrieve cables. In New Mexico, they picked up the wire from Marvin McIntyre confirming their visit to Hyde Park on Tuesday and sent a message to Jim Farley requesting a meeting with him in Washington. A labor group in Chicago invited Sinclair to deliver a speech at the World's Fair. Nearly thirty years after *The Jungle,* this would represent quite a homecoming for the old muckraker.

Devouring newspapers purchased at every stop, Sinclair recognized that Henry Mencken's anti-EPIC gibes attracted a lot of notice. Sinclair often hid behind the mistaken notion that when Mencken ridiculed him he was only "kidding." Mencken's fiercest punches barely bruised him—Uppie called them love taps. Responding to one Sinclair polemic, Mencken had informed the author: "As always you are right—save on matters of politics, sociology, religion, finance, economics, literature and the exact sciences." It didn't faze Sinclair one bit when Mencken, reviewing *The Wet Parade,* observed that the author's "cunning as a literary artist does not diminish," quoting several embarrassingly banal lines of dialogue as evidence.

Occasionally Sinclair recognized that the master's verbal darts bore poison but welcomed their promotional sting anyway. He once begged Mencken not to "ever restrain your impulse to ridicule me. That is the way my reputation was made. Do anything but ignore me as you have been doing of late." Sinclair claimed in 1932 that his play based on *The Wet Parade* was published only on condition that Mencken poke fun at it. His friend did not fail him. "Poke fun at it?" Mencken wrote in response. "You really shock me. I think it is a masterpiece, and put it far above such immoral plays as Ibsen's *Ghosts* and Shakespeare's *Hamlet.*"

But that was then and this was now, and this was no time to accept criticism meekly. Sinclair believed that his literary standing, such as it was, had survived Mencken's assaults, but he knew that cynical attacks on EPIC would have political effect. He was a big man, he could take the kidding, but it might dishearten the little people, some of whom still idolized Mencken. (Their enemies were Mencken's enemies, but their friends were Mencken's enemies, too.) And so, hurtling eastward, Sinclair composed a statement for immediate release to the newspapers. "My old friend Mencken," he wrote, perhaps with a tinge of sadness, "is a brilliant artist with words, but just now we need action, and his witticisms do not fill the stomachs of the hungry." Even Mencken might agree that Upton Sinclair had not written this eloquently in years.

SEPTEMBER 1

SATURDAY

The New York Times didn't hand over part of its front page to William Randolph Hearst very often. Hearst put out a rival newspaper in New York. His political views were often reprehensible, and then there was the matter of style—both personal and journalistic. So when the gray lady of the press asked journalism's bad boy to express himself on a pivotal issue of the day, one would have expected the subject to be Franklin Roosevelt or labor strife or (since Hearst was in Germany) the menace of Nazism. Instead, W. R. Hearst was asked to expound on Upton Sinclair.

The *Times,* through its Berlin bureau chief, F. T. Birchall, found Hearst at Jeschke's Grand Hotel in Bad Nauheim, where he had settled in for one of his periodic sessions at the spa. Hearst needed to drop a few pounds. Now seventy-one, he had developed a minor heart murmur—virtually his only health ailment—and physicians at Bad Nauheim were experts in the field. The year before, when Irving Thalberg sought treatment in Europe following his famous heart attack, Hearst introduced him to his personal physician at the spa. That visit proved to be a medical success but a psychological horror. Battalions of Brownshirts, goose-stepping past the hotel shouting anti-Semitic epithets, thoroughly unnerved Thalberg, who returned to Hollywood determined to take part in the film community's nascent movement against Nazism.

Hearst had no qualms about returning to Bad Nauheim himself and found the carbon dioxide baths as welcoming as ever, even as half a million Hitlerites converged on the ancient city of Nuremberg for the National Socialist party pageant, set to begin on September 4. Rudolf Hess, recently named chief deputy to Hitler, denied rumors that he was about to issue an order forbidding Nazis to fraternize with, or even speak to, Jews. "There has been no such order," Hess declared, "there will be no such order—in fact, I haven't yet even thought of such an order."

Provoked by *The New York Times,* Hearst was ready at last to spell out exactly where he stood on Upton Sinclair. He couldn't quite bring himself to endorse Frank Merriam, whom he considered an illiterate boob, but that was no reason to hold his fire on Sinclair. Hearst, after all, had helped ensure Roosevelt's election in 1932 by attacking Hoover rather than by expressing unqualified praise for FDR. He did the same thing in 1928 on Hoover's behalf in demonizing Al Smith. This was Hearst's way of maintaining his independence from the candidates he helped elect, and it allowed him to criticize them freely once in office with little fear that hyperbolic campaign rhetoric would come back to haunt him.

Concerning Upton Sinclair, Hearst saw no reason to mince words. Early in the campaign, Sinclair had made personal comments about the Chief, so now it was open season. Sinclair claimed that he was sick of watching "our richest newspaper publisher keeping his movie mistress in a private city of palaces and cathedrals, furnished with shiploads of junk imported from Europe, and surrounded by vast acres reserved for the use of zebras and giraffes." (The crack about W.R.'s taste in antiques surely went *too far.*) Hearst used his newspapers merely to celebrate Marion Davies's "changes in hats." Sinclair revealed the reason he had never reprinted his 1907 book *The Industrial Republic*: In it he prophesied Hearst as a left-wing president of the United States. "He really looked like a radical then," Sinclair recalled, "and I was too naïve to imagine the depths of his cynicism and depravity."

The Hearst papers had responded by thoroughly ignoring Sinclair's campaign. When the candidate wrote to the Chief to complain, he promised to no longer make "attacks on individuals," but he warned that if Hearst continued his blackout of EPIC activities it would amount to suppression of news, "and of course I shall be driven to fight back."

Sinclair closed by expressing the hope that Hearst would align himself with "the people" and not with reactionary *Los Angeles Times* publisher Harry Chandler.

The Hearst papers continued to ridicule EPIC anyway, and today the Chief himself would have his say. W.R. composed his remarks, solicited by *The New York Times,* with his customary verbal flair. Sinclair, he wrote, was "but a visionary," an impractical theorist "whose remedies, like his writings, are pure fictions." This utopianisn was all too typical of Americans today, and therefore Sinclair had "a very fair chance" of being elected.

This, it might surprise some readers to learn, did not particularly disturb Hearst. "If children are determined to play with fire," he wrote, "perhaps the best thing is to allow them to get their fingers good and well burned. They will remember that lesson." If they want to follow the siren song of discredited communism or socialism, "let them do it. It's their funeral. At least when they have counted the costs we may be sure that they will not want to repeat the experiment." Then he called for abolishing the NRA, which he said stood for Nonsensical, Ridiculous, and Asinine. (He was down on the New Deal—this week.)

His statement completed, Hearst turned it over to an aide, who telegraphed the message to Berlin. From there it was dictated over the telephone to Paris, converted to Dictograph, and sent by wireless to New York, where it was set in type for tomorrow's *New York Times.* Technologically, politically, and journalistically, it was a virtuoso performance, uniting the nation's two greatest names in newspapers.

Mission accomplished, F. T. Birchall, the *Times* man on the Kochstrasse in Berlin, informed W. R. Hearst that he had enjoyed "sending along so wholesome a piece of gospel truth." Just this morning the *Times* had carried on its front page the self-fulfilling headline SINCLAIR VICTORY SCARES CALIFORNIA. Tomorrow, in the same spot, it would broadcast the Hearst missive. Defeating Upton Sinclair was no longer solely California's responsibility. It was the nation's.

Hollywood harbored more than a thousand professional screenwriters. It was the heyday of the writer in Hollywood: there were just too damn many of them for their own good. Eighty writers at MGM toiled on hundreds of scripts simultaneously. Screenplays were revised so often, and by so many hired hands, that a single author rarely got credit for what appeared on screen. This process provided a lot of work for writers, no small thing in the Depression, but it also meant that remuneration was spread thin. A few well-known writers, such as Scott Fitzgerald and Anita Loos, earned two thousand dollars or more a week, while most hacked away at subsistence wages or faced months-long layoffs. Few were surprised when the frustrated scriptwriter Sidney Lazarus made, and kept, a suicide pact with his wife. The only wonder was that some producer didn't assign four writers to turn Lazarus's misfortune into a screen tragedy.

Unlike the rest of Hollywood, the scenario writers tended to be liberal in their politics, sometimes passionately so. This often brought them into conflict with the reactionary studio executives, especially after the creation of the Screen Writers Guild in 1933. Many of the writers were left-wing Jews from New York, former Socialists, or budding Communists. The moguls considered them necessary evils and treated them as social pariahs. "Jews are the writers of this business," the saying went, "and writers are the Jews of this business." Their sense of isolation was acute, especially with the East Coast papers and literary journals arriving five days late. Stranded in what one melancholy writer called "a warm Siberia," the celebrity writers were ripe for a radical cause, any cause, and the EPIC movement, led by an intellectual, somewhat snobbish writer who also hailed from back East, was a perfect fit, at least to Frank Scully's way of thinking.

Francis Xavier Scully had only recently arrived in Hollywood, but he was hardly an unknown quantity. Over the years, his villa in Nice, France, had served as a rest stop for Isadora Duncan, Ernest Hemingway, and Scott Fitzgerald, among others. Scully wrote the "European Runaround" column for *Variety,* collaborated with Frank Harris on his biography of George Bernard Shaw, and ghosted a book for former New York mayor Jimmy Walker. He had dozens of famous friends, who prized his wit, courage, and generosity in the face of almost constant pain.

Since contracting osteomyelitis at the age of seventeen, Scully had walked with a cane or a crutch but rarely let the handicap get him down. He spent sixteen years in Europe undergoing numerous operations and chasing cures for various ailments, including tuberculosis, and finally he had lost a leg. Still, Scully was an impressive figure, over six feet tall, with a prominent nose, firm jaw, and wavy, blondish hair. It was often said that the person he most resembled was George Washington.

Due to surgical complications and chronic illness, Scully spent an average of three months of every year in bed. He made the most of it, penning a popular book of puzzles and stories for shut-ins called *Fun in Bed.* Sam Goldwyn wanted to turn the book into a movie musical starring Eddie Cantor, but the Hays Office, the final arbiter of celluloid morality, blocked the deal, charging that the title was too suggestive. Scully, a devout Catholic, threatened to sue just to find out whether Will Hays, a Presbyterian elder, had fun in bed himself.

When he returned to the United States in 1933, Scully proclaimed that he was down to one leg, one lung, and one idea: to make good with the suitcase of writings he had brought with him. Hired by Twentieth Century in the spring of 1934, he moved his wife and two children to Burbank, near Toluca Lake, eight hundred feet up a hillside and just beyond Hollywood's stagnant air. He called his home Frank Scully's Bedside Manor. Among his neighbors were W. C. Fields, Bing Crosby, and Walt Disney. According to Scully, his three-year-old son's reading of the Lord's Prayer always included the line, "Hollywood be thy name."

Upton Sinclair was one writer Scully had never met, but he admired him enormously, and following his victory in the primary, he set out to assist the candidate as an organizer and propagandist. Had any other writer, Scully marveled, ever imagined an almost perfect state, as Sinclair had done in *I, Governor,* and then climbed out of his ivory tower to make it happen? This was too big a task for Plato or Thomas More. The EPIC plan was the New Deal with a lemon scent—and was more workable, confined to just one state. Sinclair had only one fault. "The literati read him in translation in forty countries," Scully told screenwriter J. P. McEvoy a few months before the primary, "but the striking stevedores in Frisco never heard of him."

"That's it," said McEvoy. "He knows how to write about the underdog, but has never met him."

Since then the candidate had made great strides with the stevedores of the state, so Scully decided to plunge into politics and establish something called the Authors' League for Sinclair, or ALFS. He drew up a long list of writers and celebrities he considered likely to support the candidate: Robert Benchley, Edgar Rice Burroughs, Charlie Chaplin, Irvin Cobb, Gene Fowler, Lillian Hellman, Nunnally Johnson, Anita Loos, Groucho Marx, Dorothy Parker, S. J. Perelman, Will Rogers, Lincoln Steffens, Donald Ogden Stewart, and others—as Scully would put it—too humorous to mention. He didn't know exactly what ALFS would do, but surely such a talented group would come up with something outrageous.

Until they did, Frank would write articles booming Sinclair; but with little time left to place stories in national publications, he had to get straight to work. In the glassed-in porch facing south that doubled as his office, Scully dictated a telegram to Arnold Gingrich, editor of the new magazine *Esquire,* in Chicago:

> WHAT ABOUT A HILARIOUS SQUIB ON UPTON SINCLAIR'S ADMISSION-CHARGING ROAD SHOW TO LAND HIM THE GUBERNATORIAL NOMINATION? WOULD THE FIFTH BE TOO LATE FOR THE NOVEMBER ISSUE?

Scully already had a working title: "Author! Author! For Governor." Gingrich's reply arrived posthaste:

> SINCLAIR IDEA SOUNDS GOOD. YOU CAN HAVE UNTIL THE TWELFTH. BUT FOR THE SAKE OF YOUR FUTURE HAPPINESS IN CALIFORNIA BEAR IN MIND THAT THE GUY MAY BE GOVERNOR SOON.

———

If there was one man in California more pleased with the prospect of Sinclair's election than the candidate himself, it was inmate #31921 at San Quentin, Thomas J. Mooney, whom *Vanity Fair* had admiringly dubbed "the world's most famous prisoner." Early and often in the primary campaign Sinclair had promised that his first act as governor would be to pardon Tom Mooney, setting him free after eighteen years behind bars. He'd do it as fast as he could put pen to paper, "and," Sinclair reminded his audiences, "I've had a lot of practice in that." It was hard to say whether this vow gained or cost votes. Mooney was widely viewed as a dangerous radical but generally considered a victim of gross injustice. No one knew which perception carried the most freight.

Sinclair was not one to vacillate, or to consider the consequences of taking a controversial stand, but still Mooney was happy to learn that just hours after winning the primary, the candidate had renewed his pledge. Today, when the prisoner's mother, Mary Mooney, visited her son at San Quentin, she found him in a jubilant mood. For the first time, Tom told her, he could see freedom at the end of the tunnel.

Mooney's troubles began on July 22, 1916, when ten people were killed and forty wounded by a bomb that exploded amid a crowd of spectators on Market Street during the Preparedness Day parade in San Francisco. Assorted anarchists, pro-Germans, and pacifists had threatened to disrupt the march, but when the perpetrator of the spectacular blast was not immediately apprehended, Tom Mooney, long a thorn in the side of the local oligarchy, seemed as good a suspect as any. Mooney, a militant labor agitator and a friend of Emma Goldman's, was arrested with four others and charged with murder. At his trial a few months later, a surprise witness identified Mooney as the man who had carried a suitcase, presumably containing the bomb, to the site of the explosion.

Convicted on dubious testimony and sentenced to hang, Mooney became a cause célèbre around the world, even for many who hated his politics. Fremont Older, the legendary San Francisco editor who had once trumpeted Mooney's guilt, published evidence showing that the chief witnesses had committed perjury. A federal report commented on "the general flimsiness and improbability" of the testimony, "together with a total absence of anything that looks like a genuine effort to arrive at the facts in the case . . ." After the California Supreme Court refused the state attorney general's request for a retrial, Governor William Stephens, at the request of President Wilson, commuted Mooney's sentence to life imprisonment, saving Tom's neck.

Still the storm raged, for Mooney remained imprisoned at San Quentin as one governor after another refused appeals for a pardon and legal technicalities prevented a new hearing. The trial judge, the ten surviving jurors, the chief of the detective bureau that organized the evidence, and the district attorney of San Francisco all petitioned the governor to pardon the prisoner. Numerous committees circulated petitions for Mooney's release, solicited contributions, organized protests. They rallied around Tom's kindly mother, now immortalized as Mother Mooney, nearly blind and inarticulate but nevertheless a faithful campaigner for her boy.

A Free Mooney rally drew fifteen thousand to the San Francisco Civic Auditorium on November 7, 1932, with Theodore Dreiser as keynote speaker and James Cagney as celebrity guest. By then, Communists and Communist sympathizers, like Dreiser and Lincoln Steffens, were in the forefront of the Mooney fight.

Despite Mooney's growing Communist orientation, Upton Sinclair supported him, if not without qualms. Sinclair was an expert on martyred prisoners. His most accomplished work of fiction, *Boston,* depicted the Sacco and Vanzetti case. The author interviewed the two anarchists in jail a few months before they were put to death in 1927.

Sinclair considered their trial a sham and their execution a crime but came to believe that although Vanzetti was probably innocent, Sacco was likely guilty as charged. In what he called the most difficult literary challenge of his career, Sinclair added shades of ambiguity to his re-creation of the case. Predictably, *Boston* earned Sinclair the wrath of the Left, but many mainstream critics, previously unfriendly, praised the novel, with *The New York Times* declaring that it demonstrated "a craftsmanship in the technique of the novel that the author has seldom displayed before." The chairman of the 1928 Pulitzer Prize Committee declared that only the novel's "socialistic tendencies" and "special pleading" had kept it from winning that year's award.

A novel about the Mooney case seemed a natural for Sinclair, but he resisted. Although Mooney was clearly innocent of the Preparedness Day bombing, he was guilty of certain other transgressions, Sinclair told Fremont Older, which the author would feel compelled to disclose. Tom Mooney, in truth, was a better symbol than he was an actuality. He was headstrong, irascible, immodest. After meeting the short, solid Irishman with the bold glow in his eyes, Lincoln Steffens had confided to a friend that as Mooney talked, "we all felt that he was not only innocent; he had become a righteous bore, an offense with his rights and his wrongs."

Although they corresponded over the years, Sinclair and Mooney had not met until February 24, 1934, the seventeenth anniversary of the prisoner's sentencing. Sinclair told Mooney, in the visiting room at San Quentin, that he would pardon him as his first official act as governor. "That's a little hard to believe," Mooney said.

Mooney's cynicism didn't discourage Sinclair from meeting with the state's new governor, Frank Merriam, to appeal for his release. Merriam said he'd consider it.

"You know," Sinclair told him, "the Mooney people have defeated every governor who refused a pardon."

"I greatly appreciate your interest in my election," Merriam replied.

Any chance that Merriam might move in Mooney's behalf evaporated with the onset of the San Francisco general strike in July. Strikers carried FREE MOONEY banners and distributed messages of support from the prisoner smuggled out of San Quentin. When Merriam called in troops to restore order, Mooney's fate was sealed, at least for the duration of this governor's term. Impressed with Sinclair's tenacity, Mooney ordered his defense committee to help the muckraker win the election. Mary Mooney even stumped for Sinclair and on August 28 spent primary night at EPIC headquarters.

Now, four days later, Mother Mooney chatted with her son in the visitor's room at San Quentin, accompanied by her daughter Anna. For the first time, she felt, Tom seemed genuinely optimistic. Leaving San Quentin, set to begin the long and tiring return trip to San Francisco, Mother Mooney told her daughter that although she felt her boy's release was imminent, she feared she wouldn't live long enough to witness it.

If EPIC was indeed unstoppable, it was only because the special interests had waited too long to mobilize against Upton Sinclair. Only the powerful California Real Estate Association, which represented two thousand real estate offices statewide and claimed to speak for eight hundred thousand property owners in California, had the foresight to prepare a battle plan. Announcing the association's goals in an open letter to his fellow realtors, Robert A. Swink, longtime president, warned that Sinclair would "confiscate homes and farms, irreparably injure real estate, impair, if not entirely destroy, the real estate brokerage business."

So what was the California Real Estate Association going to do about it? It was not a political organization, but it simply could not sit idly by when a grave danger threatened property rights and American values. Already it had organized brokers and property owners in key cities. Swink challenged all twenty-five thousand realty employees to step forward "to protect their commodity and defend our present system of government." William May Garland, the so-called Prince of Realtors who in 1932 helped bring the Olympic Games to Los Angeles, would direct the drive.

Organizers devised a strategy likely to provoke an anti-Sinclair panic. Realtors would warn the tens of thousands of Californians attempting to sell their homes that no one would even look at their property until after the election—and that if Sinclair won, their holdings would be worthless. Those looking to buy would be informed that virtually everything was off the market until November. It would be a self-induced real estate crash.

The *Santa Fe Chief* stopped for a spell in Emporia, Kansas, but not long enough for Upton Sinclair to visit the man who made the town famous. William Allen White, editor of the *Emporia Gazette* since 1895 and sometimes called the conscience of small-town America, was a Republican and a close friend of Herbert Hoover's, but called Sinclair a friend. A former Bull Mooser, he opposed reactionary Republicans almost as much as Uppie did. He had even run for governor himself back in 1924 as a way of fighting the Ku Klux Klan, and had won a quarter of the Kansas vote.

This past spring, Bill White wrote a column praising Sinclair's platform, indicating that its promise to put the unemployed to work at productive labor "is not far from where Hoover stands and near where Gov. Alf Landon will stand in the Kansas election." White stated flatly that Sinclair deserved to win the Democratic nod and privately considered signing a formal endorsement letter.

During his stopover in Emporia, Sinclair told reporters that he was looking forward to assuring President Roosevelt "that we are not going to run wild out here" and that EPIC is "safe and sane." During another layover, this one in Kansas City, Sinclair was greeted by Al Finestone, correspondent for two of the leading movie-industry trade magazines, *Motion Picture Daily* and *Motion Picture Herald.* Finestone wanted to know what the EPIC plan promised for the movie industry in California. Sinclair had always been pretty vague on this score. He wasn't quite sure himself what the implications were, and no one seemed interested until he won the primary.

A prudent man would have continued to dodge or hedge, to qualify, to declare that Hollywood in any case had nothing to fear. As one of California's leading employers and taxpayers, the movie industry, Sinclair might have explained, was part of the solution to what ailed the state, not the problem. But Upton Sinclair was not a prudent man. *Caution* was one of the few words not in his vocabulary, and at the present moment, flushed with victory he felt even more full of himself than usual.

No group held the candidate in lower regard than did the motion-picture moguls. There was the matter of ideology, of course. Then there was the biting-the-hand-that-feeds-you aspect. After the success of *The Wet Parade* in 1932, Irving Thalberg had signed Sinclair to a ten-thousand-dollar deal to produce scenario ideas for MGM. Thalberg, who hated socialism the way only a former true believer could, despised Sinclair's views but recognized a man with an eye for potboiling melodrama. It was an even better fit for the author. He didn't much care about the political implications of working for reactionary MGM; he just wanted to establish a beachhead in Hollywood. But Sinclair, as usual, self-destructed. After meeting with Thalberg four times to discuss a project called *The Star-Spangled Banner,* he changed the title to *The Gold-Spangled Banner,* and in November 1932 MGM terminated his contract.

About the same time, Sinclair rubbed the moguls the wrong way by attempting to salvage Eisenstein's American expedition after the studios, who had invited the Soviet director to California in the first place, balked at one project after another. The moguls wanted the flamboyant Russian to head home in defeat. Instead, Upton Sinclair stepped in and financed a wild, prorevolutionary Eisenstein epic in Mexico (which Edmund Wilson, after viewing rough footage, termed a masterpiece in the making). It was OK when Eisenstein was the studios' favorite homosexual Communist; it was quite another when he was sponsored by Upton Sinclair. That the entire *Qué Viva México!* episode eventually ended in disaster for both Sinclair and Eisenstein did little to assuage the studio bosses.

Then came Upton Sinclair's coup de grace, a direct assault on the movie executives themselves, in the form of a biography of William Fox, one of the most hated men in Hollywood. In the book, Fox charged that he had lost control of his studio thanks to a conspiracy fueled by his fellow moguls. The Fox book exploded in the movie colony like the Preparedness Day bomb. Sinclair was finished in Hollywood, but Hollywood might not be finished with him.

A prudent man . . . well, there was no chance that Sinclair, just days after his greatest electoral triumph, would pander to the studios. So when Al Finestone asked him about EPIC and the movies, Sinclair proclaimed that it was time for the motion-picture industry, perhaps the most profitable business in California, to contribute a fair share of the state's tax revenues. The moguls would be taxed as individuals at a higher rate, too.

As if that wasn't frightening enough, Sinclair then promised, if elected, to put the state of California in the movie-making business. "We will make our own pictures," he said, "and show them in our own theatres with our own orchestras." (This was doubly threatening: the studios owned most of the theaters their movies were shown in.) EPIC would provide employment for thousands of out-of-work actors, musicians, and craftsmen, and cheap, wholesome entertainment for their families. If there was sufficient demand, the movies would be released to the general market. Not satisfied with targeting the studios' economic base, Sinclair attacked their aesthetics. The EPIC movies, he said, would be culturally superior to studio fare, which was generally "in bad taste." EPIC would elevate the present standards of quality "without much difficulty." And, he hastened to add, "you can be sure there won't be anything Communistic in them."

Interview over, Sinclair reboarded the train, and as the *Santa Fe Chief* headed for Chicago, Finestone composed his report for *Motion Picture Daily.* "The motion picture industry in California—the state's dominant industry—faces the prospect of state-operated studios and theatres," Finestone wrote as his lead, pulling no punches, "if Upton Sinclair is elected governor of California. . . ."

———

Charlie Chaplin returned to Hollywood from Lake Arrowhead with neither a public endorsement for Upton Sinclair nor a private explanation to Alistair Cooke concerning his absence. When Cooke called him at his Benedict Canyon home, Charlie acted as if nothing had happened. He simply suggested that Alistair and his new bride, Ruth Emerson, join him and Paulette Goddard in a rare evening of nightclubbing at the Coconut Grove. They would dress in white tie and tails for the occasion.

When the two couples arrived at the Ambassador Hotel for the midnight show, they were bubbling. Paulette Goddard was as frisky as the young newlyweds, thrilled to be out on the town, for once, with the reclusive Charlie. In a moment alone, Chaplin finally explained to Cooke why he had failed to appear as his best man: Paulette was miffed because the ceremony was a painful reminder that Charlie would not set a date for *their* wedding.

The high spirits of the evening began to dissolve when crooner Gene Austin, a kind of castrato, took the stage. Chaplin started to sulk. "Revolting," he whispered. On the way home in the car, the comic genius derided "eunuch" music, modern jazz, and nightlife in general, driving Paulette to tears. "One night a year is enough of this rubbish," Chaplin announced.

Back in Benedict Canyon, the belated wedding celebration continued without a drop of drink. Like his political mentor, Upton Sinclair, Chaplin would not imbibe, nor would he serve liquor to guests. After ordering a servant to assemble a pitcher of water and four tumblers, Chaplin began lecturing on politics, socialism, and the decadence of the Republic. This was one of Charlie's favorite sports. "If you want to get yourself a load of economics, with a sidecar of theories," Will Rogers once observed, "why, Charlie can give 'em to you. . . . What that little rascal knows will just surprise you." Tonight Chaplin dissected several ponderous subjects while his guests yawned—between sips of ice water.

SEPTEMBER 2

SUNDAY

Rex Tugwell awoke early at Hyde Park and lay in bed a very long time. His thoughts may have drifted to the big softball game that afternoon, when he would take the mound for the Washington White Hopes against Lowell Thomas's Saints and Sinners. He might have meditated on his latest assignment from the President: ushering Upton Sinclair around Washington later this week. But mainly he reflected on how Roosevelt was not a made president but a born one. Gazing out the window at a giant oak standing in a meadow, Tugwell experienced a kind of epiphany: FDR, he realized, embodied the collective personality of the American people much as a great tree absorbs the entire intricate arrangement of nature.

What prompted Tugwell's early-morning reverie was the chaos surrounding the National Recovery Administration. After soaring spectacularly, the NRA's Blue Eagle had swooped noisily to earth, carrying thousands of codes of fair competition with it. Its hard-drinking, temperamental director, General Hugh Johnson, had allowed business interests to subvert the agency to such an extent that terminating the NRA itself seemed inevitable.

Tugwell finally got out of bed, dressed, and made his way to the

President's bedroom. He found FDR in an old sweater, surrounded by the Sunday papers, a cigarette secured in its signature holder. Roosevelt spoke frankly about his errors concerning the NRA. Now it was time to make a graceful exit, to reorganize government planning and spending so that the recovery effort itself could recover. "We ought to do more for the poorer farmers," Roosevelt told Tugwell. "Put a floor under wages. Build more dams for power." And so on. He knew Tugwell needed no persuading but that others wanted to balance the budget instead of spending billions putting people to work. Roosevelt would find a safe middle way out of the wilderness, Tugwell believed. But in this case, was that good enough? Tugwell, an original Brain Truster, now undersecretary of agriculture, wanted to make one more plea for saving the NRA.

Thin, suave, and silver-haired, Rexford Guy Tugwell was, at age forty-three, "the beau of the Administration," John Franklin Carter had observed, its principal economic philosopher, and "the chief target of all the foes of change." The former Columbia University economist profoundly distrusted big business and felt it incapable of spearheading recovery. Tugwell endorsed the early NRA, seeing in it a great collective effort into which the boundless energies of America might be directed and disciplined. He loved the great parades, the Blue Eagle hanging in shop windows, WE DO OUR PART. Then he watched General Johnson turn over power to business interests who saw in the NRA the chance to establish a supertrust that could fix prices, manipulate supplies, and diminish competition.

From this morning's conversation, Tugwell sensed that FDR wanted to discard the NRA right along with General Johnson—throw out the baby with the bath water. Tugwell wanted to salvage the NRA. A managed economy was the only way out of the Depression. The question was, who would manage it—government or business? Tugwell continued to push his point as FDR got ready to leave for church. The President seemed to question whether the nation was ready to breathe as one, gaining the advantages of cooperation while eliminating the wastefulness of needless competition.

Ready for church, the two men walked outside into the sunshine, and Tugwell helped lift the President into the backseat of his car. FDR patted the seat beside him, and Tugwell sat down. As they rumbled along the the Albany Post Road in the open air, Roosevelt's cape blew a little in the wind. Arriving at St. James Episcopal Church in Hyde Park, an ivy-covered building little larger than a chapel, the President struggled with his braces before reaching a pew, where he would happily remain seated while everyone around him rose for hymns and responses.

Glancing sideways at the President, who listened attentively to the sermon, completely at peace, Tugwell suddenly realized that he had lost his argument for a revival of the NRA as bulwark of a coordinated economy. He was asking too much too soon. Roosevelt, he sensed, was possessed not so much by an urge for reform as by a striving for the Christian notion of the brotherhood of man. FDR would compromise here, experiment there, but he could not make the nation more than it was. Franklin Roosevelt could only make it conscious of what it was trying to become.

Fiorello La Guardia wanted to know all about EPIC. "You should try it in New York," Upton Sinclair told him. "You have the same situation we have in California. The same population, six or seven million, the same number of unemployed workers, the same deficit, the same clamor by the taxpayers against the piling up of debts. Take over some idle factories in the city and exchange shoes and clothing for farm produce from upstate! Surely an elaborate trucking system could be devised."

The two mavericks met for the first time in La Guardia's hotel room in Chicago before Sinclair left for the Century of Progress exposition. La Guardia, mayor of New York only since January, would deliver a Labor Day address at the Fair tomorrow, and he threatened to "drop a lot of bombs." When he was through, "nobody will talk to me," he predicted. This was a man after Upton Sinclair's heart.

So different on the surface—Sinclair the reserved WASP, La Guardia the feisty half-Jewish Italian—the two men actually had a good deal in common. They were scrappy fighters who rarely gave a damn what anyone thought of them. Like Sinclair, La Guardia had created a crisis for the Socialist party when his 1933 campaign for mayor drew many prominent Socialists to his Fusion ticket. La Guardia also knew what it was like to be called a Red in an election race—that was Jimmy Walker's word for him. Another odd and distant occurrence that connected them: eight years before *The Jungle,* La Guardia's father had died after eating putrefied meat.

La Guardia expressed deep interest in EPIC but feared it would take forever to institute such a system. Sinclair, typically, saw no reason for concern, declaring that a delay would occur only if public officials were paralyzed, worrying about what big business might do to subvert them.

When the meeting ended, La Guardia suggested that now he would have to revise his Labor Day speech. Sinclair promised to set up a New York EPIC Committee. They agreed to meet again in Manhattan in forty-eight hours.

—

Upton Sinclair did not share Franklin Roosevelt's skepticism about fundamental change. He thought he could make California over, turn it upside down. That's precisely what worried motion-picture executives. Rumors circulated in Hollywood that leaders of the film industry, meeting privately, had vowed to close down operations and move back East if EPIC became a reality. Now the moguls were about to go public with this threat. *Variety* prepared a front-page story that promised to produce panic not only in Hollywood but across California when it hit the newsstands on Tuesday.

Today that seemed very far away, as Hollywood, feverish and self-fascinated as ever, passed its final idyllic hours before trouble came to paradise. The holiday weekend barely slowed the juggernaut of movie production. After a momentary downturn in the early 1930s, business was booming. Movie attendance shot up 15 percent in 1934, and most studios had increased their earnings 100 percent over the previous year. MGM showed a profit of about $1.5 million for the second quarter alone. Dozens of stars, old and new, brightened the Hollywood skies. Émigré writers and directors arrived nearly every day—some escaping impoverishment or chilly weather on the East Coast, others fleeing Hitlerism in Europe.

Unpredictable but profitable, Hollywood was, in the words of Walter Winchell, "a nut farm on a paying basis." It was hard for even the daily trade papers to keep track of all the activity. C. B. DeMille, whose *Cleopatra* had just opened in New York, contemplated *The Crusades.* MGM rushed ahead with a sequel to its successful *The Thin Man.* Over at Columbia, Frank Capra started shooting *Broadway Bill.* Sam Goldwyn completed *We Live Again* and promised *The Wizard of Oz.* Darryl Zanuck bought Jack London's *The Call of the Wild.* Warner Brothers prepared Sinclair Lewis's *Babbitt,* and Fox was set to remake *A Tale of Two Cities.* After the most extensive talent hunt in history—over two thousand kids considered—David Selznick picked Freddie Bartholomew to star in *David Copperfield.* Over on the Left side of town, King Vidor was finally ready to serve up *Our Daily Bread,* and Charlie Chaplin would soon start shooting his long-awaited factory film.

Putting his own political troubles aside—he had just been branded a Communist sympathizer—Jimmy Cagney starred in *The Perfect Weekend.* Garbo shot *The Painted Veil.* Shirley Temple seemed to finish a movie every month as the studios attempted to exploit her sudden preeminence at the box office. Clark Gable and Joan Crawford were *Forsaking All Others* for Woody Van Dyke at MGM. Harry Cohn tried to sign tennis star Fred Perry to a Columbia contract. Max Baer, the heavyweight champ who claimed movie fame in *The Prizefighter and the Lady,* was set to make a pic for Paramount. Young Mickey Rooney, about to appear as Puck in Max Reinhardt's fanciful Hollywood Bowl production of *A Midsummer Night's Dream,* had just inked his first movie contract, a seven-year deal with MGM.

This being Hollywood, gossip was rife and well circulated, thanks to that new phenomenon, the gossip columnist. Louella Parsons, Hedda Hopper, and Sidney Skolsky pretended to know it all, and sometimes Walter Winchell (who referred to himself as "hot air in a hurry") even got it right all the way from New York. This week Douglas Fairbanks and Mary Pickford were thinking of getting back together, but Cary Grant's marriage was in trouble and the Robert Riskin–Glenda Farrell "thing" was over. Loretta Young, no longer stuck on Spencer Tracy, was now dating racqueteer Fred Perry.

The fabulously popular Mae West planned to purchase a house next to Jean Harlow's in Westwood, making this the "hottest block" in Los Angeles. Jokes, innuendo, and publicity stunts surrounding the buxom star ran rampant. William Wyler, on learning that Miss West did all of her writing in bed, purportedly sent her a telegram offering to collaborate on a screenplay for nothing. ("What a sensayuma!" as Walter Winchell would say.) Prime target, perhaps even raison d'être, for the censorship boards, the actress had to change the title of her latest movie from *It Ain't No Sin* to *Belle of the Nineties.*

Some reports emanating from "the land of sunshine and poses" (Winchell again) were actually based on certified fact. California's first drive-in cinema was set to open September 9 at Pico and Westwood, with Will Rogers's *Handy Andy* the inaugural feature. "This is the theatre," *Variety* explained incredulously, "at which patrons view the show from seats in their automobiles." Another dubious innovation, something called Technicolor, was being refined over at Pioneer Pictures, which had produced several shorts utilizing the process and promised to finish eight full-length features over the following year. And a young playwright by the name of Preston Sturges was in town to test the Hollywood waters.

With so much sunshine to enjoy, gossip to absorb, and money to make, why would the moguls, most of whom had fled the dark and dirty East Coast years ago, give it all up because of one crackpot politician? Producers and high-bracketed Hollywood salary earners, according to *Variety,* feared that under Upton Sinclair's EPIC scheme, taxation would fall "particularly heavy" on the film industry. And so "switching of much film production from California to New York" was now being contemplated.

How would the readers of *Variety* react? Would they pigeonhole this report as fact, rumor, or propaganda? Would they even care enough to take it seriously? Contrary to popular perception, the number of high rollers in Hollywood was minuscule. Of the thirty thousand movie workers and moviemakers, perhaps only 1 percent fit this bill. The great mass of bit actors, assistant directors, prop makers, sound men, and wardrobe people each made less than three thousand dollars a year. Hollywood was, in addition, notoriously—proudly—apolitical. Its social consciousness was admittedly askew. It was a town where the only discussion of the Mooney case revolved around what kind of movie deal the convict might get when he emerged from San Quentin; whose concerns about Nazism extended little further than Germany's threat to ban Shirley Temple's latest picture. Will Rogers didn't call Hollywood "cuckooland" for nothing.

The bases were loaded in the bottom of the fourth, and the lead was down to one run, twenty-six to twenty-five. The President had to face this fact: his moundsman, Rexford Guy Tugwell, who thought left but threw right, didn't have it today. Singles fell in front of center fielder Harry Hopkins; doubles flew by on either side, a home run sailed over his head. Hopkins came into the game mentally exhausted from arguing with the President in favor of instituting a phenomenally costly public-works program. Now his ideological comrade, Rex Tugwell, was killing him on the ball field. Hopkins finally fell to the ground and screamed to the manager, who was sitting in his car near home plate, "Take him out, take him out!"

Tugwell had seen better days, but at least he'd had the satisfaction of striking out Kenneth C. Hogate, president of *The Wall Street Journal.*

The boys in the press would have a good time with that. Hogate handled second base for Lowell Thomas's Saints and Sinners, a group of writers and businessmen who owned summer homes near Pawling, New York. Played on a golf course four miles north of Hyde Park, this was the latest in a series of grudge matches between the Saints and Sinners and the White Hopes, a team of newspaper correspondents and other members of the Roosevelt party.

Roaring with laughter but determined to win, FDR ordered Rex Tugwell to the showers. When the White Hopes held on to a narrow victory, everyone agreed that rangy, loose-jointed Harry Hopkins, a star basketballer back in Iowa, had saved the day, his performance marred only by an incredible baserunning blunder: Hoppy stopped to tie a shoelace instead of racing around the bases on a teammate's hit.

Norman Thomas, arriving in Milwaukee for a meeting of the Socialist party's executive committee, knew that disaster for his party in California could no longer be averted. Upton Sinclair, the party's most famous deserter, had rolled up an astounding vote, and he had done it with the aid of vital California Socialists like J. Stitt Wilson (the mayor of Berkeley), young schoolmaster Jerry Voorhis, and ACLU activist John Packard. Membership in the California party, which tripled between 1931 and 1933, had been reduced by half since that fateful day last September when Upton Sinclair changed his party registration from Socialist to Democrat. Thomas, the party's candidate for president in 1932, tried to stop the hemorrhaging, denouncing Sinclair's switch in no uncertain terms, but with absolutely no success. Had Sinclair lost on August 28, Thomas might have been exonerated: See, he would have said, a Socialist can sell out and still not win a major-party nomination. Instead, it was his dear friend and colleague Upton Sinclair who earned vindication.

Like nearly everyone on the Left, Norman Thomas considered Sinclair an early influence, and he loved Uppie as a friend. The feeling was mutual. Practically from the moment he declared his candidacy, Sinclair cultivated Thomas's support. Yet Thomas let him down. His opposition was based purely on means, not ends. Thomas remained convinced that Sinclair was "still a Socialist at heart and in intention" but was doomed to failure. A separate EPIC economic system within capitalist California could not work; even if California went entirely socialist, "in blissful disregard of other states," it would fall apart.

The reason? The economy of the country was too intradependent. Socialism had to reign everywhere or nowhere. Despite these reservations, Thomas informed Sinclair, he would have welcomed the EPIC experiment "if you still held aloft the banner of Socialism." Instead, he wrote, Upton had chosen to wound the Socialist cause:

> Words are symbols. You alone, or you with the help of a certain number of California voters, cannot make the word Democratic a symbol for Socialism. That word with its capital D is a symbol for the party which bitterly discriminates not only against Negroes but white workers in the South, for the party of Tammany Hall in New York, and Hague in New Jersey. There are not words enough in the dictionary for you to explain to the great masses of common folk who have looked to your books for leadership the different sense in which you are Democrat. Still less will you be able to explain your defection to the multitudes in Europe who have hailed you as prophet and spokesman of their hopes.

In a letter to a comrade, Thomas insisted that it was "infantile" for Sinclair to feel he could "conquer poverty in two years. . . . You can't beat capitalism by colonizing the unemployed." When other candidates in California publicized these views, Sinclair protested that it was Thomas who was setting back socialism. This thought weighed heavily on Norman Thomas. He assured Sinclair that he felt "nothing but goodwill and friendship" for him. He even wrote, quite movingly: "Above all, let me tell you how very keenly I feel your loss."

Nothing much had changed since then—except that Sinclair had swept the Democratic primary, and hundreds more Socialists had left the party to join EPIC. Thomas had been hearing it loudly and often all week. Letters arrived from across the country. *Now* what do you think? a party member from Ardsley, New York, wondered. A man in Salt Lake City pointed out that Sinclair had proved that a socialist *can* win as a Democrat. A woman in Los Angeles begged Thomas not to say another bad thing about Upton. "He is our emancipator," she wrote. Others pointed out that Sinclair, running for governor of California on the Socialist party line in 1926 and 1930, had amassed only around fifty thousand votes each time.

Thomas, a candidate for the U.S. Senate in New York this fall, admitted that there was something appealing about Sinclair's triumph. "There are good and bad elements in his victory," he told reporters upon arriving in Milwaukee today. "He is not a socialist and is not supported by the Socialist party. But it is encouraging that a state cursed by reaction and industrial feudalism should nominate for governor a man like Sinclair."

Still, Thomas wouldn't, or couldn't, admit that the Socialist party's opposition to EPIC was wrong or should be modified. Jerry Voorhis, now an EPIC candidate for the California state assembly, had petitioned for a change of heart months ago. "My conviction is that the Socialist party as such will never gain power in America," Voorhis told Thomas. "I feel that we are in a great crisis right now and that only the most bold and unfettered action can possibly save us. We never know when we may be passing up the great opportunity. And the Sinclair movement is the nearest thing to a mass movement toward socialism that I have heard in America."

Most of the SP members sympathetic to Sinclair had already left the party. Those who remained were staunch in their opposition, and they controlled the party mechanism. The SP's state leadership had just issued its strongest attack on EPIC yet, asserting that Adolf Hitler "promises to achieve by dictatorship what Mr. Sinclair promises wildly to achieve peacefully."

Still, Thomas was unsure of what to do next. But as the executive committee convened in Milwaukee, it was apparent that self-discipline would prevail. Party leaders declared that Sinclair was not a Socialist and that he had neither the open nor the tacit support of the party. The SP would stand by its nominee in California, Milen Dempster, a former Unitarian minister.

Out in Stockton, California, Milen Dempster wasn't so sure he wanted all this support. Just last year, Sinclair had let Dempster, visiting Pasadena on Socialist business, sleep in his bed while Upton and his wife were out of town. Now Dempster was thinking of writing Norman Thomas, a man he idolized, asking for permission to quit the race and throw his support to Upton Sinclair.

When he reached the fairgrounds, Upton Sinclair found that a persistent rain had driven the ceremonies indoors. Only a fraction of the thousands who had gathered at the Chicago World's Fair to hear him could fit inside the auditorium. No matter: the nationwide radio hookup would enable him to reach millions. "If you had known what Roosevelt would do after you elected him, most of you would have voted for Hoover," Sinclair told his audience. "But now that he's in office, you see the wisdom of his acts. It's a stroke of luck almost more than the voters deserve."

Far from home, Sinclair felt emboldened. He took this occasion to expose California election practices. The "sand and gravel" industry, he revealed, promised fifty thousand dollars if he'd look after their interests. Gamblers in San Francisco offered him fifteen thousand dollars a month to leave them alone for as long as he was in office. Promoters of an illegal lottery offered the candidate a portion of their thirty-five-thousand-dollar-a-day take, but he was incorruptible. "Christ drove the money changers from the temple with whips," Sinclair declared. "We are doing the same thing with ballots."

After an exhilarating day, the three-man Sinclair entourage boarded another train heading east. At a stop along the route, Bob Brownell, recent Stanford graduate, now personal secretary to the Democratic candidate for governor of California, disembarked briefly. What state was he in? He was in the state of euphoria. Brownell wired a message back to EPIC headquarters in Los Angeles.

> TRIUMPHANT TRIP TO CHICAGO, REPORTERS EVERY STOP, EVEN ROUSING SINCLAIR FROM BED DEMANDING EXPLANATIONS OF EPIC. EASTERN AND MIDDLE WESTERN NEWSPAPERS PLASTERED WITH PHOTOS, STORIES AND EDITORIALS. PEOPLE IN EVERY STATE THRILLED AND ENVIOUS. WHOLE NATION TREMENDOUSLY STIRRED OVER EPIC MIRACLE AND UPTON IS TELLING THEM ALL HOW TO DO IT IN THEIR OWN STATES.

Grand Central Terminal was less than twenty hours away.

Against her daughter's wishes, Mother Mooney planned to appear at tomorrow's Labor Day parade, which promised to be the biggest in San Francisco history. Trudging over to Market Street was no big deal; she had sailed to Russia for her boy and journeyed to New York to visit Governor Roosevelt. When John Mooney came home for dinner his mother seemed optimistic.

"Do you really think they'll let Tom out?" she asked him.

"I know they will, Mother," John Mooney replied.

After dinner, John Mooney returned to work, leaving his mother alone in the house on Clipper Street. She fed their dog, Blackie, then collapsed. About half past five, a neighbor, hearing someone moaning next door, found Mary Mooney slumped in a chair, victim of an apparent heart attack. In an ambulance en route to Mission Emergency Hospital, she uttered her last words. Close to death, she still could think only of her son. "Poor Tom," she said. When Tom Mooney heard that she had passed away, he collapsed in his cell as if struck by a sledgehammer.

SEPTEMBER 3

MONDAY

"Rex Tugwell thinks Sinclair has a chance," Eleanor Roosevelt scribbled in a letter to Lorena Hickok. "I hope Franklin gives him a good politician!" A year spent cultivating the First Lady appeared to be bearing fruit for Upton Sinclair.

Eleanor's note to her dearest friend provided one of few political exclamations of this holiday at Hyde Park. She had arranged the Labor Day picnic herself, centered at Val-Kill, the little Dutch cottage two miles west of the main house. More than fifty guests attended, including White House staff, newspapermen, chauffeurs, state troopers, and assorted wives and children. The newsmen noticed that ruddy-cheeked Franklin Roosevelt looked healthy, laughed heartily, and hugely enjoyed the fun, proving that his extended vacation was clearly in the national interest.

When the revelers departed, the First Lady retreated to her room, where her thoughts turned to Lorena Hickok even more than they usually did. Hickok was Harry Hopkins's chief field investigator. For the past year, she had traveled around the country, studying conditions in depressed areas and the relief efforts meant to alleviate them. This summer, touring California, she had labeled Los Angeles "the blackest spot in the U.S." and called state relief efforts "very bad. . . . What's needed out here in the California desert," she informed Hopkins, "is some plan whereby these people can support themselves, here or elsewhere. They don't want relief. They hate it." Now Hick was sick in bed somewhere out West, her return East—Eleanor was knitting her a sweater—delayed. Eleanor feared that Hick had picked up typhoid fever from drinking water at a desert spring.

Hickok, a former journalist, sent reports to Harry Hopkins as perceptive, vivid, and gossipy as any administrator could hope for. They were populated by children ashamed to go to school in ragged clothes, women walking the streets to make ends meet, men too proud to take a government check. Just this week she related the poignant story of a California woman who claimed to speak for countless others facing a grim paradox. Already surrounded by babies, poor mothers couldn't afford to conceive any more children, but they also couldn't afford "protection," the woman had explained. Many times, sex was "the only way" to keep their husbands from "going crazy," even at the risk of producing an unwanted child.

Two days ago at Hyde Park, Harry Hopkins predicted that Hickok's field reports would one day be considered the richest history of the Depression. He routinely forwarded the best of them to the President and to key congressmen. The reports hardly needed the verdict of history: by influencing policy they were already making history.

In her letters to the First Lady, Hick passed along the same gritty anecdotes and salty advice. But Eleanor Roosevelt had arrived in Washington already primed for social service. Reviewing E.R.'s 1933 book, *It's Up to the Women,* Mary Beard found that "the implications of some of her economic statements reach to the borderland of political, social and cultural change." Eleanor admitted that she was "not a philosopher," let alone an economist; she was a moralist and something of a utopian. In a magazine article, she sketched her ideal community: every family would have an adequate income, selfishness would be a thing of the past, and the entire community would pull together as one. She called this "a really new deal for the race."

One day, after hearing about the wholesale destruction of hogs to maintain prices, Eleanor called a federal administrator and asked, "Why do you dump all these little pigs into the Mississippi when there are thousands of people in the country starving?" Not long afterward, a reporter commented that surplus farm products were being fed to the hungry instead of being destroyed because Eleanor Roosevelt "asked a government official a question." Eleanor called these and other New Deal innovations "revolution without violence."

Like her husband, Eleanor encouraged the poor to tell her their troubles, and tens of thousands of letter writers took her up on it. Impressed with her kind deeds, many called her the "mother of the country" or simply Mother Roosevelt. At one public appearance, the First Lady told the story of a man sentenced to jail for filching food to feed his family. Upon being released, he informed the warden that he would do it again if necessary. "I wouldn't blame him," Eleanor said. "You would be a poor wishy-washy sort of person if you didn't take anything you could when your family was starving." Newspapers denounced the statement, angry letters arrived at the White House, but she didn't back down.

Then, in the fall of 1933, Upton Sinclair, having just declared his candidacy, asked Eleanor if he could pay her a visit. "I will probably not be governor," he wrote, "but at least I hope to get some new ideas at work in this state." They met at the White House in November 1933. Citing illness, FDR declined to attend, but Eleanor was most cordial and impressed Upton with her emphasis on the need for economic security for all.

A few weeks later Sinclair wrote to ask whether the rumor he had heard was true: the First Lady was about to endorse him. Eleanor replied, in a note marked "not for publication," that she had read *I, Governor, and How I Ended Poverty* and found that she was "heartily in favor" of some of the things he advocated. Others she found impractical, "but then what is impractical today is sometimes practical tomorrow." Still, she was not "sufficiently in accord with your entire idea" to make a public statement in Sinclair's behalf. She handed *I, Governor* to her husband, however.

Like FDR, the First Lady, in the wake of Sinclair's stunning primary win, was bombarded with mail from California. She received a telegram from Edna Heney, wife of the great Progressive Francis J. Heney, asking her to persuade her husband to repudiate Sinclair, whom she called an "anarchist communist" and a follower of Stalin. Now Sinclair was coming to Hyde Park. What to do?

Contrary to her public image, Eleanor felt not entirely self-assured. "No dear," she had written just last week to Lorena Hickok, "I'm not at peace with God and man, not even at all times with myself." Eleanor hoped the President would send an experienced political operative to California to assist Sinclair, but she planned to pass up a chance to give the candidate a personal boost right in her own home. Her schedule was set. Tomorrow, when Upton Sinclair headed up the Hudson to Hyde Park, she would leave for New York—to see her dentist, get her hair done, and appear on a national radio broadcast.

Fear of communism swept Metro-Goldwyn-Mayer, sparked more by labor strife—inside the studio and out—than by the present election campaign. No one in the front office could identify any Communists, or even knew for sure that any existed at the studio, but there were so many Jews on the writing payroll, and so many Jews were Communists, that there almost had to be some Reds on the lot. Further evidence: several leading MGM writers, including Frances Marion and Joseph L. Mankiewicz, had played formative roles in organizing the left-wing Screen Writers Guild.

Hollywood was still chattering about reports linking four of its most prominent stars—James Cagney, Ramon Novarro, Dolores Del Rio, and Lupe Velez—to Communist activities in the state. And it was abuzz with news that the sons of two of its most prominent executives, B. P. Schulberg and Harry Rapf, were presently touring Russia and finding it much to their liking. The college students, Budd Schulberg and Maurice Rapf, would probably head to Hollywood in a year or two to pursue screenwriting careers. Surely they wouldn't emigrate to Russia: everyone knew that the Russians had ordered all American Communists to stay in Hollywood, where their pro-Red propaganda efforts would be most useful.

According to the Hollywood rumor mill, an informal blacklist was already in effect, and Luis Buñuel, the director from Spain, was said to be on it. When George Cukor interceded on Buñuel's behalf, Irving Thalberg denied that a blacklist existed, and then added, "But I'll see he's taken off it."

In declaring that Upton Sinclair's maggotlike horde of Reds was about to take over the state, the *Los Angeles Times* warned readers that even "the movie star whom you admire on the screen" might be a Communist dupe. The number of well-known figures who had endorsed Sinclair was still small—Charlie Chaplin, Victor Jory, Irving Pichel, Dudley Nichols, Frank Scully, and a few others—but struggling actors and writers, as well as trade unionists, were flocking to the EPIC banner. Sinclair, after all, had promised jobs for everyone in his state-run movie studio.

Los Angeles was an open-shop town. Of all the studio execs, Irving Thalberg was one of the most anti-union. The idea that writers needed protection was positively repugnant to him. "Those writers are living like kings," Thalberg once proclaimed. "Why on earth would they want to join a union, like coal miners or plumbers?" Responding to the Communist menace, MGM troubleshooter Eddie Mannix had ordered studio police chief Whitey Hendry to place a number of employees under surveillance. There was no telling what this would turn up.

Carey Wilson was not on the original watch list, and for good reason. Coauthor of *Ben-Hur* and dozens of other scripts, and a close friend of Thalberg's, he was an unlikely candidate for conversion to radicalism. But when the studio Red Squad got a tip that he was doing considerable work at home at night, they decided to investigate. Wilson was supposed to be completing his script for *Mutiny on the Bounty,* but he seemed to be making little progress. He must be moonlighting, but on what? Hendry put Wilson's home under surveillance. Detectives heard the chatter of a typewriter through much of the night. This went on for days. One morning a messenger arrived, then left with a large envelope under his arm. The gumshoes followed him to Sam Goldwyn's studio over on Melrose, where former MGM producer Walter Wanger had set up shop.

Mannix and the other studio execs put two and two together. One of Wilson's most celebrated (and politically liberal) scripts was *Gabriel Over the White House,* the controversial 1933 Wanger parable that featured additional dialogue by W. R. Hearst. Wanger, one of the few Democrats in upper-echelon Hollywood, was preparing a kind of follow-up to this fantasy, called *The President Vanishes,* but now he was no longer with MGM. Louis B. Mayer was still mad at Wanger for serving as best man at Jean Howard's wedding, so Carey Wilson couldn't very well ask L.B. for permission to free-lance for him. Mannix sent the report to Thalberg, urging that he fire Wilson immediately.

Called to Thalberg's office, Carey Wilson admitted that he had been moonlighting for the previous three weeks. Mannix saw this as an opportunity for MGM to send a message to every high-rolling, ungrateful writer in Hollywood. Instead, Thalberg ordered Wilson simply to hurry up and complete his work on *Mutiny on the Bounty.* He casually instructed his functionaries to bill Wanger for Wilson's salary, which was a thousand dollars a week. And, Thalberg added, "I want no more snooping on my staff."

From the study on the second floor of his home, Herbert Hoover could gaze out the window and, on a clear day, observe the full expanse of the bay, the top of Mount Tamalpais, the silhouette of Mount Diablo. Every time he looked down the Santa Clara Valley from another window, Hoover once told a reporter, he thanked God he lived in California.

The stucco house on Mirado Road in Palo Alto had been Herbert Hoover's retreat for years, his home for the past eighteen months. It was an eclectic structure with exterior stairways, airy rooms, and flat, Algerian-style roofs converted to terraces. Hoover loved Stanford, and he generously invited students to impromptu gatherings at his nearby home. As a university trustee, he raised money for the institution and helped build the collection of books in the Hoover War Library.

Upon leaving the White House in March 1933, Hoover announced, "On economic and political matters I am silent. Even on fishing I am silent." Since then, he had spent a lot of time alone. He played solitaire for hours, and collected stamps. A friend who called on the former president a few months after he left office found him "lonely beyond measure." Privately, Hoover complained about smears in the press and criticized the New Deal as "fascistic"—part of an attempt to erect a "Fascist-Nazi state"—but for eighteen months he had maintained a public silence.

Most of his advisers urged him to go on the attack, but Hoover followed the advice of his friend William Allen White, who instructed him "to emulate Brer Fox and the Tar Baby—lay low and say nothing." The popular Disney song "Who's Afraid of the Big Bad Wolf?" seemed to celebrate the end of the Hoover era, and encampments of the homeless known as Hoovervilles stood outside several American cities. Recognizing the stigma attached to his name, Hoover felt it would be fatal to attack Roosevelt—meaning every knock from him would be a boost for FDR. "We must reserve our fire until we can make it effective," he told a friend.

With FDR suddenly on the defensive as the autumn of 1934 approached, the time to open fire arrived. Hoover had promised "one final blast" to conclude his service to his country, and now he was about to explode—or, quite possibly, implode. He had completed a book, *The Challenge to Liberty,* and sold two excerpts to the *Saturday Evening Post* for ten thousand dollars. The first blast would hit the newsstands Wednesday. Several of the former president's friends who perused the manuscript called it a relic of the eighteenth century. Still, *The Challenge to Liberty* was a Book-of-the-Month Club selection, and Hoover had purchased twenty-five thousand copies to distribute himself.

His writing chores completed, the former president could now pay attention to the unfinished business of keeping Frank Merriam, who had managed Hoover's California campaign in 1928, in office. The hated Roosevelt seemed to favor Upton Sinclair, so this was an opportunity for Hoover to exact a small measure of revenge. He wasn't called the Great Engineer for nothing.

Letters from concerned Republicans around the country arrived at Hoover's home every day, begging the former president to help eradicate the Sinclair epidemic in California before it spread eastward. It was a strange place to look for reassurance, since Hoover had so miserably failed to save the Republicans from Franklin Roosevelt. Hoover was uncertain of the outcome in any case, so his words today were tempered, even a bit pessimistic.

"Altogether, the situation is one of a great deal of anxiety," Hoover advised a correspondent in Cleveland. "A great deal depends upon the attitude of Hearst." He noted that Hearst was "out this morning with a violent attack on Sinclair"—the California papers had picked up the *New York Times* article—"that does not, however, disclose where he will ultimately get to." If Hearst decided to support Ray Haight, Sinclair's election was "a foregone conclusion." The implication was clear: someone had better get to Hearst, the loose cannon in this battle, and soon.

———

Clem Whitaker couldn't quite bring himself to work for Frank Merriam. The GOP had offered him five thousand dollars to help out with the governor's campaign in northern California, but Whitaker thought Merriam was an incompetent fool. Also, he had no intention of following someone else's orders. He would run the show—every bit of it—or find another candidate, or skip a campaign entirely. That's what he had done in the Republican primary. None of the candidates would let him call the tune. Fine. They would *learn.*

Upton Sinclair was a friend of the Whitaker family's, but under no circumstances would Clem manage a socialist's campaign. So Clem Whitaker was sitting out the governor's race. Instead, he would handle George Hatfield's contest for lieutenant governor against Sheridan Downey, Sinclair's running mate. Downey happened to be one of Whitaker's best friends in Sacramento, but Sheridan was on the other side now.

This would be Whitaker's first statewide election race. Just last year he had established Campaigns, Inc., the country's first political consultancy firm. Whitaker had created a new category of political operative. The fact that he was one of a kind gave him supreme confidence. There wasn't even any competition on the horizon, and this made him smile.

Whitaker offered a candidate what he called full-service campaign management. This meant that he would attend to every aspect of the campaign. The candidate just had to *be*—neither the candidate nor party headquarters had to *do.* Whitaker would draw up a tight budget and blueprint a battle plan, establish the themes and invent the slogans, set up an itinerary and arrange the radio addresses, write the speeches and place the advertising.

Nothing like this had previously existed in American politics. Until recently, the party organization handled every campaign task, much of it focused on precinct work—drumming up, getting out, or simply buying votes. If the party boss was king, then the ward heeler was the worker ant. The political party acted as the principal link between candidates and voters, and communication depended primarily on face-to-face contact. The ward heeler's job was to be personally acquainted with as many voters as possible within his territory. Most voters relied strictly on party labels when they cast their ballots. Because there were relatively few undecided voters, political advertising was not pervasive. Newspapers were so partisan that advertising was often considered superfluous. Rather than buy space in a newspaper, a political party sometimes bought the newspaper.

Campaigns were directed by party officials. Some, like Mark Hanna, who put William McKinley in the White House, were good at it. Party hacks handled the detail work. With a party machinery in place, there was little cause to call on mercenaries from outside to tell the worker ants what to do. Party discipline was all.

By the 1920s, however, this system had started to wear thin. The party no longer spoke to the voter unobstructed. Newspapers, at least in some parts of the country, asserted their political independence. The new medium of radio became popular, not just for entertainment but as a source of news and opinion. Advertising was ubiquitous, and a new breed of soap salesman known as the press agent had arrived on the scene. Thanks to muckrakers like Ida Tarbell, Lincoln Steffens, and Upton Sinclair, corporations that once cared little about what appeared in the press now set up publicity bureaus. It didn't take long for the press agent to appear in politics. Party officials started hiring outsiders to promote causes and candidates. Woodrow Wilson hired the writer George Creel to direct his wartime propaganda office.

In 1928, after another crushing electoral defeat, the Democratic party in Washington hired Hearst reporter Charles Michelson as its first full-time publicist. The bureau he established hounded Herbert Hoover into bouts of pettiness, fits of anger, and, eventually, involuntary retirement. So the idea of the publicist in politics, while new, was no longer novel.

What Clem Whitaker had seized on in 1933 was the notion that free-lancers could, should, and (if he had anything to say about it) would handle every aspect of a political campaign, not just public relations. Whitaker did not want any part of a campaign that he did not control, all the way down to writing the checks.

It was no accident that California inspired the first experiment in professional campaign management. Political machines, even Tammany Hall, were beginning to break down everywhere, but they had already collapsed in California, for several reasons. The state had absorbed so many émigrés—if America was the melting pot of the world, California was the melting pot of America—that loyalties were not long-standing. The political party had never been king in California politics anyway. That position traditionally belonged to the Southern Pacific Railroad, and politics hadn't been the same in the state since Hiram Johnson and the Progressives came to power in 1910 and broke that control. The measures they passed promoting citizen-led activism (initiative, referendum, and recall) and permitting a candidate to run as the nominee of both major parties (cross-filing) led to a precipitous decline in party influence.

Like lobbyist Arthur Samish, Clem Whitaker recognized a political vacuum in the state that he could partly fill. Samish and Whitaker might even work out a jurisdictional agreement: Artie could control the legislature, while Clem would take care of public opinion.

George Hatfield, a prominent San Francisco attorney (and a political novice), served as Whitaker's guinea pig; his race against Sheridan Downey in 1934 was the first campaign to test the Campaigns, Inc., concept. It would be a challenge, because in California the votes for governor and lieutenant governor were tabulated separately. Merriam and Hatfield were running mates, but voters could split the ticket. Whitaker felt that Hatfield, in contrast to Old Baldy, was a thoughtful, intelligent statesman. But so was his opponent, and unlike Upton Sinclair, Sheridan Downey had led a controversy-free life. Voters might reject the radical Sinclair but elect the sane, sensible Downey as a check on Frank Merriam. Of course, the reverse was possible: voters would dismiss Merriam but elect Hatfield as an anchor on Sinclair. That was why Hatfield was keeping his distance from Frank Merriam—and why he had hired Clem Whitaker.

One of Clem's maxims was "You can't wage a defensive campaign and win." That was another reason he wouldn't assist Merriam directly. But that didn't mean Clem couldn't contribute to the cause of keeping state socialism out of California. The Republican party had offered Whitaker a generous sum to help organize a bipartisan front group in San Francisco that would stir up anti-Sinclair sentiment in the state. Whitaker had some new ideas—utilizing modern advertising and publicity techniques—he wanted to try out. To attack meant more than just stating the obvious. It was a way of defining the political situation.

For starters, Clem wanted to find out exactly what ammunition he had at his disposal. And so, having obtained dozens of the old muckraker's books and pamphlets, Clem Whitaker and his redheaded associate, Leone Baxter, left their office in the Forum Building at Eighth and K streets in Sacramento and went into seclusion, setting as their unenviable goal an examination of virtually every word Upton Sinclair had ever written.

Duke beckoned, so Richard Nixon would miss the fall campaign in California. Having turned twenty-one in January, he was eligible to vote in his first election, but it looked as if he would spend November 6 in Durham, North Carolina, instead. Nixon had graduated second in his class at Whittier College, earning a B.A. in history and a full-tuition scholarship to Duke Law School. In a couple of days, accompanied by his younger brother Donald, who planned to finish high school in Greensboro, Richard would start driving east. It would be his first trip across the Rockies.

Nixon, a firm Republican, considered himself a "practical" liberal; his heroes were Teddy Roosevelt and Woodrow Wilson. He admired some aspects of the New Deal but often argued with his girlfriend, a Democrat, about Franklin Roosevelt. As president of the student body at Whittier this past year, Richard "led us through the year with flying colors," according to the school yearbook, but that did not satisfy his political ambitions. He told friends that he wanted to run for Congress someday. One of his professors, in recommending him to Duke, praised his "human understanding, personal eloquence and a marked ability to lead." Walter Dexter, the Whittier College president, declared in his recommendation letter that one day "Nixon will become one of America's important, if not great, leaders."

———

When Upton Sinclair arrived at Grand Central Terminal, publisher Stanley Rinehart and dozens of reporters, photographers, and newsreel cameramen greeted him. Weary from his travels, Sinclair fended off interviews until he settled in at the Algonquin Hotel over on West Forty-fourth Street. It was early evening and chilly, and the candidate was glad he had carried his heavy overcoat all the way from California.

"I don't want to involve the President in our program," Sinclair told the reporters who crowded into his comfortable two-room suite. "It is our program and we are going to try it out." Asked what he and the President would talk about if politics were excluded, Sinclair read aloud a satiric newspaper column that portrayed the two men genially discussing the weather. "Perhaps it will be like that, at the start," Sinclair said mischievously. "All I know is that I will tell the President what I've been telling my audiences in California—that we love him for the enemies he has made and continues to make." Pressed to predict the outcome of the election, Sinclair would only allow that the odds presently favored him, and that the gamblers were "usually right."

Sinclair's two young aides and a secretary from New York were already busy answering telephones, arranging interviews, and accepting writing assignments. Tomorrow would be even more hectic, Sinclair knew. Now he had to get some sleep. He asked the reporters to leave. Before exiting, one of them wanted to know what Upton thought of William Randolph Hearst's characterization of him as "but a visionary."

"I appreciate the compliment!" Sinclair responded, imperturbable as always. "I think vision is one thing that is sadly needed in American politics."

SEPTEMBER 4

TUESDAY

Robert Benchley, Dorothy Parker, and Alexander Woollcott were lolling about in Hollywood as Heywood Broun, another former knight of the Round Table, rang the Algonquin from his home in Connecticut, trying to reach Upton Sinclair. Broun, the nation's leading liberal columnist, suspected his old friend Uppie was heading for victory in November. How else to explain the *Los Angeles Times*'s equating Sinclair supporters with termites, maggots, and wolves? The *Times* advised readers to keep an eye on their cooks, who might be agents from Moscow. Not even a bowl of alphabet soup, Broun pondered, was safe from Communist manipulation. What if the cook, under orders from Stalin, arranged the letters to read "Arise, ye prisoners of starvation"?

Broun was anxious to get out to California to witness this spectacle, for he had hastened down the electoral path once himself, running for Congress in Manhattan as a Socialist in 1930. Theodore Dreiser had wondered why Broun would want to descend to Congress but endorsed him anyway. So did Lunt and Fontanne, Walter Winchell, Fred Astaire, Helen Hayes, all of the Marx Brothers, and dozens of other celebrities. Racing to campaign appearances, Broun was quite a sight, a bear of a man, sloppily dressed, bushy hair blown back—"an old mattress," in

Winchell's words. Broun finished a poor third, but unlike many of his friends, such as Dreiser, he stuck to socialism instead of wandering off toward communism.

With Norman Thomas, Broun tried to persuade Upton Sinclair to run for president on the Socialist party line in 1932, but Uppie demurred, explaining that the way things were going, he might just win, and he did not consider himself enough of "a practical man and an administrator" for the job. Broun regarded Sinclair with profound ambivalence. He claimed he always took him seriously but never liked his work. As a writer, Sinclair was "among the most boring of the bores," but politically he was an "advanced thinker." Broun, like H. L. Mencken, often poked fun at his friend's eccentricities. When Broun declared in *Life* magazine that Sinclair was living on nuts and lettuce, Uppie begged him to advise readers that "I used to live on nuts, now the nuts live on me." Sinclair not only wanted you to read his books, Broun complained, he also wanted you to eat your spinach, and the columnist wished to do neither.

When Broun finally reached Sinclair today at the Algonquin, he informed him that he had written a column for tomorrow's New York *World-Telegram* lampooning the *L.A. Times.* It would be syndicated around the country by Scripps-Howard. Broun promised to come to California in October to cover the last weeks of the campaign.

That was terrific news, Sinclair responded, but the trip was by no means assured. Roy Howard, once a crusading New Dealer, seemed to be turning to the right. Broun's commitment to Scripps-Howard had waned considerably, to the point where he was considering an offer from Arthur Brisbane to jump ship and, like Mencken, join the cursed Hearst family. Brisbane considered Broun something of a baby—he was a hypochondriac and had a neurotic fear of riding on trains—but offered him a thousand-dollar-a-week salary and a twenty-five-thousand-dollar bonus anyway.

Broun's close friend, political opposite, and *World-Telegram* stablemate Westbrook Pegler was sure to put in for a California trip himself. Among readers, fellow journalists, and the New York literati, Broun was a beloved figure; but as national president of the American Newspaper Guild, he was an unpopular fellow in the front office. Pegler, on the other hand, was militantly antilabor. His cynicism was so complete it was almost heroic. The man Broun called Peg was as caustic as battery acid. His most famous column defended a lynching—in California.

W. R. Hearst, immersed in his health-cure routine in Bad Nauheim, had passed up a chance to attend the opening of the Nazi party congress at Nuremberg, thereby missing an opportunity to observe his friend Dr. Hanfstaengl welcoming the world's press to Nuremberg with his customary savoir faire. "May the good spirits of Nuremberg," Hanfstaengl instructed them, "dwell among you in the coming days." This may not have been as soothing as Hanfstaengl intended.

Bugles blared, church bells rang, and more than one hundred thousand Nurembergers roared a welcome as Herr Hitler's motorcar raced through the streets to a ceremony held in the festival hall of the Rathhaus, the scene of state rallies in centuries past. The chancellor, who had flown up from his summer home at Berchtesgaden, expressed the hope that the week's events would spread Nuremberg's fame around the world. A heavy cordon of black-uniformed Special Guards surrounded the Deutscher Hof, headquarters for Hitler and his staff.

The party congress would get down to business tomorrow with the first of Hitler's seven scheduled speeches. More than half a million of the party faithful were expected to arrive, including eighty-eight thousand storm troopers and sixty thousand Hitler Youth. Hitler's favorite movie director, Leni Riefenstahl, assembled an enormous film crew to document the event for propaganda purposes. Partly for her benefit, rally organizers choreographed every session for visual effect.

Angling for an invitation to meet Hitler, W. R. Hearst continued to correspond with Putzi Hanfstaengl, apparently undisturbed by his friend's recent remark aimed at British critics of Nazi detention camps. "I'll send some of our swine to burn down their Oxford!" Putzi had promised.

Today Hearst was busy with other matters, such as finally replying to Jack Neylan's urgent cable of August 30. Neylan, Hearst's political fixer, had wondered whether the Chief wanted him to try to get either Frank Merriam or Ray Haight to quit the California governor's race. Hearst replied that neither should drop out, as it was impossible to say which candidate would attract progressive Republicans and disaffected Democrats and thus emerge as the strongest candidate. "We can decide later whom to support," Hearst pronounced.

This was precisely the strategy Herbert Hoover prayed Hearst would avoid. The publisher's refusal to back Merriam meant that he took Haight seriously. The public couldn't help but recognize this, and it mandated fair coverage of the Haight campaign by the Hearst press. The Chief's message to Neylan indicated, moreover, that he thought Haight could, and probably should, become Sinclair's main opponent, with Merriam dropping by the wayside. But what if, as seemed likely, GOP support for Merriam remained firm, resulting in a three-way split in November, with Sinclair almost certain to gain a plurality? Hearst could "decide later whom to support," but that decision might come too late to propel Ray Haight to victory or save Frank Merriam from disaster.

By midmorning, perhaps half of the nation's 650,000 cotton, silk, and wool workers were out on strike. Unprecedented mass picketing crippled mill towns from Maine to Alabama. The state militia took over two South Carolina plants. Strikers imprisoned three hundred workers in a Fall River, Massachusetts, mill. It was the largest strike ever directed by American labor, and both sides in the battle predicted a wave of violence if President Roosevelt did not intervene soon. Calling it a "fight to the finish," Thomas F. McMahon, president of the United Textile Workers, advised the strikers not to turn the other cheek but "hit back if you are hit" and "fight back even if you are shot down. . . . I know that President Roosevelt would rather see mill workers fight for the justice he demands for all labor." McMahon added, "We have a friend in the White House."

Aides kept FDR abreast of developments as he prepared for another busy vacation day at Hyde Park. Harry Hopkins issued the administration's only statement on the strike, announcing that federal relief funds would not "underwrite" the labor stoppage.

Before sitting down with Upton Sinclair, the President played host to another distinguished guest. Joseph P. Kennedy, en route from Hyannis to Washington, stopped by for lunch, providing political ballast for the President's day. By all accounts, the boyish millionaire from Boston was doing surprisingly nimble work as head of the new Securities and Exchange Commission, gradually overcoming the suspicions of those who likened Kennedy's appointment to putting the fox in charge of the henhouse. Joe Kennedy was a prima donna, FDR complained to his aides—he always wanted the President to hold his hand—but he was a useful public relations tool and a profanely entertaining conversationalist.

Kennedy and Roosevelt went way back, to the days when Joe was in the shipbuilding business and Frank was assistant secretary of the navy.

They met again in 1930, after Kennedy had made his mark as Wall Street manipulator and Hollywood mogul. Joe promised to support FDR's presidential try. This was surprising, since Al Smith also planned to run. Like Smith, Kennedy was a self-made Irish Catholic, but Joe knew a loser when he saw one, and after a decade of accumulating money, possessions, and children, he now sought power. He wanted his nine kids to respect him not just as a rich man, but as an influential one.

At the 1932 Democratic convention, Kennedy helped swing the support of William Randolph Hearst, who controlled the make-or-break California delegation, to Roosevelt. As head of the party's finance committee, he raised an estimated one hundred thousand dollars from his Wall Street cronies, donated twenty-five thousand dollars of his own money to the FDR campaign, and lent the party another fifty thousand dollars. He wooed A. P. Giannini, the leading California banker, out of the Hoover camp and into Roosevelt's. During a vacation trip with FDR, Kennedy's secretary, Edward Moore, amused fellow guests with the prediction that if everyone lived long enough, they would witness one of Joe's sons taking office as the nation's first Catholic president.

When Roosevelt won, Kennedy took credit. He expected to be named secretary of the treasury, but FDR's top aide, Louis Howe, opposed him. Kennedy refused the administration's best offer, U.S. ambassador to Ireland, on the grounds that it was insultingly predictable. Feeling betrayed, he lashed out at the President in long telephone conversations with W. R. Hearst. Kennedy, with the President's son James, went to England to secure liquor franchises in anticipation of the repeal of Prohibition and returned with a vengeance to Wall Street, where he had made his fortune as one of the most unsavory speculators of the 1920s.

Then, in 1934, Congress passed the Securities and Exchange Act, setting up a commission to combat fraudulent trading. To the surprise of nearly everyone, Roosevelt named Joe Kennedy, the so-called "King of the Street," to be its chairman. It takes a thief to catch a thief, FDR joked to intimates. Others were not amused. Roy Howard wrote a front-page editorial for the *Washington News* attacking the appointment. *The New Republic* denounced Kennedy as "that worst of all economic parasites, a Wall Street operator." Harold Ickes considered Kennedy nothing but a "stock-market plunger" and was dubious of Roosevelt's explanation that Kennedy wanted nothing more than to make a name for himself for the sake of his family.

But, in fact, things worked out astonishingly well. Since assuming office on July 2, Kennedy had proposed tough rules while sweet-talking the Street into believing the New Deal wished it well. He also assembled one of the brightest staffs in Washington, led by William O. Douglas of Yale Law School. The press found amusing Kennedy's attacks on "stock market gambling" and other unethical practices he had engaged in so recently himself. But in securing Wall Street acceptance of the SEC, Kennedy helped restore business confidence, and this might speed recovery. FDR also appreciated Kennedy's continuing efforts to keep W. R. Hearst and Father Charles Coughlin in line.

Pleased with his emergence as a Roosevelt intimate, Kennedy installed an elevator at his Marwood estate outside Washington to allow easy wheelchair access. This autumn he planned to entertain the President with good Scotch, Maine lobsters, and films flown in from Hollywood. Warm, easygoing, political to the core, the two men always had a good time together. FDR would tease Joe about his affair with Gloria Swanson, and Kennedy would make snide references to the President's stenographer, Missy LeHand.

Today, emerging from his lunch with the President at Hyde Park, Kennedy limped outside—he was nursing a broken leg—to announce that by October 1 the SEC would officially take over supervision of stock exchanges. Then he resumed his southward trek to Washington. After vacationing with his famously large family on Cape Cod, Kennedy was happy to return to work. He also looked forward to a trip out West at the end of the month. Joe would be returning to his old haunts in Hollywood, all arrangements provided by movie czar Will H. Hays.

After only a few hours' sleep and a hectic morning in Manhattan, a peaceful ride up the Albany Post Road to Hyde Park was looking pretty good to Upton Sinclair. He had courted reporters. He had entertained Dale Carnegie, who was writing a book called *Little-Known Facts about Well-Known People.* And he had swept down to City Hall for another meeting with Fiorello La Guardia.

Sinclair had congratulated the mayor on his Labor Day speech in Chicago, which had earned La Guardia the wrath of *The New York Times,* just as the mayor had hoped. La Guardia had called for "a new order in this country" and a more equitable division of profits. "The American people," he had declared, "are not satisfied with any system which causes and permits millions of willing workers to remain idle. . . . It may be necessary to make drastic changes." La Guardia pledged that in 1936 the country would witness "the last contest between the two great existing political parties, and in that campaign I venture to predict that there will be the greatest political upset ever seen in the history of American politics." Who would produce that upset? La Guardia himself? One of the La Follettes? Upton Sinclair?

It was two o'clock and time to leave for Hyde Park, eighty miles due north. Sinclair wore a white double-breasted suit. Bob Brownell and Crane Gartz accompanied him, and young William Loeb, Jr., took the wheel.

Sinclair had known Loeb's father back in the days of *The Jungle,* when Loeb Sr. was President Teddy Roosevelt's personal secretary. No fan of muckrakers, T.R. credited the author with drawing attention to the meat-packing problem but grew exasperated with his ceaseless demands for a Pure Food and Drug Act, finally instructing publisher Frank Doubleday to "tell Sinclair to go home and let me run the country for a while." Loeb later bought an estate in Oyster Bay, Long Island, near T.R.'s home. William Loeb, Jr., born in 1905, had Teddy Roosevelt for a godfather.

Loeb Jr., a brash youth, attended Williams College, where he majored in philosophy and resigned from a fraternity after it refused to admit a Jewish applicant. He also created a stir when he invited William F. Green, president of the American Federation of Labor—then considered a left-wing organization—to address a student group. After two years at Harvard Law School, Loeb turned to journalism, working as a cub reporter for Hearst, among others. His long-standing ambition was to own a daily newspaper in New England. Upton Sinclair was a shade radical for Loeb's taste, but the two men had this in common: they feared and hated American Communists with a passion.

Driving north along the Hudson, the Sinclair party passed through Tarrytown, where controversy still raged over the Jere Miah II mural. Today a town justice denied an appeal for John Smiukese's release while expressing sympathy for his motives in torching the anti-FDR painting. Sinclair and his friends continued northward, through Putnam and into Dutchess County, and were surprised to see the sumac already turning red. Sinclair recalled that in woods like these, not far away, he used to hunt rabbit and deer. That was back in his days as a struggling young writer in New York City. Once he rode a bicycle on this very road, long before it was paved, all the way up the Hudson to the Adirondacks.

Loeb, an expert on presidents named Roosevelt, had one bit of advice. "The whole country is waiting to know how Roosevelt receives you," he explained. "No matter what he says, and no matter how you really feel, you must look cheerful when you come out. The reporters will be watching every sign."

Just outside Hyde Park the party spotted a long line of trees and the entrance to the President's estate approaching on the left. A state trooper greeted them at the gate.

As Upton Sinclair headed for Hyde Park, the French liner *Ile de France,* carrying a Democrat whose support he coveted almost as much as the President's, docked in New York Harbor. New York held a special place in the long and remarkable life of Senator William Gibbs McAdoo of California. McAdoo built the first tunnel under the Hudson River connecting New York and New Jersey. And it was in New York, at Madison Square Garden, that McAdoo was denied his party's presidential nomination after 103 ballots at the 1924 Democratic National Convention. He came so close to the nomination, H. L. Mencken later wrote, "that the memory of its loss must still shiver him." Mencken found it amusing that eight years later McAdoo would deliver the convention delegates that put FDR over the top, for he was "certainly worth a dozen" Roosevelts.

The past two months had treated McAdoo poorly. He suffered from a variety of ailments, including carbuncles and a bad back. His wife, Eleanor, the daughter of Woodrow Wilson, divorced him, and his candidate, George Creel, lost in a race for governor. Now the Republicans, believing Mac had one foot in the grave, were offering Ray Haight his seat in the U.S. Senate.

On arrival in New York, the tall, rawboned McAdoo told reporters that he knew Upton Sinclair to be "a fine fellow and one of genuine sincerity," but that some elements of his EPIC plan were clearly preposterous. Mac planned to visit Hyde Park later this week. Two years had passed since he personally delivered the votes that put FDR on the road to the White House, and he felt the President still owed him a favor.

Logs crackled in the fireplace. The President occupied a large leather chair in his library; a block of documents a foot high rested on the table before him. "You see how far behind I am in my work," Franklin Roosevelt said.

"Actually," observed Upton Sinclair, sitting directly across from him, "we all marvel that you're so far ahead with it."

"I cannot go any faster than the people will let me," Roosevelt said.

"The people of my state," Sinclair responded eagerly, "will soon let you know what they are thinking!"

So much for keeping politics out of the conversation.

A servant brought two glasses of iced tea, then exited, leaving the two men alone. The President had rejected Jefty O'Connor's idea of having someone monitor the meeting. Since there were only two parties to this discussion, Roosevelt could afford to trust Sinclair. His visitor might actually keep his vow of secrecy; and if he didn't, FDR could always say that Sinclair recalled a particular statement or detail wrong. Whom would people believe: Franklin Roosevelt or Upton Sinclair? There would be no transcript, no third party, for Sinclair to appeal to.

Still, it wouldn't hurt to flatter Sinclair. The President was not above it—in fact, he was famous for it—and this fellow was known to take flattery to heart. FDR told Sinclair that he admired his work. When Franklin was a child, his mother used to read *The Jungle* to him at the breakfast table.

"And it spoiled your lamb chops?" Sinclair offered.

"Yes," the President said, throwing his great head back in a hearty laugh.

The story, of course, was suspect, since Roosevelt, at the time *The Jungle* was published, was married and a student at Columbia Law School. Apparently he thought his guest would gather this chestnut, and Sinclair obliged.

The President started telling stories out of school. He gossiped about some of his aides, his enemies in Washington, and Democratic politicians in California. He referred to John Elliott, the Democratic leader in Los Angeles, as "Black Jack" and warned Sinclair to be wary of him.

"I have met two presidents named Roosevelt in my life," Sinclair responded. "The other was Theodore, and I don't know which of you is the more indiscreet." Roosevelt threw his head back again and roared.

It was time to get down to business. Sinclair was determined not to settle for vintage Roosevelt. He had come to Hyde Park for political effect, but now that he was here, he discovered he was intensely curious about FDR. Was he a wise man, learning by his own blunders, or a blind man groping his way? He wanted to know how much the President really knew about conditions in California—and how familiar he was with the EPIC campaign.

Soon the candidate discovered that the President had either read *I,*

Governor or had been well briefed on the EPIC plan. They discussed EPIC's effect on unemployment, capital investment, and inflation. Sinclair finally found a detail Roosevelt seemed unfamiliar with—the so-called EPIC tax. Companies or utilities strapped for cash could pay their state taxes in the form of goods and services. This would provide materials (such as lumber and steel), as well as heat and electricity, for public-works projects. Roosevelt leapt right in, as if, Sinclair observed, firecrackers were going off in his head.

"Yes, it could be that way," he said, "but what if you did this . . ." Roosevelt asked questions, and before Sinclair could respond, FDR took the answers right out of his mouth. This was the President's own mind working, Sinclair discerned; he wasn't following a script.

Sinclair started off in another direction.

"Yes, that's important," FDR said, cutting him off. "I was just talking to someone about it yesterday."

Finally the old muckraker laughed. "I see you don't need me," Sinclair said. He would have understood if Roosevelt had responded to any particular point by saying, "I couldn't support that," or "You're right, but I can't say so right now." But the President never fell back on these staples of political obfuscation. If Sinclair was causing FDR any embarrassment, the President was doing a good job of concealing it.

This seemed an appropriate moment for Sinclair to urge his new friend to ignore reports about a third-party EPIC campaign for president in 1936. Roosevelt cheerfully informed his guest that he was itching to get back to writing and suggested that it might not be a bad idea for them to trade jobs for a while.

The two men had been scheduled to meet for sixty minutes, and the hour had long passed. It was now early evening, and the sky outside was darkening. The butler brought another tray of iced tea. Sinclair didn't know the proper etiquette. Should he rise, apologize for keeping the President so long, and leave? Or wait for FDR to terminate the conversation? The longer the discussion, the better it would appear for Sinclair; afterward he could use it as a yardstick of presidential interest and support. The meeting continued.

After a lengthy discussion of production for use, the President startled Sinclair with a revelation. "My advisers tell me that I have to talk to the people again over the radio and explain to them what I am doing," he said. "I am going to give that talk in two sections." The first speech would concern "general problems"; the second, unemployment. FDR seemed to suggest that he would deliver a fireside chat endorsing production for use sometime around October twenty-fifth—two weeks before Election Day.

Sinclair could hardly believe his ears. Ratification of his most important platform plank—the whole basis of the EPIC plan—would be almost as valuable as an endorsement of his candidacy.

"If you will do that, Mr. President," Sinclair said, barely able to contain his gratitude, "it will elect me."

Charles Chaplin motioned Alistair Cooke to join him on the terrace outside the writer's room at the Highland Hotel. Cooke and his new bride were set to return to the East Coast by train in the morning. On his last night in Hollywood, Chaplin had come for dinner, without Paulette Goddard.

Out on the terrace overlooking the hills, Charlie asked Alistair if he would stay on and act as assistant director on his new film. Cooke was startled, flattered beyond measure, but he had to decline. He explained that one of the conditions of his Commonwealth Fund fellowship was that after two years he must spend time in some part of the British Empire. Cooke was heading back to England to serve as film critic for the BBC. His creative goal, in any case, was not to conquer Hollywood but to be the next Eugene O'Neill.

Chaplin was disappointed. Then he revealed that what he really had in mind for Cooke was not filmmaking but performing. "If you stay with me," Charlie said, "I'll make you the best light comedian since Seymour Hicks."

As he stepped through the double doors and down the four stone steps leading to the waiting automobile, Upton Sinclair did not forget to broadcast a smile to express satisfaction. This was one smile that Sinclair did not have to force. Waving off reporters, he headed for a press briefing at the Nelson House in Poughkeepsie, a few miles south of Hyde Park. He couldn't wait to tell the world exactly what had transpired, but knew he shouldn't.

At the Nelson House, Sinclair sat down at a front table and stripped to his shirtsleeves. A mob of reporters, photographers, and newsreel cameramen crowded around. "Well," he said, still panting from a walk up the stairs, "I just had the most interesting two-hour conference I ever had in my life." Sinclair brushed aside requests for specifics but pointed out that the President had entertained him for two solid hours, or twice the scheduled allotment.

If Roosevelt's aim was to keep a potential rival off his back, he clearly succeeded. Sinclair treated FDR like the Great White Father. He called him "a marvel," "open-minded and lovable," "a very cheerful-hearted man and a tonic to the whole nation." While refusing to quote the President on any topic, Sinclair slyly suggested that it was apparent that the New Deal was "catching up" with EPIC. "I don't think I ought to say anything about what he said about the California or national political situation," Sinclair added, coyly confirming that the two men, contrary to the party line, did talk politics.

A newsman, perhaps sensing that the candidate was one gaffe away from committing political suicide, called Sinclair's attention to the tall, almost emaciated figure of Marvin McIntyre sitting inconspicuously off to the side. Happy that he hadn't yet disclosed anything of importance, but uncertain of it, Sinclair nervously fingered his glasses and asked McIntyre if he was being a good boy. The President's assistant nodded his approval, so Sinclair continued in this coquettish vein for another fifteen minutes.

"We folks out in California speculate as to what the President knows about what we are doing," Sinclair said, fairly radiating. "I am very happy to tell the people of California that he knows."

Managing to complete this performance without a fatal faux pas, Sinclair motored back to Manhattan. It was now well past eight o'clock, and the candidate had a nationwide radio date at ten-fifteen. Unfamiliar with the road, William Loeb broke the speed limit barreling through the Bronx and down Riverside Drive. Sinclair figured that if they were stopped by a cop, he would simply explain that he was late for an appointment because the President of the United States had kept him for so long. When he reached the WMCA studio, he was seven minutes behind schedule, but no one seemed to care. They encouraged him to talk as long as he wished. But the candidate had one more appointment to keep before catching the midnight train to Washington.

Sinclair rushed over to the Biltmore Hotel to meet James Farley at the Democratic headquarters. When they shook hands, the tall, strapping Democratic leader unexpectedly said, "Call me Jim." For a moment, the diminutive Sinclair pictured himself as a blushing maiden being introduced to a new beau. He felt like saying, "Jim, this is so sudden!" Sinclair was surprised to find Farley so rosy in appearance, so genial in manner. Farley offered a little political advice, some of it smacking a bit too much of Tammany Hall for Sinclair's taste.

After twenty-five minutes behind closed doors, the two prominent Democrats emerged, smiling broadly. "Mr. Farley," Sinclair announced to the waiting press mob, "told me he was pleased that I shared his opinion of our Chief Executive. Further than that you will have to talk to Mr. Farley."

"We had quite a pleasant chat," Farley added. "We did not discuss politics."

With that statement, which brought his visit to New York full circle, Upton Sinclair left for Grand Central, believing for the first time, after twelve months of campaigning, that the governorship was within his grasp.

SEPTEMBER 5

WEDNESDAY

At ten minutes to eleven, the President's 141st press conference got under way with the usual verbal horseplay. This time the subject was Monday's softball victory over Lowell Thomas's team.

"There is only one way we can be sure of winning," FDR observed. When the *Crimson* battled the *Lampoon* at Harvard, he confessed, his team always put one keg of beer at second base and one at third base.

"How did you get anybody to home plate?" one newsman asked.

"Oh, we had two kegs there," the President explained.

When the laughter died down, another reporter posed the question of the hour. "Speaking of kegs," he said, "what did you feed Upton Sinclair?"

The first fatalities in the textile strike had just been recorded. Someone had fired five shots at Huey Long's house in New Orleans. At Nuremberg, Adolf Hitler was predicting a thousand-year *Reich* and blaming "Jewish intellectualism" for the degeneration of German art into cubism, dadaism, and futurism. Yet FDR's meeting with Upton Sinclair was the subject most on the mind of the press gang gathered in the President's study.

The whole country was talking about yesterday's tea chat at Hyde

Park. SINCLAIR IS ELATED BY ROOSEVELT TALK, *The New York Times* boomed on its front page. SINCLAIR IS HAPPY MAN, *The Washington Post* observed. The *Post* also published a poem by humor columnist H. I. Phillips, entitled "Rooseveltian Soliloquy":

> This is the question that's
> Thinning my hair;
> What'll I do about
> Upton Sinclair?
>
> If I embrace him
> The slams will be hot.
> And I'll be roasted
> If I do not.
>
> Choosing a course is
> Not such a snap;
> Why did they put that
> Guy in my lap?

California newspapers covered the story under banner headlines—they could hardly ignore it—but often in an unflattering light. Ted Gale's editorial cartoon in the *Los Angeles Times,* called "The Unwanted Child!," portrayed INNOCENT LITTLE UPTON in a baby basket on the doorstep of THE SUMMER WHITE HOUSE, while a bearded fellow, labeled THE REDS, hid just out of sight of a worried FDR.

"Do you know what I fed him?" Roosevelt said, responding to the reporter's question about Sinclair. "Two long glasses of iced tea."

"You must have had something in them," one correspondent quipped. Another added, "He was babbling when he came back." A third chimed in, "Mr. President, can you tell us anything more than Sinclair told us yesterday in five thousand well-chosen words?"

"He promised you were going to tell us," another interjected, making mischief.

"Did he, really?" the President said, raising his eyebrows and grinning.

"Yes."

"Then he must have had *something* on the way to Poughkeepsie."

Laughter again.

"There is nothing that you can say about it, Mr. President?"

"No."

"Cannot you discuss the EPIC plan along purely nonpolitical lines?"

"No."

The President volunteered little else. He took a few jabs, however, at both sides in the textile walkout. He criticized Norman Thomas for allegedly instigating the strike with an ill-timed speech but suggested that management had practically begged for a confrontation. FDR also aimed his ire at critics who belittled the administration's budgetary problems. Some of the newsmen had never seen the President this irritated. Roosevelt said he would have to amend his famous statement that America had nothing to fear but fear itself. "I would now say," the President declared, "that there is a greater thing that America needs to fear, and that is those who seek to instill fear into the American people."

Otherwise, FDR commented, "we are feeling very well this morning."

As good as the President felt, no one was feeling any better than Upton Sinclair. Making his way through the enormous crowd at the National Press Club, Sinclair was as sunny as a California lemon.

The Press Club auditorium was packed with several hundred curiosity seekers. Even tables placed in the gallery failed to accommodate the throng. Besides scores of journalists, many prominent New Dealers turned out, and Henry P. Fletcher, chairman of the Republican National Committee, sat right down front, no more than fifteen feet from the candidate. This would be a tough audience, mixing as it did the suspicious, the expert, and the antagonistic. A nationwide radio audience would eavesdrop on the proceedings.

As the luncheon crowd downed cocktails and consumed ham and beans, Sinclair sipped milk and munched on lettuce. William C. Murphy, president of the Press Club, introduced the speaker as "a man who made political history in recent days," and Upton Sinclair, dressed in a tan double-breasted suit, stepped before the microphone to polite applause and delivered his standard stump speech. Reporters, to their surprise, found Sinclair professorial and unthreatening. He sketched the EPIC plan and explained production for use, calling this "the next stage in civilization that lies before us."

When Sinclair finished, the questions flew hard and fast, sometimes with tricky topspin. Like the expert tennis player he was, Sinclair volleyed brilliantly, displaying unexpected humor. The jaded journalists were impressed. Next to practically any Roosevelt press conference, this was, nearly everyone agreed, the grandest political performance in recent Washington history. Like FDR, Sinclair had a "famous" smile. One correspondent thought the little man was downright puckish.

What did Roosevelt tell him yesterday? "I thought my ideas were original until I talked to the President," Sinclair replied brightly. "Last night I slept like a baby, because I said to myself, 'For the first time we are safe, Roosevelt can run the country.' "

Was he still a Socialist? "I haven't changed my principles, but I have changed my technique. For thirty years I had been drawing the picture of an ideal commonwealth, but nothing happened. Socialists have been using long words like 'collectivism' that no one understands. I say 'abolish poverty.' That is plain language that everybody can understand."

Would production for use one day replace capitalism entirely? "I say in California let's try it as an experiment and see how it works. . . . What we are doing in California *you* can do when you wake up and get ready!"

What if EPIC scared businessmen into leaving the state? "It is hard to drive people out of California."

When Sinclair was asked about his campaign fund-raising schemes, the candidate made them sound like a concert tour or an Aimee McPherson revival show. Tickets for his most recent midday appearance in Oakland, for example, cost seventy-five cents, with each ticket holder responsible for selling an additional ten tickets for another gala meeting that night. At the jam-packed evening rally, they passed the hat, shaking another six hundred dollars out of the pockets of the faithful. Politicians were not in the habit of charging people admission to see them, knowing that if they did they might speak to an empty hall. Sinclair's novel, yet in his case necessary, approach to campaign finance showed that with the right candidate some of the techniques of show biz and evangelism could be applied to the art of raising money. Observers at the Press Club luncheon swore they saw a wicked glint in the eyes of Henry Fletcher, the embattled GOP chairman.

After an hour of questioning, Sinclair was still standing, and only about a dozen of the curious had departed. Applause rang through the auditorium. Even the representatives of high finance seemed more amused than outraged when Sinclair referred at one point to "bankers and other parasites."

Stepping down from the platform, the conquering hero was introduced to Henry Fletcher, a sturdy white-haired gentleman wearing a bright, pin-striped suit. The conversation was cordial for a moment, but the mood changed when Sinclair, with a smile, said, "Well, Mr. Fletcher, I guess you and I will be crossing political swords pretty soon."

Fletcher scowled, and in a voice that sounded like sandpaper on concrete, growled, "Any time, any time."

Dorothy Parker was happy to be back in California. Signing a new contract this morning with Paramount, at a salary of five thousand dollars a week, she also felt a bit sheepish, for she was the latest in a long line of literary figures to arrive in Hollywood with much fanfare, having once vowed never to return.

For several dozen celebrity writers, Hollywood was truly the land of milk and honey. Since the dawn of the talkies, the studios had lured star newspapermen, playwrights, and novelists with sunshine and fat paychecks, which most of the writers were wholly unaccustomed to. Some, on arrival, bought automobiles for the first time. The émigrés from the East looked down their noses at the crude moguls and posturing actors, then knocked off early and headed for the pool, the racetrack, or the beach.

"Millions are to be grabbed out here," Herman Mankiewicz had wired his friend Ben Hecht, "and your only competition is idiots." It was an invitation few could resist—not John Dos Passos, not Scott Fitzgerald, not even Thomas Wolfe. MGM grabbed the lion's share: Robert Benchley, Anita Loos, Joseph and Herman Mankiewicz, George S. Kaufman and Morrie Ryskind, Frances Marion, P. G. Wodehouse, S. J. Perelman, Charles MacArthur, Carey Wilson.

Some came and left quickly, in disgust. "It's slave labor and what do you get for it?" one writer complained. "A bloody fortune!" After working on eight scripts for MGM in 1932, only two of which were produced, William Faulkner happily returned to writing stories in Mississippi, announcing that he had "not forgot how to write during my sojourn downriver." The only reason anyone would ever go to Hollywood, Faulkner announced, was "to get what money he could get out of it." Following this dictum, he returned in July 1934 to work on *Sutter's Gold* for Universal.

Departing Hollywood in 1931, Dorothy Parker boasted that she hadn't actually written a single word. Hollywood was the Klondike, Sodom-in-the-Sun, Poughkeepsie with palms. Streets were paved with Goldwyn, she sighed. The pay was good, but in Hollywood money was like congealed snow in your hand. She likened Beverly Hills, where she lived, to a woman in a Cadillac dangling a mink-clad arm out the window and holding a bagel.

Although her initial stay in Hollywood lasted only three months, stories about her season in the sun were legion. "Where does my contract allow time to fornicate?" she supposedly asked one MGM executive. . . . Upon occupying her office at MGM, she stripped the nameplate from the door and replaced it with MEN. . . . After completing a script and then waiting for days to see Irving Thalberg, she abandoned her office to meet a gentleman in Santa Barbara. When Thalberg, suddenly unable to reach her, wrote to complain, she replied that the only excuse for her absence was that she was "too fucking busy and vice versa."

Now, three years later, the sparkling critic, poet, and short-story writer, often called, to her horror, "American's only female humorist," was back, with her two Bedlington puppies and new husband Alan Campbell, to supply witty dialogue for Paramount. Dottie and her handsome bridegroom, who at age twenty-nine was twelve years her junior, would write in tandem. Their first assignment: a piece of fluff entitled *One Hour Late.* Dottie considered scriptwriting a bore, a strenuous bore—you sat there and sat there and sat there—but she thought they might be able to toss it off in about a week. Then they would relax and enjoy themselves. Everything about California that wasn't writing was fun.

While looking for a mansion to call their own, the couple, like so many transplanted literati before them, pitched their tent at the Garden of Allah on Sunset Boulevard. This garish stucco bungalow hotel was home, at the moment, to Dottie's old friends Bob Benchley, Aleck Woollcott, John O'Hara, and Donald Ogden Stewart.

Hollywood was happy to have Dorothy Parker back, and though Parker might deny it, she fit right in. She was a celebrity herself, and on her arm she wore a tattoo in the shape of a star. Her life-style was suitably flamboyant. She had engendered numerous affairs (with Charlie MacArthur, Ring Lardner, and Scott Fitzgerald, among others), at least two suicide attempts, and a marriage to a much younger man that had Hollywood tongues clucking already. Like her fictional character Hazel Morse, she was socially promiscuous and always good for a few laughs. At parties, some guests demanded, others dreaded, one of Parker's famous put-downs, always delivered in a soft, pleasant voice. This was one person whose bite was frighteningly worse than her bark.

Alexander Woollcott called her "so odd a combination of Little Nell and Lady Macbeth." When George Bernard Shaw attended a party of international celebrities on the Riviera, the one person he asked to meet was Dottie Parker. Surprised by her girlishness, he admitted that he had "always thought of her as an old maid." Only five feet tall, and no Garbo or Dietrich, she was nevertheless interesting to look at, with her cute bangs, wide brown eyes, and huge hats. "A tired Renoir" was how her friend Sheilah Graham described her. Dottie never wore her eyeglasses when men were around, proving that her most famous couplet (concerning men, passes, girls, and glasses) was heartfelt.

What Hollywood didn't know about Dorothy Parker was that she had a hidden political agenda. Back in New York she was, with Lillian Hellman, a chief organizer of the Screen Writers Guild. Even worse, she had privately declared herself a Communist. All she meant by this, friends believed, was that she felt sympathy for the poor and wanted to help them, and was mad at the rich (who wouldn't). Several years ago, Parker had been arrested, with Robert Benchley and John Dos Passos, for protesting the execution of Sacco and Vanzetti. Now she had taken up a new cause, the Scottsboro Boys—nine young blacks arrested in Alabama on charges of raping two white women—and planned to throw a fund-raising bash for them when she got settled in Hollywood.

Dottie had come a long way from her prosperous but lonely childhood as Dorothy Rothschild. As a young woman, she began to identify with the underprivileged. Her slashing wit, said to be the product of mere cynicism—Mencken in verse—actually reflected a kind of crushed idealism. As self-contemptuous as she was critical of others, Parker found that the left-wing politics of the 1930s gave her life new purpose.

Naturally she supported Upton Sinclair's EPIC crusade. Like so many of Upton's admirers, she was no fan of his fiction. His muckraking, she once remarked, was marred by his inability to "keep himself out of his writings, try though he may; or, by this time, try though he doesn't." Also, he had become a confirmed bellyacher. Many socialists get to be that way, she observed, "and I say it though my heart and soul are with the cause of socialism."

Still, she loved Sinclair as a symbol, as a cause. "To me," she had written back in 1927, "Upton Sinclair is one of the American great. I have no words worthy of being laid before his courage, his passion, his integrity." As she signed on at Paramount for another tour of duty, Parker was determined to put some of her own passion into politics, Hollywood-style.

They had fifteen minutes to get to Harry Hopkins's office, so Upton Sinclair suggested to Bob Brownell, Crane Gartz, and *Washington Post* reporter Robert T. DeVore, "Let's hike it." This was how he got his exercise, he explained. With Sinclair leading the way, the four men left the Department of Agriculture, where the candidate had called on several officials, cut across the grounds of the Washington Monument, and arrived at the Federal Emergency Relief Administration (FERA) with thirty seconds to spare.

Hopkins, a professional social worker with the zeal of a reformer, greeted Sinclair warmly. They agreed on the fundamental importance of getting people off relief and into productive jobs. Hopkins had just come from lunch with Harold Ickes over at Interior, where the two had discussed Hoppy's proposed five-year, twenty-five-billion-dollar public-works initiative. Sinclair found Hopkins to be frank and clearheaded and well aware of conditions on the West Coast. (Hopkins's brother was running for the post of coroner in Tacoma, Washington, as a Republican, causing Harry to comment, "I thought that party was buried two years ago.")

When he emerged, Sinclair was jubilant, for Hopkins had informed him that federal funds could be allotted to the governor of any state for the purpose of putting the unemployed to work. Sinclair wanted not one penny more than two hundred million dollars. "As the result of our conference," Sinclair told reporters, "I have every reason to believe we will get our money."

One of Hopkins's assistants showed Upton the fruits of the Ohio Plan, which the President had told him about yesterday. Sinclair examined a couple of pairs of shoes, a rather well-made coat, and a ragged catalog picturing hundreds of other items produced by workers in Ohio. The government had leased twelve idle factories and put more than five hundred people to work. The laborers produced clothing, furniture, and other necessities and in return received credit that could be applied to selections in the catalog. A factory worker in one town might trade the time he spent making some dishes for a mattress a comrade assembled across the state.

"It is the EPIC system and the New Deal is helping it out," Sinclair advised reporters. There were some differences to be sure, but the cooperative groundwork was the same: the unemployed would produce goods and exchange them among themselves outside ordinary business channels. FERA promoted similar experiments in several other states, and big business was already howling at Hopkins. Every set of trousers selected from a FERA catalog, they charged, was one fewer pair of pants purchased from a store. Soon the clothing factories run by private industry would be forced to close, they warned, swelling the ranks of the unemployed. A process would begin that inevitably would end in the bankruptcy of private business and the absorption of all labor into one big co-op.

This, of course, was the unstated premise of the EPIC campaign. It was Upton Sinclair's unspoken rebuttal to Norman Thomas and other critics on his left. EPIC was nothing less than a roundabout route to socialism.

———

The clerk at Boccanfuso's fruit and vegetable store at Third Avenue and Eighty-ninth Street in Manhattan remembered very clearly how he had secured the incriminating ten-dollar gold note. A customer had offered Salvatore Levitano the ten-dollar bill in payment for a six-cent purchase. If business wasn't so lousy, Levitano would have told him to get lost. Instead, he handed over the change. Then he deposited the gold note, with other bills, at the National Bank of Yorkville.

This afternoon the FBI informed the clerk that the rare ten-dollar gold note had been traced to the Lindbergh ransom money. Could he describe the man who had passed the bill? He could, and did, and the description matched the shadowy murder suspect known only as John. FBI chief investigator Thomas Sisk assigned several plainclothes officers to the Upper East Side. For two and a half years, the nation had been obsessed with the Lindbergh kidnapping. Now it appeared that a breakthrough in solving the century's most heinous crime was finally at hand.

———

Upton Sinclair was coming for dinner, so Rex Tugwell wanted to shoot off a memo to the President in a hurry. Tugwell had the unpleasant task, after meeting with Henry Wallace and Donald R. Richberg, of informing the President that the feeling was unanimous: NRA chief Hugh Johnson had to go. FDR should arrange it so that "the break comes on a personal question" rather than on a policy that Johnson could then appear to champion.

No matter how the President framed it, Tugwell would probably get blamed for the firing anyway. Tugwell had served as lightning rod for the administration practically from the moment he joined Raymond Moley and A. A. Berle in the original Brain Trust triumvirate. The only way FDR got Tugwell's appointment as undersecretary of agriculture past the Senate was by making a deal with Senator Ellison D. ("Cotton Ed") Smith of South Carolina: FDR would get Tugwell, and Smith would be allowed to appoint as a U.S. marshal an old friend who happened to have a homicide record. At a cabinet meeting a few days later, Roosevelt announced that he had "traded Rex Tugwell for the favorite murderer of Senator Smith of South Carolina."

When W. R. Hearst asserted that some of Roosevelt's aides were more "Communistic than the Communists themselves," he was referring, notably, to Tugwell. (Of course, if the New Deal actually succeeded, Tugwell would probably be credited with helping to save capitalism in America.) More than once Tugwell offered to resign to save the President embarrassment, but FDR wanted him close at hand. Among other things, he served as FDR's emissary to the Populists and Progressives, making them feel a part of the New Deal family.

Now the President had assigned him to keep Upton Sinclair "sweet." (Ironically, Tugwell hailed from a small town in upstate New York called Sinclairville.) Tugwell once fancied himself a poet, and he liked to hobnob with Sinclair Lewis and other writers. When Tugwell met Upton Sinclair at Hyde Park yesterday, he found him to be a pale and pleasant gentleman with a kind manner and soft voice. The New Deal pretty much fulfilled Sinclair's hopes, Tugwell believed. And after a lifetime as a political outcast, the writer seemed pleased to be regarded as respectable.

Unlike most of Roosevelt's associates, Tugwell admired the nation's many leftist governors. He felt they were fighting FDR's battles right at the front lines—and the least the administration could do was to support them. FDR encouraged his friendship with the radicals and expected him to help forge some sort of coherent liberal movement. Like Woodrow Wilson, Roosevelt believed that the greatest challenge for the head of a democracy was not to fend off reactionaries but to reconcile and unite progressives.

This effort to forge a liberal alliance was constantly sabotaged, however, by Jim Farley's insistence on Democratic "regularity" and cronyism, Tugwell felt. Farley had become what Tugwell called an "ultra-party man," not FDR's man. Big Jim continued to use patronage to strengthen the Democratic organization, even in places where reactionary Democrats were running against progressive Republicans friendly to the New Deal. At this rate, Tugwell feared, FDR would never succeed in his avowed goal of reforming and liberalizing the Democratic party.

Since Upton Sinclair was running as a Democrat—no matter how irregular—he at least had a fighting chance of gaining the administration's support. To prime this pump, Tugwell added a few sentences, seemingly an afterthought, at the end of his memo to the President. "Upton Sinclair talked with the newspapermen this noon at the Press Club and seemed to have taken them completely into camp," Tugwell wrote. "They tell me that he can have a large majority vote from them if they were asked to decide on his election. He is coming out to my house tonight quietly and I hope to have a talk with him then.

"I think the situation has been handled beautifully so far," Tugwell observed, "and from his behavior I think he can be trusted to do exactly as you direct. . . ."

SEPTEMBER 8

SATURDAY

"Harry, I told them I'm tired and I don't need this nomination for myself," Upton Sinclair said, leaning over the table to address his friend Harry Hansen, who was busily probing a lobster. "I said that I could always make enough money to live on writing books and that I had enough fame and publicity for one man." From the far end of the table, red-haired Johnny Farrar shouted out, "Upton, you've never looked better in all your life!"

Sinclair laughed and settled back in his chair at the Harvard Club in Manhattan, where his publishers, Messrs. Farrar and Rinehart, had invited a knot of book critics to meet the candidate over lunch. The lobster, everyone agreed, was excellent. "It looks very much as though I am going to be elected governor of California," Upton announced. "In all the city of Washington I could find no government official who disagreed with our plan or purpose. Even Secretary Ickes was favorably impressed. I've been welcomed into the family."

For forty-eight hours, Upton Sinclair had indeed captured the imagination of official Washington. On Thursday night, he could not get a single guest at Rex Tugwell's dinner party to identify any fault with the EPIC plan. FDR should endorse him, Harry Hopkins said, and forget all the other "bunk." Even Justice Louis Brandeis, an ardent anti-socialist, seemed friendly. The following day Henry Morgenthau advised Upton not to be afraid to ask him for "anything." (Hearing that in the United States Treasury made Sinclair laugh.) Then the candidate discussed with Secretary Ickes his plans for reviving the Central Valley Project, which involved damming the Sacramento River and diverting water to the dry San Joaquin Valley. EPIC could handle it on the cheap by sending fifty thousand unemployed workers to construct the system, Sinclair said. Revitalized farms would feed them, and the "EPIC tax" on corporations would take care of the goods and services. "That is a novel and important idea," Ickes replied, "and if it succeeds it can be applied all over the country."

Yesterday, back at the Algonquin, Sinclair found *The New York Times* declaring that he seemed to be "in love with his new role as Democrat." That was true enough, but by now he wearied of the attention. Someone wanted to make a feature film about EPIC. Someone else wanted to lead a caravan of EPIC supporters from New York to California. Flashbulbs popped, newsreel cameras whirred. Telephones rang in three different rooms, secretaries delivered messages, magazine editors arrived with assignments while an artist sketched his portrait, and old friends like Neil Vanderbilt hung around waiting to say hello. Now, as one of his last official acts in the East—he was booked on a a midnight train heading west—Sinclair was wooing New York critics, hoping they would be kinder to his politics than most of them had been to his books.

"The machinery of the present regimen is worn out, stale," Sinclair said, brushing a few crumbs of bread off the white tablecloth. "It needs refurbishing and we in America have our own way of putting a fresh jacket on this book. We're not book collectors—not most of us, anyway. We don't want a foreign edition. We want our own edition, presented in the type we recognize and enjoy and with our idiom and our terminology.

"You know, 'epics' may also be written in the annals of statecraft. For all we know, they may even outlast the literary variety."

Henry Mencken was one literary critic who found the EPIC saga as indigestible as most of Upton Sinclair's novels. The two writers' political views were no more compatible than their personal habits. Until recently, they at least shared an aversion to the party in power. Now they even argued about Roosevelt. Once they were both political outcasts.

Now Sinclair was in vogue, and it was Mencken who was dancing on the fringe.

From the beginning of their friendship in 1918, there was about as much chance of Sinclair converting Mencken to socialism as there was of Mencken leading Sinclair to drink. Sinclair wanted to remake society; Mencken, the individual. Sinclair had faith in the common man; Mencken felt most people were "imbeciles" who could do next to nothing to change history. "So long as there are men in the world," Mencken told Sinclair, "ninety-nine percent of them will be idiots." That was why a democracy, for Mencken, was in many ways the worst form of government.

To Mencken, any scenario for social change was mere quackery. (Sinclair once had an idea for a short story about a young Menckenite who witnesses the crucifixion of Christ and goes away muttering about what a "dumb-bell" Jesus was.) A fiscal conservative, Mencken considered Sinclair's "government-worship" unmanly. "To hell with Socialism!" he once told Sinclair. "The longer I live, the more I am convinced that the common people are doomed to be diddled forever. You are fighting a vain fight."

During the 1920s, when both men skewered Republican presidents and their wealthy patrons, it was easy to think that they shared a distaste for plutocracy. This was not exactly true. Mencken mourned the passing of a true aristocracy in America, one based on the qualities of intelligence, nobility, refinement—the makings of "the first-rate man." He yearned for Jefferson's aristocracy of talent and virtue. The country was now run by cads and Babbitts, not gentlemen.

The coming of the Depression confirmed each writer's worldview, in spades. To Sinclair, it proved that fundamental change was necessary, while for Mencken it provided ample evidence that the human condition was hopeless. The gods of public opinion were now with Uppie. No matter how hilariously Mencken mocked the status quo, he was, de facto, siding with it. Sinclair admired Mencken "for his fighting qualities, but scolding is not enough; you have to know what to do to remedy affairs, and Mencken does not know. He is ignorant of the revolutionary movement, and that is the cause of the sterility of his work."

For a short time, the two writers shared a reluctant curiosity about Franklin Roosevelt. A month before FDR's inauguration, Mencken wrote Sinclair, "I hear confidentially that the end of the depression is in sight. The moment Roosevelt gets into the White House the bankers will pass the word along and their slaves and everyone else will begin to buy radios and Fords again." But by the middle of 1934, Mencken was mocking Roosevelt in unusually strident tones. This turnabout didn't surprise a soul: in his entire life, Mencken had never supported a sitting president. Perhaps Roosevelt's greatest sin was that he had gone back on his patrician upbringing. FDR, it turned out, believed in helping the little people. Worst of all, he brought college professors to the White House as advisers. Mencken declared that planned economies were fine, but they were possible only in dictatorships. "Give the people time to watch the tax bills roll and pile up," he predicted. "They'll throw out the quacks." To Mencken the "slimy false pretenses and idiotic contradictions of the Brain Trust" were no better than "the blind, envious fury of Upton Sinclair."

This kind of commentary, however, was now rare for Mencken, who recognized that his heyday as a political analyst and literary critic had passed. The young lions no longer admired him. When he gave up editing *The American Mercury* in 1933, it marked the end of an era. H. L. Mencken had become, of all things, a columnist for W. R. Hearst.

Seeking refuge, Mencken retreated to his study of language, and that was why 704 Cathedral Street in Baltimore was currently littered with notes, books, and manuscripts relating to his favorite subject. He couldn't resist zinging Upton Sinclair, though—everyone expected it, Uppie most of all. So he put off his demanding mistress, *The American Language,* to hunt and peck at the keyboard for the proper words to express just the right tone of fondness and indignation.

Sinclair would defeat Frank Merriam, Mencken predicted in this essay for the *Evening Sun,* simply because it was "a zoological fact" that there were more nontaxpayers than taxpayers in California, and the bogus Democrat was offering each and every one of them "forty acres and a mule." For years, the mentally halt and blind had been pouring into Los Angeles, making the southern third of the state "one vast home for incurables." Nowhere else on earth were its collection of idiots and incompetents matched. Every sort of lunacy ever heard of was preached there, and hundreds of new ones had been hatched. Such things as Holy Rollerism, osteopathy, and chiropractic, hooted at in the East, were almost orthodox in California. Aimee McPherson was "as high-toned as a presiding elder." According to police records, some of the cults advocated human sacrifice.

A movement to save humanity was always under way simply because so many in Los Angeles were constantly in need of saving. They arrive from the Midwest and "invite their souls on the dole." The weather is so balmy, they don't even need a roof over their heads. "But no one, of course, ever heard of a mendicant who believed he was getting enough," Mencken declared. "They all aspire to more, and the New Deal metaphysic has taught them that what they aspire to is theirs by right. Upon this teaching Sinclair grounded his campaign in the primary." Like the New Deal, EPIC was based on the theory that it was immoral to earn any more than a bare subsistence "and that the only virtuous property right is the right of the improvident and indigent to the property of the thrifty."

> Such are the main outlines of the EPIC plan for converting California into an earthly paradise. It had only to be announced to win the hearty support of the melancholy misfits now accumulated in the southern part of the State. To the northward there was skepticism, but south of Bakersfield and San Luis Obispo it came as a revelation from Sinai. All the played-out farmers from Iowa and the Dakotas were for it instantly, and all the veterans of greenbackism, free silver and the single tax, and all the students of the swamis, and all the miscellaneous clients of naturopathy, faith healing, rosicrucianism, astrology and the New Deal. Sinclair himself was known to be a Prohibitionist, a vegetarian, and a believer in both mental telepathy and the spondylotherapy of Dr. Albert Abrams. Thus he was a proved wizard, and there was no resistance to EPIC.

This was vintage Mencken, misanthropic and consciously exaggerated but not entirely off the mark. He might be losing his audience but he was not losing his sting. The sage of Baltimore dismissed his friend Uppie with a poisonous kiss on the cheek:

> The campaign promises to make a gaudy show. Merriam, who is a hack politician of the hollowest sort, will try to hang on to the Governorship by raising a Red scare, and Sinclair will try to wrest it from him by crowing the dawn of the New Jerusalem. For one, I hope that Sinclair wins. It is always amusing to see a utopian in office, and this one is far bolder, vainer and more credulous than the general. Certainly he will perform with more dash and deviltry than the decaying and over cautious pedagogues of the New Deal.

An elderly lady walked into a downtown Los Angeles theater, *Variety* reported this morning, and spotting a poster proclaiming a new Fox film an EPIC, demanded to know from the doorman whether the Fox studio was backing Upton Sinclair. The question was not as absurd as it seemed, for Hollywood appeared dazzled by the Sinclair candidacy. Rumors, reports, and threats splintered off in a dozen futile directions. With Louis B. Mayer detained in Europe by his wife's illness, Hollywood was the proverbial chicken with its head cut off.

Awaiting directions from King Louis, the moguls were lying low, allowing the trade press to lead the charge. *Variety* mocked Sinclair's plan to offer jobs to actors and others who wanted to avoid "manual work." The *Hollywood Reporter* poked harmless fun at Sinclair's "EPIC Pictures Corporation." The studios hinted they might leave town if Sinclair won—so why did the *Motion Picture Herald* report that MGM was launching a massive expansion program? This would not do. Hollywood was foundering as badly as the Republican party in devising a coherent anti-Sinclair strategy. Someone had to take charge until Louis Mayer returned, and it had to be a heavy hitter, not some flack or trade-magazine flunky.

Fortunately, a man who fit the bill had decided to step forward. Today he was partying on his one-hundred-foot yacht, *The Invader,* with Clark Gable, but he planned to swing into political action soon. It was none other than that inveterate womanizer, master of the malaprop ("Don't cut off the hand that lays the golden egg"), and exemplar of Hollywood decadence—United Artists president Joseph M. Schenck.

One of Joe Schenck's favorite partners in intrigue was the secret boss of California, Artie Samish, and why not? What were vices for Schenck—gambling and drinking—were clients for Samish. Some claimed that Joe's name was pronounced "Skenk, as in skunk," but Samish considered him a real sweetheart. Whatever Schenck wanted, Artie tried to get for him—little things, like legalized racetrack betting in California and the repeal of Prohibition.

Schenck himself was something of a pioneer in the art of lobbying: during the 1920s, he had the bright idea of providing every state legislator a free movie pass, the first time this type of perk was awarded in California. When daylight saving time caught on in several states in the early 1930s, Schenck and Samish organized Hollywood's first full-scale lobbying effort ever—and kept it out of California. The moguls feared the extra hour of daylight would drive people away from movie theaters.

Samish performed other legislative favors for Louis Mayer, Jack Warner, and Harry Cohn, but it was the beer and liquor industry, not Hollywood, that provided his bread and butter. It not only awarded him a huge stipend with which to defend its interests in Sacramento, it also offered Samish a network of forty thousand taverns and liquor stores that could be organized in behalf of a political candidate. During political campaigns, the industry also lent Samish thousands of billboards. Some of his other clients did the same. This made Samish the political commissar of outdoor advertising.

Upton Sinclair and Frank Merriam were both drys—they supported Prohibition—but there was no question whom the beer and liquor interests favored. Sinclair was infinitely more dangerous. He was an anti-drink crusader and was likely to impose new taxes on the brewers. And so, as a favor to the beer barons, Samish called a meeting of southern California newspaper publishers in San Bernardino.

It was top secret, but one of Sinclair's friends in the press called EPIC headquarters and described what transpired. According to this source, the brewers, operating under the name Steadfast Californians and including such giants as Rainier and Anheuser-Busch, offered to provide generous amounts of paid advertising to members of the California Newspapers Publishers Association if each paper would run a series of editorials under the general title "Stand Fast—America." The press campaign against Sinclair would change from week to week, following the flow of the campaign.

First, the newspapers were to institute a blackout on all EPIC activities. The following week would be Ridicule Sinclair Week. After that, Distort EPIC Week. Then, Sidetrack Sinclair Week, during which voters were to be fed irrelevant and false issues, such as communism and religion. As part of Minimize Sinclair Week, he was to be merely laughed at, but in mid-October, Discredit Sinclair Week would lay down the heaviest barrage of the campaign. Finally, the battle won, Merriam Week would arrive at last. The incumbent governor, no more than an apparition until then, would suddenly materialize as the sane, steady pilot of California's ship of state.

W. R. Hearst personally took charge of derailing the comeback hopes of his old friend Herbert Hoover—all the way from Europe. Ignoring Louis B. Mayer's pleas on Hoover's behalf, Hearst ordered his newspapers to prepare editorials pushing the former president "back into his political tomb." Hoover was the "most conspicuous failure in American history," Hearst cabled his editors.

Hearst was not alone in reacting furiously to the excerpts from the former president's new book published in this week's *Saturday Evening Post.* Hoover disappointed several different audiences: those who hoped for a vindictive attack on FDR, those who thought he might offer some fresh insights into what went wrong during his presidency, and those who expected concrete suggestions on how to end the crisis inherited by his successor. The Great Engineer was now all rhetoric. Government intervention in the economy was "regimentation" based on the thesis that "man is but the pawn of the State." He decried the "usurpation of the primary liberties of man by government," terming this "a vast shift from the American concept of human rights."

To his credit, the former president did not dredge up any dirt. He never even mentioned Franklin Roosevelt by name. On the other hand, he expressed no essential idea that he had not already revealed back in 1928. His capacity for self-delusion appeared undiminished. He clung to a belief that the American economic system possessed "fundamental correctness." Like communism, socialism, fascism, and Nazism, the New Deal involved "the servitude of the individual to the state." He still believed that federal relief programs were largely unnecessary, that people would voluntarily help their neighbors through bad times.

Hoover's opponents responded to *The Challenge to Liberty* almost with glee. The only liberties Hoover ever cared about, Upton Sinclair charged, were "the rights of millionaires." Henry Wallace quipped that the kind of liberty Hoover preferred in the economic world "is the liberty one takes in running a red light in an automobile." Harold Ickes said he agreed with Hoover about fighting for liberty. "We must fight to return it to the great masses of the people who have had it taken from them by exploiters," Ickes insisted.

It was already clear that *The Challenge to Liberty* would not herald Herbert Hoover's return from Elba. It might accomplish something quite different, however. Raymond Clapper, top *Washington Post* analyst, observed that until now both political parties "tried to straddle the conflict of interest and played both sides." Now the Democrats were settling in on the left and the Republicans on the right. Hoover's book would sharpen and define this cleavage. "Those who often have lamented that there was no difference between the two old parties shortly may have no further cause for complaint," Clapper declared, "because there is a strong tendency for the first time in recent political history for the two parties to stop shadow-boxing and get down to fundamentals."

The hearse bearing the body of Mary Mooney pulled up to the front gate of San Quentin and by its very presence demanded entry. Behind it snaked a procession of automobiles filled with mourners. High above the gate, Tom Mooney took a break from peeling potatoes and walked to a window to bid his mother farewell. First the warden, then Governor Merriam had denied his request to be let out for the funeral or to allow the hearse in. Now Mother Mooney was denied one last visit.

The procession doubled back to San Francisco, where it moved slowly, somberly, down Market Street in the bright sunlight, eerily following the path of the Preparedness Day parade. It was a sight like none in the city's history. Over five thousand union men and women followed the hearse, marching eight abreast behind a brass band and wearing white armbands with FREE TOM MOONEY stitched in. At the Civic Auditorium, members of the Young Communist League moved the coffin down the long aisle to the stage for what was billed as a worker's funeral. Someone read a tribute penned by Mary's "loving and grateful grief-stricken proletarian son," Tom Mooney. Her other son, John, labor leader Harry Bridges, and Socialist minister Robert Whitaker—Clem Whitaker's uncle—delivered the eulogies. (Upton Sinclair had been invited to join them, but he sent his regrets from New York.)

Following the funeral, the procession, now consisting of only family and friends, made its way back across the bay to Mount Tamalpais Cemetery, only miles from San Quentin. At the grave site, John Mooney asked the mourners to raise a clenched fist and swear an oath. "Mother Mooney," they roared, "we'll finish your fight!"

———

Uppie looked like a tired child, Helen Woodward thought. His eyes were ringed with red from lack of sleep. She meant to put drops in his eyes, even if she had to use force, but he was about to scurry away, and in the confusion she forgot. Sinclair had come to East Fifty-seventh Street to call on two of his dearest friends, the historian W. E. Woodward and his wife, Helen, just before catching a train home. Helen told him he would be elected for certain and offered to help William Loeb organize the New York EPIC Committee. What she kept to herself was the strong feeling that she didn't actually want Uppie to win. She was afraid that in office he would be stymied by his enemies. They would not let him do what he wanted. If he fought them, he might lose his life.

Sinclair had considered the benefits of defeat many times himself. Right now, however, he was thinking positive. Sinclair judged his East

Coast trip an unqualified triumph. Press coverage was tremendous, and FDR's apparent promise to come out in favor of production for use was nothing less than providential. And when Uppie took office (only a formality now) his new friends in Washington—Harry, Harold, and Henry—might actually loosen the federal purse strings and give EPIC a real chance to succeed.

After five days in the East, Sinclair was as upbeat as could be, blissfully unaware that in an off-the-record comment at yesterday's press conference, President Roosevelt had finally taken a potshot at EPIC. The EPIC program, FDR told reporters shortly after meeting with Senator McAdoo of California, was "impossible, absolutely impossible, on a scale anything like" Sinclair had in mind. Citing the Ohio experiment, the President added that "there is real merit and real possibility in the community plan based on the same principle. . . . If Sinclair has any sense in him he will modify at least in practice this perfectly wild-eyed scheme of his and carry it on as a community experiment. It will do a lot of good work that way."

Tuesday's fatherly embrace had turned to skepticism by Friday. Within three days, EPIC went from reasonable to fanatical, and the President now questioned its creator's political sanity as well. Upton Sinclair headed west having won a public relations battle, not a war. The struggle for the soul of the President had only begun.

PART II

HOLLYWOOD TO THE RESCUE

SEPTEMBER 9

SUNDAY

Royal Oak, Michigan, thirteen miles from downtown Detroit, was an odd place for the nation's most famous priest to call home. Many of its residents hated Catholics, and it was a bastion of the Ku Klux Klan. The Reverend Charles E. Coughlin, shortly after coming to this community of autoworkers in 1926, discovered a cross burning on the front lawn of his little church. He stamped out the fire himself, vowing to build a new church with a cross so high no one would be able to harm it.

When Upton Sinclair, rushing from the Detroit train station, arrived in Royal Oak this morning just before noon, he beheld Father Coughlin's new church and tourist attraction, the Shrine of the Little Flower. An architectural miscellany, it featured a granite and marble tower over 150 feet high bearing a giant stone figure of Christ on the cross. A service station and a hot-dog stand occupied a corner of the church property. Parishioners sold souvenirs inside and outside the shrine.

Father Coughlin was conducting a Sunday service. It seemed the least of his earthly endeavors. Coughlin's weekly radio sermons reached an estimated audience of forty million listeners in every part of the country except the West Coast. *Fortune* magazine called Coughlin "just about the biggest thing that ever happened to radio." In many working-class neighborhoods, his Sunday afternoon sermons rang out from nearly every window.

"Perhaps no man has stirred the country and cut as deep between the old order and the new as Father Charles E. Coughlin," the *Literary Digest* commented. Blessed with a musical, spellbinding voice touched with an Irish brogue, Coughlin was, like Franklin Roosevelt, a master of the new medium—a "religious Walter Winchell," according to one observer. He could make a four-syllable word like *dictatorship* go on forever. Listeners loved to hear a priest using street-corner expressions like *swell* and *lousy.* Coughlin's voice, in this time of trouble, was caressing, fatherly, reassuring. "I think I know the pulse of the nation. . . . I get 150,000 letters a week," Coughlin boasted. He once told his radio flock that "the dictionary describes 'demagogue' as 'the leader of the people.' I plan to be a demagogue in the original sense of the word."

His audience responded viscerally. Coughlin received more mail than anyone in America—as many as a million pieces in a week following a fiery sermon. He had to hire a hundred clerical workers to handle it all. Coughlin was selling hope, and it was a seller's market. *The Golden Hour of the Little Flower* was as profitable as it was popular. Listeners contributed five million dollars a year to Coughlin's ministry. He asked his followers to "put a dollar in an envelope," and one morning he personally lugged twenty-two thousand dollars in one-dollar bills to a local bank. Some of the cash was used to run his local relief operation, God's Poor Society. Some of it went into his own pocket. He denounced Wall Street in no uncertain terms but kept a personal account at Paine Webber. A Hollywood studio offered Coughlin five hundred thousand dollars to play himself in a film called *The Fighting Priest,* but he declined.

The message he broadcast was often self-contradictory but never inconsequential. "International bankers" were "modern Shylocks." In their greed for money, they created the Depression; now they prevented recovery. "Oh rob, steal, exploit and break your fellow citizens," Coughlin cried. "Every time you lift a lash of oppression you are lashing Christ!" Hating modern forms of capitalism and socialism with equal force, Coughlin had arrived at an unworkable hybrid, "state capitalism." He was sweet on the New Deal one moment and sour the next. One of his famous catchphrases was "It is either Roosevelt or Ruin!" but he also declared, "It is Tugwell or Christ." He blamed Rex Tugwell for agricultural policies that destroyed hogs and crops while millions went hungry. He denounced the administration for not moving quickly enough to control industrial profits and feed and clothe the poor. His solution? Nationalize public utilities and the banks.

Despite his growing criticism of the New Deal, Coughlin remained in personal contact with the President. FDR considered the arrogant priest a pest, nothing more than an occasionally useful propagandist. "He should run for the Presidency himself," Roosevelt told Jim Farley. "Who the hell does he think he is?" The President flattered Coughlin and called him Padre but instructed Farley and Joe Kennedy, the administration's leading Irish Catholics, to keep a leash on him. There was no telling where Coughlin was headed. Spearheading a third-party presidential slate in 1936 was not out of the question.

While Coughlin finished Mass, Upton Sinclair, the agnostic, sat in the modest cottage where the priest lived with his mother. He chatted with one of Coughlin's assistants, who informed him that the radio priest was studying production for use and was keen on it. Coughlin arrived and led Sinclair into his study. Like Sinclair, he was far more attractive in person than he appeared in pictures. He was, at the age of forty-two, gray-haired, plump, genial, pink-faced—altogether priestly, except that he chain-smoked cigarettes and dotted his conversation with *hell*s and *damn*s.

Quickly he informed Sinclair that he was all for putting the unemployed to work, producing for their own benefit, not someone else's profit, and he promised to broadcast this view to the nation. Sinclair told him it was the backbone of his EPIC plan. Coughlin asked him what else EPIC proposed. Sinclair ticked off each point of the program: establishing "land colonies" and co-ops, increasing the inheritance tax, hiking taxes on public utilities and banks, creating an old-age pension of fifty dollars per month, and all the rest. Responding to each point, Coughlin said, "I am for that," or "That is right," and at the end he declared, "I approve that program, and you are authorized to state that I endorse it." That was welcome enough, but then Coughlin added, "You may say that I am willing to forgive you for anything you may have written against our church seventeen years ago." This was a reference to Sinclair's scathing *Profits of Religion.* "Tell them about Paul who persecuted the Christians and later joined them," Coughlin instructed.

This ended the interview, and the two men joyfully sat down to Sunday supper. Sinclair looked at his watch and suddenly discovered that he had only a few minutes to catch his train. One of Coughlin's young associates offered to drive him to the station. Halfway to Detroit the car ran out of gas. The young priest flagged down a passing automobile, which pushed the car to a service station a mile down the road.

Clem Whitaker returned to Sacramento loaded for bear, having subjected himself to Upton Sinclair's literary rantings for three solid days. With less than two months remaining until Election Day, Whitaker knew he had to effect a drastic shift in public opinion. The only thing that could defeat Upton Sinclair at this point, Whitaker presumed, was the author's own pen. Sinclair had nothing to fear but fear himself.

The biblical Job, unable to fathom what was happening to him, cried out, "Would that mine enemy had written a book!" Upton Sinclair had written not one but dozens of them.

For three days Clem Whitaker, pioneer in the art of campaign management, and his top aide, Leone Baxter, had pored through Sinclair's books, identifying paragraphs, sentences, and phrases—most of them written years ago, even decades ago—that might come back to haunt the candidate over the next eight weeks. They knew this was fertile ground; still, they were astounded by what they found. There didn't seem to be a single religion, institution, or interest group that escaped Sinclair's muckrake. He had criticized, often spectacularly, the American Legion and the Boys Scouts of America, Christian Scientists and Baptists, the University of California and the entire city of San Francisco. What he actually wrote was incriminating enough, but by editing the quotes with creative flair or simply wrenching them out of context, the author's words became positively incendiary. Wedded bliss was nothing but "marriage plus prostitution." Every religion was "a mighty fortress of graft." And so forth. Sinclair might have outgrown these sentiments, but in these excerpts he would retain the blush and brashness of youth.

In rare cases, Sinclair's own views proved disappointingly mild. No problem! Whitaker and Baxter simply retrieved provocative lines of dialogue spoken by some of the unsympathetic characters in his novels. Uppie might not favor a violent revolution or free love, but some of the one-dimensional characters he created did, and they would do just as well. Taking phrases from three different sentences in a letter written by a character in Sinclair's 1910 novel *Love's Pilgrimage,* for example, Clem and Leone compiled this quote: "The sanctity of marriage . . . I have had such a belief . . . I have it no longer." The quote was real enough—that is, the words actually appeared on the page—and it could be attributed to an actual book. Readers of these excerpts in 1934 wouldn't recall which books were novels and which were nonfiction.

Sure, the quotations were irrelevant, Whitaker and Baxter agreed, but the political consultants had one objective: to keep Sinclair from becoming governor. Because they considered Sinclair a good man, they regretted they had to do it this way.

Whitaker liked Uppie personally, but this was politics, California-style, and so he was eager to get on with what he called "the show." For a typically stiff fee, he had agreed to promote a "nonpartisan" front group in San Francisco called the California League Against Sinclairism. In response, the socialist side of his family, led by his famous uncle, Robert Whitaker, had stopped talking to him. Clem, a registered Republican, often argued politics with Uncle Rob, a Baptist preacher, socialist poet, and noted orator—and an old friend of Upton Sinclair's. Two of Clem's brothers also favored Sinclair.

Clem's father was a Baptist minister, and his son shared his sense of moral uplift. Clem passionately opposed the death penalty and claimed that he wanted to clean up politics. He just thought EPIC was a dangerous program that threatened American institutions.

Born in Arizona and raised in Willits, California, Clem Whitaker wrote his first news story at thirteen and at eighteen covered the state capitol for the *Sacramento Union.* Then he founded the Capitol News Bureau, which provided eighty newspapers with political news from Sacramento. Tall, spindly, a chain-smoker and demon typist never at a loss for words, Clem was the prototypical newshound. He had only rarely thought of a career in politics until his barber complained that his trade association was having trouble getting a certain bill through the legislature. For a fee of four thousand dollars, Clem agreed to turn the trick, which he accomplished not by twisting arms in the legislature but by trying a new approach: he organized the barbers themselves into a potent army of lobbyists.

Clem decided to manage election campaigns next. He loathed amateurism in anything. Well, the amateur hour was over; he would be the first professional campaign manager. His initial client was John B. McColl of Red Bluff, and Whitaker got him elected to the state senate.

In 1933, the legislature passed McColl's Central Valley Project Act, which authorized the issuance of $170 million in bonds to launch an ambitious irrigation and public power project. The Pacific Gas & Electric Company, its power monopoly threatened, sought to repeal the act by referendum: it was the California way. Hired by local interests to defend the Central Valley project, Whitaker formed his groundbreaking political consultancy firm, Campaigns, Inc.

It was David versus Goliath. PG&E had unlimited campaign funds; Whitaker had forty thousand dollars. Sheridan Downey introduced Clem to Leone Baxter, manager of the Chamber of Commerce in Redding, California. Whitaker hired her as his top associate and together they tried out some new campaign tricks, bypassing the political parties and going directly to the voter—through the media. They coaxed their propaganda into practically every small-town newspaper in the state and made extensive use of radio, handling everything from the production of scripts to sound effects. Whitaker and Baxter defeated the referendum by thirty-three thousand votes.

Now Clem was ready to take the next step in his career as professional mastermind: elect one statewide candidate, George Hatfield, and demolish another, Upton Sinclair.

Attorneys for the state EPIC committee were close to cracking the case of the Bogus Campaign Circular, and the Los Angeles district attorney's office advised that the distributors would be prosecuted if additional evidence could be assembled. To that end, the *EPIC News* published a call for anyone with information to step forward.

The case traced back to August 26, the Sunday before primary day. Two young members of the Communist party rushed into EPIC headquarters in Los Angeles demanding to know how that social fascist Upton Sinclair dared claim their party's endorsement. They produced a flier that was being distributed in front of churches throughout the city. It featured a photo of Sinclair next to a red flag stamped with a hammer and sickle. The heading screamed, WE APPEAL TO THE EXPLOITED MASSES! "HELP US SAVE THE STATE!" Below that, UPTON SINCLAIR FOR GOVERNOR. The following notation appeared at the bottom: "Sponsored by the Young People's Communist League. Vladimir Kosloff, Secy., 234 N. Chicago St., Los Angeles."

The EPICs hastened to assure the Communists that they had nothing to do with the document and set out to solve the mystery. They soon discovered that the circulars had been distributed simultaneously all over southern California and up north in San Francisco and Oakland. The Young Communist League was a rather popular organization at the moment, but there was no such thing as a Young *People's* Communist

League. The address printed on the circulars led them to a lodging house. Vladimir Kosloff did not live there, but a person who worked at George Creel's headquarters did.

Following a trail of clues, the EPICs tracked the circular to a printshop and found that, indeed, the document had been designed by Creel personnel. EPIC attorneys proceeded with a legal case, since the flier did not comply with the state law requiring that the name of the true sponsor appear on every campaign document. The appeal for additional evidence in the *EPIC News* quickly bore fruit. A young man who worked for Los Angeles's most prestigious law firm, O'Melveny, Tuller & Myers, provided the name of the attorney who had created the circular for George Creel. The trickster's name, he said, was Albert Parker.

Rob Wagner was in a quandary. Along with Dorothy Parker, he was listed as an organizer of Frank Scully's Authors' League for Sinclair. He had also promoted Sinclair's candidacy in his weekly magazine, *Script.* Now *Literary Digest* had identified *Script*—the *New Yorker* of the Hollywood set—as the one and only California publication supporting Sinclair, and the canceled subscriptions started to mount. Wagner's wife, Florence, the magazine's business manager, pressured him to pull back from Sinclair or risk putting *Script* out of business. Wagner was editor of *Script,* but his wife was affectionately known as Ye REAL Ed.

A native of Detroit, Rob Wagner came to Los Angeles in the early 1900s after studying art in Paris. He wrote about the infant film industry for the *Saturday Evening Post* and *Collier's,* and in 1923 he directed one of Will Rogers's most memorable shorts, a parody of the Western epic *The Covered Wagon* entitled *Two Wagons, Both Covered.* A year later he directed Rogers's satire of the election process, *Going to Congress,* which was shown at both the Republican and the Democratic national conventions.

Wagner founded *Script* in Beverly Hills in 1929, and it soon became a Hollywood institution, favored especially by expatriates from the East. In a sprawling studio town where writers, actors, and executives usually went their separate ways, it was one thing that brought them together, once a week. Wagner tried to show the film colony that it was a community. Mayer and Thalberg subscribed; so did Joan Crawford, Eddie Cantor, and Jean Harlow. Wagner billed it as the magazine of the Pacific Coast, "a literary freak, with an editor who says whatever he pleases (if it gets by Ye REAL Ed!) and writers who do the same." *Script* was intelligent without being smart-alecky. Like *The New Yorker,* it featured cartoons, poems, fiction, reviews, and literate articles by well-known authors, but its paper was not glossy, and it carried few ads. Sometimes the same cartoon appeared year after year—only the caption was changed. Wagner supplied the editorial commentary, mixing high-minded gossip with easygoing, liberal politics.

Script published the work of newcomers like William Saroyan, Louis L'Amour, and Ray Bradbury, as well as old-timers like Upton Sinclair. Neil Vanderbilt was a regular columnist. Many Hollywood celebrities known for their work in front of or behind the camera—people like Tom Mix and Ernst Lubitsch—got a chance to put pen to paper. Charlie Chaplin, one of Wagner's best friends, once submitted a "scenario" about a scientist who developed a cure for all diseases. When thousands flocked to his lab, he announced that he would treat them on the basis of their contributions to society. The scientist placed poets ahead of doctors and industrialists because they were "high priests of the soul. . . . They make men want to live for more than bread alone." This mirrored *Script*'s view that it was the writer, not the mogul, who was the soul of Hollywood.

"Just goes to show how far you can go with a sense of humor," Frank Capra observed in *Script*'s fifth-anniversary issue. Neil Vanderbilt arranged for FDR to write a similar note, but Marvin McIntyre, incensed by a recent Ogden Nash poem in the magazine that poked fun at the President, killed the idea.

White-haired and kindly looking, a wearer of wire-rimmed spectacles, Wagner was a tall version of Upton Sinclair. He and Uppie talked about the EPIC campaign during long Sunday morning walks in the hills behind Sinclair's house. Wagner advised the candidate how to approach Chaplin and other possible Hollywood supporters. He appeared at a Sinclair rally and wrote an editorial that called Uppie "utterly incorruptible" and "the greatest 'brain-truster' in America." He even created EPIC's official emblem, a golden bee.

There was a limit to Wagner's support, however. He never actually called for Sinclair's election and he declined Uppie's invitation to become contributing editor of the *EPIC News.* "I've never said in *Script* I'm a Socialist," Wagner once told him, "with the result I can slip over Socialism. I'll be able to boost your candidacy better that way." He compared his position with Chaplin's. "As it is now," Wagner observed, "his Red stuff leaks out, helps the cause and doesn't crab his profession."

Still, by writing favorably about his friend while satirizing the other candidates, Wagner did not disguise his true feelings very well: hence, the canceled subscriptions. *Script* needed every reader it could muster, so Wagner now felt required to state clearly, in his latest issue, exactly where he stood on "the most picturesque campaign in the history of America."

Script never endorsed Sinclair in the primary, Wagner pointed out. The magazine merely treated his candidacy fairly, while other papers ignored him or treated him contemptuously. While *Script* had a tremendous regard for Upton's intelligence, sincerity and, above all, "his almost ridiculous honesty," Wagner explained, "we personally did not wish him to run, and we dreaded his victory. Not for what he might do to California, but for what California might do to him. We did not wish to see a sensitive artist crushed in the political mill."

Besides, if *Script* lined up strongly behind Sinclair, "we'd lose half our readers," Wagner admitted unashamedly. "Thus *Script* stands today—on the sidelines of the snappiest campaign in the history of America." Sinclair's media support, always next to nothing, was now nil.

SEPTEMBER 10

MONDAY

The tumultuous Nazi party congress in Nuremburg concluded with a sentimental mob serenading Adolf Hitler from the public square facing the Deutscher Hof. Hitler listened at his window as eight bands played outside the hotel, which was decorated with swastikas. The concert concluded with German taps played by a single bugle, then a somber drumroll and the chorus, "*Ich bete an die Macht der Liebe.*"

The week-long party gathering—half rally, half pageant—had exceeded even its organizers' expectations. More than six hundred thousand party faithful attended, swelling the medieval city to twice its normal capacity. Some foreign observers believed the week's events might mark a turning point in the evolution of the Nazi regime. Hitler had proclaimed, to thunderous applause, a number of bold initiatives previously suggested but not officially sanctioned until now. He grasped for state control of religion, calling for the creation of one *Reichskirche,* and announced that Germany's free press had been placed at the service of the government. The Nazis, henceforth, would also be the custodians of German culture. (They were already burning books. On July 19, the Berlin government had ordered all of Upton Sinclair's volumes confiscated and burned in Prussia.) Hitler also threatened to "demolish the opposition," referring to the four million who recently voted against his assumption of presidential powers.

Equally disquieting were the many references to "race and national health." One prominent Nazi health official, Dr. Gerhard Wagner, asserted that the greatest danger to the nation was the survival of the unfit. Those afflicted with congenital diseases and mental illness were bleeding the state dry. Dr. Wagner proposed drastic action to curb this problem, though he did not suggest a specific solution.

Foreign diplomats found especially chilling the massive display of German weaponry. Soldiers brandished machine guns on this final day of pageantry and fired artillery shells at distant targets on Zeppelin Field. As a grand finale, all branches of the army joined in mass maneuvers. This whipped the three hundred thousand spectators into a frenzy: it was the first time since the Versailles treaty that Germans had observed their armed forces in exercises.

What many observers feared was not so much the immediate political or military effects of Nuremberg as the psychological impact. Never had a party gathering in Germany or anywhere else been so well orchestrated for its propaganda effect. Stage managers used visual tricks to hypnotize those who attended the congress, and radio and press reports attempted to mesmerize the masses. The *Reich*'s obvious aim was to replace religious devotion with ideological emotion, through ritual. What none of the diplomats and foreign journalists could calculate, however, was the effect of Nuremberg on Hitler himself. An Associated Press reporter, after witnessing thousands of citizens wiping away tears as der Führer's motorcade passed by, observed that unless Americans "understand this Messiah-complex, they are bound to be wrong in the estimation of the German situation."

Friday night might have driven Hitler right over the edge of megalomania. Organizers timed his address so that his closing statements coincided with the arrival of nightfall. Acolytes lit bonfires along the horizon as searchlights scanned the sky, creating the impression of a heavenly field surrounded by ghostly columns. Then two hundred thousand party functionaries took an oath of allegiance to der Führer, raised torches, and followed Hitler's car to his hotel along a ten-mile route lined by half a million spectators. One German journalist likened the torch parade to "a river of molten, bubbling lava which slowly finds its way through the valleys of the city." Adolf Hitler may have felt, at the conclusion of this week in Nuremberg, that no task was impossible, no hysteria beyond his command.

"Congrats on nomination," Ezra Pound wrote to Upton Sinclair from his decaying palazzo in Rapallo, Italy, on the Mediterranean near Genoa. "Now beat the bank buzzards and get elected." Pound scrawled his message in black ink on Hotel Vittoria Bolzano stationery and dated the letter *10 Sept XII*. This was not a poetic affectation. The Roman numeral stood for the twelfth year of Mussolini's reign.

Pound, born in Idaho, had lived in Italy since 1924. He started corresponding with Sinclair, whom he had never met, in 1929. They were both amateur economists and enemies of American capitalism—"we are both firing in the same general direction," Pound once informed Sinclair—but radically divergent in temperament and outlook. Sinclair, the poet believed, was not a monomaniac but a polymaniac with way too many "fixations." He proposed that they conduct an open debate on monetary matters and find a publisher for it.

Like so many others, Pound admired Sinclair for his spirit, his courage, and his literary output but decried the lack of subtlety in his work. "I believe you are at yr/best when you are LEAST trying to put over any partic. idea," he informed Sinclair back in 1930. Since writing that, however, the poet had turned even more didactic than the muckraker.

The burly, red-bearded Pound had lived more than half of his forty-eight years abroad. For almost that long, he had enjoyed a reputation as "the greatest single influence on American poetry"—that was how Carl Sandburg had put it. He was a master experimenter, trying out every verse form known in English. He translated Chinese poets and created a new appreciation for the Greeks. His many protégés, including T. S. Eliot and William Carlos Williams, often complained of his despotic and capricious criticism yet appreciated his promotion of their work. He could be arrogant and generous at the same time, without contradiction.

Tiring of France, Pound fled to Italy in 1924 and published the first volume of his celebrated *Cantos* the following year. Pound still had immense influence, T. S. Eliot wrote, but no longer any disciples. "Influence," Eliot wrote, "can be exerted through form, whereas one makes disciples only among those who sympathize with the content." Pound's philosophy, he added, was "just a little antiquated." Paeans to the values of America's founding fathers started turning up in his poetry. He also published essays under titles like *ABC of Economics* and *Jefferson and/or Mussolini.* This long-time foe of all forms of censorship now revealed himself to be an admirer of il Duce.

"The heritage of Jefferson, Quincy Adams, old John Adams, Jackson, Van Buren, is HERE, NOW in the Italian peninsula at the beginning of fascist second decennio," he wrote. And: "Dictatorship is not in our time a word current in Italy. The idea here is leadership." He called Fascist Italy "freer than anywhere else in the Occident." While other world leaders were talking about turning their economic systems around, Mussolini was already doing it, and Pound pointed with pride to the new homes being built in Italy and the famous smokeless trains. (Pound met Mussolini in January 1933, and presented him with a list of suggested economic and fiscal reforms.) Like Father Coughlin, Pound attributed all the economic troubles of the world to the money and banking systems in Europe and America, which left the individual consumer with "insufficient purchasing power." He propounded Social Credit economic nostrums, which called for public ownership of a nation's money supply.

When Ernest Hemingway denounced Mussolini, Pound told him he was "all wet" but asked the novelist if he knew a way for the poet to make money writing campaign songs for American political candidates. President Roosevelt's Brain Trust, Pound informed Hemingway, was lacking some of the best brains from abroad, and he offered to come back to America and straighten out "Frank" himself. Twice during 1934 he wrote directly to President Roosevelt. In one letter, Pound identified a misprint in FDR's recent book *On Our Way* (which the President made sure was corrected). On the second occasion, he sent FDR a facsimile of the scrip currency once issued to workers by his grandfather Thaddeus Pound, the owner of a logging company. Workers could exchange the scrip for lumber or other materials. Pound instructed the President:

> Lest you forget the nature of money/i.e. that it is a ticket. . . . Certificates of work done. That is what these notes were in fact/before the bank swine got the monopoly.

As 1934 unfolded, Pound's friends became increasingly concerned about his mental health. The poet denounced Roosevelt's "Nude Eel" and struck up a correspondence with the American leader of the profascist Silver Shirts, William Dudley Pelley. Liberalism, he proclaimed, was a "running sore," and usury was "the cancer of the world, which only the surgeon's knife of Fascism can cut out of the life of the nation." James Joyce asked Hemingway to accompany him to dinner with Pound, who was visiting in Paris, because he felt the poet was "mad" and he was frightened of him. During dinner, Pound spoke irrationally, Hemingway noted.

When news of Upton Sinclair's victory in the California primary reached Rapallo, Ezra Pound was delighted. Yes, Sinclair was pigheaded and set in his ways. Pound considered Sinclair, George Bernard Shaw, and H. G. Wells to be "3 conceited and braying asses" who hadn't recognized a new idea since their adolescence. Despite these misgivings, Pound wished Uppie well in his campaign, perhaps figuring that any setback for the bankers was a victory for fascism.

EPIC's "best item," Pound informed Sinclair in today's scribbled note from Rapallo, was its reliance on scrip to pay workers in production-for-use co-ops. "But you are a bloody ass," he continued, "to go on with doles and relief etc. . . ." Doles, he commented, were "a bloody insult . . . if you cd. once understand money and banks you cd. get rid of a lot of clutter.

"Any how here's luck," the poet concluded, "but try to modernize. . . ."

Upton Sinclair, leaving Chicago for points west, sent the following report to California, via the newspapers: "I came, I saw, I'm bringing home the bacon." That was an odd way, indeed, for the author of *The Jungle* and a vegetarian to phrase it.

Speeding across the plains, Sinclair decided to send a message to his wife, Craig. She worried about Uppie's health whenever they were apart, and feared that the strain of the campaign, or an assassin, might kill him. Albert Einstein once told him that Craig "is bound to you by anxiety even when she is physically separated from you." As EPIC's popularity grew, so had Craig's fears. She started keeping all of the shades in their house drawn, and she warned her husband to stay away from windows. Sinclair suffered his wife's paranoia gladly. Preoccupied with writing and politicking, he needed someone to protect him from his most gullible instincts, and Craig provided this service in spades.

Shortly after meeting Upton Sinclair in 1910, Mary Craig Kimbrough identified him as a little boy in need of a mother, and this profoundly shaped their relationship. Years later, Uppie cheerfully confided, "It's all right to be henpecked, but be sure you get the right hen!" No two people more dissimilar had ever been yoked together in marriage, Sinclair admitted: Craig was all caution, while he was all venture. She endorsed his political beliefs, but rather than attempting to change the world she favored hiding her husband from it.

But Craig was more than a mother protector. Daughter of a plantation owner—a judge who handled Jefferson Davis's estate—she was also a shrewd businesswoman. Terrified of becoming poor, she bought, sold, and traded property for profit. (Craig once sold two lots in Long Beach, near an oil field, for ten thousand dollars each—to William G. McAdoo.) Sometimes she donated the proceeds of her sales to her husband's political causes.

When the EPIC campaign began, Craig had to extend her leash. Sinclair traveled widely, often in unfriendly territory. Someone, she feared, was bound to take a shot at him sooner or later. On the road, Sinclair often wrote little notes in pencil to assure her that he was eating sensibly and taking his afternoon nap. Today, he simply reported that he would arrive in San Francisco on Wednesday and hoped to be home for lunch on Thursday. The trip east, he gushed, had probably "cinched" his election, adding: "Surely be glad I came!"

Signed, "Love, Uppie."

Nearly two weeks had passed since the August 29 primary, and the power structure of southern California still had not pulled itself together to form a united front against Upton Sinclair. Surely this was one cause on which nearly every civic and business leader could agree. But except for the California Real Estate Association and the press caucus organized by Artie Samish, the special interests did little more than wring their hands. They wondered what Franklin Roosevelt was going to do, while waiting for a brilliant Republican tactician to appear on the horizon. It sure wasn't going to be Frank Merriam.

Then, out of Ventura County rode Charles Collins Teague.

C. C. Teague came to Los Angeles this morning to whip his conservative colleagues into shape. Hell, they owned the state—why didn't they start acting like it? Teague was just the man for the job. He had wealth, integrity, and sturdy political connections. Teague was the most important farmer in the state—maybe the most influential of all time. He ran the world's biggest lemon ranch in Santa Paula and controlled sixty-five hundred acres of vegetables up in Salinas. But his influence extended way beyond that. Teague headed the largest cooperative marketing association in the country, the California Fruit Growers Exchange, also known as Sunkist. He was president of the California Walnut Growers Association, creators of the Diamond brand. And he was chairman of the state Chamber of Commerce.

A close friend of Herbert Hoover's, Teague was no redneck, so he could work with California's ambiguous breed of moderate Progressives and reactionary Democrats. He was, in fact, one of those self-proclaimed liberal conservatives that political columnist David Lawrence claimed actually existed. When Hoover, shortly after Labor Day, urged him to accept Harry Chandler's invitation to level a blast at Sinclair in the pages of the *Los Angeles Times,* Teague happily complied, and this morning the *Times* published his broadside. "I have never been so concerned for the future as I am at the present time," Teague wrote. If Sinclair was elected, "all capital now here, where it is possible to do so, will be withdrawn." Sinclair, he predicted, "will destroy the prosperity and industry of this fair State of ours, and his poor misguided followers will find their standard of living and their ability to make a living greatly lowered."

To prevent this, Teague declared, every single citizen who believed in law and order, individual initiative, and property rights had to unite behind Frank Merriam, regardless of race, creed, or political party. These were only words, of course; other prominent Californians had said much the same thing. Teague was different, though. He staked his reputation on it. This afternoon, with the ink barely dry on his statement in the *Times,* he met with Harry Chandler and southern California's other giants of finance at the California Club, headquarters of the elite in downtown Los Angeles, attempting to turn his personal vision into a political miracle.

C. C. Teague's idea was as simple as it was practical: raise hundreds of thousands, even millions, of dollars (illegally if necessary), direct it to a nonpartisan front group in Los Angeles, retain a crackerjack advertising firm to churn out propaganda, and go to work, ignoring Frank Merriam's reactionary tendencies and basing the entire campaign on saving the state from Upton Sinclair.

Like C. C. Teague, Jimmy Cagney started life with practically nothing in the East and ended up with almost everything in California. Jimmy could afford to throw lots of parties on his yacht, even though he often got seasick, gossip columnist Sidney Skolsky reported this morning, and his buddies sometimes had to take him ashore to recover.

This was a season of choppy seas for Cagney. He was going through yet another contract tussle with Jack Warner. Jimmy wanted to tackle a different type of role. Fisticuffs had made him famous. It was said that cops searching for fugitives need to do nothing more than visit a theater screening one of Cagney's gangster movies and arrest the patrons shouting the loudest approval. His current role as a truck driver in *The St. Louis Kid* required the usual number of punch-outs, but he was tired of smacking people around in his pictures. When his squawking did no good, Cagney suggested as a compromise that his character knock the bad guys out using his skull. "If I must continue to smack guys," Cagney said, "let me try to do it differently."

What troubled the star even more was the continuing controversy over his alleged Communist affiliations. While Charles Chaplin picked Upton Sinclair as his political mentor, James Cagney had selected another old muckraker, Lincoln Steffens. Sinclair was a Socialist; Steffens favored the Communists. The choice of mentors was in keeping with the actors' characters. Chaplin had assumed the bearing of an aristocrat, and so he chose a relatively safe political path. Cagney, a street kid from Avenue D at heart, decided to play with fire. Now he had got burned.

Cagney had been something of a radical and a rebel his entire life. Before he even reached his teens, he was listening to rabble-rousers in New York's Union Square and at the neighborhood settlement house. As a copyboy at the *New York Sun,* he began a lifelong association with hard-bitten left-wing journalists. Cagney, up from the slums himself, identified with the downtrodden. By the time he arrived in Hollywood in 1930, he was a Communist sympathizer.

The following year, Theodore Dreiser, John Dos Passos, and a few other writers launched an ad hoc investigation of injustices inflicted on coal miners in Harlan County, Kentucky, and were arrested for their troubles. Cagney stepped forward with a donation to the Harlan County miners' fund and struck up a close friendship with the Marxist screenwriters Sam Ornitz and John Bright. They got him involved in the Scottsboro Boys Committee and the movement to free Tom Mooney, among other leftist causes. It was at a huge Mooney rally at the Civic Auditorium in San Francisco that Cagney met Lincoln Steffens. The sight of thousands of wild-eyed Mooney partisans shaking their fists gave Cagney the creeps, but he and Stef hit it off right away. Jimmy visited the courtly Steffens, then in his mid-sixties and in ill health, at his house in Carmel and eventually bought a vacation home nearby.

Because, unlike Chaplin, Cagney took so many public stands, he was singled out for criticism by the anti-Red press in Los Angeles. Jack Warner assailed Cagney as a Communist dupe and ordered him to reduce his political activity. He called Cagney a "professional againster," and there were rumors that the studio put some of the star's salary in escrow, to be released only if he kept his nose clean. Cagney's wife also pleaded with him to pull back. But Jimmy pushed on, taking on new responsibilities as a vice president of the Screen Actors Guild.

By this time, *The Public Enemy* and other gangster pictures had made Cagney a celebrity. He was that rare creature in Hollywood, the Everyman star; a tough, red-haired Irish ethnic so true to type, *The New York Times* observed, "it is a natural thing to suspect that he is not acting at all." On screen, he fought cops and capitalists, making himself a symbol of hope and rebelliousness for millions of Depression-racked Americans. His movie *Taxi,* written by John Bright, was perhaps Hollywood's most pro-union picture.

Then, in August 1934, Cagney's politics put his future in Hollywood in jeopardy. The story broke on August 18, when the *Los Angeles Times* reported on its front page that police in Sacramento had named James Cagney and sculptor Jo Davidson as financial supporters of certain jailed "Communist" agitators. Investigators had discovered evidence in letters written by Ella Winter, the wife of Lincoln Steffens, seized by the local Red Squad in a recent raid on Communist headquarters in the state capital.

"I have Cagney's money again," Winter allegedly wrote to Caroline Decker, secretary of the Cannery and Industrial Workers' Union and one of twenty-six radicals held in jail in Sacramento on criminal syndicalism charges for attempting to organize farm workers. "Cagney was fine this time and is going to bring other stars up to talk to Stef again." In another letter seized by the Red Squad, Winter informed Decker—one of the state's most prolific young pamphleteers—that Cagney had offered to provide her with all the typewriter ribbons she needed.

Decker, in yet another confiscated letter, told a friend that perhaps it was worthwhile getting arrested "if one meets Jimmy Cagney, who offers to go one's cash bail regardless of amount. Nice, huh? And he'd better get a nice lump sum ready." The names of three other Hollywood stars, all of Mexican descent, also turned up in Decker's writings: Ramon Novarro, Dolores Del Rio, and Lupe Velez (wife of Johnny

Weissmuller). The Sacramento district attorney announced plans to seek an injunction that would restrain the four film stars from advocating communism or financially supporting it.

Steffens immediately stood up for his friend. He explained that the entire affair stemmed from an article on a cotton strike in the San Joaquin Valley that his wife had written for a national magazine the previous year. Ella Winter had seen a baby turn black and die of starvation. "When she told people, including Cagney, of the utter misery she had seen there," Steffens said, "he gave some money to help. So did other people who gave food or clothing or money for food or clothing. That's all."

The newspapers exploited the controversy but gave Cagney a chance to defend himself. Jimmy claimed that he was a "100 percent American" and against all "isms." He would never aid "anyone trying to upset our government. . . . This old country of ours has been pretty good to me. I started with nothing, worked hard and today am very comfortable." Cagney allowed that he knew Steffens and Winter but asserted, laying it on a bit thick, that he was "not in sympathy with their tenets" and had never contributed to a radical cause or individual. (Tom Mooney must have been surprised to read that.) Cagney said he would "spend every dollar I have in the world" to defend himself against these charges.

For once, the shy actor had adopted his tough-talking screen persona in his private life, and it worked. Perhaps afraid that Cagney might smack him in the nose, the Sacramento D.A. backed off, at least until he developed further evidence. Still, Cagney's career hung by a thread. The studio bosses and adoring movie fans had shown they would accept almost any behavior in Hollywood: divorce and adultery, public intoxication, brawling and betting, even associating with radicals. But assisting Communists was still forbidden.

Upton Sinclair was no Communist, so normally Jimmy Cagney would not have been afraid to lend him a hand. But the *Los Angeles Times* and other newspapers were painting Sinclair Red, so at this point the candidate's true colors hardly mattered. The picture was further confused by the fact that Cagney's mentor, Lincoln Steffens, while publicly supporting the Communist party candidate for governor, had privately offered to assist his old friend Uppie. Stef informed EPIC headquarters that he was willing to make a great show of denouncing Sinclair as a right-wing "fascist." Coming from one of the state's most famous Communist sympathizers, this might undercut the *Los Angeles Times*'s Red-baiting of Sinclair.

Cagney couldn't afford to play that kind of game. In fact, at the moment, given his political troubles, he couldn't afford to do much of anything in this campaign. Perhaps unintentionally, the Red Squad had managed to neutralize, at least for the moment, another one of Upton Sinclair's most likely, and potentially most useful, supporters.

SEPTEMBER 11

TUESDAY

Huey Long padded around his suite in peach-colored pajamas. It was two o'clock in the afternoon at the Roosevelt Hotel, but the Kingfish had no particular place to go or reason to get dressed. A radio transmitter connected him to the outside world, and he held that world seemingly at his command. Huey tramped, barefoot, from bedroom to microphone to deliver one of his hourly blasts over the radio. He urged followers of his Share Our Wealth plan to accept the ten or twenty dollars that each would be offered to support the regular Democratic ticket—and then vote for *his* candidates in today's election. Huey extended his kind of bribe, a promise that every citizen would save $250 a year based on reductions in utility rates. Then he returned to his bedroom to chew on a sandwich and shout instructions to bodyguards and aides. Outside, two thousand National Guardsmen under his control threatened to provoke, or put down, a disturbance—or both. Canal Street might run red with blood before sunset.

Primary day, New Orleans, 1934.

After ten days of violence, the bloodiest labor dispute in the nation's history reached a climax in Saylesville, Rhode Island, just north of Providence. Striking textile workers pushed over a gatehouse and twice attempted to set fire to the Sayles Finishing Plant. The mob, three thousand strong, repeatedly assaulted state troopers and local police who were defending the mill and the eleven hundred scabs working inside. Two hundred National Guardsmen arrived at the scene on horseback, dismounted, and used nightsticks to club their way to the mill. Then, hurling tear gas, they attempted to push back the crowd, which responded by ripping up paving stones and heaving them at the steel-helmeted troops. A nearby cemetery became a war zone, with rioters ducking behind gravestones for cover. Terror-stricken residents barricaded their homes as a battle raged up and down Lonsdale Avenue. When the fighting ended, eight strike sympathizers had been shot, including a seventy-three-year-old woman cut down by a volley of buckshot from a deputy sheriff's gun. Over 130 others, including 18 Guardsmen, suffered less serious injuries.

Another riot broke out at a mill in Salem, Massachusetts, and the National Guard dispersed combatants in Augusta, Maine, and Hartford, Connecticut. Twenty people were injured at a mill in Lancaster, Pennsylvania, where women used hatpins to attack strikebreakers on their way to work. Soldiers and policemen meted out punishment, but the conflict was essentially between workers—unionists versus scabs. Hundreds of thousands of workers had walked out, but hundreds of thousands remained on the job or rushed to fill the ranks. No matter how righteous the rhetoric or just the cause, it was impossible, during a depression, with jobs at a premium, to achieve working-class solidarity. The textile strike was ill-fated from the start. Not even martyrdom could save it.

The mood at Hyde Park, despite the intensification of the textile crisis, remained buoyant. Late this morning, Jim Farley joined FDR, the President's family, and several guests for lunch at Hyde Park. It was a pleasant occasion. Franklin Jr. tried to talk his grandmother into purchasing a Packard roadster for the family, but she insisted that they buy an Oldsmobile instead.

Afterward, speaking privately with FDR, Farley suggested it might be time to give up his cabinet duties to devote full time to the Democratic National Committee. With a reelection campaign only two years off, that might be his best way to serve the President. Farley had his own political ambitions to look after, as well. According to White House insider John Franklin Carter, Farley hoped to run for governor of New York in a few years, and then "on to the Presidency in 1940!"

Roosevelt squelched Farley's offer to resign, "for now." Then they discussed Farley's upcoming political tour of the Midwest. He would visit Illinois, Iowa, Nebraska, Minnesota, and South Dakota.

"You are not going to Wisconsin?" FDR asked mischievously.

"That's one state," Farley said, "I'm going to try to keep out of!" The brothers La Follette were friends, and at the same time victims, of Franklin Roosevelt. The New Deal had doomed their brand of progressive Republicanism, perhaps forever. As the Democratic party in Wisconsin revived, the GOP turned to the right. Unwilling simply to switch parties, the La Follettes instead reestablished the Progressive party, which had sponsored their father's race for the presidency in 1924. The Progressives would run a full ticket across the state this fall, headed by Phil La Follette's attempt to regain the governor's office and Bob La Follette's bid to win reelection to the U.S. Senate.

This presented a difficult choice for FDR and Farley. Did they want regular Democrats or their maverick friends, the La Follettes, to run Wisconsin? Several weeks ago, the President had wistfully expressed the hope that Democrats in Wisconsin would somehow find a way to embrace Bob La Follette as their own. La Follette had been "very helpful" in the Senate, but FDR refused to endorse him. Wisconsin, like California, was just too hot for the White House to handle.

Louis B. Mayer longed to join the fight against Upton Sinclair in California, but today his wife's illness went from bad to worse. Margaret Mayer was reported in critical condition at the American Hospital in Neuilly, just outside Paris, suffering from pneumonia. L.B. spared no expense in meeting the emergency. From London he summoned Lord Horder, physician to the Prince of Wales, and Lord Dawson, physician to the King.

Still feeling guilty because of the Jean Howard affair, Mayer refused to leave Paris and return home without his wife. Instead, he ran up an astronomical phone bill at the Hôtel George V, keeping tabs on studio production and politics back home. Sometimes he kept three conversations going at once, jumping around the suite from phone to phone like a cue ball rocketing off the cushions. One problem, impossible to resolve at the moment, festered right there in Europe. It concerned W. R. Hearst.

As usual with Hearst, business and politics collided. Mayer was mad at Hearst for responding so abusively to his suggestion that he support Herbert Hoover for president in 1936. L.B. felt that W.R. should be plenty disillusioned with FDR by now, but Hearst, calling Hoover "selfish and stupid," instructed Mayer to "suppress this hoodoo" if he wanted to save the Republican party. Hoover's name, he wired Mayer from Bad Nauheim, "is anathema to the American public."

This enraged Mayer just when a confrontation over Marion Davies's movie career appeared at hand. Earlier in the year, Mayer had backed Irving Thalberg in his decision to cast his wife, Norma Shearer, instead of Davies as Elizabeth Barrett in *The Barretts of Wimpole Street.* Hearst howled. The film became one of the biggest hits of the year, and Hearst responded by ordering his newspapers to ignore Miss Shearer. Now, after touring castles in Europe all summer, W.R. had decided that another MGM property, *Marie Antoinette,* was a perfect vehicle for Miss Davies. (After all, she had a gift for light comedy.) Once again, however, MGM had promised the role to Norma Shearer.

On returning from Europe, Hearst might force a showdown. A confrontation would be unpleasant. With Upton Sinclair, the common enemy of Hearst, Mayer, and Thalberg, threatening to take over the state, this was no time for nepotism to come between them.

"Even at long range," Norman Thomas wrote from New York to Socialist party leader Milen Dempster in California, "I have felt some of the pressure that is being brought to bear upon you to withdraw your candidacy for Governor and to give tacit support to Sinclair." Thomas was still being pounded by party members deploring his position on the California race. Some accused him of taking money from reactionary interests. A woman from Los Angeles told him that he was just jealous because Uppie had made Thomas's two campaigns for president "look weak by comparison." If Thomas followed Sinclair's lead, she wrote, he could be elected governor of New York, then president. "Do you, as a minister," she wondered, "need to be booted into it?"

A leading California Socialist informed Thomas that only fourteen members had attended the last meeting of the SP in San Francisco, while the most recent Sinclair rally in that city drew nine thousand people "and was dominated by socialists. . . . Practically all class-conscious socialists will vote for Sinclair," he predicted, "and no one can stop them. . . . This is possibly the start of the revolution. Do not try to stop the bandwagon—it is going places." Dempster's candidacy was "entirely empty" and might only succeed in defeating Sinclair.

It was time for Thomas to send a clear signal to Socialists in California, who in the wake of EPIC's primary sweep feared the train to Utopia was leaving the station without them. A few days ago, Thomas received a desperate note from Milen Dempster asking him to make a personal appearance in California and to send money so he could buy radio time. Dempster explained that with Sinclair going all out to win mainstream Democratic support, "the situation is clarifying to our great advantage. Of course," he added, plaintively, "we are losing considerable membership." Half of the party's thirteen hundred members in California had quit to join EPIC.

Norman Thomas was far and away the Socialist party's most popular and influential figure. In 1932, he had gathered almost nine hundred thousand votes for president, roughly fifty times the party's actual membership. Internally, however, the SP split along ideological lines. In New York, the so-called Old Guard managed most of the party's resources over on Fifteenth Street, just off Fifth Avenue, home of the *New Leader.* Thomas worked out of the "Militant" stronghold on East Nineteenth Street, headquarters of the League for Industrial Democracy, a group founded long ago by Upton Sinclair (with his friend Jack London).

Returning to Manhattan from his many trips, Thomas always found on his desk a stack of letters from admirers around the country. As a symbol of socialism in America, he was as beloved as Upton Sinclair, and attracted a lot fewer cranks. Today, among other missives to the faithful, he dictated a lengthy letter to Milen Dempster. In his most recent note, Dempster gave no indication of quitting the race, but Thomas could read between the lines. He informed Dempster that it was his sober judgment that to withdraw now would represent a "virtual abdication" for the Socialist party, set a bad precedent, and "sign your death warrant in California." Then he ticked off the points Dempster must make in explaining his decision to stay in the fight:

- "Our friend, Upton Sinclair, may have started out to make the Democratic Party Socialist. He seems to be ending up making himself Democratic." All progressive movements within established parties have failed. If Uppie had formed a third party, like a Farmer-Labor alliance, this at least might have raised "a different question for Socialists."

- EPIC is "quack medicine." People don't really understand it but support Sinclair as "a new and clever version of the 'good man' in politics theory."
- Only by opposing Sinclair can Socialists be in a position to "avoid the blame for his failure" when he finally takes office and actually tries to institute EPIC.

Thomas knew these explanations, flying in the face of a wildly popular mass movement, might ring hollow. Preoccupied with his own hopeless campaign for U.S. Senate in New York, Thomas couldn't do much to help Dempster's cause except provide moral support. "So comrades," he closed, "keep up the fight!" Perhaps realizing the absurdity of this exclamation, Thomas added, in a postscript:

> In attacking Sinclair we do not need to deny his credit for organizing discontent. Neither need we deny credit to the California people for revolting against reaction. It is something, I suppose, to learn that California is sick. It is the job of the Socialists to show the Californians what the right remedy is.

The promising young actress Helen Gahagan opened in the Maxwell Anderson play *Mary of Scotland* at the Belasco Theater in Los Angeles last night, and the *L.A. Times* weighed in with a positive review this morning. Gahagan's performance in the title role, the critic declared, was a "signal triumph," although the play included "flamboyant vulgarities, presumably typical of the period." The actress, whom Heywood Broun considered "ten of the twelve most beautiful women in the world," planned to join her husband, Melvyn Douglas, in New York in a few weeks, where they would appear together in another play.

A native of Brooklyn and a former opera singer, Helen remained ambivalent about pursuing a movie career in Hollywood, and paid little attention to California politics. But her political philosophy was changing, the result of an eye-opening trip to California with her husband following their marriage in 1931. During that drive across the country, the Douglases had observed thousands of transient workers and homeless families living in caves and boxcars, and Helen's lifelong Republicanism had finally started to march to the left.

At midafternoon, Huey Long suddenly put on some clothes, left his suite at the Roosevelt Hotel, rushed home to collect his wife, and escorted her to a polling place. Huey's personal detail of militiamen had to stand outside in the rain, thanks to his recent deal with Mayor T. Semmes Walmsley: Long would prohibit armed troops from challenging voters if the mayor kept the local police from doing the same. The result: the most peaceful election in years and, according to Huey, the first honest one.

The Kingfish returned to his citadel to await the returns; and when they started arriving at the Roosevelt shortly after seven o'clock, he was one happy cracker. Huey had won what many called the most spectacular battle of his career. All four of the local candidates he supported—two congressmen and two state officials—prevailed. This represented public ratification of the dictatorial powers recently conferred on the Kingfish by his state legislature. The Walmsley machine, the last remaining obstacle to Long's complete control of Louisiana, lay in pieces, and it was likely that Huey would order a special session of the legislature to impeach the mayor—the man he called Turkey Head. Walmsley, Huey predicted, would be taking "an early trip to China."

Long had accomplished all this despite opposition from every important newspaper in the state. Around nine o'clock, in the offices of the *Times-Picayune,* Hilda Phelps Hammond, leader of a women's movement to unhorse Huey, conceded defeat but promised, "We'll get him yet." No one could count the days.

Huey Long's electoral sweep was impressive, but it did not hold a candle to what the Commonwealth Builders accomplished twenty-five hundred miles away in the state of Washington. Back in 1932, this coalition of technocrats, unemployed citizens, and production-for-users had elected a U.S. senator and two congressmen. Today their candidates, running on an End Poverty in Washington platform inspired by Upton Sinclair, swept dozens of state and local Democratic races. A young left-winger named Warren Magnuson won the prosecutor's race in King County. Lewis B. Schwellenbach, a forty-year-old radical attorney, earned the Democratic nod for U.S. Senate. With Democrats now owning a comfortable edge in registration in the state, it appeared likely that Schwellenbach would soon join fellow Washington progressive Homer Bone in the Senate.

Also in Washington, Harry Hopkins's brother won the GOP primary for coroner of Pierce County. "I just wanted to be in a position to give Harry a job in 1936," Dr. Lewis Hopkins explained. Judging by the way things were going, Harry wouldn't be looking for a job anytime soon.

SEPTEMBER 13

THURSDAY

The critics were right: Upton Sinclair's schemes, however well intentioned, never seemed to work. Take today, for example. Sinclair knew that a mob of reporters would want to meet him on his triumphant return to Los Angeles, so he got off at Glendale instead. Somehow the newshounds caught wind of it, and several were there to greet him with open notebooks.

Alighting from the Southern Pacific *Lark,* Sinclair announced that he was confident of victory and certain of winning FDR's support. Then he rushed to his headquarters in Los Angeles at 1501 South Grand. Ironically, Grand Avenue was once known as Calle de Caridad—Charity Street; residents were teased about "living on charity." A crowd of EPICs had gathered for a welcome-home celebration. It was more like a coronation. Sinclair, dressed in a gray suit, ascended a platform to tumultuous applause. A huge American flag served as a patriotic backdrop for photographers. Stripping to his shirtsleeves to address the crowd, Sinclair revealed that he had completed another campaign booklet, *Immediate EPIC,* on the westbound train.

Completing his remarks, Sinclair took a quick tour of the bustling End Poverty League offices, shaking hands with supporters as he passed.

Among those he met was a young man named Stan Gordon, who had come to the office to pick up some compaign material. He was no Sinclairite, however. A few days ago, Ralph Trueblood, managing editor of the *Los Angeles Times*, had asked Gordon, who worked in the newspaper's morgue, to visit the public library over on Fifth Street and skim through some of the candidate's books, searching for self-incriminating prose. Gordon had some sympathy for Sinclair's cause but considered EPIC crazy, so he was only too happy to comply. And he looked forward to getting out of office to do some serious research.

So for two days, he had sat at a table in the library, jotting down quotes from Sinclair books on a yellow legal pad. After thumbing through just six volumes, he felt he had verified enough extracts to scare conservative voters out of their wits. Then he went back to his office, typed up the notes, and passed them along to Trueblood. This morning, Gordon visited EPIC headquarters to acquire additional material that might interest his editors—and ended up meeting the candidate himself.

While Stan Gordon trudged back to the *Times*, Upton Sinclair, weary from two weeks on the road, motored home, declaring on arrival, "Pasadena looks mighty good to me."

Upton Sinclair would need all the rest he could get, for his return to California marked a turning point in the campaign. Until now everything had gone his way. The California newspapers could not put him on the hot seat while he was hobnobbing with federal officials far from home. Local Democrats battled over whether or not to support him, while above the fray Uppie kept his dignity. Now that he was back in California, he would be right in the thick of things.

Two nights ago the directors of the San Francisco Democratic Club, representing twelve thousand members in the Bay area, had voted to endorse Frank Merriam for governor by a nineteen-to-twelve count. A riot almost broke out right there in the meeting room at the Palace Hotel, and the losing faction was promptly expelled from the group. "I do not care to be identified with a socialist," J. Pendleton Wilson, club president, declared. Now the Sinclair supporters were seeking an injunction to prohibit Wilson and his gang from using the Democratic Club's resources to support a reactionary Republican.

Democratic defections were not limited to San Francisco. In most counties, the party's central committee declared neutrality or came out for Merriam. The Monterey County committee voted unanimous opposition to the EPIC plan. A Democrats-for-Merriam Club formed in Santa Barbara. Major Charles C. Tilden chaired the "nonpartisan" Merriam Club in Oakland. Democratic councils in Orange, Riverside, and Imperial counties repudiated Sinclair. EPIC supporters took command in Los Angeles, but in San Bernardino almost half the central committee quit when a Sinclair supporter was elected party chairman. A fistfight between EPICs and Merriamites broke out in San Diego as the Democratic committee debated an endorsement.

One of the first GOP insiders to advocate a bipartisan strategy was Murray Chotiner, a young, brilliantly combative Los Angeles attorney who had toiled mightily for Hoover in '32. Shortly before the August primary, he advised his candidate, C. C. Young, that the only way the GOP could win in November was to rally the support of Progressives, "labor groups who are not radical," liberal young Republicans, and anti-Sinclair Democrats. Now Chotiner lined up beside Frank Finley Merriam, who was doing everything he could to encourage Democratic defections. Today, in a letter to a prominent San Francisco Democrat, Merriam pledged that if elected he would "recognize all groups and both parties."

To stop the bleeding, Upton Sinclair, against his every instinct, would have to start courting the man who controlled the balance of political power in the state, George Creel. His bloc of almost three hundred thousand primary votes could elect Sinclair or Merriam—or give Ray Haight a fighting chance.

Senator McAdoo, the state's other leading Democrat, would return home from Washington this weekend. McAdoo had just received a frantic cable from Ham Cotton, one of President Roosevelt's favorite California Democrats, informing him that the situation in California was "chaotic. . . . Tenets of the Democratic Party completely destroyed. . . ." McAdoo had wired back, "Don't blow up yet."

The *Hollywood Reporter* presented further evidence this morning that Upton Sinclair's return to California signaled a change in season a full week before autumn actually arrived. W. R. Wilkerson, the editor, joyfully reported in his "Tradeviews" column:

> The first shot of the State political campaign, so far as the motion picture industry in Hollywood is concerned, was fired last night by Joe

> Schenck, who came out flat-footed for Frank Merriam for Governor against Mister "Epic" Sinclair.

Schenck had told reporters that Sinclair's election "would be the end of California. . . . Republicans and Democrats alike must unite to save the State." He derided Sinclair's production-for-use idea as "one man trading a bunch of onions for a dozen eggs" and claimed that Sinclair had "besmirched" the state's reputation throughout the country, giving the impression that "California is in a state of poverty."

With Louis B. Mayer detained in Europe, Joe Schenck apparently took it upon himself to unsheathe the studios' political sword. Or maybe Joe felt heartsick and simply lashed out at Upton Sinclair out of frustration. Earlier in the day Walter Winchell had reported from New York that "the Merle Oberon–Joseph Schenck merger plot is off." That was Winchellese for: no wedding.

Norman Thomas already had second thoughts about the advice he had passed along to Milen Dempster on Tuesday. Word arrived that the Socialist party in California was seriously considering ordering Dempster's withdrawal from the race. Thomas was in the same position as Franklin Roosevelt. He was skeptical about EPIC, but he wanted to be on the winning side in California—and was paralyzed by the impossibility of predicting a winner.

For now, like FDR, he had to cover all the bases. He didn't want Dempster to quit the race, but he could open the door for the state party to act as it saw fit. And so he wrote Dempster again, indicating that it would be acceptable if he dropped out so long as a cross section of the party, not just a few excited members, favored it. If he did quit, he should acknowledge that Sinclair was the lesser of two evils but reiterate that EPIC was not socialism and that the SP would continue to fight on.

William Randolph Hearst, of all people, fumed about sensationalist press coverage. Hearst had explained to reporters in Europe that he liked President Roosevelt personally but didn't always agree with his policies; the British press quoted him saying just the opposite. In Spain, the newspapers pictured him traveling with two hundred dogs when all he had was one tiny dachshund. "I guess American journalism is best in world," Hearst wired E. D. ("Cobby") Coblentz, one of his top editors in New York.

For several days, Hearst had fed Coblentz a steady diet of cables. Arthur Brisbane had sent Hearst some ideas on how to beat Upton Sinclair in California, and Hearst wanted Coblentz to transmit them to his papers on the West Coast. Today, however, Hearst was looking at the big picture. After pussyfooting around the issue for several months, he decided to lay siege to American communism in all its forms.

Fascism had come to Italy and Germany purely to prevent communism, Hearst maintained. Now Communist movements and "atrocities" haunted America. The only way to stop communism was "by arousing public to its dangers," Hearst instructed Coblentz.

It was a landmark day for W. R. Hearst in Bad Nauheim. He launched a new holy war against communism—and Putzi Hanfstaengl informed W.R. that Hitler was finally ready to see him.

———

W. R. Hearst was a force to be reckoned with, even in Europe. Louis B. Mayer had to deal with him; so did Adolf Hitler. Across the ocean, Harold Ickes had his own day of reckoning. The secretary of the interior used all of his powers of intellect and reason, over dinner near DuPont Circle with two of Hearst's top associates, to keep W.R. in FDR's camp.

The three men talked at length about the recent primary elections. The trend was distinctly radical, Ickes remarked. In fact, the voters were more radical than the administration, and the President, if anything, would have to move even further to the left to hold the country together. If FDR couldn't accomplish that, no one else could hope to do it; and if he was prevented from doing it, the result would be a left-wing movement beyond his control, "the extent of which no one can foresee," Ickes insisted. If newspaper publishers now so busy attacking the administration had any regard for their own interests, they would recognize this. "I would a whole lot rather give up fifty percent of whatever property I might possess," Ickes argued, "than be forced to give up all of it, and the latter is a distinct possibility if affairs are permitted to get out of hand."

It seemed to be the emerging Democratic line. On Wednesday, Representative Sam Rayburn of Texas, currently campaigning for the position of Speaker of the House, declared in a nationwide radio speech that the New Deal "makes property safe." This assertion was about to be put to a test, however, in dramatic fashion. Business leaders demanded that

President Roosevelt act to end the textile strike. The situation continued to deteriorate. National Guard units converged on Gastonia, North Carolina. Three men were beaten and two automobiles overturned when strikers attacked special guards in Pennsylvania. National Guardsmen fired into a crowd of five thousand protesters in Woonsocket, Rhode Island, killing one striker and wounding seven others. Looters and rioters destroyed much of Woonsocket's business district. Governor Theodore F. Green ordered six mills in the state to shut their gates.

Today Governor Green, claiming that "the situation that confronts us now is not a textile strike, it is a Communist uprising," took what he labeled the most drastic action of the past century. "We must put the Communists down here," he declared, "as they were put down in San Francisco when the longshoremen went out on strike." Governor Green ordered the arrest of all known Communists in the state and asked the commanders of the state American Legion and Veterans of Foreign Wars each to mobilize one thousand former soldiers, who would be armed to defend the state against a Communist insurrection.

At Hyde Park, President Roosevelt weighed his options. General Douglas MacArthur, his chief of staff, drew up plans for the use of five thousand federal troops. Regular army detachments at several bases in the East prepared for possible strike service. Moving fast to quell the emergency, FDR announced plans to call a conference of leaders on all sides in the strike in an attempt to enact a truce, perhaps even a settlement. Negotiations would be carefully studied by Roosevelt watchers. Was the President, through manipulation and personal charm, still capable of keeping both the working man and the industrialist in line? Did he still have the Roosevelt touch—or, with huge segments of his constituency marching steadily leftward, was FDR now *out* of touch?

When Rex Tugwell sailed for Europe, the usual cloud accompanied him. The official reason for his trip was to attend the International Institute of Agriculture convention in Rome, but journalists and political wags in Washington weren't buying this explanation. Why was Tugwell leaving now, when the meeting was still more than a month off? Speculation centered on the political advantages of getting him out of the country during the election season. Tugwell, in any case, would not return until mid-November.

The President, in his meetings with the press, continued to sidestep California. Today, however, he personally contacted J. Edgar Hoover, director of the Federal Bureau of Investigation, concerning something Sinclair had mentioned to him when they met. FDR asked Hoover to look into Sinclair's charge that Los Angeles "interests" had set up a fifteen-thousand-dollar fund in New York to hire East Coast gangsters to come to California and break up the EPIC organization.

It was one of the strangest meetings in San Francisco history. On the one side: A. P. Giannini, founder and president of the Bank of America and the Transamerica corporation. On the other: Hjalmar Rutzebeck, a former sailor, novelist, Christmas-tree salesman, and federal prisoner. Giannini was known variously as the Bull of the West and the J. P. Morgan of California. Rutzebeck was just "Hans." They were both big, strong ethnic Americans with a taste for blunt talk. Upton Sinclair had brought them together, if only briefly.

Rutzebeck, a red-haired giant from Denmark said to be descended from the Vikings, wore several hats in the EPIC organization. He advised Uppie on self-help cooperatives. He served as Sinclair's bodyguard whenever the candidate came north. And he ran an intelligence unit in San Francisco that infiltrated Republican organizations. Sinclair admired Rutzebeck's autobiographical novels, *Alaska Man's Luck* and *Mad Sea,* even though Hans was as rough as Uppie was gentle. Rutzebeck, now forty-five years of age, told friends that he had once killed a man in a street fight in Chile. In *Alaska Man's Luck,* he suggested that he had served eighteen months in a federal prison in Juneau. "I have often been on the ragged edge of outlawry," Rutzebeck wrote. But Sinclair appreciated his most recent experience, working for Harry Hopkins in Alabama, and he planned to make Hans state relief administrator after the election.

For some reason, Sinclair entrusted Rutzebeck, not exactly a smooth operator, with the herculean task of winning over A. P. Giannini. Well, Rutzebeck was a Hercules, of sorts. His intermediary was a man named Ferrari, a Bank of America official and a Democrat. Rutzebeck sat down with Ferrari today before meeting Giannini at his office in San Francisco. Ferrari informed Rutzebeck that in top business circles it was "generally conceded" that Sinclair would be elected if he could make peace with George Creel. Some businessmen were even starting to swing in Sinclair's direction; only a series of serious blunders could stop the EPIC express.

Giannini, Ferrari explained, was truly neutral in the race, and so at all cost EPIC should refrain from attacking him or his bank. A.P., he said, was a natural fighter and would never turn the other cheek if attacked. Eventually he might even come out for Sinclair, simply because he believed that EPIC could restore good times to California and that the Bank of America would be bound to benefit from it. If Giannini decided to put money into the EPIC campaign, the sum might be staggering.

Just one thing, Ferrari added. Giannini needed to know whether Sinclair *wanted* his support. Rutzebeck thought he heard a quid pro quo approaching like a freight train round the bend.

"Sinclair," Hans the Viking replied, "hasn't made a single promise to anyone except to end poverty for everyone."

"That's one of the things Giannini likes about Sinclair," Ferrari responded, "and there would be no strings attached to his support, if he gave it." Ferrari explained that other banks treated the BOA as an "outlaw bank," so it would be natural for Sinclair to act friendly toward Giannini, the only New Deal banker in the state. It would enrage the other banks—but they were already deployed against EPIC.

Finally Rutzebeck met the great Giannini. He found him to be his mirror image, a huge, friendly, likable man. A.P. told Rutzebeck that he hated to be classified with the city's other lords of finance, all backward Republicans, such as Herbert Fleishhacker. But when Giannini had the temerity to misquote Upton Sinclair, Rutzebeck brusquely informed him that he didn't know what he was talking about. Giannini blinked and frowned—no one talked to him like that—but he appeared more amused than angry. Rutzebeck, convinced that Giannini had a streak of fairness in him, decided that he would advise Sinclair to write the banker a note, stating clearly that he wanted him on EPIC's side.

When Rutzebeck departed, Giannini called Jefty O'Connor. Jefty was Giannini's man in Washington and, as comptroller of the currency, a well-placed friend indeed. Giannini had tabbed O'Connor to run for governor of California this year, but Jefty, dubious of his chances of winning, decided to stay in Washington. After Sinclair won the primary, Giannini started exploring the possibility of supporting Raymond Haight. Like W. R. Hearst, Giannini was a wild card in the race.

One of the few bankers to support Roosevelt in '32, Giannini remained willing to toe the FDR line. But what, in regard to the California governor's race, did FDR want? When Giannini reached Jefty O'Connor this afternoon in Washington, he informed him that he hadn't taken a position on the governor's race. What, he wondered, did Roosevelt plan to do? About a million other Californians, including Jefty O'Connor, were asking the same question. Jefty couldn't help his friend on that one, but he wired a message to FDR up in Hyde Park. "Mr. Giannini," he informed the President, "said he was marking time waiting for us to speak and I told him that I had not taken any position as yet as I did not know exactly what the administration wanted done." They were all in the same boat. Roosevelt didn't know what he wanted the administration to do either.

SEPTEMBER 14

FRIDAY

Putzi Hanfstaengl, with four storm troopers in tow, arrived at Bad Nauheim to take W. R. Hearst to meet Hitler. Hearst was almost as excited as Marion Davies, who had been trying to see Hitler for weeks. Last month in Munich she had visited a hotel, an airfield, and the opera, trying to catch one of the chancellor's public appearances, but Hitler failed to show. Captivated by his voice on the radio, the actress was anxious to see how he performed in person. Also, she wanted to be able to brag to friends back home that she had seen him.

"Have a heart," Marion said, begging Hearst to let her tag along, "I've gone every place to see this man." She suspected that, in person, Hitler looked like Chaplin's Little Tramp, "only worse." Now she was buttering up Hanfstaengl, the Harvard-educated foreign-press officer, angling to be included in the pilgrimage to Berlin. Putzi responded warmly. Ever the propagandist, he praised Marion's films. But it was Hearst, his old friend and fellow art collector, he was after. He didn't want W.R. to back out now.

Hanfstaengl, with an assist from an American official, had played a key role in Hitler's ascent. Back in 1922, Captain Truman Smith, an assistant military attaché at the American embassy in Berlin, was sent to Munich by his superiors to check up on an obscure political agitator by the name of Adolf Hitler. "Never saw such a sight in my life!" Smith scribbled in his diary after attending a Hitler rally. He interviewed Hitler in his "little bare bedroom on the second floor of a run-down house" and found him to be "a marvelous demagogue." That evening Smith advised his friend Hanfstaengl to witness the Hitler phenomenon himself, handing him his press pass to that evening's rally. Overwhelmed by the experience, Putzi became a convert and sought out Hitler afterward.

The following March the wealthy Hanfstaengl, whose family owned an art-publishing house in Munich and a gallery in New York, lent the fledgling National Socialists one thousand dollars to enable the party's daily newspaper, *Völkischer Beobachter,* to keep publishing. This was crucial to the Nazi cause, as Hitler needed the newspaper to spread his views. The Hanfstaengl family was one of the first to embrace the young, rough-hewn politician. It was to their country home that Hitler fled after the failed putsch of 1923, and where he was arrested.

Putzi Hanfstaengl was a tall, gangling man and not especially bright, but his sardonic wit and virtuoso piano playing pleased Hitler immensely. When Hitler came to power, he made him his foreign-press officer, and in this role Putzi wooed the West, with mixed results. It was Hanfstaengl who arranged Dorothy Thompson's 1931 interview with Hitler that later led to her expulsion from Germany. (Hitler reportedly found Thompson's pro-Jewish sentiments especially intolerable because she was not Jewish herself.) Another one of Putzi's ill-fated schemes involved getting Churchill and Hitler together in 1932. He enticed Churchill as far as Munich, but the encounter never came off. "Tell your boss from me," Churchill told Hanfstaengl "that anti-Semitism may be a good starter, but it is a bad sticker." Two years later it was still sticking, as Hanfstaengl arranged to fly W. R. Hearst and his party to Berlin.

———

"I would like to write the thing about Upton Sinclair very much," Theodore Dreiser informed Arnold Gingrich in Chicago, "because I know his books and I know that he was twenty years ahead of the rest of the critics of America who are now so loud in their condemnations. His foresight, in my judgment, is only to be matched by their vociferous hindsight."

Esquire magazine was on an EPIC binge. Frank Scully's article,

"Author! Author! For Governor," had arrived for the November issue, and now Gingrich, editor of the new monthly, had asked Theodore Dreiser, one of America's foremost novelists and public figures, to contribute five thousand words about his friend for the December number. Dreiser was working on a novel called *The Stoic,* but he was more interested in fact than fiction these days, and he needed the money, so magazine assignments were always welcome. At present, he divided his time between his suite at the Ansonia Hotel in New York City and a courtroom in Wilkes-Barre, Pennsylvania, covering a murder case many compared with his celebrated 1925 novel *An American Tragedy.*

Dreiser and Sinclair went way back, back before *The Jungle,* back near the turn of the century, when they met as struggling fiction writers. Dreiser hailed from Terre Haute, Indiana, home of Eugene V. Debs. He was an imposing figure, over six feet tall, "swaying above the heads of others" (as Edgar Lee Masters would put it a few years later). He found young Upton to be wide-eyed, poetic, and bursting with vanity. Like Sinclair, Dreiser was a realistic writer whose motto might have been "I'll fit it all in!" They shared a publisher, but with a difference: Doubleday censored Dreiser's remarkable first novel, *Sister Carrie,* in 1900 because of its profanity and sexual content but six years later beat the publicity drum loudly for *The Jungle.*

The two writers also had in common a strong association with Sinclair Lewis. Upton Sinclair's link was based mainly on the confusion surrounding their too-similar names. Dreiser and Lewis, however, had a kind of blood feud going, each seeking the mantle of greatest living American novelist. When Sinclair Lewis, author of *Main Street, Babbitt,* and *Dodsworth,* won the Nobel Prize in 1930, the first American to be so honored, matters came to a head.

One evening in March 1931, Lewis drank a bit too much before delivering a speech at a Metropolitan Club dinner in New York. He lamented that he had to dine with two writers—Heywood Broun and Arthur Brisbane, apparently—who considered him undeserving of the Nobel Prize, and he accused Theodore Dreiser, who was also present, of stealing "three thousand words from my wife's book." (Dreiser and Dorothy Thompson had toured the Soviet Union at the same time in 1927, and each wrote about the experience.) When the meal ended, Dreiser asked Lewis to meet him in the anteroom.

"You made a statement about my taking stuff from your wife's book," Dreiser said. "I know you're an ignoramus, but you're crazy." Then he asked Lewis to retract his charge. Lewis, only half as hefty as Dreiser, repeated it. Dreiser smacked him in the face. Lewis, more bemused than angry, said it again. Dreiser slapped him again. Lewis was about to say it a third time when someone intervened. As Dreiser was being led away, Lewis said, "I still say you are a liar and thief." Dreiser shouted, "Do you want me to hit you again?"

The next day the story made front-page news across the country. "Rash and unwarranted insults were rewarded with two slaps upon the face," Dreiser commented. Fight promoter Jimmie Johnston wired Dreiser with an offer to stage a fifteen-round bout in Ebbets Field, the writers to receive 50 percent of the gate. Westbrook Pegler suggested that next time the two men use "ghost-fighters." It was the slap heard round the world, and astonishingly, Lewis was pictured as the villain, despite Dreiser's pro-Soviet politics. (Lewis's nickname was Red, but Dreiser *was* Red.) Some Americans were still angry that Lewis, in his Nobel acceptance speech in Stockholm, had bewailed the intellectual and artistic shortcomings of his own country. Dreiser, in any case, was deluged with congratulatory messages: "No face ever deserved it more than his." "Why didn't you use your closed fist?" "You did just what many thousands of Americans would like to do." And so on.

Although they both aspired to a Nobel Prize, Dreiser never felt competitive with Upton Sinclair, perhaps because he recognized that the old muckraker was simply not in his class as a novelist. That was becoming less apparent, however, seemingly by the day. Dreiser had discovered the Communists, and vice versa, and neither side gave the other any rest. The writer championed the Soviet cause. He wrote a statement for *Izvestia,* calling the American system "rotten to the core." He topped the bill, above even James Cagney, at the mass rally for Tom Mooney in San Francisco, and he gave money to Emma Goldman, among other radicals. The Communist party manipulated the novelist on many occasions, but when he formally applied for membership, CP leader Earl Browder turned him down.

Despite this setback, Dreiser continued to allow politics to overwhelm his prose. He was an activist, a public figure, an influential pamphleteer, but no longer much of a novelist. Since *An American Tragedy,* he hadn't written any fiction worth reading. His statistic-filled broadside *Tragic America* proved an embarrassment. Sexually and politically the author consistently acted without regard for consequences, behavior that could only be called Dreiserian.

It reached a kind of apogee in 1931 when he conducted ad hoc hearings in Harlan County, Kentucky. Dreiser, along with fellow left-wing novelist John Dos Passos, uncovered some of the most pitiful working and living conditions in America. But his Dreiserian reputation preceded him. On the night of November 7, 1931, detectives observed a woman entering the author's hotel room at 11:00 P.M. They leaned some toothpicks against the door, went away, and discovered that the slivers were still standing in the morning. Two days later Dreiser was indicted by a local grand jury on charges of adultery. This made news across the country, crowding out the revelations Dreiser's own probe had uncovered. How Dreiserian!

Then Dreiser topped even himself, releasing to the press one of the most remarkable documents ever penned by a major American writer. In an attempt to save his neck, Dreiser confessed that "at this writing" he was "completely and finally impotent."

> In fact, today, you may lock me in the most luxurious boudoir with the most attractive woman in the world, and be convinced that we are discussing nothing more than books or art or some aesthetic problem of one kind or another.

"I told them I was impotent," Dreiser informed a friend. "They can't prove I'm not." He had little to fear. Kentucky wasn't going to extradite him from New York to face a misdemeanor charge.

"Like most peasants," H. L. Mencken commented, "[Dreiser] is bearing money very badly. . . . True enough, he can't write, but nevertheless he is a great writer, just as Whitman was . . . he wastes his time clowning. . . . he has become too tragic to be borne." Mencken had been Dreiser's greatest booster and esteemed friend in his early days. Now he wrote, "Seeing him would be like visiting an old friend who had gone insane. . . ."

Dreiser was on better terms with Upton Sinclair, although the two men had met only three times since 1904. One of the occasions was completely bizarre. During the 1920s, Uppie and Craig, passionate believers in mental telepathy, often invited famous guests, including Charlie Chaplin, to their home for seances. One night the guests included Rob Wagner, editor of *Script,* Theodore Dreiser, and their wives. Conducting the seance was the famous medium Arthur Ford, who summoned to the Sinclair's semidark living room a spirit named Fletcher. Among other things, the spirit re-created a conversation between Dreiser and a newspaperman that purportedly had taken place years before. Did it really happen that way? Dreiser couldn't say. He had nodded off and missed the whole thing.

A more memorable day found Sinclair driving Dreiser and Gene Debs—two left-wing Hoosiers—to a rally at the Hollywood Bowl. The most recent meeting had occurred in the fall of 1933. Dreiser's publisher, Horace Liveright, had passed away, and the two writers attended his funeral in New York. Afterward they walked downtown together. Sinclair blamed Liveright's early demise (he was only forty-nine) on alcohol and suggested that Dreiser was headed in the same direction.

Dreiser once informed Sinclair that "the brotherhood of man" was "mere moonshine to me. I see the individual large or small—weak or strong—as predatory and nothing less." Nevertheless, he supported Sinclair in his election campaign and had even signed a fund-raising letter in his behalf. Dreiser had unresolved political aspirations of his own, and they were much in line with Sinclair's; he even thought about running for governor of New York. Like Sinclair, he felt the American people lacked the class consciousness necessary to embrace communism but would accept a socialist system if it arrived in the right gift wrapping and under a different name. Dreiser wanted to form a national organization called the American League for National Equity. He also liked the idea of creating Dreiser clubs across the country, using *Tragic America* as their bible, although he dropped the idea temporarily in 1933 "because I am interested to see how this Roosevelt experiment works out."

Now Dreiser wished EPIC well. He considered the creation of a Sinclair cult in California the most impressive political phenomenon America had yet produced. Sinclair articulated what no other politician even recognized: the capitalist system had run its course and was finished. Sure, Sinclair was an egoist, but the best reformers, Dreiser believed, must always be. So Dreiser agreed to write the *Esquire* article, but he had one request of Arnold Gingrich. He had met Sinclair only a few times, Dreiser informed the editor, "and never have I seriously discussed anything with him. If he, or you, through one of your devils, will furnish me with a little intimate character data about him I could take care of the intellectual and other phases and imports of his work in America so far."

While Theodore Dreiser wrote his letter to Arnold Gingrich, his nemesis, Red Lewis, just down from his farm in Vermont, was greeting his wife at a Hudson River pier. Stepping off the liner *Leviathan,* Dorothy Thompson told the New York press that the position of Jews in Germany was now "hopeless," but what worried her most was that the German people "have lost the traditional German respect of law."

Unlike Dreiser, Mencken, Broun, and many other compatriots past and present, Sinclair Lewis remained silent on the subject of Upton Sinclair. Back in 1906, young Sinclair Lewis dug ditches and tended the furnace at Helicon Hall, the controversial cooperative colony in Englewood, New Jersey, organized by Upton Sinclair. Lewis had run away from Yale to rub elbows with John Dewey and William James, among others, at Sinclair's commune. He romanced Sinclair's golden-haired secretary, Edith Summers, and later wrote that he learned many "new things" at Helicon Hall, not the least of which was "how little worth I am in manual labor." Helicon Hall burned to the ground in 1907 under suspicious circumstances—none having to do with Sinclair Lewis's furnace tending.

The two Sinclairs remained friends thereafter. They often received each other's mail and cheerfully exchanged it cross-country. Upton Sinclair avoided meeting Red Lewis when the latter was hitting the bottle, which was most of the time. Lewis claimed that *The Profits of Religion* influenced his *Elmer Gantry,* but in 1928 he reacted with outrage to *Money Writes!,* Sinclair's blast at compromised authors (that is, nearly everyone but Sinclair himself). "I love Upton," Lewis confessed to a friend, almost weeping. "But look what he writes about me. He says I am one of those writers spoiled by money. He says, 'Sinclair Lewis has a million dollars.' I give you my word, I haven't got more than six hundred thousand dollars and he calls me a millionaire." Lewis then shot off an avowedly "cruel" letter to the old muckraker, charging Sinclair with "smug sadism" and propagating inaccuracies.

> If you would get over two ideas—first that any one who criticizes you is an evil and capitalist-controlled spy, and second that you have only to spend a few weeks on any subject to become a master of it—you might yet regain your now totally lost position as the leader of American socialistic journalism. . . . My God, Upton, go and pray for forgiveness, honesty and humility!

Two years later, in his Nobel acceptance speech, Lewis mentioned Upton Sinclair, among a handful of others, as being worthy of consideration for the prize. No matter what anyone thought of Sinclair, he was "internationally better known than any other American artist whatsoever, be he novelist, poet, painter, sculptor, musician, architect," Lewis insisted. Another writer he touted to the Nobel committee: Theodore Dreiser.

Red Lewis didn't seem intrigued by Sinclair's EPIC struggle, however. "Miss Thompson is the political expert," Lewis typically responded, disingenuosly, when asked to comment on current events. Lewis followed politics closely enough to consider writing a novel about the growing threat of a right-wing takeover in the United States. He once threw a party for Rex Tugwell in Washington. And he indirectly contributed to one of the high points of the California primary campaign. Speaking at a banquet last summer, Justus Wardell, a Democratic candidate for governor, charged that Upton Sinclair had "defied the power of Almighty God." Sinclair, he revealed, once stood in the pulpit of a church, took out his watch, and declared, "If there is a God let him prove it by striking me dead within the next minute." Uppie sent Wardell a letter informing him that he had gotten him mixed up with Sinclair Lewis. *Elmer Gantry,* in fact, was a "terrible book," Uppie wrote, adding that he was on the outs with his old friend Sinclair Lewis because he had said so.

Herbert Fleishhacker, the great Giannini's archrival in San Francisco, called on Chester Rowell at the *Chronicle* this afternoon. Oscar Sutro accompanied him. It was a gathering of famous names in San Francisco history, and the subject was appropriately weighty. Was it time, the three men wondered, to toss the GOP's albatross, Frank Finley Merriam, overboard?

Fleishhacker, president of the Anglo National Bank for the past quarter century, was a reckless financial titan. He had his finger in big projects up and down the coast and from the Rockies to the Philippines—hydroelectric plants, paper mills, you name it. Neil Vanderbilt called him "the richest man on the Pacific Coast" and claimed he ran San Francisco. Fleishhacker personally endowed the city with a zoo and the world's largest saltwater swimming pool. His political connections were impeccable. Sunny Jim Rolph, the flamboyant five-term mayor of San Francisco, was heavily indebted to Fleishhacker in every sense of the word, and when he became governor in 1931, he performed many a favor for his favorite banker. Now Fleishhacker had Rolph's successor, Frank Merriam, in his pocket.

Oscar Sutro was descended from Adolph Sutro, a former mayor of San Francisco who once owned 10 percent of the city and built the public bathhouse that still bore his name. Chester Rowell, once a Progressive hero, now a Republican wheelhorse—Hiram Johnson referred to him as "an intellectual prostitute"—was a member of the state Board of Regents and a close friend of Herbert Hoover's. He was, in addition, editor of the *Chronicle* and an influential columnist. Chet could jerk a lot of strings.

Sutro and Fleishhacker informed Rowell that Raymond Haight had just paid them a visit. (Haight's was another great name in San Francisco.) They were impressed with the young attorney's argument that Merriam could not beat Upton Sinclair and that *he* could. The reason: if Merriam quit, all of his votes would flow to Haight, while Haight's votes, in the event he left the race, would not slide easily to the reactionary governor. Merriam was not averse to quitting, Haight asserted, and was only staying in the race because Harry Chandler told him that he owed it to the GOP. Haight wanted someone to take a poll to determine which of the two candidates would perform better, face-to-face, against Sinclair.

At Oscar Sutro's request, Rowell agreed to call a meeting to raise the Haight option with a wide range of civic and financial leaders, such as real estate tycoon Culbert Coldwell. Privately, however, Chet held steady for Merriam—despite serious reservations. Back in August, Chet's boss, George T. Cameron, had ordered him to write an editorial endorsing Merriam in the GOP primary. Rowell argued against it:

> Merriam's whole record, and the lack of it, will be flung at him constantly. Some of that record is bad; much of it is negative, and all of it is reactionary. . . . Merriam is charged with deserting his first wife (in Oregon, I think). He left Iowa . . . after he had been up for indictment regarding the disappearance of certain funds. He was not indicted, but he preferred not to remain. The real-estate license of his company was revoked in California, for unprofessional conduct, though his personal license was not.

Rowell charged that Merriam was "habitually affiliated" with those who oppose unionists even to the point of shooting them. "Merriam," he added, "would appoint Southern California pinheads to the Regents."

Cameron, for some reason, backed off from endorsing Merriam in the primary. Nothing, however, would prevent Cameron, Chet Rowell, and the *Chronicle* from supporting the governor in his showdown with Sinclair. Merriam was in the race to stay—Rowell was certain of it.

Haight was nothing more than a distraction, but a dangerous one. Something had to be done to cut his legs out from under him. Rowell decided to write a party platform for Frank Merriam progressive enough to win broad support. Chet's friend Herbert Hoover agreed to lend him a hand.

———

Upton Sinclair, after a two-week hiatus, returned to his favorite spot: the study in his home on Sunset Avenue. Hundreds of letters were heaped on his big old wooden desk. Sifting through the correspondence was a gratifying but humbling experience. Dozens of strangers from around the country, and as far away as Europe and the Soviet Union, sent best wishes, along with donations ranging from one to five dollars. Some thanked God for Sinclair's victory in the primary. "I am going to be perfectly frank," a man wrote from Philadelphia, "and tell you that although I pride myself on being a regular 'he-man,' when I heard the wonderful news of your success in California I just sat down and cried like a little baby." Some offered to come to California to stump the state for Sinclair or to perform odd jobs for him. Many sent along their own plans for curing poverty.

A man from Staten Island said that Sinclair's nationally broadcast speech from the Chicago World's Fair had a tremendous impact in the East, and "they are predicting you will be our next President." An old friend from Jacumba, California, the author of a new book, *Nudism, the Child and Nutrition,* offered to campaign for Sinclair at half a dozen California nudist camps. "The great majority of nudists are with us, however," she commented. "Not much more to do there except possibly among the wealthier movie people who often visit our colonies." Cyril Clemens, a nephew of Mark Twain's, sent along his best wishes and revealed that FDR had told him that he took the expression "New Deal" from *A Connecticut Yankee in King Arthur's Court.* A man named Willoughby, owner of a photography store in New York City, congratulated Sinclair on his victory. And Upton was pleased to learn that he had the support of Fremont Older, the crusading San Francisco editor.

Some ordered copies of his books. For the past seventeen years, Sinclair had operated a self-publishing business, using a small frame house on his property in Pasadena as a combination storeroom and office. It gave him the option of writing exactly what he wanted: if a mainstream publisher wouldn't put out a controversial or subpar Sinclair book, he would do it himself. It also enabled Sinclair to keep nearly all of his books in print. Presently he offered for sale editions of forty-five of his books. Some editions sold ten copies a year, others two hundred. Sinclair lost at least a couple of thousand dollars annually in this pursuit, a loss he accepted happily.

A secretary handled the book orders but passed along to Uppie the personal notes that accompanied them. Added to his other mail, it made quite a pile on his desk. Since he eschewed form letters, Sinclair would have to compose or dictate more than fifty responses a day to catch up. Today he informed the out-of-staters who offered to come to California that "this is a people's crusade, and all work is being done voluntarily by the people most deeply interested, the residents of the state." To those who sent along their own end-poverty panaceas, he commented, "It is interesting to get so many different plans, and yet dovetailing into one another more or less. . . ." But mostly Sinclair warned against complacency: "Our opponents are only dazed. . . . We're in for a war dance. . . . We know what a fight we are going to have between now and November. . . . You know the forces which will be arrayed against us!"

Mixed in with Sinclair's fan mail was a disquieting message from an old friend who was vacationing out at Lake Arrowhead. "The talk of rich men at these resorts," he reported, "is that poor people on relief rolls must be deprived of their voting privileges if possible." Sinclair had lived in California long enough to know this was not just idle chatter.

SEPTEMBER 16

SUNDAY

The ploy worked. W. R. Hearst was about to meet Hitler, and Marion Davies was nowhere in sight. Marion had made it as far as the Berlin airport, where her friend Ruth Selwyn awaited her. Ruth begged for help—she needed seven hundred dollars to pay off a hotel bill. Hearst told Marion to run along to the hotel; he would meet up with her later, and then they would visit Hitler. Marion dashed off while W.R. and Putzi Hanfstaengl rushed to the presidential palace on the Wilhelmstrasse. Hanfstaengl would serve as interpreter.

Adolf Hitler, on meeting this legend of American journalism, had to be impressed by his stature. Hearst was twenty-five years older, several inches taller, and perhaps a hundred pounds heavier than his host. But when Hitler heard Hearst speak for the first time, he was probably surprised, as others always were, to hear a soft, high-pitched voice emanating from this bulk, "a voice like the fragrance of violets made audible," as Ambrose Bierce once described it.

After a brief exchange of pleasantries, the chancellor quickly came to the point, demanding to know why he was so "misunderstood" and despised in the United States. Hearst explained that Americans loved democracy; it was as simple as that. Hitler replied that he was product of democracy, having been elected by an overwhelming vote of his people.

Hearst didn't know quite how to respond to this logic. As recently as four weeks ago, Hearst himself had praised Hitler for rallying the public will. Now he informed Hitler that it was not the structure of German government but some of its policies concerning a certain unnamed group of citizens that smacked of dictatorship. W.R. was speaking in code, but Hitler got the message. He reminded the publisher of how poorly America treated the Indians. He also assured Hearst that discrimination against particular groups in Germany was disappearing, and that it was government policy to wipe it out entirely.

Hearst, gratified, assured Hitler that this would raise his standing in America considerably, and W.R. left the meeting convinced that he had accomplished something. Stepping outside, he found photographers waiting, not something he had particularly counted on. They had him pose with Dr. Alfred Rosenberg and other influential Nazis. Asked to comment, Hearst replied, "Visiting Hitler is like calling on the President of the United States. One doesn't talk about it for publication."

Then Hearst and his party drove over to his hotel. He rang up his mistress from the lobby. "The plane's ready," he said.

"What about Hitler?" Marion asked, furious, smelling a rat.

"I just went in for five minutes and then I left," Hearst explained meekly. Marion was not mollified. She vowed not to speak to W.R. for the rest of the day.

Dr. Robert A. Millikan, en route to an international conference of physicists in London, paused long enough in Chicago to denounce Upton Sinclair as a "demagogue." Millikan, director of the Norman Bridge lab at Cal Tech in Pasadena, was the nation's leading native-born scientist, but Sinclair was not concerned. He had on his side the most famous egghead of them all, Albert Einstein.

When Einstein, at the invitation of Dr. Millikan, came to the United States in the early 1930s to spend a few months at Cal Tech, one of the Americans he most wished to meet was Upton Sinclair. He had read some of Sinclair's books and corresponded with the author from Germany. He even wrote a preface for a German edition of Sinclair's *Mental Radio,* declaring that while this report on telepathy might seem fantastic, it was inconceivable "that so conscientious an observer and writer as Upton Sinclair should attempt a deliberate deception of the reading world. His good faith and trustworthiness cannot be doubted. . . ."

Einstein had promised to visit Upton in Pasadena. Sinclair, nevertheless, was surprised one day in the winter of 1931 when his sister-in-law informed him that there was "an old man walking up and down the street, and he keeps looking at the house."

"Go out and ask what he wants," Sinclair's wife instructed.

A moment later the sister-in-law returned with this report: "He says he's Dr. Einstein."

Sinclair found Einstein to be one of the kindest, gentlest, sweetest men he had ever met. The scientist had a keen wit and expressed sharp opinions about war and other evils of the world. Uppie had him over for dinner. Like Sinclair, Einstein did not drink. They played violin duets, which listeners found scarcely bearable. Einstein told Sinclair that one of the joys of his life was Uppie's "wicked tongue." He compared Sinclair to Voltaire and introduced him to Robert A. Millikan.

When Sinclair complained that critics were always calling him "undignified," Einstein took note. The next time the physicist visited the jerry-built house in Pasadena, he brought along an enormous photograph of himself. On it he had inscribed six lines of verse in colloquial German. Translated, they read:

> Unfazed by even the grimiest pots and pans
> No tender nerve escapes his probing scans;
> Who scorns the Now and swears by What's Ahead—
> Who thinks "undignified" is better left unsaid—
> Sinclair is the valiant man
> If anyone's to vouch for it, I'm the one who can.

Sinclair had the portrait framed and displayed it prominently on the wall by his desk.

Einstein enjoyed his stay at Cal Tech and returned again the following winter. He expressed his political views freely, and Sinclair learned that Dr. Millikan, a staunch Republican, and other Cal Tech officials were not pleased that their honored guest was socializing with a celebrated radical. Einstein detected a certain snobbery. He also felt that he and his wife were slighted at times due to anti-Semitism. "The Jews have got Harvard, they are getting Princeton," one Cal Tech instructor told Sinclair's wife, "and they are on the way to getting Cal Tech."

When Hitler consolidated his power in 1933, Einstein fled his homeland. He accepted a lifetime position at the Institute for Advanced Study in New Jersey, but requested a salary so small his patrons had to increase it. (Einstein once used a fifteen-hundred-dollar check from the Rockefeller Foundation as a bookmark and then lost the book.) Arriving in America for good, Einstein spent a night at the White House, chatting with FDR about their common interest, sailing. When a women's organization protested his presence in the United States, asserting that he was a Communist, Einstein delivered a classic rejoinder: "Never yet have I experienced from the fair sex such energetic rejection of all advances; or if I have, never from so many at once."

Upton Sinclair had just launched his EPIC campaign, and Einstein, after reading *I, Governor,* sent him the following message from Princeton:

> Your anticipatory report over your activity as Governor of California has interested me greatly. You know, indeed much better than I, that nothing annoys people more than if one tries honestly to help them. I heartily wish that in your case the matter may come out otherwise.

Einstein favored production for use as a means of stopping "the intolerable tyranny of the owners of the means of production (land and machinery) over the wage-earners," but insisted that private enterprise be "left its sphere of activity."

Poles apart politically, Albert Einstein and Robert Millikan shared scientific interests. Millikan's own work closely intersected with Einstein's early studies of relativity and light quanta. The first American-born physicist to win the Nobel Prize, Millikan was the catalyst in establishing Cal Tech as a center of scientific education and research. He did more than study cosmic rays—he coined the term. In the field of practical science, Millikan helped develop the three-electrode telephone relay and speech amplifier, which came to underlie much of the science of communications and the motion-picture "talkie."

At sixty-four, Millikan was a small, sturdy man with white hair, sparkling gray-blue eyes, and a charming manner. Eleven years older than Einstein, he believed, like many of his class and generation, that the United States was meant to lead the world to a glorious new era with science playing a key role. Millikan was America's spokesman for science at science's pinnacle of prestige. "There is no voice in the cosmos more persuasive than yours," a *New York Times* writer told him.

One of Herbert Hoover's strongest backers, Millikan often derided the New Deal. The Depression, he said, was merely a temporary jam in the social machinery "which makes it impossible at the moment to reap the benefit of the scientist and the engineer in creating more wealth." As for the millions on relief: "Call unemployment 'leisure' and one can at once see the possibilities," Millikan observed.

Upton Sinclair was not caught by surprise, therefore, when Millikan, during his stopover in Chicago, attributed EPIC's triumph in the recent primary to "a period of confused thinking." Sinclair's plan to end poverty in California, Millikan commented, was "just as desirable and effective as the program for the elimination of disease throughout the world which he advocated ten years ago based on the Abrams theory of electronic reactions. That was a stupendous medical fake which the public fell for to its detriment."

With Einstein in his corner, Sinclair was not concerned about Millikan. He considered Millikan's opinions infantile outside the field of physics, and he had been attacked for so long for endorsing Dr. Albert Abrams's magic vibrating machine that the barbs barely registered. But something did trouble Sinclair: he had heard from friends at Cal Tech that faculty members at the school who supported EPIC were afraid to speak out, fearing reprisals.

Aimee Semple McPherson preached her first sermon in Los Angeles in almost six months this morning. Sister Aimee filled her homecoming service at the Angelus Temple with new songs she had written for the revised version of her *Rich Man and Lazarus* opera. "It is so good to be home again," McPherson declared. "I have not wasted a moment."

After meeting with promoter Guido Orlando in New York, she had vacationed in Atlantic City, then took a train to Montreal and set off for a series of appearances across Canada. Aimee took a side trip to Ingersoll, Ontario, to visit the old family homestead and her father's grave, then headed back to California. It promised to be a hellish autumn. Aimee would have to appear in court to explain why she had backed out of a commitment to portray herself in a motion picture. There was grumbling within the congregation concerning her extended absences, and now she planned a visit to Foursquare Gospel missions in Africa, India, and China. This sparked rumors that she intended to become a missionary and leave the temple in the hands of her top aide (and rival for the affections of her flock), Rheba Crawford Splivalo.

Then there was the California governor's race. Sister Aimee couldn't very well declare for a candidate, but she could take a stand against radicalism and atheism and let people jump to their own conclusions. God had appeared to her in a dream, she told Guido Orlando, and commanded her to do something to stop communism. But God did not command her to do it for nothing. She instructed Orlando to start raising one hundred thousand dollars for a national road show starring Sister Aimee as America's Joan of Arc, based on the theme "America! Awake! The Enemy Is at Your Gates!"

———

Sherrill Halbert, an attorney in Visalia, happily received word from Los Angeles that the GOP had selected him to spearhead Governor Merriam's campaign among younger voters throughout the state. There was some irony in this. Just that spring Halbert had helped organize a new group, the California Republican Assembly, or CRA, with the express aim of injecting new blood into a party too long dominated by tired old war-horses like Frank Finley Merriam. Halbert, in a letter to a friend that summer, had denounced Merriam with the epithet "professed reactionary." Now the old man was about to hand him at least fifteen thousand dollars to ensure his election, and Halbert wasn't turning it down. This was the CRA's chance to make its mark and perhaps become a permanent fixture on the California political scene.

The CRA trumpeted itself as a champion of good government and a militant foe of corruption, expediency, compromise, and incompetent leadership. It held that the majority of Californians favored neither radical experimentation nor standpat conservatism but "can and will be enlisted in the cause of intelligent liberalism." A moderate up-and-comer like Oakland's Earl Warren was just its cup of tea. Already the CRA had gained four thousand members while seeking tens of thousands more to operate a sophisticated precinct network throughout the state.

While the group's ideals were lofty, it was not above rabid anticommunism. In the latest issue of its publication, the *Assembly News,* Ed Shattuck, chief of the group's Los Angeles office, called the governor's campaign a case of "Americanism vs. Moscowism" and declared war on EPIC. "We must fill our ranks with fighters," Shattuck wrote. "This is a call to arms!"

But how to finance it? The CRA was not an official GOP organization. Halbert learned in a letter from Gerald Toll, the group's treasurer, that Governor Merriam had promised that the CRA would receive between fifteen thousand and twenty thousand dollars to wage its war. This was a surprisingly generous sum, but what was even more eye-opening was the name of the fund-raiser who would arrange the gift: *Los Angeles Times*'s political editor Kyle Dulaney Palmer. The man known as the Little Governor apparently would be doing double duty for Frank Merriam this autumn—and Halbert didn't know the half of it.

———

Today, Cecil B. DeMille became the first creative artist in the movie colony to publicly declare for Frank Merriam. Surely this marked the first time the legendary director ever turned his back on an epic.

Fresh from his success with *Cleopatra,* his sixtieth film, DeMille was spending a lot of time on his schooner, the *Seaward,* off Catalina, working on a script about the Crusades and doing a little fishing on the side. He still had to cast the two leads and plan the costumes and sets for his next picture, no small consideration in a DeMille movie. *Cleopatra* had cost a whopping $750,000 and featured a one-acre swimming pool for the Romans and a sumptuous "love barge" for the queen, played by Claudette Colbert. "He is almost the only director in Hollywood who still uses a megaphone," *Time* magazine had observed recently. "Bald, ruddy-faced, he wears riding breeches and puttees made especially for directing."

Best known for his historical and biblical spectacles, which always featured steamy bath scenes and scantily clad women, DeMille held conservative social views that were reflected most clearly in his topical films. The titles said it all: *Don't Change Your Husband, Why Change Your Wife?, Forbidden Fruit, The Godless Girl.* His 1933 movie, *This Day and Age,* provoked a round of protest. DeMille intended to portray the evils of racketeering and the idealism of youth, but many observers felt that he unintentionally endorsed lynching: the youngsters in the film kidnap the heavy and slowly lower him into a pit full of rats to extract a confession. Responding to charges that the film was fascist, DeMille pointed to its favorable portrayals of Jews and Negroes.

A lifetime Republican, DeMille supported Herbert Hoover in 1928 with the largest donation he had ever made to a political candidate. He prized Hoover's uncompromising principles and honesty, but in 1932 he backed Franklin Roosevelt for one reason: C.B. opposed Prohibition. The director remained on good terms with the man in the White House;

his friend J.F.T. O'Connor had introduced him to FDR in December 1933, and C.B. later told Jefty that it was "a privilege to follow such a leader." DeMille, through O'Connor, promised to arrange a private showing of *Cleopatra* at the White House this fall when the President returned to Washington, and FDR was eager to take him up on the offer.

DeMille reverted to Republicanism and the self-interest of the movie industry in opposing Upton Sinclair. "Few people in Southern California," he commented today in the newspapers, "realize that they are in danger of having this industry move out of the state. The hundreds of thousands of persons directly and indirectly employed in pictures and those engaged in trading with them face the prospect of being thrown out of work. . . . Increased taxation of the motion picture industry is just what the eastern financiers are looking for as an excuse to move the industry to New York." Frank Merriam, C.B. said, had "proven ability as an economist and a leader who . . . can and will save the industry for us."

This put the DeMille brothers on opposite sides of the political fence. C.B.'s older brother, William C. deMille, a prominent writer and director in his own right—and father of Agnes deMille, the young dancer—had come out for Sinclair. He was the only Hollywood personality to join a distinguished list of Americans—Clarence Darrow, Theodore Dreiser, Archibald MacLeish, Dorothy Canfield Fisher, Margaret Sanger, and Morris Ernst, among others—appealing for donations to the EPIC campaign. William deMille was erudite and brilliant, but in Hollywood there was only one Great DeMille, and he favored Frank Finley Merriam.

For this week's *Script,* editor Rob Wagner playfully asked his old friend Charlie Chaplin what he would do after the Revolution came. "People would still want moving pictures, Rob," Chaplin replied. "I'd work if they gave me a little cottage . . . but it would be nice if they discovered I worked better on a yacht!" Then, addressing the burning issue of the day, Wagner wondered if Charlie would let the Little Tramp speak a few words in his next picture. "I don't know what he'd *say*!" Chaplin protested.

The Democratic convention in Sacramento was only four days off, so it was time for leading Democrats to decide whether to sink or swim with Upton Sinclair. That decision, naturally, would not be based purely on principle or policy. Everyone wanted to cut a deal. Senator McAdoo, back in Los Angeles, scheduled a meeting with Sinclair on Monday to advance his law partner, William C. Neblett, as state Democratic chairman. Today George Creel, down from the north, trekked to Pasadena to present his own demands.

George Creel, an inch shorter than Sinclair and considerably more caustic, was always part bantam cock. As head of Woodrow Wilson's wartime Committee on Public Information he created more enemies than Upton Sinclair ever dreamed of having. Creel was called "pro-German," a "depraved hack," and a "licensed liar." The journalist Mark Sullivan had greeted Creel's appointment as Wilson's propaganda chief by labeling the crusading journalist "temperamental, excitable and emotional to the last degree . . . the most aggressive and daring of newspaper men . . . the most violent of muckrakers. Creel is a bearer of the fiery cross." Seventeen years later George Creel was still a writer—he claimed to earn about thirty thousand dollars a year at it—but muckraking was a thing of the past; he bore no crosses.

Joining Sinclair and Creel in Uppie's living room was the inner circle of the EPIC campaign: Sheridan Downey, candidate for lieutenant governor; Culbert Olson, front-runner for the post of state Democratic chairman; Dick Otto, campaign manager; and two attorneys, John Packard (a former Socialist party leader) and John Beardsley (an ACLU stalwart). Creel took off his coat and hung it over a chair, stripped off his tie and draped it over his coat, rolled up one sleeve and then the other, sat down, and explained what he wanted.

Sinclair, he argued, should restrict himself in the party platform to a statement of general principles, with details, programs, and promises left vague. That way he could attract the broadest support, and non-EPIC Democratic candidates could run on the platform as well. Creel proposed dropping from the platform explicit mention of a fifty-dollar-a-month pension for people over sixty, the establishment of farm colonies and the use of scrip, the repeal of the sales tax, and the state takeover of idle farms and factories. He also demanded that he write a major portion of the platform himself, including the section dealing with labor. This would give Creel a chance to rewrite Upton Sinclair—something he, and countless other authors, had longed to do for years.

Perhaps to Creel's surprise, Sinclair agreed to all of this with alacrity. Sinclair thought to himself, *The platform is not that important. When I'm governor, I'll have charge of the programs and the details.* Creel agreed to chair the upcoming convention, which might still prove riotous, and endorsed Culbert Olson as party chairman, calling Senator McAdoo's candidate for this post a "dead cockroach."

The meeting ended on a cordial note. Sinclair's performance even surpassed the surprisingly favorable opinion offered by *The New York Times* on its front page this very morning. "Mr. Sinclair," a *Times* correspondent wrote from San Francisco, "has developed since the election a tact that is amazing to those who knew him in other years as personally amiable but publicly intransigent to the last degree." Shrewd observers, purred the *Times,* were predicting a Sinclair victory in November. Now George Creel had climbed aboard the glory train. "I don't think there is any doubt anymore of my being elected," Sinclair informed his publisher John Farrar.

The state committee of the Socialist party met in Bakersfield this afternoon to decide whether to continue an active campaign in the race for governor. Milen Dempster, the party's candidate, did not reveal the contents of the two letters he had just received from Norman Thomas, fearing that the committee would object to any out-of-state intervention. He was ready, even eager, to quit, but he would be a good soldier and carry on if so ordered. After a stormy three-hour debate, the Socialist leadership voted five to two to keep Dempster in the race and maintain the party's all-out opposition to EPIC.

"Hello. Hello. Is this you, old America? What? Hello. This is Will. Will!" It was six-fifteen in the evening in California but a quarter past two in the morning in Great Britain when Will Rogers phoned in his first nationwide radio broadcast of the fall season from London. Rogers had been abroad since July on an around-the-world trip that took him to Hawaii, Japan, Manchuria, Siberia, Russia, Scandinavia, Austria, Romania, and Hungary. Now he was about to board a slow boat for New York.

Cameras were ready to roll on the set of Rogers's next Hollywood vehicle, a political satire called *The County Chairman,* but he was one movie star who kept his own schedule, no questions asked. Will Rogers was, beyond a doubt, the most beloved man in America. Charlie Chaplin once claimed that distinction, but a stormy private life and a declining number of film appearances had taken their toll. (It was the Little

Tramp, not Charlie, whom the people loved anyway.) A popular new figure, Franklin Roosevelt, now vied for the position, and while millions adored FDR with a heartbreaking ferocity, many Americans despised the President with equal passion; they called him Franklin Deficit Roosevelt or "the cripple in the White House." No one called Rogers anything but Will or Bill.

According to popular legend, Will Rogers never met a man he didn't like. What was closer to the truth was that nearly everyone liked Will Rogers. He was the country's most popular newspaper commentator and radio personality, and (in 1934) its favorite motion-picture star. If Roosevelt hadn't come along in 1932, Will Rogers, a prairie populist and avowed Democrat, might have claimed the White House himself. He was the Will of the People and, at the same time, the biggest landowner in Hollywood.

Back in January the humorist had spiked a request from Democrats in San Jose that he run for governor of California, explaining that he would rather be a poor actor than a poor governor. "After rawboning these fellows for so many years," he added, "I'm satisfied to remain fancy free to go where I please when I please." Rogers, in fact, wasn't even registered to vote. On his trip abroad this summer, he sent daily dispatches to hundreds of newspapers in the United States, including the *Los Angeles Times* and *The New York Times,* but failed to comment on what was happening back in his home state. Tonight, on his "Good Gulf" radio show, which aired semiregularly on Sunday evenings, he broke that silence.

"Oh, quit crying," Rogers advised in his stuttering cowboy drawl, pretending that the party on the other end of the telephone was a dejected "money man" in America. "Tell me how things is going over there? Oh, they're terrible, are they? Yeah. Oh, I know about Sinclair being nominated. I heard that in Siberia. In Siberia! Yeah. That's the place they send all the rich men in Russia. Yes, I know—*we* send them to the Senate. 'Bout the same thing.

"Do you live in California?" Rogers inquired. "Oh, you don't, huh? What are you howlin' about, then? *I* live there. You hold the phone a minute while I do some cryin' myself. . . ." From thousands of miles away, it was hard to tell whether Will's tongue was in his cheek, but one thing was certain: California would hear a lot more from its favorite citizen when he returned to his ranch in Santa Monica next month.

SEPTEMBER 17

MONDAY

MAJOR THREAT TO CLOSE. The *Hollywood Reporter* banner headline sounded the alarm throughout the film colony this morning. At least four and possibly six of the major studios would shut their doors and move all production to the East Coast if Upton Sinclair was elected. There were no ifs, ands, or buts about it. "Major studio heads," the movie journal revealed, "claim it will be impossible to operate here with Sinclair in the chair in Sacramento. Rather than try the experiment they will move bag and baggage by the first of the year."

United Artists, Universal, Paramount, and Columbia were ready to leave town, with MGM and RKO likely to join them. Paramount would move back to its studio in Astoria, Queens. United Artists was "dickering" to rent a studio in the Bronx. Universal calculated the costs of revamping its old Fort Lee, New Jersey, plant; Columbia planned to rebuild another site in Fort Lee. MGM would use the old Hearst factory in New York City, while RKO would probably head for Long Island. If this came to pass, the journal reported, twenty thousand people in Hollywood would lose their jobs.

Although the threat to move had been raised previously by major figures like Joe Schenck and C. B. DeMille, this was the first report that pretended to speak for a majority of the moguls. The *Hollywood Reporter,* not one for understatement, declared that "the first serious shot at Sinclair's campaign has been fired, and the belief is that all the other big California industries will soon be following suit."

Variety was on top of the situation, too. It prepared an editorial, scheduled to run tomorrow, that called on Hollywood executives to "stop that moaning" over Sinclair and start "whipping their friends and employees into line." Even better, they should carry their message directly to moviegoers. "With theatres available to provide Sinclair opposition, so far as propaganda is concerned," *Variety* advised, "let the picture business assert itself against this encroachment."

Melvin Belli couldn't believe he was actually working for Frank Merriam. His recent experience riding the rails with hoboes and misfits had changed his life, he thought, placing him on the side of the underdog forever. Then along came the Merriam men, offering him the best-paying job the young attorney had ever had, utilizing his considerable oratorical skills to smear Upton Sinclair.

Like many other offspring of the well-to-do, Mel Belli was scuffling through the Depression. Born in Sonora and raised in Stockton, he was the son of a banker and the grandson of the first female pharmacist in California. By the time he received his degree in 1933 from Boalt Hall, the University of California's prestigious law school, few firms were hiring. So when a classmate told him about a job that paid a robust seventy-five dollars a week and involved a lot of traveling, Belli took notice.

"What is it?" he asked.

"Bums," his friend replied. "We'll have to ride the rods with the bums and the hoboes for the government and see what's up."

The two men would be undercover tramps for Harry Hopkins and the federal relief administration, hopping freight trains to find out how the hoboes really lived. They adopted new names—Belli became Louis Bacigalupi. In their pockets they kept a phone number in Los Angeles to call in case of an emergency; but if they were arrested on simple vagrancy charges, they were on their own. The two young attorneys put on Levi's, ambled over to the Oakland rail yard, and caught a freight heading south.

When the train slowed near San Jose, Belli jumped off with the rest of his ragged companions. Club-wielding railroad employees, known as "bulls," approached, so the bums ran through the cottonwoods and took refuge in a hobo camp next to a creek. Men in tattered jackets stood around the campfires talking. Some drank coffee out of tin cans; others ate beans or chewed on stale bread. Belli and his buddy were surprised to see entire families, including infants and nursing mothers, as well as young men much like themselves—former stockbrokers, struggling artists, college dropouts. The next night they got picked up in the stockyards at Manteca and were jailed for vagrancy, but they were released quickly: there were so many "vags" the judge had no place to keep them all.

Belli traveled up and down the San Joaquin Valley. He learned how to beg yesterday's bread at a bakery and old vegetables at the market. The Salvation Army made him chop wood and say his prayers before serving him watered-down soup and milk. In Fresno, he discovered a kind of hobo hotel where transients could pick up mail, post messages, buy a bowl of mulligan stew for fifteen cents, or huddle in the corner and catch some sleep. That night President Roosevelt delivered one of his fireside chats, and Belli was surprised when everyone stopped what they were doing to listen intently to the patrician voice booming from the radio.

Despite the hardship, Belli considered the experience something of a lark, knowing that a career in law still awaited him back home. Then things got rough. As the hoboes traveled south over the Tehachapis, the boxcars turned cold, and Belli had to stuff newspapers in his trousers to stay warm. The train shook so violently he almost wet his pants. Arriving in Palm Springs, the two undercover tramps invaded the town's only golf course and fell asleep on a cushiony green.

Belli was arrested again in San Diego with about a hundred of his fellow travelers. Outraged by conditions in the jail, he decided that rather than plead guilty and promise to leave town, he would fight his case all the way to the Supreme Court if necessary. "The only thing I'm guilty of," he told the judge, "is being caught in this Depression and not being able to work."

"Oh," said the judge, frowning, "we've got one who pleads not guilty, huh? A Communist." Belli changed his plea when the judge set the trial date six months down the road. Escorted to the edge of town, he resolved to devote his career to fighting for the dispossessed.

After a few more weeks of bumming around the Southwest, Belli and his friend returned to Berkeley in time to take the bar exam. They wrote up a report describing the hoboes as basically a vagabond army of wayward youths. (The following year, when the state organized a youth corps out in the Sierras, the two men felt they had something to do with it.) Despite passing his bar exam, Belli struggled to find work and finally was hired to do legal research for a firm in San Francisco at twenty-five dollars a month. He and his wife, Betty, who worked as a secretary, resided in a tiny cottage in Berkeley, practically living on canned spinach. So when someone connected to the Merriam organization offered Mel a two-month job at one hundred dollars per month, maybe more, he leapt at it.

His assignment: travel around the state—he had a lot of experience at that—speaking to factory and office workers, alerting them to the menace of Sinclairism. Belli called himself a liberal and an idealist, but his political principles were completely unformed. He had voted for Hoover in '32 and currently was leader of a Young Republicans group, yet he considered Frank Merriam a right-wing know-nothing. Still, Merriam's money was good, and Mel didn't have to ride the rails to earn it.

———

Charles C. Teague left what he called his "lemon Jerusalem" in Ventura County and journeyed south once again to Los Angeles for three days of meetings with the group he had whipped together to lead the fight against Upton Sinclair. He wouldn't return home until he was certain that a propaganda network was in place and business leaders were ready to dig deep into their pockets to guarantee the success of the endeavor. All the rest—naming the organization, renting an office, hiring a staff—was nothing but "scenery," Teague believed. The vital work would go on behind the scenes.

A visiting writer once described Teague as a teetotaler with a homespun quality, a "stocky, pleasant man . . . sonorous of voice" with "a weatherbeaten complexion, and a good command of English." C. C. Teague had arrived in tiny Santa Paula from Maine in 1892 and never left. "You aren't going to find anything spectacular in my story," Teague once told an interviewer. "I simply began in a small way and grew into bigger things as the years went by."

With an assist from his great-uncle Wallace L. Hardison, cofounder of the Union Oil company, Teague had transformed the modest forty acres he planted with his father in 1893 into the Limoneria ranch, the largest citrus orchard in the world, two thousand acres strong. Teague was a citrus entrepreneur, prophet, experimenter, and promoter all in one. He invented new irrigation, storage, and shipping methods that helped California lemons compete with imports from Sicily. Teague's gospel: pick lemons before they ripen, select a brand name, and most important of all, belong to a cooperative.

No matter how productive, any single grower was still at the mercy of the market, Teague pointed out, arguing for cooperation. He revived the California Fruit Growers Exchange, became president in 1920, and established its Sunkist brand as the leading produce label in the country, controlling supply and distribution to keep prices up. Thanks largely to Teague, by the 1930s the California exchange had enlisted eleven thousand growers, representing 75 percent of California's oranges and 97 percent of its lemons. It operated nearly two hundred packing houses and annually distributed more than one hundred million dollars' worth of Sunkist oranges, lemons, and grapefruits. Teague accomplished much the same success with the California Walnut Growers Association.

When Herbert Hoover appointed Teague to the Federal Farm Board in 1929, he faced strong opposition from conservatives, who felt his cooperative arrangements smacked of Sovietism. Teague won converts with his argument that the cooperative concept was valid if initiated by businessmen to guarantee profits—not by the government to benefit workers or consumers. Like nearly all of the allegedly socialistic growers, Teague was a Republican and fiercely anti-union. He chaired President Hoover's reelection campaign in southern California and helped write the 1932 Republican platform. The following year Hearst's *Los Angeles Examiner* hailed Mr. Citrus in verse:

> 'Tis C. C. Teague of GOP
> director of its destiny
> beside this sunny southern sea . . .

In early 1934, Teague was mentioned as a possible GOP candidate in a hopeless U.S. Senate race against Hiram Johnson. "I am not in politics and never expect to be," he announced, quieting the rumors.

EPIC represented the kind of government-mandated cooperation that Teague despised. He saw it as a threat to individual initiative, property, the right to engage in business at a profit, "and everything else that has made our average citizens better off than those of any other nation on earth." But people down on their luck could not reason soundly, Teague believed. They didn't understand explanations by Republican economists that the Depression was inevitable, necessary, momentary. They foolishly believed that anything was better than what they had and were willing to follow anyone who promised relief. Unemployment was making Communists and Socialists of the people.

Someone had to save the citizens of California—from themselves. It was often said of Teague that his strongest characteristic was a willingness to take responsibility. Faced with an impossible task, he would say to his associates, "Well, boys, what are the facts?" Then, facing the facts, he'd instruct, "Let's get at it." Teague once explained that "when someone tells you a thing can't be done, he means under the conditions he has in mind. The conditions under which you expect to undertake the thing may not be the same at all." Now he simply had to change the conditions under which EPIC held voters in thrall.

To that end, he had commissioned a study of Upton Sinclair's writings and discovered, to his amazement, that the muckraker had insulted almost every interest group in California. The only way to beat Sinclair, Teague decided, was to "convict" him on this evidence, however musty some of it might be. And the way to do that was to assemble his statements on campaign leaflets, produce the circulars in unprecedented numbers, and direct them at narrowly defined audiences.

To accomplish this, Teague would have to get his friends at Southern Pacific, Southern California Edison, Standard Oil, Pacific Mutual, and dozens of smaller corporations to commit to at least half a million dollars in donations. It would be like buying an insurance policy to protect against devastating losses. Teague informed newspaper publisher Joseph R. Knowland, GOP strongman in northern California, that this was the only way "a losing fight may be won." The next three days would be make-or-break time for the anti-Sinclair campaign.

———

No matter what Teague, Knowland, and the other power brokers did, they could not avoid this fact: Where Hiram Johnson led in the governor's race, California would likely follow. On August 29, he had won the Republican, Democrat, and Progressive primaries, assuring his reelection to a fourth term in the U.S. Senate. Now Johnson could act as kingmaker without any political qualms, but "Old H'arm" gave no indication of favoring any of the gubernatorial candidates.

Back in June, when Governor Rolph passed away and Frank Merriam replaced him, Johnson complained to a friend that the state was now "absolutely in the hands" of the *L.A. Times*'s Harry Chandler. Yet Johnson uttered not one kind word for either Ray Haight (a fellow

Progressive party nominee) or Upton Sinclair. It was impossible to predict what he would do. Party labels meant almost nothing in California. Johnson was nominally a Republican, but until recently the GOP was considered the liberal party in California. It was Johnson, after all, who overthrew the Southern Pacific machine in California in 1910 and ostensibly gave the state back to the people. But with the decline of the Progressive movement in the 1920s, liberals now comprised, at best, a *wing* of the state GOP; while the Democrats, in the wake of FDR's election, drifted leftward.

Although he remained popular with the electorate, Johnson had disappointed liberals since leaving the governor's office in 1917 and ascending to the U.S. Senate. He remained a powerful foe of privilege, but proposed no positive programs of his own—that is, he was nothing but an obstructionist. He supported FDR over Hoover in 1932, but like many of the other great Progressives, he had calcified with age. Rudolph Spreckels and Franklin Hichborn presently supported Sinclair; most of the rest of the original Hiram Johnson gang, including Chet Rowell and John R. Haynes, backed Merriam.

As the state political conventions approached, Senator Johnson remained annoyingly neutral on the governor's race, but privately he struck a blow against Sinclair. In a letter to his old Progressive colleague Harold Ickes, Johnson described Sinclair as "erratic" and "irresponsible," adding that the EPIC program was "simply damned foolishness." Now, if Hiram Johnson took the next step, endorsing Ray Haight, EPIC was probably dead.

———

Charles and Anne Morrow Lindbergh landed at Clover Field in Santa Monica, concluding a rather leisurely trip, by this pilot's standards, from the East. With his powerful low-wing plane grounded for repairs, the colonel had rented a small blue monocoupe, which was not equipped for night flying. Yesterday, the couple landed in Roswell, New Mexico, where rocket scientist Dr. Robert H. Goddard showed Lindbergh some of the equipment he hoped would one day inaugurate a new era in flight.

The Lindberghs came to California to discuss business affairs with airline officials and to see Anne's sister in Pasadena. It was, as it turned out, a less than opportune time to fly far from home. Telltale gold notes—kidnap money—continued to turn up back in New York. Walter Winchell broke the news last night on his popular NBC radio show. "Boys, if you weren't such a bunch of saps and yaps," Winchell said, addressing local bank tellers and detectives, "you'd have already captured the Lindbergh kidnappers." The colonel and his wife had just started to get their hopes up, and now Winchell had probably sent the kidnapper right back into hiding.

The gala premiere of Max Reinhardt's production of *A Midsummer Night's Dream* was spectacular even by Hollywood standards. A rare highbrow event in Los Angeles, the opening attracted a knockout crowd. John Boles, the voice of countless movie premieres, called out the names of civic leaders, society matrons, and celebrities as they arrived at the Hollywood Bowl. Many wore tuxedos and evening gowns. When darkness fell, a torchlight procession of more than four hundred actors made its way down the aisles to the stage, and the Los Angeles Philharmonic played selections from Mendelssohn. Almost from the start the audience knew two things for certain: the child actor Mickey Rooney, playing Puck, was going to steal the show from the better-known performers, and Max Reinhardt, the great German director, would be pelted with movie offers by the end of the evening.

Several miles to the south, just off Figueroa next to the U.S.C. campus, a decidedly less affluent crowd gathered at the Shrine Auditorium for a radically different purpose: a homecoming rally for the Democratic candidate for governor, Upton Sinclair.

The Shrine Auditorium was a hulking, ocher-colored, mosquelike structure crowned with twin minarets. Built in 1925 to house the Shrine club's Al-Malaikah Temple, the fortress was frequently used for concerts and political gatherings and could seat sixty-five hundred guests, almost three thousand of them in its enormous balcony. EPIC supporters, and others curious to find out what Sinclair was all about, paid twenty-five cents for tickets until the tickets ran out, leaving several thousand milling outside. Vendors worked the crowds, peddling *I, Governor* (at twenty cents a throw) and the new issue of the *EPIC News,* featuring the front-page headline PARTY TO ADOPT EPIC PLAN; CREEL MEN COME OVER.

Those who managed to get inside the Shrine congregated in the carpeted lobby, conspiring with old friends. Like the crowd out at the Hollywood Bowl, they dressed to the nines for a special occasion. Virtually all of the men, even those on relief, wore sport jackets or suits, and the women displayed colorful cotton dresses. Upton Sinclair's first public appearance in California since winning the Democratic nomination represented the high point of their crusade. Many had worked tirelessly for months without monetary reward to arrive at this moment, and now they were ready to whoop it up with Uppie.

The EPICs gathering at the Shrine Auditorium came from every strata of society, although nearly all were white. It was not, despite what many thought, a poor people's movement. Most of the activists were middle-class and middle-aged. They either held jobs or had just been laid off and expected to work again soon. Many were down-on-their-luck businessmen. In any given EPIC club one was liable to find Utopians, technocrats, Townsendites, progressive Republicans, New Deal Democrats, ex-Socialists, and secret Communists, all united by a belief in a perfectable society. Some of the most resourceful volunteers emerged from the cooperative movement; they called EPIC "the Big Co-op."

The majority of staff workers at headquarters were women—recent college grads or housewives. Men on relief provided a solid core of workers to distribute campaign literature. Some made a fair living hawking the *EPIC News* on the street or selling Sinclair's *I, Governor* booklets at mass meetings. None of the other EPICs, including the top leaders, earned a cent from their labors.

By now, the Sinclairites had founded nearly two thousand End Poverty League chapters across the state. Each assembly district had at least one chapter, and Los Angeles boasted several dozen. There were youth clubs, veterans' clubs, and women's clubs. Members paid a dollar, a penny, or a collar button to join (lifetime membership went for a hundred bucks). One EPIC leader estimated total statewide membership at one hundred thousand. Each club was self-sustaining. From state headquarters on South Grand in Los Angeles they purchased each week's copies of the *EPIC News,* which the locals then sold to finance their own activities. Regional conferences, letters from League director Dick Otto, announcements on the radio, and the *EPIC News* itself helped coordinate the far-flung activities (and break the press blackout).

Several factors curbed EPIC's appeal to blacks. Most blacks still considered the GOP the party of Lincoln. Nearly all of the black preachers had close ties to the local Republican establishment. They warned that EPIC would force businesses to shut down and that blacks would be the first to lose their jobs. Sinclair did not court a black following; Negroes, he said, should support EPIC simply because, as the poorest citizens, they had the most to gain. In many areas, the End Poverty

League directed blacks to form their own EPIC clubs rather than integrate existing chapters. EPIC supported young Augustus F. Hawkins, who was attempting to unseat Fred Roberts, the state's only black legislator, in L.A.'s "black belt," but Hawkins did not embrace Sinclair.

Although it was a broad-based and decentralized people's movement, EPIC was far from democratic. Dick Otto appointed all of the chapter secretaries. The End Poverty League's board of directors, known as the Twelve Apostles—ten men and two women—held daily meetings in L.A. (rarely attended by Sinclair) to decide policy, with little input from outside. Some EPICs considered organized labor reactionary, others felt it was too radical, so not a single trade unionist sat on the board. Northern California headquarters, on Haight Street in San Francisco, operated much the same way.

To raise funds, the EPICs sponsored bake sales and rummage sales, picnics, dances, and rodeos, and sold matchbooks with Sinclair's picture on the cover. Members contributed what they could, often a nickel or dime or a two-cent stamp. Then they would go door-to-door to raise enough money to purchase that week's allotment of *EPIC News*—which they then sold to raise more money. They were like a huge army living off the land. At local rallies, EPIC fund-raisers would cry, "I don't want you to have a damn thing in your pocket but the car fare home!" causing some people to stand up and turn their pockets inside out to show that they were already empty. Some EPICs hocked the gold fillings in their teeth to raise money. Occasionally a wealthy patron would donate a vacant lot or a diamond ring for EPIC to sell.

Lacking funds for newspaper ads and billboards, EPIC resorted to labor-intensive promotion. The EPIC symbol, a buzzing bee, was aptly chosen. To answer charges that Sinclair was not a real Democrat, members of the Palma club decorated a donkey with EPIC signs and paraded him to Culver City and back. An EPIC bus toured the state, stopping in communities to show the silent film version of *The Jungle* on a makeshift screen. Tire covers imprinted with the EPIC bee adorned the backs of automobiles. A baseball team equipped with EPIC uniforms took on all comers in Los Angeles. Windshield stickers, colorful banners, and lapel buttons printed in navy blue and white were displayed everywhere. One popular window poster read:

THIS HOUSE (ASSESSED AT UNDER $3000)
WILL BE TAX EXEMPT UNDER
THE EPIC PLAN

Another banner cried out: THINK OR SINK! Sinclair's official portrait (available for ten cents) occupied a special place in many homes. EPICs held parades complete with cornucopias, Sinclair look-alikes, girls in bathing suits, and gaily decorated floats. They performed EPIC plays and put on pageants that rivaled Aimee McPherson's. An auction to benefit EPIC was held every week on South Vermont Street in Los Angeles.

EPIC songs proliferated. There was "The EPIC Plan Song" ("It's up to you and up to me/To free ourselves from poverty"), "End Poverty" ("Vote the plan that is not slow/Vote Sinclair to make it go"), and "Hail Upton Sinclair" ("U.S. stands for Upton Sinclair/U.S. stands for us, I do declare"). "The Coming Day" was sung to the tune of "The Battle Hymn of the Republic":

> We'll build our homes by thousands
> On the most productive lands,
> We'll open many factories, employing
>   idle hands.
> The aged shall have pensions, if you
>   vote for EPIC plans,
> Sinclair is marching on.

The official campaign song, "End Poverty In All America! (And Upton Sinclair Will Show the Way)," had a lively march tempo as it sounded a "battle cry of the real democracy" that meant "the end of all hypocrasy." But the most popular EPIC anthem was "Campaign Chorus for Downey and Sinclair." Made into a phonograph record, it featured Sheridan Downey, among others, singing:

> Good times are surely coming,
> Soon business will be humming,
> And we'll give old poverty the air.
> If EPIC is a phony,
> Then the rest is all baloney,
> So vote for Downey, and Upton Sinclair.

While the EPICs took their seats in the plush-red, dimly lit auditorium, Upton Sinclair arrived at the stage entrance on the Jefferson Boulevard side of the building. Frank Scully and Morrie Ryskind accompanied him, hoping to beat the admission charge. Scully had met Sinclair for the first time over dinner. His first impression of Sinclair was that he looked like a Woodrow Wilson who got left out in the rain and shrank. Scully brought Ryskind along as his guest, hoping to recruit him to his Authors' League for Sinclair. After dinner, Scully and his wife piled into their car and let Morrie ride down to the Shrine Auditorium with Sinclair.

Ryskind had risen to fame during the 1920s writing plays for the Marx Brothers with his pal George S. Kaufman. Later the pair helped turn the plays, *The Cocoanuts* and *Animal Crackers,* into movies. *Of Thee I Sing,* a Kaufman-Ryskind burlesque (written with George and Ira Gershwin) satirizing the government, opened on Broadway in 1931 and became the first musical to win the Pulitzer Prize for drama. Ryskind was currently scripting an MGM movie called *Repeal,* but the Marx Brothers had just signed to do a picture for Irving Thalberg, of all people, set in an opera house, of all places, and Morrie would likely team up with them again.

A first-class cynic, Ryskind was not likely to jump on the Sinclair bandwagon, but there he was, sitting onstage a few feet from the candidate himself. Ten rows of chairs had been assembled on either side of the podium. Ryskind, Scully, and Sinclair sat in the front row, facing a bright red curtain. A band played a few numbers, and then, at precisely seven-thirty, the curtain rose, and Sinclair stepped lightly to the podium.

The crowd cheered wildly, but Sinclair silenced the roar with an upraised hand, explaining that his speech was about to be broadcast throughout the state over the Columbia Broadcasting network, and they couldn't waste a second of valuable airtime. Reading from a script, Sinclair calmly delivered his standard EPIC stump speech, which he concluded in precisely ten minutes, just before his radio time elapsed.

Then an EPIC finance chairman got up and explained that those ten minutes had cost one thousand dollars, and it was up to everyone in the audience to subsidize it. "Those up here have to pay, too," he announced, passing the hat to the guests seated on stage. Ryskind dropped a five-dollar bill into the hat, Scully followed suit, and Frank's wife, Alice, chipped in another dollar. *I thought we beat the admission charge,* Scully mused, *and now we've been nicked for eleven bucks.*

Sinclair popped up again and informed the audience that now they could make as much noise as they wanted, and their cheers nearly shattered the five-ton chandelier hanging from the ceiling. The candidate resumed speaking in his arid but engaging way, rambling here, joking there, economical in his movements but spellbinding through the force of his intellect. He addressed the crowd as if they were members of his family, as indeed they were, and performed with the confidence of a man who didn't have a care in the world because he knew all the answers. He was Savonarola, "leading the Hallelujah Chorus with a slide rule," as one observer put it.

From now until Election Day, they would hear no end of political poison, Sinclair warned. He lashed Hearst's *Examiner* and tweaked the "stupid, little bad boys" of the *L.A. Times.* The newspapers would be full of fabrications, and it was up to the EPICs to know a lie when they saw one, and carry on. It was "sheer lunacy" that money could buy the election. "Our opponents have already got millions from the big banks and from Wall Street," he said, "but some things are not for sale, among them the intelligence and conscience and Democratic soul of the voters. . . .

"Here in my pocket," he announced, "I have an article that was given to me at dinner by Frank Scully, and it will appear in the November issue of *Esquire.* It will come just before the election and might help us." He took out the rumpled manuscript, waved it, and told Scully to rise (on his one good leg) and take a bow. Sinclair recalled that the *Literary Digest* had put EPIC on its cover a week before the primary and "every copy on every newsstand in California disappeared. Maybe the opposition will buy up all copies of *Esquire,* too. But they can't buy up every publication in America! And if they do, what difference will it make? They now have every important paper in California against us and the result is, more people believe in our EPIC plan than ever."

The crowd went crazy again. Even Morrie Ryskind was impressed. Driving back to the Beverly Wilshire with the Scullys, he threatened to write a favorable squib about Sinclair. Ryskind would have to go a long way, however, to top Frank Scully, who had closed his *Esquire* piece by declaring that if Sinclair won, "what a novelty it will be to have a political leader who not only can read and write, but knows what the country needs, and can even spell it!"

SEPTEMBER 19

WEDNESDAY

At five minutes to nine, the front door of the small frame house on East 222nd Street in the Bronx opened, and a thin, dark man dressed in a gray double-breasted suit emerged. He walked briskly down the steps into the sunshine and strode across the lane to his garage, opened the doors, backed his blue Dodge sedan into the street, and headed south. Lieutenant James J. Finn gave the signal, and three police cars set off in pursuit, carrying a small posse of federal agents, New York City cops, and New Jersey state troopers. After two years of frustration and embarrassment, they felt confident they had the Lindbergh kidnapper in their sights at last.

The case had cracked open yesterday afternoon when a teller at the Park Avenue and 125th Street branch of the Corn Exchange Bank came across a pair of ten-dollar gold certificates in a pile of deposits. The serial number on one of the bills identified it as Lindbergh ransom money. The teller called a special Justice Department office in New York, and three detectives, including Lieutenant Finn of the NYPD, came to take a look. Usually in these cases the trail ended at a teller's window. But this time one of the detectives discovered a notation written in a margin of one of the bills: *4U-13-41, N.Y.* It looked like a license-plate number, most likely jotted down by a gas-station attendant. Going through the day's deposit slips and finding three from service stations, Lieutenant Finn excitedly set out to solve the crime of the century.

First stop was a Warner-Quinlan gas station four blocks away. Finn showed the bill to the manager, Walter Lyle. Did he recognize it? He sure did, Lyle replied; he had accepted it on September 15 from a man driving a blue Dodge. Fearing that the bill might be counterfeit, Lyle had taken down the car's license number. He described the man, who called himself John, as having dark hair, a V-shaped face, and a pointed chin and speaking with a foreign accent, probably German. This matched the description of the chief suspect in the Lindbergh case.

Finn could barely maintain his professional calm. Racing back to the bank, he called the state motor-vehicle bureau. Finn recited the license number and asked for the registrant's name and address. A moment later came the answer: Richard Hauptmann, 1279 East 222nd Street, the Bronx.

Now, eighteen hours later, the same Hauptmann was driving just a few yards ahead of Lieutenant Finn and his three-car convoy. The cops were playing it cautious, fearing that the suspect might be heavily armed: if he'd killed a little baby, he might do *anything* if cornered. Hauptmann drove through Bronx Park and down Park Avenue in the Fordham section. A block before reaching busy East Tremont, the Dodge slowed, blocked by a truck. One of the police cars shot forward and angled alongside. An officer flung open the right front door of the Dodge, slid in next to the driver, and stuck a pistol in his ribs. Hauptmann, apparently in shock, pointed the car to the curb. An officer pulled him out of the car and clamped a pair of handcuffs on his wrists.

"What is this? What is this all about?" Hauptmann stammered. Finn detected a German accent. A twenty-dollar gold note turned up in the suspect's wallet. The serial number linked it to the Lindbergh ransom money.

Heading back to East 222nd Street to look for more gold notes, a detective turned to Hauptmann, sitting beside him in the backseat of one of the police cars, and said, "You're going to burn, baby."

His wife's recovery assured, Louis B. Mayer announced in Paris that he would board a boat for New York at the end of September. He also issued his first public edict on the California governor's race. Joe Schenck and C. B. DeMille had lit the fuse, and now Mayer was set to explode. L.B. predicted nothing less than "chaos" for California if Sinclair was elected. "I am a Republican only because I believe a Republican Administration is better for the business and economic conditions of our country," Mayer told reporters in Paris. "But I am first of all an American and, in the interests of America, would forsake any political party. I believe Californians should and will forget partisanship and vote for the best interests of the state." And why should they do that? "The election of Sinclair would plunge California further into debt," Mayer explained.

This outburst would surely reverberate in Hollywood, still shaking from reports that six major studios would flee the state in the event of Sinclair's election. Harry Cohn had just affirmed that his studio, Columbia, would "close in a minute" if Sinclair won.

—

It was the day before the political party conventions in Sacramento, and two of the candidates for governor found themselves on the same train heading north out of Los Angeles. Ray Haight came to Upton Sinclair's stateroom for a chat. The two men liked and admired each other. They were honest, clean-living, self-styled crusaders, and they had both voted for Norman Thomas for president in 1932. Their backgrounds, however, were radically different. One was an old Socialist from the East Coast, the other a young Republican whose great-grandfather drove an oxteam to California in that watershed year, 1849.

Sinclair respected Haight so much that he had once suggested that Haight run for attorney general on the EPIC ticket, but Ray wanted to try to whip Merriam in the GOP primary. Now, for reasons that were not entirely clear to Sinclair, Haight was continuing his campaign. The two political parties whose endorsements he expected would meet in Sacramento tomorrow, just like the Republicans and the Democrats. The Progressive party caucus would draw a few dozen members. Besides Haight, they had Hiram Johnson on their ticket. Only one delegate would attend the Commonwealth party gathering—Ray Haight himself. Haight would serve as chairman, secretary, and sergeant at arms. "He also will be able to draw up a platform that will be pleasing to him," the Associated Press noted.

Speeding northward this morning, Haight informed Sinclair that one of his friends had seen the actual checks, totaling some thirty thousand dollars, sent to Frank Merriam by California businessmen to reward the governor for calling out the state militia to quell San Francisco's general strike in July. One of the checks, Haight said, came from Standard Oil, another from the Crocker First National Bank. Haight also entertained Sinclair by describing the Merriam camp's increasingly desperate bid to get him to quit the race. On four different occasions, businessmen or politicians had approached him, bearing gifts. Speaking on behalf of the governor, they offered Haight (1) as much state legal business as his law firm cared to handle, (2) any state office he wanted, (3) William G. McAdoo's seat in the U.S. Senate when Mac passed away, (4) the governorship in 1938, and (5) one hundred thousand dollars in cash. Haight lovingly described one scene, in which a group of prominent northern California businessmen promised him a place in the U.S. Senate. "They told me exactly how old McAdoo was and the diseases he suffered from," Haight revealed. "They laid him out cold in his coffin, right there before my eyes!"

Sinclair responded with a bit of Scripture. "The devil taketh him up into an exceeding high mountain," he recited, "and showeth him all the kingdoms of the world, and the glory of them; and sayeth unto him, 'All these things will I give thee, if thou wilt fall down and worship me.' "

C. C. Teague wound up three days of meetings in Los Angeles convinced that he had achieved his objective: the formation of a lavishly funded apparatus outside the feeble grasp of Frank Merriam that would destroy Upton Sinclair. Teague had assembled some of the biggest names in southern California at the California Club and declared that to do the job right, he would need at least half a million dollars *just from Los Angeles.* It would go for radio programs, newspaper support, public speakers, the financing of a nonpartisan front group, money for Merriam's own committee, and possibly a small sum to buy off the remnants of George Creel's organization.

The elite group did not fail him. It included Harry Chandler, patriarch of the *Los Angeles Times* and perhaps the richest man in California; Asa V. Call, vice president and general counsel of Pacific Mutual; Byron C. Hanna, a top Chamber of Commerce official; James L. Beebe, partner in the leading law firm of O'Melveny, Tuller & Myers; Mendel Silberberg, attorney for Louis B. Mayer; and Sam Haskins of the Merchants and Manufacturers Association. They immediately subscribed fifty thousand dollars just to get things rolling. Teague named a finance committee to raise additional funds and an executive committee of five to disburse the money, with himself as chairman.

So there would be an organized anti-Sinclair effort after all, revolving around a front group called United for California, which would provide cover for the real work of the campaign. Robert M. Clarke, a respected local judge, would head the group.

What would United for California do? First, it would transform into campaign propaganda the quotes Teague had dredged from Sinclair's writings. Teague told his associates he was certain that if these quotes were carefully edited and convincingly attributed, then printed in pamphlets by the millions and mailed "to the full extent" to the various groups attacked, United for California would "build up a great group of crusaders against Upton Sinclair between now and election time—and what our campaign is lacking is crusaders." Teague asked his friends to solicit mailing lists from the Knights of Columbus, the Boy Scouts, the American Legion, the Mormons, and so forth. A precisely targeted direct-mail effort of this intensity had never previously been attempted in politics.

Who would head the propaganda effort? Teague tapped an old friend, Don Francisco, chief of the West Coast office of one of the nation's top advertising firms, Lord & Thomas. Francisco, a dark-haired, dapper man in his early forties, was rumored to be Albert D. Lasker's heir apparent at the ad agency. If C. C. Teague made the citrus business tick, it was Albert Lasker and Don Francisco who had made it unusually profitable—and, in the process, mythologized California in the heartland of America.

Sunkist and Lord & Thomas went way back. In the early part of the century, oranges were still considered something of a luxury item. California growers packed each orange sent East in lovingly designed tissue paper. In 1907, at the urging of Lord & Thomas, the growers attempted to change that perception and turn oranges into a staple. As an experiment, the California Fruit Growers Exchange sent a special Orange Train to Iowa, promoting "Oranges for Health—California for Wealth." Orange sales picked up dramatically in that state. One unexpected side effect was the mass migration of Iowans to California. (One Iowan who trudged west: Frank Finley Merriam.)

Lord & Thomas developed sophisticated advertising and marketing techniques for Sunkist. The agency pioneered direct mail as a promotional technique—to sell oranges. By 1914, orange consumption had jumped almost 80 percent. Sales soared still higher after Albert Lasker conceived the idea of encouraging people to drink orange *juice.* Millions ate oranges, but few took the trouble to squeeze them into a drink.

Lasker felt that orange juice would not only increase profits but would also contribute to a healthy populace.

During this period, Don Francisco, a young horticulturist employed by Sunkist in Los Angeles as its advertising manager, helped develop the groundbreaking "Drink an Orange" campaign. Francisco also promoted the use of colorful labels on orange crates, which as much as anything affixed in the American imagination the idea of California as a sinfully lush and healthful paradise. And he invented a system whereby each lemon, orange, and grapefruit could be stamped with the name Sunkist without damaging the fruit. No one had imagined that individual labeling was possible, or even desirable. Working at home, Francisco performed experiments, heating a metal flyswatter and burning an impression into an orange. No wonder Albert Lasker wooed Francisco away from C. C. Teague in 1921 and made him director of California operations for Lord & Thomas three years later.

When C. C. Teague asked Don Francisco to handle the Sinclair account, he essentially put a professional advertising agency in charge of the Merriam campaign—the Republican party be damned. This was an unprecedented step based on fear and desperation. Admen had contributed to political campaigns before: Lasker advised Harding in 1920, Henry T. Ewald supplied the winning slogan in the 1924 race ("Keep Cool With Coolidge"), and Bruce Barton wrote parts of Hoover's acceptance speech at the '28 GOP convention. But no one had ever put an ad agency essentially *in charge* of a campaign. The Sinclair threat provoked the breaking of every rule. Up north, Clem Whitaker became the first political consultant to be enlisted in a major campaign. Now Don Francisco heeded the call to handle the creative chores in the south and appointed his top associate, Don Belding, to oversee the effort.

Walter Johnson, president of the American Box Company, which owned sixteen lumber mills in California, summoned his office personnel to a special meeting today at company headquarters on Montgomery Street in downtown San Francisco. The topic: the California governor's race. Johnson informed his forty office workers and salesmen that if Upton Sinclair was elected, American Box would move out of the state. If they wanted to retain their jobs, they'd better see to it that Sinclair was defeated. "If you don't believe you are going to lose your jobs if you don't fight Sinclair," Johnson added, "just support him and see what happens!" One woman at American Box, threatened with dismissal if she continued to support Sinclair, managed to keep her job only by recanting her endorsement to the satisfaction of the company manager.

———

While Don Francisco and Don Belding took charge of the smear-Sinclair drive in southern California, their boss, Albert Lasker, jumped into the fray half a continent away. Lasker, at a meeting in the office of Frank Knox, publisher of the *Chicago Daily News,* proposed using radio in the California campaign as it had never been used before.

Innovation was nothing new for Lasker. It was said that Albert Lasker made more money than anyone in the history of advertising, spent more, and gave more away. The son of a prosperous German immigrant, he had joined Lord & Thomas in Chicago in 1898 at the age of eighteen. (One of his duties: cleaning out the spittoons.) A few years later, he bought the company and soon made it the biggest ad agency in the country.

An intuitive genius, Lasker had little use for market research. Lord & Thomas's carefully crafted ads pinpointed the unique qualities of the product and the reason it should be purchased. Despite its appeal to reason, Lord & Thomas copy had to be catchy. Schlitz was "the beer that made Milwaukee famous." Quaker Puffed Oats were "shot from guns." Goodyear made the "all-weather tire." The "Reach for a Lucky Instead of a Sweet" campaign, on behalf of Lucky Strikes, probably had more to do with getting women to smoke cigarettes in escalating numbers than any other factor. Lasker also helped develop the concept of celebrity endorsements. If Lord & Thomas was the MGM of advertising agencies, Lasker was Madison Avenue's Louis B. Mayer.

When the era of radio unfolded in America in the 1920s, Lasker was the first adman to recognize the medium's potential. David Sarnoff established NBC in 1926, and William S. Paley followed suit with CBS, but it was advertising agencies, not the networks, that produced the prime-time programming—as showcases for their clients. Albert Lasker took the lead. His radio people conceived the idea of daytime serials for women, soon to be known as soap operas. To promote Pepsodent, Lord & Thomas created *Amos 'n' Andy,* the most popular program of them all. There was a period in the 1920s when Lord & Thomas placed almost half of all the national advertising on NBC. Billings later reached as high as fifty million dollars a year.

Heady with success, Albert Lasker became an overbearing, irresistibly magnetic man. His personal motto: "There is no advertising man in the world but me!" During the early years of the Depression, Lasker cut all of his employees' salaries by 25 percent while taking home about three million dollars a year himself. He collected Renoirs, Matisses, and Picassos. His five-hundred-acre estate near Lake Forest, Illinois, was possibly the grandest property between the two coasts. It harbored a herd of prize-winning Guernseys and sported six miles of clipped hedges, a sundial that told the time in fifty-seven cities, an ice cream parlor, a movie theater, and an eighteen-hole golf course. Lasker entertained NBC executives, tycoons, athletes, the columnist Walter Lippmann, and numerous politicians. He loved to play golf for high stakes and once lost forty thousand dollars to the California financier Herbert Fleishhacker.

Few Democrats made it to Lasker's parties. He was a dyed-in-the-wool Republican who worked on numerous GOP campaigns and served as a delegate to national conventions. He backed Hiram Johnson for the GOP nomination in 1920 but later went to work for Will Hays, who managed the Harding campaign. According to some accounts, one of his duties involved passing twenty thousand dollars to one of Harding's mistresses in exchange for her silence. He later became a regular member of Harding's White House poker gang. But when Herbert Hoover asked for his help in 1932, Lasker told him, "You haven't got a dog's chance of getting elected." Lasker had no taste for hopeless causes. He once observed that "David's victory over Goliath was such an exceptional event that people are still talking about it two thousand years later."

Clearly, then, Albert Lasker considered Frank Merriam electable, otherwise he would not have committed a significant portion of his agency's resources on the West Coast to the fight against Upton Sinclair. Now he was considering a major role for radio in that campaign, as part of a national anti-Democrat propaganda drive. Radio had not been kind to the GOP so far. The party always had more money to spend than the Democrats but hadn't figured out how to use the new medium to its advantage. Neither party employed radio professionals, so they did little more than broadcast speeches by their candidates. This orientation favored the Democrats, who had a man in the White House with a matchless radio personality.

Frank Knox, a former Rough Rider who had his eye on a run for the White House in 1936, called the meeting of Republican stalwarts at his *Daily News* office in Chicago to chart a creative new radio policy for the GOP. For weeks, he had been corresponding with Herbert Hoover concerning the Sinclair menace and other GOP headaches. Something had to be done to reach out to what Knox called "the unthinking masses." What was needed, he believed, was a "simple, homely appeal that will get under the skins of the man and woman who are too lazy to think for themselves."

Albert Lasker proposed drawing on the popularity of the radio serial and the soap opera, which he had helped develop himself, to soft-sell GOP candidates and lampoon the New Deal. Why not hire writers to script simple radio dramas that communicated in everyday terms the dangers of the New Deal and other forms of radicalism? Even the most "unthinking" listener would get the message.

Everyone agreed this was a terrific idea. Lord & Thomas, of course, had solid experience in putting together radio programming. And where better to test Lasker's new political merchandising concept than in a state rich in writing and acting talent, a state presently playing host to the most melodramatic election campaign in the country: California.

SEPTEMBER 20

THURSDAY

The textile strike, after a period of relative calm, again turned violent. The worst labor riot in the history of Maine broke out in Waterville. Two companies of National Guard troops rushed to the scene as strikers overturned automobiles and stoned buildings. National Guardsmen bayoneted two strikers in Charlotte, North Carolina; one of the men died, bringing to thirteen the number of strike-related killings in the Carolinas. Strikers in Belmont, North Carolina, attacked a car carrying a local sheriff, tore the doors off, and were about to carry him away when rescuers arrived.

Despite cries of "Hitlerism," Governor Eugene Talmadge of Georgia interned several hundred alleged rioters at Fort McPherson, outside Atlanta. Women prisoners occupied a barn; outside the men huddled behind barbed wire, guarded by soldiers with rifles slung over their shoulders. *The New York Times* published a photograph of what it called the "concentration camp" at Fort McPherson. "Roosevelt got us into this," one prisoner told the *Times,* "he's got to get us out."

Hoping to do just that, the President, just back at Hyde Park after a yacht trip to Rhode Island to observe the America's Cup races, finally ordered Secretary of Labor Frances Perkins to personally mediate the textile dispute. Strikes and riots were one thing. Bayoneting protesters and putting them in concentration camps simply would not *do* in America.

———

Dawn brought cool comfort to Los Angeles following several days of sweltering heat. The *Los Angeles Times* greeted the day with an attack on Upton Sinclair's bourgeois life-style. Under the headline EX-SOCIALIST LEAVES PALATIAL RESIDENCE FOR BALLOT BATTLE, the *Times* published photos of three homes purportedly owned by Sinclair: the rambling dwelling on Sunset Avenue in Pasadena, a humble bungalow in Hollywood that he used as an office, and a Spanish-style "mansion" on Arden Drive in Beverly Hills.

Sinclair had anticipated that his enemies would make hay over the Beverly Hills house. In his recent booklet *The Lie Factory Starts,* he explained that during the unfortunate Eisenstein affair he had to visit Hollywood nearly every day and found the trip to and from Pasadena wearing. Looking for a house to rent, he discovered that Beverly Hills was filled with foreclosed mansions. So his wife bought one a block below Sunset at a bargain price. Now she was attempting to sell it; in the meantime he would use the house as a quiet retreat. According to the *Los Angeles Times,* however, Sinclair actually resided in the mansion but found it "prudent" to meet the "common people" at the other sites, afraid to let his followers know how he really lived.

The *Times*'s brilliant new political cartoonist, Bruce Russell, produced his first anti-Sinclair drawing today. It pictured the candidate walking a big, ugly bear (labeled EXTREME LEFT DOCTRINES) on a leash, and finding the gate to California barred by an elephant and a donkey. The caption read, THEY MUST GET TOGETHER TO KEEP HIM OUT!

Hollywood studios joined the *Times* in drumming up electoral support for Frank Merriam. This morning, for the first time ever, the studios allowed election officials to invade the movie lots, set up tables, and register would-be voters, all under the watchful eye of front-office personnel. The task took on added urgency when the results of KNX radio's first straw poll started circulating. Upton Sinclair, KNX reported, presently held a two-to-one lead over Frank Merriam.

———

On this date in 1878, Priscilla Harden Sinclair gave birth to a boy in a boardinghouse on Biddle Street in Baltimore. She named him Upton Beall Sinclair, Jr., after his father, an itinerant salesman and an alcoholic. Uppie had distinguished and wealthy ancestors, mostly from the South, including a great-grandfather who commanded American naval forces in Lake Huron during the War of 1812. His immediate family was not so fortunate, however. When the Sinclairs moved to New York City in 1888, Uppie was forced to live in one wretched apartment after another, and spent hours smashing bedbugs. One day he discovered his drunken father in a gutter down in the Bowery.

His mother periodically sent Uppie away to stay with rich relations in Maryland, but he despised their snobbery. Returning to the slums, he would ask his mother, "Why are some children poor and others rich? How can that be fair?" She had no answer. Years later, his novels would obsessively probe the clash between social classes. Asked to explain how a rebel emerged from a conservative Southern family, Sinclair described his "psychology" as that of the poor relation. He constantly confronted the ruling class "apologists" with the same questions he had asked his mother, Sinclair observed, and still he received "no answer."

Now, fifty-six years from his inception and twenty-five hundred miles from the hovels and mansions of his youth, Upton Sinclair was about to receive what he considered a most appropriate birthday gift: the nomination of his party for the office of governor of California.

By law, all political parties in California had to meet in the state capital on the same day in September. This was rarely a pleasant task, for Sacramento baked in the sun at this time of year. Policemen on traffic duty donned white helmets, like African explorers. Capitol Park, a forty-acre preserve that held more than a thousand trees and shrubs from all over the world, provided the only refuge from the heat. The nearby capitol building dominated the cityscape. Completed in 1874, it was an impressive E-shaped Roman classic edifice made of California granite and brick, painted white, and adorned with Corinthian columns and pilasters. An inscription read, "Give me men to match my mountains." A gold dome over two hundred feet high topped the rotunda. The governor's office was on the first floor, the legislative chambers on the second. The Democrats, with the most convention delegates, took over the state assembly hall this morning, while the Republicans convened in the smaller senate chamber to the south.

When Upton Sinclair, accompanied by his retinue, arrived at the capitol, he happened to bump into Hamilton Cotton, a wealthy Democratic leader in Los Angeles and former Creel supporter who helped engineer Franklin Roosevelt's election in 1932. "I appear to be the only Democrat willing to fight you," Cotton remarked. This was not altogether comforting, for Cotton cut a lot of ice throughout the state.

Inside the assembly chamber, more than one hundred delegates—most of them incumbent officeholders and only about a third of them avowed Sinclairites—started taking their seats. EPIC activists in shirtsleeves filled the gallery to bursting. The EPICs buzzed nervously: what should they do if Sinclair tried to sell their movement down the Sacramento River? To blow off steam, they chanted slogans, such as "We want the EPIC plan!" as if cheering on a college football team. Observing this, Kyle Palmer of the *Los Angeles Times* wondered what politics in California was coming to.

Suddenly, just past the stroke of ten, Upton Sinclair strode down the aisle. The EPICs screamed their lungs out, not so much to celebrate their hero as to intimidate his opponents, who might still be plotting some kind of coup. Just as they quieted down, someone shouted, "We're all behind you, Upton!" producing another roar. EPICs in the gallery hung a huge banner over the railing facing the podium. It read:

EPIC
460,000 VOTES
NO COMPROMISE!

It was hard to say whether this was aimed at Sinclair or the old-line Democrats.

Convention chairman George Creel, dressed in a white double-breasted suit, took the microphone just as one of the delegates near the podium hoisted up a huge portrait of Franklin Roosevelt. "Our first order of business," Creel proclaimed, "is to ask our distinguished Senator and our equally distinguished candidate for governor to come to the platform."

The hall shook with cheers. Sinclair, wearing a light gray suit and dark polka-dotted tie, reached the platform first, at Creel's left. Smiling, the two famous authors shook hands, and then McAdoo, in a dark suit and trademark high collar, arrived from the right, completing the tableau. There they stood, together at last (symbolically if not ideologically), grinning goofily, McAdoo half a head taller than his partners. It was a Democratic propagandist's dream, and the photographers captured it all. Whether the newspapers would actually publish the photos remained to be seen.

Sinclair appeared to have Creel and McAdoo in his camp. Still, there was the platform to consider. Sinclair, in dropping a few planks and fudging on others, risked the wrath of the multitudes in the balcony. The convention recessed while the framers of the document considered last-minute adjustments.

While the two major parties met at the capitol, Raymond Haight assembled fifteen of his political supporters in a hotel room across town and convened the Commonwealth party convention. Haight, as sole delegate, adopted the party platform unanimously. Things did not go according to plan at the Progressive party gathering, however. The Progressives had no problem endorsing Hiram Johnson as their nominee for the U.S. Senate, but violence broke out when the chair announced that Ray Haight, who had won the party's nod in the primary, would address the delegates. L. R. Foster, one of the party's congressional candidates, protested on the grounds that Haight had embarrassed the Progressives by accepting the nomination of the Reverend Bob Shuler's Commonwealth party. A delegate from San Francisco protested the protest, in the process decking Foster with a right uppercut. The convention recessed while the two men battled around the chamber and out into the corridor.

When the delegates reconvened, they voted not to endorse Ray Haight—who by law would nevertheless appear on the November ballot as the party's candidate for governor.

"How does he do it?" Artie Samish exclaimed to a group of reporters as they strolled through the capitol, crossing over to the Republican meeting after witnessing the opening moments of the Democrats' lovefest. Samish, who along with nearly everyone else in Sacramento assumed that William G. McAdoo was on his deathbed, expressed amazement that the senator looked so fit and well groomed.

Arriving at the senate chamber, Artie found the GOP gathering funereal compared with the Democratic circus. The gallery, only half-full, was quiet during Goodwin J. Knight's keynote address. The meeting was not without significance, however, for a reading of the platform revealed that Chester Rowell and Herbert Hoover had succeeded in putting a moderately progressive stamp on it. Oakland political boss Joseph Knowland confessed to the crowd that the document was hard to swallow, "but it will be better than the catastrophe that will overtake us" if the party failed to inch to the left. The GOP proposed a bond issue to provide jobs, tax relief for those about to lose their property, some form of unemployment insurance, and a ceiling on utility rates. It called on the Democrats to bolt their party, and it even promised that Governor Merriam would eschew partisanship in making political appointments. One speaker after another hailed Hiram Johnson, long considered the black sheep of the party. "We urge an active and aggressive campaign of Americanism and liberalism against radicalism and the threat of a communistic adventure in California . . ." the platform proclaimed.

In case anyone missed the message, Governor Merriam spelled it out for the delegates in his acceptance speech. "I have never visited Russia," he insisted, "and I have no inclination or desire to instruct the Russian people as to the mode and manner of their civic ideals and governmental processes. But I am as equally firm and decided in my view that we in California and in America need no introduction to theories and aims which have their inspiration in an atmosphere foreign not only to our shores, but to our basic aspirations and impulses as a people."

Then George Hatfield, Merriam's running mate, added a delicious twist, quoting at length from a recent statement by Norman Thomas that referred to EPIC as "fantastic" and crazy. "Much as we may differ with Norman Thomas," Hatfield explained, "it is interesting to have his analysis of the plan submitted by our opponents." Months ago, Upton Sinclair had warned Thomas that his attacks on EPIC would one day be used by reactionaries to dash the hopes of Socialists in California, and now it had come to pass. Right-wing Republicans attacked Sinclair from the left, at a GOP convention, no less.

Sheridan Downey, candidate for lieutenant governor, read the party platform to the Democrats in the assembly chamber, in his friendly, country-lawyer voice. George Creel stood behind him, smiling triumphantly, smoking a Camel through a seven-inch cigarette holder. The easy part—fidelity to FDR and scorn for the "racketeering" Republicans—came first. Then Downey recited the party's program. The document waffled on the issue of old-age pensions, asserting that President

Roosevelt was about to introduce his own program. Downey did not breathe a word about farm colonies, state-run factories, or anything called EPIC. The phrase *production for use* was notable by its absence. Upton Sinclair, down to his shirtsleeves in the stifling heat, sweated it out on the platform.

Finally Downey came to the paragraph on unemployment. "As the greatest possible measure of tax reduction," he read, "and also as a means of industrial and social rehabilitation, employment of the unemployed, and of ending poverty in California—" The EPIC partisans in the chamber leapt up and shouted, stamped their feet, and waved their handkerchiefs. The screams shook a screen off a third-floor window and interupted the GOP proceedings down the hall. Creel took a bow, Sinclair took a bow, and then McAdoo appeared in the middle and put a long arm around each of them.

At last, Downey continued. "We pledge ourselves," he said, "to a policy of putting the unemployed at productive work—" The cheering resumed. " . . . Enabling them to produce what they themselves are to consume. . . ." This was production for use, in so many words. "Progress versus reaction, public welfare against private greed—this is the issue in the present campaign," Downey declared. "We are going forward upon a new road to reorganize our society by peaceful, orderly, constitutional, and Christian methods. . . ." Anticipating what would no doubt become the real issues in the campaign, the platform expressed wholehearted opposition to communism and unalterable support for private property, freedom of religion, and the "sacredness of the American home."

Sinclair had won his gamble; his EPIC support held. But what about the mainstream Democrats? A small renegade group led by Ham Cotton displayed keen wit and a taste for the jugular by introducing an alternative platform: Sinclair's original EPIC plan! This was hard for the gallery to hoot down and impossible at this point for Sinclair to swallow, but Creel managed to force a straight up-and-down vote on the official platform, which carried resoundingly. Even Sinclair's critics on press row were impressed with his steamroller control of the proceedings.

During his half-hour acceptance speech, Sinclair pointed at George Creel, who was strolling around the hall, and commented, "He is a little fellow in stature but the eyes of the nation are upon him today because he has chosen to be a big man." Sinclair drew cheers by proposing the campaign slogan "Put Merriam with Hoover." Then Creel and McAdoo rejoined Sinclair on the platform. McAdoo called him Governor and urged every Democrat to "get busy and go to work." The celebration drew to a close at four o'clock.

Finally the newsreel men marched Sinclair and Creel out to the capitol's porch. The convention, Creel told Sinclair, as the cameras whirred, "removed every doubt and it has released full enthusiasm," and the two old muckrakers shook on it.

It was evening in the East when presidential press secretary Steve Early received a telegram addressed to Franklin Roosevelt at Hyde Park.

> WE INFORM YOU OF OUR COMPLETE HARMONY AND OVERWHELMING ACCLAMATION FOR THE NEW DEAL IN CALIFORNIA AND CALIFORNIA'S HELP FOR YOU IN BRINGING THE NEW DEAL TO THE WHOLE NATION. OUR SUCCESS COULD NOT HAVE BEEN MORE COMPLETE.

It was signed by George Creel, Sheridan Downey, and Upton Sinclair. Early took a pencil and scribbled a note to Marvin McIntyre. "Mac—Do you think we ought to answer this?" Early asked. "If so, how?"

After twenty-four hours of secrecy, news that the police had apprehended a suspect in the Lindbergh case startled and delighted the nation. Reporters and photographers mobbed the Greenwich Street police station in lower Manhattan, where Bruno Richard Hauptmann was being held. The police called a press conference, and J. Edgar Hoover arrived to take part and take credit. Although Hauptmann had not yet been charged with any offense, Hoover said, there was no question that he was the Lindbergh kidnapper. Detectives had uncovered another $13,760 in ransom money stashed away in his garage up in the Bronx.

Police expected Hauptmann to confess, but the thirty-five-year-old carpenter continued to maintain his innocence. A friend named Fisch, now dead, had lent him the money, he explained, and he was keeping it hidden as a hedge against inflation. (Hoover and the other officials pooh-poohed the story.) Hauptmann had not yet retained an attorney, and so he was literally defenseless when police led him into the makeshift pressroom in handcuffs and placed him in a chair on a raised platform for the benefit of photographers. He sat there sullenly, like a sideshow freak, dressed in a dark suit and tie, his eyes defiant one moment, hangdog the next. By the end of the night, Hauptmann was, in every sense, a beaten man. Detectives, attempting to extract a confession, handcuffed him to a chair and pummeled him about the legs, shoulders, and back of the head. Still he stuck to his story.

What was an ordeal for Hauptmann proved to be an opportunity for others. For the first time ever, the newsreels made good on their pledge to beat the press to a major story. Footage shot this very afternoon made it onto movie screens in New York City around nine o'clock tonight and caused a sensation, for the newsreels showed detectives actually interrogating the prisoner.

Across the country, Charles and Anne Morrow Lindbergh sought seclusion at Will Rogers's ranch high above the Pacific Ocean in Santa Monica. Rogers was still in Europe, but the Lindberghs were always welcome there. The rocky hillside reminded the couple of Cuernavaca. It was a good place to hide out, collect their thoughts, and gird their emotions. They knew what awaited them in New York: swarms of reporters and cameramen and a face-to-face meeting with the man accused of killing their son.

It didn't take long for reality to shatter Upton Sinclair's fantasy of complete harmony. The outgoing state Democratic chairman, Maurice Harrison, came out against Sinclair this afternoon. William Jennings Bryan, Jr., son of the great Commoner and a prominent Los Angeles Democrat, denounced Sinclair as a "socialist interloper." Reports circulated that many local Democratic committees—perhaps the majority—still wouldn't endorse their nominee. San Francisco Democrats charged that the party platform "sugar coated" Sinclair's socialist pill.

Once the convention ended, Democratic leaders seemed to scurry from Sinclair's side. George Creel said he couldn't help much in the fall campaign; he was "broke" and needed to head East to pick up some magazine assignments. William G. McAdoo revealed that he would be out of the state almost continuously, campaigning for fellow Democratic senators in other states. An EPIC victory banquet in Sacramento tonight drew few Democratic bigwigs, and Upton Sinclair, after dining, became ill. "Among Mr. Sinclair's other difficulties," the *San Francisco News* declared, "is convincing small-town people he didn't make fun of them in *Main Street.*"

SEPTEMBER 21

FRIDAY

After spending a few days in Great Britain, W. R. Hearst left St. Donat's castle and boarded the German liner *Europa* for his long-awaited return to America. Criticism of his meeting with Hitler mounted. Associates advised him to book his passage on a British boat, but as usual the Chief paid little heed. W.R. wired a message to New York, assuring his critics that Hitler's minister of labor had just declared that the German government would not permit discrimination against "Jewish workers or Jewish business houses. . . ."

Another famous Californian set sail from England today, aboard the *Ile de France.* "Europe's awful quiet now," Will Rogers cabled his newspaper syndicate in America. "Don't hear much war talk so I guess that means one will break out. That's when they have 'em when there ain't any reason."

In London, meanwhile, the Fabian Society announced that for the first time since 1914, George Bernard Shaw would fail to deliver his annual address. The playwright was simply "growing old," the society explained today. Still, Shaw at seventy-eight felt sprightly enough to sit for an interview with the *London Sunday Chronicle.*

Just last year, Shaw managed to mount a major American tour.

W. R. Hearst even threw a gala party for him in Marion Davies's fourteen-room bungalow at MGM. Louis Mayer, Charlie Chaplin, Clark Gable, and dozens of other celebrities attended. Odd-looking and eminently quotable, Shaw had become a favorite of American newsreels. "Take an opium eater's dream to Los Angeles," Shaw observed, "and they will realize it for you; the more it costs, the more they believe in it." Observing his behavior during this visit, Edmund Wilson complained that Shaw had allowed himself to suffer the fate of Mark Twain: he had become a public "character."

G. B. Shaw and Upton Sinclair were among the world's most famous socialists. Shaw had praised Sinclair's work as far back as 1905 in his preface to *Major Barbara,* but his interest may have faded with time. "My wife reads your books with great devotion," he informed Sinclair in 1931, implying that he did not. Shaw considered Sinclair a historian, a poet of facts, a valuable proponent of socialism—but not a novelist. He even recommended Sinclair for the Nobel Prize, finding in his favor the fact that many Americans wanted to put him "in the pillory."

Based on his interview with the London newspaper—soon to be syndicated by the Hearst news service—it was hard to tell exactly where Shaw presently stood, politically speaking. He seemed to call for a one-party Socialist dictatorship in England, with a parliament retained merely to air grievances. It was impossible for any government under a two-party system to accomplish anything, Shaw explained, because the party in power was always prevented from governing by the other party. One-man rule was already an international phenomenon. Stalin, Hitler, Mussolini, and Roosevelt were all dictators, he observed, but none of the dictatorships was like any of the others.

"You are all on the rocks," Shaw said. "What must you do to be saved?" Accept revolution, gladly. "With the exception of capitalism," he observed, "there is nothing so revolting as revolution. Unless you are prepared for revolution and know what the change means—a certain amount of wreckage and the throwing away of old ideas—the effect of revolution is to make many revolutionaries reactionary."

Then he expressed a view that would no doubt resonate in California. "Nobody believes in revolution, but when it comes it will surprise everybody," Shaw advised. "When it comes, many will not know a revolution has taken place."

A tiny man carrying a metal card file arrived at the *Los Angeles Times* building on the corner of First and Broadway. The dilapidated four-story structure, built in 1912, had just about outlived its usefulness; a block away, at First and Spring, rose a massive stone fortress that would soon serve as the newspaper's new home. The inconspicuous-looking visitor walked upstairs to the newsroom and asked the receptionist who guarded the portals, known as Aunt Het, if he could see Mr. Hotchkiss. Why did he want to see Mr. Hotchkiss? He had something that might interest him concerning Upton Sinclair.

Soon the visitor was sitting next to city editor L. D. Hotchkiss and managing editor Ralph W. Trueblood. He extracted from his file a stack of three-by-five index cards. On each he had written an excerpt from one of Upton Sinclair's books, along with a citation, right down to the page number on which the quote appeared. The mystery man's detective work was exhaustive. He had caught Sinclair thumbing his nose at everyone from Calvin Coolidge to Jesus Christ. That clinched it. Along with the extracts unearthed by their own researcher, Stan Gordon, the editors now had a Sinclair quote for every occasion. Hotchkiss and Trueblood decided that they would run one of the quotes in a special box on the front page of their newspaper every morning between now and Election Day—starting tomorrow.

Five blocks south of the *L.A. Times* building, the executive committee of the Pacific Mutual Life Insurance Company convened at eleven-thirty this morning in their home office, near Pershing Square. The company's embattled president, George I. Cochran, presided. Missing, but very much present in spirit, was Asa V. Call. In addition to serving as Pacific Mutual's vice president and general counsel, Call was rapidly emerging as a Republican fixer and as a leader of C. C. Teague's United for California.

Pacific Mutual, founded in Sacramento in 1868, was California's leading native-born insurance firm. Railroad tycoon Leland Stanford purchased its initial policy and served as its first chief executive. Among its early stockholders were railroad magnates Mark Hopkins and Charles Crocker, pioneering newspaper publisher James McClatchy, and Governor Henry H. Haight. The company thrived for decades, establishing offices in more than forty states. George Cochran, a dogmatic executive and a stolid Republican, took over in 1908 and built a new headquarters, a six-story earthquake-proof structure on Sixth Street in Los Angeles.

By 1934, Pacific Mutual, while retaining twenty-five million policyholders, was close to collapse. Claims climbed swiftly during the Depression, putting the entire company in danger of bankruptcy. The company's board of directors, which included such luminaries as Herbert Fleishhacker, William H. Crocker, and George Gund, wanted Cochran out and Asa Call in.

For the moment, Cochran remained in charge, and when it came to politics, he and "Ace" saw eye to eye anyway. Cochran and Call had already instructed their branch offices to use whatever tactics necessary to whip up opposition to Upton Sinclair. Pacific Mutual also took the unprecedented step of mailing out leaflets to its stockholders, warning that the election of Upton Sinclair would imperil their investments. Cochran personally contacted B. C. Forbes, a Hearst columnist and founder of *Forbes* magazine, seeking to interest him in the campaign.

Today the executive committee decided that even though Pacific Mutual was approaching insolvency, it was not bankrupt in spirit. And so the executive committee voted unanimously to contribute the hearty sum of seventy-five hundred dollars "to aid in stabilizing our present form of government."

Walter Wanger started shooting *The President Vanishes* for Paramount this morning. It would be months before the picture appeared in theaters, but it was already the most closely watched film in Hollywood. Wanger received an unwelcome reminder today of just how well observed it was: another long memo from Joseph E. Breen, head of the Production Code Administration. Breen insisted that Wanger make additional changes in the script if he wanted *The President Vanishes* to receive Will Hays's seal of approval. This was no empty threat. Joe Breen had recently revealed that his office, besides forcing countless revisions, had rejected twelve scripts and five completed films "in toto."

Because of its pedigree, *The President Vanishes* was doomed to close scrutiny. While at MGM, producer Walter Wanger and writer Carey Wilson had created *Gabriel Over the White House,* the most sensational political film of 1933. Directed by Gregory La Cava, it told the story of Jud Hammond (played by Walter Huston), a political hack who becomes president by paying off the right people and then shows little interest in dealing with the Depression. An automobile accident places him at death's door, where the archangel Gabriel offers him a second life as a benevolent leader committed to solving the nation's problems by utilizing the full powers of his office (and then some). Using radio extensively, the President rallies the people. He bullies Congress into enacting his programs and proceeds to eradicate hunger and unemployment. Then he suspends Congress, declares martial law to eliminate crime, and sends out the army to execute gangsters without the benefit of trial. After forging an international disarmament agreement, he blows up the entire U.S. fleet. Presumably to save America from dictatorship, Gabriel kills off the President, who nevertheless dies a hero and a martyr.

Filmed before Franklin Roosevelt took office, *Gabriel Over the White House* outlined public-works programs that later came to pass. It bore the unmistakable stamp of William Randolph Hearst, an early FDR partisan sometimes accused of flirting with fascism. W.R. loved the scenario and insisted that Wanger produce it out of Hearst's Cosmopolitan studio at MGM. He also rewrote significant sections of Carey Wilson's script, making *Gabriel* an explicit expression of the authoritarian impulse.

L. B. Mayer and Will Hays saw early screenings of *Gabriel* and felt it was downright subversive. The early part of the picture seemed to parody their political mentors, Harding and Hoover, and the second half pointed Franklin Roosevelt in some dangerous directions. Mayer strode from the theater, grabbed his henchman, Eddie Mannix, and shouted loud enough for everyone to hear, "Put that picture in its can, take it back to the studio, and lock it up!" But MGM knew a moneymaker when it saw one, and though Wanger resisted, the studio reshot several scenes to remove a bit of its bite.

When *Gabriel* came out in April 1933—Mayer delayed the opening until after Hoover left office—the *Hollywood Reporter* declared that it would "probably go down in the history of motion pictures as the most sensational piece of film entertainment the world has ever known. . . ." While criticizing its profascist flavoring, *The Nation* noted that it was Hollywood's first attempt to appeal to "the current popular interest in social and economic ideas. . . . Now for the first time Hollywood openly accepts the depression as a fact." Although some politicians complained and *Variety* called it "flag-waving flapdoodle," the film reached a wide audience which, it was safe to say, longed for strong political leadership.

FDR screened it several times at the White House. The President, in a personal note to Hearst, revealed "how pleased I am with the changes you made" and asserted obliquely that the movie "should do much to help." Later, when the Chief attacked the President for using some of the very tactics W.R. had advocated in *Gabriel,* the *Christian Century* commented, "We hate to think what might happen to Gabriel if Mr. Hearst could get his hands on him now!"

Upton Sinclair, shortly after announcing his candidacy for governor, compared his *I, Governor* to *Gabriel Over the White House.*

"Sort of 'Gabriel Over Sacramento'?" a reporter queried.

"Yes, it is a little like that," Sinclair replied.

Now, a year later, Walter Wanger, a liberal Democrat who had served on President Wilson's staff at the Paris Peace Conference, prepared a sure-to-be-controversial follow-up. In *The President Vanishes,* a right-wing assortment of businessmen, corrupt politicians, and native fascists plot to drag the United States into a European war to produce profits for the arms industry. They manipulate public opinion and beat up protesters. As Congress prepares to declare war, the peace-loving president (Arthur Byron) fakes his own kidnapping to distract attention. The public loses all interest in war, and by the time the President returns, the "forces of selfishness and greed" are in retreat. Carey Wilson's script, while overtly antifascist, pictured a submissive public that could easily be brainwashed by one cause or another. Again, a strong leader takes radical action to save the nation.

One week ago, Wanger sent the completed script to Joe Breen at the Production Code office, seeking "advice and cooperation." He was being a good sport about it, but he knew he had reason to worry. *Film Weekly,* the English trade paper, had just labeled Will Hays a "mere Hindenburg" compared to Joe Breen—"the Hitler of Hollywood." Wanger got even more than he bargained for. Today he "got Breened," as the saying went.

In his memo, Breen declared that he did not want the vice president in the picture to seem like a "tool" of the "capitalists." He objected to making the "heavies" of the picture a steelman, an oilman, a banker, and a newspaper publisher. "This characterization," Breen chided, "is likely to give the [movie] industry no end of trouble because it is certain to be resented quite forcefully." Breen suggested turning the bad guys into "*international* munitions men with an *international* viewpoint." If Wanger insisted on making them Americans, he must indicate that these men were not "characteristic" of their professions but, rather, exceptions. "It should be definitely brought out that the steel people in this country," Breen wrote, "would not have a part in any such nefarious business."

For some reason, Breen raised no objection to the steel baron from

Pittsburgh being named Andrew Cullen, but he condemned other sections of the script, down to individual lines of dialogue. Referring to a scene where someone asks the police to beat up demonstrators, Breen commented, "Any references to excessive brutality on the part of the police, or law enforcement officers, is always deleted."

Now the ball was in Wanger's court. Should he try to mollify Breen? Shoot the picture and deal with the consequences later? Wanger decided to proceed as originally planned. And he vowed that the first person to see his completed picture would be Franklin Delano Roosevelt.

Joe Breen's office was new, but Hollywood had flirted with self-inflicted censorship for more than a decade. Rocked by scandal in the early 1920s—most famously when a former starlet died after a wild Fatty Arbuckle party—the movie industry put its house in order before the government got a chance to do it. Studio executives banded together to form the Motion Picture Producers and Distributors of America, and in 1922 hired Will H. Hays as its president at the almost unheard-of salary of one hundred thousand dollars per annum.

Hays served several functions, all aimed at keeping the government off Hollywood's back, but he was best known as the point man in the fight for morality in movies. By policing itself, the movie industry might avoid government sanctions. Charlie Chaplin, who claimed that he was against all censorship, "particularly Presbyterian censorship," was one of the few industry leaders to oppose the czar. At Chaplin's studio, a pennant reading WELCOME WILL HAYS was tacked over the door of the men's toilet.

During the following years, the so-called Hays Office, based in New York, proposed guidelines for moviemakers to live by. One set of commandments outlined eight *don't*s and twenty-six *be careful*s, listing profanity, nudity, "illegal traffic in drugs," "ridicule of the clergy," "deliberate seduction of girls," and "excessive or lustful kissing" among them. But this was little more than window dressing; the studios often ignored the codes, and Hays had little means of enforcement. And many moviegoers actually enjoyed sex and violence—part relief, part release for an audience ravaged by the Depression.

But then the studios went too far. Gangster movies proliferated. Mae West's *She Done Him Wrong* and *I'm No Angel* attracted huge crowds in 1933, and also mass protests. A committee of Catholic bishops formed the Legion of Decency. Millions signed a pledge to boycott impure movies. State censorship boards excised offending scenes. Box office receipts fell.

Once again, in July 1934, Will Hays rode to the rescue. With much fanfare, he organized a new office in Hollywood, known as the Production Code Administration, and hired as its head a stern Catholic ex-journalist, Joe Breen. This time the studios gave Hay police powers. They agreed not to distribute any film that did not win the official seal of approval and to pay a fine of twenty-five thousand dollars if they broke that pledge. Cecil B. DeMille, who had earlier complained that he was being accused of inventing sex, now claimed that he was happy that "vulgarity" was being driven from the screen.

Ironically, the movies' new morality cop, Joe Breen, was something of an anti-Semite who secretly despised his employers, the Jewish studio chiefs. "They are simply a rotten bunch of vile people with no respect for anything beyond the making of money," Breen wrote in a letter to a friend in 1932. "Here we have Paganism rampant and in its most virulent form. . . . These Jews seem to think of nothing but money making and sexual indulgence. . . . They are, probably, the scum of the scum of the earth."

Producers submitted scripts or finished films to Breen and his seven associates and accepted major revisions in content, characterization, and dialogue. The Production Code office tied up hundreds of scripts and suppressed some of them. MGM, after laying out twenty-five thousand dollars for the film rights to James M. Cain's *The Postman Always Rings Twice,* killed the picture before it even reached the script stage. This wasn't censorship, Will Hays argued, it was simply recognition, long overdue, that the public was sick of filth and wanted moral uplift. "I am extremely happy the film industry has appointed a censor within its own ranks," Eleanor Roosevelt told a nationwide radio audience. Business picked up at the box office, so the moguls were happy. The only people who complained were independent producers, like Walter Wanger, and writers.

Now that the Production Code office had settled in comfortably at the Hotel Roosevelt, it was ready to confound the state political campaign. Back in New York, Will Hays had just sent his right-hand man, Charlie Pettijohn, to California to ensure the defeat of Upton Sinclair. "There is a cuckoo in the Democratic nest out here," one of Hays's West Coast associates wired him today, "but Charlie and I will shoo it out."

SEPTEMBER 22

SATURDAY

Of all the opinion shapers in the nation's capital, no one could spot a Bolshevik behind every bush as readily as Mark Sullivan, perhaps the nation's preeminent political columnist. "Mr. Sullivan," Heywood Broun once wrote, "is convinced that the revolution is not only here but almost consummated." Today, after thirty years in journalism, Sullivan hit the panic button, and Upton Sinclair was the cause. At his office in Washington, he composed a cry of alarm aimed not at his large readership in California but at an influential few on the East Coast. Forget everything else happening in America; the outcome of the election in California, Sullivan wrote in his syndicated column, would affect the future of the country more than "any other one event."

A Sinclair victory, he insisted, would drive Roosevelt, a notorious follower of fashion, to the left, the last thing the country needed. It would influence Democrats in Congress to step to the left along with their leader and accede to his every wish. And it would prevent a nationwide recovery, for Big Business would cut investments, fearing that California's experiment would spread elsewhere. This might lead to economic paralysis throughout the country. But, ah, should Sinclair be defeated, "both Mr. Roosevelt and the Democrats in Congress would feel that the tide of radicalism had reached its highest point and that this point is higher, more radical, than the country as a whole is willing to go to. Defeat of Mr. Sinclair might be a turning point, might be the beginning in the White House, in Congress and throughout the country of a turn in the direction of economic orthodoxy and political conservatism." It would indicate that "America as a whole is not going to adopt state socialism," encouraging business to begin to "expand normally" at once. "Defeat of Mr. Sinclair in California," Sullivan concluded, "might be like the defeat of William Jennings Bryan in 1896, a sign of the climax and beginning ebb of a period of radical proposals in government and social organization." It might be the one event that "would start the country forward in a business way."

Following a personal appeal from President Roosevelt, the executive council of the United Textile Workers of America voted unanimously to end their nationwide strike. The basis for the settlement: the creation of a new board to handle grievances. FDR called on the textile industry to take back striking workers without prejudice. Union leaders declared victory, calling it "one of the greatest in all labor history," but it was difficult to judge what they had won. The promise of further mediation paled alongside the paychecks forfeited and lives lost.

It was, in fact, another setback for labor, following failures earlier this year in the steel, rubber, and automobile industries. The reasons for labor's decline were many: weak leadership from the American Federation of Labor; the perplexing requirements of the NRA codes, and perhaps most of all, the fighting spirit of management. Employers hired scabs, spies, and agents provocateurs in unprecedented numbers. They stockpiled tear gas, rifles, even machine guns, and weren't afraid to use them. In some cities, a class war seemed imminent. A young reporter named Eric Sevareid, covering a protest by striking truckers in Minneapolis that left sixty-seven of them injured, many shot in the back, wrote that suddenly he understood "deep in my bones and blood what Fascism was." Horrified, Sevareid's father saw it a bit differently. "This," he said, "is *revolution*!"

It was the first full day of autumn. Yesterday the capture of Bruno Richard Hauptmann dominated press coverage in California, as it did everywhere else. Today newspapers in Los Angeles and San Francisco cleared the decks for a declaration of war. For starters, they christened the Democratic ticket "Uppy & Downey."

According to one tally, 92 percent of California's seven hundred newspapers supported Merriam, 5 percent backed Haight, and the rest were neutral. If any paper besides the *EPIC News* had declared for Sinclair, no one knew about it. The anti-Sinclair press had a stranglehold on virtually every major city; few papers even acknowledged EPIC activities. Haight's lift came almost exclusively from C. K. McClatchy's chain of "Bees," concentrated in the Central Valley. The *San Francisco Chronicle* clearly would lead the reactionary charge in the north; the *Los Angeles Times* in the south. The two newspapers even seemed to coordinate their strategies. Today they kicked off the fall campaign by running front-page editorials against Sinclair, expressing their views in similar language.

"The issue is now drawn in California," the *Chronicle* heralded, suggesting that in the wake of the political conventions the governor's race was clearly a contest between socialism and "progressive Liberalism." Upton Sinclair, "a master of propaganda . . . has hypnotized himself into a fanatical sincerity for the cause." The *Chronicle*'s star political reporter, Earl Behrens, didn't even try to hide his bias behind thoughtful analysis. Behrens, a courtly gentleman known as "Squire," referred to Sinclair's recent triumph in Sacramento as "the rape of the Democratic party." His stylistic contribution to the campaign was the phrase "erstwhile Socialist," which he attached to Sinclair's name at every opportunity.

Obviously this sat well with Behrens's boss, Chester Rowell, and publisher George Cameron, who had made a fortune in the cement business long before he inherited the *Chronicle* from his father-in-law, Michael de Young, in 1925. Cameron had recently presented jeweler's boxes to 161 of his employees for courageously carrying on during the San Francisco general strike, despite threats and rocks thrown through windows. Without their help, Cameron couldn't have gotten the *Chronicle,* which viciously attacked the strikers, onto the street.

Elsewhere in San Francisco, Hearst's *Examiner* could be counted on to roast Sinclair, while the *News,* a Scripps-Howard paper, and the *Call-Bulletin,* owned by Hearst but edited by the maverick Fremont Older, would provide at least a measure of moderation.

Fremont Older, in fact, favored Sinclair, but the Chief would not allow him to editorialize on Upton's behalf. That would have enraged Older years ago, but the crusading editor with the sweeping mustache—

probably the greatest newspaperman in the state's history—had mellowed considerably. Last month he informed Lincoln Steffens, another old muckraker in failing health, that he intended to never again be "deeply stirred emotionally" by any cause.

Across the bay, Joe Knowland's *Oakland Tribune* eagerly joined the battle against EPIC. Knowland had taken the extraordinary step of ordering his attorneys to research the question of how boldly the *Tribune* could lie about the EPIC candidate and legally get away with it. Citing a 1921 court ruling, the lawyers told Knowland that "misstatements of fact by newspapers are qualifiedly privileged when made on a matter of public concern. . . . when made without malice, with reasonable grounds of belief, and when not in excess of the occasion."

Opposition from the Bay-area press would damage Sinclair's chances, but EPIC's core support rested in Los Angeles. Unfortunately for Sinclair, the press was even more viciously aligned against him in the south. The three largest papers in L.A.—Harry Chandler's *Times* and Hearst's morning *Examiner* and afternoon *Herald-Express*—were sure to slam him unmercifully. Manchester Boddy, editor of the iconoclastic tabloid the *Daily News,* championed technocracy and the Utopian Society but was skeptical about Sinclair. "A man is not necessarily an outstanding champion of the people," Boddy observed, "simply because the press is against him." The *Daily News* covered the campaign evenly—the only paper in L.A. to do so—but its circulation trailed the *Times* and the Hearst papers by a considerable margin.

With Hearst yet to declare for Merriam, it was up to the *L.A. Times* to rally the troops in southern California. In a front-page format strikingly similar to the *Chronicle*'s, the *Times* today termed the election a clear-cut choice between "sane progress" and "fantastic experimentation." It was a "battle for the future of California that must bring her every loyal son and daughter into the fighting line." The editorial, however blunt, was predictable. What caught the eye was the newspaper's all-out commitment to its cause. Overnight, the paper had become the repository of literally dozens of pro-Merriam or anti-Sinclair news items. Democratic leaders Ham Cotton and Maurice Harrison attacked Sinclair. One business leader after another, including executives of Lockheed Aircraft, the Los Angeles Brewing Company, and the Golden State Milk Company, announced opposition to EPIC.

Most effective of all: the debut of the front-page Sinclair excerpt, published in an eye-catching box. Today's blurb, lifted from the candidate's 1926 pamphlet *Letters to Judd,* was called SINCLAIR AND INDUS-

TRY, and in it the author vowed to "take over" railroads, banks, telephone companies, and the entire "industrial plant of the U.S."

Troops were being rallied and cries raised against Upton Sinclair, and Herbert Hoover, for one, was impressed. The GOP convention had endorsed Hoover's fumigation of Frank Merriam, C. C. Teague had finally got things percolating in the south, and now the newspapers were throwing caution to the wind. Hoover wrote to his old friend Frank Knox in Chicago:

> The situation here is getting a little better. The action of Creel and McAdoo rather helps the Republican candidate, as it has so effectively disgusted the old line Democrats. Haight is fading from the picture somewhat and we are getting a good organization and will be able to put up a first class battle.

Hollywood expressed second thoughts today about pulling up stakes to avoid EPICism in California. Movie colonists never took the threats seriously anyway. Rob Wagner offered a year's subscription to *Script* and the telephone number of twelve tall blondes "to the first fellow who makes good on that threat. It's the old political hokum," Wagner observed in an editorial, "and lost its effectiveness way back in the time of Rutherford B. Hayes." Wagner recalled that Henry Ford had once vowed to stop making automobiles if Prohibition was repealed.

Industry insiders knew the studios had too much to lose. Paramount, for example, had just reported $3.9 million in profits for the first half of 1934, a 33 percent increase over the previous year. And what about the social sacrifice? Would the Jewish moguls abandon the Promised Land, a paradise in the sun they called their own, and flock back to New York, the grimy city they once fled? *Motion Picture Herald* this morning raised an additional obstacle, stating that it would be amiss not to point out that "what with lotteries, city income taxes and the like in New York, it may be well to look over the landing places before taking off. The revolution is not localized."

Billboard offered an equally bleak analysis. The entertainment industry in New York was "not excited" with the prospect of the movie industry's return. Facilities in New York could grind out no more than fifty flicks a year, compared with the current output of five hundred in California. "The solution to the problem as seen from New York City," the journal reported, "is for the producers to use all their influence to defeat the candidate in the November election and, should they fail in this, to take it and like it" during Sinclair's tenure.

Realizing that the threats were making them look foolish, two of the moguls backed off. Harry Cohn of Columbia now denied he intended to move, and Carl Laemmle of Universal announced that he had "never mixed business with politics nor have I ever cared a rap who was or was not Governor as far as business is concerned." The studios' initial threats still played well outside the movie colony, however. The farther one got from Hollywood, the more credible they seemed. Newspapers publicized the moguls' warnings and ignored the retractions, so the threats still stood and they packed an emotional wallop.

Now Joe Schenck aimed to add credibility to the original threats and maybe even make Cohn and Laemmle disavow their disavowals. Schenck flew East, where he'd made his first fortune. Joe and his younger brother Nick had come a long way from their days as owners of Palisades Amusement Park in New Jersey. Besides chairing United Artists, Joe had just founded Twentieth Century Pictures (with Darryl Zanuck); Nick was president of MGM's parent firm, Loew's, Inc.

Before visiting Nick in New York, Joe intended to spend a couple of days with the Chamber of Commerce boys down in Miami, inspecting real estate that might provide refuge for the studios after November 6. Why Florida? Miami was sunny, it had palm trees and ocean, it was relatively unsettled, and best of all, state officials promised to give the moguls a tax break if they made the move. Florida even had a town called Hollywood.

Bodyguard, political organizer, newspaper editor, expert on self-help cooperatives—Hjalmar Rutzebeck did it all for his friend Upton Sinclair. He even stood up to A. P. Giannini. Rutzebeck's service to the Sinclair campaign also included running an undercover intelligence operation. EPIC couldn't match Merriam's payroll, but it could match wits.

Rutzebeck, the Great Dane, had recruited a number of operatives, and in his memos to EPIC headquarters he referred to them only by their I.D. numbers (e.g., "I am enclosing herewith No. 12's reports . . ."). Rutzebeck himself assumed the code name "M." He had been busy the past week, writing several accounts of below-board activities in San Francisco.

September 14: Rutzebeck revealed that No. 12 had identified a new front group called the Citizens Loyalty League, backed financially by the *Chronicle* and Standard Oil. It would, in the words of No. 12, "fight the Reds, College Professors who teach 'Red Doctrine,' and Upton Sinclair." No. 12 added that "it may be possible for me to get on the inside of the organization."

September 17: A Rutzebeck agent visited the new Citizens Loyalty League and discovered an office consisting of five well-furnished rooms, an organizer named Holmes, and a secretary, Mr. Ward. Before exiting, he helped himself to some letterhead. In a few days, the group would open another office, "unknown to outsiders," the spy disclosed, "and in it will be maintained a staff of secret investigators." From another operative, Rutzeback received the names of twelve individuals who had taken part in vigilante raids on communist groups during the San Francisco general strike and would likely be employed in a similar fashion against EPIC chapters, if so directed. The list included each suspect's address, a description of his automobile, and the car's license-plate number.

September 20: Rutzebeck had come across a seminal document produced by the Non-Sectarian Voters League, which sported excerpts from Sinclair's *Profits of Religion.* He found the quotes to be "true and accurate" and predicted that they might cause many "lukewarm" EPICs to lose faith. Sinclair, he suggested, should address this circular in a statewide radio address.

Rutzebeck also related a conversation he'd had with the manager of the American Smelting and Refining Company on California Street. This company now belonged to a "very confidential" organization called the Commercial Employers Association, whose policy was to impress upon workers that their jobs would disappear and they would become "state slaves" if Sinclair was elected. "He told me," Rutzebeck wrote, "that he, personally, is convinced that Sinclair can be defeated by this method. . . ."

At midnight, the movie elite gathered at the Pantages Hollywood Theater for a benefit screening of *We Live Again,* Sam Goldwyn's latest star vehicle for Anna Sten, "the Russian Garbo." At the urging of director Rouben Mamoulian, Goldwyn had hired the young playwright Preston

Sturges to doctor the script. Goldwyn called him "Sturgeon" and thanked him for providing some "snappy nineteenth-century dialogue." Maxwell Anderson and Thornton Wilder contributed to the screenplay, as well.

Unfortunately, the music that accompanied a Russian Orthodox Easter service in *We Live Again* was recorded backward by mistake. Goldwyn didn't notice, but because of his enthusiasm for this scene no one dared tell him of the error, and the sequence stayed in. But then almost no one stood up to Sam Goldwyn, one of Hollywood's founding fathers. A compulsive gambler, he took chances in every phase of studio life, from the casting couch to the soundstage, and bullied talented directors to the point where they would no longer work for him. With the exception of Harry Cohn, he made more enemies in Hollywood than anyone else.

"You can't really resent Sam's vulgarity," a writer once said, "when he himself has never learned the meaning of the word." The famous producer lent his name to a spectacular species of malaprop known as the Goldwynism. Who could forget "I'm sticking my head in a moose" or "You need Indians, you can get 'em right from the reservoir?"

Goldwyn was politically conservative, like the other moguls, but had such an independent streak—the most famous Goldwynism of them all may be "Include me out"—that he sometimes marched in a different direction just to show up the others. So far, he had remained silent on the subject of Upton Sinclair. He welcomed Walter Wanger's *The President Vanishes* to his Melrose lot, but that was just business. So was *We Live Again,* another film with leftist touches.

One of those attending the midnight preview at the Pantages was Rob Wagner, editor of *Script.* Goldwyn's film, he discovered, charted a tragic romance based on Tolstoy's *Resurrection.* A prince impregnates, then abandons, a servant girl, who turns to prostitution. The prince by chance sits on the jury that inadvertently convicts the girl, condemning her to Siberia. Realizing that he has caused her downfall, the prince gives away all of his land and possessions and accompanies her to Siberia, telling her, "All I ask is to live again with your forgiveness and your help and your love."

What Rob Wagner found interesting about the picture was not the melodrama but the politics, such as they were. The prince, he observed, was a traitor to his class, like Franklin Roosevelt, who reads the pamphlets of some local Upton Sinclair and then proposes a Russian reconstruction program that out-EPIC's Uppie.

Following the screening, Wagner sidled up to Goldwyn and half-seriously inquired, "And *you* made that picture, Sam?"

"Yes, and I'm for Merriam," Goldwyn replied, a broad grin crossing his face.

Then Irving Thalberg, listening in, interjected, eyes twinkling, "But you won't release it before the election, will you, Sam?"

Wagner watched as Goldwyn smiled back a silent reply: *Not a chance.*

SEPTEMBER 24

MONDAY

Harry Rapf, a producer and vice president at MGM, greeted his son Maurice and Maurice's best friend, Budd Schulberg, when the liner carrying them home from Europe arrived in New York. Rapf had come all the way from Hollywood, and not entirely out of affection for his son. Maurice and Budd, undergraduates at Dartmouth, had traveled to Russia this summer under the auspices of the left-wing National Students League. According to reports reaching Hollywood, the experience had radicalized them both.

This was an embarrassment, and possibly a problem, for the movie industry. No one doubted that Maurice Rapf and Budd Schulberg (son of B. P. Schulberg, former head of production at Paramount and now an independent producer) would end up in Hollywood after they left college. Even worse, they were in the line of succession to head major studios themselves one day. "Get Harry Warner to talk to them," someone had advised Harry Rapf. But another associate commented, "Those kids will make mincemeat out of Harry Warner."

The moguls had reason to worry; the kids were smitten with the Soviets. From Yalta they informed Dartmouth they would be enrolling a little late this fall: they had to attend the World Writers Congress chaired by Maxim Gorky. The Soviets seemed to tolerate Jews, and evidence of opposition to Hitler was everywhere. One wall poster showed a red fist raised against the image of a storm trooper and the slogan KEEP THE NAZI SLOP OUT OF THE SOVIET GARDEN. Ring Lardner, Jr., a Princeton student they met in Russia, was impressed by all the construction going on at a time of economic standstill in the West and felt that the Soviets represented the best hope for mankind.

While abroad, Maurice and Budd followed developments in the California governor's race as best they could. They wanted Sinclair to win, of course—the concept of an author-politician appealed to these would-be writers. Before leaving for the Soviet Union, Schulberg had made a special trip to San Francisco to observe the general strike, and it was still vivid in his mind. Schulberg's mother, from whom his father was separated, knew Upton Sinclair and Lincoln Steffens personally and had flirted with socialism. Sinclair had even visited the Schulbergs' home, impressing Budd with his surprisingly boyish manner.

B. P. Schulberg was a liberal Democrat and tolerant of Budd's behavior. Harry Rapf, on the other hand, was a conventional, hardworking man baffled by his son's trip to Russia. His attitude on meeting Maurice in New York was one of sadness, not anger. He listened respectfully to his son's tales, certain that he didn't know enough to counter them. Then, following the advice he received in Hollywood, he sent Maurice to meet Harry and Albert Warner, who had offices in New York.

"I don't want to talk to no goddamn Communist," Harry Warner told Maurice. "Don't forget you're a Jew. Jewish Communists are going to bring down the wrath of the world on the rest of the Jews." Maurice replied with a report on the anti-Semitism he had observed in Berlin during a stopover there and said the Soviets seemed to be the only ones taking a strong stand against the Nazis.

Then he met Albert Warner, known as the Major. He called Maurice a traitor, and when the young man tried to reply shouted, "Don't come into my office and start spouting any of that!" Maurice didn't get much of a chance to make mincemeat of the studio execs, but he knew he'd get another chance in California during Christmas recess. His father planned to get Irving Thalberg and Louis Mayer to give him a good talking to.

Like Maurice Rapf, Theodore Dreiser once visited Russia and came away impressed. Uptown in Manhattan, in his suite at the Ansonia, he might have enjoyed hearing about the young man's travels, but at the moment he was focusing his attention on a college student of the fairer sex. Dreiser was one of the satyrs of American letters. Not much had changed since the day in 1917 when he wrote in his diary, "I must give up so much screwing or I will break down." For the past year he had been trying to bed a certain Bryn Mawr sophomore—"an armful of sweet girlieness," he called her. Now he brought matters to a climax.

"The trouble with you," Dreiser instructed in a lengthy letter, "is that you are not a bad girl but rather an unthinking and indiscreet one." The coed had recently visited Dreiser at the Ansonia uninvited, waited in the hallway for his return, then slipped a note under the door. What if Dreiser had arrived with another woman or someone else found the note? "You know that you have no business doing a thing like that," he scolded, "whatever your charm or mental gifts. . . . I admit that you are interesting, that you are entertaining and witty and a lot of things that men like," Dreiser confessed, "but there is really such a thing as common sense and fairness to others underlying even free love." What Dreiser was really worked up about was this: he had learned that on a recent visit to New York, the girl had slept with someone else.

Dreiser was back in New York for a few days, waiting for the so-called American Tragedy murder trial he was covering in Wilkes-Barre to resume. He also had to get to work on his Sinclair article for *Esquire.* Arnold Gingrich had sent over the biographical material the writer had requested, and Dreiser was impressed anew with Sinclair's productivity, his integrity, his vision, and—most of all—his track record. The man was nearly always right, or so it seemed to Dreiser. *The Brass Check:* ten years ahead of the American public's realization of how they are betrayed by newspapers. *The Profits of Religion:* forty years ahead of its time. *Mammonart:* dangerously wrongheaded but still a hundred years ahead of its time in describing what was politically wrong with the literature of the world.

One of the great mysteries in life, Dreiser felt, was what makes a man like Upton Sinclair? He could have earned a fortune rowing along with the other literary boatmen on the surface of the swamp. Instead, he chose to wade, jump, *plunge in.* He was that rare manifestation: the painfully honest writer. Sinclair had written more true words about his country than anyone else. America almost didn't deserve him, but there he was! This was Dreiser's view. Consider Sinclair's life: the struggle, the enthusiasm, the openness to new ideas, the opposition to brutality, stupidity, and injustice. He had more guts than any six writers, Dreiser maintained. Yet he was belittled by trashy critics and petty liberals, and despite his recent triumph in California, he remained a literary and political jest. Hearst, of all people, accused him of misleading the masses to serve his own ends! Sinclair was called a crank, an egoist, a falsifier of facts. And yet look at him now! Even James A. Farley told him to "Call me Jim."

That was theme enough for any *Esquire* article. It would practically write itself.

———

For old-line Democrats in California, the convention in Sacramento settled nothing. They weren't going to take direction from ciphers like McAdoo and Creel; they would carry their fight directly to Roosevelt. Letters from increasingly desperate California Democrats continued to arrive at the White House. The warden at San Quentin urged FDR to crack down on "these communistically-inclined gentry." A woman in Hollywood suggested that Roosevelt get the names of the Communist groups supporting Sinclair and confiscate their literature. Many simply begged FDR to save California, the Democratic party, or both from disaster.

Sinclair supporters were also busy. They sent along EPIC circulars and politely implored the President to board the Sinclair bandwagon. A man named Harry Colpus assured Roosevelt that Upton Sinclair was a friend of the New Deal. Colpus, who lived in Pasadena, identified himself as Grover Cleveland's chief butler in the White House.

Some correspondents didn't give FDR advice; they sought it. These Democrats would follow the Great White Father wherever he led. But when would they break camp, and where were they heading? One Democratic office seeker in California wired Jim Farley fourteen times, seeking direction.

Despite his high rank and his recent visit with FDR, Senator William G. McAdoo was as perplexed as anyone. He didn't want to stick his neck out at a time when his own popularity was sinking in California. Mac was surprised by the intensity of the revolt against Sinclair; he had never seen anything like it. So he decided to query the President directly.

From Los Angeles, he wrote a letter, marked "Personal," to the man he called Frank. He informed FDR that he found Sinclair reasonable about the party platform and felt that if he stood flat-footedly on it, "his chances for election are exceptionally good." The state's senior senator, Hiram Johnson, had complimented McAdoo on the "good job" he had done in Sacramento. This was significant. "I don't think Hiram will say anything during the campaign," McAdoo wrote. "He has the nomination of all parties and can, with propriety, remain silent." Since McAdoo was not so fortunately situated, he wondered if the President wouldn't mind telling him "to what extent the ticket and platform may have the blessing of the administration."

While McAdoo wavered, his law partner, William C. Neblett, executed an astounding political backflip. Neblett had endorsed Sinclair following the primary, fully expecting to be named state Democratic chairman in return. When it became apparent today that Sinclair planned to endorse Culbert Olson instead, Neblett suddenly had a change of heart. Sinclair, he now suggested, intended to scrap the Democratic platform and "replace it with its only substitute, Communism."

So there were three groups of Democrats in California: Democrats for Sinclair, Democrats for Merriam, and Democrats for themselves. Actually there was a sizable fourth group, as well: Democrats for Haight. One of the most passionate was the young San Francisco attorney Edmund G. Brown.

Known as Pat to one and all, Brown seemed destined to a life in politics. He earned his nickname at the age of twelve after reciting Patrick Henry's "Give me liberty, or give me death" speech during a Liberty Bond drive. At Lowell High School in San Francisco, he held no fewer than eleven student offices. Lacking the money to enter college, Pat worked in the Tenderloin district in his father's cigar store, which doubled as a poker club, and studied law at night, finally receiving his degree in 1927.

The following year he ran for the state assembly as a Republican on the slogan "Rid the state of bossism and elect an independent and progressive young attorney." He lost the race but remained politically active, joining the New Guard, a group of reform-minded attorneys and businessmen, as well as helping to direct the local Taxpayers Association. Street-smart, he knew where a fellow could gamble and a girl could get an abortion, yet he lived comfortably on top of Twin Peaks with his high-school sweetheart and their two daughters.

Brown shared an office in the Russ Building with his friend Norman Elkington. They both supported Hoover in 1932, but by 1934 the sands were shifting. Pat was impressed by FDR's fireside chats. It occurred to him that the Democrats, unlike the Republicans, actually *wanted* the government to do things for people. A political switch was not in his best interest, however, since the GOP had promised him an assistant U.S. attorney's post.

One day in the spring of 1934, Mathew Tobriner, an attorney down the hall, told Brown he was going out to change his registration to Democrat.

"You can't do that," Pat responded, "it's like changing your religion."

"But what if you stop believing in your religion?" Tobriner answered, and that settled it.

"I'm going with you," Brown replied, and off they went.

Upton Sinclair was too radical a Democrat for Brown's taste. Pat had just started to feel comfortable with Roosevelt—supporting Sinclair would be going too far too fast. Yet he considered Frank Merriam a weak sister. For Pat Brown and others like him, Ray Haight was an appealing alternative. Brown knew Haight and considered him a good lawyer with a bright future in politics. Pat became a leader of the local Haight campaign, traveling far and wide across northern California. He went out campaigning almost every night and sometimes during the day. Often he spoke to three or four "improvement clubs"—associations of store owners—in a single night. This was Pat's first bite of politics at the gubernatorial level, and he liked what he tasted so far.

Joseph R. Knowland was among the the handful of men who ran California unashamedly. Publisher of the *Oakland Tribune* since 1915 and a former six-term congressman, Knowland threw his weight around with the best of them. It was often alleged that he conspired with George Cameron of the *Chronicle* and Harry Chandler of the *Times* to dictate state policy. They were known as the Unholy Triumvirate and the Republican Axis. Knowland, achieving the age of sixty, engineered the election of his son, William F., to the state assembly in 1932. Billy was only twenty-five at the time. Now the younger Knowland was running for the state senate and facing strong opposition from local EPICs.

Hardly a progressive, Joe Knowland spoke loudly for liberalization at the recent GOP convention, and he recognized the importance of channeling anti-Sinclair enthusiasm (and money) through bipartisan front groups, such as C. C. Teague's United for California. Knowland wrote today to thank Teague for keeping him abreast of activities in the south, and to inform him that he was organizing a United for California–type group in the north. It will "take a tremendous effort" to defeat Sinclair, Knowland acknowledged.

Joe Knowland had another message for Teague, and it was something of a shocker. The Republican leadership, with absolutely no direction from a befuddled Frank Merriam, had decided on a new state chairman: Earl Warren, the Alameda County district attorney. The man everyone expected to get the post, John McNab, had declined under pressure from Kyle Palmer of the *L.A. Times.* Palmer, who often wrote about GOP policy he himself had established, feared that McNab's reputation as a Hooverite would taint the entire GOP ticket.

"Earl represents the younger group," Knowland told Teague, "and is a man of splendid character, and the kind of leader we could well put to the front this year."

The *Oakland Tribune* was only one of seven hundred newspapers across the state opposing Upton Sinclair. Today, at last, a lone voice in the journalistic wilderness stepped forward in Sinclair's defense. It was no Knowland, Chandler, or Hearst but, rather, one Stephen F. O'Donnell, editor and publisher of the Huntington Park *Signal,* who blew the whistle on the propaganda campaign against Sinclair launched by the California Newspaper Publishers Association.

EPIC organizers had learned about some of the trade association's campaign activities weeks ago, including the fact that they were financed by California brewers (via Artie Samish) and directed by Governor Merriam's private secretary, Justus Craemer. Now O'Donnell emerged with additional details, as well as copies of the first of many anti-Sinclair editorials that the association expected its several hundred members to publish. One editorial warned of the dangers of communism and included a nightmare vision (ironic, under the present circumstances) of newspapers' being allowed to print "only those items of news and expressions of opinion as might be permitted" by the powers that be.

Infuriated, Stephen O'Donnell wrote a letter to the avowedly nonpolitical association, threatening to resign his membership if this outbreak of "bilge" continued, and said he would encourage other publishers to do the same. "Until this occasion arose," O'Donnell added, "I was unwilling to admit such a thing as a 'kept press.' Now I am convinced."

It was a dirty little story, but unlikely to affect public opinion: the only newspaper that would touch O'Donnell's scoop was the *EPIC News.*

This week's edition of the *EPIC News* was characteristic in all respects. The front page of the hard-boiled, eight-page tabloid featured—in addition to the O'Donnell exposé—a report on the Democratic convention, Ray Haight's colorful account of the latest bribes offered by the "Merriam Men," and photographs of a mountain of oranges being set ablaze in Orange County "to keep the prices up." Inside, the crisply designed paper carried the usual array of material: national politics (LA FOLLETTE SWING TO LEFT RUMORED); breathless news items (FROM EPIC FRONT LINE TRENCHES); an excerpt from Sinclair's new booklet, *Immediate EPIC;* editorials and political cartoons; and witty one-liners known as *EPIC*grams. Small ads promoted Square Deal shoe repair and politically correct piano tuning ("By an 'EPIC' Blind Man"), among other services.

The formula obviously worked. After a slow start last winter, back when it was known as *Upton Sinclair's End Poverty Paper,* the tabloid, which sold for a nickel, had achieved weekly distribution of over a million copies, with no ceiling in sight. Unlike most of EPIC's other activities, it operated at a profit, owing to its strict cash-on-the-barrel-head policy. No matter who you were—ten-year-old newsboy, unemployed laborer, or EPIC leader—you paid a dollar for thirty-three copies. That meant you made two cents on every issue sold. Many EPIC chapters produced inserts for local editions, selling regional advertising to pay their way. Sometimes the locals sold so many ads they were able to place a free copy of the *EPIC News* on every doorstep in town.

The newspaper's editor, Rube Borough, was an excitable fellow with bushy hair described by a former colleague as "a wild man from the Borneo of newspaperdom." As a Socialist reporter in the Midwest, he had been close to Carl Sandburg (whom he knew as "Sandy")—until he panned the poet's *Good Morning, America.* Rube came to Los Angeles and started working for the pro-worker daily the *Record* in 1917.

Borough was a natural choice to edit the *EPIC News,* operating out of state EPIC headquarters in L.A., but lately he had started to look ahead. EPIC had become so much more than Sinclair, and yet the *EPIC News* was little more than Uppie's campaign sheet. Borough wanted it to promote the entire progressive movement, from co-ops to technocracy. He loved Sinclair, but recognized that he was only the catalyst of the insurrection, not its cause. Win or lose in November, EPIC's priorities (with no election to mobilize around) would change. Borough's goal was to make the *EPIC News* a daily newspaper, and go toe-to-toe with the *Los Angeles Times.* It would be the People versus the Interests, seven mornings a week.

———

Upton Sinclair took the stage at Dreamland Auditorium in San Francisco tonight still feeling the effects of the ptomaine poisoning he'd come down with following his triumph at the Democratic convention. San Francisco was by no means an EPIC stronghold; Creel had carried the city in the primary. Yet the *Chronicle* and the *Examiner* had so far failed to generate anti-Sinclair hysteria. Perhaps July's general strike, which cost several lives and ended in stalemate, had drained the city of its political passion, and neither Left nor Right had recovered yet.

Rather than worrying about the election, some San Franciscans simply counted the days until the October 1 opening of Max Reinhardt's *Midsummer Night's Dream* at the Opera House. Others looked a bit further down the road to the completion of the two wondrous bridges under construction—one, already dubbed the Golden Gate, to Marin County, the second across the bay to Oakland.

Sports fans pondered the future of San Francisco Seals' star Joseph Paul DiMaggio, known as Dead Pan Joe. Young Joe, a product of the city's North Beach sandlots, had hit in sixty-one consecutive minor league games in 1933—at the age of eighteen—and was off to a fine start this season when he tore up his left knee getting out of a taxicab. Now his future as a big-league star was in doubt. Most scouts questioned Joe's ability to rebound from his injury, but the New York Yankees' Bill Essick advised his boss George Weiss otherwise. "Everybody out here thinks I'm crazy," Essick reported, "but I think he's all right." The Yankees, consequently, had just struck a deal that would make San Francisco proud and happy, purchasing DiMaggio from the Seals for twenty-five thousand dollars. As part of the agreement—which the Yankees wished to keep secret until after the World Series—they would send the Seals five players and, best of all, allow DiMaggio to play one more season in San Francisco before ascending to the major-league level.

This evening in San Francisco, Upton Sinclair was in a feisty mood despite his illness, and the crowd of over six thousand in the overflowing auditorium urged him on. Sinclair warned that the coming campaign would be "one of the most bitter in the history of our country." He predicted a civil war, "followed by fascism and ultimately by Bolshevism," if the people didn't rise up and drive the money changers from the temple. And he issued a challenge to critics of his religious views. "Which would you rather have as governor," he asked, "an atheist who acts like a Christian or a professed Christian who acts like an atheist?" In typical Sinclair fashion, he had tried to dispel fears, only to confirm suspicions.

SEPTEMBER 26

WEDNESDAY

Franklin Roosevelt, ending his monthlong vacation at Hyde Park, returned to the White House today still wearing his summer straw hat. By custom, such headgear could not be worn past September 15. FDR smiled as photographers snapped his picture and said he hoped no one would notice the faux pas. Then he ducked into a luncheon meeting with Joseph P. Kennedy, who brought him up to date on the Securities and Exchange Commission. Kennedy was about to travel to California with some visiting royalty from Europe.

After lunch, Harold L. Ickes arrived at the Oval Office for his first meeting with the President in weeks. "Hello, Harold, I liked your book, it was grand," the President said as they shook hands, referring to Ickes's *The New Democracy.* FDR looked tired despite his long vacation and lacked his typical carefree spirit, Ickes observed.

Roosevelt and Ickes had some important decisions to make. General Johnson had finally quit as head of the NRA. The five-man National Emergency Council, which included Ickes and Harry Hopkins, would run the NRA for now, but Roosevelt had to select a new director. Later a reporter reminded FDR that he had called himself the quarterback of the New Deal and wondered whether any new plays were in prospect. Roosevelt grinned and replied that might not be necessary, because his team was still scoring.

He had reason to boast. Turner Catledge of *The New York Times* had just outlined an amazing phenomenon. Despite the strain within the administration and a rising chorus of criticism from without, the "Smiling Squire of Hyde Park" and his policies were "destined for one of the greatest demonstrations of popular approval ever accorded to an American administration," Catledge insisted. The Democrats, he predicted, would pick up from four to seven Senate seats in November and lose far fewer seats in the House than was customary in an off-year election.

The major White House announcement of the day brought news nearly every American longed to hear: FDR would deliver his first fireside chat of the season on Sunday to explain where the apparently directionless New Deal was actually heading.

W. S. Van Dyke was one of hundreds of Californians great and small trying to stop FDR from embracing Upton Sinclair. Van Dyke had the lean, brush-cut appearance of a former marine, which indeed he was, and made movies as if they were military assaults, bowling over every obstacle in his path. He had no time for perfection, earning himself the nickname One-Take Woody, but his style suited itself well to adventure films such as *Trader Horn* and *Tarzan the Ape Man.* His most recent film, *The Thin Man,* was an unqualified hit, but the movie he was most famous for was *Manhattan Melodrama,* a gangster movie so compelling that John Dillinger came out of hiding in Chicago on July 22, 1934 to see it—and was gunned down by FBI agents on leaving the theater.

Woody Van Dyke could outshout and outcurse anyone. He drank gin for breakfast and threw wild parties at his home in Brentwood, stationing marines at the door to handle gate-crashers. He spanked the actress Lupe Velez and threw the boxer Max Baer into a swimming pool. "I'm a little tamer now," Van Dyke had told the columnist Sidney Skolsky back in August, "but I have gotten away with murder."

One of the most militant anti-Sinclair directors in Hollywood, Van Dyke was eager to lend his talents to the big fight. Last night he spoke on the subject "Elements of Economic Chaos" at a meeting of the California Crusaders at the Biltmore in L.A. Afterward, this rambunctious gang of rich, young go-getters adopted an eight-point platform and vowed to rally thirty-five thousand Crusaders across the state against Upton Sinclair.

Today Van Dyke started shooting his new MGM movie, *Forsaking All Others,* written by Joseph L. Mankiewicz and starring Clark Gable and Joan Crawford, but still managed to find time to write a personal letter to President Roosevelt. Van Dyke was politically conservative, yet he supported FDR. He alerted Roosevelt to Sinclair's eccentricities and warned that support for Sinclair would be used as political ammunition by FDR's Republican opponent in 1936. In closing, Van Dyke identified himself as head of the "MGM branch" of the California Crusaders.

Charles C. Pettijohn had been in Hollywood only two days and already the anti-Sinclair struggle, which was in disarray when he arrived, was coalescing nicely. *Variety* noticed the new air of confidence, observing that the GOP had enlisted the aid of "picture and show biz folk" to scuttle Sinclair "and incidentally, to cover up the personality of its own candidate, Frank Merriam." MGM, the journal said, would lead the fight, while Warner Bros. found itself "straddling the fence." The Warners yearned to distribute patronage under a Democratic governor, but EPIC's evil taxation schemes might outweigh that honor.

Variety also disclosed that Hollywood was in the process of creating "radio playlets" showing what California would be like if EPIC came to power. Participation by actors and writers was "a cinch from practically all studios."

Charlie Pettijohn, general counsel for the Hays Office in New York, was just the man to compel cooperation in Hollywood. A Democrat, he had helped Will Hays, a fellow Hoosier, elect Republican presidents throughout the 1920s. Pettijohn's job with the Hays Office, which paid him fifty thousand dollars a year, was to fight off legislation in Congress, and in any of the forty-eight states, that might curb the movie industry's power or profits. Over the years, he had made countless political contacts in California and compiled lists of theater owners and managers who could be called on for lobbying purposes. These connections would be invaluable in the fight against Sinclair.

Arriving in Hollywood this week, Pettijohn made lunch with Mae West the first order of business. This was the favorite sport of many important visitors, but Charlie had a finer purpose in mind. The new Production Code had put West's career in jeopardy. It had already forced her to rewrite her latest movie, *Belle of the Nineties.* The film did OK at the box office, but nothing like her off-color pictures, thus ratifying one of her most famous quips: "It pays to be good, but it don't pay much." Mae was miffed, and the producers didn't want her to leave town in a huff.

After lunching with Pettijohn, Miss West announced that she thought she could adapt to the changing moral clime. "If you can't go straight," she commented, "then you've got to go around." She promised to use more innuendos.

With that settled, Pettijohn set out to unite Hollywood on a three-pronged anti-Sinclair strategy involving fund-raising, coercion, and propaganda. (One new recruit, Kyle Palmer of the *Los Angeles Times,* could contribute on every level.) If the election were held tomorrow, Pettijohn wrote Will Hays, Sinclair would win, but he labeled the candidate "self-destructive" and predicted that he would "ruin himself between now and election day." Pettijohn would return east in another week, but Fred Beetson, a West Coast aide, had the anti-Sinclair campaign under control.

One of Pettijohn's allies saw it a little differently, however. Pat Casey, head of labor relations for the Association of Motion Picture Producers in California, informed the Hays Office in New York that Sinclair would win easily unless something drastic was done. And if Sinclair won, he warned, the Warner brothers "will be in the driver's seat instead of Mayer."

———

Upton Sinclair knew that he faced an array of powerful enemies almost unparalleled in American politics, but that couldn't be avoided. He also knew that words he had written years or even decades ago would be thrown back in his face; there was nothing he could about that either. What he could control were his statements and actions between now and November 6. It would be hard enough to win even if he ran an error-free campaign. A race strewn with mistakes would surely undo him.

Today Sinclair made his first major blunder, and he was so tired he didn't even recognize it.

Arriving home on the overnight train from San Francisco, worn out from his week-long trip, he learned that EPIC headquarters had arranged a press conference in Pasadena at 11:00 A.M. Craig begged him to rest, but it was too late. A dozen reporters arrived at their house, and Sinclair started speaking.

Uppie was bushed but in a happy frame of mind, with much to talk about. For example, did the newsmen know that gamblers in San Francisco had promised to pay him sixteen thousand dollars *a month* during his term in office if he'd leave them alone? That worked out to something like eight hundred thousand dollars over four years, he calculated. Sinclair went on and on, and his wife started slipping him notes, instructing him to cut it short. But her husband loved to talk, and when he gazed at the knot of reporters before him, he saw a bunch of affable young men, some of whom actually seemed interested in what he was saying. That's the way it had been throughout the campaign. Sinclair may have loathed the editors and publishers, but the beat reporters seemed a decent lot—oppressed workers, one might say. Like FDR, Sinclair enjoyed banter and repartee.

"What good is the EPIC plan to me?" one reporter barked. "I'm not unemployed."

"You go back and tell your boss what you think of him," Sinclair cracked, "and you'll be eligible under the EPIC plan."

The questioning seemed unusually persistent today. Finally one reporter asked what would happen if EPIC actually went into effect. Wouldn't a great number of unemployed scurry to California from other states?

Sinclair replied with a grin, "I told Harry Hopkins in Washington that if I am elected half the unemployed of the United States will come to California, and he will have to make plans to take care of them." The scribbling on notepads turned furious.

Perhaps realizing that this statement required some cushioning, Sinclair elaborated. "Of course," he explained, "I was making Mr. Hopkins a sales talk. But he recognizes the situation. The unemployed come to California every winter because it is less easy to freeze to death here. The federal government presently takes care of them where they are. If they come to California they will have to take care of them here. Mr. Hopkins knows that."

Someone asked whether there was any way to prevent deadbeats from flocking to California. Sure, Sinclair replied, make conditions in California so dreadful that no one would want to live there! This, apparently, was Merriam's plan, he added. EPIC, on the other hand, was "the best advertisement California ever had."

Finally the press conference ended, and the reporters departed. A small group walked away together, discussing, as reporters are wont to do, what the lead for their stories the next day might be. One mentioned the gamblers' offer; another, Sinclair's surprisingly strong statements against the Townsend Plan. The *Los Angeles Times* reporter disagreed. "I think the important thing was what he said about half the unemployed coming to California," he commented.

"But you know he didn't mean that," replied one reporter, who happened to be a friend of Sinclair.

"Maybe he didn't mean it," the *Times* reporter responded, "but he said it, and it's what my paper wants."

It was bad enough, from Upton Sinclair's perspective, that virtually all of the publishers, businessmen, and film producers in California hated him. That was to be expected—it was almost a badge of honor. Harder to accept was the fact that his own son opposed him.

"Almost collapsing grief," David Sinclair had wired his father in September 1933 when he learned of his defection from the Socialist party. "Insane opportunism. Is it possible you have lost all integrity as man and socialist?" Nothing had changed in the twelve months since, despite sporadic attempts by each to change the other's views.

It wasn't easy being the thirty-two-year-old son of Upton Sinclair. David even had trouble finding work as a physicist because of it. Hunter College in New York turned him down for a teaching position after the president of the school referred to Upton Sinclair as "a notorious man." (Upton had to ask Albert Einstein to help David find a job.) This was nothing, however, compared with what David's own father had put him through as a youth, including long periods of abandonment or neglect while Sinclair wrote one book after another. David even had to follow his dad's crank diets when all he wanted, probably, was a hot dog.

As a child, David had witnessed the very public breakup of his parents' marriage. After years of sexual frustration—for extended periods, Upton was literally all work and no play—Meta Sinclair had taken a series of lovers, including one of her husband's best friends, the poet Harry Kemp. For a while, Upton reluctantly went along with this, and even found a lover himself, his future wife, Mary Craig Kimbrough. Finally, when Meta flaunted her affairs in the press (and wrote letters to David describing them), Upton filed for divorce. He won custody of David—and promptly sent him off to a series of boarding schools. Later, Mary Craig virtually forbade David to visit his father in California, calling him "a child so like its selfish mother," and Upton protested the order only meekly.

Sinclair was, in short, as poor a father to his son as his own father had been to him. One father was crippled by drink, the other by ambition. At least Sinclair recognized his shortcomings, writing in his autobiographical novel *Love's Pilgrimage,* "He had made a martyr of the child he loved, he had sacrificed it to what he called his art; and how had he dared to do it?"

One thing Sinclair succeeded in doing was to pass socialism on to his son. This was something Upton and David were both proud of. David felt he had been raised Socialist the way other children were brought up Catholic. But a year ago one of them had ceased being a Socialist, at least in name. This split them badly yet provided an unusually rich opportunity for intimate discussion.

Shortly after announcing his EPIC candidacy, Sinclair had come to New York for the opening of his ill-fated Eisenstein film. When David met his father, he was lounging on a divan in the lobby of the Algonquin Hotel, talking to a *Herald-Tribune* reporter. Son proceeded gently to give Father hell for bolting the Socialist party. "I wish you'd go back and read all your books over again," David said, "and become convinced by them!" Upton smiled tolerantly. David accompanied his father to lunch with Norman Thomas, who was no more successful in changing Upton's mind. The next day the *Herald-Tribune* headline read SON REPROVES UPTON SINCLAIR AS BACKSLIDER.

So began a remarkable family dialogue.

November 8, 1933, David to Upton: "Every now and then a wave of almost misery sweeps over me when I think of how you have changed in the last 5 years apparently without realizing it at all. . . . When you were young you were a rebellious youth against old age, now you seem to be all for the old timers. You are young enuf to know better . . . it will be a waste of time for anyone to try to unconvert [me]."

November 13, 1933, Upton to David: "So long as I was a Socialist I was just one more crank; but when I call myself a Democrat, I become a man worth listening to. That may seem absurd but it happens to be the psychology out here. . . . You are entirely mistaken in your idea that I have changed. You will find that out in due course. In the meantime I can only tell you that I am sorry you take it so hard."

And so it went. Today David Sinclair, back in Manhattan after a trip to Bermuda with his wife, sat down in his apartment near Columbia University, where he was studying for his doctorate, and composed his most bitter rebuke yet. "Roosevelt must have you completely hypnotized," he wrote. He accused his father of "lying for votes" by claiming to believe in God. He denounced him for telling *The New York Times* that he had always been a Democrat at heart. "You know damn well you have been a revolutionist nearly all your life," David reminded him. And he was simply "aghast" over Sinclair's contention that he hadn't changed his political views since joining the party of Tammany.

> I am for awhile ashamed to have such a liar for a father. Then I realize that you are not lying, you really believe all this tripe. You are the sort of man who cannot act unless you believe in what you are doing 100%. In either case it's pretty hard on me.

What showed most clearly "how completely you are out of your mind," David wrote, was Sinclair's recent statement that the millions of words he had written during the past three decades would mean absolutely nothing if he didn't get a chance to end poverty in California. "The good that your books have done in showing up the evils of capitalism and the necessity of socialism," David observed, his anger suddenly dampened by sadness, "cannot be undone."

SEPTEMBER 27

THURSDAY

The German liner *Europa* docked in New York carrying William Randolph Hearst and his party home from Europe. Greeted by reporters, some from his own newspapers, Hearst revealed that Adolf Hitler did not represent a menace to his neighbors, "because I do not think he has anything to be a war threat with." He also predicted that Hitler would modify Nazi policies, "particularly with regard to the Jews. . . . I do not think that discrimination against the Jews is considered desirable by thinking Germans generally."

England seemed to be returning to prosperity, and the Chief attributed the success of Upton Sinclair in California "to the fact that we are not a calm and conservative people like the English, but are more like various European nations, disposed to go headlong into cure-all. Personally," he added, "I think it is a kill-all."

Meanwhile, up in the Bronx, Charles A. Lindbergh came face-to-face for the first time with the man accused of kidnapping and killing his son. Could he identify Bruno Richard Hauptmann as the perpetrator? It was both a dramatic moment and profoundly academic. The newspapers, even the staid *New York Times,* had already convicted Hauptmann, circulating numerous false reports that bolstered the already strong case against him. When U.S. Attorney General Homer S. Cummings was asked whether he thought Hauptmann was guilty, he didn't say that this was for a jury to decide. Instead, he commented, "I didn't know that anyone doubted it."

Yesterday, appearing before a Bronx grand jury, Lindbergh had offered little new evidence, beyond describing the night he accompanied a go-between to St. Raymond's Cemetery to hand over the ransom money. From far off he had heard the extortionist shout, "Hey, Doc!" When Lindbergh finished testifying, he agreed to come down to the D.A.'s office and listen to Hauptmann shout "Hey, Doc!" in a variety of tones.

Shortly after nine-thirty this morning Lindbergh arrived at the Bronx prosecutor's office wearing a cap and dark glasses as a disguise and was taken to a room where he joined a group of investigators. Then Hauptmann was brought in. He was asked to shout "Hey, Doc!" again and again, at varying pitch and volume. Lindbergh did not say a word, and Hauptmann did not know he was there.

HEAVY RUSH OF IDLE SEEN BY SINCLAIR roared the front-page headline in the *Los Angeles Times* this morning. The story opened:

> "If I'm elected Governor, I expect one-half the unemployed in the United States will hop aboard the first freights for California," Upton Sinclair, Socialist-Democratic gubernatorial candidate said here today.

A *Times* editorial calculated that ten million Americans were out of work, meaning that five million indigents would swamp the state once Sinclair took office.

"In other words," the editorial observed, "Sinclair expects to 'end poverty in California' by bringing in fifteen times as many poverty-stricken, jobless indigents as we have already! . . . the State would be thrown into utter chaos, at the mercy of riotous, Red-incited mobs. Instead of the 'Epic Plan' we would be under martial law; instead of being Governor, Sinclair would find himself running errands for a major-general of the United States Army. . . . Along with the 5,000,000 would come a horde of radical Communists, agitators and anarchists—the Red offscourings of the country."

Hearst's *Examiner* handled the story similarly. Its front-page headline warned, SINCLAIR SEES "UNEMPLOYED RUSH" TO STATE. The quote was a bit different ("If I am elected about half the unemployed in the whole country will climb aboard freight trains and head for California"), but the message was the same.

When Sinclair saw the newspapers, he realized that he had blundered badly. He knew that his offhand remark (embroidered with an evocative image of hoboes *hopping* the *first* freight train heading west) would be transmitted and reproduced throughout the state and that he would have to deal with the consequences for the rest of the campaign. Another quote occurred to the candidate. He thought it came from Mark Twain and that it went something like this: "A lie can travel halfway around the earth while the truth is putting on its boots."

———

According to a state report just released, poor pregnant women in California who could not afford to give birth to a baby, let alone raise one, were exchanging their newborns for cash to pay their doctor and their hospital bills. Physicians collected the babies and delivered them to adoption bureaus. In one case recently, a woman was paid $170 for her newborn; in another, $200. No one knew the extent of the practice.

This was not the kind of barter King Vidor had in mind when he conceived *Our Daily Bread,* his ode to the cooperative exchange movement. After seven weeks in England and Russia, Vidor returned to Hollywood today to find events outrunning the plot of his new picture—and California politics imperiling its future. Although Vidor was thought to be a Sinclair supporter, it was *Our Daily Bread,* not the views of its creator, that posed a problem for the Republicans. The *EPIC News* had praised the yet-to-be released film for visualizing "the remedial value of cooperative land-colonies" and predicted that it would "show millions how they, too, may help themselves."

If not the most successful director in Hollywood, King Vidor was considered one of the best. The son of a wealthy Texas lumberman, he had come to California in 1915 at the age of twenty-one and shot up the studio ladder, directing his first feature only three years later. *The Big Parade,* the story of how a Joe Anyman faced the world war, made his reputation in 1925, and another MGM film, *The Crowd,* which pictured the sad fate of a nonconformist, sealed it in 1928. Then he made *The Champ.*

A personable, fiercely independent man, Vidor toiled for the studios if they accepted his ideas and stepped outside the system if they did not.

He wanted to use the screen to express hope and faith and to show how every person, whether conscious of it or not, had some upward mission to accomplish. (He was a Christian Scientist.) Vidor envisioned a trilogy, starting with *The Crowd.* He would take the beaten-down protagonists of that pre-Depression picture, John and Mary Sims, put them through the hard times of the 1930s, and save their souls. In 1932, he came across a number of articles, including one by Sinclair Lewis, proposing rural cooperatives as a solution to urban unemployment. Workers, farmers, and professionals could exchange goods and services and find salvation, relying on one another and the bounty of the soil.

Working with his wife and, later, with the brilliant young screenwriter Joseph Mankiewicz, he fashioned a plot. John and Mary, impoverished in the city, inherit a bankrupt farm. Attempting to save it (and themselves), they invite homeless but hardworking people—a carpenter, a plumber, a bookkeeper, and so forth—to help them form a farm cooperative (or what Upton Sinclair would later call a "land colony"). They toil away, overcoming every adversity. Vidor thought his friend Irving Thalberg would jump at it. The MGM producer read the script and said it intrigued him, then reversed course, possibly after consulting with L. B. Mayer. Thalberg explained that this story was simply not appropriate for MGM; other studios turned it down also. Who wanted to watch a movie about unemployed farmers? It might be heroic, but it lacked glamour.

Vidor took the script to Charlie Chaplin, who suggested adding an important episode: a convict surrenders to the authorities so that his comrades at the farm co-op can acquire the reward money they need to survive. Chaplin also convinced United Artists, which he cofounded, to promise to release the picture. Vidor put everything he owned in hock and raised enough money to shoot the picture on an abandoned golf course a few miles from Hollywood. Drawing on life to imitate art, he hired unemployed workers as extras. Vidor had completed the picture this past spring and left for Europe.

Reviews in magazines, anticipating its release, were overwhelmingly positive, but still *Our Daily Bread* stayed in the vault. Finally United Artists, headed by Joseph M. Schenck, announced it would open *Our Daily Bread* in New York on October 3. But Vidor discovered that the studio had *no* plans to release the picture in California, at least until after the election. Like Sam Goldwyn's Tolstoy epic, *We Live Again,* it would sit on the shelf indefinitely.

This being Hollywood, ironies abounded. Vidor was about to start work on his next picture: a film for Sam Goldwyn. And Joe Mankiewicz, who contributed to *Our Daily Bread,* had just agreed to write a radio script lampooning Upton Sinclair.

———

Two of California's leading proponents of self-help cooperatives, Clark Kerr and Dean McHenry, saw eye to eye on nearly everything. Grad-school roommates at Stanford and again at Berkeley, they played hand-ball together, and fell in love with two girls who were also roommates. In May 1934, when Clark Kerr was selected to supervise fieldwork for the state's Self-Help Co-operative division, the first person he hired was Dean McHenry. But the two simply could not agree on Upton Sinclair.

Compared to Clark Kerr, Sinclair was a Johnny-come-lately to the co-op movement. During the first half of 1933, Kerr had visited 160 co-ops across California, conducting research for his master's thesis at Stanford, which he labeled the first study in the field. (Among the co-op leaders he interviewed: Oakland's Hans Rutzebeck.) Kerr, a Quaker economist, pitched right in: he worked the land, fought evictions, and, as he wrote in the thesis, ate "the rancid butter, bacon rinds and liberal seasoning of 'barter meals' in communal kitchens." Kerr asserted that some three hundred thousand people in California, or 6 percent of the population, were associated with what he called "organized barter groups," predominantly in L.A. County. Communists attempted to politicize co-ops, businessmen tried to destroy them, and Upton Sinclair planned to organize them into One Big Co-op. Kerr, on the other hand, wanted the co-ops to become self-sustaining and remain as independent as possible.

Toiling for the state in the summer of '34, Kerr and his pal Dean McHenry got a chance to fund the movement with New Deal money. In East Los Angeles, a pair of unemployed bread makers wanted to start a bakery co-op, so Kerr and McHenry secured some unused ovens, surplus flour, and a few workers. The two field agents supplied a boat and a pickup truck to help establish a fishing co-op in San Pedro. Start-up costs were only a fraction of what the state otherwise would have had to spend on relief. The dozens of co-op units traded their goods with one another via an exchange association.

Upton Sinclair compared the co-op movement to one great river fed by dozens of small streams. Unlike the EPIC plan, co-ops represented guild socialism, not state socialism. That's why Clark Kerr preferred co-ops to EPIC. What impressed Kerr the most about the co-op workers was how much they got out of so little. The bread might have been stale, but productive work made their spirits soar.

Kerr appeared to be in no hurry to obtain his Ph.D. At the end of the summer, when Dean McHenry returned to Berkeley and joined the EPIC drive, Clark had stayed at his co-op post in Los Angeles, with no plans to even vote for Upton Sinclair, whom he considered a "wild man" with impractical ideas.

The first of what promised to be a flood of leaflets, pamphlets, and circulars issued by mysterious organizations appeared on the streets and in mailboxes across the state. United for California, the best funded of the "nonpartisan" groups, would surely take the lead eventually, but Lord & Thomas was still designing its material. Dozens of other groups had already produced some provocative literature. It was a good time to own a printing press in California.

Much of the early campaign propaganda was playful or comic and almost always uncredited. A cartoonist pictured "Uppy and Downey" on a seesaw. There was seemingly no end to the clever wordplay on the acronymn EPIC: Elect Parties Indorsing Communism. Everyone Pinched in California. End Pleasure in California. Every Pauper Is Coming. Endless Publicity I Crave. Empty Promises in California. Endow Poorhouses—Injure Colleges. An anonymous group distributed a full-page sheet, printed in red, with an illustration of Upton Sinclair as Santa Claus presenting THE SEPTIC PLAN. SEPTIC stood for Soak Every Possible Taxpayer in California, and it threatened to "abolish all unpleasantness and to establish complete happiness for every citizen of California. . . ." That meant outlawing cold winters, hot summers, marital difficulties, earthquakes, immoral movies, greed, envy, hate, hangnails, fear, sin, sickness, death, freedom of speech, and freedom of the press.

Another group distributed a card printed with a poem entitled "The Ipecac Plan: Out of the Moscow Medicine Chest," said to be composed by Uproar Inair:

> O the Ipecac Plan is a wonderful plan,
> To cure every illness of beast or of man,
> So turn on the hot air, and start up the fan
> And listen while I tell of my Ipecac Plan. . . .

A takeoff on the *EPIC News* had appeared, a tabloid called the *EBIC Snooze,* selling for five cents in cash or one hundred dollars in scrip. Apparently it was the work of Haight's crowd, for it lampooned the other two candidates yet left young Raymond pretty much untouched. One headline dominated its front page: MILLIONAIRES FIGHT FOR SOCIAL AND ECONOMIC JUSTICE—HOOVER, AL SMITH AND J. PIERPONT MORGAN RALLY TO EPIC BANNER AFTER MCADOO AND CREEL MAKE CLEVER ADJUSTMENTS.

A group calling itself NUTS—the National Union of Technocrats and Socialists—produced a four-page booklet purporting to present the platform of Ulysses Stumpnale, the Pied Piper of California. Among other things, the platform promised free beer on Sundays. "Isn't it perfectly simple to tax the breweries during the weekdays enough so that the Sunday beer will be paid for?" it proposed. "And, if the breweries go broke, the state will take them over—so there you are!"

For most of the past month, Henry W. O'Melveny, founder of Los Angeles's dominant law firm, had been confined to bed with a stomach ailment. Now he was resuming his legal and political activities. He even had a go at his long-neglected flower beds out at his Sunny Slope ranch. Today he planted daffodils.

While convalescing, O'Melveny watched approvingly while colleagues at his law firm plunged into the campaign to stop Sinclair. James L. Beebe, one of the firm's partners, pressured George Creel, whose campaign he managed in southern California, to endorse Merriam. Beebe also helped organize United for California; young Albert Parker, an O'Melveny associate, served as the group's secretary. Like them, H. W. O'Melveny considered himself a solid Democrat.

The O'Melveny firm had countless financial resources and political connections to draw on. It had been a success almost from the moment of its founding in 1885 by Henry O'Melveny and Jackson Graves, mainly representing clients involved in massive real estate transactions and corporate reorganizations. During Hollywood's early days, it was one of the few large law firms that would represent Jewish moguls and flighty movie stars. By 1930, O'Melveny was the "law firm that Hollywood can talk to," according to *Variety.* Studios requested help in restructuring to survive the Depression, and stars like Bing Crosby, Mae West, Shirley Temple, and Jack Benny asked the firm to negotiate their contracts.

The firm, known in 1934 as O'Melveny, Tuller & Myers, operated out of offices in the Title Insurance Building at Fifth and Spring. Henry O'Melveny was wealthy and socially prominent: trustee at Cal Tech, friend of Will Hays's, fishing partner of Winston Churchill's. He tried to stay out of politics, if possible, but followed Upton Sinclair's emergence closely. Back in July he had predicted that Sinclair would win the Democratic primary, "and there will be a slump in California utilities," he wrote in his daily journal. Ever the sagacious businessman, he immediately sold shares in three such companies at a premium.

After Sinclair won the primary and O'Melveny recovered from his illness, Ham Cotton, the Democrats' patronage chief in Los Angeles, approached him for help. Cotton explained that the Merriam forces were in dire need of funds; they had to turn the race around immediately before Sinclair ran away with it. Like O'Melveny, Cotton had little stomach for Frank Merriam, so he had created an organization strictly for anti-Sinclair Democrats. His group's name: American Democracy.

Henry O'Melveny was president of two huge companies, the Dominguez Water Company and the Dominguez Estate Company, and Cotton wanted him to ante up ten thousand dollars from each for his group. O'Melveny thought that was a bit steep and handed over two checks for fifteen hundred dollars each instead. But that was just for starters. California's leading attorney was secretly working on a scheme that would enable corporations to skirt the campaign finance law that prohibited them from contributing directly to a political fund.

"Working and dictating on a plan to enable us to make a legal contribution to the Merriam Campaign—by declaring a dividend and then having the recipients assign to one person, who could make the contribution," O'Melveny wrote in his diary today. That way, the money would come *from* the corporation but could not be easily traced back *to* the corporation. Tomorrow, directors of the Dominguez Estate Company would meet to discuss the plan. Corporations throughout the state, if they wished, could follow suit.

Ham Cotton received additional good news today when Tallant Tubbs quit as Ray Haight's campaign manager to devote his efforts to American Democracy. The *San Francisco Chronicle* called on Haight to abandon the race, charging that he was splitting the anti-Sinclair vote. Haight responded by taking to the airways this evening in a desperate attempt to turn the tide.

Keeping his promise to Sinclair, Haight concentrated his fire on the Republicans. "Every time I have said 'no' to their lucrative offers to get me out of the race," Haight explained, "I have been amazed at their apparent shock upon discovering that I was not interested." He read from a letter in which the president of one of the leading financial institutions in the state called Haight's refusal to cut a deal "just dumb" and evidence of "a bitterness of spirit or a quality of judgment, neither of which does him credit."

Upton Sinclair also went on the radio this evening, to explain that he was only "speaking playfully" when he made the remark about half the unemployed coming to California. The reporters knew what he said, but their editors embellished the quote and put it in the morning papers, accompanied by solemn mathematical calculations. "For the first time in history," Sinclair quipped, "the *Los Angeles Times* is willing to state the number of our unemployed, and even to exaggerate it!"

But Sinclair knew that a single radio address would not undo the damage. Whether he meant the statement literally or not, it sounded like something this candidate might very well believe. It was Sinclairish enough to have the ring of authenticity, and that meant trouble for EPIC and Upton Sinclair.

SEPTEMBER 30

SUNDAY

By now, hundreds of Americans had implored Franklin Roosevelt to repudiate Upton Sinclair, but almost none of them had a chance to sit down and discuss the matter with the President. One exception was Secretary of Labor Frances Perkins. Returning from a recent trip to California, she had warned the President that Sinclair might very well win. EPIC was a fanatical program, she reported, and would ruin the California banking system.

FDR thought a minute. "Well, they might be elected in California," he had finally replied. "Perhaps they'll get EPIC in California. What difference, I ask you, would that make in Dutchess County, New York, or Lincoln County, Maine? The beauty of our state-federal system is that the people can experiment," Roosevelt commented. "If it has fatal consequences in one place, it has little effect upon the rest of the country. If a new, apparently fanatical program works well, it will be copied. If it doesn't, you won't hear of it again."

Obviously the message wasn't getting through to the President, so today Raymond Moley, the man often credited with assembling the original Brain Trust and applying the name New Deal to Roosevelt's vision, decided to put in his two cents.

If Moley couldn't convert the President, who could? As speech writer, adviser, and convener of experts, Moley helped elect Roosevelt governor in 1928 and president four years later. During FDR's first months in office, Moley was considered "the second strongest man in Washington," according to one columnist, but he avoided the press, preferring to remain something of a mystery. "A rather hard-boiled person this Dr. Moley, and about as different from the timid, absent-minded professor type of fiction as could be imagined," George Creel had observed in a magazine profile. "There is a jut to his jaw, a steel-trap effect around the mouth, and behind his glasses are a pair of clear eyes that have the bore of gimlets."

Midway through Roosevelt's first year in Washington, Moley decided to seek other employment. His wealthy friends W. Averell Harriman and Vincent Astor founded a weekly magazine of news and opinion called *Today,* based in New York, with Moley at the helm. The magazine, which frankly supported Roosevelt, proved to be a success, and Moley continued to shuttle to Washington for frequent conferences with FDR. "Moley is still a big force in the New Deal and is growing stronger," John Franklin Carter wrote in his 1934 book, *The New Dealers.* "No one has arisen to take his place as a reliable first aide and trouble-shooter for FDR in the interpretation and execution of policy. . . . His absence explains some of the terrifying lurches and wobblings of Administration policy."

As the year went on, Moley seemed to grow more critical of the New Deal and his former colleagues, such as Rex Tugwell. "I tilt at no windmills," he confessed. He helped craft a series of speeches for Roosevelt that expressed sentiments reassuring to industry. In August, he started hosting what the press called "the Moley dinners," meetings between New Dealers and businessmen aimed at smoothing their differences. One columnist friendly to FDR called the dinners fascist and suggested that the businessmen were planning to install Moley as leader of a reactionary cabal. Roosevelt approved of Moley's activities, however, and this week called on him to craft his fireside chat scheduled for ten o'clock tonight.

Moley took this opportunity to argue strongly that Roosevelt must rebuke Upton Sinclair. He believed that EPIC was dangerous and absurd. Nothing more than social and economic spiritualism, it had little in common with the pragmatic New Deal. Moley was appalled by a recent editorial in *The New Republic* that endorsed Sinclair: whatever the candidate's faults, the magazine observed, EPIC at least would prove "tremendously interesting as a social experiment." Moley was afraid this mirrored the President's own view. It was intellectually dishonest, he argued, to say that an experiment like EPIC must be tried before it could be condemned.

FDR listened carefully to Moley, as always, but appeared unmoved. Roosevelt pointed out that Frank Merriam had just endorsed the Townsend Plan, which was just as farfetched as EPIC. "Besides," FDR commented, exposing the heart of the matter, "they tell me Sinclair's sure to be elected."

Moley wouldn't take no for an answer. He had lost this argument but resolved to renew it in the pages of *Today.*

Louis B. Mayer finally left France today, heading for New York on the liner *Paris.* Before he departed, he told reporters that he was hurrying home to organize the fight of the film industry against Upton Sinclair. "Mayer already has arranged, it was said, the withdrawal of an opposition candidate from the race," one wire service reported, "in order that a unified front may be presented against the former Socialist."

Joe Knowland's plan to pass the mantle of GOP leadership in California to Earl Warren almost came unglued this weekend. Warren's supporters argued, at a meeting of the Republican State Central Committee, that he would attract progressives to the Merriam campaign, support that was now vital. But conservatives were skeptical of this strategy and suspicious of Warren, who had opposed Merriam in the primary, backing a moderate candidate instead. Also, at the age of forty-three, Earl had never managed a state campaign before, let alone a holy war.

Finally the right wing agreed to accept Warren's leadership if he would promise, as one reporter put it, to "provide the punch and leadership of the strenuous campaign being planned for Merriam." Warren said he could. In his keynote speech, Warren also reached out to disaffected Democrats. "It is the duty of Democrats," Warren said, "to vote for the best man available."

A week ago Earl Warren was just another promising young GOP officeholder. Sure, Raymond Moley had labeled him the nation's best district attorney. And yes, he was the most popular politician in

Alameda County, but he was better known in Washington, D.C., than in southern California. Now he was thrust into the limelight as a statewide star.

Warren had ambition to spare. He had already told the state's longtime attorney general, U. S. Webb, that he planned to succeed him, probably in 1938. That's why Warren's pet issue this year, an amendment to the state constitution that he personally maneuvered onto the ballot, caused such political tongue clucking around the state. The amendment called for placing each of the state's scattered law-enforcement agencies under the attorney general's control and also provided for a doubling of salary for the post. "That Warren's making a good job for himself," the political wags observed.

Earl Warren could not have had any illusions about what he was expected to do for Frank Merriam. Warren was the cleanest politician in California, but if he yearned for statewide office, he would have to get down in the muck with the rest of the Republicans.

If the number of clerics in the news was any indication, Los Angeles was experiencing a religious revival. Organized religion, rarely directly involved in California politics, answered the GOP's call to expose Upton Sinclair as a wicked infidel. Many leading clergymen came out for Merriam. "It would be better to endorse the devil than his Socialist candidate," one Methodist minister proclaimed. The local presbytery, representing 110 churches, embraced Merriam and asked for the "prayers of our constituency in this crisis hour in the life of our people."

The *Los Angeles Times* contributed to the religious hysteria, featuring Sinclair's views on the church in its now-famous front-page boxes. This morning's quote from *The Profits of Religion* found Sinclair labeling as hypocrites Methodists, Episcopalians, Baptists, and Unitarians, among others.

Several newly formed church groups sent pamphlets to thousands of homes. The California Democratic Governor's League blared from the cover of its leaflet:

> *SINCLAIR.* DYNAMITER of ALL CHURCHES and ALL CHRISTIAN INSTITUTIONS. ACTIVE OFFICIAL of COMMUNIST ORGANIZATIONS. Communist Writer. Communist Agitator. The Man Who Said the P.T.A. Has Been Taken Over by the *BLACK HAND.*

Flipping open the pamphlet, one could enjoy fourteen excerpts from *The Profits of Religion.* Sinclair had called the church a "sepulchre of corruption" and "the servant and henchman of Big Business." Religion was "a source of income to parasites, and the natural ally of every form of oppression and exploitation." Christianity was "the chief of the enemies of social progress." Evidence of Sinclair's devotion to atheistic communism included his being connected with the ACLU, "an organization to provide funds for and finance the defense of Communist agitators charged with crime."

Lincoln Steffens, still recovering from a heart attack, failed to attend the big Communist party rally in San Francisco, but he sent along a message endorsing his friend Sam Darcy for governor. Communism promised "a scientific cure for all of our troubles," Steffens proclaimed. "We cannot do it as Upton Sinclair proposes. We cannot any of us go out 'as one good man for governor' and do it individually. We must do it as the American Communist Party, taught, fortunately, by the Russian pioneers. . . ."

Perhaps more than anyone, Steffens had a sentimental stake in determining who would live in the governor's mansion in Sacramento: He grew up in that fine Victorian home, which once belonged to his parents. Stef feared that Frank Merriam would reside there for four more years, but this possibility was not entirely bad. By encouraging class warfare, Merriam "works for The Revolution," he informed writer Robert Cantwell, "without any cost to Moscow gold."

This was small consolation for Sam Darcy. If Sam had his way, he wouldn't even be running for office this year. Steffens would be a CP candidate—for the U.S. Senate—and both Sam and Stef would support Upton Sinclair for governor. But Communist party boss Earl Browder would have none of it, and now Darcy was expected to do the party's dirty work against Sinclair.

Sam Darcy, only twenty-nine but a Communist for ten years, headed the CP's District 13, which covered the entire West Coast, Arizona, and Nevada. A Jew born in the Ukraine, Darcy grew up in New York and organized the first mass demonstration of the unemployed in that city in March 1930. While studying at the Lenin Institute, Darcy showed visiting Americans, including Theodore Dreiser and Dorothy Thompson, around Moscow. Summoned to the Grand Hotel, Darcy had found Sinclair Lewis inclined on a couch, a few hits of vodka under his belt.

He wanted Darcy to serve as his eyes and ears in Moscow while he stayed in the room. "I don't want to go rubber-necking around like these goddamn fool tourists," Lewis instructed. "God, this vodka is good! Keeps your hair red. Give me the material, I'll stay here—it's comfortable and the drinks are okay."

When Darcy chose the losing side in an intraparty dispute, Earl Browder exiled him to California. Although it was the CP's stronghold after New York, the party in California was in bad shape—it was down to about fifty active members in San Francisco and perhaps three hundred across the state. Tough-minded but sensible, Darcy turned things around, and in 1933 and 1934 he helped direct union activities in California cotton and lettuce fields, the widest agricultural strikes in the nation's history.

One of Darcy's most memorable encounters occurred during this period. Driving south from San Francisco one day, he experienced car trouble near San Jose. A big black limousine pulled up, and a uniformed chauffeur offered to give him a lift back to San Francisco. Climbing inside, he discovered former president Herbert Hoover sitting in the backseat. Darcy felt paralyzed; for the past year he had violently denounced Hoover across California and was sure the former president would recognize him.

"What do you do?" Hoover inquired.

"I'm a . . . labor organizer," Darcy replied. They spoke in general terms about the problems of workers and the unemployed, and Darcy was surprised to learn that Hoover still didn't feel that the government had a strong responsibility to provide jobs and expand relief.

In the spring of 1934, Darcy witnessed a surge in EPIC strength; he admired Upton Sinclair, whose books once whetted his political appetite. Traditionally the CP attacked groups on the left that did not share its revolutionary tenets, but Darcy favored an alliance with other progressives. Communists and Socialists had just decided to work together in France, and reports from Moscow indicated that the party leadership was considering a radical change in policy. The worldwide threat of fascism was now so great it might require the formation of a united front on the left to guarantee the survival of democracy.

Darcy met with Sinclair aides and proposed a common front. But Sinclair, like a good Socialist, hated Communists and felt any alliance with them would do him more harm than good. Sinclair supported the Soviet government but considered communism "the wrong way—for this country." By resorting to violence, the Communists made the work of all progressives harder. As a civil liberties activist, Sinclair felt it difficult to defend the rights of Communists, who themselves "repudiate freedom of speech" and "do everything they can to deprive others of those rights."

The CP candidate proposed a plan, however, that would allow the two movements to cooperate secretly: The Communists would not run a candidate for governor if EPIC agreed not to nominate anyone for state comptroller or the U.S. Senate. This might enable the CP to pile up a hefty vote in at least one statewide race. When the EPICs responded favorably, Darcy met with his friend Lincoln Steffens in Carmel. Steffens agreed to run for Senate, so long as he didn't have to actually join the CP; he was too much of a "liberal-bourgeois" for *that,* he explained.

But the party leadership vetoed the Darcy plan. Until the Kremlin officially announced a united-front policy, cooperation with heretics like Sinclair was strictly forbidden. And Steffens, in any case, could not run as a CP candidate unless he joined the party. Then, to test Darcy's "discipline," party bosses insisted that *he* run as the CP candidate for governor in California and expose Sinclair as a "social fascist." Darcy protested, but he had little choice but to comply.

Although he denounced Sinclair as a New Dealer in disguise, Darcy's tone was not excessively harsh: he still hoped to tap EPIC's popularity after November 6. And during the summer of 1934, he had more pressing concerns. Working closely with longshoremen leader Harry Bridges, he helped foment San Francisco's general strike. Vigilantes wrecked the CP offices, and Darcy narrowly escaped going to jail.

Sinclair's victory in the August primary split the Communist party in California just as it shook the Socialists. Many Communists joined EPIC, while others happily heckled Sinclair and tossed CP leaflets from the balconies at EPIC rallies. From its headquarters on Grove Street in San Francisco, the party issued its major campaign document, a rather subdued booklet entitled *Sinclair: Will His EPIC Plan Work?* The cover drawing showed Sinclair riding a Democratic donkey backward. Cheap relief, the pamphlet argued, was no substitute for class struggle.

Tame, by Communist standards, this rhetoric was about as far as Sam Darcy was willing to go to appeal for votes. Little did he know that Earl Browder and other CP leaders in New York had closely monitored his conduct of the campaign and found it wanting. If Darcy refused to turn up the heat on Sinclair, they would find someone who would.

Will Rogers, just returned from Europe, took the stage at Radio City Music Hall at nine o'clock for another "Good Gulf" radio show. Will explained that he was so excited about fellow Oklahomans Dizzy and Daffy Dean pitching in the World Series that he had changed his plans, and now would make his way back to California via Detroit, site of the first two games between the Tigers and the St. Louis Cardinals. Will had even arranged to sit in Henry Ford's box at the stadium. Yesterday, Rogers revealed, he had attended a rehearsal of the new play *Jayhawker,* starring his friend Fred Stone. The play, he said, was written by "Mr. Sinclair Lewis . . . not Upton Sinclair! I got to take care of *him* when I get home."

For once, Rogers's show would not draw the biggest listening audience of the night, for President Roosevelt would be coming on in another hour. So Will acted as a kind of warm-up act, offering his own jaundiced opinions about the state of the economy. For starters, he called Radio City "the only big house in the world that ain't got a mortgage on it."

After studying up on the Liberty League and reading Herbert Hoover's new book, Will had decided what FDR should do to get the "old rich boys" off his back. He should invite all those fellows who extolled the value of "rugged individualism" down to the White House, and he should say to them, "Now, you blame your lack of present ruggedness on too much government supervision. Well, I'll take the government right off you. . . . I'm also sending the Brain Trust back to college, and the whole thing goes into the hands of big business. So back to the old days, boys. . . . After one year of rugged individualism if there's not more people rugged than there is unrugged, why then—you lose!"

Given Will Rogers's popularity, it was not improbable that President Roosevelt was listening at home, and not impossible that he would follow Rogers's advice. The nation anxiously awaited this fireside chat. Would FDR ridicule Hoover, the Liberty League, and his other critics and render them superfluous? Would he announce new and bolder reforms? Some were afraid he would swerve to the left, others suspected he was about to move right.

As it happened, the President, in his skillful way, came at least halfway around to Will Rogers's plan, signaling that he was going to give business a fair chance to get rugged. He called for an armistice between capital and labor while the reorganized NRA worked out regulations calculated to safeguard the rights of each. And he declared that the driving power of individual initiative, free enterprise, and the incentive of "fair private profit" remained the keynotes of American life. This was hardly a startling statement, except to those businessmen who were starting to fear they had no rights and could expect no profits under the New Deal.

At the same time, FDR renewed his commitment to the dispossessed and drew a deep distinction between his own philosophy and that of the rugged individualists. "I stand or fall," the President said, "by my refusal to accept as a necessary condition of our future a permanent army of unemployed." Denouncing the definition of liberty under which "a free people were being gradually regimented into the service of the private few," FDR voiced his own broader definition of freedom: "greater security for the average man." He failed to mention production for use, but the President, his aides indicated afterward, would chat with the nation again shortly before the November elections.

MONDAY

Will Hays, the movie czar, lunched with Albert Lasker, the advertising genius, in New York this afternoon. Lasker always enjoyed visiting Hays, and liked to take credit for creating his czardom. It all went back to baseball's Black Sox scandal of 1919. Lasker, a part owner of the Chicago Cubs, helped persuade major-league owners to appoint a baseball czar to clean up the game following its brush with organized gambling. The "czar" concept captured the public's fancy. Hollywood moguls figured that if it worked for one troubled national pastime it might work for the other, and they hired Will Hays to fill the post.

Though his office was in New York, Hays had his finger on the pulse of the political contest in California. His top aide, Charlie Pettijohn, was heading back to New York, having whipped Hollywood's anti-Sinclair forces into shape. Kyle Palmer had started moonlighting for Hays in Los Angeles. Through Lasker, the czar knew what Lord & Thomas was doing to defeat Sinclair, and Hays planned to meet with W. R. Hearst next week in New York. He corresponded with financial writer B. C. Forbes, who would be leaving New York in a few days to cover the California campaign. Hays's brother-in-law, Ted Herron, was traveling with Joe Schenck. His old friend Herbert Hoover had just sent him a copy of his new book. Louis B. Mayer would return to Hollywood in a few days; it was L.B. who had introduced Hays to Frank Merriam in 1932.

It was starting to look as though all roads in the stop-Sinclair movement led to, or at least through, William Harrison Hays.

———

If Herbert Hoover launched *The Challenge to Liberty* to test the climate for a political comeback, he must have felt sorely disappointed by now. The trial balloon was going over like a lead balloon. Critics complained so loudly that Hoover's friend William Allen White had to bury the former president to win sympathy. White told reporters that Hoover's book was nothing but a "posthumous protest." He recalled an old joke about a "darky" who sees a decapitated turtle in the middle of road, still kicking, and exclaims, "Dat old fool don't know he is daid!" Herbert Hoover knows one thing better than any other, White revealed, "and that is that he is for the moment, and maybe forever, politically 'daid.' "

Hoover, in his correspondence, seemed wounded by the attacks on the book, even though he expected the barbs and felt that history would absolve him. He attributed a "smear" in *The New York Times,* for example, to the newspaper's "complex of humiliation" for having "betrayed American institutions" in supporting FDR in 1932. Today he sent an autographed copy of *The Challenge to Liberty* to one of his allies, *Baltimore Sun* columnist Frank Kent, along with a note that revealed how bitter he had become. "For all that you and I, or anyone else, can do," Hoover wrote, "this country is headed for more and worse before it gets better. At least that is as much as history teaches. Incidentally, I presume that the old observation that 'revolution devours its own children' has re-occurred to you. There is perhaps some satisfaction in the assurance and the present evidence that some are being scorched at least."

Upton Sinclair, Hoover happily reported, might be the latest victim of this curse. "Sinclair will probably be beaten, not because of his economic program, but because of his sins against all organized religion," the former president informed Frank Kent. Since Hoover felt victimized by vicious propaganda during the 1932 campaign, he might have sympathized with Sinclair. Instead, he praised the efficacy of smear tactics and urged their employment in the California campaign. (In his letters, Hoover often quoted a remark by one of Lloyd George's opponents in Great Britain: "We destroyed him and his ideas not by assaulting his finely phrased objectives, not by stating our philosophy, but by detailed attack on his methods and his results. It is only these things which can be gotten over to the people.") This strategy had worked for the Democrats two years ago, Hoover felt, and it damn well better work against Upton Sinclair.

One of the kindest reviews of Hoover's book appeared this week in the *Saturday Review of Literature.* Allan Nevins didn't exactly approve of it ("an appeal to old standards, old aims, and old traditions"), but at least he considered it an "able" expression of the conservative viewpoint. Appearing with the Nevins review was a timely nine-stanza poem by Robert Frost, "Two Tramps in Mud-Time":

> Out of the mud two strangers came
> And caught me splitting wood in the yard.
> And one of them put me off my aim
> By hailing cheerily "Hit them hard!"
> I knew pretty well why he dropped behind
> And let the other go on a way.
> I knew pretty well what he had in mind:
> He wanted to take my job for pay.
>
> . . . .
>
> Nothing on either side was said.
> They knew they had but to stay their stay
> And all their logic would fill my head:
> As that I had no right to play
> With what was another man's work for gain.
> My right might be love but theirs was need.
> And where the two exist in twain
> Theirs was the better right—agreed.

H. L. Mencken contributed to the same issue an appraisal of the latest trend in fiction, "proletarian literature." Mourning the days when *The Masses* at least exhibited a sense of humor, Mencken termed the new generation of radical novelists "amateurish and preposterous, and in large part downright idiotic," mercifully failing to mention any names. He suggested that the radical writers were only in it for themselves, not for the benefit of the proletariat; that some had taken Anglo-Saxon names to disguise their Jewishness, and that many of the novels read poorly because their English "seems to be a bad translation from the Yiddish. . . ."

These propagandists were so dull they made Mencken yearn for Upton Sinclair. "There have been world-savers who had their say in very pretty terms, and some survive to this day," Mencken commented. "I need point only to Upton Sinclair. The facts he relies on so confidently are often mingled with fancy, and his arguments are seldom models of logic, but he at least knows how to snuffle and gargle words, and sometimes he is also amusing, although usually only unconsciously."

One radical novelist who transcended Mencken's critique was about to leave Hollywood and join Hemingway in Cuba, and he wanted to confer with Upton Sinclair before he left. John Dos Passos, the celebrated author of *Manhattan Transfer, The 42nd Parallel,* and *1919,* supported EPIC but due to illness had been unable to take part in the campaign or visit Upton personally.

Like Dorothy Parker and many another leftist social critics, Dos Passos could not resist Hollywood's call. Dos, as he was known, had left New York in July for a lucrative stint with Paramount, ostensibly to write a script for a Josef von Sternberg–Marlene Dietrich collaboration. Upon arrival, Dos Passos informed Hemingway that he had decided to restore his finances and take a look "at the world's great bullshit center . . . it's all very educational I suppose. . . . People you meet out here greet you with a nasty leer like the damned in Dante's inferno."

Three weeks later he wrote Hem again: "What I did the minute I got out to this dump was put on a small bout with the old rheumatic fever. . . . I've been writing my story for Mr. Von Sternberg all the time so its been a fairly profitable little illness—but never again. This place is funny to see, but it's no place for yrs truly. . . ." He told another friend that he was struck by the local citizens' capacity for self-destruction "by cap pistol, codeine, old dueling swords, drownings, castage out of windows and off bridges. . . . Like the New York literati, everybody is on the make and everything is part of something else. . . ."

Francis Faragoh, cofounder of the New Playwrights group in New York, let Dos Passos recuperate at his home on North Orange Grove Avenue in Hollywood. From there, the novelist informed Edmund Wilson that Upton Sinclair was about to win the Democratic primary, and though the "comrades" opposed him, Dos Passos found Uppie to be "damn shrewd. . . . I don't suppose he will be elected, or that even if he was he would be able to establish his double standard society. However it must be handed to him that he has been the first radical to recognize the political importance of the double standard. . . ."

At night, Faragoh and his screenwriter friends would play poker at Dos Passos's bedside, and Dos was amused to learn that the winners tithed a share of the pot to the Communist party. Weeks passed, and little changed. Still bedridden, Dos read Thorstein Veblen and listened to Upton Sinclair and Aimee McPherson on the radio. "California's a great place now," he informed Malcolm Cowley, literary editor of *The New Republic.* "You can look out the window and watch the profit system crumble." He wrote the young novelist Robert Cantwell:

> Frankly I dont see all this fatalism about fascism on the part of the communists. If you mean repressive violence, sure, we've always had that tougher than anywhere; if you mean Hearstian demagoguery, sure—Hearst is handsome Adolph's schoolteacher—but fascism organized into the state I cant see—I dont think its in the breed—I think you've got to have the feudal pattern in the social heritage to make it stick—and that's one thing we haven't got. What turns out is Al Capone—Bilbo—Huey Long—Upton Sinclair—Franklin D, the noblest Roman of them all. . . . Try to fit that group together into a fascist state. I dont mean that the monopolies aren't going to run us, but I think there's more life in the debris of democracy than the comrades do. . . .

A few days later, Dos Passos again wrote Edmund Wilson, complaining that he had learned that while he was laboring over his film script, another young man was writing the actual screenplay for *The Devil Is a Woman* behind the scenes! And so Dos Passos and von Sternberg had parted company. "I'm darn sorry I wasn't able to stagger round the studios some more," Dos Passos admitted. "It was interesting there though the horrid stalking of intangibles makes it more nerve-wracking, I imagine, than the average industrial plant."

Before leaving to visit Hemingway in Havana, Dos Passos scribbled a note to his colleague Upton Sinclair. The two writers—one not quite Communist, the other no longer Socialist—admired each other's work. Back in 1927, Dos Passos had staged Sinclair's play about the Wobblies, *Singing Jailbirds,* for the New Playwrights. They had both championed Sacco and Vanzetti (and Dos got arrested in Boston for his troubles).

Dos Passos's innovative novels, harshly critical of American society, electrified left-leaning intellectuals in the early 1930s; Jean-Paul Sartre considered him the greatest writer of his time. Yet Dos Passos called himself "a middle-class liberal, whether I like it or not," and a "camp-follower of radical politics."

Stern-looking but always amiable, Dos Passos challenged the Left to "Americanize Marx," so naturally he appreciated EPIC. Writing to Upton Sinclair today, he explained that he was hesitant even to propose a meeting because of the current demands on the candidate's time, "particularly as I have nothing particularly useful to say." Dos Passos revealed that he wanted to visit Uppie because he would "like to see how a man looks who has given up his typewriter for the microphone." Just give a shout, Dos Passos instructed, and he would hop in a car and drive out to Pasadena. "In any case," he confessed, "let me say, that I am one of those radicals who would rather see you win than lose and that I think your EPIC plan put into effect would be a much more valuable step towards socialism than its defeat and the satisfaction of the I-told-you-soers and theoretical wiseacres."

Was nothing sacred? The *Los Angeles Times* reportedly planned to convert the phenomenally popular film short *The Three Little Pigs* into a political cartoon, starring Communism as the Big Bad Wolf, Upton Sinclair as the pig who made his house out of straw, and Frank Merriam as the pig who used bricks—until the Disney studio caught wind of it and asked the newspaper to desist. Walt Disney, rumored to be planning his first full-length animated picture, *Snow White and the Fairies,* was as reactionary as anyone in California, but he wanted to keep his copyrighted stars out of politics.

Perhaps to make up for this loss, the *Times* unveiled its own cartoon feature this morning, apparently intending to run it daily right through Election Day. The four-panel comic strip, drawn by political cartoonist Bruce Russell and entitled "Wynndebagge, the IPECAC Candidate," appeared on the front page of the newspaper's second section, and starred a goofy-looking Sinclair as a government pharmacist. Today a tramp came in seeking a cure for what ailed him, and the druggist replied, "A little IPECAC ought to fix you up."

The press was still bashing Sinclair for inviting a bums' rush to California. The *Los Angeles Examiner* reported that a "jobless flow" was already streaming into California. The *San Francisco Chronicle,* responding to Sinclair's claim that his now-famous remark was meant playfully, accused the candidate of "jesting about human misery."

Working largely through the newspapers, the GOP had managed to halt EPIC's momentum. The hysterical Red-baiting and the airing of Sinclair's dirty laundry had hurt him badly, but it could only go so far—that is, hardening the position of those least likely to vote for EPIC in the first place. How could the Merriamites swing the truly undecided voters to their side?

Hollywood's threat to emigrate had fallen flat, but as a tactic it showed infinite promise. The idea was to split the state into the haves and the have-nots: anyone who had a job and wanted to keep it should momentarily ignore those less fortunate and look out for number one. That's why Sinclair's quote about the unemployed flocking to California was so provocative. Now it was time for businessmen and financiers to sound the same alarm, striking fear into the hearts of jobholders and property owners throughout the state.

Major companies notified stockholders that Sinclairism imperiled their investments. The Chrysler Corporation put expansion of its plant in Los Angeles on hold pending the results of the election. If Sinclair won, a Chrysler general manager declared, "we will begin at once to cut down in our operations in this state. . . . If California citizens realized the reaction of eastern business executives to the threat of Socialism, or worse, seizing the California state government, there would be widespread alarm over the consequences that must follow."

Financial houses in the state obliged with statistics showing that California stocks were down as much as 12 percent since the primary, and state and local bonds had supposedly dropped fifty million dollars in value. Holdings in Pacific Gas & Electric were off 9 percent and Southern California Edison 8 percent. "In other words," one analyst said, "capital is getting out of the bonds of the State and cities of California and investing elsewhere." Sinclair's call for an influx of the unemployed "spells keener competition for jobs with resultant lower wages and spread of destitution," the analyst continued, while the flight of capital indicated that there would be less wealth to pay the huge taxes Sinclair demanded.

Commerce and industry "will move out of California with all possible celerity," reported Blyth and Company, the West Coast's premier brokerage house, "and into places where the tax burden will not be confiscatory." One state already vying for California's business: nearby Nevada. Trade and banking officials in Nevada had coined a takeoff on

EPIC—Every Possible Inducement Claimed—as their slogan. Among other things, they promised to kill any attempt to levy a state income tax or inheritance tax.

The business press carried frightening news across the country. *The Wall Street Journal* ticked off EPIC's affronts to business: a state income tax on corporations, increased inheritance taxes, special taxes on large land holdings, "a large-scale effort at redistribution of wealth along socialistic lines." It was the business view in California, therefore, that the coming election "involves something so closely akin to economic and social revolution as hardly to be distinguishable from it, and that so far as constitutional and profit system beliefs are concerned, there can be but one choice."

Anti-Sinclair warnings grew so intense, *The New York Times* observed this week, that one of the Merriam camp's chief worries was that it would "overreach itself" and play into Sinclair's hands "by giving him the opportunity to charge that an enormous slush fund is being used against him."

———

Attempting to find out how well the intimidation tactics were working, Hjalmar Rutzebeck, in his role as Upton Sinclair's chief undercover operative, once again visited the San Francisco office of the American Smelting and Refining Company. "They came around and told us that if we voted for Sinclair we would lose our job," one of the young clerks informed him, "but I am going to vote for him and see if I lose my job! I am going to vote for Upton Sinclair and so is my whole family and so are many working here." Another employee echoed this assertion.

Rutzebeck's counterintelligence network was now working overtime. He had just received from a man close to Arthur Samish a long list of Bay area residents who purportedly had donated one hundred dollars or more to the Merriam campaign. (They did it off the books, of course, through Samish.) It was practically a Who's Who of northern California: Herbert Fleishhacker, William H. Crocker, Leland Cutler, Louis Ghirardelli, Francis V. Keesling, Clarence Lindner, San Francisco mayor Angelo Rossi, Chester Rowell, Matt Sullivan, Sam McKee, Clem Whitaker. Apparently, Crocker and Fleishhacker had each handed over five thousand dollars or more. Louis R. Lurie, a local realtor and financier who reputedly "owned" Merriam's running mate, George Hatfield, had chipped in fifteen grand.

Two of Rutzebeck's operatives alerted him to keep an eye on a couple of other problems. First, rumor had it that Ray Haight was ready to withdraw from the race, waiting only for a suitable excuse to do so. Second, the religious issue was going to be pressed sotto voce with increasing energy. Prominent Catholics, they reported, were pressuring Father Coughlin's bishop in Detroit to prevent the radio priest from speaking favorably of Upton Sinclair.

OCTOBER 2

TUESDAY

"A German town on Hitler day couldn't be any nuttier than Detroit," Will Rogers observed, after a quick look around. "There is only two sane, quiet, well-mannered people in the whole city today and they are visitors from Oklahoma, Jerome and Paul Dean. . . . Jealousy and not facts nicknamed them 'Dizzy' and 'Daffy.' "

Who but Will Rogers could hobnob with the brothers Dean and Henry Ford in the same day? The automobile magnate, a Tigers fan, had paid one hundred thousand dollars for the broadcast rights to the World Series, which would open tomorrow afternoon in the Motor City. Will thought Henry was daffier than the Deans for spending money like that when other rich men were buying Canadian and English bonds. "He must be plum dizzy," Rogers observed, "for he believes the country is improving and that if he had to vote tomorrow he would vote for Roosevelt." Ford told Rogers that he hadn't heard a single constructive plan from anyone else.

EPIC wasn't likely to be Henry Ford's cup of tea, and Upton Sinclair had already flubbed his chance with the great industrialist. Ford once wintered in Altadena, a few miles from Pasadena. One day in 1919, Sinclair managed to wangle an invitation to Henry's estate. Like Sinclair, Ford fancied himself an economist, a sociologist, and an expert on national policy, so they got on famously. Sinclair introduced Ford to one of his friends, King Gillette, but the Razor King failed to convert the Flivver King to socialism. One day Uppie and Henry went for a walk in the Pasadena hills. Sinclair told Ford he should start a magazine to cover topics such as production for use and self-help cooperatives. Ford said that sounded splendid. Then he went home and founded the *Dearborn Independent,* one of the most reactionary publications in America.

When Roosevelt took office, Henry Ford, independent and anti-union, refused to adopt the NRA codes. All of the other auto companies went along with FDR, prompting Ford to observe that his competitors were in league with "the bankers' international and they are running all the governments in the world." Ford didn't let the Depression get him down. When someone asked what should be done for the homeless waifs who rode the boxcars looking for work, Ford replied, "Why, it's the best education in the world for those boys, that traveling around. They get more experience in a few months than they would in years at school."

Now Henry Ford was spending millions on new auto plants, Will Rogers reported, and didn't seem to fear the future in the slightest. "What a relief," Rogers commented, "to meet the richest man in the world and him not worried. Well, I will take that back. I think these two Dean boys have got him worried."

Ray Moley resumed his argument with FDR over Upton Sinclair in the pages of his magazine, *Today.* In an article called "Looking Backward with Mr. Sinclair," published this morning, Moley compared Sinclair to Rousseau, another prophet who was an exponent of "reaction, carried to its extreme limit." Sinclair had sounded the retreat in California, back to a preindustrial structure, "back to barter, back to nature." Responding to those who said EPIC should at least be tried out, Moley described the tragic consequences of entrusting government power to an incompetent technician.

> To want to see a scrambled hodge-podge of proposals, some sound and some absurd, tried out under the leadership of a man with no experience in practical administration, is to confess the failure of whatever has been done in centuries of slow development of political institutions in the United States and abroad.

These words, emanating from FDR's speech writer, were sure to do Sinclair damage, if not in the White House, then up and down the coast of California.

It was a bad day all around for Upton Sinclair at the corner newsstand. *Variety,* addressing a Hollywood colony of one hundred thousand voters, attacked the candidate today in an editorial entitled "Payday vs. Paradise." Studio talk of moving east represented "rank stupidity," *Variety* confessed, but the collapse of the movie industry was a distinct possibility if Sinclair established an EPIC Pictures Corporation. And now Sinclair had invited "millions of boomers, bums and will nots" to the state. Every Sinclair "mendicant" was a threat to jobs in Hollywood.

The Hollywood rank and file seemed to embrace EPIC, however, not flee in fear. The annual convention of labor unions representing projectionists, stagehands, musicians, and unionized crafts at the studios voted 498 to 2 to endorse the EPIC candidate. Sinclair also had Hollywood actors and actresses on his side, columnist Sidney Skolsky reported today: they hoped that if Sinclair won, the hated Harry Cohn would make good on his promise to leave town.

Although the Hollywood campaign against Sinclair had fared poorly so far, the moguls might have a trick or two up their sleeves, Hans Rutzebeck warned today in his latest memo to EPIC headquarters. One of the best-known studios planned to film a couple of short subjects "ridiculing Sinclair and his plan in an unmistakable way" as well as conduct interviews for newsreels for release during the last weeks of the campaign.

Billy Wilder didn't like this political campaign one bit. He barely understood English, and what he knew about American politics could be described in one word: Roosevelt. The studio bosses at Fox wanted the writers to support someone named Frank Merriam for governor, but having witnessed firsthand the rise of Adolf Hitler, a true menace, Billy couldn't take seriously the Red scare raised against Upton Sinclair. It didn't matter anyway. Billy, not yet an American citizen, wasn't eligible to vote. He just wanted to be left alone and not let politics imperil his visa status.

Born in Austria in 1906, Samuel Wilder was nicknamed Billy by his mother, who liked the American ring of it. As a young journalist, Billy specialized in personality interviews (Richard Strauss was one of his subjects) and crime reporting. By the mid-1920s, he was writing scenarios for silent films, and between 1929 and 1933 he wrote scripts for German talkies, mainly lighthearted tales rife with mistaken identity. But after reading *Mein Kampf* and hearing Hitler over the radio, Wilder decided to abandon the good life in Berlin. Some of his friends were afraid to flee to a country where they didn't speak the language, so they ended up in Vienna or Prague, which Billy thought was rather shortsighted; he left for Paris shortly after the Reichstag fire.

In 1933, he directed his first feature film, *Mauvaise Graine,* starring sixteen-year-old Danielle Darrieux. But Billy didn't like directing. He wanted to write, he wanted to get far away from Hitler, and he wanted to make it in Hollywood, so he sent one of his scripts to his old friend Joe May at Columbia Pictures. The studio promptly invited Wilder to Hollywood. Billy set sail in January 1934, virtually penniless and desperate to learn English. All he knew were American song lyrics. Crossing the Atlantic, he read phrase books and novels, and danced with the ladies so he could try out his English.

In New York, he boarded a train west, which shuttled him across the fabled American landscape and through Chicago, Kansas City, Santa Fe, and Albuquerque. Joe May met him at the station in L.A. and took him out to the Columbia lot off Gower Street. Sam Briskin, Harry Cohn's top gun, introduced Billy to his office in the writers' quarters, a set of bungalows fronting a courtyard. Wilder sat down at his typewriter, but words failed him: he simply didn't know enough English to get started. To remedy this, he started listening to the radio twelve hours a day. He picked up vernacular from listening to soap operas and baseball games. The other writers—James M. Cain, Dore Schary, Robert Riskin—took the cherubic-looking Austrian under their wing.

Wilder's work did not go well. In August 1934, his six-month deal with Columbia expired, as did his visitor's visa. Billy deeply wanted to be an American, so he went to Mexicali to get an immigration visa. The man at the immigration office asked what he did for a living. Billy said, "I write movies." The official advised, "Write some good ones."

Billy got the visa, but he couldn't get a job. The studios rejected one script after another. His agent didn't return his calls. When his name popped up in the trade papers, it was sometimes spelled Billie. He was living in a tiny room at the Chateau Marmont on Sunset Boulevard; some days all he could afford to eat was a can of soup cooked on his hot plate. One night, to win an eighty-dollar bet, Billy jumped into a swimming pool fully clothed. Desperate, he accepted grisly rewrite assignments.

The one he was working on currently, at $250 a week, was one of the worst, a Raoul Walsh film for Fox entitled *East River,* starring Victor McLaglen. It was the story of two sandhogs who help build the Brooklyn-Battery Tunnel in New York. Billy didn't understand America yet, but he knew enough to know the plot was moronic; with any luck, his name wouldn't appear on the credits. The joke around Hollywood was that workers at Fox were singing, "*East River,* stay away from my door. . . ."

The Fox studio was aflame with political passion. Winfield Sheehan, the head of the studio, let everyone know he backed Merriam and expected them to tag along. Billy thought the scare campaign against Sinclair was silly. When he was growing up in Vienna, Upton Sinclair was, along with Bret Harte and Mark Twain, the most popular American author. He had read some of Sinclair's books himself. Billy let the Socialist rhetoric roll off his back, but Sinclair, he felt, left him with something far more important: a gritty view of America he couldn't get from F. Scott Fitzgerald. Now, in serving as a lightning rod for what Billy considered "Hitler-like" tactics in California, Upton Sinclair was revealing something else about America.

In his latest intelligence briefing, Hans Rutzebeck informed EPIC headquarters that an undercover operative had uncovered a Merriam plot to tie Sinclair to the Tom Mooney and Sacco-Vanzetti bomb blasts as an accessory to the killings. "They are diligently searching for a plausible fancy that can be dressed up to look like a fact," Hans explained.

Now the candidate received a similar warning from another old friend: Tom Mooney himself. From his document-cluttered prison cell at San Quentin, Mooney had sent a neatly typed message alerting Sinclair to dirty tricks ahead. The "powers of Mammon," he warned, might even resort to assassination. "And don't for one minute think that they would not do just that," Mooney advised. "They would kill a hundred people to accomplish that one thing."

This wasn't exactly a bolt from the blue. Sinclair had sounded the same alarm a few weeks back in a morbid little booklet entitled *Upton Sinclair's Last Will and Testament.* He drew up his *Last Will* after several threats, perhaps apocryphal, arrived at EPIC headquarters. A man who worked for a detective agency had sent word that the opposition had decided "if necessary, to employ a little German frightfulness"; a leading banker supposedly told a Sinclair supporter, "Don't fool yourself, we are not going to let any goddamned Communist become Governor of California."

Many of Sinclair's advisers urged him to stick close to home or hire some bodyguards. But he liked to sit in the sun, or do his thinking while going for a walk; the weather was the reason he came to California in the first place. And anyway, if someone wanted to pull up next to his car "and pour a stream of machine-gun bullets into it," as he put it, what could he do? Instead of hiding out, he published his *Last Will* to put his enemies on notice that his death would only intensify the EPIC struggle. "You can kill me any day or night that you desire," Sinclair instructed. "I am sitting on my front porch every morning from six o'clock on. Every afternoon I walk to the post office to get my mail." But if he perished, "you will find you have not killed our movement to End Poverty in California . . . The death of Upton Sinclair will steel their resolve. . . . My death would provide them a martyr, a slogan, an advertisement."

Some of Uppie's friends called the booklet dangerously indiscreet and urged him to withdraw it—he was practically inviting every nut with a gun to come after him. Repeated references to being "frail" gave the impression that if the assassins didn't get him, natural causes would. Even Tom Mooney, in his latest note, admitted that far more likely than assassination was a "rash and murderous" act by an agent provocateur that EPIC or perhaps Sinclair himself would be blamed for. It might occur just before Election Day, leaving Sinclair no time to respond. Remember the Reichstag fire, Mooney advised, before closing with this prayer: "Here's hoping for your victory and mine—freedom from this living tomb."

Sophisticated political polling had not yet reached California from the East, so the candidates and the press could only speculate about the outcome of the gubernatorial race. Haight and Merriam commissioned unscientific straw polls. The KNX poll, which last week gave Sinclair a two-to-one edge, was suspect because it was little more than a call-in survey (and EPIC had purchased more radio time on this station than on any other). A seeress from London arrived in Los Angeles today, predicting that the Cardinals would capture the World Series, Hauptmann would be convicted, and Sinclair would win the election.

Big-time gamblers were the only political prognosticators whose opinion could be trusted. They knew their stuff, for they had as much invested in the results of a California election as any politician. In fact, they were organized much like old-style political machines. They had their own ward heelers and precinct organizations, so when they took a survey they knew whom they were talking to and how much weight to ascribe to every finding. According to today's *Variety,* the "gamboleers" had so much riding on the governor's race that they had just hired one hundred young men, most of them out-of-work college graduates, to canvass house to house.

So it was major news across the state today when the state-sanctioned gambling salons in Los Angeles and San Francisco released their first official projections: Raymond Haight was out of the running, but the contest between Sinclair and Merriam was dead even.

OCTOBER 3

WEDNESDAY

Louis B. Mayer arrived in New York today, declaring that he was anxious to get out to California and find out "what all the excitement is about." He knew enough already, however, to suggest that Sinclair's election might drive the movie studios not only out of California but out of the country. England might welcome the moguls with open arms. "There isn't a meeting of Parliament that does not consider ways and means of getting the movies over there," Mayer disclosed. "New York, of course, is the logical place."

Europe was mocking California, Mayer revealed, but "it is too serious for me to laugh about. I'm going home to find out all about it." No matter what he found, he would never join ranks with Upton Sinclair, but would "take a licking if necessary to stand by my principles."

"Well, Jefty, you're putting on weight," Franklin Roosevelt told the comptroller of the currency, James Francis Thaddeus O'Connor, when they met this morning in the President's office at the White House.

"Maybe you should work me harder," O'Connor replied. Actually the President was thinking of giving O'Connor a rest—from Washington. O'Connor had been feuding with his boss, Henry Morgenthau, for months, and FDR wanted to find a new job for him out in California, his home state.

O'Connor, a native of North Dakota with a law degree from Yale, was one of Roosevelt's pets. He had managed FDR's campaign in southern California in 1932, earning his high-level position in the process. Now FDR offered to appoint him chief of the Federal Reserve in San Francisco. "The salary is pretty good," FDR pointed out. This would also put O'Connor in line to run the Democratic party in California on FDR's behalf. He said he would think about it.

The talk, naturally, turned to politics out West. Roosevelt confided that Upton Sinclair had made a favorable impression on him at Hyde Park. Now he'd learned that the third fellow in the race—O'Connor supplied the name, Ray Haight—had informed Sinclair that he was going to take a poll, and if it showed that he was drawing more votes from Democrats than Republicans, he would withdraw. So Sinclair looked like a sure winner.

O'Connor expressed a few qualms. What he wanted to know directly from Sinclair was, first, whether he would go along with the President on every issue "without question" and abide by all of FDR's decisions, and second, would he promise to appoint a U.S. senator acceptable to the President if a vacancy occurred during his term as governor? (In other words, if McAdoo died, would Sinclair select someone like Jefty O'Connor to replace him?)

"We don't want either extreme," FDR responded, "a reactionary or any extreme radical in the Senate."

Jim Farley, just back from a tour of the Midwest, also met the President today. He informed FDR that on November 6 Democrats would sweep every western state except Kansas. In New York, where Farley continued to serve as state Democratic chairman—and FDR still enjoyed calling the political shots—Governor Lehman would likely crush Robert Moses, the Republican candidate. Afterward, Farley relayed to Senator McAdoo the clearest indication yet of the President's actual wishes regarding Upton Sinclair. Farley's instructions to McAdoo could not have been more precise:

> Frankly, Mac, we want to see Sinclair elected because he won the nomination and is the Party nominee. I know the President feels the same way because, otherwise, of course, it would mean a Republican victory. Sinclair's victory will help to break the Republican organiza-

tion in California which of course will help us in '36. I don't want to be quoted on the above, but I know you will be guided by our attitude.

Had Upton Sinclair seen this letter, he probably would have sat right down and started writing his inaugural address.

FDR was happy to learn from Joe Kennedy that William Randolph Hearst, recently returned from Germany, would pay him a visit on Monday. Roosevelt sent Hearst a note inviting him to spend the night at the White House.

Hearst's friend Dr. Hanfstaengl made the front page of *The New York Times* this morning in a way that could not have pleased either W.R. or FDR. Hanfstaengl, class of '07, had confided to Harvard president James B. Conant that his years at the school had given him "incalculable advantages, not the least of which consist in a knowledge of America and the world and in the spirit of discipline and fair play inculcated on the sporting field of Harvard." He offered to endow the Dr. Hanfstaengl Scholarship, which would enable an outstanding Harvard student to study in Germany. President Conant had informed him, however, that the Harvard Corporation could not accept a gift from one so closely associated with Nazi leaders, who had inflicted so much damage on academic freedom in Germany.

This morning he had breakfast with Will Rogers and Damon Runyon. This afternoon Dizzy Dean, a thirty-game winner during the regular season, pitched the Cardinals to an eight-to-three shellacking of the Tigers in the opening game of the World Series before forty-three thousand startled fans in Detroit. Ducky Medwick contributed four hits, including a home run. Will Rogers reported that Henry Ford, a Tigers fan, felt he got *his* money's worth, so "certainly nobody else has a squawk."

The so-called American Tragedy murder trial in Wilkes-Barre resumed with a parade of prosecution witnesses. Evidence indicated that Robert Allen Edwards, a young man with a jutting chin, deep-set eyes, and jet-black hair, would have a hard time beating this rap. The state accused Edwards, who came from a coal-mining family, of blackjacking his childhood sweetheart and leaving her to drown in Harvey's Lake a few days after learning from a doctor that she was carrying his child. The prosecution's thesis: Edwards wished to get rid of the girl so he might marry Margaret Crain, a pretty music teacher a step up the social ladder.

This murder case was so similar to Theodore Dreiser's 1925 masterpiece, *An American Tragedy,* that *The New York Times* had declared, "Only the locale and the personalities have changed." Dreiser's book, based on a true story, depicted a lower-class youth who plots to drown his pregnant girlfriend in an upstate New York lake so he might wed a more wealthy girl. Sergei Eisenstein once wrote a scenario for a Hollywood film based on Dreiser's book but was discouraged from going forward with it when a studio hack described the plot as "the story about the guy who got hot nuts, screwed a girl and drowned her."

Naturally Dreiser was drawn to the Wilkes-Barre trial. For some reason, *The Washington Post* used this as an opportunity for a personal attack on the left-wing writer. "Life may occasionally be said to imitate art," the *Post* declared in an editorial, "but to say that it imitates Mr. Dreiser is a good deal too easy on the author and far, far too hard on life."

Today, during testimony concerning the slain girl's supposedly happy homelife, Judge W. A. Valentine admonished one of the spectators for breaking into a smile. "Mr. Dreiser," said the judge, "I cannot tolerate this facial expression in the presence of the jury. You will have to refrain." The famous novelist remained poker-faced for the rest of the day. Friends later explained that the expression to which the judge had objected was a natural and characteristic one. Dreiserian, one might say.

Every morning when he got up and saw another Sinclair excerpt on the front page of the *Los Angeles Times,* Jerry Voorhis died a little. The schoolmaster from San Dimas, one of the most notable defectors from the Socialist party in this election and now an EPIC candidate for the state assembly, feared that these boxed quotes hurt Upton Sinclair's chances more than any other factor. Day after day dreadful views arrived on hundreds of thousands of doorsteps. Sinclair on the American Legion: "They would like to take your schools and make 100,000 little West Points." Sinclair on Christianity: "shield and arrow of predatory economic might." Sinclair on violence: "We are moving toward a new American revolution." Sinclair on wedded bliss: "The sanctity of marriage . . . I have had such a belief. . . . I have it no longer." Sinclair on San Francisco: "A city without order, dignity or charm, whose standards of truth are those of a horse trader."

Sinclair belatedly recognized the damage himself. When the boxes first appeared, his friends congratulated him: the excerpts provided the most illuminating and radical commentary ever to appear in the *Times.* But after a few days of laughs, Sinclair realized that they imperiled his candidacy. "It is impossible that the voters will elect a man who has written *that*!" Sinclair exclaimed after spotting a particularly outrageous quote. He likened the *Times* editors to chemists releasing poisons into the air.

Admittedly, he had written and even believed *some* of the things they quoted. But in many other instances, the *Times* dropped the opening or closing words of the excerpt, twisting its meaning. Devoid of context, the barbs appeared to be the product of a deranged mind. Often the quoted words came from dialogue in one of Sinclair's novels; the *Times* deftly used this prodigious storyteller's own fictional characters against him. Last night, at a campaign appearance in Los Angeles, Sinclair compared this practice with seizing a quote by Lady Macbeth ("A little water will wash that out") and putting it in a box entitled SHAKESPEARE JUSTIFIES MURDER.

Gift for irony intact, Sinclair wondered aloud why the *Times* had not yet carried an excerpt from his exposé of American journalism, *The Brass Check.* One box he wouldn't object to seeing in the *Times,* he said, would be this one:

SINCLAIR ON THE "TIMES"

> This paper, founded by Harrison Gray Otis, one of the most corrupt and most violent old men that ever appeared in American public life, has continued for thirty years to rave at every conceivable social reform, with complete disregard for truth, and with abusiveness which seems almost insane.

The *Times* showed that in the heat of the campaign it, too, retained its sense of humor. Yesterday, referring to the *Times*'s editors, Sinclair had said, "I don't know what there is left for them to bring up, unless it is the nationalizing of women." This morning a *Times* box carried a quote from Sinclair's *The Industrial Republic* on cooperative child care and headed it SINCLAIR ON NATIONALIZING CHILDREN.

It was against Upton Sinclair's nature to respond to personal attacks. He liked to rake muck, not throw it. It was becoming apparent, however, that if he wanted to win in November, he would have to return fire whenever possible—and protect his flank. Informed that Father Coughlin might be under pressure to repudiate EPIC, Sinclair reminded the radio priest of his pledge to deliver a broadcast endorsing production for use. "We want to co-operate with you and get that broadcast into California," he wrote. The candidate urged EPICs to write similar letters, but Sinclair knew this effort would be wasted if one of Coughlin's prominent Catholic friends, such as Jim Farley or Joe Kennedy, argued otherwise.

Taking time out from campaigning, Sinclair finally responded to the recent letter from his son, David. He considered the reply so private that he typed the two-page letter himself instead of dictating it.

"I don't appreciate your telling me that I am lying for votes," Sinclair wrote, "and I am afraid we will just have to stop discussing politics if that is your attitude." (Sinclair often made this threat but never abided by it for long.) He charged that David relied too much on *The New York Times* for his information. Contrary to what that newspaper said, his Democratic platform contained all of the essential provisions of the EPIC plan. "*We* are the Democratic party," Uppie asserted, "and the Democrats are coming along as meek as lambs . . . you don't need to believe the capitalist newspapers in preference to your father."

Responding to another charge, Sinclair claimed that he wasn't joking when he said he believed in God. Whether David knew it or not, his father "always believed in a creative intelligence in this universe, which comprises all other intelligences and all other personalities. . . ." The candidate even threatened to write a book called *Me and God.*

W. R. ("Billy") Wilkerson had come a long way since 1930, when the movie producers tried to put his new publication, *The Hollywood Reporter,* out of business. His Vendome restaurant a success, Wilkerson had recently opened another Hollywood night spot, the Trocadero, a combination French grill and sidewalk café on Sunset Boulevard. Moguls and stars filled the Troc every night, dining, dancing, and playing high-stakes poker. Wilkerson worked the crowd wearing gray spats, expensive suits, and a waxed black mustache. He planned to develop that curiously barren strip of Sunset between Beverly Hills and Laurel Canyon and call it his own.

Just four years ago, Wilkerson was struggling to survive in Hollywood. An unsuccessful film producer in New York, he came to California to publish the *Reporter,* the first motion-picture daily based right in Hollywood. At first, he struck an independent stance, printing news about the industry and its stars that went beyond studio-fed puffery; sometimes he even told the moguls how to run their business. The moguls responded by refusing to place advertising in the paper.

Then Louis B. Mayer saved Billy's hide. Breaking the studio boycott of the *Hollywood Reporter* in 1931, L.B. promised to supply Wilkerson with a year's worth of ads. Coverage of MGM naturally grew more favorable, and the other studios soon came around. The maverick became part of the Hollywood establishment, and his daily eight-page journal, printed on shiny paper, sold enough advertising to bankroll Wilkerson's restaurant ventures.

Until today Wilkerson had let the magazine's other columnists lead the charge against Sinclair. Now he stepped front and center in his "Tradeviews" column, declaring that Sinclair would do more to "ruin the motion picture industry" than all the abuse heaped on the studios in the past thirty years. Following *Variety*'s lead, he argued that the moguls wouldn't move out, they would just shut down rather than compete with a state-run film studio. Before Hitler, Germany had a great film industry, but now there "is NO PICTURE WORK IN GERMANY," Wilkerson pointed out, "and there will be little in California if Sinclair is elected and attempts his EPIC plan in this business."

One thing was now certain: if the studios beat Upton Sinclair, the Troc would host Hollywood's victory party.

Carey Wilson had mixed feelings about Irving Thalberg, who had nearly fired him last month for moonlighting on *The President Vanishes.* "You never know whether to kiss him or kill him," he once observed in a magazine profile of Thalberg. Right now Irving was due for a kiss. Wilson, perhaps trying to regain Thalberg's trust, agreed to go off the studio payroll this month and offer his services to the Merriam campaign. Besides his skills as a writer, Carey Wilson had another talent that might prove useful in a propaganda campaign: he narrated short subjects.

Wilson was garrulous to a fault. "Ask him what time it is," one associate complained, "and he'll tell you how to make a watch." Apparently he could talk out of both sides of his mouth, politically speaking, for he had penned the leftish *The President Vanishes* and joined a reactionary political crusade practically in the same breath.

———

United for California, its bank account flush and several million pamphlets at the ready, finally went public today, releasing a statement from its headquarters on West Fifth Street in L.A. calling the Sinclair candidacy the most menacing challenge in the history of the state. His election, the statement said, "would strike at the roots of our most cherished institutions—the home, the church and the school," and it invited all citizens to join a crusade to "prevent the insidious inroad of Communism and to preserve the ideals of the Republic."

It was unclear exactly what the organization's activities would amount to, but behind the scenes it was about to launch a major initiative: direct mailings to target groups. Lord & Thomas would guide this effort. Every citizen in the state would likely receive at least one and possibly a dozen different pamphlets bearing insidious Sinclair quotes. Almost every special interest in the state deserved a circular of its own: from Catholics to doctors to Stanford University alumni. It was perhaps the most sophisticated direct-mail scheme ever attempted in American politics.

Charles C. Teague, the Sunkist man, was ill, so Pacific Mutual's Asa Call had taken charge of the organization. Call would secretly carry the ball for Harry Chandler, Standard Oil, Southern Pacific, and most of the other powerful forces in southern California. The new group had the money, it had the incentive, and it had the protection of the local press, which would turn a blind eye to any excesses. What United for California needed was an everyday manager, an idea man—maybe even a trickster. It would be an anything-goes campaign, but the group needed to know what *anything* might mean.

Albert Parker, the young O'Melveny attorney, volunteered to fill this position. He was already active in the anti-Sinclair fight as a leader of the Crusaders, a national organization of socially prominent young people. And Parker had previous experience in tricking Upton Sinclair: it was he who dreamed up the fake Young People's Communist League leaflet that endorsed Sinclair just prior to the August 28 primary.

Parker had plenty to do while waiting for United for California's mass mailings to begin. Among other things, he spearheaded a drive to get every employer in Los Angeles to help employees vote correctly in November. Asa Call's Pacific Mutual served as a kind of model for this campaign of coercion. Today, at the insurance company's headquarters across from Pershing Square, officials called together several hundred workers to hear guest speakers deliver anti-Sinclair tirades. Officials circulated pro-Merriam petitions and announced that fifty-five Pacific Mutual employees had offered to make sure their colleagues voted for the right candidate.

Afterward several troubled Pacific Mutual workers told EPIC headquarters what was happening. EPIC attorneys informed them that they could charge the company with violating Section 53 of the State Penal Code, which held that any person who influences an elector's vote by threats, bribery, "or any corrupt means . . . shall be guilty of a felony."

OCTOBER 4

THURSDAY

A throng of movie fans greeted Douglas Fairbanks as he stepped from Pan Am's *American Clipper* onto the runway at Miami Airport. Fairbanks, impossibly tan and wonderfully dapper in a white suit and black hat, waved to the crowd as he accepted official greetings from the city manager. Accompanying him on his long trip from California, via Mexico City and Havana, was Joseph M. Schenck.

Reporters crowded around the famous actor, who declined to discuss his stormy separation from his wife, Mary Pickford. Doug revealed that he was thinking of remaking his classic silent film *The Mark of Zorro* as a talkie, but doubted he would be able to "recapture the zest necessary to carry it over." Then the autograph seekers enveloped him.

Joe Schenck made an announcement of even more serious consequence. "Florida, if it is wide awake and offers tax concessions for a few years," he declared, "will be the center of the moving picture business of $150 million a year in the event Upton Sinclair is elected governor of California. Sinclair's taxation plan will drive the industry out of California. Florida has everything the industry needs," Schenck explained. "Conditions in this state have greatly improved since the time, several years ago, when attempts first were made to establish part of the industry here, and there is no handicap here now to be overcome."

Florida officials, anticipating this statement, had pushed through the legislature a proposed amendment to the state constitution that, if adopted by voters in November, would exempt the movie industry from paying taxes on its property and products for fifteen years. *The Miami Herald* and the Chamber of Commerce pledged to promote the move, recalling that the city of Jacksonville had hosted fourteen small studios early in the century until political interference drove them out of the state. Perhaps California would make the same mistake, to Florida's benefit.

If the locals thought Joe Schenck was merely grandstanding for the folks back home, they didn't show it. Neither, for that matter, did Schenck, since he spent the better part of the day driving around with Chamber officials, inspecting possible sites for his studio. One or two properties might actually do the trick, he remarked afterward. Then he and Doug Fairbanks climbed into an American Airways plane piloted by Eddie Rickenbacker and flew north to Newark.

Joe Schenck was one of several moguls who paid Will H. Hays to keep his industry out of trouble, but he was not one of the movie czar's favorite people: his life-style threatened at any moment to create a public relations scandal Hays would have to attend to. No one, on the other hand, had to worry about Hays getting caught with his pants down. The movie czar, who once referred to himself as "an unreconstructed Middle Westerner from 'the sticks,' " had attended Wabash College, the institution that fired Ezra Pound for nonconformity. H. L. Mencken contemptuously referred to him as Elder Hays, in recognition of his position in the Presbyterian church. But Hays was not exactly a prude. He loved to dance, he played penny-ante poker, and after several years of commuting to Hollywood, he had even learned to curse. What bothered him the most about sex in the movies was that the producers had hired him to keep their image clean and then did their best to circumvent his codes of conduct.

One night in New York, riding from his office to his apartment at the Waldorf, Hays turned to his college-age son, Will Jr., and said: "Cleavage, cleavage—I'm tired of fighting cleavage. I'd like to wade through a forty-acre field of breasts!" Hays's chauffeur commented from the front seat, "Say the word, sir, and I'll join you!"

Alva Johnston, in a two-part *New Yorker* profile in 1933, called Hays "America's most debatable figure." Some considered him a censor; others felt he was not censorious enough. Most observers agreed with Johnston, however, that the movie industry might have been ruined by too little—or too much—morality had its destiny been guided "by a less competent, alert, shifty, and agile Czar."

Despite his varied accomplishments, Hays seemed destined to wear the tag *bluenose.* By 1934, Hays had been movie czar for twelve years, and Americans were beginning to forget about his previous career as a political tactician. Born in 1879, William Harrison Hays took his name from President William Henry Harrison, whose grandson, Benjamin, was a friend of Will's father. Elected president in 1888, due largely to Republican vote buying and trickery, Benjamin Harrison might have appointed the senior Hays to his cabinet if the GOP had not already sold the positions to other prominent supporters. With this heritage, it was no surprise that young Will became a local GOP precinct boss before he was even eligible to vote, and then, in rapid order, county, state, and in 1918, national chairman, all the while operating as a successful attorney back home in Sullivan, Indiana. Hays masterminded Warren G. Harding's successful run for president in 1920, the most sophisticated political merchandising campaign of its day.

That campaign made Hays a political legend. Ironically, he might have been elected president himself. When the GOP convention in Chicago that summer reached an impasse, party leaders met at the Blackstone Hotel in what the press dubbed "the smoke-filled room." According to Hays's private account, they first offered *him* the top prize. "Gentlemen, I thank you," he responded, "but in Indiana we have a saying, 'A man doesn't bid at his own auction.' " It was just as well. Hays might not have won the election without Hays to run his campaign.

Harding later appointed Hays postmaster general. Hays played poker in the White House with Harding and Albert Lasker but cashed in his chips with the administration just one year into his term to accept the post of movie czar, one of the highest-salaried positions in the land. (The other two finalists for the job: Herbert Hoover and Hiram Johnson.) Journalists later speculated that Hays saw the Teapot Dome scandal on the horizon and fled Washington as fast as he could.

It was not hard to see what the moguls saw in Hays, a pious evangelist-politician with extraordinary government connections. Hays established his office and five-man staff in New York but frequently took the train to Los Angeles, where he stayed at the Chateau Elyse. The movie czar became a celebrity. The first person to talk in a talking picture was not Al Jolson but Will Hays. On August 6, 1926, in a New York movie theater, prior to the showing of *Don Juan,* the first movie feature utilizing sound, Hays spoke a few words from the screen, congratulating the Warner brothers on their invention. It was a measure of Hays's prominence that in 1929, at a gala celebration of the fiftieth anniversary of the invention of the electric light, the movie czar sat at the head table with Thomas Edison, Henry Ford, Albert Einstein, and President Hoover.

Hays was an odd-looking fellow, which only added to his public recognition. Slight of stature, he was blessed with enormous ears, which he often joked about in his after-dinner speeches. Durante had the *schnozz,* Eddie Cantor the eyes, but Will Hays was all ears. "Not matching, the right one spreads with a tendency futuristic and triangular," one writer observed, "while the left has a conservative roundness."

The first decade of czardom transpired under Republican presidents, old friends of Hays's. When FDR took power, stories circulated that the moguls contemplated replacing Hays with a Democrat such as Joe Kennedy or Jim Farley. Hays professed not to worry about it and struck up a friendly relationship with FDR. Then the Legion of Decency protests started. Some claimed that Hays, looking for an excuse to increase his power, conspired to create the new morality movement. In any case, he welcomed the uproar, for it forced the moguls to give him police powers for the first time.

Many cities had movie censorship boards that snipped out offending scenes, but Hays kept state and federal censorship legislation on the back burner. He boasted that he rang up the biggest phone bill of anyone in the country, but he did not trust the telegraph; when a particularly sensitive message had to be wired between the coasts, the czar sometimes sent it in code. He was impossibly well connected. Hays knew every prominent Republican, and was even on friendly terms with leading Democrats, such as Joe Kennedy and Will Rogers.

Naturally, when Upton Sinclair won the Democratic primary in California, the movie industry looked to Will Hays for guidance. He had saved the industry back in the 1920s during its hour of greatest need; now another threat, even more pernicious, had reared its head. Hays had sent his top aide, Charlie Pettijohn, to Los Angeles, but there was so much more he could offer the Republicans. Frank Merriam was nothing more than an elderly version of Warren G. Harding! The movie czar might teach Merriam's managers a thing or two; after all, Hays had raised an amazing eight million dollars for Harding in 1920 and spent, it was said, a million dollars more than he collected. He also devised Harding's "front-porch strategy," enabling the colorless candidate to keep his mouth shut while his aides distributed millions of brochures attacking his opponent. And he manipulated the newsreels, convincing them to picture Harding, greeting visitors on his porch, as the consummate statesman.

Another one of Hays's accomplishments back in 1920 was the artful wooing of the press, a skill he continued to display. Nearly every major publisher in California had declared for Frank Merriam—except the czar's friend W. R. Hearst. Today Hays dropped Hearst a line care of the Ritz Tower suggesting they meet while W.R. was in New York. He let the publisher know that he appreciated his recent statements cabled from overseas.

> We hear much these days in scientific circles of "remote control." The most outstanding example of "remote control" that ever happened is your own experience this summer. I wonder if you have any idea of the far-reaching influence exercised in this country by your messages sent home. . . . You out-did yourself in thought and in writing. . . .

An Associated Press dispatch out of San Francisco reported that California stocks continued to tumble. Stocks selling between thirty dollars and sixty dollars a share were down from one to three dollars, and higher-priced issues suffered more. Standard Oil, Pacific Gas, Union Oil, Transamerica, and other leading California enterprises shared in the decline. "Mr. Sinclair is not interested in the reactions of the Wall Street–manipulated stock market," EPIC headquarters commented.

No business group was more intent on electing Frank Merriam than California realtors, and they were engaged in manipulations of their own, pulling half a million dollars' worth of property off the market for the balance of the campaign (according to their own estimates). Today the state's realtors, meeting in convention at the Biltmore in Santa Barbara, voted to band together and work as one huge fist against Upton Sinclair.

During its thirty-year history, the California Real Estate Association had never taken part in electoral politics, but it had never faced an emergency quite like this. Its board unanimously passed a resolution calling on the association to "take such actions as are necessary" to elect Merriam and defeat the "socialistic and communistic" EPIC. The resolution repeated the popular charge that Sinclair had never owned an acre of real estate, ignoring the fact that his wife currently possessed several valuable parcels, including a jewel in Beverly Hills. Uppie couldn't win: the *Los Angeles Times* accused him of owning too many properties, and the realtors claimed he didn't own enough.

President Robert A. Swink called for those realtors to step forward who were "willing to pass through another Valley Forge, if necessary, in order to achieve a victory at another Yorktown. . . . In a contest between Americanism and Communism I feel confident that every realtor in California will be found standing on the side of true Americanism, under the stars and stripes, ready to die, if need be, in defense of country and home." The directors instructed two thousand members in over two hundred cities to mobilize for action, closing down their offices if necessary to organize the state's property owners against Sinclair. The association's newly formed Merriam for Governor Committee had already printed over four hundred thousand posters and bulletins for distribution, posing questions such as these:

> If Sinclair's plan is adopted, could you borrow a nickel on a home in California?
> Could you borrow to build a house?
> Would you if you could?
> If you had a dollar would you lend it in California?
> If you had a dollar would you invest it here?
> Further, if Sinclair's invitation to 5,000,000 of the Eastern unemployed is accepted, what will it cost you to entertain them?
> Now are you going to vote for Sinclair?

The association's campaign slogan: "It's Merriam or Moscow!"

The Merriam for Governor Committee was headed by the elderly William May Garland, who once owned much of Los Angeles. His committee operated out of the Garland Building at Spring Street and Ninth. Garland had gained valuable experience in mudslinging during the 1910 campaign that crushed the mayoral hopes of Socialist candidate Job Harriman. The realtors had closed their offices to campaign that year, too.

Tonight Frank Merriam appeared in Santa Barbara to accept the group's endorsement. Glenn Willaman, secretary of the association, sent a note to FDR's press secretary, Steve Early, at the White House, predicting that Upton Sinclair would be "snowed under" in November. Why? There were 800,000 property owners in California, Willaman advised, "and these alone can elect the governor."

OCTOBER 5

FRIDAY

The *Los Angeles Times* declared this morning in a prominent editorial entitled "Stand Up and Be Counted" that organizations and individuals who had not yet joined the fight against Upton Sinclair must face the facts: EPIC represented a "threat to sovietize California" and therefore was the equivalent of "the appearance of a hostile fleet off our coast." Unified, militant patriotism was required to prevent an assault on our shores. "Gentlemen—and ladies—this is not politics," the *Times* declared. "It is war."

Upton Sinclair girded for battle, confident he could hold off the *Los Angeles Times* in a fair fight. Today, however, the newspaper added Franklin Roosevelt to its arsenal. At least *The New York Times,* in hailing Raymond Moley's recent attack on Sinclair, did not claim that Moley was the President's official spokesman on this matter. But the *Los Angeles Times*—and nearly every other newspaper in California—asserted that Moley, in his *Today* article, delivered a secret message directly from the White House. "No one able to put two and two together can doubt that the Moley blast represents the administration view of Sinclair and Sinclairism," the *L.A. Times* declared. Earl Warren, the new GOP chief, commented that he was sure Moley "has the complete confidence of President Roosevelt and remains one of his closest advisers."

This stood FDR on his head. Moley's assault came about only because Roosevelt had *rejected* his anti-Sinclair argument. And Jim Farley had just informed Senator McAdoo that the President secretly wanted Sinclair to win. But out in California, Upton Sinclair had a public relations disaster on his hands. Sinclair did what he usually did in these circumstances: he fired off a batch of letters—to the President, to Marvin McIntyre (to make sure FDR got the first letter), to Farley, to Moley.

Accompanying each of the notes: a four-page rebuttal of the Moley article. Sinclair confided that he was surprised that such an intelligent man hadn't bothered to find out what the EPIC plan really stood for. He asserted that he was at the pole opposite Rousseau, believing as he did in modern machinery as the instrument for saving mankind from wage slavery. In suggesting otherwise, Moley made himself the "champion of reaction in California."

Sinclair challenged Moley to write another editorial stating his opinion of Frank Merriam and the state GOP platform. Was it possible that Moley had overlooked the fact that the incumbent would benefit from any attack on EPIC? "This being the case," Sinclair wrote, "it seems to me of the utmost urgency that Professor Moley should state whether he . . . wishes such a man in charge of the New Deal in California for four years. If Professor Moley does not desire this, he should state what he does desire. . . . It might be worth while for me to point out to Professor Moley," he concluded, "that I am carrying on a campaign for the Governorship without the support of a single daily newspaper in the State, and so my enemies do not need the help of New York weekly magazines to put me down."

In his cover letter to FDR, Sinclair left the matter in Roosevelt's lap. "Now of course Professor Moley is a free man and says what he pleases," he told the President. "But you are in politics and you confront this practical problem. You are coming up for re-election two years from now and you will wish to carry the State of California. Is that State going to be in the hands of Sinclair, who is pledged not merely by his public statements but by his private word of honor to your ardent support, or is it going to be in the hands of Merriam, a life-long tool of the power trust, a hired man of the Crocker bank crowd, and incidentally a grafting politician who was driven out of the State of Iowa by the exposure of his public peculations?" Sinclair continued:

> I am not going to suggest what you should do in this situation. I just want to make sure you have it clearly in mind—Sinclair or Merriam—there is no other choice. . . . I do not think there is anybody in the country who can undo the damage except yourself and possibly Hiram Johnson.

In closing, Sinclair confessed that he was "cherishing your promise to come out in favor of production for use about the twenty-fifth of this month. If you make it strong enough it should serve the purpose!"

H. G. Wells once addressed his friend Upton Sinclair as "the most hopeful of Socialists," claiming that *he* was "the next most hopeful." In the autumn of 1934, Wells still had faith that Franklin Roosevelt would lead America out of the Depression. In his just-published memoir, *An Experiment in Autobiography,* he praised FDR's receptiveness to new ideas. "He is continuously revolutionary in the new way," Wells commented, "without ever provoking a stark revolutionary crisis."

Back in July, the British author had interviewed Joseph Stalin in Moscow, but newspapers in the United States only now reported details of their three-hour conversation, courtesy of the Hearst news service. Stalin had informed Wells that he admired the courage and initiative of FDR but that a planned economy and the abolition of unemployment can be realized only with the overthrow of capitalism. Wells disagreed, asserting that a "socially minded" capitalist could remodel society in the interest of the masses. In fact, Wells believed there was some similarity between New Deal America and Stalinist Russia.

Stalin rejected this notion. Roosevelt was just reacting to a crisis, he offered, not addressing the reason for the crisis. "Capitalists," he argued, "will not agree to any social progress completely eliminating unemployment because such a program would reduce the supply of cheap labor. You will never persuade a capitalist to cause himself losses for the sake of satisfying people's needs." FDR, he said, would suffer "complete defeat" if he did try to take on the capitalists, for they would simply say, "presidents may come and presidents may go, but we capitalists remain. If one president does not defend our interests, we will find another one."

Upton Sinclair often claimed, rightly or not, that he was the only American ever to receive a personal telegram from Stalin. During the

Eisenstein debacle, the Soviet leader advised Sinclair that the famous director, who had dawdled too long in Mexico, had lost the confidence of his comrades in the Soviet Union. "Am afraid the people here would have no interest in him soon," Stalin explained. This helped persuade Sinclair to terminate financial support for Eisenstein and, later, to edit his raw footage in Hollywood rather than ship it to the director in Russia, as he had promised. The movie that resulted, *Thunder Over Mexico,* flopped at the box office in 1933, and Lincoln Kirstein charged that Sinclair had "butchered a great work of art."

Ironically, a young man named Marx was one of the few studio hands who stood up for Sinclair during the Eisenstein fiasco. Now Sam Marx was Upton's top-ranking supporter at MGM. Marx considered himself apolitical, but he had a soft spot in his heart for Sinclair.

The two men had met in 1931 when Sinclair pitched MGM on making a movie of his forthcoming novel, *The Wet Parade.* Sam Marx, story editor at MGM, liked the idea, but when he mentioned it to his boss, Irving Thalberg, the Boy Wonder thundered, "Don't let that Bolshevik inside this studio!" Louis B. Mayer warned that if "that bum" visited MGM, he would probably bring a bomb with him.

Rather than accept no for an answer, Marx invited Upton to come to his apartment and talk about it. Marx, still in his early thirties and a recent émigré from New York, had never read Sinclair's books. He decided to wait for him in the courtyard of his Hollywood apartment building, and if the Socialist breathed fire, he would shoo him away. Sinclair, of course, proved to be a polite and humorous gentleman: more dragon slayer than dragon. Observing the glittering façade of the building, Upton waved his arms and, as if pointing a sword, cried, "I dub thee—Platinum Blonde!" Sinclair had made a friend.

Thalberg eventually approved paying twenty-five thousand dollars to the "Bolshevik" for the rights to *The Wet Parade.* In Marx's view, Thalberg was obsessed with buying literary quality, whether it emanated from George Bernard Shaw, William Faulkner, or Upton Sinclair. Still, Thalberg barred Sinclair from the MGM lot, so Marx had to motor to Pasadena, contract and check in hand, to close the *Wet Parade* deal. Craig insisted that a clause be added indicating that the studio would adhere to the spirit of the book. Marx, wishing to avoid another trip to Pasadena, agreed, and wrote something to this effect in a margin.

When Thalberg saw the contract, he erupted. "Thanks to you," he told Marx, "he can take us to court and prevent our showing the film. If we follow the book word for word he could still say, after we spent a million dollars, that we did not maintain his intent—and that Bolshevik is just the man to do it. I won't make that picture!"

Fortunately for everyone involved, Sinclair agreed to drop the troublesome clause. When the film, written by John Lee Mahin, premiered at Grauman's Chinese Theatre in March 1932, the audience called for Uppie to get up and make a few remarks, but Sid Grauman prevented it, explaining that Sinclair had not had the decency to wear formal attire for the occasion. (The writer did not own a tuxedo.)

When *The Wet Parade* performed well at the box office, Sam Marx finally won permission to bring Uppie and his wife to the studio. They even called on Thalberg. Mary Craig Sinclair immediately committed a faux pas, asking Thalberg whether he was the person they called the Boy Wonder. Thalberg stared back angrily. "If so, I never heard it," he muttered, and the Sinclairs left quickly.

Although Marx didn't care for politics, he figured he'd vote for Sinclair for governor. Sam wasn't in a high salary bracket (he was making $350 a week), so the "EPIC tax" didn't threaten him the way it did most of the MGM bigwigs. The fact that all of the other ranking MGM employees supported Frank Merriam did not particularly bother Sam Marx. He and Louis B. Mayer each knew where the other stood. Standing in line one day, waiting to register to vote, Marx said to Mayer, "You know we're just going to cancel each other out, so why don't we just leave and get back to the office!"

Like everyone else at the studio, Marx was curious to see what would happen when Mayer showed up next week in Culver City. The studio hierarchy, judging by the Merriam placards posted around the lot, hated Sinclair, but it was unclear who had ordered the mobilization. Mayer could easily have directed it from Europe via his extremely efficient and politically well-connected secretary, Ida Koverman. Despite his tirades against Sinclair, Irving Thalberg was much less likely to waste time with politics. As a youth in New York, Thalberg had read Upton Sinclair's books, which helped convert him to socialism. He made speeches from a soapbox in Union Square for a Socialist candidate for mayor, but when his candidate lost, partly due to Tammany Hall vote stealing, Irving's infatuation with the Left and electoral politics ended seemingly forever.

Little did Sam Marx know that the refined Thalberg, without waiting for Louis B. Mayer's return, had just ordered an MGM production team headed by writer Carey Wilson and director Felix Feist, Jr., to start filming a series of shorts aimed at delivering the deathblow to Upton Sinclair's candidacy.

The executive committee of the financially troubled Pacific Mutual met this morning at eleven-thirty and voted to contribute another ten thousand dollars "to prevent the spread of socialism and communism in California." The committee directed the company's two top executives, George Cochran and Asa Call, to authorize payments to persons or organizations as they saw fit.

Corporations throughout California participated in the anti-Sinclair drive in a similar fashion. Funds from outside the state also flowed in. An oilman known for raising campaign money for Republicans in Texas took up a collection for Merriam and amassed eighty-four thousand dollars without breaking a sweat. Cash was tight in 1934, but the Texas oil interests feared that if Sinclair won in California, a copycat would appear in their state before long.

Wall Street also got into the act. Frank Taylor, before losing his job and going to work for EPIC, saw the results firsthand.

A native of Cincinnati, Taylor attended four colleges during the early 1920s before settling in Los Angeles and going to work for Blyth and Company, the leading West Coast brokerage house. The firm—known as Blyth, Witter and Company before Dean Witter split off to open his own office in 1924—operated in L.A. out of a magnificent eleven-story bank building on Sixth Street. Taylor directed a coterie of men who wrote stock prices on a blackboard as the figures arrived at the Blyth office via telegraph from the New York Stock Exchange. Traders and investors watched from a dozen rows of seats. Since California was three hours behind New York, Taylor had to get to the office by six in the morning, but he got off work at one o'clock.

One of Blyth's steadiest customers was Democratic leader Ham Cotton. Blyth also handled accounts for movie stars such as Douglas Fairbanks and Zasu Pitts. A familiar office routine would commence with the cry, "Clear the line, Harpo's going to trade!" This meant that Harpo Marx was on the telephone in Blyth's Hollywood office. The Blyth broker in L.A. would hold phones to his ears; through one he received Harpo's orders, and into the other he barked instructions to a broker in New York.

Starting in late summer 1934, however, a new ritual unfolded. Almost every day, Frank Taylor observed messages arriving over the telegraph, asking Blyth to transfer corporate funds to the "Sinclair account." The orders arrived in a steady stream: a few hundred dollars here, a few thousand there, sometimes amounting to twenty or thirty thousand dollars in a single day. Some of the orders came from large companies, others from individuals, most of them based on the East Coast. Charlie Blyth, the company's founder and a legendary GOP fund-raiser, knew what to do with the money. Someone from the Blyth office would write the appropriate check and run it over to a local bank before closing time.

Taylor, by this time, was spending his afternoons working for Sinclair. He had approached End Poverty League director Dick Otto a few months back and asked how the EPIC plan was going to be instituted once Sinclair took office. "We haven't gotten to that—we're busy electing Mr. Sinclair," Otto replied. "*You* tell *us* what do." Taylor volunteered to do just that. He helped found the Research Associates, a group of self-styled technicians, agronomists, and economists who acted as EPIC's liaison to the academic community. Whenever someone raised a question about Sinclair's statistics or EPIC's practicality, Taylor would confer with a group of experts and roll out a rebuttal. He also helped write Sinclair's booklet *EPIC Answers* and eventually joined the End Poverty League board as one of Sinclair's "Twelve Apostles."

Now, as the campaign entered its final month, Taylor had the luxury of working full-time for EPIC. Blyth and Company, no doubt aware of his EPIC sympathies, and perhaps fearing that Taylor knew too much about Merriam's source of campaign funds, had fired him from his job.

———

Earl Warren, a visitor from the north, was "pleasantly surprised," he told reporters, to find anti-Sinclair fervor so far advanced in Los Angeles. This boded well for the outcome of the election, since the GOP chairman believed Frank Merriam would sweep northern California. "In this election our democratic institutions will undergo trial by ballot," Warren declared. "Those institutions will be scrapped if Upton Sinclair is elected."

Sinclair did say "one true thing" the other day, Warren remarked, mentioning the comment that half the unemployed would hop freight trains and head for California. "Without waiting for his election," Warren told reporters, "the unemployed and penniless are coming in droves now, and if the movement gains proportion it can't be stopped. They will keep on coming without rhyme or reason. I regard that as the great menace of the situation."

The press hardly needed another story along these lines. Article after article had already sounded the alarm: EVERY PAUPER IS COMING. It was the Days of '49 redux. The *Los Angeles Times* warned that a "locust-swarm" was approaching, and columnist Harry Carr predicted that California's open spaces would soon "look like the interior of a box of sardines." Editorial cartoons pictured happy hoboes riding boxcars to the Sunshine State, contemplating Easy Pickings in California or crying out, "California, Here I Bum!" One cartoon showed two tramps reading about EPIC in an eastern newspaper and deciding to winter in California instead of Florida this year. Another portrayed California as a beautiful Spanish mansion with an endless stream of carefree bums, "criminals," and "agitators" entering the front door and terrified businessmen, farmers, and "home-loving Californians" exiting out the back.

Thousands of billboards across California—courtesy of Artie Samish, no doubt—now bore the slightly embellished Sinclair quote "I expect half the unemployed in the U.S. to flock to California if I am elected." Driving the countryside or walking around the city, it was impossible to avoid The Quote for long. It was a legend in its own time. Some people thought that EPIC put up these ads, because Upton Sinclair's name always appeared next to The Quote. Since EPIC promoted this message, they figured, Sinclair must truly believe it! Other billboards pictured an army of transients marching, marching, marching beneath The Quote, with the commentary DO YOU WANT THIS TO HAPPEN?

Another effective propaganda ploy was the inevitable song parody, printed in blue type on white note cards and distributed by the thousands throughout the state:

> California, here we come! Every beggar, every bum
> From New York—and Jersey—down to Purdue—
> By millions—we're coming—so that we can live on you
> We hear that Sinclair's got your State
> That's why we can hardly wait
> Open up your Golden Gate
> California, here we come!
>
> California, here we come! California, don't be glum!
> Just keep—your flowers—sweetly in bloom.
> But tell—your people—to get out and give us room!
> We'll soon be with you, you can bet
> When your Sinclair Plan is set
> Hail to Thee, our Soviet!
> California, here we come!

Reporters found compliant officials in state bureaus to attest to the sudden influx of the unemployed. Russell Bevans, registrar of the state Department of Motor Vehicles in Sacramento, a Republican appointee, claimed that "all" of the new arrivals "base their hopes of relief on the election of Sinclair." He formed this opinion, Bevans said, on the basis of reports sent to him by clerks at border crossing stations. Today, for example, the clerk in charge of a station in Blythe, California, estimated that 90 percent of the new arrivals were indigent.

This evidence was purely anecdotal, Sinclair responded. A few hundred arrivals here, a few hundred there hardly amounted to a flood of human flotsam and jetsam. There was no hard evidence that the recent upsurge was any greater than that which occurred every year as winter approached in the Midwest and the East. Even if there was a steady increase, the culprit, Sinclair charged, was not EPIC but the Los Angeles Chamber of Commerce, which had recently spent tens of thousands of dollars on advertising in eastern magazines, attempting to lure settlers to California.

OCTOBER 7

SUNDAY

Arriving in Culver City, Louis B. Mayer discovered that in honor of his return the entire MGM studio had been given a coat of white paint so bright it was almost blinding. L.B. also found Hollywood's swankiest office awaiting him on the second floor of MGM's new wardrobe building. The three-room suite featured gray wood paneling in the waiting room and main office and gray leathered walls in Mayer's inner sanctum.

Fear of what might happen in Hollywood after November 6 hadn't slowed the studio one bit. Dozens of productions were in progress. Carey Wilson had finally finished his script for *Mutiny on the Bounty,* and the big ship, a converted Alaskan windjammer, was anchored in San Pedro Harbor. This being MGM, stars were shooting all over the lot: Garbo in *The Painted Veil,* Wallace Beery in *The Mighty Barnum,* and Gable and Crawford in Woody Van Dyke's *Forsaking All Others.* Then there was the improbable matchup of the Marx brothers, Irving Thalberg, and a movie (still in the planning stages) set in an opera house.

Through Chico Marx, a partner from the poker table, Irving Thalberg had offered the boys an MGM contract. Their last movie, *Duck Soup,* had been a bust, and Thalberg felt they needed to control their manic behavior and accept more of a plot, including a love interest. Zeppo Marx had just quit to become a Hollywood agent, and Thalberg wondered whether the three-man act would demand to be paid as much as the four-man crew. "Don't be silly," Groucho replied, "without Zeppo we're worth twice as much."

This wasn't going to be an easy experience for the already-frail Thalberg, and now Harpo wanted to do a voice test. MGM had barely secured his signature on a contract when the wacky mime started talking about making arty pictures—and *speaking* on screen! Groucho and Chico announced that if Harpo started talking, they would stop; but it wasn't entirely a laughing matter. A New Deal liberal, Harpo had trekked to the Soviet Union last winter—he told the Russians he was distantly related to Karl Marx—and it may have changed his life.

Harpo was Thalberg's headache. According to reports in the trades, Louis B. Mayer's first order of business on returning to work was to put EPIC in its political grave. If anyone could elect Frank Merriam, it was Louie B. "He knows how to salvage junk," one Hollywood wag observed, referring to L.B.'s boyhood career.

Returning to the studio today, Mayer told reporters that Merriam offered the people of California "a chance to retain an able, energetic, and sincere public servant whose election will represent the rejection of radical and unsound theories and doctrines. As I see it," L.B. continued, "this is no time to consider either personal or partisan interests. The voters have too much at stake to think of anything except the welfare of California and its people."

L.B. branded as nonsense reports that he had asked Merriam to quit the race to prevent a split in the anti-Sinclair vote. "We have the best candidate we could possibly find," Mayer explained. "Why should he withdraw?" He didn't want Haight to quit either, because young Ray was going to draw more votes from Sinclair than from Merriam, L.B. predicted. Would MGM follow Joe Schenck to Florida if Sinclair won? "That is something to be considered if and when the time comes," Mayer replied.

In a campaign address, Upton Sinclair expressed his reaction to Joe Schenck's proposed move to Miami: "Think of what those big Florida mosquitos would do to some of our screen sirens. Why, one bite on the nose could bring a fifty-thousand-dollar production loss."

Sinclair was getting it from all sides. In *Izvestia,* the Soviet Union's foremost political commentator, Karl Radek, expressed the regret of Soviet readers who had long admired Sinclair's books but now found that their hero had joined the Democratic party, thus paying tribute to capitalism. "The legendary Hercules, according to tradition, was stronger than Sinclair," Radek declared, "but when he cleaned the Augean stables he did not use a toothbrush." Sinclair's campaign, Radek predicted, "will end only in bankruptcy, but may give the masses a lesson." The *San Francisco Chronicle* published Radek's analysis on its front page under the headline RUSSIAN BRANDS SINCLAIR FASCIST.

Kyle Palmer raised funds and wrote speeches for Frank Merriam, advised him on strategy, and worked on the Hollywood end of the race for the Hays Office. Somehow he still found time to direct the *Los Angeles Times*'s coverage of the campaign and write some of the paper's most ferocious anti-Sinclair editorials. Except for the Hollywood aspect, this was old hat for the man known as the Little Governor.

A native of Tennessee, Palmer had joined the *Los Angeles Times* in 1919 at the age of twenty-seven. Three years later, he was covering politics for Harry Chandler and writing speeches for Friend W. Richardson, a long shot challenging Governor William D. Stephens (and the Hiram Johnson machine) in the GOP primary. Palmer boldly predicted an upset, and when Richardson won, the short, curly-haired, bow-tied *Times* reporter was proclaimed a prophet and a genius. Before long he became a political power in California and eventually its kingmaker.

In the early 1930s, Chandler sent Palmer to Washington, where he managed national as well as state politics for the *Times.* But in June 1934, when the Sinclair menace suddenly appeared real, Harry Chandler called Kyle home. Palmer's *Times* salary was modest—only $150 a week—and his life-style lavish, but he picked up additional money moonlighting for Merriam, Hatfield, and Hays while continuing to abuse Sinclair in print.

Today, in his widely read Sunday column, "The Week in Politics," Palmer predicted that "the next four weeks will find the entire population of California drawn into a battle of ballots such as this State has never witnessed." The Merriam forces claimed that their candidate had climbed slightly ahead in the polls, an assertion Palmer used as a springboard from which to study a new development in American politics: manipulation of public opinion surveys.

Sure, these polls were made of straw. George Gallup and Elmo Roper on the East Coast were only now developing scientific approaches that might prove useful in the 1936 election. But even though the California surveys, like the famed *Literary Digest* polls, might be questionable, that didn't stop the candidates from commissioning them and then using the results to promote their candidacy. Haight produced numbers that showed he could beat Sinclair and Merriam couldn't. Sinclair pointed to his big lead in the KNX poll to rally EPICs who might be losing faith in the face of daily ridicule in the press. Trying to create a snowball effect, Merriam declared that *his* polls showed him in the lead, despite every indication to the contrary. Merriam knew that if Sinclair looked like a winner, EPIC was certain to gain additional support. On the other hand, fence-sitting Democrats (all the way up to the President) were not likely to back a loser they didn't much care for in the first place.

"Straw ballots," Palmer wrote, "which formerly were sought merely as indications of the general drift of the political winds, now have become a definite part of the general propaganda of politics, and are being employed not only to inform but to influence the voters." Each of the candidates in California, he observed, was utilizing polls to an extent never before attempted, to encourage his supporters and "add to his seeming advantages."

———

The new issue of *Script* was out, and in it Rob Wagner revealed that Will Anderson, president of the Los Angeles bar association, had urged members to vote for Merriam as "the best of two evils."

———

Herbert Hoover spoke over shortwave radio today with Admiral Richard Byrd in the Antarctic. The conversation was broadcast over nationwide radio in the United States. "Whatever the physical difficulties of the Antarctic region may be," Hoover advised from Palo Alto, "you have one advantage over us. You are at least free from the storms and contentions over social, economic and political fires which are raging through the whole temperate zones of the earth."

———

At almost any hour, day or night, one could turn the radio dial in Los Angeles and hear someone ranting and raving about EPIC, and the United for California radio drive hadn't even started. The most prominent radio personality was Martin Luther Thomas, a pistol-packing ex-prizefighter, now Presbyterian minister at the Metropolitan Federated Church on Crenshaw Boulevard. The man known to readers of the *EPIC News* as Spouting Thomas conducted his right-wing radio ministry sixteen times a week over three Los Angeles radio stations—morning, afternoon, and evening.

One program, *The Unmasking of Upton Sinclair,* broadcast every Tuesday and Thursday over KNX, was devoted entirely to the campaign. Reverend Thomas had also produced a pamphlet under the same title exposing Sinclair's communist and atheist past, and distributed it by the tens of thousands throughout the state. "Any Christian, after reading this exposé, who votes for a man of this caliber," Thomas warned, "will most certainly be held responsible at the judgment seat." He claimed that God had spoken to him, ordering Sinclair's crucifixion. Over the radio, he read affidavits he obtained from listeners who on one occasion or another had witnessed Sinclair trampling the flag or heard him curse the Constitution or call for the death of American servicemen. Socialist leader (and former minister) Norman Thomas, reading about Reverend Thomas in the *EPIC News,* felt certain that such a preacher could not possibly exist and complained to friends that Sinclair's newspaper was parodying *him.*

Today a group called the Constitution Society presented another of its Sunday evening broadcasts condemning Sinclair. Like M. L. Thomas, the host often quoted testimony linking Sinclair to all sorts of nefarious deeds, including the assassination of President McKinley. On one show, an old man with a quavering voice—probably an actor—revealed that at a Sinclair rally in the Shrine Auditorium he had stood next to the candidate himself, and Upton Sinclair, that rascal, had picked his pocket.

Broadcasts from the religious fringe struck nonbelievers as absurdly comic, but to hundreds of thousands of conservative Christians who had lately arrived in Los Angeles from the Midwest, they rang true. Recognizing this, EPIC sponsored an official response, over the radio, of course. Upton Sinclair would not do the expedient thing—recant *The Profits of Religion* and beg for forgiveness—so EPIC turned to a man with impeccable religious credentials: Horace Jeremiah "Jerry" Voorhis.

A devout Episcopalian, Voorhis was one of EPIC's most able and admirable young leaders. Son of a well-to-do businessman, a graduate of Yale, Voorhis had founded a residence for homeless boys in San Dimas, twelve miles northeast of Whittier. When Sinclair announced for governor last year, Voorhis informed Norman Thomas that EPIC would have "far-reaching consequences, none of which are likely to be good," but after much soul-searching, he left the Socialist party to run for the state assembly as an EPIC Democrat. Sometimes he even pinch-hit for Sinclair at campaign rallies when Uppie was ill.

Responding directly to Martin Luther Thomas, Voorhis titled his speech "Unmasking the Unmaskers." The worst that could be said of Sinclair, Voorhis insisted, was that he wrote with too much invective; the real issue of the campaign was whether California would answer Jesus' challenge to Love Thy Neighbor as Thyself. If church leaders actually wanted to save America from godless communism, Voorhis advised, they would "turn a deaf ear to the minions of privilege" and instead take their proper place "at the forefront of the fight for social justice."

America's greatest radio star, Will Rogers, wandered into California over the airwaves this evening from deep in the heart of Texas. It was a typical Rogers weekend. Saturday he flew from St. Louis to his hometown of Claremore, Oklahoma, to speak at a political rally, then crossed the border to keep this radio date in Fort Worth. He planned to fly out right after his nationwide broadcast, bound for Detroit and the final two games of the World Series.

"This gentleman's an old friend of mine," Rogers had remarked at yesterday's Democratic rally, referring to the party's nominee for governor of Oklahoma, "but I'm not endorsing him. I don't know whether he'd be any good." Will's policy against endorsing candidates also applied to California, but he confessed that since he had to "make a living joking about the Governor out there, it would be best for me if Sinclair's elected." This was a quip likely to be quoted in California all week.

Perhaps the question most often asked in America was *Did you see what Will Rogers said?* Some of his wisecracks had turned to cliché ("All I know is what I read in the papers"); others entered the American language as folk sayings or punch lines:

- "Every time Congress makes a joke it's a law, and every time they make a law it's a joke."

- "We hold the distinction of being the only nation that is goin' to the poorhouse in an automobile."
- "This would be a great world to dance in if we didn't have to pay the fiddler."
- "My idea of an honest man is a fellow who declares income tax on money he sold his vote for."

Will Rogers was America's "most complete human document . . . the heartbeat of America," Damon Runyon had observed. Reviewing one of his books, a *New York Times* critic insisted that "America has never produced anybody quite like him, and there has rarely been an American humorist whose words produced less empty laughter or more sober thought." The theologian Reinhold Niebuhr praised his facility in puncturing foibles "which more pretentious teachers leave untouched."

Rogers's life was an American amalgam. He liked to brag that his ancestors did not come over on the *Mayflower*—they met the boat. Rogers was born in Oklahoma Indian Territory in 1879, and he was part Indian, but his parents were prosperous Methodists. Before settling down as a political philosopher and movie star in the 1920s, Rogers worked as a cowboy, a circus performer, and a comedian. Rope tricks were his specialty, but Rogers was no bumpkin: he lived in New York City for many years while appearing with the Ziegfeld Follies, and he often traveled abroad. He hated to hunt and fish but loved to play polo.

Although he never took the trouble to vote, Rogers read newspapers and magazines voraciously and hobnobbed with politicians and foreign dignitaries, gathering material for his seemingly spontaneous political gibes. "This man Rogers has such a keen insight into the American panorama and the American people," Theodore Roosevelt told Albert Lasker way back in 1918 when Will was still twirling rope, "that I feel he is bound, in the course of time, to be a potent factor in the political life of the nation." A few years later, Rogers was mentioned as a presidential candidate, and he regularly received a strong write-in vote in state and national elections. This was one way for a populist voter to protest without turning Socialist. The humorist ran a mock campaign for president in 1928 as the candidate of the Anti-Bunk party ("He Chews to Run") in the pages of *Life,* the humor magazine. The National Press Club appointed him America's congressman at large, and others called him the Unofficial President. At the Democratic National Convention in 1932, he received twenty-two votes as Oklahoma's favorite-son candidate and was so excited he slept through the balloting. Another Oklahoman named Will Rogers, no relation, ran for Congress in honor of the comedian—and won by fifty thousand votes.

To those who complained that his humor was becoming too topical, Rogers replied, "I hope I never get so old that I can't peep behind the scenes and see the amount of politics that's mixed in this medicine before it's dished out to the people as 'Pure statesmanship.' " He proposed as his epitaph: *Here lies Will Rogers. Politicians turned honest and he starved to death.*

During the early years of the Depression, he voiced the despair of the common man and appeared at countless benefits to raise relief money. "What is the matter with our country anyhow?" he wondered. "With all our brains in high positions, and all our boasted organizations, thousands of our folks are starving, or on the verge of it. Why can't there be some means of at least giving everybody all the bread they wanted, anyhow?" He boosted FDR's election, and when Roosevelt was about to take office, Will sent along a list of soon-to-be-immortalized suggestions:

"A smile in the White House again, why, it will look like a meal to us."

"Kid Congress and the Senate, don't scold 'em. They are just children that's never grown up. . . . Keep off the radio till you got something to say. . . . Stay off that back lawn with those photographers. Nothing will kill interest in a President quicker. . . ."

"If somebody gets all excited and tells you, 'Wall Street has just done a nose dive,' tell them, 'Those Republican organizations don't interest me in the least. Why, there is 115 million of my subjects don't know if Wall Street is a thoroughfare or a new mouthwash.' "

Roosevelt, a big Rogers fan, followed his advice almost to the letter. When the President declared a bank holiday, Rogers commented:

> The whole country is with him . . . Even if he does something wrong they are with him, just so he does *something.* . . . If he burned down the Capitol, we would cheer and say, "Well, we at least got a fire started anyhow." . . . We have had years of "Don't rock the boat." Go on and sink it if you want to. We just as well be swimming as like we are. . . . For three years we have had nothing but "America is fundamentally sound." It should have been "America is fundamentally cuckoo." Every American international banker ought to have printed on his office door, "Alive today by the grace of a nation that has a sense of humor."

Rogers called the NRA "decency by government control," although he was suspicious of the Brain Trust gang and theorists in general. "I don't know what additional authority Roosevelt may ask," he advised, "but give it to him, even if it's to drown all the boy babies, for the way the grown-up ones have acted he will be perfectly justified in drowning any new ones." Some accused him of writing the President's speeches, but he explained that he was the Dumb Brain Truster and that the difference between him and Roosevelt was that "when *he's* talking he knows what he's talking about, and when I'm talking, I'm just guessin'."

Recognizing Rogers's political pull, the White House asked him this past summer to make a phonograph record of a recent column about Maine that might be used by the Democratic candidate for governor in that state. This very evening, while Will broadcast from Texas, his latest picture, *Judge Priest,* was screened at the White House. FDR enjoyed it so much he wondered if maybe he *should* appoint Rogers to the bench.

Like FDR, Will Rogers hadn't declared for a candidate in California, and wasn't likely to. He didn't take governors all that seriously. "There is graveyards in forty-eight state capitals," he recently observed, "where headstones say, 'Here lies Governor Meantwell, here lies Governor Honesty, here lies Governor Reform.' Yet the barnacles of connivance, political graft, lobbyists, and party leeches are still hanging onto the whole forty-eight." Yet even a left-handed compliment from Rogers might sway votes in California. Among Will's listeners were thousands of undecided voters, and then there was the usual bloc determined to scribble Rogers's name on their ballot no matter what. Tonight, in the course of his "Good Gulf" program from Texas, which was largely devoted to the World Series, the cowboy philosopher eventually got around to Upton Sinclair.

"You don't see me rushing home," Rogers confided. "I could have been home a week ago! The minute I go to California I got to declare myself on this guy, and I ain't made up my mind yet how I'm going to be. I don't know. Sinclair says he never did ruin the country, but he might." The studio audience laughed. "The Republican says he has, but he won't do it again." Another roar. "So that's what we're up against in California."

PART III

"ARMAGEDDON"

OCTOBER 9

TUESDAY

"The only good thing Roosevelt has done recently is to spend an hour in yr company / but as for his being kind hearted / so was that fat shit Harding. It's a lot / but it aint enuff." Ezra Pound, who had been following Upton Sinclair's antics in the international press, sat down today in the rooftop flat of his Italian villa, put a sheet of his personal stationery (with a likeness of himself in profile sketched at the top) in his typewriter, and gave the candidate a piece of his mind.

What he wanted his friend Uppie to do was forget FDR and follow Mussolini. Three days ago, at fourteen minutes past four in the afternoon, speaking to half a million Italians in the piazza and a nationwide radio audience, il Duce had not only "BURIED scarcity economics," Pound advised; he "rewrote the Declaration of Independence." Mussolini proclaimed a program to End Poverty in Italy, explaining that fascism meant nothing more than "equality of all men in respect to work and to the nation." That, Pound revealed, "damn well plugs the hole left in Jefferson's somewhat hurried 'Declaration'/ the hole thru which the buggaring banks and other exploiters have been sliding.

"Of course," Pound observed, "you and a lot of heckers will try to dodge this speech/because you are set in yr rabbits. . . . BUT you once did think. and you might have another try at it. . . ."

The poet closed with these instructions: "Here's luck/and git on with gettin elected/ BUT don't SHUT yr/ block Absolootly, when you're in office." Signed: *E.P.*

After spending the night at the White House, W. R. Hearst returned to New York this morning with a smile on his face and words of praise for FDR. Franklin Roosevelt still held him under some kind of spell. Every time Hearst broke ranks, the two lions got together and patched up their differences, at least temporarily. Roosevelt owed his election to Hearst as much as to any man, but in their meetings it was the publisher, not the President, who acted the faithful lapdog.

FDR had paid off his debt to Hearst eighteen months ago, consulting him closely on his cabinet selections. Sam Marx, the MGM story editor, had witnessed one of these conferences. Marx and Hearst were sitting in Marion Davies's bungalow at the MGM lot discussing the studio's casting choices for her next movie when a telephone call from the White House came in. Marx overheard Hearst dissecting candidates for the cabinet. "Well, Frank, he'll be okay but I think you can do better," Hearst would say, or "Personally, I'd favor him more for Agriculture than Navy," and so forth. Marion Davies turned to Sam Marx and remarked, "The Chief is casting, too." The President didn't follow all of Hearst's suggestions, but he appointed no one the publisher opposed.

Since then W.R. had conducted a love-hate relationship with the New Deal, embracing parts of it, rejecting others, backtracking and contradicting himself wildly. With Hearst presently referring to the NRA as "State Socialism, Communism, extortion, confiscation, demagogic military regimentation," it was clearly time for the two men to have another chat.

Whatever Roosevelt said last night, it appeared to work magic. Arriving in New York, Hearst declared that he now believed "we are entering upon a period of genuine recovery. . . . Conditions are improving greatly. The Government has done great work." The only cloud on the horizon, Hearst said, was the next Congress, which "will be full of reckless extremists." He closed his remarks without mentioning whether the two men had discussed the California political situation, something very much on the publisher's mind, if not the President's. Then W.R. trotted off to lunch with A. P. Giannini.

While Hearst sat down with California's leading banker, Franklin Roosevelt broke bread at the White House with Roy Howard of the Scripps-Howard newspaper chain, like Hearst an early booster of the New Deal now turning balky. Howard had just been discussing the California race with Will Hays up in New York. It was still unclear which of Howard's famous New York columnists—Heywood Broun or Westbrook Pegler—would cover the campaign.

FDR expressed his current view of the EPIC contest today in a letter to Senator Key Pittman of Nevada. Last week, Pittman had relayed to the White House a message from leading Democrats in California, who wanted Roosevelt to rebuke Sinclair for claiming that FDR secretly supported him. Of course, the President *did* favor Sinclair, judging by Jim Farley's latest letter to Senator McAdoo. Still, FDR replied:

> In regard to the gentleman in California, I suppose that if matters come to a head and he takes my name in vain the only possible answer is the one we have used before—"The President has taken no part in regard to any matter of policy, party or candidate in any State election; he is taking no part and will take no part." At this distance it looks as though Sinclair will win if he stages an orderly, common sense campaign but will be beaten if he makes a fool of himself.

While Hearst dined with Giannini and FDR entertained Roy Howard, Jefty O'Connor lunched at the Mayflower Hotel with another wavering friend of the New Deal, Father Charles Coughlin. Along with Joe Kennedy and Jim Farley, O'Connor was the administration's Catholic conduit to Coughlin. Later, O'Connor met with FDR, and the President again urged him to take the Federal Reserve job in San Francisco. "I have no one in California, Jefty," he said, implying that no matter how the November election turned out, FDR wanted O'Connor to be the New Deal's strongman out there.

Jefty O'Connor's former law partner, Senator William G. McAdoo, stopped in to see the President, too. McAdoo had just concluded his trip by monoplane through Mexico and the Southern states and didn't know what to make of a message from his associate William Neblett back in Los Angeles. A statement McAdoo made back on July 23, when he was still stumping for George Creel—"The EPIC plan is of utter and hopeless impracticality"—was apparently being published in pamphlets and plastered on billboards all over California.

Accompanying McAdoo to the White House was Santa Barbara newspaper publisher Thomas M. Storke, a wealthy Democrat who helped engineer FDR's triumph at the 1932 Democratic convention. Descended from José Francisco de Ortega, the soldier who founded the Santa Barbara presidio, stocky Tom Storke lorded over his realm in his Dakota Stetson like a benevolent W. R. Hearst. Always public-spirited, he helped rebuild the city after the devastating 1925 quake. A few years later he directed a disproportionate share of New Deal public-works money to Santa Barbara, thanks to his key role in electing both Roosevelt and McAdoo in 1932.

The two visitors from California found FDR relaxed and outgoing, so Storke ventured into what he considered risky territory. He wondered how the President was going to "combat the menace" posed by the Southern populists—Long of Louisiana, Bilbo of Mississippi, Talmadge of Georgia.

Roosevelt turned somber. "Indeed, I do know the danger, probably more than any man living," he replied. "First, though, I want to say this: I am not as 'radical' as most of my enemies say I am." FDR became increasingly reflective as he went on, revealing a side that Storke had not suspected was there. "I liken these threats to an epidemic of measles," the President said, waving one arm. "You can't halt measles when it becomes epidemic in scope, you have to let it run its course and hope for the best. That is exactly what I am trying to do. In doing this, many of my own people may misjudge me. But I feel I am right and when those self-appointed dictators have had their day, then we will be able to get on with a constructive job here in America. I pray it will not be too long."

What a day. King Alexander of Yugoslavia was assassinated in Marseille by one of his own countrymen, for reasons unknown, and the event was captured by photographers and newsreel cameramen. Spain appeared on the brink of civil war following the brutal suppression of a Socialist-led general strike that left over five hundred dead and five thousand in jail. Violence flared in the United States, and it, too, attracted wide interest and condemnation. It took place on a battlefield in Detroit, Michigan, during the seventh game of the World Series.

"We had a ball game, we had a riot," Will Rogers observed in today's dispatch, "we had Judge Landis hold court right on the field." Others called it the most appalling incident in the history of the fall classic.

It happened in the sixth inning of the deciding game. The indomitable Cardinals had blasted their way to a big lead with seven runs in the third inning, and Dizzy Dean was on the mound firing blanks. By the time the Cards' Ducky Medwick stroked a ball off the right-field wall in the sixth, the poor Tigers and their loyal partisans were in a surly mood. Medwick slid into third base, toppling Marvin Owen to the ground. For no apparent reason, Medwick aimed a kick at Owen's chest, and although it missed the mark, players from both sides rushed to the scene. After a little pushing and shoving, the umpires restored order and play resumed.

Then the fun began. Between innings, Medwick took his place in left field and was greeted first by boos and then bottles, oranges, apples, and anything else that wasn't nailed down in the bleachers. The umps called time, the grounds crew removed the garbage, and then the sky rained debris again. Four times the fans repeated the ceremony. Finally Judge Kenesaw Mountain Landis, the baseball commissioner, called together umpire Bill Klem, the players Medwick and Owen, and rival managers Frankie Frisch and Mickey Cochrane, and ordered that Ducky remove himself from the game. Medwick's manager threw a fit, but Landis wasn't called Czar for nothing, and that was that.

The final score: eleven to zero. The Cards took the Series four to three with the Dean boys winning all four games. Will Rogers, who left the third-base box he shared with Henry Ford to visit the two clubhouses, ran into Dizzy Dean wearing an Indian headdress. "Will," Diz said, "the championship remains in Oklahoma."

Worn out from nonstop speaking and traveling, Upton Sinclair took a few days off to recuperate at the remote Palos Verdes vacation home of the Lady Bountiful of the California Left, Kate Crane-Gartz, before mounting his final election drive.

The rotund daughter of plumbing magnate Charles R. Crane, a man whose name was stenciled on millions of toilets and sinks, Kate plowed her inheritance into one hopeless cause after another, believing she had nothing to give the world but money. Charlie Chaplin knew her as "Mrs. Craney-Gartz" and believed she was worth forty million dollars. Upton Sinclair called her the richest woman in Pasadena, although she actually lived in nearby Altadena. Her handsome son, Crane, had accompanied Uppie on his recent pilgrimage to Hyde Park, and she helped bankroll the EPIC campaign. She was also an inveterate letter writer, and throughout the EPIC struggle Kate dashed off dozens of letters to FDR, Joe Schenck, and Dr. Francis Townsend, among others. She even wrote *L.A. Times* reporter Kyle Palmer, informing him she could not believe that his mother, whom she knew personally, could have raised such a reactionary.

Sinclair, wary of press reports placing him anywhere near a mansion, tried to keep his whereabouts hidden, only to pick up the *Los Angeles Times* this morning and find a photograph of the two-story Spanish-style mansion where he was presently residing. "Worn out by the labors of his candidacy," the *Times* observed, "which he says is purely in the interests of the downtrodden," the ex-Socialist had taken to "living luxuriously at the Gartz home. He has been whiling away the hours sunning himself on the extensive lawns or walking on the beach."

Now that his vacation spot had been discovered, Sinclair would have to break camp; but before he did, he examined his mail. He continued to receive dozens of letters a day from admirers around the country. They sent plays, poems, anthems, economic plans, and bills in small denominations. Twenty members of the Brotherhood of Locomotive Engineers had sent a package of donations ranging from fifty cents to a dollar. A letter from his friend W. E. Woodward in New York carried the news that William Loeb, Jr., the would-be publisher and head of the New York EPIC Committee, was working on a scheme to bring Garibaldi's grandson from Italy to California to solicit Catholic votes for Sinclair. Woodward warned that this might be nothing but a publicity stunt and insisted that Loeb was simply trying to ingratiate himself with "distinguished people."

Sinclair, despite the crush of the campaign, still managed to reply to nearly all of the letters, no matter how daffy they might be. Today, for example, responding to a woman from San Diego who wanted to draw his astrological chart, Uppie revealed that he was born in Baltimore on September 20, 1878, in the morning—"hour not known!" He also shot off a telegram to Heywood Broun in New York, reminding him that he had promised to "come out here and support the campaign. It is getting red hot, plenty of news." If Broun couldn't make it, would he at least record an endorsement to air over the radio?

What bothered the candidate today even more than the *L.A. Times* exposing his hideaway was an item on the front page of the *San Fran-*

cisco Chronicle suggesting that Father Coughlin, through one of his secretaries, had indicated that contrary to Sinclair's claims he had *never* endorsed the EPIC plan. If true, Coughlin's repudiation would mark a serious reversal for Sinclair, who was already in deep trouble with Catholics. So Sinclair dashed off a telegram to the radio priest in Royal Oak, Michigan:

> VERY EARNESTLY HOPE YOU WILL STATE THE FACTS. I OUTLINED THE PLAN TO YOU IN YOUR STUDY AND YOU CHECKED IT POINT BY POINT, AND SPECIFICALLY AUTHORIZED ME TO SAY YOU ENDORSED THAT ENTIRE PROGRAM. WE ARE BEING SUBJECTED TO TERRIFIC BARRAGE BY CORRUPT AND VICIOUS INTERESTS, AND YOUR REPUDIATION IS DOING US INCALCULABLE DAMAGE.

"The masters of big business and special privilege," Upton Sinclair once charged, were "willing to spread ten million lies at a cost of $1 per lie, knowing if they can win this election they can wring hundreds of millions of dollars out of the toil and suffering of the people of California." If Sinclair was right about the ten million dollars—others made much the same guess—it would represent a staggering sum, easily the most ever spent on a campaign in a single state. But with hundreds of millions, possibly billions, of dollars in investments at stake in this race, fund-raising in California rolled on, inexorable.

Today, as the temperature reached a record eighty-seven degrees, one hundred of San Francisco's wealthiest gathered at what was described as a very private meeting to pledge additional funds for Merriam. The conference was organized by the famed realtor Culbert Coldwell.

Like A. P. Giannini, Coldwell got his big break because of the Big Quake. Where others in San Francisco in 1906 saw devastation, Coldwell identified the potential for unimaginable profit. Property owners were eager to sell, and Culbert Coldwell was savvy enough to buy. Now his firm of Coldwell, Banker dominated the local real estate market. An austere gentleman of fifty-one, Coldwell was prominent in social and civic affairs and served on the Committee of 44 that organized opposition to the recent general strike. But his firm's reach extended well beyond San Francisco. Its representative in Hollywood, Charles Detoy, handled investments for many stars, including Mary Pickford.

Whatever sum of money Coldwell raised today would surely be well spent. Northern California's two major front groups—the Merriam Democratic Campaign Committee and the California League Against Sinclairism—lagged about two weeks behind their counterparts in the south in creating anti-Sinclair hullabaloo. But with more slush money in the bank, they might close that gap in a hurry.

Millions of United for California pamphlets had flooded the mail, but the group still had its hands full. There were workers to intimidate, voters to invalidate, dirty tricks to instigate. EPIC was on the defensive, but it was a long way from dead.

Albert Parker, acting under the direction of Asa Call, dispatched a memo to "Southern California Employers," urging that "all true Americans make it their first order of business to see that those who have jobs be given proper information upon which to base a sound decision." Executives should secure a supply of anti-Sinclair literature and place it with each employee personally. Then the boss should urge them to "soberly think of the danger to their jobs if Sinclair is elected and be sure to cast their votes on election day." Attached to the directive was a list of twenty-three different leaflets that the employer could obtain by writing a letter or sending a messenger to the group's headquarters in downtown Los Angeles. "Please do not order by telephone," the memo warned cryptically.

Also enclosed in the United for California packet was a sheet labeled "Suggested Methods of Placing Information in the Hands of Employees." "The employer is in a position to obtain and analyze data on both sides of the picture," it advised, "while the average employee does not have this facility and therefore must largely base his opinions on the illogical and incorrect statements made to him by the proponents of EPIC." It then listed four ways of transmitting information, in descending order of probable effectiveness:

1. Direct contact of employer (preferably the chief executive) with employees, on a man to man basis. . . . Care should be exerted to eliminate any thought of pressure or coercion.
2. Use of trustworthy old employee to spread the facts.
3. Direct mailing of instructive literature to the home addresses of employees.
4. Speakers from outside the plant to address the employees.

One task completed, Albert Parker turned to unfinished business. United for California's investigation of Democratic vote fraud had turned up a number of illegal registrants, but nowhere near enough to cost Sinclair the election. Voters could be challenged at the polls or in court, but this was a cumbersome process and might result in striking only a few hundred names from the rolls. Scare tactics, however, might successfully keep tens of thousands from voting. Some of Sinclair's supporters were transient workers; many other EPICs, recent arrivals in the state, had signed up to vote only in the past few weeks. These types of people might be susceptible to intimidation.

Unsure of a legal precedent in California, Parker recalled that some sort of mass vote-purge scheme had been tried with some success in New York City by George Medalie, a former U.S. attorney. So he sent a telegram to his close friend Eli Whitney Debevoise, who was practicing law in New York with another one of Parker's buddies from Harvard (class of '25), Francis Plimpton. "We are bending our energies toward defeat of Upton Sinclair," Parker wired his friend. "He has secured many false registrations to bolster up his vote. Hope to attack this as federal crime." Parker said he'd appreciate it if Debevoise could find out how Medalie managed to invalidate voters in New York.

OCTOBER 11

THURSDAY

Literary Digest announced today that it was conducting another one of its famous straw polls. Known for correctly picking presidential races, the *Digest* this time turned to a statewide race, explaining that the eyes of the entire nation were trained on California. "No political development in recent years has stirred the imagination of the people of the United States as the forthcoming contest for Governor of California," the *Digest* observed. "Will the results of the election in California be a future guide to the political and economic future of the other forty-seven States?"

They would know soon enough. The *Digest* had just put 680,000 ballots in the mail to voters in every city in California, representing about one quarter of the expected turnout on November 6. On the ballots were the names Haight, Merriam, and Sinclair, as well as Dempster and Darcy. This being a magazine promotion, the cover letter also made a sales pitch—seventeen issues for one dollar—but voters were under no obligation to subscribe. *Literary Digest* even promised to pay the postage if they returned their ballots.

The *Digest* claimed amazing accuracy in previous polls, correctly predicting the past four presidential contests. It had called the Roosevelt landslide in 1932 and in 1920 had forecast the seemingly impossible: Warren Harding would carry all five boroughs of New York City. "So," the *Digest* proclaimed immodestly, "this new Poll of California will show who will be the next Governor."

———

H. L. Mencken planned to write another column attacking his old friend Upton Sinclair but couldn't find time to finish it. He was still immersed in *The American Language* and in caring for his invalid wife, Sara. Today, however, he wrote Lee Hartman, editor of *Harper's* magazine in New York, proposing an article on the fundamentals of democracy:

> My belief is that the Fathers made a tremendous error when they laid the foundations of universal suffrage. To be sure they were against it, but nevertheless they opened the way for it. We are now beginning to learn how dangerous it is to permit paupers [to] vote. I am half convinced, indeed, that the present troubles of the world are not due to the downfall of capitalism, but to the breakup of democracy. The two things are constantly confused, but they are really quite antagonistic. Capitalism is probably still a going concern, even in Russia, but certainly democracy begins to look sick.

"Would an article going into these blue matters," Mencken wondered, "interest you?"

———

The jobless marched on Washington this afternoon. When police attempted to break up the demonstration, a riot broke out. Twelve of the more than five hundred protesters were injured and had to be treated at the scene. It was merely a scene from a movie, and at the same time horribly real.

The bloody conflict occurred on the Paramount lot during the final day of filming Walter Wanger's *The President Vanishes.* The demonstration was in the script, but the riot was not. Many of the extras apparently identified too closely with the role of scruffy agitator. During the mob scene, they pounded thirty-five policemen (played by stuntmen), and studio personnel had to train fire hoses on them to cool them off. Then the director, William A. Wellman, ordered free dinners for all.

Riots were breaking out at the World Series and at movie studios but not in Washington. What was America coming to?

It was a momentous day over at the Chaplin studio as well: Charlie finally started shooting his new movie. The first scene he filmed showed a factory boss played by Allan Garcia in a futuristic office equipped with a huge screen—a prototype of the new invention, television—that enabled him to keep an eye on his workers. Chaplin continued to equivocate on the use of sound. He couldn't decide whether to keep the new film completely silent, like the rest of his movies, or to include spoken dialogue, like every other picture in Hollywood. He also considered a kind of compromise: no dialogue but a lot of sound effects, such as the rumbling noise of a hungry stomach. One might blow bubbles in a pail of water to get this effect.

Filming may have started slowly, but once Chaplin got going, he was a demon about work, making it ever more unlikely that he would rejoin EPIC. Others stars remained curiously mute about both Sinclair and Merriam, but an item in the *Hollywood Reporter* this morning suggested that screenwriters might not feel so reticent. "Joe Mankiewicz, who is one of the Young Crusaders group," the *Reporter* observed, "has written a skit against Sinclair for their bi-weekly broadcast." Mankiewicz, according to this report, intended to build the story around the talents of Ted Healy and Nat Pendleton, but the two actors suddenly "withdrew their services and it has since been found that they had received threatening letters, warning them that it would do their careers no good to appear in such a radio program."

Mankiewicz had been in Hollywood five years, arriving from New York at the age of twenty at the urging of his already successful brother, Herman, also a writer. Joe helped develop W. C. Fields's "My Little Chickadee" number, wrote several films for Joan Crawford, and earned an early Oscar nomination. Nineteen thirty-four was a busy year for Joe. He supplied dialogue for King Vidor's *Our Daily Bread* and wrote two scripts for Fritz Lang and two more for Woody Van Dyke.

The *Hollywood Reporter* item raised eyebrows, because Mankiewicz was considered a pro-FDR liberal and had been an early force in the formation of the Screen Writers Guild. It wasn't hard to imagine, however, who might have enlisted him in the radio campaign. Woody Van Dyke was the most outspoken anti-Sinclair director at Metro and head of the Crusaders' "MGM branch" (as he had put it in his letter to FDR last month). Mankiewicz and Van Dyke saw eye to eye on the dangers of Sinclairism, particularly as it applied to higher taxes, so Joe had agreed to polish GOP campaign speeches and anti-Sinclair radio scripts. One of the radio melodramas warned rich folks that Governor Sinclair might confiscate their swimming pools.

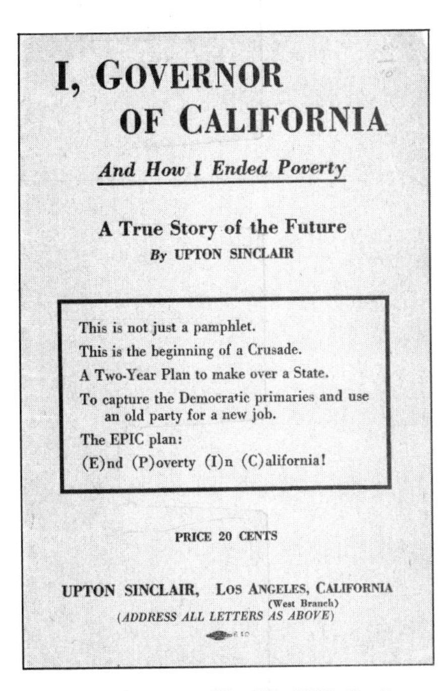

I, GOVERNOR OF CALIFORNIA

And How I Ended Poverty

A True Story of the Future

By UPTON SINCLAIR

This is not just a pamphlet.
This is the beginning of a Crusade.
A Two-Year Plan to make over a State.
To capture the Democratic primaries and use an old party for a new job.
The EPIC plan:
(E)nd (P)overty (I)n (C)alifornia!

PRICE 20 CENTS

UPTON SINCLAIR, LOS ANGELES, CALIFORNIA (West Branch)
(*ADDRESS ALL LETTERS AS ABOVE*)

The book that started it all in 1933: By the summer of '34 it was a best-seller.

Courtesy of Ray Haight, Jr.

Raymond L. Haight, third-party candidate, mocked Governor Merriam but found Sinclair too radical.

Courtesy of the Lilly Library, Indiana University

Sinclair at the Centinella Bowl in Inglewood, July 1934: a modern-day Savonarola, "leading the Hallelujah Chorus with a slide rule."

Lilly Library

Charlie Chaplin with his "mentor," Upton Sinclair.

Courtesy of the Academy of Motion Picture Arts and Sciences

Jimmy Cagney, the "professional againster," in a 1934 publicity pose: Like Sinclair, he was labeled a Red sympathizer.

Courtesy of the Academy of Motion Picture Arts and Sciences

Dorothy Parker (with new husband Alan Campbell) returned to Hollywood in September 1934 and joined the Authors League for Sinclair.

Courtesy of the Academy of Motion Picture Arts and Sciences

Louis B. Mayer, Norma Shearer, Irving Thalberg: The MGM lions roared against Sinclair.

Lilly Library

H. L. Mencken feared he'd laugh himself to death if his friend Uppie ever took office.

The Bettmann Archive

Albert Lasker, the advertising king, approved his agency's groundbreaking media campaign against Sinclair.

Courtesy of Clem Whitaker, Jr.

Clem Whitaker, the nation's first "political consultant," and the creative genius behind the California League Against Sinclairism.

The Bettmann Archive

Following his chat with President Roosevelt at Hyde Park on September 4, 1934, Sinclair met reporters at the Nelson House, certain he had just wrapped up the election.

Lilly Library

Meeting with Harry Hopkins in Washington, D.C., on September 6.

EPIC sponsored many festive pageants and parades. This one took place in Santa Clara.

The candidate with one of the many EPIC vans that toured the state.

Earl Warren (right), Alameda County district attorney (shown here with legendary San Francisco editor Fremont Older), took charge of the Republican campaign at the end of September.

California State Archives

Franklin D. Roosevelt Library

FDR delivers fireside chat, September 30, 1934: Would he keep his "promise" and endorse Sinclair?

Dizzy Dean and Will Rogers at the '34 World Series.

Will Hays, the movie czar, helped mobilize Hollywood against Sinclair.

Joseph M. Schenck and Douglas Fairbanks arrived in Miami, Florida, on October 4, 1934, to inspect new sites for studios (in case Sinclair won).

The Bettmann Archive

Courtesy of Will Hays, Jr.

Courtesy of Ruth Cashman

Albert Parker, a young O'Melveny attorney, bragged to his friend Eli Whitney Debevoise about a plan to "terrify" voters from coming to the polls in Los Angeles.

The fake Communist endorsement, reportedly the work of Albert Parker.

Anti-Sinclair leaflets handed out on street corners.

Hundreds of thousands of "SincLiar" dollars, printed in red ink, circulated throughout California.

Typical Ted Gale cartoon from Hearst's *Examiners*.

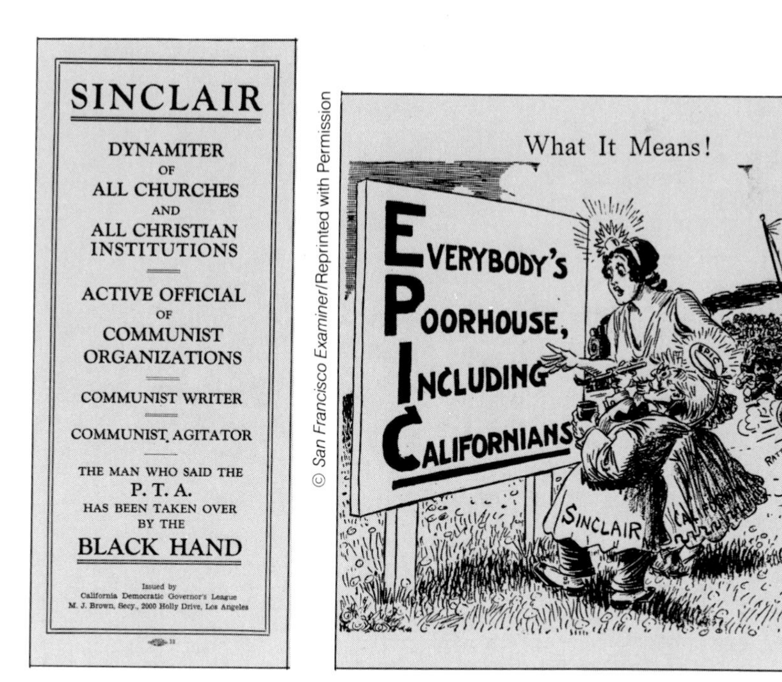

SINCLAIR

DYNAMITER
OF
ALL CHURCHES
AND
ALL CHRISTIAN
INSTITUTIONS

ACTIVE OFFICIAL
OF
COMMUNIST
ORGANIZATIONS

COMMUNIST WRITER

COMMUNIST AGITATOR

THE MAN WHO SAID THE
P. T. A.
HAS BEEN TAKEN OVER
BY THE
BLACK HAND

Issued by
California Democratic Governor's League
M. J. Brown, Secy., 2000 Holly Drive, Los Angeles

A popular leaflet from a Los Angeles front group, the California Democratic Governor's League.

Miss California warns that a migrant horde, seeking Sinclair's EPIC utopia, is about to invade the state.

The Bettmann Archive

Street scene in Los Angeles: Tens of thousands of billboards bearing "The Quote" appeared everywhere.

University of South Carolina Newsfilm Library

"Bums" arriving in California, courtesy of Irving Thalberg, from the propaganda short *California Election News No. 3*: precursor of political advertising on television.

Courtesy of the Academy of Motion Picture Arts and Sciences

Katharine Hepburn (second from left) on set of *The Little Minister,* October 1934: Pressured to oppose Sinclair?

Courtesy of Rolf McPherson

The evangelist Aimee Semple McPherson took aim at Sinclair, the Red Devil, during the last two weeks of the campaign.

The Bettmann Archive

Jefty O'Connor, FDR's emissary, takes time out during his mission to California to lunch with Shirley Temple and his friend Elissa Landi, November 1, 1934.

Governor Frank Merriam, "Old Baldy," casts his vote on election day, November 6, 1934.

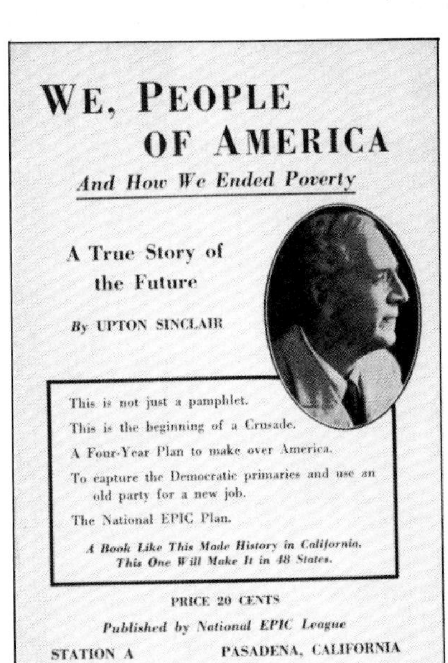

Two years after the '34 race, Sinclair attempted to start a national movement, to no avail.

—

Obviously, Joe Mankiewicz obviously was no longer a candidate for Frank Scully's Authors' League for Sinclair. Scully had fallen on hard times. Besides Dudley Nichols, Aldous Huxley, and a couple of other brave souls, few writers expressed support for EPIC. One scribe, last name Murray, was known to wear a Sinclair button away from the studio and a Merriam pin when he showed up for work. One of Scully's few recruits, *Script* editor Rob Wagner, had already asked him to take his name off the membership list, calling Sinclair "a swell propagandist," but "a bum executive." Wagner added that he had talked to Uppie over the phone recently, "and he seemed utterly bewildered."

Scully replied angrily, arguing that the candidate knew where he was going, even if he only got half way there. "Stick to Uppie," Scully pleaded, "even if he doesn't stick to himself." Gene Fowler volunteered to take Wagner's place on the Authors' League organizing committee.

At a studio luncheon today, Harry Brand of United Artists pulled Scully aside to inform him that the Republicans, believe it or not, were exploring a scheme to disenfranchise one hundred thousand Democrats. GOP canvassers aimed at obtaining a court injunction from a friendly Republican judge that would drive an entire class of voters from the polls. Knowing that Frank was close to Uppie, Harry suggested that he pass this information along to Sinclair. Scully replied that EPIC had so many sharp investigators, he was certain they'd already uncovered the plot.

—

When he received Albert Parker's telegram seeking advice on his vote-purge scheme, Eli Whitney Debevoise responded immediately, as any good friend would. Debevoise and Parker had in common a law degree from Harvard and a patrician upbringing. Debevoise was named after his great-great-grandfather, Eli Whitney, inventor of the cotton gin. After leaving Harvard, he joined a law firm headed by John W. Davis, the Democrat who snatched the 1924 presidential nomination from William G. McAdoo. In 1931, Debevoise and William E. Stevenson formed a partnership. A few months later Francis Plimpton joined the firm.

As Parker suggested, Debevoise called former U.S. attorney George Medalie in New York. Medalie, a Republican, once purged Democratic voters in an attempt to rout Tammany Hall. Debevoise wanted to know whether federal charges could be brought against illegal registrants in Los Angeles.

Medalie explained that while voting illegally might be a federal crime, fraudulent registration was not. Illegal registrants could be challenged in state court prior to Election Day, but these cases were always difficult to prove and the would-be voters usually defended themselves vigorously. Even if the GOP won, this probably would amount to nothing more than "flea bites" on a donkey, he advised.

A way to circumvent the inconvenience of voters sticking up for their rights was to draw up two separate lists of illegal registrants, Medalie suggested. One list would identify individuals who would be ordered to appear in court to show cause why they should be allowed to vote; this would signal that the Republicans meant business. But by far the more important list was the second one, which would be filed with the prosecutor and *sealed.* It might include tens of thousands of names or only a dozen: it mattered not. A cooperative D.A. might refer to this document as a "secret indictment." Any Democrat's name *could* be on it, and if that unfortunate citizen attempted to vote he or she might be arrested. Press coverage could be orchestrated to dwell on that uncertainty.

The purpose of this procedure would not be to throw a few Democrats in jail but to intimidate a mass of citizens into staying home. Medalie had tried this once and found that many voters whose names were not included in the secret indictment, but who were uncertain about the status of their registration, "were scared away from the polls." There would be no way anyone could tell in advance whether his name was actually on the secret list.

After talking to Medalie, Debevoise called his successor as U.S. attorney in New York, Thomas E. Dewey. The cocky young prosecutor "had no further practical suggestions," Debevoise reported today in a letter to Albert Parker, except to approach the FBI for support and to ask the Justice Department to appoint deputy U.S. marshals "to appear at the polls to detect and prevent illegal voting."

Upton Sinclair was already in deep trouble with Catholics in California, and now it appeared certain that Father Charles Coughlin would not ride to his rescue. The *Los Angeles Examiner* released the text of a recent letter the radio priest had mailed to a follower in Hollywood.

"May I take this opportunity," Coughlin wrote, "to assure you that I am supporting no candidate for Governor. The rumor that is being circulated in your vicinity is false and erroneous. . . ."

Coughlin elaborated in another letter published in *The Tidings,* the official organ of the Catholic diocese of Los Angeles. "Mr. Sinclair," Coughlin explained, "called at my home. Naturally, I treated him as any other stranger would be treated, with the hospitality which he deserved. I am so ignorant, I have not read any of his books and I am so provincial I have not even read his EPIC program."

———

The anti-EPIC struggle in northern California finally got rolling today with the public unveiling of the California League against Sinclairism, or CLAS. Former governor C. C. Young told a crowd of eight hundred at the St. Francis Hotel in San Francisco that EPIC stood for "End California in Poverty." Headquartered on the twenty-eighth floor of the Russ Building, San Francisco's tallest structure, CLAS was ready to put millions of pieces of handsomely printed literature (prepared by Clem Whitaker) in the mail.

A youth brigade known as the Young Liberal League, under the direction of Bert Levit, president of the California Junior Chamber of Commerce, would act as CLAS's army. Like United for California in the south, its aim was to reach every single employer in northern California. Levit appointed a "general" for each region, a "colonel" for each county or large city, "majors" for smaller cities, a "captain" for every ten companies, and a "lieutenant" for every major office. Captains were to visit each company and distribute anti-Sinclair literature. Lieutenants would survey workers, place Merriam stickers around the office or factory, and convince everyone to vote Republican. In a confidential memo to employers, CLAS asked them either to mail literature to employees' homes or to forward the workers' addresses to CLAS. It also requested that they assign as many workers as they could "to spend two days of each week on definite duty prior to November 6."

One CLAS item already widely circulated was the SINC*LIAR* DOLLAR, issued by the "Uppy & Downy Bank" and printed in red ink. According to the small print, it was "redeemable, if ever, at the cost of future generations." The so-called Red Currency was "good only in California or Russia," but "not very good anywhere." Another popular item was a parody of Sinclair's *I, Governor of California, and How I Ended*

Poverty entitled *I, Menace of California, and How I Ended.* CLAS sounded this warning: "YOU started this, Upton Sinclair. We plain American voters of every party will finish it on November 6."

All over California, shop owners coaxed customers, employers coerced workers, and newspaper editors courted readers, all in the name of "keeping California out of the red, and the Reds out of California," as one popular slogan put it. Frank A. Garbutt, president of the Los Angeles Athletic Club, sent a letter to his employees warning that they might lose their jobs if Sinclair won; when the economy collapsed, club membership would decline precipitously.

At first, doctors, lawyers, and educators sat on the sidelines of anti-Sinclair activity, reluctant to exploit their positions of trust in the community. Now that resistance was crumbling. One of the many professional groups joining the crusade was the Northern California Dental Non-Partisan Merriam-for-Governor Club. (In abbreviated form, it might be called the NCDNPMFGC.) From its Market Street headquarters in San Francisco, the club sent a letter to every dentist in the north, four thousand in all.

"Dear Doctor," the letter began, "It has never before been so necessary for dentistry to have a man of responsibility conducting the affairs of our State." EPIC raised "the spectre of a series of experiments in the important field of public health. . . . Doctor, you spent many years in building your practice and protecting professional ideals, are you willing to have these jeopardized?" Besides asking for "militant" opposition to Sinclair, the group asked each dentist to supply it with the names and addresses of fifty to one hundred patients and a like amount of letterhead. The anti-Sinclair group would then write a "suitable letter" to the patients on the *dentist's own stationery.*

Would any professional actually submit the name of a client and samples of his own stationery to a stranger, particularly for political purposes? The answer: within forty-eight hours of mailing its appeal, the Northern California Dental Non-Partisan Merriam-for-Governor Club had secured the names of more than five thousand patients.

Strangely enough, the beneficiary of the screamingly negative anti-Sinclair campaign was howling about it almost as loudly as Uppie himself. Frank Merriam rarely read or heard a word about his own moral character, his accomplishments in office, his goals for the future. Perhaps for the first time anywhere it was the front-running incumbent who was the forgotten man in a campaign.

Merriam was almost invisible. His campaign appearances were low-key, and he only spoke to friends: the Knights of Columbus, the Chamber of Commerce, a convention of policemen. Everywhere he looked, he saw signs of anti-Sinclairism on billboards, in newspapers, in his mail. "Stop EPIC" blared from every radio. "It's Merriam or Moscow"—some choice! Didn't anyone have a kind word for good old Frank, a Sunday-school teacher loved by every child and dog in Long Beach?

Frank Finley Merriam had decided: enough was enough. No more of this hold-your-nose-and-vote-for-Merriam. He wanted the GOP campaign to turn positive. He expressed this view in a meeting with Asa Call, acting head of United for California.

"A hell of a lot of money is being spent," Merriam said, "and it's all about what a stinker Upton Sinclair is. But there's nothing about me."

Call was in no mood to take any guff from the governor. Suffering from heart strain brought on by the stock market crash in 1929, Ace had quit private law practice to take what he thought was a soft job at Pacific Mutual. Now the insurance company was near collapse, and Call was virtually directing the anti-Sinclair campaign in Los Angeles. Ace had to put Merriam in his place. Who did he think he was, anyway?

"You're a tough guy to sell," Call explained, "and we're going to do it our way. We're going to continue to say that Upton Sinclair is a no good son-of-a-bitch, and we're going to spend a lot of money for that. In the last ten days of the campaign we'll promote you with billboards with your name all over the place.

"That's what we have planned," Call concluded, "and *that's* that."

OCTOBER 14

SUNDAY

For once, the stars in Hollywood would not come out. No matter what the moguls did, celebrities simply would not cozy up to Frank Finley Merriam. Except for a Sam Jaffe here, a Leo Carrillo there, few first-rank actors took a public stand for Merriam, partly because they didn't want to lose any fans, mostly because they had contracts that protected them from coercion. Of the three biggest names in Hollywood, two were off-limits to Merriam anyway. Charlie Chaplin favored Sinclair, and Will Rogers probably wouldn't endorse anyone. That left the fastest rising star of all, and it didn't matter if she was barely three feet tall and wouldn't be able to cast her first vote for another fifteen years. America was in the midst of a Shirley Temple craze, so she might swing more votes than anyone.

Little Shirley from Santa Monica had burst onto the movie scene early this year in *Stand Up and Cheer.* A Fox musical based on an original idea by Will Rogers, it portrayed a president appointing a Secretary of Amusements to lift the country's spirits. Shirley Temple, goldilocked and not yet six years old, stole the show singing and dancing "Baby Take a Bow." Next she made *Little Miss Marker,* and suddenly the curly-top was hot. Toy companies started making Shirley Temple dolls. Her latest movie, *Now and Forever,* costarring Gary Cooper and Carole Lombard, opened in September, and currently she was rehearsing *Bright Eyes.*

Shirley's timing was impeccable: she was both the squeaky-clean answer to Will Hays's prayer and an antidote to the Depression. She was a "warm sun flooding a dreary room," in the words of Walter Winchell. Even President Roosevelt hailed her arrival, observing that in tough times "it is a splendid thing that for just fifteen cents an American can go to a movie and look at the smiling face of a baby and forget his troubles."

Those fifteen cents multiplied rapidly for the studio. After making an astounding $1 million on one of her films, Fox signed Shirley to a seven-year contract at $1,000 a week. Her mother, Gertrude, got another $250 weekly for reading Shirley the script and setting her hair in fifty-six curls every night. Shirley Temple had the only contract in Hollywood without a morality clause. By all accounts, the little scene-stealer was remarkably well behaved, all things considered (she had a bodyguard and rode to work in a bulletproof limo). She even ate her vegetables. And her parents were lifelong Republicans.

By the terms of her contract, Shirley was excused from making personal appearances, but the studio made at least one exception this autumn so that she could stand up and cheer for Frank Merriam. In an official ceremony at the state capitol, the governor presented Shirley with a welcoming proclamation covered with gold seals and tied with ribbons. "Funny papers," Shirley commented. Cameras flashed.

FRANK: Are you Republican or Democrat?
SHIRLEY: What are they?
FRANK: Well, are you going to vote for me or Upton Sinclair?
SHIRLEY: I'm going to vote for the boss.

Merriam pulled Shirley up onto his lap. She found it amazingly bony, considering his girth. He told her that she was the only performer who could make him go to the "picture show." Ten thousand people were expected at his rally later this day, mainly because of her, he said.

Shirley remained uncharacteristically silent; she had a healthy respect for authority. But Mom stepped in. Shirley would not be attending the governor's rally, Gertrude Temple announced, because she didn't want her daughter to "get into politics—at least until she can spell the word."

Charlie Pettijohn was back in Hollywood and, as one of the trade papers put it, conducting a "studio look around." Will Hays's emissary to the anti-Sinclair campaign also attended a special meeting of the board of the Motion Picture Producers and Distributors of America, the outfit that paid his fifty-thousand-dollar-a-year salary. Most of the big men of the industry appeared, including Louis B. Mayer, Harry Cohn, and Jack Warner. Hollywood, with some help from New York, had finally settled on a cohesive strategy to punish Sinclair between now and Election Day. There would be no more threats to move out of the state, and the moguls would quit trying to herd their employees into line by promising a loss of jobs under EPIC. Instead, they would turn their attention to the millions of voters beyond the movie colony who would ultimately decide the contest.

The studios chose to fight the war on two new fronts: fund-raising and propaganda. Louis B. Mayer had concocted a scheme to enact a kind of "Merriam tax" on MGM personnel. Each of his employees, from the lowliest propman to the biggest star, would be assessed one day's pay to be earmarked for the Merriam campaign kitty. Depending on the salary, this would represent a contribution of anywhere from twenty dollars to five hundred dollars. Most of the other executives—even Jack Warner the Democrat—agreed to levy a similar tax at their studios. This might raise another half million dollars for Merriam.

The other new tactic had already drawn a friendly notice in *Variety*. "Trailers attacking the candidacy of Upton Sinclair for governor," the journal reported, "are being prepared at several of the studios, for screening in the theaters throughout the state during the remaining weeks preceding the November election."

The *Beverly Hills Bulletin,* one of the few papers in California that offered EPIC an even break in its political coverage, appeared to be on the verge of expiring. John McAndrew, owner of the weekly, declared that "agents have been approaching all *Bulletin* advertisers, threatening them, and warning them to withdraw their advertising immediately." Now his landlord, a large bank, had ordered him to vacate his office by November 1. McAndrew balked, then offered to pay a steep rent increase, but the bank reportedly refused his offer. "It is apparently worth a publisher's business life," McAndrew complained, "to be unbiased in printing the news."

———

Reporting from Los Angeles, a *New York Times* correspondent declared this morning that "a sense of Armageddon hangs in the bland California air." The governor's campaign, he wrote, had loosed "a whole arsenal of 'below-the-belt' strategies calculated to substitute embittering extraneous issues for the real ones." As the California campaign approached its climax, criminal mischief and violence increased. Speakers were heckled, signs torn down, loudspeaker wires cut. Street-corner arguments sometimes ended in fisticuffs. Upton Sinclair claimed that EPIC's phones were tapped and that mail arrived already opened. Clem Whitaker and Leone Baxter heard rumors that certain people planned to shoot the EPIC candidate on the steps of the state capitol if he ever took office, and they found these reports credible.

In Los Angeles, a young man named Harold M. Lewis revealed that he was assaulted late last night when he left his California Republican Assembly office on South Flower Street. Lewis, like most of his CRA comrades, had spent the day canvassing door-to-door, searching for illegal Democratic registrants. Suddenly he was accosted by a rather large, well-dressed man who politely informed him, "I'm sorry I must do this, but I have been paid twenty dollars to give you a beating." Then the stranger slugged him in the face and chest, blackening his eye and breaking three of his ribs. Newspaper photographers documented the injuries for tomorrow's editions.

So who were these California citizens whose voting status was suddenly open to question? The bulk of them fell into two categories. One bloc consisted of the homeless unemployed. When they registered to vote, many of them provided the address of the flophouse where they were temporarily staying, and then moved on. The other group: transient workers who shuttled between rooming houses in the city and migrant camps in the country, their schedule fixed by harvest. Although members of either group might move around the state willy-nilly, their registration, in most cases, remained valid. According to state law, they were legally registered to vote in their original precinct until they established a permanent residence elsewhere.

McIntyre Faries, a local CRA leader, stumbled on this phenomenon during a recent visit to a transient hotel on the East Side of Los Angeles, checking on seventy registered Democrats who had claimed it as their home. He discovered that the building could not house anywhere close to seventy men, even with several crammed into each room. But the hotel manager claimed that everything was on the up-and-up. "Most of our people are transient workers," he explained. "They come and go. They register to vote here, and get their mail and checks here."

Faries realized, with some chagrin, that many of the other "illegal" registrants fell into the same category. But canvassing was only one of his duties. Although the anti-Sinclair drive was centered on Los Angeles, young Republicans like Mac Faries were active in every election district in the south. The money might be coming out of L.A., but the foot soldiers covered the map.

An attorney in his mid-thirties, Faries was a GOP activist in the South Pasadena–Alhambra area, just north and east of Los Angeles. He had helped the upstart California Republican Assembly take over the GOP campaign in the twelfth congressional district this fall. Like his colleagues, he considered Frank Merriam a prehistoric relic but still preferred him to the socialist Sinclair. A local bank donated space over its branch in Alhambra for GOP headquarters. The Title Insurance Company in downtown L.A. sent seven secretaries (and five typewriters) to the twelfth district to work full-time on the campaign. Southern California Edison assigned fifteen employees to the GOP office, and they became its key operatives.

All of this was hush-hush and likely illegal, but it seemed to be standard operating procedure in every election district in the south, Mac Faries observed.

Mel Belli was doing some hard traveling. As a speaker for Frank Merriam, he was logging almost as many miles as he had in his days as a hobo for Harry Hopkins. From his home in Berkeley, he drove in every direction. Before he went anywhere, he would visit Merriam headquarters in San Francisco for briefings and to pick up a carload of literature. Then he would go on his way.

In factories and offices, at schools and as a guest of civic organizations, Belli used his law-school oratorical skills to promote the candidacy of the incumbent governor. He did his best to identify and emphasize Merriam's good points. For the first time, Belli felt he truly understood the legal concept that even the most unappealing person was entitled to a strong defense. Merriam, in a sense, was Mel's client—and a generous one as well. In his speeches, Mel ignored Merriam most of the time, of course. He told jokes and concentrated his verbal fire on Sinclair. It was a classic legal defense: Take the heat off your client by attacking the prosecution and questioning his evidence.

One thing unnerved Mel Belli, however. Summoned by their employers to hear him speak, workers would assemble dutifully and listen politely, but Mel noticed that despite his impassioned arguments the audience inevitably lacked enthusiasm. Their applause was patently phony—as insincere as his praise for Merriam. They were ready to convict his client, no matter what Belli did or said. But then, Mel wasn't sure he was going to vote for Merriam himself.

Another young, would-be San Francisco attorney who professed sympathy for the underdog took an entirely different approach. Charles Garry, who operated a small dry-cleaning shop in the Richmond District and attended law school at night, actively promoted EPIC.

Unlike Mel Belli, Garry came from a disadvantaged background. His Armenian parents had fled Turkey and settled in Massachusetts near the turn of the century, eventually moving to Selma, California. At the age of eleven, their son Garabed Hagop Garbedian—known as Charles—worked in a cannery and read *Les Misérables.* Like Jean Valjean, the young boy passionately believed that no one should have to steal or beg to make ends meet. Taunted with ethnic slurs, Charles became an accomplished street fighter, finally changing his name from Garbedian to Garry to escape discrimination. A union activist, he lost his job at a cannery in Berkeley for attempting to organize workers. In 1933, he took out a hundred-dollar loan and opened Garry's Cleaning and Tailoring Shop in San Francisco. At night he attended San Francisco College of Law, intent on becoming a people's lawyer.

Near the end of 1933, Garry met Upton Sinclair, one of his heroes. He had read nearly all of the candidate's books and identified completely with his social program. Somehow, while running a business, attending law school, and organizing workers in the cleaning and dyeing industry, Garry found time this autumn to stump for Sinclair in San Francisco. Privately, Mel Belli referred to Frank Merriam as "that bald-headed son of a bitch." Charlie Garry simply called him "Marbletop."

By all accounts, Lord & Thomas's radio crusade for United for California, which began airing over several Los Angeles stations this week, promised to produce better results than Mel Belli's barnstorming. Albert Lasker had passed this plum to his man in Los Angeles, Don Francisco, who had handed it to one of his top execs, Don Forker. Lord & Thomas spared no expense. Forker, a former advertising manager for Union Oil, hired top-flight radio and screen writers to script four serials, each about fifteen minutes in length, and employed thirty-five actors to play the various roles. Some of the programs aired daily, others three times a week. Every night a "board of strategy" met at Lord & Thomas's office on South Broadway to discuss reaction to each program.

One of the shows, *The Political Observer,* was a straightforward current-events program, albeit with an anti-Sinclair twist. The other three series displayed a good deal more flair. On *Turn of Events,* based on the *March of Time* concept, actors impersonated famous people. *Weary and Willie* followed the adventures of two hoboes from the Midwest who hop a train for California, answering Sinclair's call.

More in the soap-opera vein, *The Bennetts* was modeled on the popular *One Man's Family* serial. Members of a middle-class family chatted by the fireside and around the dinner table about the governor's race. In one program, Mom was fixing a meal when Sis came home from school. Beneath her carefree exterior, Sis was worried she wouldn't be allowed to graduate next year if Sinclair took over, because he was opposed to education. Then Dad came home from work and, in an aside to his wife, confessed he was afraid his factory would close down if EPIC took effect. When the Bennetts sat down to dinner, Junior urged everyone to hurry up and eat so he could go to a picture show—something he might not be able to do for long, since Sinclair promised to put Hollywood out of business. Sis was anxious to leave for choir practice at church—which would surely be suspended under the atheistic EPIC plan.

Finally settling down to dinner, the Bennetts thanked God for this fine feast. Sadly they agreed that when Dad lost his steady paycheck under EPIC, this too would pass.

James A. Farley, speaking to the nation over the new American Broadcasting Company network in New York, tonight denied rumors that the White House intended to use radio as a medium of government control. President Roosevelt, he pointed out, had recently declared that he would never permit radio to be used for propaganda purposes. Farley acknowledged that radio was playing an increasingly powerful role in politics but asserted that its effect was entirely positive. Citizens, he said, now had "a more accurate understanding of governmental problems than ever in the history of the nation. Misinformation is rapidly dissipated.

"It is common knowledge," Farley added, "that radio has revolutionized political campaigns. Millions may now be reached, compared with thousands of former days." In the old days, the political parties could easily mislead voters. Now, he pointed out, "it is comparatively easy to reach the whole electorate and to present the issues in a calm and dispassionate manner. Once the American people are in possession of all the facts the verdict will always be fair and just."

America's most famous Communist writer—discounting fellow travelers like Dreiser and Steffens—arrived in San Francisco tonight, denouncing Upton Sinclair with virtually his first breath of Bay air. The CP politburo in New York, dissatisfied with the rather gentle tone of Sam Darcy's attacks on Sinclair, had sent their chief hatchet man to California to do the job right. Although he was an old friend and colleague of the EPIC candidate's, Robert Minor was only too eager to fire both barrels at Sinclair.

No Communist had a finer lineage than tall, bald, bushy-browed Bob Minor. His father, a top Texas judge, was a great-grandson of a Revolutionary War general; his mother was related to General Sam Houston. But Minor had spurned his ancestry, leaving home in his mid-teens. After working as a carpenter, he ended up in St. Louis, where in 1906 (the year *The Jungle* was published) he landed a job on the *Post-Dispatch* as an artist. In 1913, when Minor was twenty-nine, Joseph Pulitzer, Jr., summoned him to New York to draw for the *World.* Minor contributed powerfully crude drawings exposing the European conflict as a munition makers' war, but when Pulitzer's paper came out for American involvement, he quit and switched to the antiwar *New York Call.* He also contributed to *The Masses.* In 1918, he traveled to Russia, chatted with Trotsky, and conducted a lengthy interview with Lenin that caused a sensation in the United States. When the war ended, he was arrested by the U.S. Army and accused of being a Russian agent, but the charges were eventually dismissed. Minor by now was a confirmed Bolshevik, and his career as one of the nation's top editorial cartoonists was over. He edited the CP's *Daily Worker,* lectured widely, and in 1933 polled twenty-six thousand votes running for mayor of New York against Fiorello La Guardia.

Naturally, at various points the paths of Bob Minor and Upton Sinclair crossed. In 1914, the two men were neighbors (and tennis partners) in Croton-on-Hudson, and they remained friends and correspondents for years. But as Minor turned more doctrinaire, their friendship cooled; and when Sinclair novelized Sacco and Vanzetti in *Boston* in less than saintly terms, Minor called him "a hired liar, a coward and a traitor."

That was only a taste of what Minor had in store for Uppie now. For starters, on arriving in San Francisco today, he observed that Sinclair "always deserted every cause he stood for when the moment of crisis arrived—the antiwar cause in 1917, the labor cause when Tom Mooney was arrested, the General Strike which he stabbed in the back when it most needed friends." Far from being a great progressive, Upton Sinclair, Minor asserted, was actually the most reactionary candidate in America. Conservatives in California had been painting Sinclair red for the past six weeks. Now one of the nation's top Reds was calling him a reactionary.

The nation's most popular radio voice, next to FDR's, crackled over the air from Los Angeles, "the home of sane politics," as Will Rogers put it. Will called this the "first of a series of intellectual and unreliable talks on Russia," which he had just visited. By Russia he meant the Soviet Union, not the Russia that the Republicans said was growing out in the "California orange groves."

Rogers claimed that he knew as much about what made Russia tick as anyone else, which was nothing. Russia was just like the NRA—it had some of the best ideas in the world and some of the worst. "In the first place," Will said, "the government owns everything. Well, that ain't so different than it is over here—the banks own it here." Observing Russians on the street, he had a hard time telling whether they were happy or sad. Most of them had "a dull, blank expression on their faces. . . . But I've sat in the gallery of the Senate and the House of Representatives in Washington and I've seen the same dull, blank expression.

"Then, too, it's not what you'd call a good year for happiness in any part of the world, anyhow. It's what you might call an off year on happiness."

Will was not about to take a stand on the California election race. He compared himself to W. R. Hearst, who apparently had instructed his newspapers to "wait till it's over, then I'll write an editorial about it," and W. G. McAdoo, who went to Mexico "and won't be back till two days after it's over." But the humorist indirectly helped EPIC's cause by explaining why Russian-style communism posed no threat to California: Karl Marx, who "wrote more books than Upton Sinclair and Sinclair Lewis combined," called for exporting revolution, but Russia was concentrating on its own problems now.

"There's some pretty smart birds over there in Russia," Will revealed, "and they're not sending any dough to some soap box orator over here—they know that this country is hopeless as far as Communism is concerned. You never heard of the Republicans trying to send a lot of dough to try to carry Alabama, have you? And the Baptists are not rushing any money into Rome to swing it their way, either.

"Russia's got a suit of clothes. Now it don't fit 'em very good, but it's the best one they got. And at the time they put it on, they didn't have any suit at all, and never had one. They was as naked as a fish. Now how are you going to take that suit and make it fit somebody else? No nation has the same size and build as Russia. We're used to suits, and you can't just hand us any old kind. Now maybe ours don't fit us right now, and maybe it's a little tight in places, and it's big in others. Maybe we want a lighter color, but brother you can go and bet your last dollar that the color of our new suit won't be all red."

OCTOBER 15

MONDAY

At an extradition hearing in the Bronx, Bruno Richard Hauptmann today denied that he kidnapped the Lindbergh baby. He swore that on the night of March 1, 1932, when the child was abducted in New Jersey, he met his wife at the Bronx restaurant where she worked, took her home, and spent the night there. Later, a friend named Isidor Fisch, now deceased, asked him to hide a pile of gold notes. Hauptmann did not know that the money was part of the Lindbergh ransom until after he was arrested. The suspect's wife corroborated his story.

Courtroom observers, while skeptical of Hauptmann's alibi, were impressed with his manner. For two hours, he testified calmly, losing his temper only once, when asked directly whether he murdered the child. Hauptmann leaned forward, his body tense, eyes blazing. "No!" he shouted.

A man named Frank Walker called James A. Farley's office this morning to say that William Fox would be stopping by at four o'clock and "shouldn't be kept waiting." What the devil did Bill Fox want? He was a Republican who had once told Upton Sinclair that the only reason

Herbert Hoover didn't end the Depression was because he faced a "bolshevik" Congress. Perhaps Fox wanted to discuss last week's Supreme Court decision that threatened to put him back on top in Hollywood.

Five years had passed since William Fox's previous attempt at becoming "the undisputed grand panjandrum of cinema," as *Time* put it. In October 1929, Fox ruled a two-hundred-million-dollar empire and appeared ready to wrest control of MGM's parent company, Loew's, Incorporated. Unfortunately for Fox, he owed money in short-term notes; when the stock market crashed, creditors converged on him, and L. B. Mayer helped scuttle the Loew's deal. Even his right-hand man, Winfield Sheehan, turned against him. When the smoke cleared, Fox had lost control of his studio and his chain of eight thousand theaters. Granted a salary of half a million dollars a year for five years, he retired to his apartment on Park Avenue and his estate on Long Island to plot his revenge.

Upton Sinclair, of all people, loomed large in his plans. Fox had asked the muckraker in 1932 if he could visit him in Pasadena. Smelling money, Craig urged him to accept. When Fox arrived, he explained that he wanted Sinclair to write a book describing how he had been fleeced of his fortune, and he would pay him twenty-five thousand dollars to do it. This put the Socialist author in a difficult spot. Should he risk his reputation defending a man whose cutthroat business tactics and reactionary politics were altogether repulsive to him? And could he justify accepting a rather large payoff as part of the agreement? Sinclair decided that he should and he could. Fox had been wronged, and if Sinclair stuck pretty much to 1929 he could turn this tawdry affair into an anti–Wall Street morality tale. And as for the money: Sinclair, as usual, needed it.

So Fox started visiting the humble Sinclair residence three days a week. Uppie and his corps of stenographers listened quietly as Fox told his life story. Born in Hungary, Fox grew up on New York's Lower East Side, quit school at thirteen, and made a fortune in the clothing trade. He opened his first movie theater in New York in 1904 and sponsored vaudeville at the Academy of Music. Like many of the other moguls, Fox parlayed a chain of theaters into a major Hollywood studio.

A workaholic devoid of charm, Fox had a "good Jewish nose," as Sinclair described it, a bald head, and a useless left arm that rarely prevented him from shooting a round of golf in the eighties. He was so possessive that when his two daughters gave birth to sons, he immediately banished their husbands from the family. One unlucky son-in-law came home from work one day to find his apartment empty: wife, son, and furniture were all missing. The man had a heart attack and died on the spot, according to legend. Fox legally adopted his two grandsons as his own, renaming them William Fox II and William Fox III.

Fox referred to lawyers as "reptiles" and bankers as "vultures," demonstrating a paranoia that proved prophetic, at least in his eyes, when Wall Street seized his empire. Sinclair dutifully transferred the story to paper. Fox read the manuscript, pronounced it acceptable, handed Upton a check, and fled to New York.

A couple of weeks later, Sinclair heard that Fox had no intention of publishing the book. He merely wanted to use the threat to publish as a means of getting back some of his film properties. But Fox was messing with the wrong guy. Sinclair promptly sent a carbon copy of the manuscript to his printer in Indiana. Fox threatened to sue, but it was too late, and the book, *Upton Sinclair Presents William Fox,* became a best-seller in Hollywood. Sinclair heard that a sign went up at the Fox studios warning that anyone caught with the book would be fired.

Sinclair's friends, notably Lincoln Steffens and W. E. Woodward, complained that he had made a scoundrel into a hero. Mencken congratulated him on "a magnificent job of editing" but added that by the end of the book he was convinced that Fox was "a very slippery fellow, and that putting him out of business was probably a good thing for the movies." Sinclair shrugged off all criticism, claiming that "no melodrama that I have been able to invent . . . has been more packed with crimes and betrayals, perils and escapes. . . ." The public controversy passed, but movie executives savaged by Fox (through Sinclair) had very long memories.

While Sinclair hatched his EPIC plan, Fox launched his comeback through the courts. One piece of his empire that he had retained was a patent for producing sound equipment for motion pictures. Fox pressed a lawsuit against RCA and AT&T, claiming that the sound apparatus they sold to the studios infringed on his patent. A circuit court of appeals upheld his claim. Last week, the Supreme Court unexpectedly refused to hear the case, thereby letting the lower court's decision stand.

This meant that Fox could, if he wished, bring Hollywood to a halt or charge his former enemies a fortune for any picture they produced using sound. (Charlie Chaplin might have the last laugh after all.) This morning, columnist Sidney Skolsky predicted that Fox would demand five hundred dollars *per reel* for every film produced. All over Hollywood, lawyers met with producers, devising a response. According to one rumor, Fox had already been offered eight million dollars for the patent and refused it. Instead, he eyed a triumphant return to the movie colony as its dominant figure. To put it simply: Fox was loose in the henhouse.

So what did he want with Jim Farley? Could it have something to do with Upton Sinclair? Despite the dispute over *Upton Sinclair Presents William Fox,* Uppie and Bill remained a team, according to the newspapers. The press alleged that Fox was pumping big bucks into EPIC and might increase the flow in the wake of the Supreme Court ruling. One reporter even went so far as to describe the EPIC campaign as *William Fox Presents Upton Sinclair.*

True to his word, Fox arrived at Farley's office today at four o'clock for a half-hour conference with Big Jim. A few minutes after Fox departed, Farley emerged and addressed his secretary, J. M. Duffy.

"Mrs. Duffy," he said, "strictly confidential, Bill Fox has offered me a job with him at two hundred fifty thousand dollars a year."

Duffy murmured surprise at the staggering sum. Farley's current salary as postmaster general was fifteen thousand dollars. Even Will Hays made only one hundred thousand dollars annually. Fox had offered Farley a ten-year contract, now that the courts had made him "supreme" in the industry. He told Farley he could take his time deciding.

The offer was straight out of left field. Even more startling: Farley seriously considered accepting it.

———

What did it mean that the man purported to be Upton Sinclair's financial angel had offered Franklin Roosevelt's political boss $2.5 million three weeks before Election Day? More important, what did Jim Farley think it meant? The bid, in any case, was tendered at a particularly thorny time. Farley was under siege from Democrats in California, begging him or the President (or both) to rebuke Sinclair before it was too late.

Only one man in California knew that Farley and FDR were actually inclined in the opposite direction. Senator William McAdoo had just received Farley's confidential note announcing that the White House wanted Sinclair to win. Now McAdoo asked, What are you going to *do* about it? It was time for Farley to fish or cut bait.

McAdoo, fresh from his meeting with the President last week, wrote Farley today, pointing out that it was of utmost importance that the White House, if it really sought Sinclair's election, "find some way" to signal its support. The fight in California was getting very bitter, McAdoo reported, and he had received wildly conflicting statements. A customs collector in San Diego told him that Sinclair was drawing overflow crowds and that the Red-scare tactics were backfiring. Other experts advised that Sinclair was sinking, making McAdoo's support for him suicidal. "I want to see you before I return west," McAdoo pleaded, "so that we can talk over the situation."

Several cabinet officers received telegrams today from McAdoo's friend Ham Cotton, head of American Democracy, the leading Democrats-for-Merriam group in Los Angeles. American Democracy had caught on like wildfire, establishing fifty offices in Los Angeles and a dozen more in other areas of southern California. One office opened right next door to Rob Wagner's *Script* in Beverly Hills. Cotton, who had helped engineer FDR's election in 1932, claimed to have thirty thousand names on file, with three thousand more coming in every day. The group's storefront windows displayed side-by-side photographs of Frank Merriam and Franklin Roosevelt.

Cotton had read the latest *EPIC News* with some concern. A brief item suggested that several cabinet members, including Henry Wallace, Harold Ickes, and Secretary of War Dern (who had endorsed Sinclair), would visit California in the waning days of the race to campaign for EPIC. Cotton wired the three men in Washington, asking whether this was true, and each replied: not a chance. Ickes explained that he *was* coming to California at the end of the month, but it was merely to inspect the new Hetch Hetchy water project. "Do not expect to make any political speeches in state," Ickes wired.

United for California went public today in Los Angeles with evidence that as many as two hundred thousand Democrats—about 15 percent of the party's total enrollment—had illegally registered to vote. This was said to be the result of a "conspiracy" to stuff the ballot boxes organized by Sinclair forces. "I've never seen anything to equal this, and it must be stopped," commented an attorney for the group, Walter K. Tuller of O'Melveny, Tuller & Myers.

Local and state officials explored various options, including felony prosecutions and civil suits. One list of unlawful voters, twenty thousand strong, had already been submitted to authorities. The county board of supervisors voted to deputize four hundred special agents to work on the investigation under the Registrar of Voters. Another proposal before the board called for securing two thousand police officers to restrain illegal voters from visiting the polls.

Rube Borough, editor of the *EPIC News,* called the budding vote-fraud scandal "a laugh." EPIC, he explained, had "no money to corrupt anyone—and we don't *have* to corrupt anyone to vote for us."

Although illegal registrants presumably existed throughout the state, the GOP focused its probe on the south. The party in Los Angeles, led by state vice-chairman Ralph Clock, a judge in Long Beach, tried to get the north to follow suit, but to little avail. The vote-fraud scheme was simply too complicated for the California League Against Sinclairism to undertake in the Bay area with only twenty-two days remaining until the election.

Earl Warren had plenty of other concerns, not the least of which was running the district attorney's office in Alameda County. The young D.A. divided his time between the courthouse in Oakland and state GOP headquarters in Suite 2030 of the Palace Hotel in San Francisco. He received mail at both offices, and it was abundant. His correspondents fell into four categories:

Old friends. They inevitably addressed him as "Pink" or "my dear Pinky" and congratulated him for finally gaining statewide recognition.

Republicans demanding money or favors. A man in El Centro sought two thousand dollars to start a pro-Merriam newspaper. Glenn Willaman of the California Real Estate Association requested funds to print another two hundred copies of the popular PROPERTY OWNERS BEWARE poster. A top Republican in San Diego wanted one thousand dollars for an anti-Sinclair front group. The head of the Independent Forerunners suggested that a lot of undecided votes would swing to Merriam if Warren would "appoint a Negro as a deputy." A doctor representing physicians in Los Angeles proposed an appointee for state insurance commissioner, warning that Sinclair's advisers "are holding out certain promises if we will work with them."

Candidates pleading for help. Warren had sent letters to GOP candidates seeking comments on the campaign. What came back was a chorus of complaints that Merriam was getting all the money, thereby dimming their own hopes. The GOP candidates were further handicapped by the fact that Republican funds were being channeled to Democrats like Ham Cotton, who urged his followers to back Merriam—but otherwise vote a straight Democratic ticket. Some simply asked Warren to quit knocking Sinclair and start presenting a positive picture of what the GOP stood for, if anything.

Democrats seeking support. The top Democrats-for-Merriam group in San Francisco resided just down the hall from Warren's office at the Palace Hotel. This made communication, and the transfer of funds, easy. The GOP was already funneling a thousand dollars per week to this group, but Henry Monroe, a leading Merriam Democrat, told Warren "that is not enough." Monroe insisted that it would "mean everything to the cause if you will assume the position of real leadership. If you as a young man and known progressive could only dominate the situation, it would help enormously to remove the curse of 'stand-patism' of the old reactionary regime."

As if responding to Monroe's challenge, Earl Warren today released what his publicist referred to as his first official statement on the governor's race. "This is no longer a campaign between the Republican Party and the Democratic Party in California," Warren said.

> It is a crusade of Americans and Californians against Radicalism and Socialism. The issues involved in this campaign are beyond the realm of politics. The doctrines of individual freedom and personal property rights as laid down by our forefathers in the Constitution of the United States are under dangerous attack. These attackers must be repulsed. . . . In this campaign we are no longer identified by political parties and partisan beliefs. We are Americans, loyal to the faith of our forefathers, and true to the standard of freedom and equality of individual opportunity which our Constitution so nobly represents. . . .

According to the press release, Warren hereafter would "take an aggressive part in the campaign."

Like United for California in the south, CLAS had selected a respectable civic leader to front the organization: Harold J. Boyd, assistant city assessor in San Francisco. This disguised the fact that the group was lavishly funded by big-money interests and that its key operatives were hard-knuckled politicos like Chester Rowell and Clem Whitaker. Officially, Whitaker served as CLAS's publicist, but he was that and so much more. As a free-lance political strategist, Clem was literally one of a kind.

In winning his first ballot initiative in 1933, Whitaker had witnessed the impact of direct mail and the value of accentuating the negative when there was no positive to speak of. But paramount among his political tactics was what he called "an aggressive newspaper publicity campaign to overcome public apathy." Whitaker had developed a cozy relationship with the seven hundred newspaper publishers in the state, most of whom put out small but influential weekly papers. Besides his Campaigns, Inc., operation, Clem ran an advertising company in Sacramento, and he had discovered that one operation benefited the other: it was amazing how much free coverage for his candidate he could secure simply by placing a few dollars' worth of advertising in each of the weeklies. He revealed his true purpose by insisting on paying for the ads *in advance.*

Clem also discovered that the newspapers were as strapped for articles and artwork as they were for cash. They were inclined to run his publicity releases as news stories—even as editorials. If he sent out political cartoons ready for printing, they would slap them right in the paper. And why not? Whitaker's work was more clever and more professional than anything the country editors could come up with themselves. They wanted Clem to keep advertising, too, for in a depression every few dollars counted.

This incestuous relationship, which had helped Whitaker's other client, George Hatfield, win his GOP primary race in August, was tailor-made for the California League Against Sinclairism. Clem flooded the newspapers with "suggested editorials" and "news stories" and then sat back and watched them materialize in hundreds of newspapers around the state every week. If CLAS somehow missed a couple of voters with one of its mass mailings, Whitaker was sure to hit them with the same material in a seemingly more objective package: the pages of their local newspaper.

One recent packet to the papers included, among other items, a news story about the influx of unemployed, an editorial revealing that Upton Sinclair was a free-love advocate, and a statement by a top Democrat suggesting that the EPIC candidate was suffering from hallucinations and should be treated by doctors "until he has recovered sufficient to be allowed to run at large." Whitaker even reprinted H. L. Mencken's recent column mocking EPIC. He generated so much copy that some editors complained that they didn't have time to read it all—but that didn't stop them from publishing nearly all of it.

Equally compelling were the political cartoons drawn by Whitaker's art director, Bill LeNoir. While not on a par with the work of Bruce Russell in the *L.A. Times* and Ted Gale in Hearst's *Examiner*s, LeNoir's cartoons drove the message home effectively in hundreds of newspapers every week. One showed a huge boot labeled SINCLAIRISM about to stamp out an entire town dotted with church steeples. Another pictured a bear of a man, labeled COMMUNISM, with a pistol in his belt, posing under a roll call of some of Sinclair's "Red" affiliations. In a third cartoon, Sinclair put on a Punch-and-Judy show, "Come to Utopia." And there was plenty more where that came from.

In Palo Alto, Herbert Hoover penned a note to Albert Lasker in Chicago, thanking him for sending along a speech he had recently delivered warning of incursions on free speech. Hoover closed with this message: "It is a sad commentary that we shall defeat Sinclair because of himself and not by conviction of the people that his proposals are wrong or his promises futile."

Frances Goodrich and Albert Hackett reluctantly returned to Hollywood after a six-week sabbatical in New York. The couple preferred the changes of weather on the East Coast to the relentless southern California sun. Besides, they missed Broadway. They had made their name in the theater before coming to MGM in 1932 to work for what they called "the sophisticated comedy unit." One of their plays, *Up Pops the Devil,* about a married couple that tries to write together, had been made into a movie for Carole Lombard.

Goodrich and Hackett dubbed themselves "the Good Hacks." Early this year they had collaborated on the screenplay for the very successful *The Thin Man.* Now they were about to start work on an adaptation of Eugene O'Neill's *Ah, Wilderness!* Hackett found something disturbing in his mailbox at MGM when he arrived: a check made out to Louis B. Mayer, filled in with a figure that represented a sizable chunk of Hackett's weekly paycheck. A note explained that the "donation" was intended to assist the campaign of the Republican candidate for governor of California. It instructed Hackett to date the check, write in his name and the name of his bank, sign it, and send it to the front office as soon as possible.

OCTOBER 17

WEDNESDAY

There, improbably, staring out from the cover of *Time* magazine, fists raised to his chest in a schoolboy boxer's stance, was Upton Beall Sinclair. Inside, a national affairs article entitled "California Climax" captured in a bemused and at times evenhanded way some of the character and significance of this "tense and terrible" race.

To be sure, Henry Luce's magazine painted its cover boy as a bit of a menace. *Time* hated the New Deal, so Sinclair never had a chance. "No politician since William Jennings Bryan," the article declared, "has so horrified and outraged the Vested Interests. Those whose stakes in California are greatest hold themselves personally responsible to their class throughout the nation to smash Upton Sinclair. . . .

> They hate him as a muckraker. They hate him as a Socialist. They hate him as an I.W.W. sympathizer. They hate him as a "free-love" cultist. They hate him as a Single Taxer. They hate him as an atheist.

Sinclair was as "an evangel of nonsense, . . . an agent of Moscow" preaching a "Red" state-ownership scheme.

That's what the Vested Interests thought. What did *Time* think?

"Fact is," the article revealed, "Upton Sinclair is as American as pumpkin pie." After exploring his patrician lineage, *Time* took its measure of the man in a surprisingly clear-eyed way. "He is not a crackpot," *Time* confessed, "but he is inordinately vain. . . . He is not an atheist; he is disgusted by commercialized religion. He is not a 'free-love' cultist; he is an ascetic." Even his crank diets were no cause for worry, since publicity was "meat and drink to him." In short, Sinclair was little more than an old-fashioned Socialist who "looks like Henry Ford gone slightly fey."

Frank Merriam emerged as a less-than-sterling alternative. *Time* called him "plump, round-faced and by no means inspiring. . . . A small-bore, Iowa-born politician . . . lacking personal appeal or popularity." Merriam's political appearances had been limited to football games and being photographed "talking to deaf mutes through an interpreter." He had made his first campaign speech just last week and lifted its key phrase from Herbert Hoover; he espoused the Townsend Plan, but "nobody took him seriously." *Time* even implied that the "shrewd stratagem" that won Merriam the GOP nomination involved calling out the militia to crush the San Francisco strike in return for political support arranged by "big industrialists."

Who would win? "Anything can happen in fabulous California," *Time* insisted. It was, after all, the state of Hearst and Millikan and Mooney and McPherson. Despite the drumbeat of anti-Sinclair propaganda, political observers in the state conceded Los Angeles and the south to Sinclair, *Time* reported, and looked to San Francisco to save the day for sanity.

Two days had passed, and Albert Hackett hadn't yet sent a check to Louis B. Mayer for the Merriam campaign, when the phone rang in his office at MGM and someone asked where the hell it was. Hackett had been warned by other writers that if he didn't hand over the money, the front office would "fix" him when his contract came up for renewal. That didn't particularly upset him. He and his wife would just as soon move back to New York and write for Broadway anyway.

Another Hollywood figure rebelling against the so-called Merriam tax was that "professional againster" James Cagney. He was back in Los Angeles after shooting *Devil Dogs of the Air* in San Diego. Politically, Jimmy was still skating on thin ice thanks to the flap over his alleged role in last summer's Communist uprising, so it behooved him to go along with Jack Warner's request for money for Merriam. But Cagney wouldn't sign the studio's check.

At least that's what he told Frank Scully when they met, for secrecy's sake, just outside the Warner gate. Scully found it amusing that two Americans were huddling on the street, speaking in whispers, as if plotting a revolution. Cagney told Scully not only that he had refused to sign the check delivering one day's wage to Merriam but that if the studio forced him, he would donate one *week's* salary to Sinclair. Since that represented a six-to-one advantage for EPIC, Jimmy figured *that* would stop them.

Stars in the studio system like Hackett and Cagney enjoyed certain privileges. The studio bosses at least asked them to donate to the Merriam fund before threatening to dock them. Some writers, such as Donald Ogden Stewart, went along with the request. Less established figures were given no choice in the matter.

Take the young writer Billy Wilder over at the Fox studio, for example. Wilder, who was still trying to salvage Raoul Walsh's *East River,* received his latest paycheck, normally $250, only to find $50 missing.

"There's something wrong," Billy said to the studio cashier in his heavily accented English. "There's been a mistake."

"There was no mistake," she replied. "They took fifty dollars from everyone to give to Governor Merriam. If you have any complaints, talk to Mr. Sheehan."

Billy didn't know what this was all about, but he knew one thing: he desperately needed that fifty dollars to make the rent on his tiny room at the Chateau Marmont and to pay for his English lessons. He was behind on payments on his '28 De Soto, too. In no position to approach Winnie Sheehan, Fox's top man, he cornered another studio exec instead.

"Will you please explain?" Wilder asked. "I'm just here on a visa, I'm not interested in politics."

"Sinclair is dangerous," the executive replied, "he must be defeated. The Communists want to take over."

"Shouldn't I have the privilege of making the donation myself?" Billy asked innocently.

"No, the house is burning down," the exec said, "and we need as much water as possible to put it out. That son of a bitch bolshevik Sinclair must be stopped."

"And my hard-earned fifty dollars is going to stop him?" Wilder wondered.

Billy was aghast. It seemed childish, foolish, and incipiently fascist at the same time. And he knew something about fascism. He went back to his office and asked his colleagues, red-blooded Americans all, what he should do. After all, he was just a hick from Austria and unwise to the ways of American politics. This just didn't seem like the American way, as he understood it.

They said, "It had to be done," and "There's nothing you can do." You can't fight city hall, and all that. Some of them agreed that Sinclair was a Communist. Wilder said he knew a little bit about Sinclair and he was not by any means a Communist.

"Oh, you're a Communist too?" one writer replied. "You better watch it."

Wilder was out of fifty dollars and left with two conflicting thoughts concerning the forced donations. One was: *It may not be democratic, but it's a brilliant idea. Maybe if businessmen in Germany had deducted fifty marks from their workers to stop Hitler, Europe would be a safer place today.*

The other was: *I fled fascism for THIS?*

A reporter for the *San Francisco Chronicle* interviewed Cecil B. DeMille in his room at the Palace Hotel while a barber trimmed the hair on DeMille's nearly bald head. DeMille was in town to promote *Cleopatra.* He had just cast Henry Wilcoxon as Richard I in his next picture, *The Crusades,* instructing him to spend the next two months training a falcon to sit on his wrist. Dudley Nichols, a Sinclair supporter, was helping C.B. with the script. Asked by the *Chronicle* to comment on the governor's race, DeMille replied: "Communism is all very well, but when I was in Russia I saw that the majority of people had no shoes. I have no fear that the state will permit communistic doctrines to take the place of our present laws." The motion-picture industry, he added, would never "succumb" to state regulation.

All he knew was what he read in the papers, and the papers today were full of reports of an EPIC plot to flood the ballot box with unlawful votes on Election Day. "In most places," Will Rogers commented in his daily dispatch, "it's awful hard to get folks to go and register to vote, but out here in Los Angeles, where we do everything 'big,' why, each qualified voter is allowed to register himself and ten dead friends. If he hasn't got ten dead friends, why, he is allowed to pick out ten live ones, just so they don't live in this State.

"The Republicans are kicking on this arrangement, as they claim that system of registration gives the Democrats the best of it, as very few Republicans have ten friends. You ought to come out here some time. We do have the most fun."

The Merriamites had succeeded in convincing the state attorney general, a Republican, to bring suit against the first batch of 24,136 illegal registrants. Two O'Melveny attorneys represented the plaintiffs: Walter K. Tuller, for the GOP, and Albert Parker, for United for California. A superior-court judge in Los Angeles, Frank C. Collier, accepted their argument over the objection of EPIC attorneys.

Now the burden was on the defendants to prove that they deserved to vote. But how would they even know that their names were on the disqualified list? Since many had recently moved, they couldn't be contacted by mail, even if the Republicans wanted to reach them. By law, notice must be served by publishing the names of challenged voters in a local newspaper—so United for California started searching for the paper with the smallest circulation in Los Angeles. It also spread rumors that "secret indictments" were in the works.

United for California was becoming a household name throughout the southland. One anti-Sinclair bulletin after another turned up in millions of mailboxes. Mail trucks groaned, postmen moaned under the burden of paper. Many of the leaflets were directed toward specialized audiences, but those of a more general nature reached everyone with eyes to read. Most had the same format: four oblong-shaped pages (nine inches high by four inches wide) with simple but attractive type printed in black on coated white paper. OUT OF HIS OWN MOUTH SHALL HE BE JUDGED generally appeared at the top of the first page; at the bottom, the name and address of United for California ("a non-partisan organization"), along with the names Robert M. Clarke, Chairman, and Albert Parker, Secretary. The targeted leaflets bore such titles as:

"Upton Sinclair on the Catholic Church"
"Upton Sinclair on the Legion, the R.O.T.C.
and the Boy Scouts"

"Upton Sinclair on Doctors and Dentists"
"The Proof That Upton Sinclair Preaches
Revolution and Communism"
"Upton Sinclair Calls U.S.C. the Intellectual
Sweat-Shop and Discusses its
'Jabbergrab' Courses"

There was even a circular devoted entirely to Sinclair's comments on Seventh-Day Adventists.

The copy that filled these broadsides amounted to little more than a collection of vintage Sinclair quotes, but they were priceless. Sinclair on Mormons: "Latter-Day Grafters," "weird," "pathetic," "dangerous," "grotesque." The Boy Scouts were becoming "more and more warlike every hour." Doctors performed a million abortions every year just so they could make a "thousand dollars by a few minutes' work." One pamphlet labeled Sinclair a "dynamiter of all churches," but someone must have thought that too harsh, because subsequent editions called him merely a "defiler" or a "slanderer" of churches. Most of the brochures closed with the question WILL YOU TURN CALIFORNIA OVER TO THE MERCIES OF UPTON SINCLAIR?

Some leaflets actually took the trouble to explain, even analyze, the EPIC phenomenon. One booklet, "The Truth About the EPIC Plan," ran sixteen pages. Another, "A Ruined Business Has No Payroll," quoted Raymond Moley and called EPIC "plain Communism. This is Red Russia."

A third type of leaflet appeared, identical to United for California's work but with the name of some other mysterious organization grafted on—the Veterans Non-Partisan League, Friends of Truth League, Progressive Fusion League, California Educators' Non-Partisan Committee, or Farmers Merriam-Hatfield Committee, among others—perhaps to make it appear that the propaganda blizzard emanated from dozens of sources instead of one huge storm center. Someone named Bernice H. Johnson, operating out of the Fidelity Building in Los Angeles, took responsibility for "Upton Sinclair Discusses the Home, the Institution of Marriage and Advocates Free Love." This leaflet extracted woefully out-of-context Sinclair quotes from his *Book of Life.* This was a man who once wrote: "Personally, I am prepared to go as far as the extreme sex radical in the defense of love and the right to love. . . . And when I say love, I do not mean mere affection."

The massive direct-mail operation went off without a hitch, with one known exception. United for California sent sixty thousand copies of its "Sinclair and the Boy Scouts" circular to two thousand scout leaders for distribution. When a Boy Scout executive discovered that the mailing list was obtained under false pretenses, he ordered the scoutmasters to destroy the leaflets.

The mailings even reached the White House. One United for California official sent a batch of circulars to President Roosevelt, with a handwritten explanation: "6,000,000 copies of these pamphlets have been mailed to California voters."

Up north, the California League Against Sinclairism matched United for California pamphlet for pamphlet. CLAS had so much money it could afford to distribute eleven thousand leaflets at a single work site, a dairy in Visalia. The design and content of the two groups' material was virtually identical, except that Clem Whitaker printed his propaganda in bright blue type instead of plain black. But then Clem always did things first-class.

Whitaker's candidate, George Hatfield, topped Sheridan Downey two-to-one in various polls, so it looked as if Clem would soon be able to claim a landmark victory for "full-service campaign management." Whitaker ran a media-based campaign, tightly budgeted at nineteen thousand dollars, and kept Hatfield as far away from Frank Merriam and the Republican party as possible. Movie shorts had worked especially well for Hatfield; Agfa and Eastman Kodak in Los Angeles donated the raw film and Harry Cohn at Columbia Pictures provided the prints.

Clem's subtle manipulation of the press—essentially trading paid advertising for editorial space—did not remain a secret for long. One EPIC supporter urged Sheridan Downey to inform the public that what they were reading was "not what their local editors write but what they get from Clem." Downey had sent Whitaker, his old friend, a copy of the letter containing this tip, as if warning him to cut out the funny business. Clem responded by suggesting that Downey might find it amusing if he would only "look at the situation with some detachment. Quite frankly, I have been envying you [EPIC] your nation-wide broadcast, your ability to publish your own weekly newspaper and give it state-wide circulation, your tremendous force of personal workers, etc. And now I find that you are apparently envying me my little ads in the newspapers.

"At any rate," Whitaker concluded, "it's a great fight and I imagine the reverberations will be heard for some years to come."

The big day was nearly at hand. President Roosevelt announced that he would deliver his second fireside chat of the season next Monday evening, October 22. Upton Sinclair had come away from his September 4 meeting with the President with the distinct impression that FDR planned to endorse his production-for-use formula in the second of two fireside chats this autumn, thereby sealing his election. He attached enormous credibility to the President's "promise," but any Washington political observer could have told him that FDR was notorious for leading visitors on. William Allen White once accused Roosevelt of "going a little piece down the road with anyone, backward and forward, zigzagging, covering and recovering. . . ." FDR even pandered to Huey Long; but Long, unlike Sinclair, was wise to the ways of the consummate politician. "When I talk to him, he says, 'Fine! Fine! Fine!' " Huey once reported. "Maybe he says 'Fine!' to everybody."

EPIC headquarters, nevertheless, was so sure that the President would keep his word that it scheduled radio and personal appearances surrounding Monday's speech. Last night in Fresno, Sinclair had urged five thousand acolytes to "send word to Mr. Roosevelt that you are behind the EPIC plan." He planned to send the President a telegram himself, reminding him yet again of his "promise."

After a lousy couple of weeks, Uppie felt upbeat again. "I cannot tell you how unreal the world of books seems to me now," he wrote his biographer, Floyd Dell. "I doubt if I ever write any more books!" To a local political columnist who had asked for a prediction of the November 6 vote, Sinclair submitted this tally:

Sinclair:	1,200,000
Merriam:	900,000
Haight:	300,000

Most of the state's odds makers continued to call the race a toss-up, although one betting parlor in Los Angeles quoted ten-to-eight odds on Merriam.

Sinclair rested at home, preparing to leave for his final campaign swing north. He was never idle, of course—not with a stenographer handy and a stack of mail a foot high in front of him. He sent a package of EPIC booklets to M. K. Gandhi. (The Mahatma and his son were known to read Sinclair during periods in prison.) The letter that occupied most of his attention, however, was a pained response to his good friend Rob Wagner, who had just renounced *Script*'s support for EPIC, apparently under pressure from his business manager—his wife. Sinclair assured Wagner that he harbored no hard feelings but remarked, sarcastically, that "there are hundreds of thousands of people in the state who cannot publicly take a stand and you have a perfect right to list yourself among them." He rejected Wagner's recent comment that Uppie seemed scared to death of winning. "I am happy to say," Sinclair reported, "that I am entirely cheerful at this moment and I expect to lick Merriam to a frazzle and to End Poverty in California."

OCTOBER 19

FRIDAY

The *Los Angeles Times* greeted the morning with a warning. "It is perfectly obvious," the editors stated, "that a wholesale job of ballot-box stuffing is contemplated, with the State election result at stake." Illegal registrants must be barred from the polls. Sure, mistakes will be made, the *Times* admitted, but "it would be far better for a few honest persons to lose their votes than for a hundred thousand rogues to defeat by fraud the majority will of the people."

Two days of torrential rains had destroyed several hundred homes and left seven dead in the foothills of Los Angeles, but the story dominating the front page of every newspaper was the EPIC "vote scam." Ham Cotton of American Democracy wired William G. McAdoo suggesting that Mac drop his support for Sinclair on the grounds that he was not the party's legal nominee, since he had "evidently" won the primary by fraud.

Upton Sinclair worried about a different kind of ballot stuffing, however. A disproportionate number of Republicans seemed to have received *Literary Digest* straw ballots. From talking to postmasters, EPIC investigators discovered that GOP precincts were flooded with ballots while certain Democratic strongholds missed out entirely. This wasn't necessarily intentional. Many Sinclair supporters lacked a permanent address or any other means of making themselves known to a publisher clear across the country. Deliberate or not, an undercount of Sinclair support would be damaging.

EPIC also heard that Merriam supporters were buying up *Literary Digest* ballots on the street for twenty-five cents apiece. According to one report, a pro-Merriam plant manager ended up with two hundred ballots to distribute to his workers.

W. R. Hearst returned to California to find that his leading finance writer, B. C. Forbes, had beaten him to the Coast. Hearst had many things on his mind, notably Marion Davies's gala costume party in Santa Monica tomorrow evening. B. C. Forbes, on the other hand, came to California for the express purpose of exposing the threat to the state and national economies should EPIC be enacted.

Forbes planned to travel the state interviewing experts and devote his next several columns to the Sinclair menace. At a luncheon in his honor yesterday in San Francisco, he called EPIC's cost to California "prohibitive." Today he filed his first dispatch from the front.

One of B. C. Forbes's favorite aphorisms was "Act in haste, repent at leisure." He had the energy of three men, and he needed it, writing a daily column, compiling books, and publishing a bimonthly magazine, pretty much simultaneously. Born in Scotland in 1880, Bertie Charles Forbes had come to America in 1904 and quickly made his mark as a business editor. He joined Hearst's *New York American* in 1911 and left to found *Forbes* in 1917. The magazine was something new in American journalism, a neatly packaged survey of the economic scene, "devoted to doers and doings."

Since Forbes had borrowed money to start his publication from such leading captains of industry as Henry Frick, he could hardly be objective, but his impulse was not entirely commercial. His first editorial began, "Business was originated to produce happiness, not to pile up millions." The magazine's motto was: "With all thy getting, get understanding." Forbes claimed that business and industry were run too "harshly" and that employers would gain satisfaction if they treated their workers humanely. This was practically a unique view at the time.

Forbes boomed through the 1920s, eventually gaining a circulation of more than sixty thousand and inspiring a competitor, Henry Luce's *Fortune.* B.C. wrote much of the magazine himself. His specialty was the personality profile, and he assembled many of these articles in books with titles such as *Men Who Are Making America.* He foresaw the stock market crash and saved his own neck, but afterward *Forbes* foundered. Hearst offered to buy the magazine; failing that, he hired its publisher as a columnist. Somehow Forbes kept the publication going. He put his four sons to work in the mail room at the office on lower Fifth Avenue, and one of them, a gangly, bespectacled boy named Malcolm, caught a fever for journalism.

One of B. C. Forbes's books, *Men Who Are Making the West,* revealed his high opinion of the business leaders of California. These men had the right idea: they didn't view making a fortune as an end-all. "The typical Western leader has an open-heartedness, a warmth, a friendliness, a cheeriness, a charming democracy of manner," Forbes wrote, "not equalled by the ultra-busy men of large affairs farther East. . . . They convey the impression of having time to live as rational human beings."

Now B.C. had come to California again, this time to study the EPIC phenomenon, by no means with an open mind. Even Roosevelt was too experimental for him. Back in February he congratulated Hearst for expressing misgivings about the New Deal, which in Forbes's view was "in danger of becoming altogether too dictatorial." His columns, while filled with high-minded epigrams, rarely strayed from the reactionary line. Forbes was nothing more than "a mere representative of Wall Street and the big interests," Senator Hiram Johnson once complained.

In his first column on the Sinclair race, Forbes today revealed that the "big interests" were agog over the prospect of an EPIC takeover. The eyes of the entire country were on California, and the outcome of this election, he wrote, "is expected to mark an epoch, politically, in this country. There's as much interest in the financial field as there can possibly be in California itself." EPIC could never pay for itself, Forbes declared, and because of the flight of capital, it would actually hurt the workers it was most trying to help.

Nevertheless, Sinclair's pipe dreams were "so alluring, so glittering, so fascinating to the unthinking and, of course, to the unemployed" that the candidate had a real chance of winning. In California, Forbes advised, "thoughtful, responsible, intelligent citizens" simply must find a way to overcome the votes of those "whose education and experience have been such that they themselves cannot—and cannot be expected to—dig beneath the surface and reach sound conclusions."

Moviegoers across California flocked to theaters today to see Jackie Cooper and Wallace Beery in *Treasure Island,* Ann Harding in *The Fountain,* or Crawford and Gable in *Chained.* For the price of admission, they not only got to enjoy the feature film, a newsreel, and a cartoon; they also watched a five-minute political short distributed to theaters throughout the state by MGM (although Metro's name appeared nowhere on it). Apparently the propaganda screen campaign promised by the Hollywood trade journals had finally come to pass.

In hundreds of movie theaters from Eureka to San Diego, the scene was the same. A title, *California Election News,* flashed on the screen, accompanied by a map of the state and the familiar orchestral strains of "California, Here I Come." A narrator interrupted.

"Ladies and gentlemen," he intoned richly, "I am the Inquiring Cameraman. All day I travel around California, the highways and the byways, the downtown districts, the residence districts, the farm districts, all districts." A series of sunny outdoor scenes appeared. "I stop people on the street, I pry into offices and shops and stores and restaurants. I knock on the doors of homes, all for the purpose of digging out voters of California to express their views for your edification."

Faces of laborers, businessmen, and young women appeared. "Remember," the announcer said, "they're not actors, they're *nervous.* I don't rehearse them, I'm impartial. Now for the votes."

First up: a working man in overalls, sitting on a bench eating an apple, apparently on a lunch break. Whom did he favor in the race for governor? Sinclair, because a "different man in office," he said, a bit slow of speech, might "get away from the old line."

"Do you really believe he can end poverty in California?" the Inquiring Cameraman asked.

"Well, no, I don't think so," the worker replied.

Number two: another laborer at the same workplace. "I'm going to vote for Merriam," he announced, "because I want a job. If you drive capital out of the country, who's gonna pay us?"

The setting shifted. Two stocky black men dressed in vests sat in the front seat of an old car. The passenger proclaimed that he was "gonna vote for Mr. Sinclair. He has something new, that new EPIC plan, and I think it's time to try something new out again."

"Do you think that plan will work?"

"I don't know . . . but I'm willing to take a chance on it."

Again the Inquiring Cameraman immediately found someone to offset this view. A black man, also in a vest but standing in front of a house, possibly his own, declared that he was going to vote for Merriam, "because I need prosperity."

Then a young, shifty-eyed Chicano man standing on a busy street corner endorsed "Uptown Saint-Clair" because "we need complete rejuvenation of our government system." But the next voter, a portly gentleman wearing a tie, proclaimed that Mr. Sinclair should not be governor "because of his socialistic views."

Interviewee number seven happened to be a sweet old lady wearing a flower-print dress, posing in front of a suburban hedge. She supported Merriam because the other candidate was "untried."

"You think Merriam would keep the boat from rocking?" the kindly announcer said, just trying to start a conversation.

"I do."

"Safer for you and your family and all?"

"Very much so."

Again, the next subject provided a vivid contrast. Identified as a Mr. Duncan, he was also elderly. He wore a beat-up hat and was absent his front teeth. One might call him a bum. "I'm going to vote for Upton Saint-Clair," he said.

Voter number nine, a well-dressed young chap in a dark suit, with black slicked-back hair and a natty mustache, stood on a tennis court, though not dressed for the sport, looking for all the world like an . . . aspiring actor? Maybe even an accomplished one. Merriam, he said, was "for democracy rather than socialism, and he won't involve us in any dangerous experiments."

A gentleman in a gray suit and hat standing next to him put in his two cents. "Being in the real estate business," he said, "I believe Merriam to be the ideal man. I'd like to stay in the real estate business, and if Mr. Sinclair gets in I believe there will *be* no real estate business."

A blue-collar worker in a garage confessed that he once had Sinclair "in mind" but "his plans are so far ahead of the times that it is doubtful I will vote in that way." Finally, the Inquiring Cameraman found a Haight voter, a fat old man sitting on a porch. The impartial survey concluded with another pleasant grandmother type, standing in front of her typical American home, declaring that "Sinclair's attitude towards institutions I believe are sacred don't quite agree with mine. . . ." THE END.

If intended as propaganda, *California Election News* no doubt accomplished its task. It was skillfully executed. Most of the faces and settings appeared authentic. The respectable-looking people endorsed Merriam, while those down on their luck supported Sinclair or Haight, but the contrast was just subtle enough to be effective. Almost as if reading from a script, the Merriamites in just a few soft-spoken words managed to raise virtually every major point promoted by the anti-Sinclair forces. Even the Sinclair partisans admitted EPIC wouldn't work.

This wasn't the first time producers used film shorts in an attempt to influence voters. In 1931, the Metropolitan Water District of Southern California, backing a bond issue for the Colorado River aqueduct, spent a reported one hundred thousand dollars on film trailers showing lush valleys suddenly fading into desert. ("Do you want this to happen to you?" the narrator had asked movie audiences.) The 1934 governor's race, however, marked the first time that filmmakers set out to destroy a political candidate. Until the '34 campaign, newsreels and film shorts commonly covered candidates in a dull, scrupulously nonpartisan fashion. That was not to say that political bias never appeared, but the deck was rarely stacked; both candidates in a race usually had an equal say. With that expectation firmly in place, the audience for *California Election News* probably regarded it as a fair reflection of public opinion.

Not everyone, of course, found it credible. Some Hollywood scriptwriters chuckled as they watched. The short carried no credits of any kind, surely a first in the film industry, but that Inquiring Cameraman sure sounded like MGM's Carey Wilson. Others thought they recognized a couple of actors from Central Casting up there on the screen.

Many EPIC activists unwittingly subjected to this short laughed aloud, finding it blatantly biased, even comical, and therefore ineffectual. But they missed the point. They were judging the short too much on what it said, not on what it showed. The opinion expressed by the Merriamites might not, by itself, swing votes. But this was a new political medium—a visual medium. The spoken word might rule the radio, but in a darkened theater moviegoers identified with images projected on the big screen. They imagined themselves as Mary Pickford or Douglas Fairbanks, Katharine Hepburn or Gary Cooper. Forget the lines of dialogue. It was the face—the visual evidence—that was important.

California Election News presented new faces to identify with or reject. There was the man in the three-piece suit and the grandmother in the print dress (both for Merriam); the gap-toothed bum and the sneaky-eyed foreigner (for Sinclair). Forget the words. Whom would undecided, middle-class voters in California relate to? Whom would they hate to be identified with?

And apparently, there was more to come. This edition of *California Election News* was labeled "Number One."

———

Frank Scully tried without success to get Upton Sinclair to accompany him to Hollywood dinners that might do the candidate some good. Tonight's affair, though intimate, might have proved profitable, since the lineup of guests ran the studio gamut. Dorothy Parker from Metro, Nunnally Johnson from Twentieth Century, and Joel Sayre from Warners met Scully at the home of Paramount's Ted Paramore. The dinner-table talk, as one might have expected, was scintillating—an Algonquin amid the eucalyptus.

Dottie Parker recounted a recent phone call from an MGM exec who wondered whether she was really serious about joining the Authors' League for Sinclair.

"Never more so," she'd replied.

"But you're cutting your own throat," the exec had said.

"I doubt if that's important," Dottie responded, "or anyway not as important as this election."

The exec apparently confessed that he liked Uppie, too, but felt that his EPIC plan was "devious." Dottie asked what he meant by that.

"Well," he explained, "I don't like it."

"That's a better explanation," Dottie said, "but the point is, I do. I gave Frank Scully my support and it sticks."

Then Joel Sayre informed his dinner companions that Jimmy Cagney wasn't the only one at Warner Brothers to refuse to hand over one day's pay to the Merriam fund: he wouldn't do it either. But the studio rank and file had no choice in the matter: a few dollars were simply deducted from their paychecks. "The whole gyp has everybody so sore," he commented, "it simply means one thousand more votes for Sinclair."

Nunnally Johnson topped that story. At the age of thirty-seven, Johnson was one of only three scriptwriters in Hollywood who generally received solo writing credits (the others were Robert Riskin and Dudley Nichols). A former New York newsman and *Saturday Evening Post* short-story writer, Johnson had already written scenarios for four United Artists pictures in 1934, although his script for *The House of Rothschild* was criticized by some for being too sympathetic to Jews. Johnson was a Democrat but no bomb thrower.

Tonight, for the benefit of Parker, Scully, and the others, Johnson recalled a recent conversation at United Artists. A studio executive had asked him what he was doing endorsing the Authors' League for Sinclair.

"You damned fool," the exec advised, "don't you see the Boss"—meaning Joe Schenck—"has threatened to move the studio to Florida if Sinclair is elected?"

"Fine," Johnson replied. "I own a lot of bum real estate in Miami. So I'd be a damn fool to vote for Merriam!"

Ted Paramore, who was about to leave for Washington to meet with Jim Farley on another matter, relayed an interesting rumor: he'd heard that William Fox had offered Uppie two hundred thousand dollars to finance EPIC but that Sinclair had turned it down, fearing that strings were attached.

Dottie Parker said Heywood Broun wanted to come out to cover the campaign but wasn't certain it would help. Someone else speculated that Senator McAdoo, angry that his anti-Sinclair quote from the past summer was being printed on billboards all over the state, would finally come home to stump for Uppie.

Scully contributed this gem: an EPIC partisan named Ernest J. Buttner (like Scully, a devout Catholic) happened to be in charge of the teletype machines at the local phone company. Whenever he saw confidential anti-Sinclair information coming over the wire, he would dash outside to a phone booth and relay the message to EPIC headquarters. Sinclair would then issue a denial before the charge even appeared. This mystified the Merriam forces.

The consensus around the table, however, was that Sinclair would have to go on the offensive in the next ten days to offset the impact of what someone called "the ten-million-dollar slush fund." Frank Scully said he thought Sinclair was up to it. Uppie, he predicted, would let the opposition burn itself out down the home stretch, and then Sinclair would electrify the voters in the race to the wire.

———

If the EPIC candidate was about to put a charge in his campaign, he disguised it rather well today. Upton Sinclair maintained his defensive posture. Attempting to undo the damage caused by his "bums' rush" quote, he announced that an unemployed worker would have to reside in California for at least a year to receive benefits under his EPIC plan. He wired Senator George Norris of Nebraska requesting an investigation of Frank Merriam's slush fund and the United for California vote-fraud scheme. And he dictated a telegram to George Creel asking him to please stop telling reporters that he was straying from the Democratic platform. "I beg you to believe this is campaign lie," Sinclair wired. "Am standing by all agreements."

On the radio tonight, Upton Sinclair, attempting to prove he was not an atheist, swore that Jesus was in his thoughts "more frequently than any other man who has ever lived."

At ten minutes past seven this evening an appellate court in New York denied Bruno Richard Hauptmann's last attempt to avoid extradition. Ninety minutes later he was led from his cell at the Bronx County jail to a waiting automobile. Heavily guarded by state troopers, Hauptmann was transported across the George Washington Bridge, bound for Flemington, New Jersey, where he would await trial for murder.

OCTOBER 20

SATURDAY

Harry Chandler owned a storehouse of Sinclairiana: damaging book excerpts, embarrassing biographical details, ill-considered quotes from campaign speeches. He had anti-Sinclair editorials, cartoons, and comic strips up to his ears. His newspaper, the *Los Angeles Times,* didn't have enough pages to print it all. But in Palo Alto, Herbert Hoover found the perfect gift for the man who had everything. Someone had sent the former president an article from *Pravda,* purportedly dated July 5, 1934. Hoover had a Russia expert at Stanford decipher it, and today he sent the text to Harry Chandler.

"Herewith," Hoover wrote, "the translation of a gem which we have found in the *Pravada* [sic], which is the official government organ at Moscow." According to this version, Upton Sinclair, in reply to a questionnaire sent out (on an unspecified date) by a Soviet journal called *International'naia literatura,* had written:

> I do not stop repeating that the experiment of the Soviet Union is the most important event in the whole history of humanity. I am watching with the deepest interest and am reading everything that I can find. . . .

"I will send you a photostat of the page of the paper in Russian on Monday," Hoover added.

Remarkably, Hoover and Chandler, although hundreds of miles apart, were operating on precisely the same wavelength. This very morning the *L.A. Times* had published a facsimile of a November 5, 1932, letter from Upton Sinclair allegedly printed in something called the *Moscow Daily News.* Sinclair had labeled the Russian Revolution "the most important event in human history" and predicted that if the Soviet Union could stay out of war for a few more years, its glorious example would cause capitalism in other countries to "collapse of its own physical and moral decay." The *Times* headline over the reprint screamed, CONGRATULATIONS FROM UPTON SINCLAIR!

B. C. Forbes also did his best to link Sinclair to the Soviets. In this morning's column for the Hearst papers, he observed that Stalin would heartily approve of the EPIC plank calling for private individuals to withdraw their money from savings banks and invest it in the state. Forbes had been chatting with "intimates" of Sinclair's who privately advised that the EPIC candidate was a "communist at heart" who "admires the way things are done in Russia because he proclaims that the Soviets copied their ideas from him." These same unnamed sources claimed that if Sinclair had his way, "he would turn California into first a socialistic and then a communist state—only he is soft-pedaling these doctrines."

The famed financial writer had one good word to say for Sinclair: *sincere.* "The pathway to Hades," Forbes observed, "isn't more generously paved with the proverbial 'good intentions' than is Mr. Upton Sinclair's mind and heart."

The California League Against Sinclairism had pulled off quite a coup, recruiting as a leader of its women's division tennis star Helen Wills Moody. This gave new meaning to the expression "political racket." Moody sat at the head table at a CLAS luncheon in San Francisco and heard Dr. Aurelia H. Reinhardt, president of Mills College, describe how Upton Sinclair's contempt for marriage, religion, and the American home should poison all self-respecting females against him. It was unclear exactly what Helen was going to do for Frank Merriam, but just showing up at the widely publicized luncheon probably earned the governor a few thousand votes. Next to Eleanor Roosevelt and a movie actress or two, Helen Wills Moody was the best-loved woman in America.

During the Roaring Twenties and into the early thirties, when she captured six Wimbledon championships and seven U.S. women's titles, Helen was known as the American Girl. To many, she represented the grace, spirit, and energy of America. Intelligent and uncommonly pretty, she attracted fans of both sexes. Men fell in love with her; women appreciated her relentless, big-boned athleticism. Helen was, in many ways, the New Woman. College girls sought her advice on everything from diet to marriage. Great artists, including Alexander Calder, Diego Rivera, Childe Hassam, and Augustus John immortalized her in their work. Edwin Markham wrote a poem about her. She even did a screen test arranged by Joseph P. Kennedy. (Hollywood judged her a bit too muscular, but Charlie Chaplin commented that the most beautiful thing he had ever seen was the American Girl playing tennis.) A *New Yorker* writer observed that if the Miss America title were put to a popular vote, Helen would surely win.

But now, at the age of twenty-eight, Helen Wills Moody faced an uncertain future. In 1933, Helen Jacobs supplanted her at the top of women's tennis, and this season a back injury kept the American Girl out of competition. At her home on Clay Street in San Francisco, she had time on her hands. She took English courses at Berkeley to finish her degree and covered Wimbledon for the Hearst chain. And she got involved in the California governor's race.

Helen's first exposure to politics came in 1928, when Arthur Brisbane persuaded her to chair the Hoover Women's Committee. She appeared in a newsreel in her tennis whites, reciting a speech written by Brisbane, asserting that by voting for Hoover youth might "show that its ideals are of the highest and that it has the earnest desire to be of service."

This past summer she had worked for former governor C. C. Young, a progressive Republican who bitterly attacked Frank Merriam throughout the primary campaign. One night, appearing with Young on the radio, Helen confessed that a few years ago she hardly knew that state government existed, "but now I and all the other children of my generation have grown up and we are looking around wondering what is going on about us. We cannot help but realize that these are troubled times and we are somewhat bewildered by it all. We know we cannot accept things as they are, that we certainly cannot go backwards but must be progressive." Helen had seemed to speak from the heart. She observed that unless all the citizens of the state were protected by government, "there can be no true security for any of us." Then she listened as Young called Merriam a "reactionary" with a "bad" record who believed in state government for "the protection of the few." Young predicted that progressive Republicans would "never" vote for such a man.

Two months later, C. C. Young and Helen Wills Moody were campaigning for this "bad reactionary" as the most famous members of the California League Against Sinclairism.

Outraged Sinclair supporters stormed the box office of a suburban Los Angeles theater following a screening of the first Inquiring Cameraman short, demanding to see the manager. They labeled it political propaganda and demanded that the short be withdrawn. "I'm just a cog," the manager explained. Apparently MGM and other studios had instructed theaters that they'd better run the Inquiring Cameraman short or risk losing forthcoming releases. After chatting with his boss on the telephone, the manager announced that the short would no longer be shown at his theater.

Scattered protests would not slow MGM's screen campaign, however. MGM cameramen, under the direction of Felix Feist, Jr., today visited the railroad yards out at Colton, near San Bernardino. Colton, a stopping point for settlers during the 1800s, was now a major terminus for the Southern Pacific. Feist and his crew hoped to shoot some terrifying footage of transients arriving in California by boxcar. While waiting for the hoboes to arrive, they interviewed local officials willing to attest to an "EPIC influx," including a top man with the railroad who just happened to be a Frank Merriam man.

Feist was known as a test director. He filmed screen tests for would-be actors and actresses while awaiting a chance to make a feature. Son of Felix Feist, an MGM executive in New York, he started his career as a film salesman, a cameraman, and a producer of travelogues. Feist was aggressive, opinionated, and desperate to be a big-time director, an ambition not likely to be realized at talent-rich MGM. Besides doing film tests, he worked with Carey Wilson and Pete Smith on short subjects. Now he was working with Carey again.

For Feist, this was low-pressure work. It wasn't like shooting a newsreel, which had to capture a breaking event. If Feist couldn't find any

EPIC hoboes out at Colton, why, he could create a few back home on the MGM lot. This was Hollywood, wasn't it?

———

The first defendants in the landmark vote-fraud case stepped forward today. Living up to the letter, if not the spirit, of the law, United for California had served notice by publishing its list of 24,136 alleged lawbreakers in a local newspaper. But it wasn't the *Los Angeles Times* or the *Examiner* or even the *Daily News.* It was a community paper called the *Daily Journal*—circulation fifteen hundred. That allowed one copy of the newspaper for every sixteen defendants. Perhaps that explained why only seven men appeared in court today to contest the striking of their names from the voting rolls. All seven proved they had registered legally, and were so certified.

EPIC attorneys claimed to have located five hundred others who would attempt to regain the franchise sometime next week. One EPIC lawyer called the court action "a hoax perpetrated by the Republicans to intimidate the voters of this county." Another declared that California was "not yet ready for any Hitlerism" and promised that if United for California's lawsuit was not thrown out of court, EPIC would recall from office every victorious Republican candidate. A third attorney called for federal prosecution of anyone who attempted to obstruct voters on November 6.

Threats and counterthreats—calls for police action and police protection—filled the air, but the horrifying din was music to the ears of Albert Parker. The prospect of going to the polls on November 6 was growing scarier by the day, and that would keep a lot of EPIC voters home. Los Angeles was starting to look a lot like Baton Rouge. Parker liked the way events were unfolding and recalled that he hadn't yet thanked his New York friend, Eli Whitney Debevoise, for supplying crucial advice (courtesy of George Medalie and Thomas E. Dewey).

Parker was making a name for himself in this campaign, and there was no telling where that would take him. Until now, his reputation was pretty much limited to the society page. Parker had famous relations. His great-uncle, Shelby Moore Cullom, served in the U.S. Senate. His father, Charles Cullom Parker, was a wealthy merchant on that stretch of Sixth Street in downtown Los Angeles known as Book Row. Some booksellers specialized in rare books; others promoted the latest fare. C. C. Parker, an austere man known for wearing wing collars, catered to the carriage trade. They bought what he told them to buy, or he didn't want their business. Parker at least displayed excellent taste and had acquired an impressive library, mostly fine books from England. Now the Depression threatened him with extinction. The carriage trade was dwindling, and he wouldn't condescend to selling so-called dollar books.

Albert took after his father in many ways. He was well spoken, an inveterate reader, and a bit of a snob. After getting his Harvard law degree, he had secured a top position with Henry O'Melveny, an old family friend. In one of his first cases, Parker represented Bing Crosby. Every year he presided over the Bachelor Club's annual gala at the Biltmore, an exclusive affair for the young elite. A.P., as he was called, was tall, handsome, meticulously dressed, and a good poker player, and he led the California Crusaders' fight against Prohibition. In 1929, he crashed an automobile into three sheriff's cars in front of the Hall of Justice in L.A., later pleading guilty to transporting two bottles of illegal liquor. A newspaper noted that he set "a new style for liquor law violators" by appearing in court wearing evening clothes. A local cop called him the worst driver he'd ever seen; this pleased Albert enormously.

Wellborn, Parker married better. His wife was Rosemary Harden, daughter of Edward Walker Harden, a famous reporter who later became one of Wall Street's leading financiers. (In 1934, Harden served on the boards of RCA, NBC, and RKO.) Rosemary's uncle, Frank A. Vanderlip, longtime president of the National City Bank in New York, was one of the nation's financial titans. Vanderlip once owned a major chunk of Palos Verdes, south of Los Angeles, including ten miles of oceanfront, and he developed the exclusive Palos Verdes Estates.

With these connections, Albert Parker had no trouble raising a million dollars to defeat Upton Sinclair. Today, however, he was counting illegal voters, not money, and he was no Scrooge. He wanted to share his good fortune with Debevoise.

In his letter, Parker apologized for not having written sooner, but this "bitter contest" was monopolizing his time. He thanked Debevoise for his suggestion "relating to secret indictments." The L.A. district attorney had "adopted it at once." United for California was in the process of striking an initial list of twenty-five thousand names from the register of voters, and planned to enlist police officers to challenge voters on Election Day. Most important, it was "bringing the secret indictments which you suggested in sufficient numbers to terrify many people from coming near the polls." As if that weren't sufficient, Parker boasted of raising enough money

> to support every organization which is combating the election of Upton Sinclair. We have to date distributed some 6,000,000 pamphlets of which I am enclosing a few specimens. We have also caused to be erected some 2,000 billboards upon which we are displaying suitable anti-Sinclair publicity. Altogether it has been a lot of fun and I think it will be very successful, for I honestly believe that Mr. Sinclair will be not merely defeated but demolished on November 6th.

———

The simmering feud between Louis B. Mayer and W. R. Hearst came to a head tonight in a bizarre setting: an elaborate Tyrolean costume party at Marion Davies's 110-room beach house in Santa Monica. Mayer, Hearst, and all the other male guests, including Harpo Marx, Gary Cooper, and Howard Hughes, wore short pants, knee socks, embroidered suspenders, and funny goatherd hats for the occasion. Most of the women wore puffy German dresses or bibs and aprons, although Jean Harlow modeled shorts that showed off her smashing legs. Marion Davies was so pleased with what she referred to as her "Alpine get-up" that she threatened to set off a fashion craze by wearing the outfit around town next week.

Mayer and Hearst had been sparring over Herbert Hoover, but the person who threatened to drive them irreparably apart was that sweet soul Marion Davies. Hearst had returned to California to discover that Irving Thalberg's wife, Norma Shearer, was still scheduled to star as Marie Antoinette in the forthcoming MGM film. W.R. was more intent than ever to seize this property. Marion, on one level, was a natural for the part: no other actress knew what it was like to live at Versailles.

Thalberg had avoided a similar confrontation over *The Barretts of Wimpole Street* by convincing Hearst to exchange his rights to that picture for a modest Civil War comedy called *Operator 13,* a movie that put Marion in men's pants throughout. (Thalberg called this Hearst's "sexual fixation.") But *Operator 13* had bombed, and *The Barretts* was one of the hits of the year, so W.R. was in no mood to compromise on *Marie Antoinette.*

At some point during tonight's costume party, Marion Davies asked

Irving Thalberg for the role. He claimed it was all right with him, but she should ask his wife about it. Norma Shearer told Marion that if she really wanted it, she could have it, but W.R. would have to talk to L.B. later this week. Louis B. Mayer was still furious at Hearst, however, for slandering Herbert Hoover in Europe and then spending a night with Roosevelt when he got back to the States. Hell, L.B. still hadn't forgiven W.R. for making *Gabriel Over the White House.* More to the point, Mayer had vowed that he would never approve the casting of Marion Davies—box office poison despite the shameless promotion of the Hearst press—in a costly production like *Marie Antoinette.*

When Mayer talked to Hearst, fur was sure to fly. What a time for these two heavyweights to have a falling out. Hearst still hadn't declared for a candidate in the governor's race, and now he and foremost Merriam man Louis B. Mayer were at loggerheads.

OCTOBER 21

SUNDAY

In a recent note to Upton Sinclair, Henry Mencken threatened to write another column on the California campaign, and when he finally did it, he outdid himself. The syndicated piece appeared in Hearst's *Los Angeles Examiner* under the title NATION WATCHING SINCLAIR GULPING DOWN QUACK CURES, and it was accompanied by a tiny snapshot of the unsmiling Sage. Mencken looked vaguely thuggish, an appropriate pose for someone about to mug an old friend.

Upton Sinclair had been swallowing magic potions since the turn of the century, Mencken declared, and now he was at it again in California. "It would be hard to find in all history a more assiduous consumer of goods of that sort," he observed. "The bottle is never too black for him, nor the flavor too bitter. Now he gives himself the treat of his life by compounding a cocktail of all the political shampoos and economic wart-removers ever heard of, and getting it down at one gulp with a rousing ah-h-h-h! The dose is so dreadful that even the celebrated Professor Raymond Moley, who has a platinum esophagus, refuses to touch it. But to Sinclair it is no more formidable than four fingers of radiator alcohol to a dry Congressman."

In the autumn of his years, Mencken hoped to spend a year or so compiling a list of all the great untruths Sinclair had believed in his time. It would run, Mencken predicted, to hundreds, and maybe even thousands, "a number so far beyond the bounds of ordinary probability that, aside from Sinclair himself, not more than half a dozen human beings have ever believed in them." Mencken was on one of his celebrated rolls.

> Obviously enough, a man of such talents enjoys large advantages in the field of politics, for it is the first business of every politician to find out what his constituents believe, and then to begin believing in it with loud hosannahs.
>
> But Sinclair goes a great deal further than that. He not only believes everything that his followers believe, and with greater earnestness and devotion; he also believes a lot of things they would like to believe, but can't. Thus he strikes them as a man of superior gifts, as indeed he is, and they follow him joyously. And thus he lifts himself clearly above the common run of politician, and becomes a statesman. . . .
>
> The truth is that Sinclair fits into the New Deal precisely. It almost seems to have been made for him. So far he is plainly its greatest story, with not a rival in sight. How many of its young professors get down its whole shelf of elixirs as eagerly and easily as he does? Every one of them, of course, takes tremendous swigs out of his own bottle, but all of them have doubts about the bottles of the rest, and those doubts are whispered behind every door in Washington. . . .
>
> But none of them is a believer to be put beside Sinclair. He is, at that exercise, without a peer on earth. He swallows each and every invention of the Brain Trust lads the moment it comes out, with a noble smacking of the lips, and he always adds an invention of his own for good measure.
>
> Beside him all the Moleys and Tugwells look like atheists. Thus I have no doubt that when the history of the New Deal is written at last he will turn out to have been its greatest glory. And also, I should add, its perfect *reductio ad absurdum.*

Even the thick-skinned Sinclair could not possibly consider this just another "love tap" from his friend in Baltimore. On studying the column in this morning's *Los Angeles Examiner,* he must have regretted that he had once begged Mencken to "do anything" but ignore him.

The *Los Angeles Times* celebrated a full month of excerpting Upton Sinclair's collected works by compiling a list of highlights on its editorial page. It was the best of the *Times,* it was the worst of the *Times.* Sinclair on Methodists: "children of hell." Bankers: "legalized counterfeiters."

The American Legion: "riot department of the plutocracy" and conductors of "drunken orgies." The Elks: "primitive lowbrows." Motion-picture studios: "honey-pots which gather the feminine beauty and youthful charm of the country for the convenience of rich men's lust." And on and on, thirty-six in all.

One of the *Los Angeles Times*'s most righteous Sinclair critics, Chapin Hall, also provided campaign coverage for a great newspaper across the continent. *The New York Times* hadn't bothered to send one of its own reporters to the West Coast and was still relying on stringers. Until the past two weeks, *The New York Times,* while denouncing Sinclair editorially, provided balanced news accounts of the race. When Chapin Hall started stringing for the paper, however, the *Times* began printing Merriam propaganda as fact. This morning, for example, it announced "a noticeable influx of unemployed persons into Southern California." Vote-fraud investigators had uncovered a "well-organized plot" to register "indigent newcomers"; even "dead men and women were brought to life." Hall went so far as to repeat the lie, left over from the primary, that the mythical Young People's Communist League was working for Sinclair. *The New York Times* illustrated Hall's latest article—under the heading NEEDY HEAD FOR "HEAVEN"—with photographs of transients arriving in California by boxcar and truck.

John E. Steinbeck, the *San Francisco Chronicle* reported this morning, sought reelection as treasurer of Monterey County on grounds that he had saved the taxpayers tens of thousands of dollars since taking office in 1923. Also working in his favor was the fact that he was no newcomer to California, having lived in Salinas since 1900.

Steinbeck's son, a little-known writer also named John, feared that his father would lose this time around but had little time to work for his reelection, since he was deep into his fifth novel. His first three books had sold poorly, and his fourth, called *Tortilla Flat* and set in Monterey, had been rejected left and right by New York publishers. To earn a few dollars, he volunteered for jury duty while his wife, Carol, toiled as a researcher for the State Emergency Relief Administration. He was only thirty-two but felt much older; he was turning gray.

Still, Steinbeck worked happily and productively on his next novel, which he called *In Dubious Battle.* It marked a turning point, he felt, in his development as a novelist: for a change, he was writing about contemporary events. A few months ago a friend had informed him that two strike organizers hunted by vigilantes were hiding out in the nearby town of Seaside. Steinbeck interviewed them, then spent the summer of '34 visiting migrant labor camps in the Salinas area. Almost by accident, rich new subject matter had come his way. Steinbeck had expressed concern for migrant workers before, but hadn't thought to write about them, until now.

Sidney Skolsky, the diminutive gossip columnist, marveled today at how the motion-picture industry this week had "come out in the open" against Upton Sinclair. Practically all the major studios forced their stars to donate to the Merriam campaign, although a few refused—Jean Harlow and Jimmy Cagney among them. Charlie Chaplin "is said to have made donations to Sinclair's campaign," Skolsky revealed. When a comic actor named Ned ("Cold Pan") Sparks was asked for his donation to Merriam, he was so eager to save his career that he wrote a check for one thousand dollars right on the spot.

MGM's *California Election News* had paved the way, and now political film shorts produced by other studios reached the screen. One aimed at "colored" audiences featured Oscar Rankin, a popular former boxer turned preacher in Los Angeles. Asked why he was voting for Governor Merriam, Rankin replied that he liked to preach and play the piano, and if the other fellow got elected there might be no churches left to preach and play *in.* Raymond Moley, starring in another short, charged that EPIC was "no more related to the New Deal than chloroform is to milk."

EPIC headquarters in downtown Los Angeles was aflutter with excitement. Congressman J. H. Hoeppel of Arcadia, California, had just sent over a letter written by James A. Farley to one of his constituents. It appeared to signal the Roosevelt administration's long-awaited endorsement of Upton Sinclair and could be exploited to the hilt.

The Farley letter advised that the New Deal "must have friends on guard from top to bottom." Senator Hiram Johnson would be returning to Washington for another term, and by "electing Hon. Upton Sinclair, your popular Democratic candidate for Governor, California will have a combination of leaders in Washington and in Sacramento who can cooperate in the best interest of the people of the State and of the Nation.

Each voter owes it to himself to vote not only for Johnson and Sinclair but for the entire Democratic ticket." Farley instructed:

> If there have been minor differences of opinion, I am sure they will be forgotten, and everyone will work with the State leaders in the interest of all. By working shoulder to shoulder with real team work, I am satisfied we can achieve a great victory.

In a postscript scrawled in the same green ink with which Farley signed his name, the Democratic National Committee chief added, "Friends of the administration in Washington will be grateful for all your efforts."

The recipient of the letter, Eugene Troskey, a Democratic leader in Whittier, had asked Farley for a clear statement vis-à-vis Sinclair. Farley may not have intended his message for publication, but that hardly mattered to the EPICs. Now they had to get the word out. The local press probably would not cooperate unless national publicity forced their hand, so someone hustled a typescript of the document over to the United Press bureau. And, of course, Rube Borough planned to feature it on the front page of tomorrow's *EPIC News.*

It was a Sunday morning to take the good with the bad and count one's blessings. Henry Mencken's latest blast wounded Upton Sinclair, but the Farley letter put him right back on his feet. Potentially, in fact, it was a panacea. And the best might be yet to come, for President Roosevelt would be addressing the nation tomorrow night.

In a jaunty mood, Uppie sent a note to his son, David, informing him that the wire services were requesting photos of his "family" (Sinclair put the word in quotes). This might be a sign, he said, "that they expect us to win." In a few moments, Uppie would leave by auto for four speaking dates up north. "The campaign is getting hot now," he wrote, "and the lies are amazing. I am told they have an affidavit connecting me with the San Francisco Preparedness Day bombing." The country nervously awaited the results of the *Literary Digest* poll, but Sinclair assured his skeptical son that his precinct reports indicated he had a big lead.

"I'm speaking—I'm speaking to everybody tonight from San Francisco, California," Will Rogers said, opening his radio broadcast on a typical stuttering note. "Now remember that word, California, for in a couple of weeks, after the election, if I was speaking to you from San Francisco it might not be in California.

"For in the case of Mr. Sinclair's election," he observed, "the northern end of California, including San Francisco, may secede from the rest of it." The studio audience cheered. "And in case Mr. Merriam, our Republican, is elected, why Los Angeles is going to secede from you all." They cheered again. "And in case it's a tie, why, Sister Aimee McPherson is going to take up a collection.

"Or even if it ain't a tie."

Earl Warren wisely waited until Will Rogers finished speaking before taking to the air at six-thirty this evening to deliver the first statewide address of his political career. No matter what he said, it would be momentous—for Warren, if not for Frank Merriam. Many Republicans had ruefully agreed to "hold their nose and vote for Merriam" (this had become a popular expression) while vowing that next time they wanted a fresh face like Earl Warren on the ticket. If Warren wanted to step up from district attorney to higher office, he would have to make the most of statewide exposure.

Warren had already served eight years as D.A. with another four on tap and was growing weary of it. He had turned Alameda County around, waging war on gambling, bootlegging, racketeering, and corrupt public officials, but he found that prosecuting criminals and sending them off to prison was no longer pleasurable. Warren couldn't hear the word *guilty* without thinking of the defendant's grieving family. Convictions in murder cases almost nauseated him; he knew that the path led to the electric chair.

He wanted to shape statewide policy instead. Also, he needed a higher salary: his wife was pregnant with the couple's sixth child, and their Oakland home on quiet Larkspur Road was already filled to bursting. Warren eyed the attorney general's post, knew it would be up for grabs in 1938, and planned to seize it. He might even go after the nomination of both major parties.

This year's governor's race placed Warren in a kind of no-lose position. If Merriam won, he could take credit. If Merriam lost, he might catch some flak, but at the same time the defeat would clear out the deadwood at the top of the state GOP. Tonight's speech was vital because it would reach well beyond the party councils and introduce

Earl Warren to the citizens of the entire state, Republican and Democrat alike. The speech was also important as an indication of where the Merriam campaign was heading in the final fifteen days of the race. Would Warren turn up the rhetoric against Sinclair? Or would he ignore EPIC and focus instead on whatever it was the GOP offered in its place?

Warren would do neither. He ridiculed Sinclair and his EPIC plan but attempted to blunt any backlash by appealing to bipartisanship. He could see the writing on the wall in California: the Democratic party was rising, and if he wanted to win statewide office someday it behooved him to meet it halfway.

Although recently elevated to the post of GOP chairman, Warren "by a strange twist of fate" found himself in his first major radio address "appealing with equal force to Democrats and Republicans." He asked Democrats to join him in the common cause of rescuing the state from "the most freakish onslaught that has been made upon our long established and revered American institutions of government in the history of our country. . . . This is not a partisan campaign," he declared. "It is not a contest between Democrats and Republicans. It does not involve a single national issue—it is in no sense a referendum on the administration of President Roosevelt—it is a simple issue between those who believe in the Constitution of the United States and in our Democratic institutions on the one hand, and those who would destroy both in favor of a foreign philosophy of government, half socialistic and half communistic.

"It is the issue between Americanism and extreme radicalism—a communistic radicalism which cannot be disguised by coined phrases such as EPIC or collectivism or Sinclairism. The battle is between two conflicting philosophies of government—one that is proud of our flag, our governmental institutions and our honored history, the other that glorifies the Red Flag of Russia and hopes to establish on American soil a despotism based upon class hatred and tyranny. To this fight we have called every loyal American regardless of his party affiliation in a nonpartisan struggle to preserve those institutions, rights and liberties which we cherish as Americans.

"It is imperative that Sinclairism shall not be allowed to gain a foothold, that it shall be thoroughly eradicated once and for all. I make an earnest appeal to all voters to rally to the candidates for the Republican legislature who will join in defense of our state and to elect them by imposing majorities that will be a death blow to this dangerous movement. Wherever there is an EPIC candidate it is the duty of good citizenship to snow him under by an impressive vote, for the general welfare of our state is at stake. . . . It is imperative that they shall be put down by the greatest nonpartisan upheaval in the history of this state.

"It is not sufficient that we should barely win at this election," Earl Warren said, concluding his maiden speech to the people of California. "We must win by such a sweeping majority as to serve notice not only in this state but throughout the nation that California still adheres to the fundamental principles of Americanism."

OCTOBER 22

MONDAY

The news Republicans dreaded rolled into Los Angeles with the morning haze. The White House, it seemed, had finally blessed Upton Sinclair. Since the *EPIC News*'s circulation now approached two million, nearly everyone in L.A. saw the front-page headline on the way to work: FARLEY GIVES OKAY TO SINCLAIR, SLATE, it read. The *EPIC News* asserted that the Farley letter erased all doubt "as to the standing" of the Roosevelt administration in the governor's race. Ham Cotton, leader of the Democrats-for-Merriam group, American Democracy, saw the story and at 9:55 A.M. shot off a telegram to Jim Farley in Washington demanding to know what was happening.

Ninety miles north, Cotton's friend Thomas M. Storke, publisher of the Santa Barbara *Daily News,* also composed a message for Farley. His newspaper had received a United Press dispatch on the Farley letter Sunday evening, so Storke had a night to sleep on it—except the story upset him so much he couldn't sleep. Fortunately, Storke had some pull with the Democratic boss. The New Deal had pumped millions in public-works money into Santa Barbara, but Farley still owed the portly publisher a political favor. Tom Storke had carried the ball for Farley at the Chicago convention in 1932 and helped to direct the pivotal

California delegation into FDR's corner, handing him the Democratic nomination. Storke and Farley had grown quite fond of each other. When Farley visited Santa Barbara, the publisher personally showed him around its famous mission.

So it was with no sense of futility that Tom Storke, known as T.M. to his newspaper associates and Mr. Santa Barbara to the rest of the city, sat down this morning in his office in the Spanish-style *Daily News* building on the Plaza de la Guerra and tapped out a message to Jim Farley. "I returned from Washington a few days ago," Storke revealed, "and had been sleeping the sleep of a child with a conscience that only a good Californian possesses; and because you told me I might. These are your words that lulled me to sleep: 'I never did and never will endorse him.' "

Then, last night, Storke had spotted the story about the Farley endorsement. "No sleep since," he reported grimly. "How come!! Seriously, Jim, is this authentic? It's undated and unsigned and this bird Uppie has been putting over some fast ones on us out here."

By all appearances, Jim Farley was playing some kind of strange political game, even by Democratic standards. Three weeks ago he was criticized for not taking a position on Upton Sinclair. Now he was accused of taking too many. On October 3 he privately informed Senator McAdoo that "we want to see Sinclair elected. . . ." Six days later he apparently told Tom Storke, "I never did and never will endorse him." A week or so after *that* he sent a form letter to California calling for the election of the "Hon. Upton Sinclair." Was Farley changing his mind about Sinclair every few days? Or was he simply responding to ambivalent orders from his chief? Was it just coincidence that his first flip-flop followed Raymond Moley's attack on Sinclair? And that he restored Sinclair to favor after William Fox offered him a $250,000-a-year job?

The answers might arrive soon enough. FDR would be going on the radio in a few hours, and if he kept his "promise" to Upton Sinclair, he might clarify the White House's policy on the California race. But matters were coming to a head, speech or no speech. Today the President received a personal message from Culbert Olson, the Democratic chairman in California, virtually begging him to send his best wishes "for the success of the state ticket." FDR scribbled a note to Marvin

McIntyre, and attached it to Olson's letter. "Ask Farley to speak to me about this?" the President wrote.

———

High-salaried actors and writers were no longer the only targets of anti-Sinclair fund-raising. Today the Hollywood magnates levied the "Merriam tax" throughout their realm. Executives at major studios called their rank-and-file workers together to hear anti-Sinclair speeches delivered by prominent Republicans. At some studios, the employees were politely asked to donate one day's pay to the Merriam fund. At others, they were simply told to look for a lighter paycheck this week. MGM distributed personal vouchers made out to Louis B. Mayer, and workers at some of the other studios received them as well.

At Columbia Pictures, the set department erected a huge thermometer on the patio of the executive dining room, and as studio personnel contributed to Merriam, the red bar climbed toward the 100-percent mark. Today it was nearly there. Columbia's leading writer, Robert Riskin, and its top director, Frank Capra, had resisted at first. Frequent collaborators, they made films in which characters were forced to call upon inner reserves of courage, integrity, and idealism, with social justice inevitably winning in the end. Perhaps Riskin and Capra saw no happy ending in the EPIC campaign, for they agreed finally to give money to Merriam. Creators of the year's most acclaimed film, *It Happened One Night,* starring Clark Gable and Claudette Colbert, they had the power to hold out, but perhaps not the incentive.

That left the writers John Howard Lawson and John Wexley as the last two holdouts at Columbia. Jack Lawson was a radical playwright, first president of the Screen Writers Guild, and a friend of John Dos Passos's. (He had just received a letter from Dos Passos advising that all Lawson's talk about "integrity" in Hollywood was nothing but "the purest and most mouldy mahoula.") John Wexley was another left-winger. Harry Cohn, Columbia's president, was so anxious for his thermometer to hit the top that he personally approached the two writers and demanded an offering.

Wexley was making about $800 a week, so one day's pay represented about $150.

"John," Cohn said, "just make it an even hundred."

"No," Wexley responded.

"Well, just give me fifty."

Still, Wexley wouldn't budge.

"How about ten, then?" When Wexley wouldn't even hand over a token donation, Cohn blustered, "You know, you'll be marked lousy." "Marked lousy" was another way of saying "blacklisted."

Jack Lawson, who had just joined the Communist party, fared even worse. "I am the king here," Cohn informed him. "Whoever eats my bread sings my song." After failing to convince Lawson to donate even a dollar to Merriam, Cohn decided to fire him.

Over at MGM, Louis B. Mayer faced a minimutiny. Technicians, carpenters, and secretaries had no choice but to go along with the levy, but a solid corps of creative personnel held out. Asked to submit fifty dollars to Merriam, Sam Marx, the story editor, sent off that amount to his friend Upton Sinclair instead. The "Good Hacks," Frances Goodrich and Albert Hackett, continued to resist the tax.

A studio exec told Allen Rivkin, "You better not work for Sinclair or you'll be in trouble." Rivkin, who was writing a film for Carole Lombard, did not consider this an empty threat but raised money at the studio for EPIC anyway. The studio's tactics seemed to give the Screen Writers Guild a new sense of purpose, Rivkin observed. Not every member supported Sinclair, but they all opposed attempts by the studio to control their life away from the office. The moguls' anti-Sinclair campaign symbolized the authoritarianism the writers had been organizing against for the past two years.

Louis B. Mayer was so upset he called a group of defiant writers together and advised them to cooperate. "After all," L.B. told them, "what does Sinclair know about anything? He's just a writer."

At another studio, an executive advised his workers against Sinclair by pointing out that "of forty-seven books he has written, not one has ever been filmed." (This wasn't even true.)

A reporter for an Eastern newspaper decided to have some fun. He strolled into the MGM commissary and began distributing pro-Sinclair literature, just to see what would happen. Some MGM publicity men accepted the leaflets but on discovering what they were dropped them as if they were on fire. They pleaded with the journalist never to play such a prank again, as it could cost them their jobs if they were spotted with a Sinclair circular in their hands.

Even the pro-Roosevelt studio, Warner Bros., took part in Mayer's money-raising plan. John Bright, who had written *Public Enemy* for James Cagney and *She Done Him Wrong* with Mae West, was one Warners writer who protested. A boozing, brawling ex-reporter from

Chicago, Bright had helped organize the Screen Writers Guild. He often enrolled his friend Cagney in radical causes but couldn't get Jimmy to donate to Sinclair. Bright thought EPIC was silly but respected Sinclair's integrity. He attended several EPIC rallies, rarely spying anyone else from Hollywood in attendance, except for the young writer Nathanael West.

On several occasions, Bright had offered Sinclair advice on how to counter the smear campaign. He thought Upton should meet every charge promptly and directly, using the radio as much as possible, but Sinclair acted unconcerned. On one occasion, he told Bright that the charges against him amounted to nothing more than "nonsense."

"But nonsense," Bright replied, "often rules the roost."

When the first Inquiring Cameraman short came out, Bright informed Sinclair that MGM's Carey Wilson was the creative force behind it. Bright tried to get Wilson to appear on the radio with him, without any luck.

Unlike the writers, Hollywood's acting talent, with the exception of Jimmy Cagney and a handful of others, seemed to go along with the Merriam tax without much of a fuss. Early reports that Jean Harlow planned to buck the system proved premature. But the name of another young star supposedly fighting the Merriam tax had surfaced in Hollywood. It raised eyebrows, for the actress, Katharine Hepburn, had much to lose, having just won an Academy Award. While Jean Harlow's career, in the Production Code era, appeared to be imperiled, Hepburn's was clearly on the rise.

On arriving in Sonora this morning, Will Rogers was met at the train station by the usual contingent of officials. Rogers politely accepted their greetings and then shambled over to a group of railroad tramps who had assembled off to the side, hoping to meet him. Rogers was due to start shooting *The County Chairman* out here in Bret Harte territory, but he paused to chat with the hoboes for half an hour or more. By the time he was through he had distributed three hundred dollars, all the cash he had in his pocket, to his new friends, and now he'd have to borrow money to get home.

BABIES AS DOG FOOD. The *Los Angeles Times* was at it again in its front-page Sinclair box. Today's quote came from *The Profits of Reli-*

gion. In this heavily edited excerpt, Sinclair warned that "some of our leisure class ladies" may one day discover that "the flesh of working class babies . . . is relished by poodles."

Also in Los Angeles, the GOP staged a parade featuring a fake train engine pulling boxcars filled with tramps. Pretty girls stationed throughout the city stopped traffic and slapped MERRIAM OR BUST stickers on windshields. Eugene Biscailuz, sheriff of L.A. County, met with a force of twelve hundred special deputies at the Shrine Auditorium to go over Election Day duties. He told them they would constitute the largest police force ever to watch the polls in California and that trouble was brewing.

The betting line on the election now stood at anywhere from six-to-five to ten-to-seven in Merriam's favor, depending on the bookmaker. The "gamboleers" knew their stuff, but according to published reports the odds on Merriam were highly suspect. A significant slice of the enormous GOP slush fund was supposedly being wagered on Merriam's behalf. Besides being a potentially lucrative investment, it punched up the odds favoring Merriam—which in turn drove public opinion in his direction. Heavy betting on the incumbent might produce a bandwagon effect. This was a unique way of "buying" an election, and with money to be won in the event of Merriam's victory, it gave his funders all the more incentive to see to it that they did not fail.

United for California sponsored an anti-EPIC speech over KNX radio by Dr. Francis Townsend, whose old-age pension plan Merriam had shamelessly endorsed, knowing that his approval would cost him nothing (since the plan required federal action). Sinclair explicitly rejected Townsendism, knowing it might cost him everything. An article in today's *Boston Globe* asserted that if Sinclair was beaten on November 6 "it will be because another economic doctor, sponsoring a remedy essentially antagonistic to his EPIC, has risen to replace him in the favor of many of the voters. . . ."

At a recent rally, Dr. Townsend had given Sinclair one last chance to save his political career by backing his plan. "There might come a day," he added, "when Mr. Sinclair could use two hundred dollars a month, and if he ever applies for the pension I can promise him we will do all we can to help him get it."

One Townsendite who had no use for Upton Sinclair was a young, aspiring Los Angeles politician named Sam Yorty. Like most Townsendites, Yorty hailed from the Midwest. Growing up in Nebraska, he idolized William Jennings Bryan and Woodrow Wilson and vowed to devote his life to politics. While studying for a law degree in Los Angeles in the early 1930s, Sam worked as a salesman and a movie projectionist. A born orator, blessed with a booming voice, he entered politics in 1933, making speeches that helped elect Frank Shaw mayor of Los Angeles. Then he rallied support for technocracy and, later, the Townsend Plan.

Sam had hoped to run for the state assembly this year, but found his way blocked by the EPIC-backed incumbent in his downtown district. Now he was sitting out the governor's race. Although decidedly liberal, Yorty felt he could never support a Socialist; he wasn't in any position to endorse Sinclair, anyway, since his present employer, the L.A. Water and Power Commission, bitterly opposed EPIC. Besides, it seemed to Yorty, as the campaign approached its climax, that Sinclair no longer *wanted* to win; as if he, too, recognized that the EPIC plan was unworkable. A serious candidate would never retreat under heavy fire the way Sinclair did. He would never do that when *he* ran for office, Sam decided.

When Upton Sinclair arrived in San Francisco, he was greeted by a startling story in Fremont Older's newspaper, the *Call.* Rumor had it that anti-Sinclair Democrats were considering a new "stunt": promoting a write-in vote for Will Rogers to take Populist votes from Sinclair. Had Rogers given his blessing? The article didn't say, but it claimed that the humorist would play a "surprise" role in the final days of the campaign.

Sinclair had a few other things on his mind today. First order of business was a luncheon address to a thousand members of the League of Women Voters at the St. Francis Hotel. When he was a boy, Sinclair told the audience, the thrill of his life was visiting the Eden Musee in New York City. Its Chamber of Horrors featured several trick mirrors. One made you tall and skinny; another, short and fat; a third twisted your features grotesquely. "Now, twice a day when I get the newspapers," Sinclair disclosed, "I think of the Eden Musee. I gaze at images of myself in dismay and wonder, will the people of California vote to make such a creature their Governor?"

Then, as usual, he invited questions. Dozens flew his way, and he responded cheerfully to each one. He even admitted that he talked too much for his own good. This went on for hours.

Finally, Sinclair looked at his watch to make sure he was not overstaying his welcome and, noticing that it was four o'clock, impulsively decided to make a major announcement. For seven weeks, he had somehow managed to keep secret President Roosevelt's "promise" to come out in favor of production for use. Now the big day had arrived.

And so, speaking to the League of Women Voters, Sinclair decided to reveal his secret. "The President is scheduled to speak over the radio about four hours from now," Sinclair chirped, "and if he says what he told me he was going to say, I expect to be elected."

Lawmen finally surrounded Charles ("Pretty Boy") Floyd on an East Liverpool, Ohio, farm this afternoon. Federal agent Melvin Purvis, who had nailed John Dillinger in Chicago earlier this year, moved in for the kill, along with four other federal men and four local cops. Floyd had worn the Justice Department's public-enemy-number-one label ever since Dillinger's demise.

As the famed bank robber darted for a wooded ridge, Melvin Purvis shouted, "Halt!", but Floyd kept running. Machine guns and pistols barked, and the desperado fell. When Purvis reached him, Floyd asked, "Who the hell tipped you?" Pretty Boy had earned his nickname more for his stylish manner of dress than for his good looks (he resembled Babe Ruth), but now his fine clothes had fifteen bullet holes in them. The agents carried Pretty Boy to a nearby farmhouse, and Purvis started questioning him about the machine-gun massacre of five men at a Kansas City train station in June 1933. "I am Floyd," Pretty Boy admitted, but he denied taking part in that shoot-out. Then he died. That made George ("Baby Face") Nelson the new public enemy number one.

Floyd had eluded so many manhunts that radio reports of his death startled listeners. Two women were not surprised. One was his estranged wife, Ruby, who had been supporting herself lecturing on "Crime Does Not Pay." Another was his mother, Mrs. W. F. Floyd of Akins, Oklahoma. A year ago her son had picked out a grave site near Tulsa. "Right here is where you can put me," he advised. "I expect to go down soon with lead in me—perhaps the sooner the better." Mrs. Floyd had kept the plot well tended and soon it would welcome Pretty Boy back home to Oklahoma.

Tom Mooney's appeal reached the Supreme Court today. Mooney's attorneys were seeking a writ of habeas corpus on grounds that the defendant had been convicted at trial solely on the basis of perjured testimony. Four lower federal courts had denied the motion since May. The court recessed until November 12, taking Mooney's appeal under advisement.

It was nearly half past seven, and President Roosevelt was about to deliver his second fireside chat of the season. Upton Sinclair borrowed a radio and set it up in his room at the Whitcomb Hotel in San Francisco. His bodyguard, Hjalmar Rutzebeck, attorney John Packard, and a couple of other friends joined him. Uppie had been telling his aides that he was on pins and needles anticipating this moment, and when it arrived, he was even more nervous than he had imagined.

The President's chat focused on charity. FDR sermonized about the sacredness of pity and the holiness of giving, and then, just as he got rolling, he came to an abrupt halt, without breathing a word about production for use. The speech was so short it didn't even fill the allotted radio slot, and the network had to play music to complete the program. Pain and saddened, Upton Sinclair recalled the fable of the mountain in labor and a little mouse coming forth.

OCTOBER 23

TUESDAY

George Creel came to the White House today in the guise of a journalist. Having relinquished his NRA job to run for governor of California, he had returned to writing to make ends meet. Creel secured an assignment from the *Saturday Evening Post* to interpret utopianism in California, but it was a story for *Collier's* on public works that brought him to the President's office.

It was an important day for FDR. He was set to address the American Bankers Association convention in Washington tomorrow, and the newspapers were billing it as a momentous occasion. Harry Hopkins and Henry Morgenthau argued today that it was time to draw the line and show the bankers who was boss, and Roosevelt seemed to agree. Ray Moley wanted to craft a conciliatory statement and was horrified when the President ordered a hard-line message.

FDR couldn't find time to meet with EPIC's Culbert Olson, who had come from California hoping to see him, but he happily chatted with George Creel. Exiting the President's office, Creel handed a document to press secretary Steve Early: a six-page letter, dated October 18, addressed to "My dear Sinclair" in Pasadena. Creel had either forgotten to give it to Roosevelt or, fearing disapproval, chosen not to discuss it with FDR personally.

In the letter, Creel renounced his support for Sinclair, bitterly rebuking the EPIC candidate for straying from the party platform the two men had hammered out in Sacramento. Sinclair's new *Immediate EPIC* booklet "seems to be at utter variance with our understandings," Creel wrote. "In essence it is the original EPIC Plan that I attacked as unsound, unworkable and un-American, designed to appeal to the credulities of ignorance and despair, and immeasurably hurtful in its effect on true progressivism. It is, therefore, with the very real regret that must always be stirred by lost opportunities, that I withdraw my offer to campaign in your behalf."

Creel advised Steve Early that the letter was, for now, "confidential." When he left, Early wrote a brief message to the President and attached it to the document. "George Creel left this most interesting letter to Sinclair," Early explained. "Creel is returning to California and may release letter to the press when there."

Early also penned a note to Eleanor Roosevelt:

> The President's instruction on Sinclair's candidacy in California are: (1) Say nothing and (2) Do nothing.

Senator William G. McAdoo had reached a kind of crossroads himself. Upton Sinclair, a man he had ignored publicly but defended privately for the past five weeks, now seemed to be slipping. If he lost, it would mean four more years of Frank Merriam in Sacramento. This would not help FDR's campaign in 1936 or McAdoo's own reelection bid two years later. On the other hand, why back a reviled loser? McAdoo had two choices: drop what he was doing in Washington, fly back to California, and put his personal prestige on the line to help the Democratic nominee stage a comeback, or sit out the campaign entirely.

Today he decided on the latter course. Responding to Tom Storke's recent letter, which warned that the senator's support for Sinclair was damaging his reputation, McAdoo announced that he had made up his mind "to take no part in the campaign. Frankly," McAdoo informed the Santa Barbara publisher, "I am disappointed in the way Sinclair departed from the platform. In these circumstances I do not feel that

I am under obligation to do more than I have already done." George Creel, he added, had showed him a letter he had just written, "which he is going to release soon, and which I think will be tremendously hurtful to Sinclair."

Having survived the Tyrolean revelries in Santa Monica, W. R. Hearst was back at San Simeon after an absence of five months and ready at last to select a candidate in the governor's race. Upton Sinclair might be down, but Hearst's decision would put Ray Haight out. Haight, perceiving Hearst as a fellow maverick, had lobbied long and hard for the publisher's support. Today, in a personal letter to Haight, the Chief put an end to that nonsense. "What I conceive to be the best interests of the people of California," Hearst explained, "impel me to support Mr. Merriam for Governor."

> With all respect to you, sir, the choice for Governor in this instance seems clearly to lie between Mr. Sinclair on the one hand—a man who is shockingly unstable in his opinions, and obviously unreliable in his ever-varying and conflicting advocacies—and Mr. Merriam on the other hand—a capable and conscientious American, wholly dependable in his proven devotion to the public welfare. . . . It would be unthinkable to have this great state, and the interests of its millions of worthy citizens, come under the control of an unbalanced and unscrupulous political speculator who would, in the performance of his unsound and sinister program, wreck the very foundations of all prosperity for years to come.

Hearst informed Haight that he was taking this step solely "to serve the State in which I was born" and humbly suggested that Haight reconsider his own role in the campaign. "I am sure, sir," he advised, "that you, in whatever way you think best, will co-operate in the patriotic effort to rebuke a dangerous and discreditable demagogue, and to elect an honest and experienced public servant as the Chief Executive of Our State."

Upton Sinclair talked about sharing the wealth, but Huey P. Long was actually doing it. Baton Rouge went crazy today as Senator Long handed out thousands of dollars in cash.

It started as a scheme to encourage Louisiana State University students to accompany Huey to the big LSU-Vanderbilt football game in Nashville on Saturday. Huey was scheduled to make a speech in the stadium before the contest, and according to some reports he intended to announce that he would run for president in 1936 on the Share Our Wealth platform. Long was even taking along his own sound trucks for the occasion, as well as a contingent of state police as bodyguards.

Appearing on the LSU campus, Huey took wads of bills from his pocket and passed them out, announcing that he had chartered five special trains to Tennessee and the cash was to be used to buy tickets and meals on board. That kind of news traveled fast in Baton Rouge, and when Huey returned to his hotel, he was besieged by townsfolk seeking a handout. Huey being Huey, he obliged. The senator stood in the doorway to his suite passing out bills to a seemingly endless line of supplicants. Miraculously, the line ended before the money ran out.

"Wall Street cohorts flocking here. We await you anxiously." Heywood Broun had received yet another telegram from Upton Sinclair imploring him to come out to California and save his campaign. But Broun, contrary to his promise, had not budged. His ex-wife, Ruth Hale, had passed away in September, and Broun was still up to his neck in Newspaper Guild affairs. Broun's boss, Roy Howard, opposed Upton Sinclair. Had Howard discouraged Broun from going to California? That's what Upton Sinclair had heard. This much was known for certain: this week, as the campaign entered its crucial stage, the famous Scripps-Howard columnist who arrived in California to cover the campaign was not Heywood Broun but, rather, his polar opposite, Westbrook Pegler.

Disturbed by the death of Ruth Hale, whom he considered his best friend, Broun had spent most of this autumn at his upstate Sabine Farm. Often he paced the floor and could not sleep. "Come on, Woodie," he'd say to his sixteen-year-old son, Heywood Hale Broun, "let's go to town," and off they would go to New York to hit the racetracks, restaurants, and casinos. Broun was still considering the offer from Arthur Brisbane to join the Hearst stable. "I don't know," he said to his son. "I can imagine myself sitting at the typewriter, my fingers beginning to move—and then I would think of that old man sitting in his palace out in California."

The old man had declared for Merriam today, but Broun was standing by Sinclair, albeit at some distance. It could not have been coincidence that Broun wrote a column about the California race on the very day Westbrook Pegler unleashed himself on California.

" 'Free love comes to California?' Upon this issue and others equally authentic and intelligent Frank F. Merriam is battling to save his State from the threat of Upton Sinclair," Broun observed. "No wonder lonely women shiver at night even in the mild Los Angeles climate. Nothing stands between them and dishonor save the stalwart figure of Frank Merriam.

"However, at the eleventh hour Hollywood rides to the rescue. The motion picture magnates are ready to march shoulder to shoulder with the statesman who contends that it is Upton's intention to end purity in California. The hearth, the home and Hollywood have joined hands to repel the invader. It would be very funny but for the fact that democratic government is under fire and cannot stand many more Merriams."

Reports of coerced contributions at movie studios revealed which candidate in California really believed in democracy. "No such flagrant forced levy has been known in this country," Broun wrote, "since the days when Mark Hanna bought the presidency of the United States for William McKinley." It was Merriam's candidacy, and not Sinclair's, "which endangers American tradition. If it is possible for a minority of rich men to thwart the will of the commonwealth by corruption and misrepresentation, then it will be very difficult to answer adequately the radical who says that he believes in revolution and direct action since the masses can never get a fair deal at the polls.

"Many American campaigns have been distinguished by dirty tactics," Broun acknowledged, "but I can think of none in which willful fraud has been so brazenly practiced." He dissected some of the most outrageous anti-Sinclair leaflets and then observed:

> It seems to me that it is not fantastic to say that Frank F. Merriam, if elected, will be the first out-and-out fascist Governor the United States has known. The tactics which he is pursuing in his campaign follow very closely the formulae used by Hitler in smashing the German republic. I insist again that it would be preposterous to assert that government by the people will perish from the face of the earth if government by boodle conquers in California. But the issue is sufficiently vital to enlist the support of all those who feel that democracy is not a dead and gone theory.

Arthur Brisbane, the richest columnist in the world, prized the picture of Heywood Broun hanging on the wall behind his desk in his New York office. He valued it so much that he trained a museum light on it. Concerning their mutual friend, Upton Sinclair, the two men did not exactly see eye to eye, however. Brisbane had directed a steady stream of good-natured mockery at Sinclair throughout the campaign. He was no Mencken in his use of language, but he had something the Sage of Baltimore lacked: a daily column.

Today he upbraided Upton for claiming in a recent speech that when EPIC went into the motion-picture business he would put Charlie Chaplin in charge. Chaplin, Brisbane observed, "is supposed to be a pretty good radical himself, but, with all his industry and willingness to succeed, even financially, produces only one picture in about five years. He would probably not undertake to beat the able Warner Brothers, the intelligent Schencks, and the powerful MGM, to say nothing of Lupe Velez, using the unemployed as moving picture raw meat."

United Artists continued to keep King Vidor's *Our Daily Bread* on the shelf in California, despite critical acclaim. *The New York Times,* for example, called the film "a brilliant declaration of faith in the importance of cinema as a social instrument" and a "social document of amazing vitality and emotional impact." *Our Daily Bread* had brought motion pictures "squarely into the modern stream of socially-minded art . . . it is impossible to overestimate the significance of the new work." Despite, or perhaps because of, such reviews, the movie still did not have a release date in California.

Outside the state, the film was not drawing enormous crowds, and some theater owners and distributors thought a Sinclair endorsement might help. Sinclair had just appeared on the cover of *Time,* and if all of his admirers around the country bought tickets to *Our Daily Bread,* it would be a bonanza. King Vidor today responded to a United Artists executive in New York who had urged him to screen the movie for Sinclair. "Sinclair is willing to run the picture and make a statement," Vidor revealed, "but the local picture bosses are out for his scalp and MacLaine, the local United Artists branch manager, is afraid to tie up *Our Daily Bread* with Sinclair on account of helping Sinclair and hurting the picture in addition to stirring up local opposition.

"I don't see how we can get a statement by Sinclair to use out of California without local publicity," Vidor observed. "MacLaine wants to lay low until after the election of November 6th."

Upton Sinclair got one break today. On a morning when headlines celebrated his latest pratfall (UPTON WAITS IN VAIN FOR FDR BOOST, crowed the *San Francisco News*), a delicious story involving another leading California Democrat hit the front pages. It seemed that Ellen Wilson McAdoo, the pretty nineteen-year-old daughter of Senator McAdoo (and granddaughter of Woodrow Wilson) intended to marry one Rafael Lopez de Onate. In the eyes of the McAdoo family, who violently disapproved of the marriage, this gentleman had at least three strikes against him: he was twice Ellen's age, he was a native of the Philippines, and perhaps worst of all, he was a Hollywood bit actor.

In the eyes of the law, there was one more problem. The county clerk in Riverside, California, announced today that he would require the prospective bridegroom to "establish proof that there is no Filipino or Malay blood in his veins before I issue the license." The clerk acted after a state senator informed him that the legislature had recently passed an amendment to the mixed-marriage laws prohibiting unions between Caucasians and Filipinos or Malaysians.

Ellen McAdoo complained that "all of our plans are spoiled" and threatened to elope. The handsome de Onate was incensed, proudly asserting that he bore no Filipino or Malaysian blood. "Why, it's absurd to believe because a person is born in the Philippines he is a native Filipino," he complained. His parents, he said, were Spaniards.

This story would prove only momentarily diverting, of course, so Upton Sinclair sent a telegram to President Roosevelt hoping to undo the political damage of the day before:

> ATROCIOUS MISQUOTATION BY NEWSPAPERS HERE. THEY ARE DELIBERATELY DISTORTING MY STATEMENTS CONCERNING ADMINISTRATION, SEEKING TO PUT ME IN FALSE POSITION. AM ENDEAVORING OBTAIN IMMEDIATE RETRACTION.

Sinclair told reporters that he had never asserted that FDR "would issue a statement supporting me. What I did say was that 'if President Roosevelt makes a statement on certain public policies, I feel certain I will be elected.' "

Tonight EPIC organizers planned to put on the biggest political rally in the history of northern California. But first Upton Sinclair would have to survive an encounter with Westbrook Pegler.

———

Eugene Troskey lost his job today, apparently for no other reason than the fact that he had received a letter from Jim Farley endorsing Upton Sinclair. O. K. Flood, manager of the Whittier office of the Automobile Club of Southern California, dismissed Troskey just hours after a United Press dispatch linked him to the Farley letter. According to Troskey, Flood complained that he was taking "too active" a role in electing Sinclair.

———

Strangers kept showing up at EPIC headquarters in Los Angeles with startling documents. Two days ago it was a messenger from Arcadia carrying the Farley communiqué. Today an accountant from the O'Melveny law firm appeared with a letter he had apparently pilfered from office files.

This wasn't the first time the young man had alerted EPIC to dubious activities emanating from the O'Melveny office: two months ago he'd fingered O'Melveny attorney Albert Parker as the culprit in the fake Young Peoples Communist League leaflet. Today he explained that he was so outraged by the firm's involvement in the vote-fraud case that he had demanded that O'Melveny and his partners put a stop to it. When they refused, he resigned his position—but not before rifling Albert Parker's personal papers. There he found a carbon copy of Parker's October 20 letter to his friend Eli Whitney Debevoise in New York.

EPIC staffers examined the two-page Parker letter, which was neatly typed on O'Melveny stationery, and decided it was political dynamite. It confirmed some of Sinclair's charges: "We will have raised $1,000,000 . . . distributed some 6,000,000 pamphlets. . . . It has been a lot of fun. . . ." Even better, Albert Parker verified the real aim of the vote-fraud scheme: "to terrify many people from coming near the polls." Sinclair had been shooting himself in the foot the entire campaign; now the other side was guilty of misfiring. Perhaps this letter, along with the Farley endorsement, might yet turn the tide in the governor's race.

———

Albert Parker wasn't the only United for California official under a microscope. Jay Starr, who worked in the group's office in Beverly Hills, found a placard on his desk today bearing the message YOU CLOSE UP THIS MUD-SLINGING MERRIAM HEADQUARTERS OR ELSE. . . .—then a sketch of a skull and crossbones—REMEMBER—EIGHT DAYS. Otis Ashworth, director of precinct work at Merriam headquarters in Santa Monica, also reported an attempt at intimidation. A few days ago his secretary found a threatening note on the steering wheel of his car. That convinced him to hire a bodyguard. Now the bodyguard had discovered another message, ordering Ashworth to cease his vote-fraud investigation, or else.

———

When Westbrook Pegler arrived at Upton Sinclair's room in the Whitcomb Hotel, he found the candidate sprawled across one of the twin beds, resting but still wearing a sport coat. An enormous man named Rutzebeck, whom Pegler took to be a combination of Jack London's Wolf Larsen and Popeye the Sailor, stood beside him, as if protecting the frail figure. Rutzebeck seemed like Sinclair's pet giant: at a word from his master he might return to his cage or battle an army of cops bursting through the door. Also present were attorney John Packard and a couple of EPIC factotums.

Greeting Pegler, Sinclair immediately sensed that he was one of those New York "swells" who take nothing seriously and treat everyone like a Runyonesque "guy." Dark-haired and handsome in a sulky sort of way, Pegler wore trousers creased to a knife-edge and a boldly striped tie. Sinclair considered him a young man of the demimonde but decided to treat him like a reasonable human being anyway. Some might say that was his first mistake.

Although he had been writing his Scripps-Howard column for less than a year, Westbrook Pegler was already known as the man who was "agin" everything. He wore the title proudly but never modestly. Pegler once complained that he had stored up a week's worth of ill will and found "no really worthy proposition or group to use it on." Readers turned to his daily column with hearts racing, wondering whom he was going to slam today. There were plenty of targets, since Pegler generally believed that both sides in any dispute were wrong. He socked everyone from J. Edgar Hoover ("a night-club fly-cop") to Fiorello La Guardia ("little padrone of the Bolsheviki"). One of his favorite punching bags, Harold Ickes ("house-dick of the New Deal"), declared that he would "no more think of reading Pegler than I would of handling raw sewage."

Born in Minneapolis in 1894, the son of a renowned reporter, Pegler quit high school to work as copy boy with the Hearst news service. One day Arthur Brisbane held up a few sheets of copy and asked Pegler to "run these down to the wire." Pegler responded, "Run it down yourself." For some reason, his career did not end right there. Other newspaper jobs followed, and eventually Pegler became a sports columnist for the *Chicago Tribune.* When sports news was slow, he took on other subjects, happily confiding that he was no deep thinker. He even joined H. L. Mencken in covering the Scopes case. His stories on the "monkey trial" were inconsequential because he hadn't yet developed his mature style: he ridiculed the fundamentalists without attacking the pro-Darwin city slickers with equal enthusiasm.

Near the end of 1933, the New York *World-Telegram,* owned by Roy Howard, announced the arrival of a new columnist with "the drollery of Ring Lardner, the iconoclasm of Henry Mencken, the homely insight of Will Rogers." It was Westbrook Pegler. Howard hired him to balance Heywood Broun's cerebral left-wing commentary and even placed the competing columns on opposite sides of the same page (Pegler on the right, of course). Howard instructed Pegler to write "lowbrow, rowdy, red-blooded" to offset Broun's "bleeding-heart approach." Pegler was only too eager to oblige. On his second day on the job he revealed his raison d'être: "My hates have always occupied my mind much more actively and have given greater spiritual satisfactions than my friendships. . . . The wish to favor a friend is not as active as the instinct to annoy some person or institution I detest."

On his third day, he saluted the lynching of two accused murderers in San Jose, California, with the immortal words: "Fine, that is swell. . . ." Pegler's rationale was that even if the hanged men were innocent, their deaths neatly balanced "the innocent persons who were murdered." Somehow he weathered the storm of protest—and the indignation of Heywood Broun—that greeted this column, perhaps because California Governor James Rolph had said much the same thing. Within a few months, his syndicated column was one of the most popular in the nation.

Even Broun grew to like him. They drank and played poker together at their country homes. Broun considered it a tragedy that Pegler, whom he knew as Peg, was not the man he pretended to be. Peg, he felt, had created a character named Westbrook Pegler. The fictional Pegler was hard-boiled, querulous, and materialistic. Peg was actually shy, sensitive, and generous. Like nearly everyone else, Broun admired him as a stylist but complained that it took Peg five hours to write a single column: this was far too much time for anyone to waste on the opinions of Westbrook Pegler.

Day after day the indignations mounted. Pegler attacked Father Coughlin, Communists, Nazis, all unionists, indecency in the theater, and anyone advocating an income tax. Everything was a "racket." Every public figure was "vile," "vicious, "foul," "degraded," or "immoral." Pegler once explained that the only way he could express what he was for was by showing what he was against. Ten months into his tenure, however, readers were still mystified. On October 9, his archenemy, Walter Winchell (who had already forbidden Pegler to attend his funeral), quoted Ernest Hemingway as saying that he couldn't tell what Pegler "really feels" about anything, "except to get his piece done." But Pegler's popularity was soaring, and his salary now approached sixty thousand dollars.

To a man who loved to demolish both sides in any controversy, the Sinclair-Merriam race was a dream matchup. *Time,* in its recent cover story, ridiculed both candidates, but the magazine didn't go at it with the relish one would expect from Westbrook Pegler. Now Peg had arrived on the scene to show everyone how to do it.

After an exchange of pleasantries in the hotel room, Pegler warmed to his task. He challenged Sinclair, who was still reclining on the bed, to name a single enterprise he had ever engineered to a successful conclusion. Surprised to be questioned directly about this—most reporters didn't have the guts to do it, leaving such accusations to the editorial page—Sinclair stammered an answer: "Helicon Hall." After a moment, however, Upton had to admit that his commune in New Jersey had quickly expired. When Sinclair and his associates attempted to explain the EPIC plan, Pegler responded that he just didn't get it; it sounded like socialism, which he despised.

"Tell him the one about the twelve barter transactions in which not a cent of money changed hands," Sinclair instructed Hjalmar Rutzebeck. While the candidate ate dinner, a baked apple, Rutzebeck told the tale with great gusto, spinning his arms with such force that Pegler expected at any moment to be hit with a flying limb.

Having finished his supper, Sinclair invited Pegler to attend the big EPIC rally at the Civic Auditorium, explaining that this might show him what success *really* meant. Citing a dinner engagement, the columnist declined.

They were hanging from the rafters at the Civic Auditorium. By seven o'clock, at least fifteen thousand Sinclair enthusiasts had squeezed inside, and perhaps ten thousand more milled about outside. It was standing room only—in the streets. A crowd of about five thousand refused to leave the entrance to the auditorium until Sheridan Downey and a couple of other speakers came out around nine o'clock and said hello. San Francisco was supposed to be hostile to Sinclair, but tonight no one would have known it.

After a few words from the president of the California Federation of Labor, Sinclair launched into a dire account of the vote-fraud case. He predicted that disenfranchised Democrats would attempt to vote on Election Day, so "there may be civil war in California." And he urged his followers to resist intimidation in the workplace. "If your boss threatens to fire you if you vote for Sinclair," he instructed, "bring me your boss's name, and after I am elected I will send that man to San Quentin to take Tom Mooney's place."

OCTOBER 24

WEDNESDAY

"This is the most fascinating thing anybody has ever seen," Franklin Roosevelt said, gesturing to a cellophane-covered pad on the desk in front of him. Reporters were still stepping into his White House office for the morning press conference. "I take this pad," he explained, "and I write, 'I owe you—let us suppose it is Fred Storm—one thousand dollars,' and I sign it, 'FDR.' " The President scribbled as he spoke. "Now, Fred thinks this is perfectly grand, and all I do is say, 'You want it?' " FDR handed over the pad, at the same time lifting off the cellophane, erasing the promissory note.

Everyone laughed. "Isn't it perfectly amazing?" the President said. "There is nothing incriminating." A last batch of reporters entered the room. "I am showing the crowd a gadget by which you can write something that you do not want anybody to see and then you lift up the leaf and the writing is gone," Roosevelt explained to the late arrivals. "It is very useful for politicians."

Perhaps FDR's commentary suggested the first question. A reporter wondered whether the President had received a telegram from Upton Sinclair.

"Have I had one?" FDR asked his assistant, Marvin McIntyre, who revealed that one indeed had arrived. "I haven't seen it yet," the President said.

According to one reporter, Sinclair still claimed that the President had promised to make a policy statement that would help his cause.

"What?" Roosevelt replied. "I do not know what that is. You have me. That is a little too vague. Did it refer to the Central Valley or something like that?" No one could supply an answer.

"No comment at all on the California gubernatorial test?" another newsman asked.

"No."

Someone else wanted the President to comment on a statement by Culbert Olson, who had just left town, embarrassed by his failure to see FDR. Before departing, Olson had suggested that it might be necessary for the federal government to intervene in California to prevent disorders at the polls on November 6. Had Sinclair asked the Justice Department to intervene?

"No," FDR responded. "Of course, as you know, in any national election there come in pleas from half a dozen or a dozen states and I don't know—I do not think the Federal Government has ever intervened in state elections." But purging registered voters just because they were forced to move or had lost their homes was "un-American," the President advised.

No one asked Roosevelt about Jim Farley's letter endorsing Upton Sinclair. Newspapers in the East hadn't mentioned the letter yet, awaiting confirmation from Farley, who was out of town. But a reporter did pose one final, point-blank question about the California campaign.

"Did you promise Sinclair," he asked, "you would make a statement at any time?"

"No," the President replied.

Gertrude Stein returned to America today after an absence of more than thirty years. A mob of reporters met Stein, who was accompanied by Alice B. Toklas, when the French liner S.S. *Champlain* docked in New York. The two women were now famous in America, due to Stein's recent *Autobiography of Alice B. Toklas.* Stein had enjoyed the ocean voyage, this being the first time she had traveled as a celebrity, but she found the New York skyline less spectacular than she had imagined. The writer would settle at the Algonquin Hotel for a spell before undertaking a lecture tour of the United States that would eventually return

Stein, now sixty years of age, to her onetime home, Oakland, California.

The dozen journalists who met the visitors in the shipboard lounge found them dressed for winter, Stein in a bulky gray tweed coat and Toklas in a dark fur. Reporters were surprised to find Stein, a celebrated enigma, so witty and accessible. She spoke in a language most could understand as she described her girlhood in Pennsylvania as a "born and raised Republican."

"Why don't you write as clearly as you talk?" one wag wondered.

"Why don't you read the way I write?" Stein replied, chuckling. "After all it's all in learning how to read it." The reporter sighed. "It's a matter of perception," she continued. "Youngsters with the least education get it quicker than those not set in their ways. I have not invented any device, any style, but write in the style that is me. I describe what I feel and think. I am," Stein explained, "essentially a realist."

Stein was looking forward to her first meal in New York. A friend, on returning to France from the United States, had piqued her curiosity by describing American food as even stranger than the American people and their homes. On the way to the Algonquin, she spotted the news ticker over Times Square announcing her arrival. To watch her name in lights, dancing around a building into oblivion, was a profoundly upsetting experience, symbolizing as it did the fleeting nature of fame.

The sensational high-society custody fight over ten-year-old Gloria Vanderbilt reached a climax this afternoon in New York in the chambers of John F. Carew, a supreme court judge. After four weeks of testimony, Carew wanted to know from Gloria herself whether she wished to remain with her aunt, Mrs. Harry Payne Whitney, or return to her mother, Gloria Morgan Vanderbilt. The mother had left the "poor little rich girl" with the aunt for two years but now wanted her back, and was also seeking to take charge of Gloria's $2.8-million trust fund.

The trial had produced titillating headlines but was widely condemned as insultingly trivial when thousands of less fortunate New Yorkers were living on the street. The leftish U.S. senator from Idaho, William Borah, used the trial as an opportunity to call for dismantling the country's family fortunes. "I do not think vast aggregations of wealth are healthy," he charged. "It breeds idiots, criminals and morons, with few exceptions." Borah compared the Vanderbilt scandal to the fall of Rome. "They do not know how many millions the child has," he pointed out, "but one can only question how many other children there are, equally worthy, who have not a place where they can quietly lay their heads. With such conditions a country cannot long endure."

Mrs. Vanderbilt, a fabled beauty, had taken it on the chin throughout the hearings as one witness after another testified to alleged affairs, excessive drinking, and constant disregard for her daughter during the first eight years of little Gloria's life. Mrs. Vanderbilt's own mother asserted that her daughter was unfit to care for the child. Today the dark-haired, moon-faced little girl spoke for herself. Gloria told the judge that she wished to stay with her aunt. When she was with her mother, Gloria said, she had no one to play with but her nurse; at her new home in Old Westbury, Long Island, she romped with cousins her own age and rode a pony. Mrs. Vanderbilt would take the stand on her own behalf tomorrow, but her quest for custody now appeared hopeless.

———

"Here we are again, ladies and gentleman," boomed the voice from the screen, "the Inquiring Cameraman, and we're going to give ourselves a little pat on the back." The second edition of MGM's *California Election News* had invaded the theaters. "Our first issue seems to have aroused all California," the narrator boasted. This was no lie. Some observers felt that audience response was so favorable it doomed Sinclair's chances completely.

"We've had lots of comments and suggestions and we found out that some of the politicians don't like our idea at all," the announcer explained. "They seem to want you to hear only what they have to say, but we still think you're interested in how the man in the street is actually going to vote. We let him say what he wants, we encourage him to talk freely and we try to be as non-partisan as possible. Now for the votes. . . ."

The format and general look of the film closely followed its predecessor, but this time it tossed subtlety to the wind. This became apparent about midway through when a dark-haired fellow in his forties wearing an open-collared shirt appeared. "I'm going to vote for Upton St. Clair," he intoned. "Upton St. Clair is the author of the Russian government. And it worked out very well there and I think it should do so here. Thank you."

An elderly gent in a bow tie, a youngster by his side, pointedly declared, "Sinclair is too radical. I feel that Mr. Merriam is the only man in the field today who can defeat Sinclair." Then a balding man, tie askew, standing on a street corner, shifty-eyed and speaking with a heavy Eastern European accent testified, "I have always been a socialist and I believe Sinclair will do best for working people."

The next scene seemed staged on the studio lot. An auto mechanic, wearing a bow tie and a work shirt, crawled out from beneath a car to address the camera. He wiped off his hands, but his immaculate clothes and face looked like dirt had never touched them. "First of all," he said, apparently struggling to remember his lines, "I am an American . . . and I believe Mr. Merriam will support all the principles America has stood for. . . . I have a job now and want to keep it. . . . I get paid in money and no scrip."

The film short drew to a close with an informal, open-air debate between purported Haight and Sinclair partisans. The Haight man, identified as a Dr. Griffith, was a dignified gent; his EPIC rival was bizarre looking, with a mustache, long sideburns, and gold teeth. The Sinclairite spoke first.

"The Democratic party," he said, "is staying with Sinclair."

"You're wrong," the Haight man responded. "The Democratic party is not with him, and it's not raising funds for him—you know that."

"Sinclair has interviewed the President of the United States and got a great reception."

"Sinclair only wanted to put him on the spot."

"Senator McAdoo is also for Sinclair."

"Senator McAdoo has billboarded the whole town and said that the EPIC plan is a failure. You can see for yourself!"

And that was it. While perhaps not as deft as the first edition, the latest *California Election News* just as effectively made Sinclair, his cause, and his supporters appear disreputable. An almost palpable stink drifted from the screen whenever a Sinclairite appeared. Supporters of the other candidates represented a cross section of society, and their remarks raised one key anti-Sinclair argument after another, almost as if the interviews had been scripted in advance. (In at least a couple of cases—the auto mechanic's scene and the "debate" at the end—this appeared to be literally true.) There seemed to be a method in the madness of including a Haight supporter, the filmmakers apparently believing it was time to build him up to draw votes from Sinclair.

"And by the way," the Inquiring Cameraman advised in conclusion, "lots of you don't know that it doesn't matter how you registered, Republican or Democrat. You can cast your vote on November 6 for any man or any party you want to." That could mean only one thing: Frank Merriam was about to become a New Dealer.

King Vidor, perhaps discouraged by his own studio's attempt to keep *Our Daily Bread* from a larger audience, appealed today to a higher authority. He wrote a note to President Roosevelt's press secretary, Steve Early, fishing for a favorable blurb that might save his picture from obscurity. Calling himself a "great admirer" of the President, Vidor explained that he had heard that FDR had recently screened the movie at the White House, and he wondered about his response. "I have felt since I first planned to do this picture two years ago," he disclosed, "that the idea projected was in accord with the President's plan of subsistence homesteads. Naturally the picture was made primarily for entertainment purposes but even entertainment can carry an amount of propaganda and educational elements.

"I deeply feel the screen to be the greatest power of exploitation," Vidor observed.

The California press continued to hail Roosevelt's EPIC "rebuff," and so Upton Sinclair dashed off one more wire to the White House:

> EFFORTS OF REACTIONARIES TO DEVELOP APPEARANCE OF DISHARMONY BETWEEN YOUR ADMINISTRATION AND OUR CALIFORNIA CAMPAIGN MAKE IT NECESSARY FOR ME TO STATE TO YOU EXPLICITLY, FIRST, I AM STANDING LOYALLY ON DEMOCRATIC PARTY PLATFORM WITH NO RESERVATIONS WHATSOEVER; SECOND, I HAVE NOWHERE SUGGESTED THAT YOU WERE GOING TO ENDORSE MY CANDIDACY. . . .

Sinclair was on the road most of the day, en route to a major appearance in Chico, eighty miles north of Sacramento. Reverend Bob Shuler had advised Sinclair that his candidate, Ray Haight, wanted to see him, and Haight happened to be in the area. With FDR failing Sinclair and W. R. Hearst rejecting Haight, it seemed like an appropriate moment for the two men to get together to talk about how they might salvage their candidacies and, incidentally, the cause of progressivism. So Sinclair agreed to stop at Haight's hotel in Sacramento for a strictly hush-hush conference.

The two men greeted each other warmly. Haight had kept his promise of September 19, training most of his fire on Merriam. Now his campaign was falling apart. His financial backers had mysteriously ceased all further support. Haight could no longer afford radio time.

He might be running a poor third in the race, but Ray Haight had a plan. He told Sinclair that he had conducted a postcard poll and the returns indicated that if Haight quit the race, Merriam would beat Sinclair easily; but if Sinclair dropped out, Haight would win.

The figures were highly unreliable, of course, but Sinclair was just weary and discouraged enough to take them seriously. He acknowledged that someone should consider dropping out, and the two men had a good laugh when they agreed that Merriam should be the one to go. Upton talked about the blunderbuss attacks directed against him, the emotional hardships he had endured, the physical stresses and strains. Ray revealed that the GOP planned to distribute five million leaflets on election eve announcing falsely that Haight had endorsed Merriam. So Sinclair, he argued, really had no chance.

Perhaps to his own surprise, Upton Sinclair saw the logic of Haight's argument. Haight was probably right: California would never elect the monster portrayed in the press, in the circulars, and on the movie screen. Perhaps if the bogeyman went away and Haight endorsed his platform, the other EPIC candidates might win. For some reason, Sinclair did not press the counterargument: if Haight dropped out and endorsed *him,* this surely would invigorate the EPIC cause. Instead, he told Ray Haight that his proposal had merit, and that he would sleep on it.

Westbrook Pegler called Upton Sinclair's room at the Whitcomb Hotel only to discover that the candidate was out of town. He was looking for a few details to add to the column he was writing. "That was a swell bunch of fellows I met last night," Pegler told one of Sinclair's associates. Then he added, "I wish I was so situated that I could write what I really think about them!" The Sinclair aide took this to mean that Pegler wanted to write something favorable but was prevented from doing so by his boss. This was wishful thinking. First, Pegler could write anything he wanted. Second, he never wrote *anything* positive.

"Tonight Mr. Roosevelt is to speak to the bankers," Will Rogers observed in his column this morning. "That shows a mighty broad-minded spirit on his part, for there has been times that we all thought he never would speak to 'em again. I hope he treats 'em with mercy and don't shoot, for the poor devils are licked."

After deciding on a militant speech yesterday, FDR switched gears today—the fifth anniversary of the Panic of '29—and allowed Raymond Moley to refashion his club into an olive branch. Once again he would reach out to his critics in the business community. Arriving at the ABA Convention at Constitution Hall this evening, Roosevelt seemed to be in a jovial mood. He instructed the assembly that the time was ripe for forging a new alliance of business and banking, agriculture and industry, and labor and capital, to speed recovery. He reminded the audience of nearly four thousand that in March 1933 he had asked the people of the country to renew their confidence in the banks, and they took him at his word. Now he asked the bankers to renew their confidence in the people of the country. "I hope you will take me at my word," the President urged.

In return, he offered to cut back government regulation in direct proportion to self-regulation and to reduce spending on relief as business recovery proceeded. This was music to the bankers' ears, for it signaled that FDR believed that federal interference in their activities must one day end. Five times the bankers interrupted the address with applause. What reporters found most striking was a significant deviation from the printed text of the speech. One sentence read, "That is what we call a profit system." Delivered by FDR it came out "That is what we call—and accept as—a profit system."

It didn't take long for Upton Sinclair to find out how the End Poverty League might react if its creator suddenly withdrew from the race. Driving up to Chico after meeting with Ray Haight in Sacramento, he put the proposal to two of his traveling companions and they responded with shock, alarm, indignation. When he reached Chico, he mentioned it to several other EPICs, and they felt the same way. No matter what the polls and gamblers might say, the EPICs felt that victory was in their grasp; and if Sinclair dropped out now, they would take to their graves the awful memory of their messiah abandoning them just yards from the promised land. Sinclair entertained the prospect of defeat, but now he knew that this eventuality never crossed the minds of most of his supporters.

A huge crowd greeted the candidate in tiny Chico. A thousand people, most of them farmers of the Sacramento Valley, paid twenty-five cents each to crowd into a local movie theater, and another two thousand stood outside and listened to Sinclair's speech over the loudspeakers. Among other things, Sinclair charged that Frank Merriam "has no idea how to deal with this depression, except by shooting people, like in the San Francisco strike." He also informed the audience that he had just been handed a copy of an incriminating letter written by an attorney in Los Angeles to a friend in New York. He only hinted at its contents but promised it would do EPIC some good.

OCTOBER 25

THURSDAY

"Your correspondent has just reeled away from an interview with Upton Sinclair and some members of his Brainstorm Trust," Westbrook Pegler reported this morning in hundreds of newspapers across the country. The column was short on substance but rich in Peglerisms. EPIC was "socialistic what-not." Sinclair was the "Mahatma." A gentleman who had suffered three business reversals during the Depression was "the triple-crash man." This fellow qualified as an economic adviser to Sinclair by virtue of failures in "manufacturing, finance and art."

Sinclair, the columnist complained, was "elusive as smoke." His pronouncements "drifted on like a faint odor in a light breeze. Now you smelled the merest whiff of a definite answer in his conversation. The next instant it was gone, and the discourse was only words." Pegler referred to Hjalmar Rutzebeck as "Mr. Utzebeck," and described him waving his arms in circles, explaining the EPIC plan "in terms of great wheels spinning in space and windmills, bolts and nuts.

"Nuts," Pegler observed, "seems an appropriate note on which to conclude today's installment."

A reporter in Washington asked Harry Hopkins, the federal relief administrator, whether transients were indeed flocking to California. "No, just the opposite," he replied. "We have had about fifteen percent increase in transients the last four or five months and the increase in others states runs up to seventy percent. The average for the country is far greater than California." Then he added, "I think that is a political story."

Hopkins's comment didn't faze the anti-Sinclair press in California; they simply ignored it. Indeed, after a few days' respite, press coverage of the "bums' rush" to California resumed with a new focus. Evidence of a mass invasion had seemed spotty, even contradictory. Testimony of state officials and border guards might have been coerced, but pictures wouldn't lie.

The unselling of Upton Sinclair increasingly relied on visual images. Graphics were not exactly new to politics. Sixty years had passed since Boss Tweed recognized the power of Thomas Nast's political cartoons in these words: "My constituents can't read, but they can all see pictures." But the 1934 anti-Sinclair crusade in California was perhaps the first election drive that intended to deliver its knockout punch with pictures rather than words. Editorial attacks, circulars, and radio shows all did their part, but when Californians talked about the campaign, they were more likely to mention a billboard, a cartoon, or a movie short they had seen. There were plenty of practical reasons for Californians to turn against Sinclair, but the visual propaganda appealed to the emotions and proved even more persuasive than brilliantly executed appeals to reason. Words on a page suggesting that Upton Sinclair was an atheist or a Red simply did not pack the emotional wallop of watching a middle-class family fleeing from an alien horde.

Realizing this, newspapers around the state had turned to photographs to portray an invasion of indigents that statistics could only suggest. The San Francisco *News* started a daily "California, Here We Come" series, spotlighting a different mode of transportation every day, from buggies to boxcars. The *Los Angeles Times* published two huge photos. A front-page shot of a dilapidated truck laden with household effects captured the "1934 version of the covered wagon" belonging to "the army of unemployed who have hastily packed their belongings and are rushing westward to be supported by taxpayers of California—if Sinclair wins." The second photo depicted a group of bums atop a moving railroad freight car (how the photographer got up there was anyone's guess). These men might be traveling light, but "they expect all the necessities of a comfortable existence to be provided for them in California—if their hero, Sinclair, is elected." The editors presented no evidence that any of the transients had even heard of Upton Sinclair, but these photos, in an emotional sense, hit home.

This morning the *Los Angeles Examiner* published a huge four-column photograph on page 4 under the headline ANOTHER EPIC IN CALIFORNIA ANNALS. It showed eleven men and two women climbing out of a Union Pacific boxcar. But there was something wrong with this picture. It had the dreamy focus of the cinema, not the gritty complexion of a news photo. And the caption took the unusual step of attributing the picture to an outside photographer—a member of the California Crusaders.

Sharp-eyed movie fans had little trouble identifying the real source of the photograph. "Did you see my picture in the Hearst paper this morning?" a young actor asked Albert Hackett at MGM. Sinclair supporters in the Warner Brothers' publicity department called EPIC headquarters with this tip: the *Examiner*'s photo, and at least one of the *L.A. Times*'s shots, came from the Hollywood feature *Wild Boys of the Road.*

The young screenwriter John Huston had written a screenplay for *Wild Boys of the Road* back in 1932, when thousands of youths were riding the rails. Huston traveled around California talking to kids, brakemen, and hoboes. His script ended with a youth shot to death while attempting to rob a pawnshop, and his accomplice trying to hold off onlookers with a gun. "You killed him!" the boy shouted at the crowd. Then the camera, according to Huston's instructions, was to swing around so that the gun was aimed directly at the movie audience. "You killed him!" the kid would scream again.

When Roosevelt took office, many of the wayward youths ended up in Civil Conservation Corps camps, and Huston's film treatment was abandoned. But another version appeared, created by William A. Wellman (who was now directing *The President Vanishes*), with child star Frankie Darro and a new, treacly ending. If one looked closely at the "bums' rush" news photo in the *Examiner,* one could spot little Frankie among the transients. Sources at the movie studio confirmed that it had recently sent out a batch of stills from *Wild Boys* to an unidentified office in Los Angeles.

The movie industry came under attack today when Upton Sinclair's campaign manager, Richard Otto, charged that the Inquiring Cameraman shorts contained faked or slanted footage. He characterized the films as Merriam propaganda and identified Will Hays's associate, Charles C. Pettijohn, as the engineer of a political conspiracy. "These trailers," Otto said, "are made up in the form of newsreels and depict a newsreel cameraman walking through the streets of Los Angeles, getting firsthand slants on the governorship contest from the man in the street." To produce a "decided trend" toward Merriam, the Inquiring Cameraman selected certain subjects and colored or created copy "to suit himself."

The most surprising aspect of Otto's statement was the name of the editorial genius who had allegedly created the trailers: not the reactionary Louis B. Mayer, the ruthless Harry Cohn, or the reckless Joseph Schenck, but the refined Irving Thalberg.

Upton Sinclair joined in the protest. He informed James A. Farley by telegram that Charlie Pettijohn had taken over three suites at the Roosevelt Hotel and, claiming to speak for Farley and the White House, was raising funds for the Merriam campaign. Sinclair also wired Will Hays, charging that Pettijohn was doing nothing but political work and "exploiting the candidacy of Governor Merriam," thereby violating the Hays Office code of impartiality in political campaigns.

The second issue of the satiric *EBIC Snooze* tabloid hit the streets today with a banner headline reading, MERRIAM SHOT. On closer examination, the story merely revealed that Frank Merriam used to shoot craps back in Iowa using loaded dice. Another headline reported: TOM MOONEY ESCAPES. According to this account, Mooney was happy to remain in jail, as it enabled him to avoid making campaign speeches and trudging to the polls. "Politics," Mooney said, "is a sentence much longer than mine."

The *EBIC Snooze* also reported the first election returns based on absentee ballots, with "forty thousand residents of the basement of Jake's cigar store" voting for Merriam. Another story imagined Sinclair trying to look more like a statesman by wearing one of Senator McAdoo's high, starched collars. "The governorship isn't worth it, Upton," the editors advised.

Campaign parodies continued to proliferate. Much of the material was distributed on street corners; some arrived in the mail. A takeoff on Sinclair's *The Wet Parade,* called *The Cat Parade,* portrayed "feline malcontents" flocking to California singing this song:

The Angoras are getting all the cream
There ain't no justice for cat or man
Let's get out and work for the EPIC plan.

We've reached the land of cream and mice
In fact it's the tom cat's Paradise!
So life flowed along like a beautiful dream
Till the larder was emptied of mice and cream.

A realtor in Los Angeles prepared a beautifully designed and illustrated leaflet entitled "If I'm Governor" by "Utopian Despair." He was so proud of it he sent a copy to Franklin Roosevelt. The EPIC candidate in this story promised that if elected he would become "a Saint Clair instead of a Sin Clair." His plan, which was approved by "Senator Mack A. Doo About Nothing," would permit the state "to covet thy neighbor's business, his wife, his cow and his ass and it may take all of them from him."

Thunder Over California, a widely distributed eight-page tabloid, imagined an even scarier scenario: John Hopewell flees the state after Sinclair's victory, and returns thirty years later to discover a totalitarian dictatorship. The author, Robert C. Emery, wrote the fable earlier in 1934 to scare the voters of Minnesota into defeating their radical governor Floyd Olson. The Merriamites simply changed the title, names, and locations, and dressed it up with a crude front-page drawing of a bearded Russian holding a red flag over a blood-spattered map of California.

Satire from EPIC's side also appeared on the streets. Someone produced a little booklet entitled "What Governor Merriam Proposes to Do for the People of California" and sold it on the streets for a penny. Inside were four pages of blank paper. Another Sinclairite distributed a takeoff on the Twenty-third Psalm, rechristened "The 1934 Psalm":

Merriam is my shepherd and I am in want.
He maketh me lie down on park benches.
He leadeth me beside still factories.
He destroyeth my soul. . . .
Yea, tho' I walk through the shadow of
  depression
I anticipate no recovery for he is with me. . . .
Surely unemployment and poverty shall follow me

all the days of my life
And I shall dwell in a mortgaged house forever.

An EPIC activist in Hollywood produced a twelve-page booklet called *Letters to Louie from Frank,* which claimed to contain actual correspondence between Louis B. Mayer and Frank Merriam. In one letter, a worried governor asks his favorite mogul to "go easy on this forced donation stuff. It's alright to make your employees wear pins and put stickers on their autos but takin' a day's pay outta their envelopes might be goin' a little too far." In another note, Merriam asks Mayer for *more* money. Those greedy Democrats for Merriam, he complains, were getting all the gravy—Ham Cotton taking home three thousand dollars a week all by himself. And buying up *Literary Digest* ballots was incredibly costly. "Ordinarily a seven and a half million dollar slush fund ought to be enough to put over any man's campaign," Merriam observes, "but you know Louie, this ain't no ordinary campaign."

Sinclair and Haight had agreed to keep their tête-à-tête in Sacramento a secret, but rumors were rife, and the press scurried for information about this sensational development. Acting on a tip, the Los Angeles *Herald-Express* sent a stringer to a hotel in San Francisco where Sinclair and Haight were supposedly meeting, to no avail. Using one of the oldest tricks in the book, a reporter called Ray Haight and informed him, falsely, that Sinclair had already confirmed the rumors. Haight then described the meeting, asserting that Sinclair listened to his plea for withdrawal with great sympathy. "Naturally his withdrawal and his obligations toward the progressive movement," Haight said, "are a matter of his own conscience."

Hearing that their leader might quit the race, EPIC insiders were apoplectic. This scuttled Sinclair's plan to think the matter through, confer with aides, and possibly negotiate with Haight. So when reporters reached Sinclair in Berkeley where he was about to speak, and informed him what Haight had said, he felt he had no choice but to debunk the report as firmly as possible. "I listened courteously to the arguments and opinions of the gentleman, for whom I have high esteem," Sinclair remarked. "I have consulted with our EPIC leaders who are best in a position to know, and they tell me I shall beat Governor Merriam by two to one. I am, therefore, respectfully declining Mr. Haight's friendly suggestion." Sinclair called the rumors that he was considering quitting "a Merriam propaganda plant."

Culbert Olson, back in California, called the withdrawal idea "complete bunk. . . . Sinclair has a certainty of election. He is in the governorship already. Why should he withdraw?"

Contacted in Los Angeles, Haight responded, "I was never more in the race than I am now." In fact, on a day that should have marked the low point in his campaign—the Hearst papers published W.R.'s endorsement of Merriam this morning—Ray Haight seemed refreshed and full of pep. He paid a visit to EPIC headquarters in Los Angeles and disclosed some dirty campaign tricks Frank Merriam might still have up his sleeve. Richard Otto and *EPIC News* editor Rube Borough kidded Haight about Sinclair's withdrawal. That might have ended the intrigue except for one detail: Haight had only begun to fight for Sinclair's vote, and he had a couple of important friends in the East who might assist him.

When her father threatened to disinherit her, Ellen Wilson McAdoo agreed to postpone her marriage to the actor Rafael de Onate. Senator McAdoo, who had commissioned a background check through the U.S. attorney general, alleged through a spokesman that while the actor claimed pure Spanish blood, he was, in fact, part Malay and therefore forbidden by law to marry a Caucasian in California.

"I still love Ellen," de Onate declared, "and believe she still loves me." This afternoon she proved it. The couple suddenly disappeared, elopement their apparent aim.

Attorneys for United for California and the Republican party filed a second lawsuit today alleging vote fraud on a massive scale. The suit identified more than thirty-three thousand unlawfully registered voters, bringing the total number named to almost sixty thousand. So far, however, every voter who had challenged the action in court succeeded in having his or her name restored to the rolls. A group of Republican and Democratic leaders who supported the vote purge explained that "a relatively small number of bona fide voters were inadvertently included" on the list and that the inconvenience these people faced "is far outweighed by the grave menace of one of the greatest election frauds in the history of the nation."

Democrats were not taking kindly to the continuing vote probe. Four GOP precinct workers told police they were threatened by wrench-wielding mechanics at an Ocean Park garage. At a huge Utopian Society rally at Olympic Auditorium in Los Angeles, the crowd was urged to recruit fifty thousand volunteers to protect members' voting rights on Election Day. "We're not telling you how to vote," advised one Utopian director, "but we're telling you to vote—and don't be scared out of it!" Election officials in Sacramento, meanwhile, warned that if the losing candidate in a close Merriam-Sinclair contest demanded a recount, it could cause riots and National Guard reprisals. For the Sinclairites, there was at least one positive development: EPIC attorneys persuaded the state supreme court to hear their appeal.

The architect of the vote-purge case, Albert Parker, received a message today from Whitney Debevoise declaring that he was "delighted" his suggestions concerning the secret indictments had proved useful. "I hope Sinclair will be demolished," Debevoise wrote. "He is a very dangerous type of loose thinker and loose talker." Debevoise passed along one additional piece of advice from George Medalie in New York: publicize the fact that deputy sheriffs and other police officers will be at the polls on Election Day armed with bench warrants to arrest "false registrants" named in the secret indictments.

Somehow Parker refrained from burning this message immediately. The text of his purloined October 20 letter to Debevoise, chortling over the scheme to "terrify many people from coming near the polls," had appeared verbatim this morning in the Los Angeles *Daily News.*

After relying for months on West Coast stringers, *The New York Times* finally sent a reporter to cover the California campaign. It wasn't just any newsman but one of the best, Turner Catledge.

As editor of the Tunica *Times* back in his native Mississippi in 1922, Catledge published a series of articles exposing the local Ku Klux Klan, and lost his job when the KKK burned the newspaper building to the ground. Five years later, while working for a Memphis paper, he escorted Herbert Hoover, then secretary of commerce, on a tour of the flood-ravaged Mississippi Valley. Hoover was so impressed that he recommended Catledge to Adolph Ochs, publisher of *The New York Times.* When Hoover became president, he touted Catledge again, and Ochs finally hired him in 1929. Serving under bureau chief Arthur Krock, Catledge became one of the newspaper's top men in Washington. He enjoyed FDR's press conferences but considered the President a consummate manipulator, a man who misled, deceived, even lied to achieve his ends.

Arriving in Los Angeles, Catledge checked into his hotel and, following the normal practice, bought a copy of a local paper to find out where the candidates were appearing over the next few days. The *Los Angeles Times* had plenty of news about Frank Merriam, but Catledge couldn't find a single word about Sinclair—beyond the fact that he was rabidly anti-Lutheran. Catledge scanned the paper, hoping to at least discover where Sinclair was speaking, but found no listing.

At dinner, Catledge asked *L.A. Times* political editor Kyle Palmer whether *he* knew where Sinclair was.

"Turner, forget it," Palmer replied. "We don't go in for that kind of crap that you have back in New York—of being obliged to print both sides. We're going to beat this son of a bitch Sinclair any way we can," the curly-haired, bow-tied reporter explained. "We're going to kill him."

"You are for Sinclair, aren't you?" Robert G. Sproul had inquired over the telephone, and Dean McHenry confirmed it. Sproul had known McHenry since 1931, when Dean was president of the student body at UCLA. Now McHenry was going for his doctorate at Berkeley. Sproul disagreed with his politics but felt McHenry could be trusted to represent EPIC in a moderate, respectable fashion; he was no rabble-rouser. And so Sproul had asked him to appear at the big debate in Wheeler auditorium this evening.

Liberal students at Berkeley had demanded that Sinclair be allowed to speak on campus. Sproul refused, citing the university's policy of prohibiting political speakers from appearing unless they debated an opponent. Since Merriam was not fool enough to square off against Sinclair, Sproul proposed that students speak for the candidates, and picked McHenry to stand in for Sinclair. That would allow the Sinclairites to blow off some steam, while denying a forum for their candidate.

Since returning to Berkeley from his summer job—promoting self-help cooperatives with his friend Clark Kerr—McHenry had tried to organize a brain trust for Upton Sinclair in the Bay area. He feared that Sinclair, inexperienced in state affairs and an easy mark for flatterers, might undermine his EPIC plan by making foolish appointments. So

McHenry, working with EPIC's Research Associates office in L.A., asked several brilliant and progressive-minded professors in northern California, such as Paul Taylor, to act as Sinclair advisors (or serve as appointees once he was elected). The response so far had been mixed, and McHenry learned that a young agricultural economist he hoped to enlist as an EPIC brain-truster, John Kenneth Galbraith, had just left Berkeley to take a teaching position at Harvard.

Several thousand students turned out for tonight's debate. McHenry produced the kind of thoughtful analysis Sproul expected, and the students responded politely, but none of the speakers lit any fires. It was a genteel affair. Robert Sproul, a consummate politician, had pretty well defused Sinclairism on campus: one survey showed that students backed Merriam by a seven-to-one margin. Even Dean McHenry, fearful that Sinclair might appoint an all-quack cabinet, was wondering if he still wanted Uppie to win.

OCTOBER 26

FRIDAY

The press outside California finally recognized the existence of a letter written by James A. Farley enthusiastically endorsing Upton Sinclair for governor. *The New York Times* put the revelation on its front page and printed the entire text of the document. The story broke after Sinclair headquarters produced a photostat of the letter (while keeping the original in a locked safe). Political observers declared that its language and signature indeed appeared to be Farley's. An Associated Press dispatch out of San Francisco declared that the Farley endorsement "added fire" to a campaign "already buzzing with rumors of withdrawals and plots."

Returning to the nation's capital last night after a brief vacation, Jim Farley declined comment. This morning, however, when press coverage indicated that the letter not only compromised the President but embarrassed the Democratic national chairman, Farley decided to extinguish the fire. He wasn't sure how, so he summoned Jefty O'Connor, his California expert, to his office for advice.

O'Connor was excited about something else: the sweet prospect of Upton Sinclair dropping out of the race in favor of Jefty's candidate, Ray Haight. From Farley's office, Jefty called one of Haight's leading supporters, A. P. Giannini, who happened to be in Washington for the American Bankers Association convention. Giannini had tried to get O'Connor to run for governor earlier in the year and switched to Haight only after Jefty declined. O'Connor asked Giannini to give Haight a call.

When the banker reached the candidate in Los Angeles, Haight revealed that Sinclair was ready to withdraw in his favor. Sinclair planned to discuss the matter tomorrow with his two chief financial backers, whom Haight identified as William Fox, the movie magnate, and Stanley Anderson, owner of the Beverly Hills Hotel. With Sinclair out of the race, Hiram Johnson and W. R. Hearst might endorse him, Haight said; if the White House backed him, he would "cooperate" with the Democrats on patronage.

Giannini relayed this message to O'Connor. Then he added considerable weight to the proposition by volunteering to mobilize behind Haight his two hundred thousand stockholders in California, plus employees at hundreds of Bank of America offices, if the White House so ordered. O'Connor passed this information along to Jim Farley and offered to fly to California immediately to strike the deal.

That would be up to the President to decide, of course. Farley suggested that O'Connor visit the White House and discuss the matter with Marvin McIntyre. O'Connor did that, and when he returned to his apartment at the Shoreham Hotel he found a telegram from A. P. Giannini awaiting him. Giannini reported that rumors of Sinclair's withdrawal were now "prevalent" in San Francisco and that "some important developments will take place today." Haight had canceled all speaking engagements in favor of holding a "special conference."

While Jefty O'Connor carried the ball for Ray Haight, Jim Farley turned to an even more pressing concern, salvaging his own reputation. Even though it might put him in conflict with his potential boss, William Fox, Farley decided to repudiate his endorsement of Upton Sinclair, at the same time shifting responsibility for the now-famous letter to one of his aides. Rather than release an official statement to the Washington press, he took a roundabout route, instructing one of his aides to leak the denial to Santa Barbara publisher Thomas M. Storke: he would know what to do with it.

This, then, was Farley's explanation: The letter was nothing more than a big "mistake." Early in October thousands of form letters endorsing various candidates had been prepared at Democratic headquarters in Washington. Each carried Farley's signature, stamped in trademark green ink. The DNC sent out millions of the letters but kept the ones pertaining to Sinclair on hold, waiting for the President to signal his intentions. When the White House, for whatever reason, decided to cut Sinclair loose, Farley ordered the letters relating to the California race destroyed, but some survived. One day, poor Eugene Troskey of Whittier called the DNC seeking Farley's official view on the race. The chairman was absent, and Big Jim's aides were not aware of the latest position on Sinclair. Discovering a pro-Sinclair letter signed in green ink, one of Farley's assistants sent a copy to Mr. Troskey, and the rest was history. That was Farley's story, anyway.

"Mr. Farley is greatly embarrassed by a mistake made by a subordinate," his spokesman told Tom Storke this afternoon. "He has not endorsed Upton Sinclair and he does not intend to do so."

"Would that indicate," Storke wondered, "that Mr. Farley at some time did consider endorsing Mr. Sinclair?"

"Decidedly not," the aide replied. "Mr. Farley never intended to endorse Upton Sinclair and will not do so." He confessed that Farley was "embarrassed" and "chagrined" by the incident but remained confident that no matter how much damage the letter may have caused, it would not affect the election, since Upton Sinclair no longer had much hope of success.

According to Ray Haight, Upton Sinclair was again considering quitting the race. Today, at the moment of decision, several events conspired to shove Sinclair toward the exit. Jim Farley debunked his endorsement letter. The *Literary Digest* disseminated discouraging poll results. And George Creel released a copy of the Dear John letter to Sinclair he had recently left at the White House.

The *Literary Digest* reported Frank Merriam with a two-and-a-half-to-one lead over Sinclair, based on 67,208 ballots. Sinclair and Haight drew only 37 percent of the vote between them. The results seemed highly suspect. The *Digest* had Merriam beating Sinclair two-to-one even in Los Angeles, which was patently absurd, and seven-to-one in Hollywood. Not even Merriam believed he would draw anywhere near 60 percent of the statewide vote on November 6. Still, the survey results might start the Merriam bandwagon rolling, meaning that its projection of a landslide, however dubious, would be self-fulfilling.

George Creel contributed to the downward trend by releasing his private message to Sinclair through the New York *World-Telegram*. Visiting his brother in Baltimore, Creel announced that he would not stump for Frank Merriam either. "My choice lies between epilepsy and catalepsy," Creel explained. "Merriam stands for everything I have fought against for thirty years. He is about as modern as the dinosaur age and his owners are medieval. Under the circumstances I am a man without a vote."

Sinclair was traveling between San Francisco and Los Angeles and could not be reached for comment. Asked to address Creel's "medieval owners" charge, Merriam responded: "I heard a man speak about a 'congenital liar' the other day. I don't know what that is. 'Medieval owners' means no more to me."

W. C. Fields might replace Charles Laughton, who was ill, in *David Copperfield.* Fred Astaire, the hoofer, signed with RKO to make six movies over the next two years. Ernst Lubitsch planned to direct Marlene Dietrich as his next assignment at Paramount. It was a star-studded but typical *Hollywood Reporter* front page, save for eight inches of type on the left side, where Billy Wilkerson, in his "Tradeviews" column, blew the lid off Hollywood's crusade against Upton Sinclair. "When the picture business gets aroused, it becomes AROUSED," Wilkerson observed, in an unusually excited manner, "and, boy, how they go to it!

"The campaign against Upton Sinclair has been and is DYNAMITE. It is the most effective piece of political humdingery that has ever been effected, and this is said in full recognition of the antics of that master-machine that used to be Tammany. Politicians in every part of this land (and they are all vitally interested in the California election) are standing by in amazement as a result of the bombast that has been set off under the rocking chair of Mr. Sinclair. . . .

"Never before in the history of the picture business has the screen been used in direct support of a candidate. Maybe an isolated exhibitor here and there has run a slide or two, favoring a friend, but never has there been a concerted action on the part of all theatres in a community to defeat a nominee.

"And this activity may reach much farther than the ultimate defeat of Mr. Sinclair. It will undoubtedly give the bigwigs in Washington and politicians all over the country an idea of the real POWER that is in the hands of the picture industry."

Wilkerson could have let it go at that, but eager to give credit where credit was due, he proceeded to tip his hat to some illustrious figures in the fight against Sinclair who probably preferred to remain anonymous. "Before Louis Mayer, Irving Thalberg, Charlie Pettijohn (a good old Democrat under ordinary conditions) and Carey Wilson stepped into this political battle here," Wilkerson observed, "the whole Republican Party seemed to have been sunk by the insane promises of Mr. Sinclair. With that group in the war, and it has been a WAR, things took a different turn. Gov. Merriam's party here in the South had a HEAD, something that was missing before. It received the finances it so direly needed AND the whole picture business got behind the shove.

"Sinclair is not defeated yet," Wilkerson allowed, "but indications point to it, and California should stand up and sing hosannas for their greatest STATE industry, MOTION PICTURES. . . ."

Dick Martin, the oldest living peace officer in California, took his son, Gil, into custody around noon today. Summoned to the Clover Valley Ranch, the constable found his son sitting on the running board of an automobile holding a .30-.30 rifle. A few feet away an older man, apparently dead, lay sprawled on his stomach in the dirt. The victim, the constable learned, was Robert Leighton, a sixty-four-year-old ranch hand. Gil Martin was superintendent at the ranch, located two miles from Loyalton, a lumber town in Sierra County barely fifteen miles from the Nevada border. The dead man's body lay on a path between Martin's farmhouse and the bunkhouse where Leighton lived.

Workers and townspeople arrived at the scene when news of the shooting spread. The constable covered Leighton's body with a white sheet; a shotgun stuck out from beneath the shroud. Gil Martin, thirty-four years old and the father of six, explained that Leighton had plowed the fields all morning, then came to the farmhouse around noon to rekindle an argument over politics. Martin favored Merriam for governor and Leighton supported Sinclair. Both men had been drinking. Ranch hands had previously witnessed the two men arguing over the governor's race, but today the conflict escalated. According to Gil Martin, Leighton finally said, "Well, there is no other way to settle it, so we might as well shoot it out." Martin claimed it was "him or me."

If it was a duel, it was manifestly one-sided. When the sheriff arrived, he discovered that Leighton's shotgun contained no shells and had not been fired. An examination of Leighton's wounds—a small hole in the left side of his back and a fist-sized gap over his heart—indicated that Martin had shot him in the back.

———

Upton Sinclair claimed that the Standard Oil Company of California funded Frank Merriam to a fare-thee-well. In the rhetoric of EPIC, this was essentially a payoff to enable the company to continue to exploit California's rich oil reserves, principally at Huntington Beach, with remarkably little payment to the state.

Twenty-three years had passed since the day the U.S. Supreme Court ordered the breakup of John D. Rockefeller's Standard Oil. As an independent entity, Standard Oil of California embarked on a kind of black gold rush, tapping rich new oil fields at Montebello, Elk Hills, and Huntington Beach and dispatching exploration parties to Alaska, Mexico, and South America. But, like virtually every other major company, Standard Oil struggled through the Depression. Increasingly the company looked abroad and in 1932 discovered oil two thousand feet under the sands of the tiny island of Bahrain. Casting a covetous eye at nearby Saudi Arabia, the company struck a deal with Ibn Saud, purchasing the rights to 320,000 square miles of desert for the next sixty-six years in exchange for a $150,000 loan and future royalties if it actually struck oil. The results were so far disappointing, but the search went on.

Kenneth R. Kingsbury, president of Standard Oil of California since 1919, was proud of the fact that despite the company's economic downturn he had never failed to issue a dividend. Today, however, from his office in the Standard Oil Building in San Francisco, Kingsbury delivered something quite different to his thousands of stockholders: a California League Against Sinclairism pamphlet entitled *SINCLAIRISM MEANS The Destruction of All Business and Property in California.* In a cover letter, he asked the stockholders to read the circular and suggested that the election of Sinclair would imperil the "business of this company and the value of your stock." Kingsbury added:

> We urge you to give the matter of Mr. Sinclair's candidacy your earnest consideration, and believe that you will conclude, if you have not already done so, to oppose his election. Sinclairism must not only be beaten but the defeat should be overwhelming—a complete California repudiation of radicalism.

"We have never talked politics to our stockholders, and this is not a political issue," Kingsbury observed in conclusion. "It is a business issue that affects you and your company."

L. D. Hotchkiss, city editor of the *Los Angeles Times,* dropped by the local United Press office this afternoon. Walking past the desk of a UP editor, who was talking on the telephone, he noticed the latest issue of *Time* magazine opened to the Sinclair cover story. The UP editor happened to be speaking to someone at *Time* at that very moment. Hotchkiss bent over the copy of the magazine, drew a circle around its claim that W. R. Hearst had dubbed EPIC "Ipecac," and in the margin scribbled a vital correction he wanted the UP man to pass along: "Tell him Wrong Again. It's the *L.A. Times,* not Hearst, that calls it Ipecac."

According to the so-called gamboleers, the odds on Frank Merriam's election had jumped from ten-to-seven to two-to-one since W. R. Hearst endorsed him. The Hearst papers, never shy when it came to claiming credit, published a dozen statements from leading Republicans and Democrats hailing the Chief. Robert Clarke, chairman of United for California, called Hearst's letter to Ray Haight a "masterpiece . . . its influence will be tremendous." William C. Neblett, Senator McAdoo's law partner, described it as "a great document, the greatest this campaign has developed."

Hearst, at San Simeon for a spell, plunged into the details of the anti-Sinclair press campaign. He had a lot of catching up to do. Besides ordering or writing editorials, he devised page layouts and even supplied copy for cartoons. Today, for example, the Chief examined sketches for ten cartoons for his afternoon papers and approved four. Hearst's top aide, Joseph Willicombe, sent a note to George Young, editor of the *Los Angeles Examiner,* concerning one of the cartoons, which showed Sinclair firing a cannon at a church. Willicombe commented that Hearst felt that the cannonballs should be labeled with "quotations from Sinclair's attacks on different religions." Willicombe generously provided a leaflet filled with suitable quotes but asked Young to return the pamphlet to him "as it is the only one I have and Chief may want to refer to it himself."

Young wired back, suggesting that Hearst hire Jimmy Hatlo, creator of the popular "They'll Do It Every Time," to provide additional anti-Sinclair ammunition. But W.R. already had his hands full. He approved the layout for a full-page feature to appear in all of his papers (and any others in the state that wished to reproduce it). Entitled CALIFORNIA AND SINCLAIRISM, it assembled in one place two favorite cartoons, three Hearst editorials, and W.R.'s recent letter to Ray Haight. The Chief also OK'd a Ted Gale cartoon for tomorrow's *Examiner:* Stalin, Hitler, and Mussolini on horseback with Sinclair, riding a hobbyhorse, rushing to catch up. "Wait for me, Boys!" Sinclair shouts.

Returning home from the north this afternoon, Upton Sinclair discovered a telegram from Will Hays responding to his wire from the previous day. Hays explained that he would never presume to tell his chief aide, Charlie Pettijohn, what to do politically, especially since they belonged to different parties.

Sinclair also learned that EPIC headquarters in Los Angeles had received the scandalous six-page letter from George Creel repudiating his candidacy. Creel seemed to base his attack on the fact that Sinclair's *Immediate EPIC* countermanded many of the compromises the candidate made at the Democratic convention. That booklet, Sinclair informed Creel by letter, was written "before I met you, and before we cooperated on the Democratic platform. . . . I have loyally kept every agreement with you. You now publicly charge me with breaking faith. It is you who have broken faith with the Democratic party of California and with the New Deal, which we support. You have done all in your power to elect a reactionary Republican." Betraying anger for once, Sinclair closed with: "Good-by."

Two weeks had passed since Frank Merriam asked Asa Call when the Republicans would be allowed to say something about their own candidate for a change. Call had replied that Merriam's day would come, and now it appeared to be at hand. United for California circulated half a million pamphlets describing Merriam's "progressive" program. The incumbent finally increased his campaign appearances. Today he spoke to insurance agents in Sacramento and addressed both the Kiwanis Club and a Junior Republican convention in San Francisco. His state chairman, Earl Warren, joined him at the latter affair.

Following Warren's lead, Merriam not only appealed for Democratic votes; he declared himself an authentic born-again New Dealer. This overnight transformation amused even the governor's own supporters. "I am heartily in accord with the President's recovery policies," Merriam explained, "because he is definitely trying to maintain American institutions and our existing system of economic and social civilization. President Roosevelt is building for recovery on an American foundation. . . . I think that Providence has raised up the proper man to meet a situation, and that he is doing it magnificently." Merriam claimed that if elected, he would be "a governor for all the people," even if that meant taking from the EPIC plan anything "that will work."

The most outrageous remark of the day, however, came from the normally placid George Hatfield. Upton Sinclair had recently warned that his enemies might assassinate him, and the bad guys knew exactly where to hire gunmen willing to carry out the deed "for as little as two hundred dollars." This evening, Hatfield took exception to that statement. He asserted that the egotistical Sinclair had put much too high a price on his head. There were men in California, he revealed, who would charge even less than two hundred dollars for the pleasure of shooting Sinclair. Even so, Hatfield confessed, he personally "wouldn't give six bits for a dozen Sinclairs, alive or dead."

OCTOBER 27

SATURDAY

Huey Long took Tennessee by storm. Throngs cheered as five trainloads of Louisiana State University football fans pulled into Nashville's Union Station at 9:00 A.M. The Kingfish pulled down his hat, straightened his tie, and plunged into the adoring crowd. Five thousand Louisianans formed an army behind Huey and the school band as they strutted two miles to Memorial Square in the heart of the city. Some called it the biggest parade in the city's history. Onlookers occupied every foot of pavement along the route. Huey grabbed a comely brunette, placed her between himself and the mayor, and continued the march.

When he reached the square, Huey declared that, contrary to rumor, he did not intend to use this occasion to announce a run for president in 1936. "This reception," he said, "has given me a swell idea. I plan to take my army and go to Mexico first and then annex Mexico to Louisiana, and then annex the United States to Louisiana." After strolling to Vanderbilt Stadium, Senator Long climbed the speaker's platform set up on the five-yard line. Everyone expected a thumping speech, but Huey merely waved, thanked his hosts, and then ordered everyone to enjoy the game. As LSU rolled up the score, Huey played cheerleader, his natural position. Final score: Louisiana State 29, Vanderbilt 0.

ROOSEVELT SEEN HOSTILE TO SINCLAIR'S CANDIDACY, shouted a headline at the top of *The New York Times*'s front page. CREEL TURNS AGAINST HIM. And: FARLEY LETTER A "MISTAKE." The White House, after nearly two months of ambiguity and qualification, "definitely turned away from Upton Sinclair today," the *Times* declared, "with unmistakable indications that it does not care to have the former Socialist elected as Democratic Governor of California."

It was not a good day for James A. Farley either as the GOP gleefully attacked the slapstick explanation of his now-famous Sinclair Letter. The Republicans and the EPICs, in the end, had this much in common: they all believed Farley's endorsement was heartfelt and that someone had ordered him to disavow it.

"It now turns out, according to the cock-and-bull story manufactured at Democratic headquarters, that it was the work of a dumb stenographer," a GOP national official insisted. "Mr. Farley has no one but himself to blame if this is true." Citing two similar incidents in 1932, the official observed that Big Jim was "without doubt the world's leading expert on collecting dumb stenographers. Isn't it about time for the Roosevelt Administration and Mr. Farley to find another alibi and give the poor dumb stenographer a break? Anyway, maybe she wasn't so dumb. How was the dumb stenographer in Mr. Farley's office to know that the President was willing to take two hours telling Sinclair bed-time stories, but is not willing to have him elected Governor of California?"

Hamilton Fish, GOP congressman from New York, likened Farley to a hapless substitute on the New Deal football team. "The fact is," Fish observed, "that Captain Farley, like a former California football player, has run the wrong way to score a touchdown against his own side." *News-week,* meanwhile, reported that FDR had reprimanded Farley for being careless. The New York *Herald-Tribune* declared that it was "not without humor to find the strutting, bragging Farley suddenly as elusive and silent as a rabbit." But the newspaper found disgraceful the antics of the Roosevelt administration in falling over itself to prove that it "never, never, never" endorsed a wicked Socialist:

> We do not expect sincerity or good faith from a Farley. But we think the country is entitled to a higher standard of political candor from its President. The inescapable truth is that Mr. Roosevelt, with his usual desire to avoid unpleasant decisions and please everybody with

a vote, was glad to give the appearance of blessing Mr. Sinclair without actually doing so in binding words. Now that a blessing becomes politically embarrassing he disclaims any endorsement. Mr. Farley follows as fast as he can extricate his heavy feet from the mud of the record, and the faithful Creel brings up the rear.

It was a beautiful Saturday morning in the nation's capital, albeit uncommonly cool, so Jefty O'Connor walked to work from his apartment at the Shoreham. When he got to his office at the Treasury Department, he found several telegrams from California on his desk congratulating him on reports that FDR had offered him the top Federal Reserve post in San Francisco. The morning's newspapers suggested that some sort of Haight-Sinclair deal might indeed be in the works, so Jefty decided to rush a memo to the White House summarizing yesterday's conversations.

"Things are moving rather rapidly in California," O'Connor reported. Sinclair was to meet today with William Fox and Stanley Anderson, and Jefty would be "advised of results." He outlined four reasons why the White House should work for Sinclair's withdrawal: It would save Democratic congressmen in California from defeat. It would "eliminate the bitterness and ill will that would follow Sinclair's defeat among his supporters who would probably blame the administration for not taking a more active part." It would keep hundreds of thousands of Democrats in California from drifting, perhaps permanently, to the GOP. Last, and surely not least, a Haight victory "would practically assure" the state's electoral votes for FDR in 1936.

O'Connor had a long chat with Senator McAdoo and found him extremely agitated by his daughter's impending marriage to a mixed-race movie extra. Then Jefty went home and listened to college football games on the radio. It was a great afternoon for Huey Long's LSU but a dark day for Southern Cal, drubbed by Stanford 16-0.

Rexford G. Tugwell, apparently exiled to Europe in mid-September, was back in the news, controversial even from afar. Addressing the International Institute of Agriculture meeting in Rome this week, Tugwell had called for a world-planned economy based on cooperation. He predicted that the nations of the world would eventually adopt a new system of commerce to obviate the present extremes of free trade and protectionism. International trade, no less than domestic industry, he observed, must be placed under social controls for the sake of all citizens. According to the Associated Press, Tugwell's remarks drew both "bouquets and brickbats," but he was used to that.

The White House had decided it would no longer try to "sell" Tugwell to his constituents in the agricultural community, *The Washington Post* had reported, and would keep him in the background from now on. So Rex was in no hurry to sail home. In Italy, he met with Mussolini. Today he came to Germany to confer with U.S. Ambassador William E. Dodd. To avoid press comment (and possible government surveillance), the two men met in Konstanz instead of Berlin.

Dodd, like Tugwell, was a distinguished scholar. A former professor of history at the University of Chicago, his favorite saying was "Democracy has never really been tried." As ambassador to Germany during the rise of Hitler, he encouraged moderate elements in the society and, using all the influence he could muster, attempted to curtail persecution of Jews. So far he had experienced little success, but he continued to sound clear warnings. For this, he was branded an alarmist by some of his colleagues.

While Dodd met Tugwell in Konstanz, the German press reported that Dr. Ernst Hanfstaengl had sent a letter to President James B. Conant of Harvard University protesting the school's refusal to accept his scholarship offer. Hanfstaengl called Conant's charge that the Nazi government was destroying academic freedom in Germany "unbelievable and unjust."

Recently, in his diary, Ambassador Dodd had observed that Hanfstaengl was "the subject of much jesting in diplomatic circles." Dodd was more concerned about Putzi's friend W. R. Hearst. The ambassador was deeply troubled by reports, which he considered authoritative, indicating that while in Berlin to meet with Hitler, Hearst had discussed a deal with Joseph Goebbels to feed his International News Service to the German Propaganda Ministry for four hundred thousand dollars a year. This was many times the actual value of the service, which Hearst provided elsewhere for fifty thousand to seventy-five thousand dollars annually. Dodd, therefore, did not consider this a legitimate business deal. The story, if true, suggested that Hitler might be attempting to buy off W. R. Hearst.

At their meeting in Konstanz, Dodd and Tugwell exchanged views freely. When they finally got around to the California gubernatorial race, both men expressed sympathy for the EPIC cause, particularly since big business had poured so much money into the state to discredit Sinclair. This evening Ambassador Dodd observed in his diary that Sinclair's election "would be a solemn warning to the extreme capitalistic people who still think they know how to govern the country."

Upton Sinclair's curse became Frank Merriam's affliction today when Westbrook Pegler trained his gunsights on the incumbent governor. Pegler had interviewed Merriam and found the experience profoundly disorienting. He had the weird feeling that he had met Merriam before.

Then it dawned on him: Merriam was the glorious, final composite of all the popular cartoon representations of the hack politician. He was bald, his face was plump, his smile dull, his figure stocky and rumpled, his manner that of the inveterate office seeker. Pegler realized that he had seen the likes of Frank Merriam depicted in political cartoons a thousand times, usually with an arm around the shoulder of a fat man in a plug hat labeled THE INTERESTS or THE TRUSTS. Merriam, Pegler decided, was Warren G. Harding come to life.

"He is a statesman," Pegler observed in today's column, "who can be relied on to condemn the housefly and the common cold in no uncertain terms. You will never find him straddling the proposition that right is right and wrong is wrong. Naturally, if Mr. Merriam is elected, his official cabinet will be composed of statesmen of similar character and ideals, just as Mahatma Sinclair must be expected to surround himself with a staff of political and social hypochondriacs like himself."

Meeting Pegler, Merriam made the mistake of repeating his recent claim that FDR had been sent by Providence to govern the country at this time. "He did not offer any excuse, however," Pegler commented, "for attempting to obstruct God's work in the last Presidential election when he supported Herbert Hoover and Prohibition. That is something which is between him and his conscience." Finally, Pegler advised:

> It is too bad for California that the choice is down to Sinclair and Merriam, but it can't be helped now. It is an awful thing to have to vote for Merriam as the only means of standing off the Mahatma and his Brainstorm Trust composed of soap-boxers, incompetents and constitutional bellyachers who want to set the whole population to trading undershirts for parsley and old jokes for new laid eggs. But it seems the only way to prevent the sudden overthrow of government in California.

Variety, confident that the Sinclair threat had expired, turned playful this morning in discussing charges that local newspapers were publishing pictures of actors and passing them off as tramps. "When is a hobo not a bum?" *Variety* asked. "When is a bum an extra? When is a 1929 tourist a 1934 Sinclair-attracted bum?" These were just some of the questions that had the movie colony "all dizzy and whoozy" since the appearance of suspicious-looking photographs this week in the *Times* and *Examiner.*

Elsewhere in Lotusland, Sam Goldwyn finally announced the date for the California premiere of *We Live Again,* the movie based on Tolstoy that Sam had indicated he would not release until the campaign ended. Goldwyn was as good as his word. The film would open in San Francisco on November 7: the day after the election.

"It may hearten the cause of conservatism," a wire service reported, "to know that Shirley Temple has decided, after grave deliberation, that she disapproves of the Sinclair EPIC philosophy and is backing her opposition with a day's salary, even if she can not with a vote."

Albert Parker's vote-purge crusade had turned into a public relations fiasco. It might yet terrify thousands of Sinclair voters from going to the polls, but in the meantime it was giving Parker and his candidate, Frank Merriam, a pair of black eyes. Indignation across the state grew so intense that some Republican leaders muttered that it might cost Merriam the election.

Today one of the sixty thousand challenged voters, William A. Mann, a member of the Utopian Society, filed a federal court action seeking to restrain Albert Parker, the Los Angeles district attorney, the state registrar of voters, and the attorney general from taking further action in the case. The disenfranchisement scheme, Mann said, violated due process and the Fourteenth Amendment to the Constitution. Mann also initiated a civil suit, seeking fifty thousand dollars in personal damages from the coconspirators.

Meanwhile a revolt broke out at the court handling the registration cases. Two of the assistant court commissioners resigned, charging that the proceeding was nothing but a political sham. One of them, Rollin L. McNitt, charged that many voters were being placed on the list because of tips from "next door neighbors" who presumably disagreed with their politics. Yesterday three hundred "illegal" voters appeared in court, and all but fifteen cleared their name.

This only added to Albert Parker's sudden notoriety. What a spot for the son-in-law of Edward Walker Harden! The wire services had picked up his so-called terror letter to Whitney Debevoise, and even worse, William Mann had cited it in his lawsuit. Parker admitted he wrote the letter but told reporters that when he referred to scaring people away from the polls, he meant only illegal registrants, not Sinclair supporters as a class.

Since the letter acknowledged Debevoise's assistance, it put the New York attorney in an unfavorable light as well; it might even be "actionable." So Albert Parker sent his friend a clipping about the controversy this afternoon, along with a hastily scribbled note. Parker explained that an office clerk he had befriended had rifled his files and stolen a carbon copy of the letter. As a postscript, Parker observed, deadpan: "I write in long-hand now."

Until today, Robert Gordon Sproul had managed to refrain from taking an active role in the governor's race. He had enough political troubles as it was, keeping tabs on Communist professors and student vigilantes. Although he strongly opposed Upton Sinclair, he did not wish to antagonize him: if elected governor, Sinclair would control the university's purse strings. United for California freely circulated the text of one of Sproul's anti-Communist speeches, but that was out of his hands.

This afternoon, however, when two members of the California Crusaders came to the president's Berkeley office, Sproul greeted them warmly. They explained that they were trying to get Governor Merriam to attend this week's Stanford-UCLA football game so they could orchestrate a spontaneous outpouring of enthusiasm for him. There was just one hitch: Merriam wasn't convinced it was such a hot idea. Maybe if Sproul gave Merriam a pep talk and personally invited him to the game, Old Baldy might change his mind.

Sproul, who probably no longer feared that Sinclair would ever come back to haunt him, readily agreed to do it.

Democrats for Merriam staged a grand event at the Biltmore Theater in downtown Los Angeles this evening. All of the leading dissident

Democrats spoke. Dick Powell, Rudy Vallee, and Al Jolson, who were scheduled to appear, failed to show, but four actors from Warner Bros. warbled a tune called "The Sinclair Blues." The star of the program, however, was its organizer, William Jennings Bryan, Jr., head of the newly organized Loyal League of Democrats. Bryan intended to use his statewide radio slot to attack the scandalous notion, now circulating, that his late father would have endorsed Upton Sinclair.

No chip off the old block, Junior was a Democrat but a reticent one. He made few waves as an attorney in Los Angeles and was not imposing in appearance. With a thin face, short black hair, and mousy black mustache, he looked rather like a villain of the silver screen. His sister, Ruth, a feminist who served two terms in Congress and in 1933 became America's first female foreign ambassador, was the real heir to the Bryan name.

Junior's only claim to fame came in 1925, when his father sent him a letter asking him to come to Nashville to help prosecute "that young Tennessee teacher whose name I keep forgetting." The place, of course, was Dayton, not Nashville, and the defendant's name was John Scopes. Bryan Jr. had little experience as a trial lawyer but agreed to help because he knew his father was ill. When the Commoner met him at the Dayton train station, he cried, "Hello, Willie—God bless you!"

And so there they were: the two Bryans, Westbrook Pegler, Henry Mencken, and Heywood Broun.

William Jennings Bryan actually had little to say during the Monkey Trial, until that famous moment when Clarence Darrow called him to the witness stand. But his son took center stage at another key moment—and missed an opportunity to make an impression. Colorless and slack-voiced to begin with, Junior was also suffering from a cold as he began the prosecution's summation. His voice barely carried to the judge and jury. Clarence Darrow gave up trying to listen and read documents instead. Spectators snickered: this was the great Commoner's son? Following the trial and the death of his father, Junior accepted the presidency of the Anti-Evolution League of America. It didn't work out, and he returned to the shadows.

Then, in 1934, Bryan ran for lieutenant governor in the California Democratic primary, only to be trounced by Sheridan Downey. Unlike many of his fellow Democrats, he never flirted with endorsing Sinclair; instead he formed the League of Loyal Democrats, essentially duplicating Ham Cotton's American Democracy. There was no need for two such groups in Los Angeles except to satisfy ego, but there was plenty of slush money to go around, so why not?

By mid-October the Loyal Democrats, based in the Subway Terminal Building, had organizers in twenty-seven cities. Bryan sent out a quarter of a million letters, and soon he had assembled a mailing list that would have made Mark Hanna (who masterminded McKinley's victory over Bryan's father in 1896) proud. From this position of influence, he warned James A. Farley that Sinclair planned to run for president in '36, and if FDR didn't stop EPIC, "you will make the mistake of your political lives. . . ."

As Bryan's group gained strength, so did EPIC's suggestion that the Commoner must be rolling over in his grave. Tonight, William Jennings Bryan, Jr., chose to put that notion to rest. This would be no "Cross of Gold" speech, but it might suffice.

"It has been charged that I am a traitor to my name," Bryan said, "that if my good father were here today he would lend his full support to Upton Sinclair. I want to answer this libel of the dead. Can any man believe that, were he here today, that he would support Communism, that he would lead the people into bondage, where freedom is gone and man becomes a chattel of the State?" Defending his decision to abandon the party of his father, Bryan quoted from a speech the Commoner delivered in 1893 at a Democratic convention in Nebraska:

> Gentlemen, I know not what others may do, but if you declare in favor of the impoverishment of the people of Nebraska, if you intend to make more galling than the slavery of the blacks the slavery of the poor, if the Democratic party indorses your action and makes your position its permanent policy, then I shall go out and serve my country and my God under some other name, even though I go alone.

The funny thing was, this didn't sound like Ham Cotton, George Creel, or even William Jennings Bryan, Jr. It sounded like Upton Sinclair.

OCTOBER 28

SUNDAY

Upton Sinclair, staggering across the desert, spotted a rescuer approaching. The stout, bald-headed man, who might be a mirage, was dressed in a postal uniform. In his hand he held a letter which read, *Dear Uppie. I'm with you. Call me "Jim."*

Newspaper readers in the nation's capital searching for laughs could turn to the editorial page instead of the Sunday comics on this frigid fall morning. The easily caricatured figure of James A. Farley appeared in political cartoons in both *The Washington Post* and the *Star.* The *Post* answered the *Star*'s "mirage" cartoon with an image of Jim Farley carrying a bouquet of flowers to the door of the Elite Public Insane Center. EPIC madmen gestured at Farley through bars on the windows, inviting him to come in, causing Big Jim to scratch his bald head. MY ERROR, GENTLEMEN, the caption read.

The New York Times, which lacked both cartoons and comics, nevertheless found a reason to chuckle over the California race. Upton Sinclair, the *Times* declared, had accomplished an authentic miracle in transforming Frank Finley Merriam into a New Dealer. "When a standpat Republican politician abandons a lifetime of party regularity at 70 to come out in hearty praise of a Democratic President," the paper noted, "it is time for connoisseurs of the unusual to stand by and take notes." Another notable aspect of the Merriam campaign, *The New York Times* observed in a second article, was the effective way it pitted jobholders against the jobless. That's what the paranoid warning about an invasion of indigents—transmitted via billboard, radio, and movie screen—was all about. In fact, the entire Merriam message was aimed at "the great white-collar class of the State. It is a unique sort of campaign," the *Times* commented, "as it probably marks the first attempt at a large scale and effective organization of this class in the history of American politics."

The *Times* hinted, however, that the election of Sinclair was not out of the question. The EPIC movement remained formidable, and public outrage over the vote-purge drive had aroused "resentment and suspicion." The *Times,* which trumpeted news of the bums' rush earlier, now labeled as propaganda the GOP's charge that the unemployed were flocking to California. "These excesses by Merriam agents," the *Times* stated, "are probably the best remaining hope of the Sinclairites."

Among Republicans in California, certainty was giving way to worry, even trepidation. The smear campaign had peaked too early, some feared; intimidation tactics backfired, others believed. The GOP had a bad case of political jitters over reports of a Haight-Sinclair union, the *Sacramento Bee* observed, upsetting the "cocksure complacency" of the Merriam crowd. Kyle Palmer observed in his *Los Angeles Times* column that Merriam had benefited from tremendous "breaks" but now faced a letdown. Palmer provided an additional reason for concern, suggesting that Sinclair may have instructed his supporters to vote for Merriam in the *Literary Digest* poll to "fool the enemy" and lull the GOP into overconfidence.

Jefty O'Connor picked up the ringing telephone and found Ray Haight on the line. Their plan had hit a snag, Haight explained. Upton Sinclair, on the verge of quitting yesterday, met last night at his Beverly Hills residence with hotel magnate Stanley Anderson and campaign manager Richard Otto. (William Fox, it turns out, was still on the East Coast.) They heatedly informed Sinclair that if he quit, the EPICs would feel he had acted cowardly and had been "bluffed" out of the race by the Republican press. They demanded that he stay in the hunt to the end, and Sinclair relented.

But Haight clung to hope. Disheartened by the *Literary Digest* results, Sinclair now knew he couldn't win, Haight said. Because Sinclair was such an "egotist," an appeal to his self-importance might convince him to step aside. If Jim Farley called Sinclair and politely asked him to drop out of the race to save other Democratic candidates—and hence the New Deal—in California, he might just go along with it. Haight gave O'Connor Sinclair's home telephone number.

"Sinclair will get out," Haight said, "if he can save face."

"I don't believe Farley can take the initiative," O'Connor replied, "but Sinclair could wire Farley asking if his withdrawal would help the progressive cause."

Haight hung up, and O'Connor called Marvin McIntyre, Jim Farley, and A. P. Giannini in succession. So much for Sunday as a day of rest.

———

Contrary to Haight's assertions, Upton Sinclair remained hopeful of a miracle finish. Returning this week to Southern California, EPIC's hotbed, had lifted his spirits. And every time he thought about quitting, someone came along to put him back on track.

This morning he received a telegram from a man named George Brasfield, who had lost his job Thursday at a biscuit company in San Francisco for objecting to the distribution of "nefarious, intimidating" anti-Sinclair literature at his office. But Brasfield seemed more concerned about Sinclair than himself. "Stay in and fight," he wired the candidate. "You are the next governor of California. . . . Change your plan or anything that will gain confidence of white collar employed and hold confidence of unemployed—but don't withdraw."

How could Sinclair respond to a message like this except to fight on? If the candidate left the race, a prominent career as a writer awaited him, but then George Brasfield would have sacrificed his job at the biscuit company for nothing. Dozens, perhaps hundreds, of EPICs had made similar sacrifices. So when Stanley Anderson called the candidate late this morning in Beverly Hills and sketched a scenario for victory, Uppie was all ears.

Sinclair had met Anderson in the early 1930s, when Uppie was writing his book about Stanley's friend William Fox. Now Anderson was an adviser to the EPIC campaign. He often entertained the candidate with celebrity gossip over dinner at his Benedict Canyon home. He was certainly well placed: Rudolph Valentino, Harold Lloyd, and Doris Duke were neighbors at one time or another, and his kids used to play with Will Rogers's kids up the block. Anderson had developed much of Beverly Hills, an area that until recently had been mainly bean fields and wilderness. He owned both the Hollywood Hotel and the pink-cheeked Beverly Hills Hotel. How rich was he? His Benedict Canyon estate covered forty acres of some of the most expensive real estate in the world.

For whatever reason, Anderson tried to help Sinclair in ways large and small. After Uppie won the primary, Stanley wrote a note to Craig offering to lend the Sinclairs his new Buick for the remainder of the campaign. He knew that Sinclair's rickety old car was always breaking down. (The Sinclairs declined the offer.) But Anderson had bigger things in mind. Months ago he informed Sinclair that he thought he could raise three hundred thousand dollars from friends for Upton's campaign.

At the top of his list: A. P. Giannini. All by himself, Giannini had donated $150,000 to Hiram Johnson's campaign this year—and Johnson didn't even need it. Anderson considered Giannini the only banker in California with a social conscience and believed that if A.P. got a chance to chat with Sinclair, he would end up supporting him. Several times he tried to arrange a meeting between the two men, but one or the other was always out of town.

Now EPIC was in desperate need of funds, and Giannini was again across the country. But Stanley Anderson reached the banker in Washington this morning and discovered that Giannini was, one, in close contact with the White House concerning the California race and, two, eager to speak to Sinclair, perhaps with an open mind. This was the same Giannini who yesterday had plotted with Jefty O'Connor to get Sinclair out of the race.

Anderson rang Sinclair and suggested that he come up to his house and talk to Giannini himself. A.P. was ready to give Uppie ten thousand dollars—or so Stanley Anderson said. Sinclair jumped in his old car and headed for Benedict Canyon, a short drive from his Beverly Hills retreat.

On a clear day, Stanley Anderson could see Catalina from his hillside home. The mansion boasted a conservatory, a four-thousand-square-foot living room, and a private waterfall, making it an odd place for Upton Sinclair to try to salvage his anti-capitalist, grass-roots movement. Anderson, a tall, husky man who had just turned fifty, led Uppie into his library.

"Giannini is sick of the corruption in the affairs of this state," Anderson instructed Sinclair, "and he doesn't want Merriam to be governor. He wants to hear just one thing—if elected you will appoint an honest man as bank examiner."

"That's all right," Sinclair replied, "but does *he* expect to name that honest man?"

"Maybe that's what he wants," Anderson responded, "but if he assumes that and later on finds that he was mistaken, that will be his hard luck! In politics you don't have to be too particular about letting other people make mistakes."

"I'll go even further," Sinclair said. "I'll tell him I'm going to appoint an honest man to *every* office."

Soon Sinclair was repeating this over the telephone to Giannini himself. A.P. said that Sinclair needed to get the White House behind him, however belated its support might be. He suggested that Sinclair call Marvin McIntyre and ask FDR to dispatch J.F.T. O'Connor to the Coast—and say it was Giannini's idea.

The conversation ended. Sinclair, somewhat encouraged, called Marvin McIntyre but didn't reach him. A. P. Giannini, meanwhile, rang Jefty O'Connor. Upton Sinclair had just asked him for ten thousand dollars, Giannini reported, but he didn't plan to give it to him. "Sinclair is beaten," Giannini said.

A. P. Giannini never had any intention of supporting Upton Sinclair with the coin of the realm or anything else. He merely wanted to raise Sinclair's hopes high enough to get him to call the White House and ask for Jefty O'Connor's "help." Stanley Anderson may have been an unwitting party to the ruse, or a coconspirator.

Giannini was used to getting his way. It was often said that the leading banker west of the Mississippi would rather fight than eat. B. C. Forbes once observed that Giannini thrived on obstacles and opposition. "His chief thrill in life," Forbes commented, "is in tackling and accomplishing what others declare to be impossible. . . . He has never been licked in anything he set out to accomplish." Sinclair, to Giannini, was just one more obstacle to be eliminated.

At the age of seven, Amadeo Peter Giannini, the eldest son of Italian immigrants, watched a ranch worker murder his father in San Jose in a dispute over a single dollar. Six years later he dropped out of school to work for his stepfather in the produce business in San Francisco.

Strong and tireless, he became a full partner in the business before he was out of his teens. A dozen years later he suddenly lost interest in the profitable enterprise and retired, at the age of thirty-one.

It was then that his real career began. Named to the board of a San Francisco bank, he argued for risky policies that would benefit what he called "the little fellow." When A.P. failed to get his way, he opened his own bank across the street and called it the Bank of Italy. Innovative from day one, he made loans to merchants, farmers, and workers, and—even more heretical—went door-to-door for accounts. He lowered interest rates and simplified the loan process. Character was his collateral. "We've cut out the bunk," he declared. "We've humanized banking." Singlehandedly he revolutionized the banking business in America.

The turning point came on April 18, 1906, just hours after the great San Francisco earthquake. A.P. reached his bank only minutes ahead of the fire. Commandeering two horse-drawn carriages, he loaded one with two million dollars in currency and securities from the bank vault, the other with business forms and stationery, hid his bounty under a cover of produce, and set off through the flames and drunken crowds of looters. Proceeding south, he reached his home in San Mateo, where he buried the money in his backyard. The next day, with the ruins of his bank still smoldering, he sent a letter to his customers, informing them that their deposits were intact and offering to lend money to all who wished to rebuild. Giannini reopened for business almost immediately, putting a clerk behind a desk in a shed on the waterfront. Hundreds lined up for loans, with the result that the North Beach section—the Italian quarter—rose from the ashes before any other.

A few years later, Giannini began buying up small banks and converting them into branches of the Bank of Italy, thereby instituting the first successful branch banking system in the country. Between 1908 and 1922 his holdings grew from $2.5 million to $254 million. By 1927 one of every five Californians had deposits in the Bank of Italy. Giannini furnished vast loans to movie producers, including Chaplin, Zanuck, DeMille, and Sennett, at a time when other local bankers refused to finance films; in this way he helped make Hollywood viable. (DeMille returned the favor, serving as a director and loan officer at the bank's Hollywood branch.) In 1928, Giannini formed the Transamerica Corporation as a holding company for all of his financial interests.

During the Depression, Giannini's institution—its name was changed to the Bank of America in 1930—allowed depositors to borrow two hundred dollars against any automobile they owned, no questions asked. A progressive Republican, Giannini soured on Herbert Hoover's handling of the Depression. At a meeting with candidate Franklin Roosevelt in September 1932 arranged by Joseph P. Kennedy, Giannini offered his support and a $2500 donation. He was virtually the only major banker in California who sincerely identified with FDR's sympathy for the underdog. The move paid off for both men: Roosevelt carried California, and the following spring the Bank of America became one of the first institutions allowed to reopen following the "bank holiday."

Two years later, Giannini struggled mightily to find a candidate in California to carry the ball for him. First he tried to get Jefty O'Connor to run for governor. Then, a little more than a month before the August 28 primary, he sent a four-page telegram to top Democrats virtually begging them to unite on a candidate to stop Sinclair, predicting that EPIC would "aggravate conditions and irreparably impair the credit and heavily handicap the development of California." At one point, Giannini even considered supporting Frank Merriam. One of Giannini's associates devised a scheme whereby Merriam, in exchange for A.P.'s support, would promise to appoint the banker to the U.S. Senate when an ailing William G. McAdoo stepped down. Giannini replied that he was "delighted" to consider "putting over" this idea. Three days after the August primary, the associate suggested they finalize the deal. By this time, however, Giannini entertained the notion that Ray Haight might win as a third-party dark horse, and so he pulled back, claiming that he preferred "to remain outside" the "political game."

Throughout the fall, bank directors, employees, and leaders of both parties implored Giannini to jump on the Merriam bandwagon, or at least induce Haight to quit the race. Giannini was uncertain how to respond. In early October, he told bank employees in Tulare that Southern Pacific and Pacific Gas & Electric were putting as much as a million dollars into the campaign to defeat Sinclair, but he doubted that would be enough. He kept in close contact with Jefty O'Connor, hoping to find out which way the wind from the White House was blowing, to no avail. Giannini was still "100% with the President," he wired the White House in September, and was willing to mobilize his considerable resources—not to mention the votes of 140,000 Italian Americans in the state—behind the candidate FDR favored.

When Giannini learned that Jefty O'Connor was attempting to rally the White House behind Haight, he offered to grease Sinclair's skids. Since Sinclair was broke and still hopeful of pulling off an upset, Giannini knew that he could be manipulated more easily than ever. Through their mutual friend Stanley Anderson, A.P. might be able to trick Sinclair into calling the White House and agreeing to accept a brokered endorsement: Giannini and FDR would throw their combined weight behind either Sinclair or Haight—but the unfavored candidate would have to withdraw from the race.

What Giannini didn't tell Sinclair was that the White House choice had indeed narrowed to two candidates in the governor's contest in California, and Uppie was not one of them.

After lunch at Stanley Anderson's house, Sinclair phoned Marvin McIntyre several more times without success. It was Sunday, after all, even at the White House, so Uppie passed the time dashing off telegrams. He demanded from Will Hays "an explicit repudiation from your organization of Mr. Pettijohn's activities." He asked the movie czar "whether your organization sanctions the making of lying motion pictures to defeat a people's candidate. . . . I intend to let the people of California know that crooked political motion pictures are being made and who is making them and who is sanctioning them."

Making good on this threat, Sinclair fired off telegrams to Senator David Walsh of Massachusetts and Representative Wright Patman of Texas, who headed congressional investigation committees. Citing Billy Wilkerson's column in the *Hollywood Reporter,* Sinclair charged that Louis B. Mayer, Irving Thalberg, Carey Wilson, and Charles Pettijohn had "entered a 'war' against me and are aiding the Merriam campaign" by creating "false propaganda in motion pictures." Congress, he suggested, should mount a "complete investigation of the political activities" of the movie industry, comparing this in importance to the probe of the meat industry sparked by publication of *The Jungle* in 1906.

If Charlie Pettijohn was worried about a congressional inquiry, he gave no sign of it today as he accepted the thanks of five hundred prominent Democrats at a gala American Democracy picnic. The setting: Ham Cotton's San Clemente estate. "Upton Sinclair is like the cuckoo bird which lays its eggs in another's nest to be hatched," Pettijohn told the crowd. "This time the Democrats won't oblige."

Father Charles Coughlin inaugurated his fall radio season this afternoon with a full-throated attack on the Liberty League and other cowardly "perverters" of financial ruin. As usual when Coughlin spoke, commerce, discourse, even conversation came to a complete halt in many working-class neighborhoods around the country. Coughlin had been off the air since the spring amid rumors that he was about to break with President Roosevelt. The White House had expended a lot of energy attempting to keep the radio priest in line. Joe Kennedy, Jefty O'Connor, and Henry Morgenthau, among others, had met with Coughlin recently.

So when the good father declared today that "more than ever I am in favor of a new deal," the President's men might have sighed with relief. Skeptics could have pointed out that Coughlin endorsed a new deal, not the New Deal, and that he warned the President to stay aloof from the "money changers." Father Coughlin remained hostile to Upton Sinclair, despite the candidate's recent plea for support. "Today we have a nominee for the office of governor in one of our states," Coughlin said, "who is advocating production for use and not for profit. As irrational and nonsensical as is this theory, who knows how many persons two years from now will support it with their ballots unless the equally nonsensical and equally irrational theories of capitalism be rectified."

Upton Sinclair never did get through to the White House. But he met with Ray Haight and, stimulated by his conversation with A. P. Giannini, again refused to forge an alliance with the third-party candidate. The two men just couldn't work it out. Each still entertained the fantasy of FDR bestowing a last-minute blessing on his candidacy. Paralysis in Washington had prevented compromise in Los Angeles. On cue, Haight might have yielded to Sinclair or Sinclair to Haight, but the signal from the White House remained dim.

Tomorrow promised to be the key day as the campaign approached its climax. Upton Sinclair had told Ray Haight he would attempt to reach Marvin McIntyre at the White House at nine-thirty in the morning Pacific time. Haight decided to beat him to the punch, courtesy of Western Union.

OCTOBER 29

MONDAY

Ray Haight, rising early in Los Angeles, phoned Jefty O'Connor in Washington and then shot off a five-page telegram to Marvin McIntyre at the White House. Haight warned McIntyre to expect a call from Upton Sinclair at midday seeking to "secure strong endorsement" of his candidacy. Before he talked to Sinclair, he should know the "real situation here."

Sinclair was headed for defeat by a two-to-one margin, Haight declared. But with Sinclair out of the race, Haight (according to his polls) would beat Merriam easily. Haight felt certain, he wired, that "we can swing ticket in week's time." The Scripps-Howard papers and the Los Angeles *Daily News* would cooperate, he explained, and even Hearst might get caught up in the excitement.

Haight then suggested how McIntyre should handle Sinclair when he called. "Emphasize fact even if his campaign successful," Haight instructed, "little national administration can do to help his program or any program if support lost in Congress. Then ask about newspaper reports of possible fusion. Remember in asking that every egotist likes people to believe he is willing to do the dramatic and courageous thing. Then ask him if he is willing to have representative of Chief come West to review situation before aiding, with understanding he will cooperate in abiding by Chief's decision as to what's necessary [to] save California from continuing in hands of opposition. If he agrees and confirms request by wire, send Farley or O'Connor for quick survey.

"Depend on my cooperation to do whatever seems best for state," Haight advised.

It was budget day at the White House. The President would discuss tax measures with his economic advisers and planned a working lunch with Secretary of the Treasury Morgenthau. Dozens of letters and telegrams continued to arrive at 1600 Pennsylvania Avenue every day asking, urging, or begging the President to save Upton Sinclair. From Berkeley: "Can our chief executive remain silent and see truth and decency murdered as the Merriam forces are now doing in California?" From Pasadena: ". . . send the Marines to the Pacific Coast to protect the California election." From Los Angeles: "Please pay no attention to the fake news reports from California. Upton Sinclair is our GOD."

FDR even heard from his in-laws. Eleanor Roosevelt's aunt, Edith Hall, affectionately known as Aunt Pussie, wired the President from Red Bank, New Jersey: "Consider the present attitude on Upton Sinclair lacking in the honest realization that Sinclair no matter what his ideas or ideals may be is a courageous and intelligent man. Is there nothing you can say that will help make people stop and think?"

The White House expected a call from Upton Sinclair at midday. Marvin McIntyre went upstairs and talked to the President. When McIntyre came back down, he arranged to have his telephone conversation with the EPIC candidate recorded—a highly unusual procedure in the Roosevelt White House, reserved for only the most sensitive discussions.

The telephone rang. It was Sinclair, calling from his home on Arden Drive in Beverly Hills. For the first time since September 4, the candidate and the White House talked directly. It was high noon for Upton Sinclair.

"I don't know how much you know of the situation in California," Sinclair began.

"Nothing except hearsay and newspaper reports," McIntyre replied.

Sinclair told him about the vote-purge scheme and other forms of wholesale intimidation. "They have started a campaign of lies," Sinclair reported, "and now have centered all their attacks on the proposition that the Administration is against us, and they are going to beat us with that argument unless we can get real action from you folks. Farley wrote us a letter and they now claim that it was a rubber-stamped letter, sent by accident, and they are publishing statements given directly from Washington, apparently from Farley, to that effect. I don't know whether that's true or not but if Farley doesn't contradict it we are sunk."

"That's a matter you will have to take up directly with Farley," McIntyre said.

"If something isn't done," Sinclair threatened, "you will find when 1936 comes that you have made a mistake."

McIntyre responded firmly. "So far as the President and the White House is concerned," he explained, "there has been nothing except a constant repetition of the President's original statement that neither the President nor the White House is taking any part in local political campaigns. The President said that a long time ago and he has reiterated it in practically every state in the union, and as a matter of fact he told you that in Hyde Park, and he has not changed—"

"He also told me definitely," Sinclair interrupted, "that not later than the twenty-fifth of October he was going to make a speech about production for use. He said that to me with all possible emphasis."

"Of course I don't know anything about that," McIntyre said. "I was not in on the interview."

"I wish you would point that out to him and tell him the seriousness of the situation," Sinclair implored. "As far as Farley is concerned, he is not the President nor is he a member of the cabinet. He is chairman of the National Committee."

"Of course that matter you should take up directly with Jim Farley."

"I know that, but I know also that you have a little influence—"

"We are not in a position to use any of it," McIntyre replied. This was disingenuous, to say the least, but Sinclair knew he had hit a stone wall, so he shifted course.

"What we want is to have O'Connor step into an airplane and come out here and help us put down these lies," Sinclair declared, "and if you will do that it will make the necessary—"

"Obviously that suggestion is one the Administration couldn't have any part in," McIntyre interjected. "If you want O'Connor out there the thing to do is to take it up with O'Connor personally, and as an individual. As a Californian he can take an interest in conditions out in his own state, and as an individual he can make any suggestion or do anything he wants to do. I suggest you take that up with O'Connor."

"The only thing I can ask you to do is to remind the President of the promise he made to me and tell him of the condition," Sinclair responded. "Really, the Attorney General ought to do something about this intimidation. They are disenfranchising a hundred thousand voters."

"I wasn't in on that conference you had with the President," McIntyre reminded him, "but I really don't know that it should be classified as a promise. He doesn't make promises of that kind. I think what he made was a statement that he contemplated such a speech."

"I just ask that you remind him of it for me," Sinclair said for the third and last time.

"As I say," McIntyre replied, apparently ignoring him, "Mr. O'Connor as an individual can make whatever decision he wants and take whatever action or steps he wants to take. The Administration obviously could not ask O'Connor to step into the situation because that would per se bring the Administration into it, so I would advise you to take that phase of it up with O'Connor."

And so the Haight plan to erase Upton Sinclair from the race ran according to script. Haight softened him up, A. P. Giannini convinced him to call the White House, and Marvin McIntyre placed him in the capable hands of Jefty O'Connor. What Sinclair didn't know was that O'Connor had a hidden agenda: to flatter, cajole, or bully him out of the race.

When Sinclair called and asked him to come to California, Jefty agreed, so long as his boss, Secretary of the Treasury Morgenthau, approved. A few minutes later Morgenthau told Jefty that it was not only all right with him—the *President* wanted him to go. O'Connor made plane reservations and wired his schedule to Sinclair: at ten minutes past five this afternoon he would be on Trans World Airways out of Washington bound for L.A.

"If Sinclair is elected I'll surely come out on a newspaper enterprise," H. L. Mencken wrote to a friend in California today. "Four years of him would be certainly too rich. I fear I'd laugh myself to death."

Shooting on location out in Sonora completed, Will Rogers returned to Hollywood to finish *The County Chairman.* Among Will's costars: Mickey Rooney in his first screen appearance since gaining fame in Max Reinhardt's *A Midsummer Night's Dream.* Rogers played the role of Jim Hackler, a political-party chairman in the fictional Tomahawk County, Wyoming, who masterminds an election campaign for his young law partner, Ben Harvey.

Jim, an old pro, tells Ben, a neophyte, that there are only two important issues in political life: promises and personality. "You have the personality," he points out, "and I'll equip you with a full set of promises." Say anything to get elected, he advises, so long as it offends no one. In every campaign speech, for example, Ben must remember to denounce the Turks for massacring the Armenians.

"What's that got to do with anything?" Ben inquires.

"Why, that's good politics," Jim explains. "You see, your opponent may not mention it, and that puts him in the position of favoring the massacre!"

Frank Finley Merriam, a stock character straight out of this movie, visited *The County Chairman* set at the Fox studio today. Unable to secure Will Rogers's support, Merriam figured the next best thing was to get his picture taken with the star. So there he was, smiling up at Rogers from behind a big desk on one of *The County Chairman* sets. Merriam looked as though he were auditioning for a part and expected to get it.

The justice of the peace in Loyalton Township, California, conducted an inquiry today into the death of ranch worker Robert Leighton, who died last Friday following an argument with his boss, Gil Martin, over the governor's race. Martin admitted that he shot Leighton, a Sinclair supporter, but claimed it was in self-defense. Testimony indicated that Martin shot Leighton in the back, but there appeared to be no eyewitnesses to the crime. The local district attorney, J. M. McMahon, sympathized with the defendant, at least politically. McMahon had recently organized a Democrats-for-Merriam club, and informed Earl Warren that he intended to "fight the red menace that threatens the state." Today he decided to reduce the charges against Gil Martin from murder to manslaughter, and the town justice ordered the prisoner released on two thousand dollars' bail.

Clyde C. Marshaw of West Ninety-ninth Street in Los Angeles rushed his two-month-old baby, Upton Sinclair Marshaw, to General Hospital with a severe eye infection. Doctors projected a one-week hospital stay for the boy, who was born on the day his namesake swept the Democratic primary. The father, out of work since February, his weight down to ninety-eight pounds, and with three kids besides young Upton to feed, addressed a letter to EPIC headquarters this afternoon. "The boy got infection in eye from some source, but by being too damn poor caused by the parisites that have caused the workingman to be pauperized, we were unable to give child proper medical attention," Marshaw disclosed. "Any rate I know disease and undernourished children are prevailing all over town right now . . . and if people do not vote for Upton Sinclair let 'em get and expect just the same treatment they are getting now."

In his personal correspondence, which today was voluminous, Herbert Hoover transmitted news of EPIC's likely demise across the continent. One comment appeared in nearly every letter: "The people here are realizing that this is only a skin eruption from the poison which has been poured into the national blood stream."

The former president elaborated on this sentiment in a note to Walter B. Mahoney of *The North American Review* in New York. "For the first time in our national history," Hoover observed, "sane Democrats and sane Republicans of all breeds of thought have openly and avowedly combined in a campaign." But Hoover still harbored some misgivings. "The campaign of opposition to Sinclair is based upon the New Deal technique of abuse," he noted. "It may be effective, but it saddens one as to the advancement of civilization."

Robert Minor, the Pulitzer cartoonist turned Communist propagandist, took to the airwaves today in San Francisco to deliver his latest assault on Upton Sinclair from the left. Minor had been been blistering Sinclair in the pages of the *Western Worker* and in numerous speeches around the state, but the man he was making most miserable was Sam Darcy, his own candidate.

Darcy, an early believer in "united front" activities, had tried to stay on friendly terms with EPIC leaders; now Minor was going around calling them incipient fascists. Minor charged that the CP had allowed EPIC to steal its thunder on the left by failing to expose the fact that Sinclair was doing the bidding of California's bankers by directing the disenchanted to the "safe" New Deal instead of to revolutionary communism. He was outraged when he learned that Harry Bridges's longshoremen—whose strike the Communists had championed and Sinclair soft-pedaled—had voted to donate two thousand dollars to EPIC and only five hundred dollars to Darcy. And one more thing: Darcy's headquarters hadn't even bothered to attempt to penetrate the EPIC organization.

In his manuscripts for the *Western Worker,* Minor dubbed his old friend Uppie "Adolf Sinclair of Pasadena," and accused him of spouting "imbecilic anti-capitalist drivel" while "building up an openly Fascist movement."

> The Fleishhackers, Chandlers, Crockers and Hearsts are rejecting and fighting the political runt who serves as their more-or-less Hitler. . . . Sinclair can comfort his sleepless nights with the recollection that Hitler, too, was not only rejected but was even jailed by the steel and coal magnates by whom he later was placed in power.

Only a "big Red vote for Darcy" would frighten the "ruling bankers' dictatorship" in Sacramento and Washington, Minor wrote.

Until tonight, Minor had preached only to the Communist converted. Now he took his message to a wide radio audience. He called Sinclair's plan to dump the unemployed in cooperative colonies "socialization of the junk pile" and "the most reactionary proposal that any candidate has made in this whole economic crisis." Hitler also used socialistic phrases to save capitalism; he even proposed sending the unemployed to live off the land in East Prussia. "Plain men and women of California, workers and farmers," Minor pleaded. "Do you not remember Hitler raised the cry *'Deutschlands Armut Verenden'*—'End Poverty in Germany'?"

At nearly the precise moment Jefty O'Connor's TWA airliner lifted off the runway, bound for Los Angeles, Raymond Haight telegraphed

A. P. Giannini at the Willard Hotel in Washington. Haight explained that a top Hearst official had just phoned, requesting that "McIntyre's chief" (i.e., FDR) telephone W.R. and personally deliver the following message: if Sinclair does not step aside, the White House will take "no favorable action" on Upton's behalf; if he does quit, the Haight candidacy "will have friendly Administration interest." The Hearst official had advised that if this was done, Haight could "expect some sympathetic cooperation from Hearst." Haight asked Giannini to convey this request to the "highest source in strictest confidence."

At about the same time, Giannini received a second telegram, this one from New York. An aide to William Fox informed Giannini that the movie magnate was coming down to Washington "and would like to see you there either Tuesday or Wednesday."

Jefty O'Connor had barely left the ground, and already his trip to California was the worst-kept political secret in America. The *Sacramento Bee* printed a New York *World-Telegram* dispatch from Washington quoting a "well-authorized" source who revealed that Jim Farley had drafted J.F.T. O'Connor to fly to California and convince Sinclair to withdraw.

In a statewide radio broadcast from Los Angeles tonight, Sinclair declared that the "hour of the great decision draws near for the people of California. They are going to give an answer which the whole world is awaiting: Can Democracy be made to work? Can the people manage their own affairs? Or can they be cheated and made fools of by greedy, lying exploiters and wholesale thieves?" Sinclair took this opportunity to declare:

"I am not an atheist, and never have been one. . . .

"I am not a Communist, and never have been one. . . .

"I never trampled on the American flag. I never cursed the constitution—or anybody or anything else. I never did any of the grotesque and hideous things which the hired liars are now shouting to you over the radio. . . .

"They tell you that I will take your job; that all the factories will close down if I am elected. My friends, that is the same bunk they have used to defeat every friend of the people since the Civil War. Give them a laugh, and go on and vote as you please; and rest assured that if the factories close down, a people's governor will find ways to reopen them. The people will not sit around and starve while I am in office."

But the most important message Upton Sinclair delivered to his hundreds of thousands of followers across the state was this: "Pay no attention to reports of my withdrawal from the contest. I have not withdrawn, nor shall I." If he kept that pledge, Haight, O'Connor, and Giannini—and, presumably, Franklin Roosevelt—were in for a surprise, perhaps as early as tomorrow.

OCTOBER 30

TUESDAY

"All good people will rejoice to learn that the devil, who has not been feeling at all well lately, has determined to change his ways and take up a monastic life," Westbrook Pegler observed this morning in his syndicated column. "This is plainly apparent in the campaign utterances of prominent Republican statesmen in California as the contest between Governor Frank Merriam, the old horseshoe pitcher, and Mahatma Upton Sinclair draws to a close."

Pegler intimated that Merriam's sudden emergence as a New Dealer virtually guaranteed his election. "It will be Mr. Sinclair's tragic fate to go down in the history of California as the savior of his loathed enemy—the regular Republican party," Pegler declared. "He undertook to destroy the Republican party, and threw such a terrific scare into the statesmen in charge that they turned square and will now proceed to be as decent as they have to be in order to save themselves."

It was Sinclair's cockeyed destiny, Pegler pointed out, always to do favors for his enemies. Perhaps one distant day Republicans in California "will erect a monument to the vegetarian Mahatma sitting at his typewriter and gnashing a gentle tooth at a dish of wild berries or a bag of nuts," Pegler proposed. "That would be the unkindest cut."

—

The day dawned cloudy and cool in Los Angeles after two weeks of blistering heat. Arriving at Grand Central Airport this morning, Jefty O'Connor encountered a swarm of reporters. They were happy to see him. Jefty cut a rakish figure—for a bureaucrat. A debate champion at Yale, he had a golden voice and was something of a raconteur. Pushing fifty but still a bachelor, Jefty was dating Elissa Landi, a Hollywood actress presently starring in *The Count of Monte Cristo.*

But Jefty was not in the mood to meet the press today. He angrily denied reports that Jim Farley had dispatched him to his home state to secure Sinclair's withdrawal. Jefty had sat in on informal discussions about the California race, he confessed, but had not met Farley for days. "I'll see Sinclair if he wishes to see me and for that matter, I'll see Merriam if he so wishes," O'Connor announced, "but my plans do not include a visit to either." Describing his trip as "ninety-nine percent personal," O'Connor revealed that he would address bankers' groups, visit his private law office in Los Angeles, and trek to the polls with his fellow Californians on November 6.

Whom would he vote for? "Boys, I don't think that is a very fair question," O'Connor replied, thereby indicating that he would not necessarily vote the straight Democratic ticket. That, in itself, was headline news.

When he reached the Ambassador Hotel on Wilshire Boulevard, O'Connor confronted another crowd of reporters. He waved them off with the explanation that he planned to catch up on the sleep he missed flying across the country. Moments later Stanley Anderson paid Jefty a visit. The two men ducked out of the Ambassador and headed for Anderson's mansion in Benedict Canyon, where Upton Sinclair awaited them.

—

"About everything is being adapted to radio in the 'beat Sinclair' campaign now in progress," *Variety* reported this morning. "For the final weeks of the campaign every device known to opinion management and the artisans of propaganda is being employed." As the contest entered its final week, the Merriam campaign intensified its reliance on radio. The *Los Angeles Times* refused to run the schedule of EPIC programs but published United for California's lineup in a special sidebar every day. Today's box listed ten pro-Merriam programs; yesterday the count was eleven.

Two of the Lord & Thomas serials aired nearly every day: *The Bennetts* (the soap opera aimed at housewives) at three-thirty in the afternoon and *Weary and Willie* (starring the boxcar tourists) shortly after ten at night. The long-winded Frank Merriam rarely got a word in edgewise, which was precisely the point. Copywriters and professional pitchmen dominated the unprecedented radio campaign. Albert Lasker's ad agency had reduced the candidate to merchandise.

"Novelty of the presentations is surefire," *Variety* commented, "and a check of the listening audience shows that a tremendous wedge is being driven in spots where other agencies of promotion have failed to make much more than a superficial dent. . . . It's a cinch that if the Lord & Thomas promotion is successful in keeping Upton Sinclair out of Sacramento this new text book in political campaigning will gain wide circulation." Another *Variety* article lent further credence to this thesis. Politicians in Chicago—home base for Albert Lasker—were now using show business talent to "bait" radio listeners and "take away the sting of bald stumping," *Variety* revealed.

It was a historic day in Los Angeles, not so much for what occurred, but for what it symbolized. Charlie Chaplin, still shooting his new picture, had used the same open-air movie lot at La Brea and Sunset for the past twenty years. Today he ordered workers to wall it and roof it, transforming the lot into a typical studio soundstage that sealed off all outside distractions. Traffic at the intersection of La Brea and Sunset had doubled lately, Chaplin explained. Los Angeles was simply becoming too noisy to film indoor scenes outdoors.

A political bombshell exploded on the campus of UCLA this morning with the news that the campus provost, Dr. Ernest C. Moore, had suspended five popular students for one year for using their campus offices "to destroy the university by handing it over to an organized group of Communists." The radical quintet included the president of the student body and the student leaders of the men's board and the scholarship committee.

Although political tensions had existed on campus for some time, the spark that precipitated this crisis was the circulation of a petition calling for an open forum on the governor's contest. Dr. Moore, a United for California partisan, claimed that the university president, Robert Sproul, forbade any debates or straw votes. This morning, however, the *Daily Californian* pointed out that Sproul had allowed a student forum on the governor's race at Berkeley, with a second debate scheduled for this very evening (and a straw poll to follow).

When news of the suspensions spread, three thousand students gathered in front of Royce Hall near the campus library. A member of the radical National Students League, Victor Leviskis, ascended the steps and started railing against the administration. "You all know what we are here for," he shouted. "All we want is a square deal." A plainclothes cop grabbed him by the leg and tried to pull him down. Unsuccessful, he smashed Leviskis in the face. A student tackled the cop, and the riot was on. Students attacked three campus policemen, tossing one of them over a hedge. Fifty cops from the LAPD arrived in riot gear. In the back of the crowd, a group of husky athletes and ROTC cadets joined in the mêlée. Only the appearance of the dean of men appealing for calm prevented a pitched battle. The rally ended with the singing of the alma mater.

Afterward Dr. Moore pledged that he would reinstate no one until the campus was purged of radicals and left-wing organizations, such as the National Students League. Today's disturbance, he observed, showed that students should take matters into their own hands and "clean house."

EPIC attorneys took their fight against the vote-purge plan to the state's highest court today, not entirely confident of the outcome. It was another David and Goliath confrontation. John Packard, former Socialist party national committeeman, argued for the EPICs. Defending the vote purge: state attorney general U. S. Webb and nearly a dozen high-priced lawyers, including Southern Pacific's Isidore Dockweiler and O'Melveny's Walter Tuller. Webb argued that if the court sustained the procedure, he was prepared to file suits all over the state, affecting more than two hundred thousand voters. According to one estimate, 99 percent of the challenged registrants happened to be Democrats.

The seven supreme court justices heard the arguments, which one judge characterized as "complicated," and announced they would rule tomorrow.

Upton Sinclair found Jefty O'Connor to be a surprisingly easygoing gentleman and frank about everything except California politics. In the course of a two-hour conversation at Stanley Anderson's house, the EPIC candidate made his last, best bid for White House backing. Despite everything, Sinclair spoke warmly of Franklin Roosevelt and claimed that he had never expected the President to endorse his candidacy; but he bemoaned the Farley letter and FDR's failure to keep his "promise" to speak in favor of production for use.

Appealing directly for administration support, Sinclair pledged fealty to the state Democratic platform, the New Deal, and FDR's run for president in 1936. EPIC was out of money, but he offered to arrange radio time for O'Connor to broadcast in his behalf throughout the state.

Jefty didn't bite. Personally, he explained, he was more interested in "causes and good government than individuals." There was nothing the White House could, or at least would, do for EPIC. But if Sinclair felt doubtful of victory or was certain he couldn't win . . . then some kind of "arrangement" should be made.

That could mean only one thing: accommodation with Ray Haight. But Sinclair didn't fall for it; he meant to fight to the finish, win or lose. Sinclair seemed steadfast, so Jefty didn't push his proposal. Clearly Haight and Giannini had underestimated Sinclair. The "egotist" would not bow out merely to earn martyrdom and a pat on the back from James A. Farley.

Jefty promised to consult with others. He chatted a bit with the state Democratic chairman, Culbert Olson, and then returned with Stanley Anderson to the Ambassador Hotel. News of a secret meeting with Sinclair had already leaked out. "Sinclair did not ask me for my support and I did not ask him to withdraw," O'Connor told the press mob at the hotel. "The visit was personal." But then he added defiantly, "I am still a citizen of California—they haven't taken that away from me by giving me a federal job. If I want to take part in the campaign I have the same right to do that as any other voter."

Asked, therefore, if he planned to speak at the EPIC rally at Philharmonic Hall later today, O'Connor snapped, "Absolutely not."

A few minutes later Ray Haight came to Jefty's hotel room for a one-hour conference, now meaningless. Then one of Frank Merriam's associates phoned to inform O'Connor that the governor wished to see him. The initial stage of Jefty's mission had failed. Now he would activate Plan B.

Helen Wills Moody wasn't the only authentic American sports hero to support Frank Merriam. The man many people called the greatest baseball player who ever lived, Ty Cobb, announced today that he had enrolled himself as a leader in the northern California nonpartisan Merriam campaign.

Tyrus Raymond Cobb, called the Georgia Peach, quit the game in 1928 at the age of forty-two, having won more batting titles than any player in history. Cobb, who loved fishing, hunting, and golf, retired to Augusta, Georgia, where he rediscovered, somewhat unpleasantly, the long, hot summers of his youth. Recalling a trip to cool, northern California, he decided to move his family to Menlo Park and later purchased a summer home at Lake Tahoe.

Cobb had earned a lot of money in baseball—a total of three hundred thousand dollars by one estimate—but he made a fortune on Wall Street. An early investor in Georgia-based Coca-Cola, he came to own twelve thousand shares of stock in the company. Not a well-educated man, he nevertheless read a lot of history and collected pictures and statues of Napoleon, whom he admired. "Napoleon," he once said, "was a big leaguer, all right."

Describing his philosophy of life, Cobb liked to recall his father's advice: "Align yourself on the side of right and fear no man." Now the rich, reactionary Georgia Peach was aligned with Frank Merriam. In fact, according to a press report, Cobb was "one of the busiest campaigners for the Governor" on the peninsula south of San Francisco.

In the aftermath of Earl Warren's first statewide radio address, dozens of friends and strangers wished him well. "It was the sanest, soundest note in the oratorical chorus that accompanied the campaign," observed a Southern Pacific official in San Francisco. "Some day I hope to have the pleasure of voting for you for governor of California." This sentiment was widely shared, at least among Warren's correspondents.

The only negative feedback arrived in a letter from a wealthy Republican in Modesto. Listening to Warren's "appeal of fear" in behalf of Merriam, this gentleman felt "disappointed in the Earl Warren that I had pictured in my mind as a true Californian who in the past has been outspoken in behalf of clean government and citizenship." He professed to be at least as opposed to Sinclair as Warren was, since he owned a quarter of a million dollars' worth of property, "but I cannot subscribe to the policies of the old machine in California. In your talk tonight, you simply repeated the age-old Republican hokum without offering any program or pledge or any cleanup or change in the rotten machine which now exists in California."

Despite this criticism, Warren continued to promote a Red scare, and other fears, in attacking Sinclair during the waning days of the campaign. He endorsed the vote-purge scheme and called on federal relief officials to deny benefits that "follow the wanderer wherever he goes." Flights of rhetoric aside, Warren concentrated on the nuts and bolts of the party machinery, consulting closely with Billy Knowland. Congressional candidates continued to raise hell over the lack of funds for their campaigns. One candidate for Congress complained that Republicans had raised eighteen thousand dollars in his district, and only five hundred dollars went to his campaign. Admitting that local candidates had been shortchanged, Warren called on party workers to spend more time on these races, for if EPIC candidates won, "legislative riots" might break out. Following orders from Frank Merriam, Warren called for a massive get-out-the-vote drive as the top priority in the final days of the struggle.

Through it all, Warren worked closely with the leading Democrats-for-Merriam group in northern California, located just down the hall from his office at the Palace Hotel. When Warren sent GOP literature to the hinterlands, he always included reams of material from the Merriam Democrats. Yesterday he directed a telegram to the Republican national chairman, Henry P. Fletcher, informing him that since "our campaign is now in satisfactory condition," he should not make "partisan mention" of the California race in his nationwide broadcasts.

Words meant something, but money counted for everything, especially in this campaign, and Warren had proved to be a good provider for the anti-Sinclair Democrats. Warren had recently called on Republicans to put "our own house in order" and "attain standards of the best idealism. . . . The cheat and the trickster whether in government service or in private business must be scorned. . . . The virtues of honesty and justice and the code of worthy men and sincere citizenship must be upheld." Yet he appeared to have no qualms about funneling slush money to a political front group. Today he sent another check to his Palace Hotel neighbor J. Pendleton Wilson, head of the Merriam-Hatfield Democratic Campaign Committee, expressing the hope that with it "the problems that have confronted the fine work you are accomplishing have been solved for the balance of this campaign."

Ray Haight wasn't the only candidate who wanted Upton Sinclair out of the governor's race. Milen Dempster today called on the EPIC candidate to withdraw and deliver his votes to the Socialist party, where they belonged. "Come back to a sound Socialist platform," the SP candidate wrote in a letter to Sinclair, released today in San Francisco. "What you do now may swing the course of history. You have become a man of greater power than ever before. Now you are at the peak of that power." If Sinclair returned to the fold, Dempster argued, he would instantly make the Socialist party the second party in California and "set it on the road to go places" nationally.

Informed of Dempster's request, Sinclair laughed heartily. "I will have a million votes and Mr. Dempster has about five thousand," Sinclair observed. "If I withdrew in favor of him that would make a Herculean task of switching a million votes. I think it would be easier for Mr. Dempster to throw his votes to me." Replying to new rumors that he planned to quit in favor of Ray Haight, Sinclair declared, "I want to reiterate with enough negatives to fill a paragraph that I am not going to withdraw in favor of Haight, Merriam, Dempster or anyone else."

Despite his disappointing meeting with O'Connor and all of the other campaign hubbub, the candidate still found time at his Beverly Hills hideaway to dictate more than fifty letters. Sinclair finally resorted to boilerplate, at least for part of each letter:

> In these last days of the campaign do not let anything that you hear or see disturb you. If it is for us, it's true; if it's against us, it isn't true, and that's all there is to it. We are in this campaign to the finish. . . .

If Sinclair really wanted to pull off a political miracle, he now knew whom to call. George Baker, the New York preacher and philanthropist known to thousands of disciples as Father Divine, had sent Sinclair a lengthy letter offering to guarantee his victory. Divine, who fed thousands of poor people at his Peace Missions in Harlem and other sites, was one of America's great Negro leaders. For the past nineteen years this sharecropper's son from the South had preached the cause of integration to a needy and devoted audience on Long Island and in New York City, achieving God-like status. He campaigned for a federal antilynching bill and pressured white Harlem businessmen to hire more black workers, yet he usually stayed out of electoral campaigns. He never publicly endorsed Fiorello La Guardia in his run for mayor in 1933 but later claimed to have interceded with the Almighty on his behalf in the election.

Now he offered to do the same for Upton Sinclair, providing the candidate recognized Divine's "Ever-Presence." Divine, writing from New York, affirmed that he and Sinclair shared many of the same ideals—and this was the reason each had been attacked by organized religion. But if Sinclair, in the days ahead, openly committed himself to "cooperate with ME" in the struggle for brotherhood and social equality, "YOU CANNOT LOSE," Father Divine declared.

OCTOBER 31

WEDNESDAY

The California Supreme Court issued a writ this morning prohibiting the wholesale purging of registered voters in Los Angeles. "It is perfectly clear now that this action is a sham proceeding and a perversion of court process, absolutely void," Justice William Langdon commented, "and it can have no effect other than to intimidate and prevent eligible voters from going to the polls. It outrages every principle of justice and fair play." The vote-purge plan, endorsed by every prominent local and state Republican official as well as the president of the Los Angeles County Bar Association, attempted to "abrogate and cut off" the constitutional rights of twenty-four thousand voters, Justice Langdon observed, without notification of any kind save for "publication of this mass of names without addresses and not even in alphabetical order, on a single occasion, in a newspaper of some fifteen hundred circulation."

Democrats hailed the decision, although one EPIC leader complained that the Merriamites had succeeded in planting the idea that a voter was liable to a penalty of seven years' imprisonment "if by any chance his right to vote is challenged." Actually there was every chance that would happen. Election officials and GOP activists would personally challenge

150,000 voters at the precinct level on November 6, the Merriamites promised, despite today's court ruling. If they did that, the EPICs warned, violence was sure to follow.

———

Victorious in Sacramento, EPIC attorneys fought back along another front, aiming their fire this time at Hollywood. Already alarmed by reports that Congressman Wright Patman planned to investigate political chicanery in Hollywood, the movie executives learned today that EPIC lawyers had requested a grand jury probe into the intimidation of studio workers. Even more startling: the district attorney's office agreed to pursue the matter, providing EPIC furnished some leads.

David A. Sokol, one of the EPIC attorneys, was only too happy to oblige. He named the actress Katharine Hepburn as "an example of an employee" threatened with dismissal if she voted for Sinclair. Sokol demanded that the D.A. summon eight studio officials before the grand jury, including Winfield R. Sheehan, Carl Laemmle, Harry Cohn, Louis B. Mayer, Darryl F. Zanuck, and Jack L. Warner. Other Hollywood figures who might have a story to tell the grand jury, Sokol suggested, included Clark Gable, Douglas Fairbanks, and Will Rogers.

No subpoenas would be issued at the present time, explained Daniel Beecher, the deputy district attorney, but he announced that he was sending an investigator to question Miss Hepburn as to whether she had been "intimidated."

No one in Hollywood was more likely to speak her mind than young Kate Hepburn. It was a genetic predisposition. Because of her cultivated accent and icy demeanor and the fact that she was the daughter of a famous surgeon, Katharine Hepburn was perceived as a product of high society and conservative to the core. The stereotype, however, didn't fit. Growing up in Hartford, Connecticut, Kate was more tomboy than debutante. Her parents were well-off, and Kate did attend Bryn Mawr, but dinner-table conversations in the Hepburn household did not revolve around teas and tennis but, rather, feminism, Marxism, Fabianism, even nudism.

Her mother, Katharine Houghton, known as Kit, had a master's degree from Radcliffe and was a prominent suffragette, feminist, and birth-control advocate. Kate's father, Dr. Thomas N. Hepburn, pioneered urologic surgery as a medical specialty, established the American Social Hygiene Association, and enlisted the support of George Bernard Shaw in publishing Eugène Brieux's *Les Avariés,* a controversial play about venereal disease—later novelized by Upton Sinclair as *Damaged Goods.*

When Sinclair Lewis moved to Hartford in the early 1920s, he interviewed Tom Hepburn extensively for background material for *Arrowsmith* and took long walks with Kate. A feisty girl, Kate was tall, athletic, red-haired, and open-minded. Her childhood was gay until the day she discovered her older brother Tom hanging from the rafters in an attic. It was unclear whether his death was accident or suicide, but it caused carefree Kate to withdraw from the world and contributed to what critics would later label a "flinty" personality.

Steely determination helped Katharine Hepburn through her early years of acting. After only mild success on the New York stage, she landed her first movie role in 1932 in *A Bill of Divorcement.* Some studio executives called her "horse-faced," but she became an almost instant star, known for what one critic called her "boyish lines and the nonchalant red locks." Hepburn helped make *Little Women* a smash hit in 1933 and contributed an Oscar-winning performance to *Morning Glory.*

But 1934, by and large, was not kind to Kate. Her return to Broadway in *The Lake*—she costarred with George Creel's actress wife, Blanche Bates—was a flop, providing Dorothy Parker with the opportunity to observe that Hepburn's performance "ran the gamut of emotions from A to B." Hepburn's next movie, *Spitfire,* also fared poorly, and suspicion arose among Hollywood insiders that she was not a star in the Lombard or Garbo sense, someone who would draw fans to the movie theater on the strength of her name or her looks alone. Hepburn did a screen test for *Joan of Arc,* but the movie was shelved, partly due to the controversy surrounding the actress's recent divorce from Ludlow Ogden Smith, the stockbroker husband few in Hollywood even knew existed.

With her career stalled, criticism of Hepburn's cool manner and unconventional dress mounted. Gossip columnists referred to her as La Hepburn. One writer dryly commented that she "occasionally has human impulses and she is not all snobbery and self-satisfaction." On October 7, Louella Parsons revealed that "photographers have agreed not to take a single pix of her because she's been so rude."

Yet, if anything, Hepburn took herself less seriously than others did. When her habit of wearing men's pants caused a stir in Paris, she commented, "I couldn't be dignified if I tried." She hated reading references to Kit Hepburn as the mother of Katharine Hepburn. "My mother is important," she explained, "I am not." Kate wished she could paint, play music, or write books instead of act, but "alas, I'm not talented at all." With her friend Laura Harding she lived in an isolated home in Coldwater Canyon.

As the California governor's race heated up this autumn, Hepburn was filming *The Little Minister,* based on the J. M. Barrie play, for RKO. It was a big-budget production, and the studio expected the film to put Hepburn's career back on track. With that much invested, RKO executives could not have been pleased when rumors circulated that Kate Hepburn favored Upton Sinclair or would not pay the "Merriam tax," or both. Now the Los Angeles district attorney had sent an investigator to find out what Hepburn really believed—and whether RKO had threatened to punish her for those beliefs.

———

The other top story in Hollywood today concerned the inevitable W. R. Hearst–Louis B. Mayer divorce, sparked by irreconcilable political and commercial differences. The two powerhouses finally had their showdown over *Marie Antoinette,* and when Mayer still refused to make the film with Marion Davies as queen, Hearst took his troubles to Jack Warner. Today word came down that W.R. would soon move his Cosmopolitan studio from Culver City to Burbank.

Hearst columnist Louella Parsons called W.R.'s agreement with Warner Bros. "by far the most important motion picture deal of the year, in fact in many years." Even more excited, Jack Warner called this the "greatest forward step" for the studio since it developed talking pictures, and he praised Hearst as "the most important and uplifting influence, not only in the journalistic field but also in the motion picture industry."

Despite this rather momentous development in Hollywood, Hearst remained in San Simeon, tightly focused on his newspaper empire. Today he killed an editorial scheduled to run in the *Los Angeles Examiner* that labeled Upton Sinclair "a fanatical bigot," "an egomaniac," and "a mountebank." Hearst instructed Joseph Willicombe to notify his editors that W.R. considered Sinclair "beaten" and that continuing to abuse him in print would only create sympathy and votes for EPIC. "I would not be severe with him," Hearst told Willicombe.

———

Like W. R. Hearst, Hamilton Cotton, the state's leading anti-Sinclair Democrat, just wanted to let sleeping dogs lie. He notified the White

House that press coverage of Jefty O'Connor's activities had revived Sinclair's chances. "Best let Sinclair alone," Cotton advised. "He is badly beaten."

A short while later came this reply from James A. Farley: "I have had nothing to do with J.F.T. O'Connor's visit to California."

Farley had consulted O'Connor on his trip, of course, but Big Jim could be forgiven for forgetting. He still confronted questions, cartoons, and jokes about his famous letter endorsing Upton Sinclair. *Washington Post* columnist Carlisle Bergeron congratulated Farley this morning for agreeing to be the administration's goat in *l'affaire Sinclair* but then revealed "the plain truth" of what actually transpired. The "rubber stamp" episode was not a mistake, Bergeron disclosed. Rather, it reflected "a change of heart on the part of the Administration. It had intended to go along with Sinclair. Finally, it decided it had better not do it. Its reasons, I suppose, are manifold. And it may be significant," Bergeron observed, "that the decision not to go along was made after the authoritative information came back here that Sinclair's goose was cooked."

After a week in California, Westbrook Pegler finally warmed to his task. The man who proudly proclaimed that he was agin everyone and who loved to attack both arguments in any dispute had so far taken a decidedly one-sided approach to the governor's race, directing most of his conspicuous ire at Upton Sinclair. In today's column, however, he displayed the kind of ecumenical meanspiritedness that made him famous.

The California campaign, Pegler declared, had "developed into a spectacle such as never has been seen before in American politics. This is the first time the citizens of any community have been asked to choose between two candidates, each of whom has been denounced by leaders of his own party as no fit man for the office. . . .

"Democratic statesmen have been going around warning the citizens that their candidate, Mahatma Sinclair, does not know enough to pour paint out of a plug hat and would be sure to ruin the State if elected. Republicans, on the other hand, insist with equal enthusiasm that their man, Mr. Merriam, is a rare combination of all the qualities which make for all-around, free-style unfitness in public office and if left to himself would make one of the worst Governors in the history of the State.

"Of course, they do not plan to leave him to himself. Anyone who is at all familiar with the records of some of California's Governors of the past will realize that this bold claim on behalf of the horseshoe pitcher takes in a lot of territory. However, they know their man, and they have reason to feel confident of his qualities. Anyone who has had the privilege of a talk with Governor Merriam on important issues of the day or has studied his career will have to agree that if it is possible to outawful the worst of California's Governors up to now the old horseshoe pitcher should be the man of the hour."

Merriam, Pegler revealed, "remarked rather proudly to your correspondent that in all his years in various offices nobody ever had made an attempt to bribe him and he took this as a mark of deference to his high honor. It did not occur to him that when anyone wished to buy him that person would not go to him but to those whom George Creel described as his medieval owners. One does not buy an ox from an ox.

"Mr. Merriam not only looks the part," Pegler continued, refusing to let go of the red meat he clasped in his teeth, "but his whole career justifies the extravagant claims of those Republican statesmen who insist that he has absolutely no mind or will of his own and therefore ought to be elected. It is a strange thing to hear a political party speak thus of its candidate, but the Republicans go even further. For the first time that your correspondent is aware of there is talk of recalling a Governor from office before he has been elected in the event that he should refuse to obey the suggestions of the medieval owners referred to by Mr. Creel.

"Rather strangely, but in keeping with the generally goofy character of the present campaign, the Democratic statesmen are doing their worst to defeat Mr. Sinclair, whereas the Republicans are doing their utmost to elect a man whom they frankly acknowledge to be an unfortunate mistake in a difficult time and for whom their most enthusiastic endorsement is a frank 'Excuse it, please.' "

As so often was the case, Westbrook Pegler's commentary hit home. The *Oakland Tribune,* published by Joseph Knowland, a man widely believed to be one of Merriam's "medieval owners," found Pegler's latest column so offensive the newspaper refused to run it.

On a damp day in Los Angeles, quiet reigned on the UCLA campus the day after Dr. Ernest C. Moore suspended five radical students, but violence was in the air. A self-avowed "vigilante" group made up of campus athletes promised to rid the campus of radicalism "with force if necessary." Dr. Moore praised the formation of the group and called on university officials and organizations throughout the nation to "become active helpers of the United States in its day of difficulty." Apparently following Dr. Moore's lead, the president of the University of Santa Clara today expelled the editor of its student newspaper for insubordination and urged students at the school to "kick Communists off campus."

All fifty-seven fraternities and sororities at UCLA today came out in support of Dr. Moore's action against the five radical students. So did a group of civic leaders, including the head of the Los Angeles Chamber of Commerce and the chief of police. Up at Berkeley, however, liberal students organized a student strike starting Friday. Robert G. Sproul, president of the University of California, announced that he would travel to Los Angeles in a few days to initiate his own investigation, not having received what he called a "full explanation" from Dr. Moore.

When Frank Merriam arrived at room 622 of the Ambassador Hotel for his audience with J.F.T. O'Connor, the possibility that the White House might actually express support for his candidacy, once so farfetched it was laughable, now seemed within reach. From the events of the past week it was clear that FDR had retreated irrevocably from Sinclair, and with the EPIC candidate remaining in the race, Ray Haight was finished. For several days now, Frank Merriam had proclaimed himself a New Dealer, and Earl Warren had devised a nonpartisan closing strategy for the campaign. That set the stage for the White House to signal that California Democrats could vote for Merriam without offending FDR.

Almost immediately upon meeting O'Connor, Frank Merriam expressed his appreciation for Democratic support throughout the state. "In fact, our Republican organization was shot and the Democrats gave us our most effective leaders," he confessed, mentioning Ham Cotton by name.

O'Connor responded by saying that Merriam shouldn't take this as an endorsement of standpatism. State leaders must try new programs and "stay a step ahead of the crowd." O'Connor was surprised to find Merriam agreeing with him.

"We must do something for our people or they will take it away," Merriam said, adding that he had once told Herbert Hoover it was fortunate that the former president was defeated in 1932, "as the country needed a new kind of leadership." Merriam claimed he wanted to work closely with the New Dealers. "You can assure the President of my cooperation," he said.

The elements of a deal then emerged. "If you are elected," O'Connor said, "will you make a statement to the press of this nation that your election is not a repudiation of the Roosevelt policies, but that your election was brought about with the assistance of many of the Roosevelt leaders in California?"

"Yes," Merriam answered emphatically. He also promised that "the Democrats will not be forgotten" when it came time to dispense patronage. In fact, Merriam boasted, he had recently appointed two Democrats to the bench.

The *Bridal Call Crusader* revealed today that Aimee Semple McPherson would participate in the climactic anti-Sinclair rally Friday night at the Shrine Auditorium in Los Angeles. An organization called the Allied Churchmen had put together a program that included nearly all of the top clerics in the city, the first time in anyone's memory that Catholics, Protestants, and Jews would share a political stage. They even invited radio rabble-rouser Reverend Martin Luther Thomas. They *even* invited Aimee McPherson, whom the staid church leaders of southern California normally treated as a pariah. Not only that, they asked her to stage a full-blown pageant, *America! Awake! The Enemy Is at Your Gates!*

Upton Sinclair had made Sister Aimee respectable again. Perhaps her appearance might help erase the stain of Aimee's infamous "kidnapping." The *Bridal Call Crusader,* McPherson's weekly publication, observed that her participation in the Allied Churchmen rally revealed "the high esteem in which Sister is held in the city."

Sinclair heard the story another way. Early in the campaign a Sinclair associate apparently had called Sister Aimee and suggested that she and Uppie hold a public debate on the EPIC plan. Surprisingly, Aimee commented that she actually favored EPIC and suggested that they hold the debate at the Angelus Temple. She would pretend to oppose EPIC, then be converted and direct her followers to vote for Sinclair. Everything was an opera to Aimee McPherson.

But Aimee never set a date, and Sinclair later heard, through his sources, that "the bankers" supposedly had threatened to foreclose the mortgage on the temple if she endorsed EPIC. So she took no stand on the race. Later, according to the same sources, "the bankers" ordered her to come out against EPIC and offered her money to put on an anti-Sinclair pageant just before Election Day. Of course, this may have just been idle campaign gossip.

For whatever reason, Aimee was now involved in a big way. This Sunday, two days after the Allied Churchmen meeting, she planned to preach not one but two sermons related to the current campaign, including one entitled, "EPIC: Enemy Power Invading Christianity."

———

The Los Angeles Chamber of Commerce today virtually ordered all member businesses to close up shop on Election Day and get out the vote for Frank Finley Merriam. The Chamber had formed a unit called the All-Party Election Day Coordinating Committee, and in a letter today to local committeemen, Arthur G. Arnoll, the general manager, asked for volunteers to report to headquarters on November 6. If employers couldn't participate, they should "assign some of your employees to answer the urgent appeal."

The president of the California Real Estate Association, Robert A. Swink, called on realtors to shut their offices on Election Day and asked that "every broker and his entire staff place themselves and their automobiles at the service of Merriam for Governor headquarters." Spurred on by Francis V. Keesling of West Coast Life, insurance agents by the thousands attempted to place anti-Sinclair circulars in the hands of every policy holder in the state.

Hollywood wouldn't think of shutting down for an entire day, but the studios announced that they would suspend movie production for two hours on November 6 to encourage workers to vote. This suggested that the top brass felt confident that, one way or another, they had secured an overwhelming vote for Merriam. Just to make sure, an official at one studio posted this sign next to a time clock: IF YOU EXPECT TO PUNCH THIS A WEEK FROM NOW DON'T VOTE FOR SINCLAIR.

———

So far, Katharine Hepburn had refused to comment on the district attorney's investigation of political intimidation in Hollywood, but across the country in Hartford, Connecticut, her father, Dr. Thomas Hepburn, spoke on her behalf. It was impossible to say whether she had asked him to make an announcement or, indeed, whether he had even talked to her lately. He spoke, however, with all the authority of a father who normally kept in close contact with his children. Dr. Hepburn called reports that Kate had been "intimidated" to contribute funds to defeat Upton Sinclair "nonsense." Kate, he asserted, "has no intention of voting for Sinclair for governor of California.

"On the contrary," he added, "she will vote exactly the opposite."

Between campaign appearances, Upton Sinclair returned to his home in Beverly Hills, a more comfortable and convenient haven than the rambling house in Pasadena. Once again he took time to catch up with his mail. It was part reflex, part relaxation. Wires and letters continued to pour in, most of them urging him not only to stay in the race, but now, with George Creel against him, to discard all of his compromises and return to the original EPIC plan. Mixed in with the mail was a five-dollar campaign contribution from Paul H. Douglas, the University of Chicago economist.

Of all the setbacks that had turned certain victory into probable defeat, Upton Sinclair ranked his two-to-one drubbing in the *Literary Digest* poll at the very top, however inaccurate it might yet prove to be. Sinclair wrote the editor of the *Digest* today, not to complain that the survey targeted a disproportionate number of Republicans, but to ask when the magazine was going to pay him for an article he had submitted a while back. He also wrote to a fan in Yokohama who offered to translate the EPIC books into Japanese. And he dropped a line to David Sinclair explaining that because of the "hurly-burly" he had been unable to correspond earlier. "I have no idea," Upton Sinclair told his son six days before Election Day, "whether I am going to win or lose."

NOVEMBER 2

FRIDAY

A herd of reporters turned out for the President's press conference this morning, causing FDR to inquire why they were still hanging around Washington when they should be heading home to vote. They ought to follow *his* example, the President argued. FDR would depart tonight at eleven o'clock on a train bound for Hyde Park, where he planned to cast his ballot on Tuesday for Herbert Lehman for governor of New York.

This was the major news out of the White House today. Because New York was his home, FDR explained, he made an exception to his rule of staying out of state politics. In fact, Roosevelt had helped guide the Lehman candidacy and regularly discussed the race with Jim Farley. "Moses did a pretty good job on parks in Long Island," FDR recently informed Farley, referring to Lehman's Republican opponent, "and it might be a break if he were to get lost in one of them." Farley suggested that they take Robert Moses for a walk in Central Park and dunk him in the reservoir. Although he endorsed the Democrat in New York, FDR told reporters they would probably be amused to learn how many times he had voted for a candidate from another party. Some interpreted this as a signal to Democrats across the nation that it was permissible to vote for Hiram Johnson and the La Follette brothers, among others.

Roosevelt timed his escape from Washington wisely. Tension had flared all week at a number of pressure points. Debate continued over the question of how much money to allocate to the new public-works program in 1935. Five billion dollars still seemed to be the popular figure, but the high-level discussion, conducted more or less secretly for the past month, had turned difficult when details appeared in the press. At lunch today, the President expressed anger about leaks to the newspapers. He told Harold Ickes that some people were trying to sabotage the public-works plan and named as likely suspects businessmen who had planted informers in federal agencies.

When the President chatted with Ickes about his recent trip to California to dedicate the Hetch Hetchy water project, it was clear to Harold that FDR had swung clear away from his earlier support for Sinclair. FDR had his man, J.F.T. O'Connor, on the scene in Los Angeles to extinguish any last-minute brushfires. Jim Farley had instructed Jefty to abandon any efforts to effect a Sinclair-Haight merger. If a fusion ticket lost, "it would be worse" than Merriam winning, Farley argued.

Today when Farley told FDR about O'Connor's negotiations with Frank Merriam, the President pronounced himself entirely satisfied with Jefty's work.

John Dos Passos had enjoyed his stay in Havana. His room at the Hotel Ambos Mundos faced Morro Castle and the sea. Ernest Hemingway, who claimed to have discovered thirty-six new varieties of fish, kept Dos Passos abreast of his attempts to harpoon a humpback whale. Opponents of the dictator Batista were blowing up department stores, butcher shops, and Chinese laundries, but Dos Passos stayed on. He liked Cuban food and savored sitting in the sun on the roof of the hotel to combat his rheumatism. Soon he would sail for Key West and more of the same.

Today he wrote his friend Edmund Wilson to express appreciation for his recent essay on Anatole France, although Dos Passos doubted that the late French writer deserved as much space as Wilson had devoted to him. "At least," Dos observed, "nobody will ever have to bring him up again in our lifetime—and I hope that goes for Joseph Conrad too. . . ."

According to Dos Passos, the world might not hear much more about Upton Sinclair either. "Looks like Uppie was slipping in California—obviously he didn't sell out," he told Wilson.

> I guess nobody'll go around anymore saying they are out to abolish poverty—it's too patently kicking the props out from under the capitalist system—It makes a pretty bunch of two timing jellyfish out of Farley/Roosevelt/Creel—swine I call 'em. AAA ought to pay mothers not to raise boys like that.

Albert Parker had mailed Whitney Debevoise a copy of the latest *EPIC News,* and it threw the young attorney into a rage. One article referred to Debevoise as the "New York financier active in political manipulation" who had originated the vote-purge "plot." The wire services picked up on it, and so Debevoise's name was covered with dirt in nearly all forty-eight states. Now California's top court had labeled the disenfranchisement scheme a sham, even a "perversion." Debevoise couldn't appeal that decision or mail protests to hundreds of newspapers, but he could reply to the *EPIC News.*

So Debevoise wired editor Rube Borough, informing him that he was neither financier nor manipulator. "Am American citizen," he related, "interested in honest ballot as essential under any system, EPIC or otherwise." He explained his involvement in the California case this way: "On request from Parker indicating fair election threatened by illegal registrations I relayed to him methods used here to fight vote frauds. Only voters [who] know their registrations illegal could be intimidated by secret indictments."

Then Debevoise, displaying his Harvard Law training, turned the whole case around. "Had not realized," he observed, "any candidate anywhere these days willing [to] lend open support to illegal voting." The *EPIC News* article, he said, "unintentionally gives this impression. Do you tolerate and rely on illegal and fraudulent voting, and what are you doing to fight it?" Debevoise asked Borough to print his telegram in full in his next issue. Then he wired a copy of it to Albert Parker in Los Angeles and advised him to "use this as you see fit."

It was four days before Election Day, but the first vote in the California governor's race had already been tabulated. According to published reports, a seventy-three-year-old gentleman named Ivan Benbow Hobson, who was visiting North Carolina, phoned a court clerk back home in Los Angeles to say that he was mailing his absentee ballot, and "it's against that fellow Sinclair." Appropriately, he did not mention which candidate he had voted *for*.

Despite Merriam's early lead, his supporters grew nervous. Attempting to halt an anti-Merriam backlash, Earl Warren and W. R. Hearst pleaded for emotional restraint, but their appeals fell on deaf ears. The GOP had fomented so much frenzy it was impossible to curtail it. "A reign of unreason bordering on hysteria has this sprawling city in its grip as the nation's ugliest campaign approaches zero hour," Max Stern, star Scripps-Howard correspondent, observed today in Los Angeles. The stop-Sinclair movement, he wrote, "has become a phobia, lacking humor, fairness and even a sense of reality. Here one feels himself dwelling in a beleaguered town with the enemy pounding at the gates."

Planes flew over downtown L.A. dropping leaflets and circulars. Representatives of a nonexistent New Citizens' Cooperative Relief Committee passed out pamphlets calling for donations of clothing, food, money, and living space for 1.5 million indigents expected to arrive in Los Angeles within a few days of Sinclair's victory. The number of United for California radio shows listed in the *Los Angeles Times* peaked at fourteen today, including an address by prosperous Los Angeles attorney Goodwin J. Knight.

The anti-Sinclair forces deluged downtown Los Angeles with "Thunder Over California" leaflets showing a Russian figure waving a tattered red flag with hundreds of bums trailing close behind him. EPIC artists grabbed some samples, pasted the face of Frank Merriam over the Russian's, and inserted pictures of babies under his feet.

Kathleen Norris, perhaps California's favorite novelist, rallied to the Republican cause. "The election of Sinclair," she said, "would be a blow from which California would take years upon years to recover." Look how the Nazis were soiling Germany's reputation, she added. The *San Francisco Chronicle* reported, without sarcasm, that a local man named Charles Smith was attempting to organize the biggest Merriam club of all. "To become a member," the newspaper announced, "your name must be Smith," adding that it wasn't too late for the Johnsons, Browns, and Joneses of the state to form their own Merriam clubs.

Ray Haight, now resentful, predicted that "blood will flow" no matter which side won on Tuesday and called on President Roosevelt to prepare to send federal troops to California to prevent civil war.

Despite Merriam's apparent strength—betting odds on the incumbent shot up to three to one—speculation in the press focused on an EPIC comeback. Sinclair was "thundering down the stretch," a Los

Angeles *Daily News* columnist noted. "He may not win, but it's going to be too close for comfort." Other newspapers detected simmering anti-Merriam sentiment because of the Parker "terror" letter and the vote-purge case. According to one report, detectives investigating charges of coercion questioned workers at one large company and found that 60 percent of those wearing Merriam buttons planned to vote for Sinclair.

An L.A. attorney named Frank C. Hoyt distributed a booklet describing the boomerang effect of various acts of coercion. The stories were by now familiar: sixty workers in Long Beach forced to plaster Merriam stickers on their car windshields; an employee of a large utility ordered to supply the names of twenty-three prospective Merriam voters or lose his job; a man who worked for an oil company compelled to contribute one dollar of his wages each week to the Merriam fund. What these individuals all had in common, according to Hoyt, was that secretly they still favored Sinclair.

Variety, no friend of Sinclair, reported today that gamblers were lying low on the election, citing conflicting poll results. "Downtown Spring Street mob and Hollywood sure-thing boys," *Variety* observed, "are keeping their purse strings taut." Radio station KNX reported several calls from listeners asking for the names of bookmakers offering three-to-one odds on Merriam, because they wanted to bet on Sinclair. A local auto dealer claimed he would bet a grand on the EPIC candidate. One group of citizens raised fourteen hundred dollars to wager on Uppie. The mood at EPIC headquarters in Los Angeles remained upbeat. Turner Catledge of *The New York Times* had to push and shove his way through a group of zealots to even get through the door.

Earl Warren warned Republicans about a sudden surge for Sinclair. "We appear to be close to the goal line, but there has been many an upset in the last quarter," the GOP chief said today. "We must beware of an opposition that is resourceful and capable in all the political arts. Eleventh-hour stunts are to be expected. Look out for the little poison pamphlet designed to mislead and to appeal to this prejudice and that."

Sinclair insisted that victory was now within reach. Donations from Hollywood stars, protesting studio strong-arm tactics, would allow him to quadruple his radio budget in the final days. "I am entirely cheerful about the campaign," he explained, "and will be the same on election night regardless of whether the results justify the *Literary Digest* or our own precinct canvassers."

Announcing a new policy, Sinclair said he would no longer answer questions from reporters, since newspapers insisted on misquoting, libeling, or ridiculing him. He would reply only to written questions, and the answers likewise would appear on paper. When the United Press submitted four queries, Sinclair composed a two-page response.

"If I were going to be embittered," he wrote, responding to one question, "it would have happened long ago. This campaign is just a somewhat larger dose of the same medicine which I have been swallowing all my life." If he lost, he would attribute it to the inability of people to tell the difference between lies and truth "when the lies have several million dollars behind them to promote their circulation." But, having done his best, he had a clear conscience "and shall rest upon the verdict of history."

Asked about his personal feelings, Sinclair declared that "defeat would be more pleasant than victory. I have offered to do a long, tiresome, dangerous and exhausting job, not because of any trace of personal ambition in my make-up, but in a mood of self-sacrifice, seeing a crisis and understanding it and offering the people the benefit of that understanding if they want it. If they do not want it I shall wake up on the morning of November 7 a writer of books. But all our people are confident that we are going to win; so I am in the position of a man on shipboard who sits and waits until he finds out whether the ship is going to sail or whether he is going back on shore."

Sinclair's written dialogue with another reporter went like this:

"Will you stick in the campaign to the end?"

"Our people would cut my throat if I deserted them."

"If defeated, will you retire from politics or again seek public office?"

"Our movement will go on. I personally am too vulnerable as a candidate. Will promote others."

"Will you drop EPIC?"

"Certainly not; the people will keep it going, for it is the way out."

"Do you have any hope that your EPIC program eventually will figure prominently in national politics?"

"Yes, certainly; it will take the entire West by 1936."

"What is your attitude toward President Roosevelt, and the administration as a whole, since both declined to address the voters in your behalf?"

"President Roosevelt is a great and wise man, a far wiser political leader than I am. He wants to carry this election, and I want him to, and I am a very small episode in the national problem. EPIC will come later."

His heavy lifting over, Jefty O'Connor swung into the fun part of his trip to California. There were movie stars to meet, not the least of whom was Elissa Landi, a socialite actress. And now that the Sinclair-Haight merger scare had passed, leading Democrats in the state wanted to thank Jefty for throwing in with Merriam.

Over breakfast with three prominent anti-Sinclair Democrats, O'Connor suggested they publicly state that their party owed the GOP a favor: many wise Republicans had bolted their party in 1932 to embrace FDR, and now the Democrats should pay off this debt by voting for Merriam. The three Democrats liked the idea and said they would use it in statewide radio addresses.

Then O'Connor visited *The County Chairman* set at Fox and lunched with Will Rogers. Jefty told Will that in college he had acted in the play on which the film was based. They talked about O'Connor's pet idea: limiting presidents to one six-year term. Will said he had favored that for a long time. The entire studio seemed to be for Merriam, O'Connor observed, but Will Rogers continued to reserve judgment.

Returning to his law office in the Title Insurance Company Building, O'Connor dictated a three-page letter to Marvin McIntyre, Jim Farley, and Henry Morgenthau marked VERY CONFIDENTIAL. Assessing the "Sinclair situation," O'Connor declared that never in the history of California "has there been such a united press against one individual." All the papers "with the exception of one little paper in Chino" opposed Sinclair. Churches, radio stations, business interests, and the "most prominent Roosevelt leaders in the State" were united against Sinclair. "The entire movie organization, which is a terrific power, and has raised $150,000—and I know this to be a fact—has thrown their whole weight against him."

Jefty's conversation with Frank Merriam on Wednesday held "tremendous significance in relation to the National Administration," he boasted. "My most important work on this trip was what we can expect if Merriam is elected governor." A Merriam victory, however, meant the Democrats would have to rebuild their party "from the bottom" after the election.

Now that FDR's course was set, it was time for reflection, possibly regret. "We missed the greatest opportunity in the history of California in having a Democratic governor and putting the State 100% under the Roosevelt banner," O'Connor complained. The President's popularity remained sky-high in California, Jefty observed, "and these people and other voters would have been extremely happy to vote for any man who had the enthusiastic endorsement of our great leader."

———

As was customary, Will Rogers tapped out tommorrow's column right on the set at the Fox studio during his lunch break. "Just had a long chat with Mr. O'Connor, Comptroller of the Currency, who is a mighty big man in the Roosevelt administration," Rogers wrote. "He is out here to vote? 'Yeah,' and try and do a couple of other little odd chores for the boys back at the big county seat. . . ."

———

Five thousand University of California students showed up at the entrance to the Berkeley campus to protest the suspension of five radical students at UCLA. Dick Criley, an EPIC worker who helped organize the protest, mounted the balustrade at Sather Gate and attempted to speak, but his voice was drowned out by jocks and fraternity leaders who had assembled at the front of the crowd. The football players were truly menacing. Coach Bill Ingram had mobilized a squad of players over the summer to serve as strikebreakers in San Francisco, so obviously they knew no fear.

Criley invited one of the hecklers to speak, but he disappeared into the crowd amid cries of "Yellow! Yellow!" Another took Criley up on his offer and addressed the assembly. "I don't know what this is about," he said, "but I'm against it."

Then Criley started to speak. "Fellow students," he said, stopping in midsentence to duck a flying tomato. The next speaker, an earnest young woman, refused to duck, and soon she was drenched in tomato juice as the scene turned ugly. Watching the incident from Telegraph Avenue across the street, a Berkeley merchant ran back to his store, grabbed an American flag, carried it to one of the leftist leaders, and said, "Hold this next to your speaker, because I think *you* represent Americanism."

This didn't stop the tomato throwing, and soon the flag, too, was drenched in red. This rallied some members of the crowd to the protesters' side and also provoked a number of fistfights. Finally the crowd dispersed, and the strike committee left for a meeting with the university president, Robert Gordon Sproul.

A few hours later, two students—one of them active in the anti-Communist crusade on campus—reported that someone had just fired shots at them in front of International House. The bullets apparently only grazed them.

Six thousand Angelenos packed the Shrine Auditorium this evening for the Allied Churchmen rally, perhaps the greatest ecumenical gathering in the city's history. "The church is nonpartisan in politics," Bishop Charles Edward Locke said in opening the program, "but now it is aroused because of the vociferous and blasphemous attacks made upon it by Upton Sinclair." Another speaker stated the theme of the rally in almost biblical terms: "Defeat Upton Sinclair so badly he will leave the state in shame."

It was part church service, part Ziegfeld Follies. Edgar Magnin of the Wilshire Boulevard Temple—"the rabbi to the stars," whose temple congregation was the wealthiest in the nation—shared the spotlight with the slightly disreputable reverends Gustav Briegleb and Martin Luther Thomas. Irvin Cobb, next to Will Rogers the nation's most popular humorist, told a few anti-Sinclair jokes. The Bilbrew Jubilee Singers parodied a spiritual, reminding the crowd that "All God's Chillun Got Votes." A Presbyterian pastor insisted that there was only one excuse for preachers' taking part in a political election: "We stand at Armageddon and we battle for the Lord." Then, as the curtain parted and an orchestra played, it was time for one of Aimee Semple McPherson's illustrious pageants. . . .

It began with Pilgrims in period costume landing at Plymouth to found a nation based on religious freedom. Then a change of scenery, as the Founding Fathers composed the Constitution. When the Civil War came, President Lincoln got down on his knees and prayed to God for guidance. Then the mood onstage turned sinister. Mobs roamed the streets. Aliens excised the words "In God We Trust" from a huge dollar bill and blotted out the words of the national anthem with red paint.

The U.S. Capitol, built on sturdy stones labeled GOVERNMENT, ORDER, FAITH, AND HOME, with the American flag flying proudly atop its dome, materialized on stage. But alas, while Miss Liberty dozed on the Capitol steps, Satan snuck past, and with a diabolical grin and jeering laugh, he chiseled out the foundation stone marked FAITH. A Communist extracted the HOME stone and scampered off, and it seemed that the entire foundation would be stolen while America slept.

But then, with a piercing cry, an avenging angel, dressed all in white, her golden hair shining, paraded on stage. "America! Awake!" she shouted in a familiar, musical voice. "The enemy is at your gates! They have penetrated your walls! America! You are in danger! An enemy power is penetrating your strongholds! There is death in their hands. Defend your own!" Awakening, Miss Liberty rubbed her eyes, recognized the danger, and unsheathed the sword of Faith. She drove Satan from the Capitol as Uncle Sam shackled the Bolshevik and handed him a ticket back to Russia. . . .

At the conclusion, the Shrine Auditorium audience—Jews, Catholics, and Protestants alike, many of whom under normal circumstances considered the yellow-haired angel, Aimee Semple McPherson, something of a buffoon—roared their approval. "Is America in the market for a new flag?" Sister Aimee responded, stepping front and center, not quite finished. She reached out to catch two ropes. Slowly she lowered the Stars and Stripes and raised a Communist flag.

"Do we want that Red flag?" she inquired. "Do we want it with all that it means—intolerance, atheism, licentiousness, rebellion, annihilation, anarchism?" The audience leaned forward, breathless, some shouting, "No, no!" and then with a dramatic sweep Sister Aimee pulled the Stars and Stripes to the top of the mast while lowering the Red flag to obscurity.

"No! Never shall another flag take the place of Old Glory!" Sister Aimee shouted to wild approval. "Our forefathers poured out their blood to protect it—and we will pour out our votes to maintain its integrity!"

Outside the Shrine Auditorium, a small prayer group carrying signs protesting preachers' taking part in politics watched silently as Uncle Sam, still in costume, emerged from the auditorium to purchase popcorn from a vendor.

It was another banner night for the revived EPIC campaign. The largest crowd in local memory, nine thousand strong, jammed the Civic Auditorium in Pasadena—"my pious home city," as Upton Sinclair put it.

Organizers turned away six thousand more, and when a thousand disappointed EPICs refused to leave, Sinclair came out to address them from the front steps.

Inside he spoke in a spirited, mocking way that harkened back to the high-flying days of September. "I've had a lot of laughs out of the elderly statesman they've put up against me," he confessed. "While denouncing my 'communism' he suddenly found that peaches were rotting on the ground in the north. He begged the growers to donate the fruit to be canned for the unemployed. If he were not so stout, so rosy, and so good-looking, you would have thought it was Upton Sinclair!"

Turning serious, Sinclair revealed, with thrilling specificity, that he had received information that "two hundred and eight experienced gangsters" had been imported from New York to fix the election. The scheme allegedly involved substituting stuffed ballot boxes for real ones just before the votes were counted on Tuesday.

After orating a while longer, Sinclair examined a note from his wife. "Mrs. Sinclair says the people are becoming tired," he explained. The crowd's roar pleaded, *Go on!*

"It's your poverty, not mine," he continued. "If you elect Merriam I'll again be a writer. I won't need to think about what Pasadena thinks of me. I can go back to that blessed state of not being recognized on the streets." Then he threw down the gauntlet. Sinclair explained that he had argued long and hard with H. L. Mencken about the wisdom and true nature of "the people." For twenty-five years, Sinclair said, "I have been Mencken's prize boob because I believed in you. Now," he said, "we shall find out which of us is right."

NOVEMBER 3

SATURDAY

The train from Washington arrived in Highland, New York, at half past eight carrying an unusually small party from the White House: Marvin McIntyre, two secretaries, and the President of the United States. Since FDR planned to do little more than rest and vote, he required little staff support. An automobile whisked the President over the misty Hudson River and across frost-covered hills to Hyde Park, where Sara Delano Roosevelt, as was her custom, greeted her son at the doorstep of her home.

Clearly FDR was leaving the last-minute politicking to the able James A. Farley, who remained behind in Washington. Farley issued a formal statement on Democratic prospects, which clashed violently with the assessment of his counterpart, Henry P. Fletcher, the GOP national chairman, who claimed the New Deal was "on the way out." To prepare the President for a huge celebration on the evening of November 6, Farley composed a private memo.

"I am going right out on a limb now," Farley related, "and make some very radical predictions as to what is going to happen next Tuesday," even though it might give the President a chance to "have a lot of fun kidding me" if the results did not turn out as planned. He maintained that not a single Democratic incumbent in the Senate would lose and that the party would pick up several new seats. Farley seemed pleased that the Democrats now had a better-than-even chance of unseating Senator Bronson Cutting of New Mexico, a progressive Republican—and a Sinclair supporter—whom many New Dealers favored.

"As far as governors are concerned," Farley observed, "I believe we are all right in most of the states," and he proceeded to tick off some of the highlights, including a possible triumph over Floyd Olson, the Farmer-Labor incumbent in Minnesota (a self-proclaimed "radical").

> As to the California situation—I do not know whether to give it to you, McAdoo or back to the Indians. As far as that state is concerned, I refuse to predict. Seriously, the slump in the Sinclair vote is likely to affect some of our congressional nominees, although they may be able to weather the storm. If we lose any congressional seats at all, it will be for other causes than Sinclair.

———

The tenth and final Westbrook Pegler column from California appeared this morning in newspapers around the country. After bashing Sinclair and Merriam with equal force for a solid week, Pegler closed with something of a tribute to the man he called the Mahatma. Like a block of granite left out in the sun, Pegler had warmed toward Sinclair in recent days. He allowed that Sinclair often spoke the truth, and because of that he should never have run for office. Wasn't there a story in the papers once about a girl who rammed an engagement ring down the barrel of a gun and fired it at her philandering fiancé?

"Any man who ever undertakes to tell the people the truth about themselves," Pegler observed, "should forever renounce his hope of public office. Mr. Sinclair should know that the people, the chronic joiners, the men who march in parades wearing feather duster hats, tripping over tin swords or the hems of nightshirts, will never forgive a man who derides their foolishness. He ought to know that he could not tell even half of the truth about the history of Stanford University and expect to receive the votes of the Stanford alumni, who are now an influential element, seeded into the citizenship of California."

The only thing Pegler found surprising and regrettable was that Sinclair had denied, or at least moderated, many of his cherished beliefs, thereby "stooping to be that which he always held to be the most loathsome creature on earth, a 'practical,' which means a compromising, politician." Sinclair, he said, might have won more votes if he had simply had the political gumption to admit, "Yes, I said it" or "I wrote it" and then added, "It goes as it lays." He should have tried to instruct the Catholics and the American Legion and the Stanford alumni instead of attempting to entice them.

"There is no doubting that he loves them more than his opponents do," Pegler explained, "and that he has logic and honesty on his side in many of the arguments, which he is now trying to hush up. But there are arguments which Mr. Sinclair can never win. He licked himself with his own typewriter many years ago and it is sad to see a crusader recant and trim for the sake of the votes of people he may love much but whom he respects but little."

But at least, Pegler remarked, in concluding his memorable California saga, Upton Sinclair had thrown such a fear of revolution into the complacent Republicans that they "now realize that they had better be good—or else."

Just when it appeared that the screen campaign against Upton Sinclair had dimmed, *California Election News,* No. 3, arrived in movie theaters this weekend. The most partisan movie short yet, it represented a breakthrough in political advertising on film, discarding the pretense of objectivity in favor of a naked appeal to the emotions.

"Ladies and gentlemen," narrator Carey Wilson began as a train pulled into a station in Niland, California, "your Inquiring Cameraman decided to look into this much-discussed situation of the unemployed of the United States flocking to California." A Colton sign appeared. "Let's see what we can see in actual scenes. . . ."

The movie short, directed by MGM's Felix Feist, Jr., under instructions from Irving Thalberg, unfolded in documentary style. This was no man-in-the-street survey but a hard-hitting exposé of the "bums' rush." Many moviegoers had read about the hobo influx or seen it captured in photographs. Experiencing it in the movie theaters, where horrific images leapt off a huge screen, was something else again.

First to appear on camera was a Mr. Healey, who identified himself as a switchman at the Southern Pacific yard at Colton. He claimed that every freight train coming into Colton carried about two hundred transients with it. "What kind of fellas are these men?" the narrator asked. "Well, they're men of all classes," the switchman replied. "Only last week I pointed out to the chief of police in Colton two men who were wanted in Yuma for burglary."

Then a local constable, a short man with a hat and bushy mustache, appeared in front of a government quarantine station, where officials inspected every car coming into that part of California. He reported "quite an increase in traffic lately." "Why is that?" the narrator innocently asked. The constable struggled to remember his lines: "They say that—they read in the papers—that California's going to be—cleared of poverty and—and they're going to get something for nothing."

Next to testify: a local judge, dressed in a white, open-collared shirt and white hat, filmed against a backdrop of a freight pulling into a train yard. He had lived in Niland for nine years, and "this situation is far beyond anything I've experienced. Since last August when conditions were improving this hobo situation has gradually grown worse." What kind of men were these tramps? "I consider most of them have radical ideas," the judge insisted, "some communist. If they stay in California, I don't know what will become of the working man." Then Russell Bevans, the state motor vehicles official who had been widely quoted in the newspapers lately, cited figures, unconfirmed by anyone else, that the number of arrivals had tripled recently and marked an increase of one hundred thousand over the previous year.

Interviewing over, Carey Wilson introduced a rush of images of indigents riding the rails. The first clip showed a couple of dozen tramps, or perhaps actors, walking along a train track directly toward the camera, some stopping to pose. "Because of the tremendous importance to you Californians of this influx of visitors," Wilson said, "your Inquiring Cameraman went even as far as Phoenix, Arizona." A federal relief administrator in Arizona had declared that so many people were heading west they had to feed an additional one thousand people a day. "Your Inquiring Cameraman," Wilson revealed, "interviewed *thirty* who said they were on their way to California to spend the winter and remain there permanently if the EPIC plan went into effect."

The images came rapidly now. Some might actually have been filmed at a rail yard: men running to catch a freight or jumping off. Others appeared to come from feature films; they might have been outtakes from *Wild Boys of the Road.* Less grainy than the other footage, these film clips portrayed men climbing up the sides of moving freight trains or reclining on the roofs. "They ride the boxcars, they ride the gondolas—not the kind of gondolas you float the canals of Venice in—but these boys don't seem to care," the narrator said, "because they're California bound." One of the bums on the screen waved to the camera.

"When they're not living on trains most of them live in jungles," the Inquiring Cameraman continued. "A jungle is a hobo camp"—not to mention the title of a famous book. "And now we're going to give you a real inside view, an actual interview in a genuine hobo jungle. Look at them," Carey Wilson advised, as close-up portraits of hoboes—or movie extras—appeared. Some of the men smoked cigarettes, others chatted or washed out their clothes. "Listen to them," he added, "and *think.*"

Suddenly it was night, and fifteen travelers were huddled around a campfire. It could have been a scene from the Wild West, but it was just a hobo jungle—or a movie set. "You fellas come a long way?" our Inquiring Cameraman asked. "Yeah!" "Where?" "Texas . . . Pennsylvania . . . Montana . . . New *Joisey.*"

"What are you doing out here, bud?" the narrator asked one middle-aged tramp.

"That's my business, pardner," he replied, but others, much younger, played along.

"Out here for the climate."

"I'm just riding."

"I know someone who is going to give us all a job."

One young man, not much more than a teenager, with blond, wavy hair, made an attempt at humor but stumbled over the punch line. He must have ad-libbed it earlier off camera, or more likely, it was written for him. Perhaps Carey Wilson, that wryly comic scriptwriter, couldn't resist ending the *California Election News* series on a purely Hollywood note. Explaining why he was headed for Los Angeles, the young tramp said: "I hear U.S.C. needs a quarterback."

At a United for California committee meeting this morning, Albert Parker read the letter of protest Whitney Debevoise had just sent to the *EPIC News.* The committee agreed it was masterly but felt they shouldn't publicize it themselves, as the less said about the entire vote-purge affair at this point the better. "This is not an especially courageous position to take," Parker explained in a letter to Debevoise this afternoon, "but it is probably the only prudent one, since the election seems to be fairly well in the bag."

Parker apologized for unwittingly injecting Debevoise's good name into such a "vicious mud-slinging contest." The whole affair was "rather bad altogether," since his wife was pregnant, and she "has been worried about my physical safety." But revenge would be sweet. Merriam might demolish Sinclair, and Parker promised to see to it that the fanatic who filched the copy of his October 20 letter from his files would never become a certified public accountant. "I think that to be my plain duty," Albert Parker declared.

Rob Wagner published his last *Script* before Election Day, and true to his word, he remained on the sidelines of the governor's race, waiting for the fires to burn themselves out. In an editorial entitled "Darkness before Dawn," Wagner praised his friend Uppie for shooting the most gorgeous oratorical fireworks the country had ever seen but lamented that the campaign had turned into a brawl. By next week, he predicted, "you'll all be breathing easier and *Script* can go on its jaunty way, kidding this and that and behaving like its own foolish self."

Actually, Wagner got a jump on frivolity in this issue, presenting a scoop on the new Chaplin picture. Wagner revealed, based on inside information from his buddy Charlie, that he was shooting from a script for the first time, had created his biggest and most expensive sets (there were twenty-four in all, and one cost sixty thousand dollars), and had tried to comply with the NRA, working on a schedule of six-hour days and five-day weeks. "It is," Wagner reported, "the biggest, most original and funniest picture he's ever made—Charlie jousting agin the monsters of a regimented machine age!"

Script also provided what it called a Chaplin beauty note: instead of blackening his hair each morning on the set, the fair-haired genius finally had it dyed. Since he hated to appear in public looking anything remotely like the Little Tramp, this pushed Charlie even further into social eclipse than before. "When the day's work is done, he jumps into his car, baggy trousers, big shoes and all," Wagner disclosed, "and beats it home to wash up. What an eyeful he'll give the crowd if he gets into a traffic jam!"

As Election Day neared, threats of violence increased, according to organizers in all camps. Frank Merriam now traveled with bodyguards, an unusual practice for politicians not named Long. Police protected EPIC headquarters in San Francisco after opponents smashed windows and slashed the tires of campaign workers' cars. In a radio address, Upton Sinclair claimed that "society people are throwing pillows at one another in the drawing rooms," arguing over whether Sinclair lived "in a harem or not."

William Kerr, the state's registrar of voters, derided Upton Sinclair's charge last night in Pasadena that gangsters from New York planned to substitute stuffed ballot boxes for real ones. This hoary practice was used, he explained, back in the days when ballots were shipped to a central station to be tabulated; partisans of one side or another could switch ballot boxes en route. But now, he said, ballot boxes "cannot be stuffed in California," because the votes were counted right at the polling place. "Any citizen," he added, "may be present at any voting place before six o'clock next Tuesday morning and make sure the ballot box is empty."

After four solid days of drizzle, it was apparent that the rainy season had arrived in San Francisco. Frank Merriam met with Earl Warren during his last day in the north and reported that he was more encouraged than ever that he would triumph on Tuesday. The *San Francisco Chronicle* praised the governor for presenting his program in a dignified manner while his opponent, who had a messiah complex, tossed restraint to the wind. The *Oakland Tribune* sounded the GOP's new theme. Warning that the EPICs were certain to turn out in frightening numbers, Joe Knowland's newspaper called on Merriam partisans to flock to the polls to take a stand against "freakishness" in California.

Earl Warren received a note from J. Pendleton Wilson, head of San Francisco's leading Democrats-for-Merriam group, thanking him for arranging another payment from the GOP slush fund. This would enable local Democats to continue their anti-Sinclair activities "unimpaired" right through Election Day. Wilson closed on a whimsical note, predicting that when his party nominated "some Red" for president in 1936, he and Earl would collaborate "as pleasantly as we have in this campaign."

Another one of Frank Merriam's prime supporters, lobbyist Arthur Samish, resurfaced with an upbeat note to his network of political associates. California's "secret boss" had raised perhaps two hundred thousand dollars for Merriam, but as was his wont, he had operated behind the scenes and let others stick their out necks in public. Because the state legislature was his personal fiefdom, Artie cared more about the senate and assembly races anyway. ("To hell with the governor," Artie often boasted, "I own the legislature.") Today, however, he mailed postcards to his thousands of friends, calling on them to work hard right up to November 6 to make Merriam's victory so huge it would show the world that California would "never permit the invasion of communist propaganda."

A realtor named Philip Norton expressed confidence in a Merriam victory in quite a different way. Norton placed ads in Los Angeles newspapers predicting that the election results would clear the way for one of the greatest home-building booms Los Angeles had ever seen. Norton offered forty lots in Brentwood, some for as low as $750. After Tuesday, he stated, "the boulevards will be filled with cars full of people on their way to select lots," so speculators should act NOW while the market was still Sinclair-depressed. "Select your lot," he advised, "pay a returnable deposit and if Sinclair is elected, take back your money!"

Although two full days remained until November 6, the Sinclair campaign climaxed today in a wonderfully representative way: an ambitious series of grass-roots rallies. EPICs gathered this evening at auditoriums in Bakersfield, Fresno, Sacramento, and San Francisco, with Sinclair himself appearing at Olympic Auditorium in Los Angeles. Promoters staged prizefights in this arena, so Sinclair, quite fittingly, would speak from the boxing ring in the center. The miracle of modern radio would transmit his remarks to EPIC supporters gathered in other cities and to a statewide radio audience.

A. P. Giannini had failed Sinclair, but Uppie's friend, oil heiress Aline Barnsdall, had come through with the ten thousand dollars necessary to rent the halls in Los Angeles and San Francisco and pay for enough radio time to attempt one last turning of the tide. Barnsdall was one of Sinclair's most conspicuous supporters. She lived just off Hollywood Boulevard in the famous Hollyhock House, designed by Frank Lloyd Wright in a pre-Columbian style. (Sinclair considered the house bizarre and laughed whenever Aline complained that the roof leaked or the furniture was uncomfortable.) Like Uppie's other wealthy benefactor, Kate Crane-Gartz, Barnsdall had recently been labeled a "parlor pink" by James E. Davis, the L.A. police chief. Barnsdall responded by erecting huge EPIC billboards on her property, facing the boulevard.

The EPICs in Los Angeles kicked off their program at eight-thirty, singing "The Star-Spangled Banner" as technicians trained a spotlight on an American flag raised over the arena. That took care of the charge that Sinclair was a Communist, or so the organizers hoped. Then Sinclair, standing in the boxing ring facing one quarter of the crowd at a time, read the Twenty-third Psalm, to prove that he was not an atheist. Then he said, "Take it away, Bakersfield!" and the radio show shot north. Subsequently it marched up the state, to Fresno, to Sacramento, and finally to Dreamland in San Francisco, where Sheridan Downey took over. Then back to Los Angeles, where Sinclair held forth for another fifteen minutes. The EPICs at each location cheered like crazy, scenting sweet victory on Tuesday.

"We still have a chance to settle our problems with ballots instead of bullets," Sinclair explained. "It may be the last chance. The issue of this campaign is: can they fool you with their lies, and get you to vote in their interest instead of in your own?" Sinclair finished the speech as he had closed so many others during the past fourteen months. "It's up to you!" he said, cheerful but resigned.

Disturbances broke out tonight at dozens of motion-picture theaters following screenings of the latest Inquiring Cameraman short. Patrons scuffled among themselves, and EPIC supporters, who thought they had seen the worst of the screen campaign already, stormed box offices to demand refunds or insist that house managers pull the offending trailers from their schedules. Near-riots were reported in several locations.

NOVEMBER 4

SUNDAY

On this last Sunday before Election Day, *The New York Times* published no fewer than five articles on the California campaign, ranging from political prognostication to Hollywood gossip. In an account of the movie-industry crusade against Sinclair, *Times* correspondent Douglas Churchill described Los Angeles as one huge movie set where studios filmed anti-EPIC trailers and newsreels every day. "Low paid 'bit' players are said to take the leading roles in most of these 'newsreels,' " Churchill revealed, "particularly where dialogue is required. People conversant with movie personnel claim to have recognized in them certain aspirants to stardom."

Having spent a week in California, Turner Catledge confidently predicted a Merriam victory by two hundred thousand votes. Still, he found sober elements in California worried about the future, apparently fearing that the election signaled the start of a vicious class war. Victorious or not, Sinclair would be the man "to whom nearly 1,000,000 people turned in their stress and who were led by him into the first serious movement against the profit system in the United States," Catledge observed.

Had Sinclair stopped with the enunciation of his principles, he could not have been halted in his march to the governor's chair, Catledge explained, but he went into method and this proved his undoing. Yet Sinclair's defeat might actually add impetus to his crusade. Defeat would fuel his persecution complex, according to Catledge, and it would leave him free to tear down the government from outside rather than having to shoulder the responsibilities of governing.

Shortly after dawn, the *Lady Southern Cross* emerged from the offshore fog a full two hours ahead of schedule, completing perhaps the greatest flight since Lindbergh's Atlantic crossing. Thousands who intended to greet the blue monoplane at Oakland Airport were still asleep when it arrived. The famed aviator Sir Charles Kingsford-Smith shattered all Pacific flying records, hopping from Australia to California in fifty-one hours, needing only fifteen hours to cover the last 2,408-mile leg from Hawaii. "Please, a cigarette," Sir Charles muttered into a microphone as he prepared to climb out of the cockpit. Five hours later, a crowd of ten thousand waved good-bye when the *Lady Southern Cross* lifted off, bound for Los Angeles.

Rejecting Raymond L. Haight's last-minute appeal, William Randolph Hearst issued his final statement on the California governor's race today. Haight, in a letter to Hearst, had charged that Frank Merriam's election "solves nothing" and predicted that Sinclairism would ultimately "sweep the entire nation, leaving in its wake a destroyed liberalism. . . ." Replying privately to Haight today, W. R. Hearst expressed exactly the opposite view, suggesting that if a hack like Merriam could stop Sinclair, EPIC had no future whatsoever.

Tuesday's vote, Hearst maintained, "will show that while it is easily possible to defeat a reactionary candidate with a sound progressive, it is not possible to accomplish this with a political psychopathic case." EPIC's defeat would be infinitely educational, not in the manner Sinclair imagined, "but by teaching the politicians that the American people in the last analysis are always sound and sane and judicious. They will not follow will o' wisps into economic quagmires. They will not allow the pied pipers of politics to lead them into the ditch of disaster." By the same token, the American people did not want reactionaries in office, and if Merriam "proves not to be as progressive as he promises, he will be defeated at the succeeding election; but not by an unbalanced and impractical theorist like Sinclair."

Hearst wrote this letter too late to make today's newspapers, but it was just as well. The Hearst papers provided enough political excitement this morning, publishing the first installment of a promised series of articles by the Nazi leader Hermann Göring.

To the surprise of many readers, and the disappointment of the EPICs, Manchester Boddy of the L.A. *Daily News* shook off his cloak of neutrality as Election Day neared and came very close to endorsing Frank Merriam, a man he often mocked. Boddy declared that Merriam at least would allow the New Deal to finally establish itself in California. Commenting on reports that thousands of people had stampeded the grave of Pretty Boy Floyd in Oklahoma, snatching flowers and dirt, Boddy predicted that no matter who was elected in California, "the next governor will have the battle of the century protecting himself from the crackpots within his own organization."

Most newspapers in California held their fire today, waiting to ambush Upton Sinclair one last time tomorrow. The exploits of Charles Kingsford-Smith dominated many front pages. The *Los Angeles Times,* on the other hand, devoted half of its first page to a blistering attack on the EPIC candidate. "Both sides have been heard," the *Times* insisted in a statement that must have shocked some readers. In just forty-eight hours, "California will make the most momentous decision in all her history."

Refusing to take the high road, even in the campaign's final mile, the *Times* labeled Sinclair a "literary dynamiter," "apostle of hatred," "collaborator of radicals," "admirer, defender and instructor of Communist Russia." California will smash EPIC, the *Times* predicted, "if the legal voters vote and the illegal voters be kept away from the polls." An editorial cartoon pictured the Stars and Stripes flying high over a prosperous city, while the hammer and sickle marked a dingy freight yard. UNDER WHICH FLAG? the caption inquired.

For just the second time in his life, A. P. Giannini announced his vote in advance. During his recent trip to the East Coast, he was "besieged" by Transamerica stockholders concerned about the outcome of the race in California. Now he was ready to pledge his vote to Frank Merriam, "although he leaves much to be desired." Giannini's support for the governor was couched in backhanded compliments. Merriam, it seems, had promised that he would *no longer* be dominated "by the sinister individuals who were too close to him heretofore," Giannini advised.

Upton Sinclair picked up some eleventh-hour support, as well, and it was just about as genuine as Giannini's endorsement. When Senator William G. McAdoo returned to Los Angeles today, just in time to miss the campaign, he told reporters that he was backing "all Democratic candidates in California as well as the whole country."

"Does that mean that you are for Upton Sinclair?" one reporter asked.

"Is he not a Democratic nominee?" McAdoo replied sheepishly.

A Catholic priest, not a politician in California or a president at Hyde Park, delivered the most surprising and possibly far-reaching political pronouncement of the day. This afternoon, in his weekly radio broadcast heard by millions, Father Charles Coughlin intimated that he had finally soured on the New Deal. For the past eighteen months, Coughlin had stammered, "It's Roosevelt or ruin," but now he suggested a third alternative: organizing new political parties to challenge the Democrats and Republicans and "rescue our country" from the Depression.

"These old parties," Coughlin said, "are all but dead. As happened to Ananias and Sapphira, the hypocritical liars of scriptural fame, the young men are waiting at the doors to carry out their corpses." The time was fast approaching, therefore, "when these two obsolete parties, both of which were formerly controlled by the unseen masters, must relinquish the skeletons of their putrefying carcasses to the halls of a historical museum. The time has come," Coughlin announced, "when sober men of a progressive mind, be they former Republican or Democrat, and equally sober men of a conservative mind indifferent to their old party affiliations, must begin building two great new parties."

This did not augur well for FDR in 1936.

Gracie Allen looked befuddled, as usual, so her partner, George Burns, explained what was happening at the Astor Hotel in New York City.

"This," he revealed, "is a testimonial dinner to the postmaster general, Mr. Farley."

"Why?" Gracie wondered.

"Why, because in just a short time," George replied, "he has been Boxing Commissioner, campaign manager for Mr. Roosevelt, chairman of the Democratic National Committee and postmaster general."

The light of recognition broke across Gracie's face. "Oh, then I think it's fine to give him a dinner," she decided. "The poor man can't hold a job."

Jim Farley joined in the laughter at the Friar's Club roast. Jack Benny and toastmaster George Jessel tossed a few barbs, but it was pretty gentle stuff, since Farley had asked that political satire be kept to a minimum with Election Day only two days off. In his own remarks, Big Jim predicted that New York Democrats would "take care" of the Republican candidate for governor, Robert Moses, but he pointedly declined comment on California, letting stand a comment by the actor Bert Lytell, who lamented the "embarrassing situation" created by the mailing of a certain "rubber stamped letter."

California audiences were roaring at the latest adventures of the Inquiring Cameraman, Sidney Skolsky reported today, particularly when one "hobo" announced that a job as football quarterback awaited him in Los Angeles. "They are the best comedy shorts in town," Skolsky raved.

For theater managers in California, the Inquiring Cameraman trailer was no laughing matter. Patrons continued to protest, demand refunds, and threaten to tear up movie houses if MGM's propaganda short remained in circulation. Finally this evening the chief of Fox's West Coast chain of theaters in Los Angeles ordered its managers to stop screening *California Election News,* No. 3. The short was also pulled from all Warner Bros. movie houses and most independent theaters. Distributors accused the EPICs of fomenting terrorism and using the trailers as an excuse to mount demonstrations in support of Upton Sinclair.

Opposition to the screen campaign against Sinclair was expressed in quite a different way when H. L. Sacks, a prominent Los Angeles attorney, denounced Louis B. Mayer as a traitor to the Jewish race for producing the Inquiring Cameraman shorts. "These pictures," Sacks wrote in a letter to Mayer, "are intended to show that while intelligent gentiles are supporting Merriam, Jews express themselves in Hebrew accents as Sinclair supporters because, as they are made to say, 'we won't have to work.' I sincerely hope that your effort will have been in vain," Sacks observed, "for unless Merriam is defeated and Upton Sinclair and ticket elected, I and many others of the Jewish race fear that we in America are but one step nearer to cruel and barbarous Hitlerism."

On this Sunday before Election Day, preachers thundered *Go and Sinclair no more!* one last time. A Methodist minister in Los Angeles addressed the question "Shall California Set Up a Soviet Government Tuesday?" The rabbi at Hope of Israel called for "Salvation not Sinclairism." From his bully pulpit, the Reverend Gus Briegleb of St. Paul's Presbyterian declared, "This is California, Not Russia," and passed out "suggested ballots" after the service.

The radio preacher Martin Luther Thomas arrived at station KNX with two bodyguards, one to guard the studio, the other to watch the entrance to the building. When he began his program, he took a large pistol from his hip pocket and plunked it loudly on the table, explaining that his life had been threatened and he was taking no chances.

Up at the Angelus Temple next to Echo Park, the faithful were in an absolute frenzy. For the first time in years, Aimee Semple McPherson promised to preach three sermons in a single day. The morning service was rather churchy and traditional, but the later programs provided the kind of gala pageantry Sister Aimee was known for.

When the curtains on the Angelus Temple stage swept open this afternoon, more than three thousand parishioners viewed a giant pot bubbling on a fire. On one side stood Uncle Sam; on the other, Columbia, smiling benignly. A colorful array of immigrants in native dress filed past, tossing different kinds of "fruit" into the melting pot. Each object represented a distinctive contribution to America: Japanese silk, the Germans' mechanical genius, the Jewish aptitude for business, and so forth.

But then a raggedy man crept across the stage and tossed a red flag into the pot. As the audience gasped, Aimee Semple McPherson emerged to exacerbate, then calm, their fears. "A few years ago," she said in her ringing, singsong voice, "we laughed at the Bolshevik, we laughed at those who became alarmed and predicted trouble with communism in this country. We said it couldn't happen in America." But now, she explained, "our laughter has turned to concern, and our concern to fear as we have seen the ugly-headed monster becoming bolder. I tell you, there is death in the pot!" she bellowed, gesturing at the receptacle onstage. "Someone has cast in the poisonous herb and if we eat thereof we shall all perish, and the glory of our nation as it has stood through the years shall perish with us." Then, in a thinly veiled reference to EPIC, Sister Aimee announced her theme: "Enemy Power is Invading Christianity."

And that was just for starters. At the evening performance, Sister Aimee presented her third pageant in three days, using many of the props and costumes left over from Friday night's Allied Churchmen rally and closing with an appeal to followers of every religious faith to unite behind the word of God in the holy war against communism.

These Sunday shows at the temple often attracted Hollywood celebrities, but tonight was something special. When the pageant ended, Jean Harlow, Clark Gable, Norma Shearer, Jeanette MacDonald, Ramon Novarro, and Charles C. Pettijohn of the Hays Office all sent floral arrangements to the stage.

After an exciting night in a boxing ring, Upton Sinclair spent most of a lazy Sunday hiding out at his Beverly Hills residence prior to an EPIC rally this evening in Ocean Park. Frank Scully, accompanied by an entourage of writers, including the left-wing journalist Cedric Belfrage, stopped by. Shades were drawn throughout the house in deference to recent death threats.

Belfrage was amazed to find the reputed Communist ogre sitting prim and solemn in a rocking chair amid rather dowdy surroundings. Uppie looked like nothing so much as a pious Methodist minister, Belfrage thought. The outcome of the election was in doubt, Sinclair insisted; but if he lost, it would not mean that socialism could never be introduced in a capitalist democracy. It would only mean that he had written too many books.

Carey McWilliams also paid Sinclair a visit. The two men had fought side by side on civil liberties issues for years, and when distinguished visitors from the East, such as Edmund Wilson, came to Los Angeles, Carey always brought them around to Upton's house. EPIC had tested their friendship, however. McWilliams, a young lawyer from Colorado now living in L.A., had covered the campaign for the Baltimore *Sun* and *The New Republic* with a skeptical eye. While other liberals got carried away after the primary, predicting an EPIC landslide in November, McWilliams insisted that Sinclair would lose owing to Democratic defections—and accurately forecast that the White House would snub him. In the latest *New Republic,* he blasted all sides in the campaign. "The blunders have been about even: both Merriam and Sinclair have generously tried to elect the other," he observed.

Sinclair bristled at this criticism, but as was his custom, forgave the critic, and this afternoon welcomed him into his home. After talking with Uppie for a while in his living room, McWilliams became convinced that the candidate was resigned to defeat and perhaps even welcomed it: as if Sinclair, in his literary imagination, had already served a term in office and eradicated poverty, and now felt ready to retire.

Tonight in Mariposa, way out in California mining country, police found a dummy hanging from a telephone poll, a huge placard dangling from its neck. DOWN WITH BOLSHEVIKS! the sign read. UTOPIANSKI SINKUSALL, BOLSHEVIK! SO PERISH PUBLIC ENEMIES!

Will Rogers claimed he "always had it in for politicians" because he was born on Election Day in 1879. Today, to take his mind off politics, and his birthday, he played polo and roped calves at his Santa Monica ranch. He also wrote a newspaper column in which he thanked the flying hero Sir Charles Kingsford-Smith for diverting attention from the local election. The people of California, according to Will, were getting entirely too serious about the governor's race. "They think this election is making history," he observed, "when as a matter of fact it's only marking time."

Opening his radio show tonight in Los Angeles, Rogers promised some "good news for you tonight. Only two more days now and things is going to start picking up." The audience laughed knowingly. "You know," the humorist explained, "elections is just one of these things that upsets everything, and then benefits nobody anyhow. Every two years . . . they're just like a drought. They come along and devastate the country and stop business—and no matter who's elected we always seem to be able to kind of live through 'em."

Rogers finally turned to the California race. "In our local election out here," he commented, "it seems acknowledged by most everybody now that Mr. Merriam, the Republican, will win. But say, this old Sinclair has throwed such a scare into these rich folks they won't stop shiverin' till this thing is over." Even if he won, Sinclair wouldn't be allowed to do much of anything, Rogers observed, "but he's put wrinkles in brows out here that won't be out for years."

NOVEMBER 5

MONDAY

Polls would open in less than twenty-four hours, and California still hadn't decided whether to hold its nose or cross its fingers. Corbett's, Inc., a San Francisco betting agency, called the state a "gambler's paradise" this morning. Wagering on the governor's race produced the most action brokers had handled in years; Corbett's alone took in one hundred thousand dollars this morning. "If things keep going," one of the local betting commissioners said, "this will be a one-million-dollar betting race." Odds favoring Merriam dropped sharply throughout the morning, from five-to-one to three-to-one. Did the gamblers know something the pollsters, the public, and the candidates didn't?

For what it was worth (and in California, it was worth a lot), a New Jersey astrologer named Gustav Meyer predicted that Merriam would hang on and win, but Sinclair and Haight would run better than expected.

POLICE TO GUARD POLLS IN L.A. blared the banner headline in the *Herald-Express.* Election officials feared bloodshed, with the Merriam forces expected to challenge thousands of illegal registrants. "An air of tenseness pervaded political headquarters and the ranks of law enforcement officers," the newspaper reported, "as the zero hour of 6 A.M.

tomorrow approaches." Sheriff Eugene Biscailuz coordinated the deployment of at least one police officer or deputy sheriff to each of 3,574 polling places in Los Angeles County. Police in Sacramento promised to protect GOP poll watchers, who planned to challenge three thousand Democrats in that city. San Francisco's police chief assigned thirteen hundred cops to Election Day duty and dispatched radio cars to key precincts.

The *Los Angeles Examiner* suggested that every voter—"unless he is an unbalanced fanatic who is not ruled by reason"—should rebuke Sinclair. Like most of the pro-Merriam newspapers, the *San Francisco Chronicle* called for a huge turnout to "let the Nation know that California is sane." Its editorial cartoon showed Sinclair about to be crushed by a giant snowball rolling down a mountain slope. *Chronicle* editor Chester Rowell, in an article that appeared in several newspapers, revealed that friends just back from the Orient had informed him "that the chief topic of conversation in Tokyo and Shanghai is the California election. The Moscow papers are full of it. Mussolini has given an interview on it." The reason: fascism and communism were now worldwide phenomena, and everyone was curious to see which way California would turn, if indeed it turned at all.

"IF YOU ARE A REGISTERED VOTER IN THE STATE OF CALIFORNIA—BE CERTAIN TO CAST YOUR BALLOT TOMORROW," W. R. Wilkerson, publisher of the the *Hollywood Reporter,* implored his readers. Wilkerson cited a litany of EPIC bunk, including Sinclair's promise to put Charles Chaplin in charge of a state movie industry. "VOTE TOMORROW!" Wilkerson demanded. "CAST A VOTE TO SAVE YOUR JOB. VOTE TO SAVE THE MOTION PICTURE INDUSTRY."

The most powerful anti-Sinclair statement appeared in the *Los Angeles Times,* where the young political cartoonist Bruce Russell had saved one of his best for last. His sketch showed Miss California holding a ballot and a rubber stamp labeled A LANDSLIDE VOTE FOR MERRIAM. On the ground next to her crawled ugly spiders marked RADICALISM, ECONOMIC CHAOS, HATRED OF EVERYTHING, and so on. The caption advised, STAMP IT OUT TOMORROW!

On this morning before Election Day, W. R. Hearst's thoughts drifted from Sacramento to Hollywood. With the shift of his movie studio from Culver City to Burbank now in progress, he instructed his editors and gossip columnists to give the same favorable treatment to Warner Bros.

they had once lavished on MGM. And in a signed editorial in all of his papers, Hearst announced that he was ready to lead a new crusade. Indecent motion pictures were on the wane, but "a new fault and an equally serious one" was developing: the "communistic character" of movies. Hearst warned that the government might have to step in to suppress Red films (and possibly even take over certain film companies). For the moment, he would not publicly identify any of the offensive pictures, "but it may be necessary to mention them," Hearst said, "and arouse the public to the danger of them and possibly stimulate the government to take action."

As it happened, Washington generated important Hollywood news this morning, but it had nothing to do with squelching left-wing pictures. The Supreme Court today reversed itself, agreeing to review the lower-court decision that allowed William Fox's patents to stand. This temporarily knocked Fox off his throne in Hollywood and likely put his job offer to James A. Farley on hold until the high court settled the dispute.

"Tomorrow is election day and all California is agog," Herbert Hoover wrote to a friend in Washington. "But Sinclair will be defeated."

Two years ago, almost to this day, Hyde Park had voted overwhelmingly for Herbert Hoover. While it remained predominantly Republican and therefore reserved about practically everything, the town had learned to take pride in the family that made Hyde Park one of the most famous villages in the world. Anticipating President Roosevelt's first trip to the polls since taking office, workers hastily dressed up the town hall for FDR, the press, and the newsreel cameramen. One of the oldest structures in Hyde Park, it was also one of the most drab, its colonial exterior yellowed by the elements. Today workmen painted it white with green trim, redecorated its interior, and groomed its lawns and gravel walks.

Three miles away FDR spent much of the day with Heywood Broun and a delegation of American Newspaper Guild activists. This wasn't a press conference but a discussion of ways to extend the NRA's code to cover small-circulation papers and protect union agitation. Broun described management crackdowns on labor organizing in Manhattan, on Long Island, and in other areas, and cited the importance of establishing minimum-wage scales and a five-day week. Emerging from the meeting, the hulking, bushy-haired Broun happily announced that the President had listened sympathetically to his pleas.

Other reporters at Hyde Park did not fare so well. The President provided the correspondents almost nothing to write about, and he refused to admit to even a trace of nervousness about tomorrow's balloting. When Jim Farley phoned FDR, he found the President in a happy frame of mind. Farley was confident about the outcome, too, but in going over the final draft of his election-eve radio address, Big Jim spotted a sentence that predicted a "decisive and emphatic endorsement of the policies of Franklin Delano Roosevelt," and crossed out the words *and emphatic.*

EPIC leaders also expressed optimism as zero hour approached. Dick Otto, campaign manager, envisioned a Sinclair victory by three hundred thousand votes. The candidate forecast a margin half that wide, basing his prediction on the latest odds out of Lloyd's of London, which favored him by a two-to-one margin.

The final pre-election issue of the *EPIC News* hit the streets, boasting an astounding circulation of two million copies—a total only slightly less than the number of Californians expected to vote tomorrow. This made the *EPIC News,* at least for today, one of the nation's most popular newspapers. "California reactionaries fell aside today," the *EPIC News* reported, "up to their knees in 'Hate-Sinclair' literature, waving a handful of synthetic newspaper headlines, and watched the Sinclair-Downey state Democratic cavalcade sweep on to victory. . . . Purported odds of 5-1 in favor of Merriam were found to be baseless camouflage, all bettors having to place money at even odds in order to find takers at all."

The final KNX radio straw poll gave Sinclair a three-to-one lead over Merriam. Reports out of San Diego, the *EPIC News* asserted, put Uppie in front by two-to-one in that city. He would carry Los Angeles by at least 150,000; Merriam would run behind both Sinclair and Haight in the San Joaquin Valley. "An amazing swing to Sinclair has taken place in the Bay region," the newspaper disclosed, "where organized labor's strength has made it certain that Sinclair will carry San Francisco and Oakland." Sinclair rallies in these cities last week drew crowds of 20,000.

Meanwhile, the frantic Merriam forces, "unable to get more than 50 persons even at meetings where Merriam personally appeared, were forced to take motion pictures of huge Sinclair meetings and misrepresent them as crowds attending Republican rallies. So admitted a newsreel man found taking shots outside an EPIC meeting this week." Among other fakeries, according to the newspaper: a Hollywood studio hired two hundred empty boxcars and paid three hundred "bums" a dollar a head "to stage a railroad scene in which the bums were supposed to be arriving from the east at Sinclair's invitation."

Finally fighting fire with fire, the *EPIC News* printed in a front-page box a non sequitur worthy of its opponents: EVERYBODY IN LONG BEACH REMEMBERS WHEN FRANK F. MERRIAM USED TO PRANCE AROUND BIXBY PARK IN THE KLEAGLE NIGHTSHIRT OF THE KU KLUX KLAN.

Upton Sinclair made his final campaign appearance at a noon rally in downtown Los Angeles. The auditorium's proximity to the *Los Angeles Times* building provided the candidate with a chance to deliver one of his best quips of the entire campaign. After denouncing the *Times*'s graphic depiction of a hobo invasion of California, Sinclair told the crowd that as a jobless youth, Harry Chandler, now the owner of the newspaper, himself rode to Los Angeles on a freight train. Turning in the direction of the *Times*'s office, Sinclair shouted, "Harry, give the other bums a chance!" The roar of the audience might have shaken Chandler out of his chair.

Franklin Hichborn, a journalist famed for covering the California legislature, took a walk this afternoon with his wirehaired dog, Guinea, on a Santa Cruz beach near his home. There he met two unemployed laborers with thick Italian accents digging clams for their supper. Hichborn, one of the few prominent Progressives supporting Sinclair, wondered whom they favored in the election for governor. One of the men explained that they had switched their party registration so they could vote for Sinclair in the Democratic primary.

"And tomorrow you will vote for Mr. Sinclair again?" Hichborn queried.

"Oh, no," the clam digger replied, "we no vote for Mr. Sinclair, we vote for Mr. Merriam. If Mr. Sinclair elected it would offend the Virgin."

"You mustn't offend the Virgin," Hichborn said sadly, shaking his head. When he returned home for supper he informed his wife that Merriam would be overwhelmingly elected tomorrow.

"How do you know, way out here?" his wife objected.

"Two Italian clam diggers told me," he answered.

"And what do they know about it?" she asked.

"They know *all* about it," Hichborn replied.

"I am going to read what I have written to read, because in a general way it is easier even if it is not better and in a general way it is better even if it is not easier to read what has been written than to say what has not been written," explained Gertrude Stein, beginning a lecture at Princeton University this evening. "Any way," she added, "that is one way to feel about it."

Stein addressed a rather small audience in McCosh Hall. She had asked that the crowd be kept to five hundred because she did not believe she could hold the interest of a larger number. When the doors closed, police struggled to keep disappointed curiosity seekers at bay.

This was the writer's second lecture in America. Four nights ago she had talked about art, or "Pictures" as she called it, at the Colony Club in New York City, under the auspices of the Museum of Modern Art. The next day *The New York Times* headlined its review of the affair MISS STEIN SPEAKS TO BEWILDERED 500, with a subhead, SPEAKER'S DRESS, ALMOST LIKE A NUN'S, FORMS CONTRAST WITH BRILLIANCE OF AUDIENCE.

Stein enjoyed herself enormously in New York. She loved eating honeydew melons and oysters and green-apple pie. Walking the streets, she was amazed how many strangers recognized her. People in drugstores and luncheonettes fascinated her—sometimes she stopped and bought a detective novel just to be able to observe the characters sitting at the counter. Studying the tall buildings, she decided that the word *skyscraper* was a misnomer, for there was no sky in America, only air, and that was why there was no real painting in this country. She also attended the Yale-Dartmouth football game in New Haven with her publisher Alfred Harcourt.

Unfazed by criticism of her conservative apparel, Miss Stein appeared at Princeton garbed in a tan jacket, fawn-colored tweed skirt, and tan shoes, and without introduction walked onstage and began to talk about what she called "The Gradual Making of *The Making of Americans.*"

For the next hour, she attempted, in her distinctive, ofttimes puzzling way to make that book understandable to the audience.

When Stein concluded the lecture, she asked if there were any questions. No one raised a hand.

Esquire's December issue finally went to press, featuring "The Epic Sinclair," Theodore Dreiser's lengthy take on the California campaign. "Probably when this article appears, Upton Sinclair will have been elected governor of California," Dreiser asserted. "I hope so."

Out of time, money, and hope, his campaign in disarray, Ray Haight raced to San Francisco today for one last radio address. His opponents had booked all of the affordable radio time in Los Angeles, so Haight had to leave town to deliver his last blast.

Frank Merriam concluded his campaign with a rally in his home city of Long Beach. A crowd of nearly five thousand assembled, drawn at least in part by reports that Will Rogers would appear. But the humorist didn't show, and by the end of the affair much of the audience had walked out.

As the clock wound down, GOP officials stuck to predictions of a landslide victory. In his final radio address tonight, Merriam said he faced the election with a clear conscience. "Despite many personal affronts and the spreading of malicious lies concerning myself and my plans," Merriam complained, "I have retained my sense of values and my good nature in this campaign. At all times we have placed honesty of purpose and expression ahead of any desire to win; for it has been our conviction that the interests of the State of California and of its people are paramount to any person or any party or any political advantage or victory. If, upon such a basis, we triumph in this contest, we shall have the satisfaction of knowing that we won our fight by clean and courageous methods, and that none supported us through misapprehension or through the influence of passion or prejudice."

Rumors aside, Will Rogers survived the California campaign without shattering his policy of never endorsing a political candidate. Tomorrow he would keep another record intact: he would not vote. But today he wrote an Election Day column for his millions of readers from coast to coast. "This last night before election," Rogers observed, "California puts you in mind of the young husband waiting at the maternity ward for news of the first born. They are walking up and down, lighting one cigarette after another, and looking anxiously toward the voting booth."

At half past six this evening, a massive crowd of EPICs assembled in front of the Angelus Temple at Echo Park. Brass bands, thousands of torchlit marchers, and hundreds of gaily decorated floats angled through downtown Los Angeles en route to Hollywood in what EPIC organizers called the largest parade in the city's history.

While the EPICs marched one last time, Upton Sinclair delivered his final statewide radio address. Once again he reminded listeners, "It's up to you!" Contrary to what his opponents charged, he was a firm believer in democracy, Sinclair argued, in the right of the people to decide their own destiny. And if the people felt they hadn't suffered enough, it was their God-given right to suffer some more: all they had to do was elect Merriam, and he would see to it. But regardless of the outcome, Sinclair promised to continue to educate the people. Sooner or later, he predicted, voters would learn to act in their own interest.

Later, after delivering two more speeches over local radio, an utterly exhausted Sinclair met with reporters one last time, just moments before November 6 finally arrived. "I talk too much," he confessed wearily. After pausing a moment in deep reflection, he added, "I write too much, too."

TUESDAY

Thousands lined up to vote even before the polls opened at 6:00 A.M. in Los Angeles. Balloting commenced one hour later in San Francisco, and by 8:00 A.M., according to election officials, twenty-nine thousand had already marked their ballots in that city, so far without incident. Early reports indicated a record vote in Sacramento and Fresno, two Haight strongholds. Perfect weather—sunny and warm with low humidity—enveloped most sections of the state.

Hollywood studios stopped shooting pictures for two hours so that workers could traipse to the polls. By state law, taverns shut their doors, but liquor stores remained open. Schools and public offices closed, which was typical, but so did many private businesses (such as stores and insurance companies), which was not. Some employers, following Chamber of Commerce instructions, ordered workers to spend their holiday getting out the vote for Frank Merriam.

Across the top of its front page, the *Los Angeles Times* warned:

TODAY'S ELECTION MUST NOT BE DECIDED
BY UNCAST VOTES, DISHONEST VOTES
OR VOTES OF A MINORITY

"No one who is entitled to cast a ballot and who neglects to do so," the *Times* declared, "will have any right to complain if his future paychecks are Sinclair scrip, payable—if at all—in carrots and potatoes. . . ." An editorial cartoon portrayed the whole world watching Miss California go to the polls carrying a ballot marked AMERICANISM VS. RADICALISM. Now that the campaign was over, the *Times* published one of its first accounts of a Sinclair speech: the candidate's final radio appearance last night.

VOTE—NOTHING ELSE YOU CAN DO THIS DAY CAN BE SO IMPORTANT, the *San Francisco Chronicle* advised. Merriamites must turn out in phenomenal numbers to overcome the EPICs, who "will vote if they have to be carried to the polling places on stretchers." Heeding that demand, a feeble and near-blind eighty-six-year-old gentleman literally groped his way from his home on Van Ness Avenue in San Francisco to a local election office, explaining, "I just have to vote for Governor Merriam."

United for California in the south and the California League Against Sinclairism in the north led the Merriam vote drive, sparing no expense with automobiles, phone banks, and reminders on the radio. They even went door-to-door, but only in middle-class neighborhoods. EPIC organized what it called flying squads of attorneys, who rushed to precincts where Republicans were harassing voters. The Sinclairites posted signs as close to polling places as legally possible. REMEMBER: THE BALLOT IS SECRET, one placard affirmed. Another boasted, I'M NO COWARD—THE LYING SPECIAL INTERESTS ARE NOT FOOLING ME.

The most unique get-out-the-vote trick belonged to Merriamites in Piedmont, California, who set off cannons in the middle of town at hourly intervals "to bomb out the voters."

At half past ten, Franklin D. Roosevelt, accompanied by his wife and mother and several aides, arrived at the town hall in Hyde Park to cast his ballot. FDR wore a brown tweed suit but eschewed a topcoat despite the damp, chilly weather. About fifty townspeople standing in the rain applauded his arrival. Greeted by a friend as he emerged from the car, the President observed that it was "good weather for ducks—Democratic weather. We should win."

Sara Delano Roosevelt preceded her son but waited in the doorway while attendants helped FDR conquer the five steps. Entering the hall he met more applause. The chief of the election board looked up at him with feigned indifference and asked, "Name, please?"

"It's still Franklin D.," he replied while the newsreel cameras whirred.

Then, leaning on the arm of Gus Gennerich, his personal attendant, the President walked past the cameras to one of the curtained voting machines. Roosevelt remained in the booth for half a minute, then pulled the lever and turned around, facing the cameras. The newsreel men asked the President and the First Lady to pose in front of the booth, but FDR vetoed the suggestion. "I decline to have it appear that my wife is telling me how to vote," he said with a laugh as he stepped away, but he assured reporters that he had voted the straight Democratic ticket. Returning home, FDR asked the correspondents whether he could participate in their Election Day betting pool. By all means, they responded.

Across the Hudson River from Hyde Park and a few miles downstream, James A. Farley, following tradition, visited political friends in his hometown, Stony Point, New York, and said a prayer at his mother's grave. Then he returned to his Biltmore Hotel headquarters in New York to monitor election returns with Governor Herbert Lehman. Later in the evening he would transmit tallies to Marvin McIntyre in Poughkeepsie, who would pass them along to the President. Farley expected the teletype to chatter noisily with good news.

———

Election Day in Louisiana was no big deal this year, Huey Long having seized complete political control in primary contests back in September. So Senator Long had other things on his mind today. "The only way for us to get out of this here depression," Huey raved, "is to secede from the United States—sever all connections and make a clean start. We ain't goin' to get any place until we get rid of all those damn bureaucrats, hobocrats, autocrats and all those other 'crats up there. Leave us alone and we'll have forty-five million people in Louisiana."

How long would that take? a reporter wondered.

"Oh, it'll take us five or six years, I reckon," Huey responded, "but we'll set up a real Utopia in the state. But we've got to get out of the United States."

———

Attempting to skirt the newsreel men, Upton Sinclair left his home on Sunset Avenue in Pasadena at 10:00 A.M., a full hour before his promised time of departure. When he reached the polling place for Precinct 92 at 1412 Lincoln Avenue, the cameramen were waiting. Sinclair, dressed in his usual tan double-breasted suit, didn't encounter many voters.

"How are they voting?" he asked an election official as he stuffed his ballot into a box marked GENERAL TICKETS.

"We've had more than one-third already of the entire registered," the official responded.

"Is that right?" Sinclair said, smiling broadly. "Well that shows people are taking our advice." Then, shaking the official's hand, he said, "Good morning," and waving to the cameramen he announced, "Good-bye."

When Uppie returned to Sunset Avenue, he found that reporters had staked out his house, so he agreed to meet with them for fifteen minutes. He insisted that he had voted the straight Democratic ticket. Newsreel stringers, citing deadline pressure, asked him to deliver two sets of remarks: one they'd use if he won, the other if he lost. So Sinclair stood in the shade under a tree in his backyard, jacket buttoned to his chest, squinting at the cameras.

"Of course, I appreciate the tremendous compliment the people of California have paid me in electing me their governor," he began, eerily. This might be the only chance he'd ever have to make a victory speech. Referring to the EPIC plan, he said, "We think it is a valid program for the whole United States and we feel certain that the whole United States will adopt it as their idea of the New Deal before very many months have passed." After finishing a feisty concession speech, Sinclair ordered the cameramen off his property.

Frank Merriam left his home on East Sixteenth Street in Long Beach and walked unaccompanied to the polling place on Lime Avenue. As he climbed the steps of the old house, he turned to the cameras, took off his dark hat, and waved, exposing his bald head, then greeted three friends on the porch. After casting his ballot, Merriam posed for the cameras and, in his usual long-winded way, turned a brief remark into an oration before concluding, "I certainly think it's the duty of every citizen to vote, and no one should tell him how to vote. . . . We are free, free to determine these matters by ourselves." Merriam confessed he was pleased that everyone in the great commonwealth of California had the right to vote.

"Early reports are very encouraging," Ray Haight reported as he cast his ballot in Los Angeles. Political observers conceded Haight at least 10 percent of today's vote. In a close contest, therefore, Haight might still be a spoiler.

Herbert Hoover voted at the Women's Clubhouse at Stanford, accompanied by his wife, Lou Henry, and doffed his hat to reporters as he emerged. Did he vote for Merriam? "Yes," the former president answered without hesitation, but he declined to reveal whether he ratified his party's Senate candidate, Hiram Johnson. Upton Sinclair seemed to be the only politician in California proud to have voted a straight ticket.

J.F.T. O'Connor cast his ballot in Los Angeles at 750 South Mariposa, where he met some old friends. "No question in my mind but state will elect Governor Merriam," Jefty wrote in his diary.

It was lunchtime at San Simeon. In the great refectory hung with European tapestries, William Randolph Hearst sat at the center of a long dining table with blond Hollywood starlets on either side. The women twitted the baronial publisher as a roguish smile flickered across his huge, jowly face. Hearst's eyes, Cedric Belfrage observed from across the table, were those of an octopus at play.

Belfrage, a young London critic who spent years in Hollywood writing celebrity profiles for British publications, had arrived at San Simeon last night with his wife, Molly Castle, a feature writer for Lord Beaverbrook's London *Express.* Molly had met W.R. in England recently, earning this invitation. When the limousine brought the two writers from the station, they were impressed with the DANGER, WILD ANIMAL and ANIMALS HAVE THE RIGHT OF WAY signs and with the herds of camel, buffalo, and other beasts roaming the Hearst ranch. The Hearst castle, Casa Grande, looked like a casino on the Riviera, twinkling with hundreds of lights, as the two writers were led to a guest bungalow.

Treat Hearst as a modern Louis XIV and one can rationalize his actions, Arthur Brisbane once advised. The Hearst ranch, nearly the size of Rhode Island, extended fifty miles along the the coast. "The days of palaces in Democracy are over," Brisbane once observed. "I've tried to tell him that, but he's going to die like a king." Like a monarch, Hearst set the rules in his castle. One rule: lunch would be served buffet-style no earlier than one o'clock. Another: no politics at mealtime.

But this was not an ordinary day. "Sinclair is beaten," someone at the lunch table said. Everyone looked at Hearst, anxious to gauge his response. For a moment W.R. frowned petutantly, unhappy with the prospect of four more years of Frank Merriam or, more likely, the poor manners of his guest. Then his face resumed what Belfrage considered a kind of seraphic complacency, which left no doubt what the outcome of the election would be—and that Hearst would be regally satisfied with it.

By noon, according to press reports, more than 430,000 citizens of Los Angeles had trudged to the polls under sunny skies. True to their word, the Merriamites challenged thousands of voters throughout the state. At one Sacramento precinct, for example, the GOP disputed eighty-three of the first nine hundred voters; seventy-seven were eventually allowed to vote, while six left without voting. This was the general pattern. Few would-be voters were ruled ineligible, but thousands—uncertain, intimidated, or scared—fled rather than risk being arrested by the cop or deputy sheriff present at most polling places.

In La Canada, when a voter loudly objected to the presence of "foreigners," two men ran out before casting their ballots. An Altadena woman, refused permission to vote, took up a position outside the polling place and shouted, "Nobody can vote here!" Police lodged a sanity complaint against her. Sixteen officials manning telephones at the registrar's office in Los Angeles fielded thousands of inquiries and complaints.

San Francisco remained relatively quiet, but officials elsewhere reported dozens of "incidents," including fistfights between Sinclair supporters and Merriamites who challenged them. Police raced to a polling place in Oakland when an election clerk claimed she had been slapped by a woman whose credentials had been contested. Cops seized a man in Los Angeles for attempting to vote illegally—and for having too many political stickers on the front windshield of his car—and took a woman into custody after she scratched and bit a deputy sheriff in a struggle. Police redoubled patrols in Culver City and in two areas on the east side after receiving reports that Communists planned to block entrances to voting places.

EPIC complained about the heavy police presence, but campaign workers informed Sinclair that reports of East Coast gangsters coming to California to stuff ballot boxes had not materialized. Supposedly some New York EPICs talked to these "boys" and convinced them not to take money from West Coast interests. This news confirmed Sinclair's cherished belief that the underworld had more scruples than the business cabal that ran California.

Robert Gordon Sproul met with the five suspended UCLA radicals and their parents this afternoon amid calls from a hundred faculty members for the dismissal of the school's provost, Dr. E. C. Moore. Debate raged. Student vigilantes continued to patrol the campus, and the *Daily Californian* reported that a local American Legion official admitted he had hired twenty-two students at the school to monitor radical activities. Today UCLA students attempting to foment a sympathy strike at San Mateo Junior College were pelted with tomatoes, and police took into custody one of the speakers, a fruit-spattered coed, ostensibly for her own protection.

After meeting with the suspended students, Sproul offered to reinstate four of them. The sole exception: firebrand Celeste Strack. But Sproul attached several provisos; and since the four students vowed to return unconditionally or not at all, the crisis was far from over.

At half past six California time, James A. Farley issued a victory statement from the Biltmore in New York on behalf of the Democratic National Committee. "The figures are not yet complete for us to go into detail of the States we have carried," Farley proclaimed, "but we do know that the New Deal has been magnificently sustained. Famous Republican figures have been toppled into oblivion. In fact we must wonder whom they have left that the country has ever heard of." Results so far exceeded even his most optimistic projections.

Farley called President Roosevelt, who contentedly sat by the fireplace at Hyde Park listening to a landslide of unprecedented proportions roll in. Farley judged FDR to be elated. The President made only one request all evening. He wanted to know how his home precinct in Hyde Park voted, and he was delighted to learn that this district, which Roosevelt carried by only eight votes in 1932, had given Governor Lehman a seventy-three-vote cushion over his Republican opponent, Robert Moses.

Polls closed in Los Angeles at 7:00 P.M., in San Francisco an hour later, and election officials estimated they might know the winner of the governor's race within two hours—if the race was as one-sided as the press and the pols expected. One precinct in Santa Ana reported a 100-percent turnout, the final registered voter having been hauled on a stretcher from his sickbed to the polls.

In San Francisco, early returns were projected on a giant screen erected on Market Street between Fifth and Sixth streets. The *Chronicle* broadcast results over radio station KGO, and eighteen movie theaters flashed vote tallies on their screens or announced results over loudspeakers.

"It's kinder early in the evening out here, and not much news yet," wrote Will Rogers, California's most famous nonvoter (at least Charlie Chaplin had an excuse, not being an American citizen).

> History has proven that there is nothing in the world as alike as two candidates. They look different till they get in, and then they all act the same. I am anxious to see how they classify these newly elected. Some are Republicans, but New Dealers; some are Democrats, but not New Dealers; some are Democrats, just to use the label; some are Republicans, just to try and keep an old custom alive. This next Congress is sure going to be a pack of mongrels.

Hollywood dozed. Excitement rippled today only when famed aviator Amelia Earhart arrived by automobile from the East after a ten-day solo drive and toured the Warner Bros. studio. Streets and movie theaters emptied this evening as studio workers trudged home to listen to the returns on the radio. Confident of victory, movie executives filled the Brown Derby and Clover Club at suppertime. Awaiting the first returns, celebrities such as Jean Harlow, Myrna Loy, and William Powell assembled in movie-star homes to place friendly bets on the outcome. Billy Wilkerson, publisher of the *Hollywood Reporter,* readied his Trocadero café for Louis B. Mayer's election-night bash.

The society crowd gathered at lavish "radio parties." At the Midwick Country Club in Pasadena, election returns arrived by direct wire from Los Angeles and were posted on a blackboard in the front of the ballroom while dozens of couples danced the night away. One member of the local elite attending the Midwick festivities: Don Francisco, West Coast manager for Lord & Thomas.

Down at Philharmonic Hall, Gene Daniels, a famous seeress, announced election results before they were even tabulated. Thousands turned out in the streets of downtown Los Angeles to listen to the returns over loudspeakers or to watch raw numbers posted on signboards. One election-night street party, sponsored by a local newspaper, took on the trappings of a Merriam victory party, with a fire-fighters' orchestra playing on a flag-bedecked platform. A huge crowd gathered outside EPIC headquarters on South Grand. The EPICs acted nervous, subdued, almost dazed. It was as if they had been running on nothing but adrenaline and hope for months and suddenly realized that their utopian dream was about to disappear.

Upton Sinclair awaited the outcome at his poor-man's mansion on Arden Drive in Beverly Hills in the company of his wife and a handful of friends. Certain that he had done his best against impossible odds, Sinclair felt serene. When the first precinct report came in and it showed Merriam leading by a four-to-one margin, Sinclair accepted it as a portent. Returns showed that he had fought the governor to a draw in his home Pasadena precinct—each candidate drew 147 votes—but Merriam swept the city by a five-to-two margin.

But as more results poured in via the radio, it became clear that the election was going to be closer than many had predicted. Sinclair rallied, fell back, rallied again. It appeared he even had a chance to win if the pockets of EPIC fanaticism in Los Angeles went big for him. Sinclair, watching his vote tally climb, felt relieved, no longer haunted by a humiliating landslide defeat. His enormous vote, possibly approaching a million, meant that many local EPIC candidates must be winning. EPIC would survive to fight another day.

Up in Oakland, William Knowland, surprised to find himself trailing an EPIC candidate in his bid for a state senate seat, studied the vote totals posted at GOP headquarters and wondered whether *any* Republican would be returned to office.

All hope for a miracle Sinclair finish faded by nine-thirty. Sinclair was winning twice as many wards in Los Angeles as his opponent, but his margins were narrow, meaning that at best he would split the county's vote with Merriam—and he was losing badly elsewhere in the state.

At last facing defeat, EPIC organizers started assembling evidence of alleged vote fraud. Closely monitored returns in precincts where EPICs had turned out in force showed suspiciously few votes for Sinclair. Some poll watchers reported that ballot boxes were opened illegally during the day. Election officials purportedly miscounted Sinclair votes here, discounted them there. Evidence was only fragmentary, anecdotal, but Sinclair nevertheless dashed off a telegram to Senator George Norris of Nebraska (who had endorsed his candidacy):

> IT IS IMPOSSIBLE TO ACCOMPLISH ANYTHING THROUGH LOCAL AUTHORITIES, AND THEREFORE ON BEHALF OF AT LEAST 1,000,000 PEOPLE OF CALIFORNIA, I URGE YOUR COOPERATION IN SENDING AN INVESTIGATIVE COMMITTEE AT ONCE. . . . WE ARE IN POSSESSION OF INDISPUTABLE PROOF OF GIGANTIC VOTE FRAUD. OUR LEGAL STAFF IS COMPILING COMPLETE EVIDENCE OF VIOLATIONS.

At EPIC headquarters, where posted figures showed Sinclair trailing by thirty-five thousand votes statewide, officials hoisted up a huge sign, which read, SINCLAIR SAYS—DON'T WORRY—THE LIE FACTORY IS STILL WORKING.

Although he believed reports of fraud, Sinclair did not think a recount would change the outcome, and the last thing he wanted was another week of name-calling and controversy. He faced defeat, in fact, with sublimely mixed emotions. While consoling his election-night guests, who appeared to take the results harder than he, Sinclair thought to himself, *I can drive my car again. I can go and take my walks. I can sleep with my windows open.*

Craig expressed her feelings more openly. "Thank God, thank God!" she exclaimed, sinking to the floor and weeping. Uppie's friend Lewis Browne approached her. "It's all right, Craig," he said. "We all understand. None of us wanted him to win."

A telegram from *Script* editor Rob Wagner arrived at the Sinclair residence. "Dear Uppie," it read, "I do not commiserate you, I congratulate you. . . ."

Henry O'Melveny, California's leading attorney, who had raised money for Merriam through a stock-dividend scheme and whose associate Albert Parker gave EPIC fits, retired early, after recording the significance of this day in his diary. The Sinclair candidacy, he observed, represented "the most serious situation I have ever known in politics." Frank Merriam, the lawyer noted, "will be elected, but not with the majority I hoped."

Other prominent Democrats brushed off EPIC's strong run in their rush to claim credit for Sinclair's defeat. "The most menacing peril to the New Deal has been definitely removed," chimed William Jennings Bryan, Jr. Ham Cotton thanked his fellow Democrats for punishing "the despoilers" and repudiating "an arrogant attempt to capture our Democratic party and Sovietize a free people." Signaling that the anti-EPIC battle had just begun, Cotton called on "all true Democrats to unite solidly behind our President and drive the interlopers back to the Socialist party from whence they came."

At a quarter to ten, Sinclair and his tiny entourage left Beverly Hills for an NBC radio station in Los Angeles. The losing candidate would speak to listeners in ninety-two cities across the country; then the winner would appear. Broadcast officials assured Sinclair that he would not confront the governor in person. Sinclair did not wish to exchange courtesies with his foe; tonight he planned to speak from the heart.

When Sinclair arrived at the station, he discovered to his chagrin that Merriam was already there. Station managers insisted that the two candidates sit together in the same studio. Angrily, Sinclair refused and waited in an adjoining chamber while Merriam spoke. Uppie sat on a couch stewing, his chin in his hand, while Craig patted his shoulder. He may have welcomed defeat, but he was still a sore loser. "They put *him* on first," Sinclair said bitterly. Then the door between the two rooms flapped open just as Merriam said, "The election is over." Fortunately for all concerned, aides hustled the governor out another door to a waiting limousine, avoiding potential unpleasantness.

At half past ten, it was Sinclair's turn to speak, and no longer melancholy, he went on a verbal rampage. Sinclair declared that he was not conceding the election just yet for reports indicated that Merriam had robbed him of 125,000 votes. "So many votes have been withheld," he said, "and so many thousand have been stolen, it may be days before we know how this election has really gone." In previous radio addresses, he had purred his message. Tonight, with nothing to lose, he growled.

"I am handicapped by not knowing just what has been the result of the election," he said. "But this we know: The EPIC party has won a colossal victory. Without the support of a single daily newspaper in the state, and in the face of a campaign of vilification, we have doubled our vote since the primaries.

"My face burns when I think of the lies and forgeries circulated by men with millions to spend to defeat me. But it won't go on. Be of good cheer. We're not going to stop. This is only one skirmish, and we're enlisted for the war."

Sinclair promised to "hang the threat of a recall as a sword over Merriam's head" and vowed to establish the End Poverty League throughout the nation. And he disclosed for the first time exactly what FDR had promised during their meeting at Hyde Park. "I am not violating any confidence now," Sinclair revealed, "to say that President Roosevelt told me last September that he was going to broadcast a speech in favor of production for use. I am going to wait day to day for President Roosevelt to do that. It is our only salvation." Then he left the studio, dodging reporters and cameramen by exiting through a side door.

Sinclair had roared mightily, and this only encouraged tears to flow and anger to rage at EPIC headquarters in Los Angeles. The same scene, presumably, was played out at many of the two thousand End Poverty League enclaves throughout the state. Alarmed, Richard Otto, the League leader, felt required to issue what he called a concession statement, urging the Sinclair supporters to "accept our temporary setback with calmness." The EPICs must not let bitterness or disappointment overrule their judgement, Otto argued. "Success for our program can only be achieved through education. Education can not be forced."

Keeping his promise to J.F.T. O'Connor, Governor Merriam emphasized the bipartisan nature of his triumph. EPIC, he said in one of his radio talks, had "eliminated all strictly party issues" and turned the election into a simple question of radicalism against Americanism. Sinclair's defeat, he insisted, "does not reflect in any sense a victory for reactionaryism." Jefty O'Connor might have written this script himself. "The people of California are progressive," Merriam affirmed, "and my election was made possible by the wholehearted and loyal support of progressives of all shades of political opinion."

Speaking over KFWB, the Hearst radio station in Los Angeles, Merriam singled out one publisher for praise. "Mr. Hearst and his great newspapers," he said, "came forward as they always do in the interests of the people and the state and aided in making possible the great victory that belongs to the citizens of California tonight." Merriam asserted that in all his years in politics he had always known Hearst "to stand on the right side of the question"—a strange statement in light of the fact that W.R. had supported Roosevelt over Hoover in 1932 and just recently backed one of Merriam's opponents in the August primary.

Now that Merriam had earned a full term in office, a radio interviewer asked the governor whether he cared to describe his agenda. "To get some sleep," Merriam replied.

Louis B. Mayer's election-night party at the Trocadero drew a stellar crowd, including Irving Thalberg, Carey Wilson, and Charlie Pettijohn, creators of the landmark Inquiring Cameraman shorts. One of the few Democrats present, Senator William G. McAdoo had every reason to cheer: Sinclair lost and didn't drag other Democratic candidates down with him. A sensational slice of Hollywood celebritydom unwound after an unbelievably tense autumn. Among the partygoers: Sam Goldwyn, Harry Cohn, Howard Hughes, Clark Gable, Harry Rapf, Helen Hayes, Edward G. Robinson, Ernst Lubitsch, Gloria Swanson, and Groucho Marx. The café was sprinkled with a handful of Sinclairites—notably Dorothy Parker and Sam Marx—who apparently had decided that if you can't lick Louie B., join him.

The party's guest of honor, Frank Finley Merriam, wired Billy Wilkerson his regrets. A radio broadcast prevented him from making it to the Troc, and his official victory party at a country club in Long Beach awaited him. But Merriam asked Wilkerson to extend his best wishes to "my good friends in the motion picture industry" and to offer "my special wishes to those two splendid hard workers, Louis B. Mayer and Charles Pettijohn."

L. B. Mayer was no less effusive. "The voters of California have made a fearless choice between radicalism and patriotism." Mayer observed. "The people of the entire United States will hail California's courage."

Like nearly everyone else in California, Lola Dominguez, a twenty-eight-year-old woman who lived on Eugene Street in East Los Angeles, listened to the election returns on the radio. When commentators reported Sinclair's defeat with certainty, Lola drank some poison. Rushed to Beulah Allen Hospital, she was given emergency treatment, and attendants expected her to live.

Other Sinclair supporters in southern California reacted to the outcome of the election not with despair but with anger. Shortly before 3:00 A.M. several EPICs invaded the headquarters of Ham Cotton's American Democracy in Alhambra, and when they left, it was a shambles.

NOVEMBER 7

WEDNESDAY

Would he interpret yesterday's verdict in the national elections as an approval of what he had done, a reporter asked, or as a mandate to enact even bolder measures? Franklin Roosevelt refused to say, allowing the pundits to judge for themselves whether he planned to steer a steady course or seize dictatorial control of the government. One thing, however, was certain: the Democratic landslide caught the President somewhat by surprise. At this morning's press conference, he confessed that he had finished next to last in the betting pool on the outcome of the election. A couple of races had yet to be decided, but Marvin McIntyre appeared likely to win the thirty-dollar pot.

"The American people have placed their future for the next two years completely in the hands of the Democratic Party," the *Chicago Tribune* advised, "and have given it the power to do anything it pleases or thinks wise." No longer would Republicans be able to charge that the New Deal was imposed upon an unsuspecting electorate who didn't know what they were getting when they anointed Roosevelt their leader in 1932. Now the voters knew about the New Deal—more or less—and they still wanted Roosevelt. Clearly FDR had become a symbol of the nation's hope; refuting him would have meant losing hope.

The Democratic sweep was indeed overwhelming. The party took all but nine of the thirty-five contested Senate seats and seemed likely to pick up about ten seats in the House, the first time a party holding the White House increased its congressional margins in a midterm election. The Republicans retained but seven governorships. Among the prominent Republicans who went down to defeat were Senators Reed of Pennsylvania, Robinson of Indiana, and Fess of Ohio. A little-known Missouri Democrat named Harry S Truman toppled Senator Roscoe C. Patterson.

"The most amazing election of its kind in the history of the United States," the *New York Post* observed, "ends with a clearer political picture than this nation has ever seen before." If the shift was Democratic, the drift was leftward. Voters elected to Congress at least three dozen "radicals," such as Maury Maverick of Texas and William Lemke of North Dakota. The La Follettes, running on a platform that stated, "Our economic system has failed," captured a U.S. Senate seat and the governor's chair in Wisconsin, and the state's congressional delegation would now be made up of seven Progressives and three Democrats. The La Follettes hinted that forming a national third party might be a good idea. Lewis B. Schwellenbach, running on the End Poverty in Washington platform, won his Senate contest, and his Commonwealth Builders played a key role in electing half the state legislature and a new King County prosecutor, Warren Magnuson. Norman Thomas lost his Senate bid in New York but drew nearly two hundred thousand votes. Floyd Olson, winning another term as the Farmer-Labor governor of Minnesota, proclaimed a mandate to put his public-ownership program into effect. His platform declared that "only a complete reorganization of our social structure into a cooperative commonwealth will bring economic security. . . ."

Upton Sinclair's defeat in California, therefore, looked like a river running the wrong way on the political map. It defied both the Democratic and the leftist trends. But no one in the White House or the press was complaining.

Indeed, many newspapers warned that the radical threat was worrisome enough as it was. The *Hartford Courant* forecast that the conflict in Congress during the next two years would not be between Democrats and Republicans but between "conservatism and radicalism." The Portland *Oregonian* observed that Roosevelt now had on his hands "a Congress made bumptious by smashing victory and permeated with big ideas. The Lord help us if it gets out of hand!" The *Washington Star* predicted that the radical element in Congress would press for leftist legislation sure to be opposed by mainstream Democrats. "In which direction," the paper wondered, "will the President lead?"

From Germany, where newspapers generally hailed FDR's victory, came this comment from *Das Tageblatt:* "Roosevelt has won the power of the dictator without taking the name. More than ever he now has a free hand. This," the Berlin newspaper added, "is the century of those who must be led."

Although he failed once again to make it to the polls, Will Rogers today expressed satisfaction with his party's gains. "The Republicans," he wrote, "have had a saying for some time, 'The Roosevelt honeymoon is over.' They were might poor judges of a love-sick couple. Why he and the people have got a real love match, and it looks like it would run for at least six years.

"If there is one thing the Republican party has got to learn it is that you can't get votes by just denouncing. You got to offer some plan of your own. They only had one platform, 'Elect us, and maybe we can think of something to do after we get in, but up to now we haven't thought of it, but give us a chance, we may.' "

One of the many victims of the Democratic landslide was Harry Hopkins's brother, Dr. Lewis Hopkins, the Republican candidate for coroner in Tacoma, Washington. A few days ago, Harry had suggested that the Republicans conduct an autopsy if his brother lost. Today Dr. Hopkins complained that the local voters took literally the "so-called wit of my brother" and he offered this prognosis of the New Deal: "favorable for next two years, with possible fatal termination at that time."

William Fox, undeterred by his latest setback in court, came to call on Jim Farley again today. Farley's secretary noted for the record that Big Jim was seriously considering Fox's job offer, and that his wife wanted him to take it.

Will Hays, whom Farley might displace as movie czar if Fox ever returned to power in Hollywood, wrote a personal note, in longhand, to President Roosevelt today from New York. Hays cited the "immeasurable" importance of FDR's role in "the lives of us all and the country's future. . . . I simply must express to you how I feel. I *know* you will succeed!" Along with his note, he sent along a three-stanza poem in Negro dialect, entitled "Perspective," but did not indicate whether he wrote the cautionary message himself or simply copied it. It began:

> You look way down 'long de railroad track
> And you scratch yer crown and yer brain ye rack—
> "By gum," y'say, "How de train done gwine
> To make its way where de two rails jine?"

———

Contrary to Will Rogers's assessment, Governor Frank Merriam apparently did earn votes by "just denouncing," and plenty of them. Latest returns indicated that when all of the ballots in California were counted, Merriam would have roughly 1.1 million votes; Sinclair, 900,000; and Haight, 300,000.

Although he won convincingly, Merriam received less than 50 percent of the vote. What if one of his opponents had dropped out and endorsed the other? Few suggested that the fusion candidate would have received *all* 1.2 million anti-Merriam votes. A considerable number of EPICs would never have voted for Haight; many Haight supporters preferred Merriam to Sinclair.

The best estimate of Haight's impact on the race could be gleaned by studying the vote for lieutenant governor. Because Haight ran without a running mate, his supporters had a chance to pair him with either George Hatfield or Sheridan Downey. From the raw figures, it appeared that of the 300,000 who voted for Haight, roughly 40 percent picked the EPIC candidate for lieutenant governor, 30 percent chose the Merriam man, and the rest selected neither.

Some EPICs nevertheless speculated that the *combination* of the Haight candidacy and vote fraud on Election Day cost their man the election. Others believed that Sinclair would have picked up at least 250,000 votes across the state had FDR signaled his support. Since the two major parties boasted roughly the same number of registered voters, dissident Democrats had obviously pushed Merriam over the top.

In any case, Sinclair had received twice the number of votes of any previous Democratic candidate for governor of California. Any Democrat in the FDR era might have accomplished that, but no other Democrat would have confronted such hysteria and hostility. A. P. Giannini called the EPIC vote "nothing short of amazing. . . . You can't tell me that there isn't something wrong somewhere when a man like Sinclair without any newspaper support can get nearly a million votes." A social security system "has got to come," Giannini told reporters.

According to the press, the most unhappy man in California this morning was Tom Mooney, who had been banking on Governor Sinclair to spring him from San Quentin. Big-time gamblers also took a beating in the election. Many had wagered that Merriam would carry the state by three hundred thousand votes, and the governor had let them down.

Merriam had steamrollered San Francisco, polling roughly 110,000 votes to 85,000 for Sinclair and 20,000 for Haight. In the north, as in the south, the pattern was the same. Sinclair fought Merriam to a draw or beat him barely in most precincts; but where the Democrat lost, he lost decisively, by three-to-one margins and up. Merriam topped Sinclair 600 to 247 in Carmel, even earning the vote of poet Robinson Jeffers. In the Los Angeles area, Sinclair fared well in Torrance, San Pedro, El Monte, and Burbank and poorly in Glendale, Monrovia, Santa Monica, and Pasadena. Statewide, Sinclair seemed likely to carry only a handful of counties, all small and all in the north.

Ray Haight ran well in the Central Valley, where the McClatchy chain of *Bee* newspapers, which supported him, dominated press coverage. Haight polled 13 percent of the vote statewide but drew thirty percent in the ten counties served primarily by the *Bee*s. This suggested that if W. R. Hearst had endorsed Haight, he might have indeed made it a close, three-cornered contest.

Six thousand voters selected Sam Darcy, the Communist party candidate. Milen Dempster, the Socialist, earned just three thousand votes, a significant drop from 1930, when the vote for the party's nominee for governor topped fifty thousand. (That candidate, of course, was Upton Sinclair.) Figures on write-in votes wouldn't be released for a while, but election officials in Pasadena counted more of them this year than ever before. Huey Long polled four votes in Pasadena, Chester Rowell two, and Adolf Hitler, Karl Marx, and John Dillinger one or two apiece.

"California is vindicated," Chet Rowell editorialized this morning in the *San Francisco Chronicle.* "The bitterest campaign, over the most important issue since the Civil War, has ended in the triumphant victory of the cause of sound Americanism." Over a smiling photo of the winner, the *Chronicle* ran this headline: MERRIAM, WE ROLL ALONG.

Prepared for this eventuality, Philip Norton, the Los Angeles realtor who had predicted a post-election land rush, ran an ad in the *Los Angeles Times* this morning. "Election results clear way for home building," he declared, making a sales pitch for property in Moreno Highlands.

Addressing the Los Angeles elite this morning at the Breakfast Club, Frank Merriam thanked the Democrats who provided him with his crucial margin of support. It was a victory not for the Republican party but for "all those who love California." The state, he added, must now move forward in the interest of economic rehabilitation, human welfare, and social justice.

One man in the audience, Jefty O'Connor, must have felt like the cat that swallowed the canary: Frank Merriam had made good on his "nonpartisan" pledge. When the two men met after breakfast, Merriam asked O'Connor to tell the President that he wanted to cooperate with the White House on all relief measures. Jefty suggested that the governor come to Washington and discuss his state program with FDR, and Merriam said he might just do that. Before they parted, Merriam thanked O'Connor for helping to seal his election. "I appreciate what you did," Merriam said.

Shortly after noon, O'Connor wired Roosevelt at Hyde Park: "Governor Merriam kept faith with me. . . . My trip was worthwhile."

Later, at lunch, Senator McAdoo told Jefty that he had decided not to disinherit his daughter Ellen if she went ahead and married her middle-aged Filipino-Malaysian-Spanish movie extra. "She's nineteen," McAdoo said, and old enough to make that kind of decision. Then O'Connor, his California assignment completed, caught a flight east.

Frank Merriam, meanwhile, returned home to Long Beach, where he greeted newsreel cameramen and fielded telegrams. "California has voiced its attitude on the issue of radicalism," Billy Knowland wired from Oakland. Another telegram came from Herbert Hoover in Palo Alto. "My sincere congratulations," the former president said, "for the state and yourself."

Hollywood celebrated the end of the Sinclair scare the same way it conducted the Merriam campaign—with little fear or shame. Studio executives announced that they would "resume" normal production and expansion, although no one had noticed any slowdown during the campaign. Paramount claimed it was rehiring three hundred workers now that California had found "peace of mind" and "all threats of moving the picture industry from Hollywood to Florida [are] forgotten." Claudette Colbert, star of *Cleopatra,* who had delayed building a new home in Holmby Hills, announced that contruction would begin next week now that the Sinclair hurricane had passed.

The *Hollywood Reporter* called the GOP victory "epoch-making" and bragged that the movie industry deserved the lion's share of credit for it. "The biggest men in the business stood shoulder to shoulder against the Sinclair menace," the movie journal boasted, fighting with "every bit of their brains and energy. . . ."

For the first time in history, W. R. Wilkerson argued, the movie magnates had joined hands and fought a battle side by side. Now they must stick together, since they faced outside scrutiny in the wake of nationwide publicity about their questionable campaign tactics. Wilkerson called Sinclair's request for a congressional investigation "poppycock," but he welcomed it anyway. "Our industry leaders," he said, "would then be able to tell the lawmakers of the country why they fought Sinclair, why they cut him to ribbons, why they caused pictures to be shown in their theatres showing the fallacy of his promises.

"They would be able to impress those lawmakers that the picture business is ready and willing to fight any force that seeks to destroy it. They would be able to show that the industry has RIGHTS and it intends to protect those rights. . . . There is no force in this world as strong as the motion picture screen, a screen that has always sought to be of benefit to the nation and its people and that, until now, has always taken the slaps directed at it in a horizonal position."

In an editorial entitled "Election's Over, Go to Work," *Variety* advised the movie colony not to turn vindictive against those unfortunates who backed EPIC, for Sinclair's demise was punishment enough. Now if only the movie execs would put as much energy and creativity into making pictures as they had into "putting over Merriam," they would really have something to brag about, *Variety* noted.

When Dr. William J. Jacobs, a fifty-three-year-old proctologist, left his apartment in Santa Barbara to go to his office this morning, he got into a raging argument with A. G. Marchind, the manager of the building. Jacobs, a Sinclairite, took exception to Marchind's jubilation over the results of the governor's race. Soon he was raving mad and threatened to go out to his car, get his gun, and shoot the Merriam supporter dead. But when Jacobs reached his automobile, he drove to his office instead.

Later, still agitated, he happened to drive past his former secretary (and lover), Adelaide Flint, and her friend Lillian Newlon, who were walking down State Street about two blocks from the Fox Theater. Miss Flint, encouraged by Mrs. Newlon, had recently broken off her relationship with the doctor. Jacobs pulled over to the curb, took out a .32-caliber pistol, yelled at his former lover, "You dirty snake!" and shot Miss Flint through the shoulder and her friend in the head. Then he went home and attempted to kill himself with a lethal dose of morphine. Police arrived and took him to the hospital and then to jail, where he was charged with one count of murder and one count of assault with a deadly weapon.

What does an author-politician do the day after losing the most important election of his life? Threaten to write a book about it, of course. And so Upton Sinclair did. He even gave it a title: *I, Candidate for Governor, and How I Got Licked.* It would tell the inside story of the campaign, including details of his conversations with Roosevelt, Farley, Coughlin, Creel, McAdoo, and O'Connor. Sinclair proposed January 7, the day of Merriam's inaugural, as the publication date. Royalties would go to pay off Sinclair's personal campaign debts, but he would also self-publish a cheap edition that the End Poverty League could sell to raise funds.

I, Candidate would probably occupy all of his attention over the next thirty days. Sinclair resolved to lock himself up in his Beverly Hills home and dictate a chapter a day. He would change his phone number, let a secretary answer his mail, and refuse to see visitors. As for EPIC, he would offer spiritual guidance and political advice, but he would leave organizational decisions in the hands of his trusted colleagues. Right now the best thing he could do for EPIC, and for himself, was to tell the people of California and the entire country the real truth about the campaign—in book form, of course.

To drum up demand for *I, Candidate,* Sinclair decided to offer hundreds of daily newspapers the serial rights to the book for the modest fee of one dollar per thousand circulation. A paper with a circulation of only five thousand, for example, would pay just five dollars for this privilege. A publication such as the *Boston Post* would pay $340, still a trifling sum for several dozen installments. This sounded like an offer few could refuse, no matter how stridently Sinclair attacked the press in his manuscript. Even Republican newspapers in Los Angeles and San Francisco might sign him up: now that the Sinclair threat had passed, they could capitalize on the author's notoriety.

The election over, Sinclair enjoyed a day in Beverly Hills with no campaign appearances or radio addresses. A stack of telegrams rested on his desk. From Democratic headquarters in Glendale: "We wish to assure you that we are with you to the last man." From a Berkeley women's group: "We are further behind you for further educational campaign." From a lady in San Diego who claimed to be a descendant of Thomas Jefferson's: "You are much superior to Roosevelt. Vindicate God and truth by starting recall of Merriam and Hatfield." From a woman in Oakland: "My undying loyalty and support I pledge you as long as I live." From a man in Oakland: "I promised Debs to fight until Tom Mooney was liberated. I make the same to you to end poverty in this world." From a woman in Long Beach: "Not being able to address you as I had confidently expected, 'Dear Governor,' I shall make it, 'Dear General.' Here's to the next skirmish with the enemy!" And from a man all the way out in Monroe, Louisiana: "Workers throughout the land know you were cheated out of the election. This proves a lot of things."

Ironically, on this day after the election, Sinclair finally received his fifty-dollar article fee from the *Literary Digest,* whose straw poll predicting a Merriam landslide—wildly inaccurate, as it turned out—did so much to damage his chances.

Before racing for Los Angeles, Sinclair dictated forty letters. To Frank O'Brien of EPIC's Research Associates in Los Angeles: "My chin is up and what seems to be defeat is really a victory." To a man in San Pedro: "We are far from being licked. The crucifixion of Jesus was looked upon as the greatest failure the world had ever known and now we know it resulted in the greatest victory."

Clem Whitaker and Leone Baxter were savoring their double victory—CLAS's triumph over Sinclair and Hatfield's win over Downey—when an old friend appeared at the door of their Sacramento office. It was Sheridan Downey, whose office was practically across the street. "The vanquished," Downey said, holding his hands out in a sweeping gesture, "greets the victors."

Other EPIC candidates fared better than Uppie and Downey (perhaps because Whitaker and Baxter had left them alone). Twenty-four

EPIC-backed Democrats earned seats in the state assembly, giving the Democrats thirty-eight seats to the Republicans' forty-two. Although the state senate remained firmly in GOP hands, EPIC's Culbert Olson won Los Angeles County's sole seat in that chamber. Eight Democratic congressmen in L.A. County won with EPIC support, including Sinclair's friend John S. McGroarty, the poet laureate of California. If the GOP stole the election, one newspaper asked, how did so many Democrats win local contests?

Among the successful EPIC-endorsed assembly candidates: Augustus F. Hawkins, a political newcomer who would replace Fred Roberts as California's only black legislator. EPIC's Lee Geyer won in Gardena, his campaign managed by a saxophone-playing schoolteacher (and political novice) named Ralph Dills. But the upset victory of the day belonged to John B. Pelletier, the bum plucked from skid row by Artie Samish's office. Pelletier did more than throw a scare into the GOP incumbent Clair Woolwine: he defeated him. Another EPIC supporter, John Anson Ford, won a hotly contested supervisor's race in L.A.

Surviving an election-night scare, William F. Knowland captured a state senate seat in Oakland, but Democrats grabbed four of the seven assembly seats in that area and one of two congressional contests. The results were so unexpected, Knowland felt it was as if a political cyclone had swept through the region.

The Democratic party in California, state chairman Culbert Olson observed, now resembled the national Republican party in 1856. Formed in 1854, the GOP failed to elect a president in its first try but in 1860 won with a candidate named Lincoln. "This is our election of '56," Olson declared. "Upton Sinclair has re-founded the Democrats in this state, and we take up where he left off."

In truth, most of the new EPIC Democrats in the legislature were more Democrat than EPIC, although at least eight were firm Sinclairites. Having lost a close contest in the Pomona area, Jerry Voorhis would not be joining the EPIC bloc in Sacramento. "With bowed head and broken heart I accept it," he announced, "and shall try to be a better citizen and more loyal son of the new America, of whose birth let us hope our present troubles are but the travail pains." Voorhis could not believe that the voters in his district, no matter how affluent they might be, had rejected the EPIC cause; rather, he felt, they "voted against me."

In a letter to his friends, Voorhis predicted that the EPIC movement "is going to become one of those great forces which appear from time to time in human history and actually change the minds and hearts of people until the world is made new." And he sent a message to Upton Sinclair:

> Your speech last night on the radio was one ray of hope in a dark, dark world. It was great—the greatest speech I ever heard. Never was I more devoted to you, never more devoted to fight with you. All I want to know is—"where do we go from here?' "

For Earl Warren, victory was bittersweet. He won another term as district attorney of Alameda County. Frank Merriam took the governor's race and Warren's pet ballot initiatives, extending civil service and expanding the power (and salary) of the state attorney general, passed. But the GOP took a beating in the state assembly races, and Merriam's coattails proved nonexistent in congressional races. Losing candidates were sure to criticize the party chairman for concentrating too much money and energy on the governor's contest.

Warren wired his congratulations to Merriam in Long Beach and offered "cooperation and aid whenever possible" in the future. "The purpose," Warren added, "is to stand by you in your leadership and fortify you against an opposition which will be persistent and resourceful."

Now that a most unsavory political campaign was history, Warren decided to shake off the mud and chart a new course for Republican leadership in California. In an official statement, he called Merriam's triumph a "progressive victory" and "nonpartisan in character." The GOP now had the responsibility to solve social and economic problems by fair and just means. "If we are to succeed," he said, "we must put our governmental house in order and keep it in order. We must make common honesty our watchword. There must be no room for the grafter or the chiseler, either high or low, and all persons must be brought to realize that the government of California is interested in but one thing—the welfare of its people."

At San Simeon, W. R. Hearst teletyped a message to his editors suggesting that the combined lesson of FDR's landslide and Sinclair's defeat was this: "Continued progressivism is demanded by the public, but SOUND progressivism." He also warned that if the New Deal did not soon produce "practical results," it would spawn an opposition party based on a "more judicious progressivism" or else "an era of communist protest which may threaten our American institutions." Hearst informed his famous columnist, Arthur Brisbane, that California had avoided the Sinclair "smallpox" and was "well rid of him."

By the time Upton Sinclair reached EPIC headquarters at 1501 South Grand in Los Angeles in the early afternoon, the place was mobbed with well-wishers. The crowd spilled out of the building and into the street. Reporters took out their notepads, eager for Sinclair to amplify his just-released concession statement: "I concede that the election has been stolen."

Like their leader, the EPICs wore resentment on their sleeves. EPIC attorneys vowed to take legal action against the E. F. Hutton brokerage house. They had secured depositions from employees of a printing company in San Francisco alleging that the Hutton firm had paid for production of the bogus Young People's Communist League leaflets. According to the attorneys, this evidence "clearly shows who is really responsible for 'Communist scares' in California." They promised to charge Hutton with libel and failing to identify itself on campaign materials, as required by state law.

EPIC workers across the state continued to assemble evidence of vote fraud. In one San Francisco precinct where three votes were recorded for Sinclair, EPIC attorneys claimed to have on hand forty affidavits from registered voters who said they voted for him. And so it went. The EPICs planned to package the evidence and send it off by courier to Senator Norris in Washington. The upstanding citizen they chose for this task: the former O'Melveny employee who had pilfered Albert Parker's "terror" letter.

Upton Sinclair might have reason to yelp, but his charge that the election was stolen was little more than rhetoric on his part. Sinclair welcomed an investigation but feared a recount; he wanted to get on with the rest of his life. And he wanted EPIC to get on with its task, too.

Speaking to his campaign workers, Sinclair expressed his "eternal gratitude" to those who built the EPIC movement into a potent force throughout the state. They should consider the results of this first skirmish a great victory over opponents who spent millions of dollars to destroy them. "We are the Democratic Party of California," he said. "We are going ahead to end poverty in California and then to end poverty in civilization." The EPICs cheered wildly. Sinclair promised that after taking a month off to write a book, he would help chart new directions for the End Poverty League, encourage the formation of self-help cooperatives, and write a regular column for the *EPIC News.* And he predicted that within a year the people of California would be "ready for a movement to recall Merriam and Hatfield. The campaign promises of the Republican reactionaries are always made to be forgotten immediately. The people of California will hear no more from them about the thirty-hour week or about a pension of two hundred dollars a month for the aged."

After serving notice to the Republicans, Sinclair issued this warning to old-line Democrats who planned to take back control of the party: "Only those who remained loyal to the Democratic party during the recent campaign will remain in the party and be recognized as Democrats. Mr. Bryan is no longer a Democrat. Cotton is in the same boat. It is possible they will form a rump organization of Democrats who feed out of the Republican trough, but the real Democrats of California will not be fooled by any such false leaders."

Sinclair closed to thunderous applause. His pep talk seemed to reenergize the downcast EPICs. Earlier in the day the mood had been bleak. An unconfirmed report that two EPICs had attempted suicide, one successfully, circulated at headquarters. Now the outlook for the End Poverty movement appeared rosy again. The EPICs' worst fear, that Upton Sinclair would abandon them once the ballots were counted, had not come to pass. Some spoke of promoting Sinclair as a favorite-son candidate for president in 1936; others vowed to put him in the governor's chair in 1938 if by chance they did not succeed in recalling Merriam before then.

Speaking to reporters afterward, however, Sinclair suggested that his office-seeking days were over. "If we had a better candidate this year," he said, chuckling, "we might have won." He was, he confessed, "an author of too many books trying to be a politician." When Sinclair tried to leave the EPIC building, he discovered that the hallways were so jammed he could not get out. Upton Sinclair's campaign for governor of California ended with him climbing out a street-level window at his own headquarters to make an escape.

Later, one of his friends, a writer in Los Angeles, related a story that convinced the always credulous Sinclair that another run for office would not only be futile but possibly fatal. His friend claimed that on election night a businessman she knew wrote out his will, stuck a pistol in his pocket, and set out for a radio studio where Upton was scheduled to speak. If Sinclair had won the election, the businessman, according to this account, would have shot him dead on the spot.

EPILOGUE

Three days after the election Upton Sinclair started dictating his campaign memoir, *I, Candidate for Governor, and How I Got Licked.* "It is a revelation of what money can do in American politics; what it will do when its privileges are threatened," he stated right at the outset. Dozens of newspapers, ranging in size from the *New York Post* and the *Boston Post* to journals in Nacogdoches, Texas, and Murfreesboro, Tennessee, purchased the serial rights. Several California papers that strongly opposed Sinclair's candidacy—including Joe Knowland's *Oakland Tribune,* Chester Rowell's *San Francisco Chronicle,* and Tom Storke's Santa Barbara *News*—paid for the privilege of carrying his account of the campaign.

The *Chronicle* advised readers on November 14 to watch for "the exploding of more political dynamite than has been detonated in California since the State became a part of the union." Five days later the Sinclair series began in the *Chronicle* as a daily feature. Chet Rowell informed Herbert Hoover that he had deleted several paragraphs from the author's manuscript, fearing that the incendiary prose would set the newsprint on fire.

Hoover, claiming that he "took no vocal part" in the California campaign, professed not to worry about anything Sinclair might write. Others read the excerpts with a certain amount of dread. Westbrook Pegler took exception to Sinclair's account of their meeting in San Francisco. "I knew you for a nut, of course," Pegler informed him, "but I did think you were a square guy."

When Sinclair revealed FDR's "promise" to endorse production for use, Jefty O'Connor clipped the column from an East Coast paper and sent it to the White House. Marvin McIntyre commented that he found the excerpt "very interesting, even though it is water over the dam."

James A. Farley had much the same reaction. "There is nothing we can do, Louis," Farley advised FDR's secretary, Louis Howe. "I only hope he gives you hell the same time he is giving it to me."

Actually, in his reflections on Farley, as in much of the rest of the book, Sinclair displayed his usual generosity of spirit—at least when it came to individuals. (He thought nothing of condemning whole classes of people.) Rather than attack Farley, he blamed his enemies in California for sending garbled quotes from his books to Washington. "If I got myself into a mess, it wasn't up to [Farley] to get me out," Sinclair admitted. "He hadn't written *The Profits of Religion* and it wasn't up to him to pay the price."

While writing *I, Candidate,* Sinclair hid out at his residence in Beverly Hills and instructed Craig to deflect all invitations, guests, and telephone calls, a service she was only too eager to provide. Finally she had Uppie all to herself again. But the hermit of Beverly Hills couldn't keep letters from arriving. Entrepreneurs wanted him to endorse products. Far-flung political groups invited him to speak. Zeppo Marx expressed interest in producing a big-budget Hollywood movie about EPIC, with Sinclair playing himself. ("Mr. Sinclair's voice records well," one press account puffed, "and his stage presence was described as good.") From Rapallo, Italy, Ezra Pound provided a detailed assessment of why Sinclair lost:

> If ever a man with enough intelligence to be held responsible for his acts deserved to be beaten at the polls you are that man. You got a mind like an old family photograph album. Any idea you get, stays. . . . All this stuff in yr/book. OF COURSE, who the hell didn't expect the other side to bribe etc/IS that news? Had you got in, you might have done more harm than good/heavan knows. . . . Forget Upton Sinclair the Big big noise, and think a little about economics. Were you more anxious to BE governor, or to govern and reform California, and bring in a better economic system?

From his favorite violin partner, Albert Einstein, Sinclair received the following message:

> My son, when he was about five years old, attempted to split wood with my razor. You can be sure that it was less bad for the wood than the razor. . . . As I read that this cup had passed from you, I rejoiced even though it had not gone exactly according to your wish. In economic affairs the logic of facts will work itself out somewhat slowly. You have contributed more than any other person. The direct action you can with good conscience turn over to men with tougher hands and nerves.

Einstein, who once endorsed Sinclair's experiments in mental telepathy, might have been reading the candidate's mind. Sinclair felt as though he had coughed up an alligator, he told a friend. Once all the votes in the November 6 election were counted, he beat a hasty retreat from the front lines of the EPIC struggle; after fourteen months on the firing line, he felt he had suffered enough. Sinclair believed he could turn EPIC over to Dick Otto and other trusted advisers while he reasserted his role as intellectual muse and master propagandist. "Six months ago I could have stopped the EPIC movement," he told one interviewer. "Now it doesn't make any difference what I do."

In his first postelection column for the *EPIC News,* Sinclair thanked the EPICs for their loyalty and insisted that they had vindicated his lifelong faith in democracy. "A few fainthearted ones may drop out," he observed, "but the great multitude will stick to the end, which will be the END OF POVERTY IN CALIFORNIA."

Newspapers in California applauded Sinclair's defeat, which they had done so much to bring about. The *Los Angeles Times* pronounced Sinclairism dead and buried in the state and throughout the nation. It complained that Uppie was a "poor loser" but thanked him for running, as the election gave the people of California an opportunity "to answer the slurs, the imputations—the winks and insinuations—that have made California a laughing-stock throughout the country." Chester Rowell of the *San Francisco Chronicle* called on Frank Merriam to take heed of the enormous vote for Sinclair and promote moderately progressive measures.

Across the country, *The New York Times* discovered a moral to the California story: When a threat like Sinclairism arises, "the only way, the American way, is to challenge the whole thing directly, face it squarely, and make an end of it for good and all. California has shown the rest of the country how to go about such a disagreeable business and do it thoroughly." *The Nation* underlined the *Times*'s view from a leftist perspective, concluding that Sinclair's defeat "shows what will happen to any radical who attempts to challenge the existing order through the medium of an old-party machine."

When the *Literary Digest* asked newspaper editors to name the outstanding personality of 1934, Upton Sinclair finished a strong fourth behind FDR, Hitler, and Mussolini (and just ahead of the Dionne quintuplets).

Frank Merriam indicated in the days following the election that he did indeed respect Sinclair's big vote and that he might even keep some of the pledges he made during the final days of the campaign. When he suggested that he'd consider supporting co-ops, a state income tax, and the thirty-hour week, the *Los Angeles Times* seethed. It hadn't gone to war for Merriam, the editors raged, simply to put him in a position to legislate some of Sinclair's lunatic ideas.

On November 21, George Young, editor of Hearst's *Los Angeles Examiner,* attended a dinner in San Bernardino and listened to Frank Merriam inform a group of orange growers that the election did not settle all of California's problems. Again the governor mentioned the possibility of raising taxes and providing old-age pensions. After dinner, Merriam told Young that he wanted to meet with W. R. Hearst to solicit his advice. Young passed this along to Hearst's top adviser, John Francis Neylan, in San Francisco. Neylan wrote Hearst:

> To be brutally frank, somebody is going to have to supply the brains for the present governor of California. The old political maxim that you can't beat somebody with nothing was proved to be unsound in the recent election in California. Whoever undertakes to supply the brains will have a 365-day job each year.

Neylan maintained that Hearst should meet with Merriam. "I cannot see that it would do any harm," he advised, "and it would give us firsthand information as to what the old boy has in mind, if anything."

Hearst, in response, agreed that doing Merriam's thinking amounted to an every-day job, and he did not have "365 days to devote to the old gentleman." The publisher was preoccupied with yet another journalistic crusade: exposing Communists on campus.

When Merriam announced his new tax program in January 1935, W.R. ordered his California editors to attack the governor. "I do not think people want a secondhand Sinclair," Hearst asserted.

Shortly after Election Day, Frank F. Merriam signed an official Statement of Candidate's Receipts and Expenditures for the state elections office. The instructions stated that the office seeker was expected to supply an itemized record of "all moneys paid, loaned, contributed or otherwise furnished to him, or for his use, directly or indirectly, in aid of his election."

Under a heading asking for the names of individuals who had contributed to his campaign, Merriam wrote: "None. Certain moneys were paid to committees interested in my campaign and candidacy, the amounts, by whom paid and to whom paid are unknown to me." Merriam insisted that if any payment was made in excess of the amount allowed by the Purity of Election Law, "I disclaim responsibility therefore." Asked to account for campaign expenditures, he repeated this disavowal.

Any misgivings Franklin Roosevelt might have felt about fumbling a chance to install a Democratic governor in California were mitigated by his party's sweep everywhere else. Jimmy Walker, the former New York mayor, put it best in a telegram to Jim Farley: "That wasn't an election, it was a census taking." Farley cited as one of the most gratifying results Herbert Lehman's crushing victory over Robert Moses. New York might never hear from Moses again, Farley predicted.

A few days after the election, letters from angry Sinclair supporters poured into the White House. Some called for a federal investigation of election fraud in California, and asked FDR how he could have stood by and let it happen. Many threatened not to support Roosevelt for reelection in 1936.

Jefty O'Connor returned to Washington for a meeting with the President on November 13. After listening to O'Connor recount his adventures in Los Angeles, FDR commented, "Jefty, you must take the party leadership in California." That night O'Connor noted in his diary that the President "was amused at my interviews with three candidates for Governor."

Two days later, in a confidential letter, Roosevelt urged O'Connor to accept the top Federal Reserve post in San Francisco, stressing what he called the "political angle." O'Connor was still a young man, FDR observed, and "by going to California at this time you enter that situation at the precise psychological moment." He would have a clear shot at the U.S. Senate when McAdoo left the scene, "and there is also, of course, the Governorship to consider as well."

A. P. Giannini also urged his friend to take the Federal Reserve job, which would put O'Connor in a good position to assist California's biggest banker. "If you decide you don't like it," Giannini observed, "why we'll run you for Senator—and I'll start the campaign with a $50,000 contribution."

Early in December, FDR attended the annual Gridiron Dinner in Washington. One of the skits performed by the Washington press corps gave W. R. Hearst credit for destroying Upton Sinclair. Normally a leader of the opposition party would roast the sitting president, but instead, a writer, H. L. Mencken, was drafted for this job.

"I am put up here," Mencken explained, "to speak a kindly word for the solvent and the damned, or, as the more advanced thinkers say, for the Rotten Rich." Mencken performed the task with relish, but FDR came prepared. The President delivered an uncharacteristically bitter assault on the American press, claiming it was shot through with "stupidity, cowardice and philistinism" and staffed by reporters "who do not know what a symphony is, or streptococcus. . . ." With growing pleasure the audience realized that the President was quoting from Mencken's essay "Journalism in America."

Mencken, for once, lost his sense of humor. "I'll get the son of a bitch," he said, turning to the gentleman sitting next to him. "I'll dig the skeletons out of his closet." Arthur Brisbane later informed W. R. Hearst that FDR "literally skinned Mencken alive quoting his own former writings to him most effectively."

Before long, Mencken was calling the President an unprincipled fraud. If FDR became convinced that "coming out for cannibalism would get him the votes he so sorely needs," Mencken observed, "he would begin fattening a missionary in the White House backyard come Wednesday." In a letter to Ezra Pound shortly after the election, Mencken declared,

> All of the ideas you have labored for for so many years are now taken over by a gang of Communists (chiefly kikes) and reduced to complete

absurdity. The country reeks with quacks of all sort. Indeed, so many are in view that shooting at them becomes almost a technical impossibility. . . . The country is going down to bankruptcy at enormous speed, and the only question remaining at issue is when the crash will come.

A different sort of crash was already occurring in California. Upton Sinclair had worried about what might happen to the End Poverty League if his campaign for governor ended in defeat, but even he was surprised at how quickly it came unglued. Many EPICs wanted the organization to remain in the election business; they would challenge the powers that be in municipal elections in 1935 and compete in congressional contests the following year. But another large faction argued that they should remain outside the Democratic party, build their own base, and work closely with the co-op movement to institute EPIC-from-below.

After months of subservience to Sinclair, egos and fiefdoms suddenly appeared, and the *EPIC News* took on a life of its own. Dissident EPICs begged Sinclair to attend a rump meeting, claiming that Dick Otto, End Poverty League director, had established an "undemocratic autocracy" and that EPIC was "at the fork of the road." Sinclair replied that he had complete faith in Otto, and besides, he had a book to write that would benefit everyone. One activist commented, "In moments of crisis a pedant goes to his book, but a wise man looks at the world." Rube Borough resigned as editor of the *EPIC News* and started his own paper, the *United Progressive News.*

On November 23, Culbert Olson, chairman of the state Democratic party, challenged the End Poverty League to abandon its name and unite with other liberal groups under the Democratic banner. Essentially he advocated that EPIC become a network of reform Democratic clubs. Some EPIC chapters voted to comply; others vowed defiance. Confused EPICs dispatched telegrams and letters to Beverly Hills seeking Sinclair's advice, but his response remained the same: I trust Dick Otto; follow *him.*

Otto angrily explained the EPIC "isn't a party, it is a movement." Culbert Olson charged Otto with "dictatorship"; Otto accused Olson of conspiring with Ham Cotton to take over EPIC. Again Sinclair sided with Otto. The press had a ball with all of this, of course. The End Poverty League moved to spacious new quarters in an old mansion on

South Figueroa in Los Angeles; its board of directors now met in a solarium. But the organization had squandered the momentum gained by its strong showing in the election.

Upton Sinclair no longer seemed capable of uniting the EPICs; by now, no one could. Communists from the co-op movement, sensing an opportunity to promote the party's new "united front" policy, had thoroughly penetrated the EPIC organization. At a convention called to democratize the EPIC movement in May 1935, open warfare broke out when Sinclair's allies proclaimed that only *they* could judge the credentials of the delegates. Communists demanded that Sam Darcy, their candidate for governor in 1934, be allowed to address the convention, and they showered delegates with leaflets tossed from the balcony inviting them to JOIN COMMUNISM IN THE UNITED FRONT. Sheridan Downey threatened to throw his gavel at a man shouting "steam-roller, steam-roller." Some delegates screamed in the direction of Sinclair, "Throw him out!"

Sinclair grew visibly agitated. Verbal adroitness gone, no longer able to get by on intelligence, wit, and charm, he insisted that some way must be found to "throw the Communists out. . . . They are here in an attempt to break up the EPIC organization." Pointing to several delegates, he demanded, "Isn't it true that you are a Communist—and you—and you!" Considering the orientation of the campaign against Sinclair in the autumn of 1934, it was ironic that EPIC would finally be torn apart by its own Red-baiting.

Dispirited, Sinclair left on a nationwide lecture tour aimed primarily at paying off his campaign debts. On three occasions he debated Hamilton Fish, the Republican congressman from FDR's home district in New York. The lecture tour produced at least one enduring moment. Motoring among the redwoods of northern California en route to the Pacific Northwest, Sinclair got an idea for an ecologically aware children's book about a dwindling tribe of little men who live in a commercially threatened forest. He wrote the book in 1936 and personally handed Walt Disney a copy, suggesting it would make a mighty fine film. Walt explained that the story wasn't right for cartoon characters, but if his studio ever started using live actors, he would take Sinclair up on his offer. And years later, with *The Gnome-Mobile,* he did.

Two films with a liberal political outlook, kept off the screen in California until after Sinclair's defeat, performed poorly once they were released. The reception that greeted *We Live Again* inspired one of Sam Goldwyn's most famous malapropisms. The public, he explained, "stayed away in droves," despite (or perhaps because of) a rave from *EPIC News* movie critic Upton Sinclair.

A Hearst editor in Los Angeles, meanwhile, informed the Hays Office that "local bankers" had "held up" *We Live Again* until after the election because it was "dangerously near the border line of Russian propaganda." The Goldwyn movie apparently stimulated W. R. Hearst to write yet another editorial for his newspapers in late November attacking pro-Communist messages in movies. The Hays Office clipped the Hearst editorial and sent it to all of the studios with a warning that pictures containing Red propaganda would not be tolerated.

King Vidor's *Our Daily Bread,* despite its selection by *The New York Times* as one of the ten best films of 1934, did not open in Los Angeles until the end of January 1935. To mark the occasion, the manager of the Pantages Hollywood Theater paid Upton Sinclair fifteen hundred dollars to deliver a five-minute talk before each show for a solid week. The *Los Angeles Times* petulantly refused to carry advertising promoting these appearances. An ad in Hearst's *Examiner* billed the film this way: DANGEROUS, DESPERATE DERELICTS, CHARGED WITH HUMAN DYNAMITE!

Walter Wanger's *The President Vanishes* reached the screen only after a celebrated battle with the Hays Office. After previewing the movie on November 9, Joe Breen instructed Wanger to make several deletions if he wanted to win Will Hays's seal of approval. These included cutting a speaker's reference to "capitalistic bloodsuckers" and toning down incidents that "may be interpreted as subversive of government and contrary to the accepted principles of established law and order." On November 22, after Wanger agreed to make some of the changes, Breen issued his OK.

The following day Will Hays informed the film's distributor, Adolph Zukor of Paramount, that he was still displeased. Hays admitted that *The President Vanishes* did not violate the Production Code, so he appealed to Zukor to order additional changes in the film as a matter of personal choice. The movie industry "has no right," Hays argued, "to present a distorted view of the banking, steel and newspaper business," or to show such "banality and corruption in our governmental and political machinery."

Zukor acquiesced and ordered the cuts. Wanger commented, "Mr. Hays ought to take over censorship of the comic pages." The film finally received the Hays seal and opened in theaters. On January 31, 1935, Breen informed Hays, too late, that Wanger had slipped the reference to capitalistic bloodsuckers back into the final cut.

———

Recognizing a born storyteller when it saw one, Hollywood asked Upton Sinclair to let bygones be bygones. Two months after the election Sinclair spoke confidently about a "big-budget" movie portraying the rise of EPIC. Zeppo Marx predicted it could be a "four-star hit" because of the worldwide interest in Sinclair. And Joe Schenck's Twentieth Century Pictures made plans to film Sinclair's play *Depression Island.*

According to one report, Louis B. Mayer—at the suggestion of Will Hays—asked Sinclair to submit script ideas to MGM. "This is not the all-time high for kiss and make up," the L.A. *Daily News* observed, "but it's pretty high at that."

In another one of the many postelection ironies, the Hollywood magnates renounced Governor Frank Merriam, who had called for taxes on movie admissions and on raw and finished film, among other things. The moguls, Frank Scully observed, had saved California from Sinclair, "and what do they get for it? Their owns purses lifted! Is that gratitude?" Once again they threatened to move out of the state. Joe Schenck took another highly publicized trip to inspect real estate in Florida. MGM and Fox inventoried their property in case they decided to flee.

"Please tell them if they go to Florida, I'll go too," Sinclair warned. He said he could organize an EPIC movement in Florida before the moguls finished building their first soundstage.

Louis B. Mayer made an emotional appearance before the Breakfast Club in Los Angeles in April 1935. "I love California—I don't want to move from California!" Mayer cried. He claimed that he would become a Socialist, a Bolshevik, even a Democrat, or anything else "which will bring happiness and security, which will continue the high standards of living of the working men of our country." Afterward one of his friends started calling him Comrade Louis.

The state legislature ultimately dropped its tax proposals aimed specifically at the movie industry but (thanks to the strong EPIC bloc in the assembly) instituted a state income tax. W. R. Hearst said he could not afford to live at San Simeon under those conditions, but neither he nor any of the moguls quit the state.

Hollywood at the top returned pretty much to normal following the Sinclair campaign. But in many ways it was never the same. In a March

1935 analysis of the California race entitled "The Screen Enters Politics," *Harper's* warned that the "movies have tasted blood." The screen "offers the image, which impresses the onlooker as the fact. Therein lies its excessive danger and the fear aroused among thinking people by its total lack of responsibility. . . . Will the nation be warned by California's recent experience?"

Actors and writers outraged by the *California Election News* shorts carried huge chips on their shoulders. Shortly after the election, at a Beverly Hills party hosted by two prominent liberals, Fredric March and his actress wife, Florence Eldridge, several guests, including writer Kyle Crichton, railed against the studios' tactics in the campaign, particularly the Inquiring Cameraman films.

Suddenly, and to the surprise of nearly everyone, Irving Thalberg quietly announced, "I made those shorts."

"But it was a dirty trick!" Fredric March protested. "It was the damnedest unfair thing I've ever heard of."

"Nothing is unfair in politics," Thalberg replied, unperturbed. "We could sit down here and figure dirty things all night, and every one of them would be all right in a political campaign."

"It wouldn't be all right with me," March maintained.

"That's because you don't know politics," Thalberg answered, recalling his days as a boy orator for the Socialist party in New York. Tammany Hall, he explained, never would have let his party win an election in New York. "Fairness in an election," Thalberg advised, "is a contradiction in terms. It just doesn't exist."

Despite their affection for Thalberg, the liberals vowed revenge. "After 1934," screenwriter Philip Dunne later recalled, "we said, 'Never again.' EPIC created a liberal climate in Hollywood for the first time." Politics in Hollywood moved steadily to the left over the next few years. Liberals organized popular crusades against Hitler and Franco. Guild activity intensified, with many union activists claiming that the eye-opening Sinclair campaign sparked their enthusiasm. Some liberals moved far to the left and joined the Communist party.

In 1938, Frank Merriam came up for reelection, and this time the Hollywood liberals were ready for him. Led by Philip Dunne and actor Melvyn Douglas, they formed the Motion Picture Democratic Committee and lined up behind their candidate—former EPIC leader Culbert Olson. In a gratifying twist, Olson swamped Jefty O'Connor in the Democratic primary and then took on Merriam in the finals. Melvyn Douglas served as Olson's campaign manager in southern California.

Putting the shoe on the other foot, the Hollywood activists produced anti-Merriam radio shows and film shorts—including an Inquiring Reporter trailer called *California Speaks*—and raised large sums of money for Olson. Displaying keen wit, they demanded that Merriam contribute one day of *his* salary to the Olson war chest.

Frank Finley Merriam's tenure as governor had proceeded pretty much according to his modest plans. He cooperated with New Deal relief measures and allowed pensions for the elderly to reach the highest level in the land. Primarily concerned with balancing the state budget, he proposed no major initiatives to fundamentally alleviate unemployment. He did provide jobs, however, for friends who had helped him whip Sinclair. Among his judicial appointments: Goodwin J. Knight.

If anyone "supplied the brains" for the governor, it was Kyle Palmer, formerly of the *Los Angeles Times,* who wrote many of Merriam's speeches and pretty much dictated state policy. When Merriam balked at signing a measure that would help Asa Call reorganize Pacific Mutual, Palmer advised, "The *Times* wants you to sign that bill, Governor"—and he did.

In May 1935, *Time* magazine stated emphatically what it had only hinted at in its cover story the previous October. Governor Merriam, *Time* revealed, "black-jacked California's influential Republicans into nominating him against Sinclair by threatening to withhold State troops from the San Francisco strike last summer." Nevertheless, in 1936 Frank Merriam, with the support of W. R. Hearst and Dr. Francis Townsend, offered himself as a favorite-son candidate for president. Appalled, moderate Republicans asked Earl Warren to assemble uncommitted delegates, and Warren's slate swept the California primary. Two years later anti-Merriam Republicans promoted George Hatfield for governor, but the insurgency failed.

That set the stage for something of a rematch of the '34 election. Culbert Olson was no Socialist, but his platform endorsed production for use and called for public ownership of utilities. Olson wasn't the only former EPIC running for high office: Sheridan Downey had trounced Senator William G. McAdoo in the Democratic primary (even though FDR campaigned on Mac's behalf in California). Neither Olson nor Downey was as radical as Sinclair, but this only worked in their favor. The GOP and the press attempted another smear campaign, this time to little effect. Olson beat Merriam by over two hundred thousand votes.

Completing the EPIC comeback, Sheridan Downey captured the U.S. Senate seat. One Republican movie producer sadly remarked, "I guess we started something in 1934."

———

When Culbert Olson took office as governor of California in January 1939, he fulfilled a promise Upton Sinclair had made five years earlier: as his first important official act, he pardoned Tom Mooney. The day Mooney left San Quentin, an enormous crowd welcomed him back to San Francisco. But it was too late for Mooney, hobbled by ill health, to return to the barricades; he died in 1942. The Preparedness Day bombing has never been solved.

After the Mooney celebration, it was all downhill for Culbert Olson. Intemperate and a poor administrator, he frittered away a popular mandate. The Republicans, who still held the state senate, opposed his progressive measures while his liberal allies argued among themselves. During Olson's first eighteen months in office, bipartisan front groups launched three separate efforts to recall him from office (indicating what Sinclair might have faced had he actually managed to win in 1934). Olson squabbled with Earl Warren, the newly elected state attorney general.

Earl Warren easily defeated Culbert Olson in the governor's race in 1942. His campaign generals: Clem Whitaker and Leone Baxter. His army: the California Republican Assembly.

In contrast to his predecessors, Earl Warren blossomed in office. He reduced taxes while raising pensions and expanding unemployment insurance. Running for reelection in 1946, he managed the unprecedented feat of winning both major-party nominations. His friend Robert G. Sproul nominated him for president at the GOP national convention in 1948; when Thomas E. Dewey won the top spot, the delegates made Warren his running mate. When Harry Truman beat Dewey, Warren returned to California, where he earned a third term as governor in 1950.

Despite his popularity, the moderate Warren had plenty of critics. Conservatives opposed many of his social programs. Liberals charged that he lacked vision and rarely fought for progressive legislation. Some charged that he was beholden to the power brokers—Kyle Palmer, Asa Call, and Joe Knowland—who had groomed him for his present position. This view gained credence when Hiram Johnson died in 1945 and Governor Warren appointed William Knowland to take his place in the U.S. Senate.

On September 3, 1953, Warren announced that he would not seek a fourth term in office. Five days later Fred Vinson, chief justice of the U.S. Supreme Court, passed away, and President Eisenhower picked Earl Warren to replace him. The following May, Chief Justice Warren announced the historic decision declaring racial segregation in public schools unconstitutional.

Goodwin Knight succeeded Warren as governor. In 1958, Knight was beaten by Edmund G. ("Pat") Brown, who won reelection in 1962 by defeating Richard M. Nixon.

Upton Sinclair's longtime friendship with Henry Mencken, sorely tested during the 1934 campaign, virtually ended a few months afterward. Mencken's third and last anti-EPIC column, "Storm Damage in Utopia," appeared in the *Baltimore Sun* on January 28, 1935. A year later the two writers suffered what appeared to be a permanent break.

It began with Mencken observing in the *American Mercury* that if Sinclair ever did occupy a high office, he would crush his opponents "with a kind of ferocity that will make that of Hitler and Mussolini look puerile." If Uppie had his way, Mencken maintained, he would make it a capital offense to disbelieve his pet theories on "thought transference, vegetarianism or spondylotherapy. When you get among apostles, you get among carnivora with sharp teeth."

Sinclair, enraged for once, instructed Mencken that he ought to be ashamed of himself. "I have made freedom of discussion the basis of all my preaching," he added. Not once during the EPIC campaign, even when he was subjected to the worst abuse, did he call for "violence, illegality or confiscation."

Mencken replied, "It seems to me that you are a professional messiah like any other, and would perform precisely like the rest if you got the chance." He pointed out that while Sinclair properly denounced Hitler and Mussolini, he said nothing against Stalin. Finally he blasted Sinclair's refusal to play the political game of give-and-take:

> You are far, far better on the give than on the take. No man in American history has denounced more different people than you have, or in more violent terms, and yet no man that I can recall complains more bitterly when he happens to be hit.

Noting that the people of California had refused to follow Sinclair as a Socialist, as a Prohibitionist, and as a Democrat, Mencken advised,

"The rule is that three strikes are out. To the bench, Comrade; to the bench!"

Friendly correspondence ceased. When they did exchange notes, it was merely to discuss the fine points of semantics and other technical conceits. Finally, as elderly men, they reconciled. In 1951, when Mencken suffered a cerebral thrombosis from which he never completely recovered, Sinclair wrote to wish him well. "I remember that during the EPIC campaign or just after it," he observed, "you wrote me to the effect that I had been trying to get on the public payroll. Let us forgive each other such blindness before we take our departure from this time and place of world war, both political and military."

A few days after the '34 election, Will Rogers observed that if Upton Sinclair had only had a few more dollars in his campaign chest, "he'd have been elected." Several days later, Will proposed that Sinclair debate Huey P. Long during halftime of the Rose Bowl on January 1, with Rogers and Aimee McPherson as referees. Sinclair replied that he'd do it only if Will agreed to debate Sister Aimee.

On July 1, 1935, Will Rogers emceed the dedication of the hulking new *Los Angeles Times* building. "They had to move out of the old *Times* building because of the termites," Rogers disclosed. "The *Times* had a special kind—their columnists."

A few weeks later, Will Hays visited Will Rogers at his Santa Monica ranch. Correcting a popular misconception, Rogers told Hays that he *never* said he never met a man he didn't like. "Only an idiot would say that," Rogers confided. What he actually said, he revealed, was, "I never *kidded* a man I didn't like."

On August 15, a light plane crashed near Point Barrow, Alaska, after its engine failed on takeoff, carrying its famed pilot, Wiley Post, and his friend Will Rogers to their deaths. When rescue workers recovered Rogers's typewriter, they discovered a sheet of paper still stuck in the carriage, carrying his final written words: "Now I must get back to advising my Democrats."

The nation mourned Rogers with a display of genuine affection not witnessed since the death of Lincoln. While private funeral services were being held at Forest Lawn, twenty thousand fans met at the Hollywood Bowl to express their grief. The NBC and CBS radio networks went off the air from coast to coast for thirty minutes, and motion-picture theaters darkened their screens in silent tribute.

In 1946, Will Rogers, Jr., taking a step his father had rejected, ran for the U.S. Senate in California as a Democrat. Carey McWilliams, head of the state immigration and housing agency under Culbert Olson, wrote speeches for him. Rogers ran a strong race but was beaten by William Knowland.

A few days after Merriam licked Sinclair in '34, Charlie Chaplin filmed a voice test under the direction of his friend King Vidor. The results changed nothing: the Little Tramp would remain speechless in Charlie's upcoming film (although he did get to sing a song).

When the film, finally titled *Modern Times,* was released in February 1936, critics perceived it as a political statement, albeit an entertaining one. A reviewer for the left-wing *New Masses* felt "stunned" that such a socially conscious picture could come out of Hollywood, while apolitical critics expressed relief that Chaplin was still first and foremost a funnyman. *Modern Times,* nevertheless, did poorer business than expected, which probably had less to do with its politics than with its anachronistic "silence." In any case, it marked a turning point in Chaplin's career. Hereafter his name would forever be linked with politics in the minds of the critics and the public.

The movie Billy Wilder worked on in the fall of 1934 proved somewhat less memorable than *Modern Times.* This saga about tunnel builders, once called *Sandhogs,* then *East River,* was finally released as *Under Pressure.* Four writers received screen credit, and Billy, happily, was not one of them. Wilder joined the Screen Writers Guild, and in 1936 he married a niece of Lieutenant Governor George Hatfield's. Uncle George "was a nice fellow," Wilder recalls. "When we talked about the 1934 campaign, years later, he was still having a near heart attack over it. He made it sound like a Communist army was trying to take over Hollywood—like another *Potemkin.*"

James Cagney remained politically active in Hollywood for years, and maintained his friendship with Lincoln Steffens right up to the writer's death in 1936. At one point, he told Steffens that the studio bosses gave him so many headaches he would "come up and cry on your shoulder before long." In 1940, Cagney testified before the Dies Committee, which was investigating Communist subversion. Cagney was in hot water again for donating an ambulance to the Abraham Lincoln Brigade in Spain, among other things. "When somebody tells you a hard luck story," Cagney instructed the congressmen, "you don't investigate him first, you help him first."

When Maurice Rapf, following his trip to the Soviet Union with Budd Schulberg, came out to California during the Christmas holiday in 1934, his father, as promised, sent him to see Irving Thalberg for some political reeducation. Schulberg accompanied him. Pacing the floor, Thalberg told Maurice and Budd that "everyone" is a Socialist when young. "Even I was full of idealism," he confessed. "But as we mature," he continued, "we see things in a different light. We become more conservative."

Then Louis B. Mayer informed Maurice that he owed it to the Jews to renounce radicalism. "Everybody thinks Jews are Communists," Mayer argued. *That's funny,* Maurice mused, *everybody I know thinks Jews are capitalists.* Rapf joined the Communist party; in 1951, in the middle of his screenwriting career, he was blacklisted.

Budd Schulberg quit the CP in the late 1930s after party members criticized his first novel, *What Makes Sammy Run,* as individualistic and decadent. Louis B. Mayer, angry about the book's unsparing portrait of life at the top in Hollywood, urged Budd's father to have his son "deported." *Sammy* includes a scene in which the producer Sammy Glick attempts to bully a studio colleague into supporting Merriam during the '34 governor's race.

A leading proponent of the blacklist, W. R. Wilkerson not only named names in the *Hollywood Reporter*—he identified pseudonymns and even supplied Communist party membership card numbers. But his greatest claim to fame remained the discovery of actress Lana Turner.

Felix Feist, director of the Inquiring Cameraman shorts, made many B movies in the 1940s and 1950s, including *Donovan's Brain.* Carey Wilson helped develop MGM's Andy Hardy and Dr. Kildare movie series. Irving Thalberg passed away in 1936 before reaching the age of forty. His son, Irving Thalberg, Jr., eventually turned his back on Hollywood and became a professor of philosophy. He wrote three books, quietly funded leftist causes, and during the fabled Chicago 8 trial in 1969 allowed Tom Hayden, William Kunstler, and other radicals to bunk at his apartment in the Windy City.

In 1947, Katharine Hepburn delivered the keynote speech at a Los Angeles rally for Henry Wallace, the Progressive candidate for president. "Silence the artist and you silence the most articulate voice the people have," Hepburn said, condemning the incipient anti-Communist witch-hunt in Hollywood. When she entered the MGM commissary the next day, nearly everyone stood up and cheered. But Leo McCarey, the director, decided not to cast Hepburn in his next picture because of her speech for Wallace.

Shirley Temple, a lifetime Republican, ran for Congress in the 1960s but lost—one of the few times the Whitaker & Baxter firm failed to manage a candidate to victory. She currently serves as U.S. ambassador to Czechoslovakia.

———

Although their first meeting in September 1934 produced unsatisfactory results, Upton Sinclair attempted to schedule another conference with President Roosevelt one year later.

Nineteen thirty-five began badly for the President. The glow of the Democratic landslide in November 1934 dimmed amazingly quickly. Despite a slight decline in unemployment, ten million Americans—almost one fifth of the work force—were still without jobs. FDR finally put forward his social security and public-works initiatives, but Congress at first balked—partly to assert its independence. Conservatives charged that five billion dollars for public works was too much; progressives considered it too little. "We have come," Walter Lippmann wrote in March 1935, "to a period of discouragement after a few months of buoyant hope."

Thus emerged the Second New Deal, as it later became known. The White House sought to stimulate recovery by restoring a competitive society. The Supreme Court struck down the NRA. Rex Tugwell pretty much lost his voice at the White House as Keynes, Brandeis, and Frankfurter rose in influence. "Patching" was all the Second New Dealers knew how to do, Tugwell later commented, "or, at any rate, all their enemies, as they regained their strength, would let them do." The basic change in 1935, historian Arthur Schlesinger, Jr., later observed, "was in atmosphere—a certain lowering of ideals, waning of hopes, narrowing of possibilities. . . ."

Beyond Washington, FDR faced a grass-roots rebellion even among the people who most (or at least, once) loved him. Five days after Election Day in 1934, Father Charles Coughlin announced the formation of the National Union for Social Justice, which he hoped would lead a populist third-party movement in 1936. The following day Governor Floyd Olson of Minnesota predicted an agrarian political revolt that would bring down the "profit system." In July 1935, five radical U.S.

congressmen called a conference in Chicago in July 1935 to explore forming a new party. Upton Sinclair sent a message suggesting that they rally around production for use but warned that a third-party run for the presidency in 1936 would only result in the reelection of Herbert Hoover—"which would be the greatest calamity in American history."

The White House girded for a Huey Long race for the presidency. Taking a page from Upton Sinclair's book, Huey hired a ghostwriter to produce a volume called *My First Days in the White House.* As one might imagine, it was bit more comical than Sinclair's *I, Governor.* (President Long put FDR in his cabinet as secretary of the navy, for instance.) As the EPIC movement waned in California, the Townsend Plan and Huey Long's Share Our Wealth gained millions of adherents from coast to coast.

Near the end of September 1935, President Roosevelt journeyed west for the dedication of Boulder Dam. From there, he would travel to Los Angeles. Sinclair, claiming to speak for 879,000 Californians who "have been voiceless since last November," wired FDR, again beseeching him to embrace production for use.

Neil Vanderbilt, a friend of both men, arranged for Uppie to climb aboard the President's train at Yermo.

"Jim Farley says he's a Bolshevik," Roosevelt complained, referring to Sinclair.

"No more than I am," Vanderbilt replied, finally convincing the President to breakfast with Sinclair the following day.

Sinclair reached the Yermo station at six-thirty in the morning. Unfortunately, so did a large crowd of onlookers and a few brass bands. Neil went out to find Uppie; suddenly the train started pulling away prematurely. Vanderbilt ran and jumped back on board, leaving Sinclair stranded on the platform. "At the time, no doubt, Sinclair thought I was in on the double cross," Vanderbilt later wrote, "but Farley did it to me."

By this point, however, Sinclair posed little threat to the President. Sinclair was convinced that the Communists had gained control of EPIC, and consequently he was "out of politics," Vanderbilt advised FDR. Further evidence that the Sinclair craze had expired in California: The parents of Upton Sinclair Marshaw, not yet two years of age, announced that they intended to legally change the child's name.

But Sinclair had one last hurrah. He produced his long-promised End Poverty in Civilization booklet, a futuristic fable closely resembling *I, Governor.* Entitled *We, People of America, and How We Ended Poverty,* it described a "Four-Year Plan to Make Over America." Sinclair disavowed any interest in running for office but fantasized that EPICs would take over the national Democratic party in 1936 and *force* FDR to endorse production for use (and, ultimately, enact the EPIC plan).

Lightning failed to strike twice. In fact, it barely flickered. In the 1936 presidential primary in California, the Sinclair-led slate of Democratic delegates lost to a McAdoo slate by a seven-to-one margin.

The EPIC organization lingered for years, and mimeographed copies of the *EPIC News* appeared as late as 1946, but the 1936 primary would be Upton Sinclair's last election campaign. In the aftermath of EPIC, his wife requested—and received—from Sinclair written promises to refrain from political activity.

———

While Upton Sinclair sat on the sidelines, his leading adversaries in 1934 continued to play the electoral game with a vengeance.

Clem Whitaker married his associate, Leone Baxter, and for twenty-five years the couple divided their time between managing candidates and disseminating propaganda for and against ballot initiatives. They taught Earl Warren "how to smile in public," *Time* magazine reported, "and were the first to recognize the publicity value of his handsome family." In the late 1940s, Whitaker and Baxter tallied their score and announced that they had won 90 percent of their campaigns. By that point, when discussing any race in California, the first question most people asked was: Where are Whitaker and Baxter?

Until the 1950s, they were the only political consultants in the country. Carey McWilliams called them "something new in American politics . . . the firm has evolved a style of operation which makes the old-fashioned boss and lobbyists completely obsolete. Whitaker & Baxter has ushered in a new era in American politics—government by public relations." The couple's precepts, developed in California in 1933 and 1934 and widely publicized years later, became gospel for campaign managers across the country:

- "Never wage a campaign defensively! The only successful defense is a spectacular, hard-hitting, crushing offensive."
- "Attempt to create actual news instead of merely sending out publicity."
- "More Americans like corn than caviar."
- "The average American doesn't want to be educated; he doesn't want

to improve his mind; he doesn't even want to work, consciously, at being a good citizen. [But] most every American likes to be entertained. He likes the movies; he likes mysteries; he likes fireworks and parades. . . . So if you can't fight PUT ON A SHOW!"

When President Truman put forward his national health insurance program in the late 1940s, which seemed likely to pass, the American Medical Association paid Whitaker & Baxter a fee of $350,000 to defeat it. The pair, who had thwarted a similar plan in California proposed by Governor Warren, dubbed the Truman proposal "socialized medicine." They distributed over 100 million pieces of literature, and in a two-week period in 1950 spent $1.1 million in advertising. Congress failed to pass the measure, virtually burying the idea for forty years.

After years of success, Whitaker and Baxter started to fade in 1958 after a falling out with their candidate Goodwin Knight. Clem Whitaker died of emphysema in 1961. A few years later Baxter turned the firm over to Clem Whitaker, Jr., who steered it out of electoral politics and into corporate P.R.

Future election campaigns, writer Irwin Ross predicted in 1959, would be dominated by the brief television speech, "the thirty-second spot," and "the carefully scripted political rally." Whitaker and Baxter, he observed, "can reasonably boast that they had led the way."

Kyle Palmer enjoyed moonlighting for Will Hays in 1934 so much that he left the *Los Angeles Times* a few weeks after the election to join the Production Code office in Hollywood. Returning to the *Times* in 1939, he resumed his role as kingpin of Republican politics, a position he maintained for more than two decades. "The *Times* was not an organ of the Republican Party in Southern California," David Halberstam later insisted, "it *was* the Republican Party." Governor Pat Brown, a Democrat, complained that even he had to go to Palmer's office "to kiss his ring." When Palmer retired in 1960, the *L.A. Times* called him "the good shepherd . . . almost saintly in his attitude toward his subject matter."

In his later years, Palmer claimed a warm friendship with the man he once called Ipecac Upton. "He's an oddball, he's very peculiar, but I like him," Palmer said of Sinclair. On one occasion, Sinclair, leaving for a holiday, asked Palmer to ghostwrite a statement for him for an East Coast magazine. Perhaps Sinclair felt that because of the '34 campaign Palmer knew his writing style as well as he himself did.

Asa Call, who directed United for California in '34, became the

GOP's chief fund-raiser, playing a pivotal role in electing Warren, Nixon, and Reagan, among other candidates. "Asa was the man who made up the minds for the businessmen for forty years," one political associate recalled, and this extended to civic affairs as well. In 1986, *Los Angeles* magazine called him "the most powerful man" in the city's history.

Artie Samish's control of the California legislature reached almost absurd proportions, until his reign as the "secret boss" of California ended abruptly in the late 1940s owing to his own cockiness. The super-lobbyist agreed to pose for a photograph for *Collier's* magazine in 1949 balancing a puppet on his knee. "How are you today, Mr. Legislature?" Samish asked the dummy. The lawmakers, shamefaced at last, took away his lobbying credentials, the U.S. Senate investigated him, and in 1953 Samish went to prison for evading seventy-two thousand dollars in taxes.

Although he had nothing to do with the '34 campaign, Richard Nixon became inextricably linked to many who did play a major role in that race. After he returned from war in 1945, Nixon ran for Congress against former EPIC activist Jerry Voorhis. Kyle Palmer decided Nixon was the best GOP candidate he had seen in years and steered the *Los Angeles Times*'s crucial support his way. Palmer also helped raise campaign funds, as did Herbert Hoover. After five terms in the House, Voorhis was regarded as one of the most effective legislators in Washington; but as a former Socialist and Sinclair supporter, he was an easy target for Nixon's Red-baiting.

In 1950, when Sheridan Downey announced his retirement, Kyle Palmer, Asa Call, and others picked Nixon to challenge Helen Gahagan Douglas for the U.S. Senate. In some ways, the Nixon-Douglas campaign replayed 1934. Many moderate Democrats, including George Creel, Sheridan Downey, and Manchester Boddy, worked for the Republican candidate; so did W. R. Hearst, L. B. Mayer, and C. B. DeMille. The press mounted a Red scare against Douglas, dubbing her "the Pink Lady." Nixon called the former actress (and wife of Melvyn Douglas) "pink right down to her underwear" and vowed to "castrate her." Hollywood lined up behind Nixon and many of Douglas's celebrity friends, at the height of the blacklist, were afraid to support her openly. Ronald Reagan, a Democrat, secretly raised money for Nixon.

Joseph P. Kennedy, through his son John, contributed to the Nixon campaign. Nixon won.

A few years later Nixon purchased Ham Cotton's estate at San Clemente. The scene of the biggest anti-Sinclair bash of the 1934 campaign served as the summer White House when Nixon became president in 1969.

To account for some of the other figures who played a role, prominent or otherwise, in the 1934 campaign:

JAMES A. FARLEY attempted to wrest the Democratic nomination from FDR in 1940, believing that Roosevelt should not seek a third term. Years later Farley claimed that he *never* favored Sinclair for governor in '34 but could not recall "how the President felt personally about" the candidate. RAYMOND MOLEY denied Sinclair's assertion that *he* was responsible for turning Roosevelt against him. FDR tolerated the EPIC "heresy" when Sinclair looked like a winner but backed off when it appeared to be a "losing heresy," Moley revealed.

WILLIAM LOEB, who drove Upton Sinclair to Hyde Park to meet FDR, purchased the Manchester *Union-Leader* in New Hampshire and for decades played a key role in presidential primaries. "The only good Communist," he once wrote, "is a dead Communist."

ALBERT PARKER left O'Melveny in 1935 to join a law firm in New York and later worked for the Justice Department in Washington. One of his most cherished possessions was a copy of *I, Candidate,* which Upton Sinclair sent to him in 1935 inscribed with this message: "To an enemy, to make a friend." Parker's pal ELI WHITNEY DEBEVOISE created one of the most prestigious law firms in the country with his partner, Francis Plimpton, father of writer George Plimpton. Debevoise played a lead role when his firm represented Alger Hiss in his two perjury trials.

HUEY P. LONG was assassinated in September 1935. The following year FATHER COUGHLIN joined with Dr. Townsend and Gerald L.K. Smith to spearhead the National Union party's try for the White House; their candidate, William Lemke, drew fewer than nine hundred thousand votes. Coughlin, by then a raging anti-Semite, lost all political influence.

Because JOHN PELLETIER, the EPIC "bum" elected to the assembly, had no money, Artie Samish had to buy him a new suit and pay his train fare to Sacramento so he could take the oath of office. Pelletier was reelected four times by his constituents in Los Angeles.

Another EPIC-backed candidate, AUGUSTUS F. HAWKINS, was later elected to Congress, serving with distinction until 1991. RALPH DILLS, campaign manager for EPIC's Lee Geyer in '34, took a seat himself in the assembly in 1938—and remains there today. SAM YORTY, who opposed Sinclair in '34, won his race for the assembly two years later, with EPIC support (unsolicited, he maintains).

JOHN STEINBECK's *The Grapes of Wrath* was published in 1939. One passage in particular captured the impetus for the original EPIC movement: "And a homeless man, driving the road with his wife beside him and his thin children in the back seat, could look at the fallow fields which might produce food but not profit, and that man could know how a fallow field is a sin and the unused land a crime against the thin children." Nunnally Johnson would write the screenplay for the 1940 film based on the book.

HEYWOOD BROUN died in 1939. His old friend, the increasingly venomous WESTBROOK PEGLER, took to calling President Roosevelt "Mama's Boy." After FDR died, Pegler labeled him "the feeble-minded fuehrer" and suggested that Americans visiting London should get drunk and desecrate the statue of Roosevelt in Grosvenor Square.

ERNST ("PUTZI") HANFSTAENGL fled Germany in the late 1930s, fearing for his life, after Hitler pulled a practical joke on him. (Hitler convinced Hanfstaengl he was about to be sent to Spain to serve as a special agent for Franco.) During World War II, Putzi turned up in Washington, D.C., ostensibly as an interned enemy alien but actually as an adviser to the American government.

In 1942, ALBERT LASKER abruptly turned over his Lord & Thomas advertising agency to three of his top associates: Emerson Foote, Fairfax Cone, and Don Belding. For five years during the 1940s, Helen Gurley Brown served as Don Belding's secretary. Belding, who had managed Lord & Thomas's activities against Sinclair in 1934, later confessed, "We hired the scum of the streets to carry placards through the cities, 'Vote for Upton Sinclair.' " He also observed, "You know, if the campaign had lasted a little longer, the public might have found out and the whole thing might have backfired." In 1949, with E. F. Hutton, he founded the anti-Communist group Freedoms Foundation.

AIMEE SEMPLE MCPHERSON died in 1944 of an overdose of Seconal. The International Church of the Foursquare Gospel today operates three Bible colleges and claims over half a million members in forty-nine countries.

Six months after the '34 election, ROBERT GORDON SPROUL denounced Governor Merriam for providing "niggardly" funds—a "Gandhi diet"—for the University of California. CLARK KERR succeeded Sproul as president in 1958, but the Berkeley Free Speech protests in 1964 tormented his administration, and Governor Reagan dismissed him two years later. His friend DEAN MCHENRY, a leading political scientist, served as founding chancellor of UC–Santa Cruz.

WILLIAM KNOWLAND, one of Chiang Kai-shek's top lobbyists, was known as "the Senator from Formosa" during the 1950s. His political career ended with an ill-advised race for governor of California in '58; Knowland later took over from his father at the *Oakland Tribune.* In 1974 he was found dead of self-inflicted gunshot wounds.

EARL ("SQUIRE") BEHRENS directed the *San Francisco Chronicle*'s political coverage for four decades. In 1968, looking back on the EPIC race, he disclosed that with the assistance of George Creel he had developed and "used as straight news items anti-Sinclair statements from leading Democrats."

Following the '34 election, RAYMOND HAIGHT supported several EPIC initiatives, and when he ran again for governor in 1938, Mary Craig Sinclair endorsed him. That year, as in '34, Haight's contributors abandoned him in the middle of the campaign. Afterward he told his son, Ray Haight, Jr., that he realized he had been "naïve." He had come to suspect that in '34 some of his funders secretly supported Merriam and kept him in the race just long enough to prevent progressives from stampeding to Sinclair.

Needless to say, Upton Sinclair did not stop writing when he retired from politics. In 1936, he completed a novel called *Co-op,* as well as a theatrical sketch, *Wally for Queen,* satirizing his famous cousin, Wallis Warfield Simpson, who had just run away with the King of England. The following year in two short novels he took on Henry Ford *(The Flivver King)* and Franco *(No Pasarán!).* Although a few pamphlets and broadsides would follow, this marked the end of Sinclair as muckraker-activist, for he had in mind a new career writing historical fiction with a dashing hero, not a working stiff, at its center.

Sinclair based his protagonist, Lanny Budd, on a number of his liberal friends, including Neil Vanderbilt. Lanny, an art dealer and a free-lance envoy for FDR, would hopscotch the globe, hobnobbing with everyone from Bernard Shaw to Hitler, Mao, and Stalin. Attempting to enlarge his audience, the puritan author allowed his hero several sexual conquests (although, for some reason, Lanny rejects Isadora Duncan).

The series, starting with *World's End* in 1940, would continue in almost yearly installments until 1953. Sinclair finally won a long-sought Pulitzer Prize in 1943 for the third book in the saga, *Dragon's Teeth.* All eleven of the Lanny Budd novels sold well, bringing Sinclair his widest audience since *The Jungle.* Thomas Mann claimed that one day the Lanny cycle would be recognized as "the best informed description of the political life of our epoch"; the series introduced thousands of readers to socialist ideas. Sinclair even enjoyed belated critical acceptance. A *New York Times* review observed that Sinclair had grown as a literary craftsman: "He has mastered his earlier tendency to put the idea and the symbol first and the character last. . . . The artist in Sinclair gets the better of the old crusader."

The artist was able to keep up his prodigious pace on the Lanny Budd books only because he had cut himself off from almost all political aggravation. Upton and Craig fled Pasadena in 1942 for a villa in outlying Monrovia. The old muckraker was now in his sixties, with more than four decades of political controversy behind him. Only rarely did he speak out politically. When he finally denounced Stalin, the *Los Angeles Times* joyously reported that Upton Sinclair now considered Russia a "slave state."

During the 1950s, Sinclair spent most of his time looking after Mary Craig, now an invalid. He ate nothing but rice and fruit, three times a day. Perhaps there was something to his "crank" diet after all: Uppie was remarkably fit. The occasional interviewer found him bright-eyed, intense, good-humored. "A man who is sensible, and knows the world, can't expect to change it in a lifetime," he confided to one reporter. Introducing a new edition of *The Jungle,* he admitted that he had once "placed far too high an estimate upon the intelligence of the human race, and its moral qualities." He offered this advice to his friend Norman Thomas:

> The American people will take Socialism, but they won't take the label. . . . I think we simply have to recognize the fact that our enemies have succeeded in spreading the Big Lie. There is no use attacking it by a front attack, it is much better to out-flank them.

Another decade dawned. Craig died, and Uppie remarried, at the age of eighty-three. (Hans Rutzebeck surprised the bridegroom by showing up at the wedding.) Eleanor Roosevelt attended a testimonial dinner in his honor. As an elder statesman, Sinclair accepted accolades left and right. Arthur Koestler, stretching the point a bit, asserted that he could think of no contemporary writer "whose non-existence would leave such a gaping hole in the face of the twentieth century [as] Upton Sinclair's." John Dos Passos, by now a Goldwater enthusiast, nevertheless insisted that he wished he "could see a few young men like [Sinclair] growing up in the new generation."

He still received a fabulous amount of mail. Old EPIC comrades kept him posted on their latest endeavors. Responding to a graduate student who had studied his work, Sinclair asked, "What did the reading of all my books do to your mind? I hope they didn't do any permanent damage."

When a scholar conducting an oral history showed him a copy of the original EPIC plan, Sinclair examined it eagerly. "I haven't read that statement for almost thirty years," he cheerfully reported, "and I'm astonished to see how sound it is and how clearly expressed. I take the liberty of telling you now that it's exactly right."

In his 1962 autobiography, Upton Sinclair acknowledged several notable accomplishments of his long lifetime. The EPIC campaign, he declared, "changed the whole reactionary tone of the state." In fact, it set the Democrats on a progressive course that the party sustained for more than fifty years, possibly even to the present day. Stanley Mosk, a Sinclair supporter in '34, later a state supreme-court justice, calls EPIC "the acorn from which evolved the tree of whatever liberalism we have in California."

Years after the Sinclair race, writer Carey McWilliams remarked that he still came across New Economy barbershops, EPIC cafés, and Plenty-for-All stores "in the most inaccessible communities of California." He saw the slogans of the EPIC campaign painted on rocks in the desert, carved on trees in the forest, and scrawled on the walls of labor camps. "I think it would have been a disaster if Sinclair had been elected," McWilliams observed. "He wouldn't have known what to do. But he did have the conviction that poverty was man-made, that you didn't need it."

Near the end of 1934, Harry Hopkins proposed a comprehensive program, dubbed End Poverty in America, which *The New York Times* said "differs from Mr. Sinclair's in detail, but not in principle." Along with other regional populist movements, EPIC exerted a leftward pressure on the New Deal, no doubt influencing FDR's groundbreaking legislation on social security and public works.

It is difficult, however, to assess the effect of the 1934 campaign, either on individuals or on society as a whole. Although in many ways unique, it was also part of a general reawakening of progressive ideals on the one hand, and the growing perception of a radical threat on the other.

The impact of the '34 campaign on the election process is somewhat easier to gauge. Arthur Schlesinger, Jr., called it "the first all-out public relations Blitzkrieg in American politics." It generated campaign techniques—including the creative use of film, radio, and direct mail—that forever changed the way candidates run for office. The '34 race was also "a landmark in the development of the political consultant," as writer Sidney Blumenthal put it. What Clem Whitaker called full-service campaign management later became de rigueur. And the anti-Sinclair crusade showed that national fund-raising for a state race could generate unimagined riches. (Kenneth S. Davis, in his book *FDR: The New Deal Years,* put the sum spent in California in 1934 at "something over $10 million.") All of these developments were inevitable, of course, as the political parties declined, the direct primary proliferated, and television arrived, but the '34 race served as the catalyst.

It didn't take long for the innovations of '34 to find meaningful expression in a presidential race. The national Republican party in 1936 hired an outside advertising agency, Blackett, Sample, and Hummert, Inc., to run its public relations office. The publicists distributed printed material in astounding numbers—probably over half a billion pieces in all. Something called a "spot announcement," only thirty-five words long, started appearing on the radio. Movie directors made a twenty-minute short touting the GOP nominee, Alf Landon, and created three-minute trailers aimed at black audiences. A staff of six came up with ideas that might attract newsreel coverage—the equivalent of today's "sound bites" and "photo opportunities." Like Lord & Thomas in '34, the GOP creative team produced radio dramas that mocked the Democratic candidate. Like Clem Whitaker in '34, publicists distributed ready-to-use editorials and cartoons to thousands of small newspapers.

The significance of all this was recognized immediately. Turner Catledge in *The New York Times* called the campaign in behalf of Alf

Landon "an intensive, subtle, highly organized salesmanship drive to 'unsell' President Roosevelt and his New Deal. . . ." *Variety* observed:

> Political parties are being reduced to merchandise which can be exchanged for votes in accordance with a well-conceived marketing plan, taking stock of income levels, race, local problems, exactly as does a commercial sponsor. This differs no whit from the tactics employed by Lifebuoy, Chase and Sanborn, or any other of a thousand consumer commodities.

Yet despite its efforts, the GOP could not push Landon into the White House. One significant reason: Roosevelt used radio extensively to repel Republican propaganda.

The '36 campaign also marked the first appearance of scientific polling techniques in an election. George Gallup, Elmo Roper, Jr., and Archibald Crossley all emerged on the national scene, and not a moment too soon: the *Literary Digest* straw poll, which had badly miscalculated the vote count in California in '34, picked Landon to win in '36. Gallup and Crossley underestimated FDR's landslide but correctly forecast his victory.

The next watershed was the 1952 campaign, when the first television spot ads, in behalf of Eisenhower, appeared. Never again would newspapers and radio dominate campaigns. Adlai Stevenson objected to appearing in spot ads but, after losing in '52, changed this policy four years later. Media analyst Edwin Diamond later observed that the anti-Sinclair film shorts served "as a model for television spot advertising when TV became a dominant national force." Just as movie trailers played to a captive audience, "so did television programming collect crowds for the advertisers' brief spots," Diamond added.

Although media specialists contributed significantly to campaigns, they still did not run the show themselves, with one exception—the Whitaker-Baxter team in California. That began to change in the 1950s and accelerated in the 1960s as the second generation of political consultants, led by Herb Baus, William Ross, Stuart Spencer, and Bill Roberts, came of age and television penetrated nearly every home. These political technologists utilized opinion polling and computers and began selling their candidates in a more systematic fashion.

After winning the California governor's race in 1966, Ronald Reagan confessed that the Spencer-Roberts agency had supplied the "know-how" for his candidacy. "I'd never run for office again," Governor Reagan said, "without the help of professional managers like Spencer and Roberts."

———

In 1966, the year Californians elected Ronald Reagan as their governor, Upton Sinclair left the state. He moved to Maryland to live near his physicist son, David, who was studying aerosols for Johns-Manville, and David's wife, Jean. At the age of eighty-nine, Sinclair visited the White House to witness President Lyndon B. Johnson sign the Wholesome Meat Act of 1967, the latest revision of the landmark laws created in the aftermath of *The Jungle* in 1906. There Sinclair met Ralph Nader, a modern sort of muckraker.

Healthy and exuberant almost to the end, though largely forgotten by the American public, Upton Sinclair died peacefully in a Bound Brook, New Jersey, nursing home on December 18, 1968. Concluding his autobiography a few years earlier, this man of perhaps too many words observed that anyone wishing to examine his heart after he passed on would find a simple epitaph written there: *Social Justice.*

———

By the 1970s, political consultants were often better known than their candidates. One of them reportedly declared, "Too many people have been beaten because they tried to substitute substance for style."

Political consultants had become the new powers in the political system. "They are permanent; the politicians are ephemeral," Sidney Blumenthal wrote in *The Permanent Campaign.* "By virtue of their central position inside campaigns, consultants, through the use of media, can shape our political thoughts."

The election of Ronald Reagan, a former actor, as president in 1980 crowned a process that began in 1934. "This was a P.R. outfit that became President and took over the country," a former Reagan deputy press secretary later commented.

"Clem Whitaker and Leone Baxter are now gone," Theodore White observed in 1982. "But their kind of politics—professional image-making—has not only persisted but thrived; and, in thriving, swept East, where a politics industry has grown up—a gathering of professionals who merchandise control of voter reactions."

At one point it appeared that 1988 would be another watershed election—at least in the arena of media politics. By the end of the Bush-Dukakis contest, the issue the candidates, the press, and the public discussed most was the vicious and dispiriting nature of the campaign itself. "Voters are fed up and turned off by a hail of mudslinging," *Newsweek* declared a week before Election Day. Two out of three voters in one survey complained that the candidates were manipulated by their "handlers." On Election Day, voter turnout sank to new lows.

Afterward, Michael Dukakis commented that his biggest mistake was not realizing that the campaign centered on ten-second sound bites. Indeed, one study showed that the candidates' average speaking appearance on the network news programs during the campaign was 9.8 seconds, down from 42 seconds for the Nixon-Humphrey race in 1968. This had broad ramifications. One reason the Reagan White House paid little attention to the emerging savings-and-loan crisis was because it "was too complicated for a catchy slogan or a television sound bite," *The New York Times* observed.

Two years later, the Markle Commission report on the media and the electorate declared that American voters no longer seem to understand their rightful place in the operation of democracy. The media's focus on campaign tactics over substance, and the candidates' use of negative and manipulative advertising, had encouraged a "cynical, passive and uninformed" electorate, the panel charged.

When the 1990 midterm elections rolled around, newspapers started critiquing TV spots for hyperbole and inaccuracy. This put the creators of so-called attack ads on the defensive but did little to curtail overwhelmingly negative campaigns, particularly in North Carolina, Texas, and California. And it only drew further attention to advertising, not issues, as the central component of campaigns. How did candidates in 1990 respond to surveys showing that voters increasingly "tuned out" political ads on TV? Not by cleaning up the ads or reducing their number but by running *more* of them to make sure their message got through. Voter turnout on Election Day 1990—just 36 percent—equaled the previous low, set four years earlier.

A year later, political experts polled by *The New York Times* promised that slashing media attacks would continue to dominate election campaigns. One analyst predicted "a mudbath" in the autumn of 1992.

———

One day recently, on the popular television game show *Jeopardy!,* the following "answer" appeared on the screen: WROTE "THE JUNGLE" AND RAN FOR GOVERNOR OF CALIFORNIA IN 1934. One of the contestants rang a buzzer, eager to supply (according to the rules of the game) the correct question that fit this answer.

"Who," the contestant asked, "was Sinclair Lewis?"

NOTES

Unless specified, all dates for letters and articles are 1934.

All books cited in the Notes are listed in the Bibliography, arranged alphabetically by author. A complete list of Sources (archives, interviews, and oral histories) follows the Bibliography.

Key for sources cited most frequently:

ACADEMY: Academy of Motion Picture Arts and Sciences, Herrick Library, Beverly Hills.

B: Bancroft Library, University of California, Berkeley.

BOA: Bank of America archives, San Francisco.

COLUMBIA: Columbia University (Butler Library).

DEBEVOISE FILE: File on '34 campaign kept by Eli Whitney Debevoise.

EPIC OHS: Oral histories related to the '34 campaign at the Bancroft Library.

HARRIS BIO: *Upton Sinclair: American Rebel* by Leon Harris.

HL: Herbert Hoover Presidential Library, Ames, Iowa.

I, CANDIDATE: Sinclair's out-of-print 1935 memoir of the campaign.

LC: Library of Congress manuscripts division, Washington, D.C.

LL: Lilly Library (Indiana University), repository of the papers of Upton Sinclair and his wife, Mary Craig Sinclair (MCS).

NYPL: Norman Thomas papers, New York Public Library.

RL: Franklin D. Roosevelt Library, Hyde Park, N.Y. (OF #1165-"Sinclair" and OF #300-"California" are the key files).

SINCLAIR AUTOBIO: *The Autobiography of Upton Sinclair.*
SINCLAIR OH: Oral history in the Columbia University Oral History collection.
UCLA: Special collections at Research Library, University of California, Los Angeles.
WARREN: Earl Warren papers at the California State Archives in Sacramento, California.

AUGUST 29

3 "I don't know where": *SF Chronicle,* Sept. 1.
4 Hearst and Munich: Swanberg book. Other details of trip: Winkler book; Lundberg book; Davies book.
"Patriotic conservatism": telegram to Coblentz, Aug. 10 (B-Coblentz).
Hearst and Hanfstaengl: Hillman telegram to Coblentz, Aug. 24 (B-Coblentz).
5 Neylan to Hearst: Aug. 29 (B-Neylan).
Farley and O'Connor: O'Connor diary (B-O'Connor).
6 Howe: Howe letter to Hopkins, Mar. 5 (RL).
Farley and Sinclair: *EPIC News,* July 23.
7 Farley informed FDR: Farley daily file, Aug. 14 (LC-Farley).
Farley to Howe: note, Aug. 28 (RL).
O'Connor and Farley: O'Connor diary (B-O'Connor).
8 Waldron visit: *Today,* Oct. 6.
9 Mencken at home: Manchester book and Mencken *Letters.*
"incurable romantic": *The Smart Set,* April 1920 (quoted in Harris bio).
10 Tender-minded and "He must suffer": Mencken quoted in Harris bio.
"I am against you": Mencken to Sinclair, Aug. 24, 1923, quoted in Remley dissertation. Many Mencken-Sinclair letters in Remley dissertation and in Sinclair's *My Lifetime in Letters.* Also see Remley article and Kress article for commentary.
Description of Mencken and hand washing: Cooke book.
11 Government the "common enemy": Mencken to Sinclair, Sept. 21, 1926 (LL).
Mencken on Sinclair campaign: *LA Herald,* Aug. 30.
Early and Farley: Early diary (RL) and Early telegram to McIntyre (RL).
Farley press conference: AP dispatch, Aug. 29.
12 Early wires McIntyre: Aug. 29 (RL).
Sinclair to FDR: Aug. 19 (RL).
Sinclair to Eleanor R.: Aug. 19 (RL).
13 "A special art": Schlesinger, *The Coming of the New Deal.*
Press conference: transcript, press conference #140 (RL).
14 Cooke and Chaplin: Cooke book; Cooke letter to author.
Chaplin and film: Robinson book.

15 Chaplin and Sinclair: Chaplin autobio; Sinclair autobio; Sinclair OH; Robinson book.

16 Chaplin and Eisenstein: Harris bio.
Chaplin telegram to Sinclair: Dec. 4, 1933 (LL).
Chaplin at rally: Sinclair autobio.

17 Letters and telegrams: LL.
Wilson: *The Nation,* Sept. 28, 1932.

18 Jere Miah II: *NY Times,* Aug. 29–30.

19 Telegrams to FDR: RL.
Elliott: *LA Times,* Aug. 30.
McIntyre telegram to Sinclair: RL.

20 Early to McIntyre: RL.
Hoover to Fletcher: Aug. 25 (HL).
Hoover to Merriam: Aug. 29 (HL).
Sinclair speech: *EPIC News,* Sept. 3.

AUGUST 30

25 Brisbane and Sinclair: Carlson book; Harris bio; Sinclair OH.

26 Long on Sinclair: *NY American,* Aug. 31.
Share Our Wealth: Burns, *The Crosswinds of Freedom.*
Sinclair to White House: LL.

27 Hopkins on Sinclair: *Washington Post,* Aug. 31.
Wallace: *EPIC News,* Sept. 3.
O'Connor telegram: RL.
Telegrams to White House: RL. Tucson man: W. R. Mathews (RL).

28 Mayer and Howard: Marx, *Mayer and Thalberg;* Carey book.

29 Mayer and politics: Gabler book; Brownstein book; *The New Yorker,* Mar. 28, 1936; Crowther book.
"A small boy": Brownstein book.

30 Mayer on Sinclair: Sam Marx interview.
Hearst to Neylan and Neylan to Hearst: B-Neylan.

31 Real estate: *California Real Estate Magazine,* Sept. 1934.

32 *LA Times* on Sinclair: Sinclair, *The Brass Check.*

33 Warren: Stone book; Warren book.
Warren to constituents: letter of Aug. 21 (Warren).

34 Sproul "for the past month": daily memos (B-Sproul).

35 Legion: Albrecht.
Sproul speech: manuscript (B-Sproul).

36 FDR speech: from *The Public Papers and Addresses.*

37 Clambake: Morgenthau diaries (RL).
"We are behind President Roosevelt": Paramount newsreel footage (Grinberg).

38 "I seem to have lost interest": Sinclair letter to Fulton Oursler, Sept. 6, 1933 (LL).
"First-time historian": *I, Governor.*
Messages pour in: Sinclair letters (LL).

39 Shadid telegram: Aug. 30 (LL).
Marshaw: *LA Examiner,* Aug. 29.
Sinclair at station: *Pasadena Post,* Aug. 31.

AUGUST 31

40 Block: *LA Times,* Aug. 29.
Orlando: Orlando book; *LA Herald,* Feb. 9, 1935.

41 McPherson background: Lately Thomas book; Wilson book; Starr, *Material Dreams.*
Poem: *The New Republic,* June 30, 1926.
Wilson: Wilson book.
Rogers: Weekly columns.
Orlando: Orlando book.

42 Huston: Harris bio.

43 Jere Miah II: *NY Times,* Sept. 1.
Morgenthau: Morgenthau diaries (RL).

44 McIntyre to Sinclair: Aug. 31 (RL).
Pelletier: Samish book, *LA Herald-Examiner,* June 9, 1989.
Samish background: Samish book; McWilliams, *California: The Great Exception;* Phillips book.
Samish and DeMille: *NY Times,* Feb. 14, 1974.

45 Samish and Jasper: Samish book, *LA Herald-Examiner,* June 9, 1989.

46 Samish and Merriam: Samish book.
Senate offer: *Pasadena Post,* Sept. 1.

47 "Merriamites and their ilk": *Pasadena Post,* Sept. 1.

48 Sullivan: *NY Herald-Tribune* syndicated column, Aug. 31.
Lawrence: syndicated column in *LA Times,* Aug. 31.
Hoover and Merriam: Hoover appointments calendar (HL).
Hoover on Liberty League: Letter to Fletcher, Aug. 25 (HL).

49 Hoover to Knox: Aug. 30 (HL).

50 Rogers: Weekly articles.
Dreiser: *Esquire,* Dec. 1934.
Utopians and Townsend: Brinkley book; Creel book; Schlesinger, *The Politics of Upheaval.*

52 Love taps: Sinclair to Mencken, Oct. 9, 1930 (LL, Remley).
"As always you are right": Mencken to Sinclair, Feb. 22, 1930, in Sinclair, *My Lifetime in Letters.*
"cunning as literary artist": *The Nation,* Sept. 23, 1931.
Sinclair begged: letter to Mencken, Jan. 30, 1932 (LL, Remley).
Sinclair claimed: letter to Mencken, June 7, 1932 (LL, Remley).
"Poke fun at it?": Mencken to Sinclair, Aug. 3, 1932 (LL, Remley).
Sinclair on Mencken: *EPIC News,* Sept. 3.

SEPTEMBER 1

54 Hearst and *NY Times: NY Times,* Sept. 2.
Hess: *NY Times,* Sept. 1.
Sinclair on Hearst: *I, Governor.*
Sinclair letter to Hearst: Feb. 13 (LL).
55 Hearst on Sinclair: *NY Times,* Sept. 2.
Birchall: letter, Birchall to Hearst, Sept. 1 (B-Hearst).
56 Scully background: Scully books; *Variety* obit, July 1, 1964.
57 Scully to McEvoy: Scully article, *Esquire,* Nov. 1934; Scully books.
List of writers: Scully form letter, undated (LL).
58 Scully and Gingrich: *Esquire,* Nov. 1934.
Vanity Fair: *Vanity Fair,* August 1934.
Mooney visited: Gentry, *Frame-Up.*
Mooney background: Gentry, *Frame-Up;* Frost book.
59 Sinclair and Mooney: Harris bio; Sinclair autobio.
60 Steffens: Gentry, *Frame-Up.*
Sinclair meets Mooney: *EPIC News,* March 1934; Sinclair OH.
Sinclair and Merriam: *Sacramento Bee,* June 7, and *SF Examiner,* June 8.
Mother Mooney in Sinclair headquarters: UP dispatch, Aug. 29.
61 Swink: *California Real Estate Magazine,* Sept. 1934.
Strategy: *California Real Estate Magazine,* Sept.–Dec. 1934; *EPIC News,* Oct. 1.
62 White: *Emporia Gazette* column reprinted in *EPIC News,* June 18.
Considered signing endorsement: letter to Mary Craig Sinclair, June 3 (LL-MCS).
"Not going to run wild": *Pasadena Post,* Sept. 2.
Finestone: *Motion Picture Herald,* Sept. 8.
Thalberg and Sinclair: Harris bio; Marx, *Mayer and Thalberg.*
63 Fox affair: Harris bio; Sinclair autobio.
Finestone: *Motion Picture Herald,* Sept. 8.
64 Chaplin and Cooke: Cooke book.
65 Rogers on Chaplin: column Oct. 15, 1933 (from *Will Rogers's Weekly Articles*).

SEPTEMBER 2

66 Tugwell awoke: Tugwell, *The Experimental Roosevelt.*
67 Carter on Tugwell: Carter book.
Tugwell and FDR: Tugwell, *The Experimental Roosevelt.*
FDR in church: Tugwell, *The Experimental Roosevelt.*
68 Sinclair and La Guardia: Sinclair, *I, Candidate; EPIC News,* Sept. 17.
"Drop a lot of bombs": *Washington Post,* Sept. 2.
69 Hollywood rebounds: *Film Daily* yearbook, 1935.
70 *Variety* on drive-in: Aug. 29.
71 *Variety* on Sinclair: Sept. 4.
Baseball game: *NY Times* and *Washington Post,* Sept. 3.
73 Thomas after reading *I, Governor:* Leader article.
"Infantile": Thomas letter to Peterson, Apr. 3 (NYPL).
Thomas to Sinclair: May 1 (NYPL).
Letters to Thomas: NYPL.
Arriving in Milwaukee: *NY Times,* Sept. 3.
74 Voorhis: Leader article.
74 Dempster: author's interview with Dempster.
Sinclair in Chicago: *Pasadena Post,* Sept. 3; *EPIC News,* Sept. 17; *I, Candidate.*
75 Brownell telegram: *EPIC News,* Sept. 10.
Mother Mooney, son, collapse: Gentry, *Frame-Up.*

SEPTEMBER 3

77 ER to Hickok: Sept. 3 (RL-Hickok)
Hickok background: field memos to Hopkins (RL-Hickok); Faber book.
78 Hickok to Hopkins: field memo, July 1 (RL-Hickok).
Sex the "only way": Faber book.
Hopkins on Hickok: ER to Hickok, Sept. 1 (RL-Hickok).
Beard, "not a philosopher," "a really new deal," "dump all these pigs," "I wouldn't blame him": Lash book.
79 "I will probably not be governor": Sinclair to ER, Oct. 21, 1933 (LL).
ER at meeting: Sinclair speech, Feb. 24 (LL).
Sinclair asks about endorsement: letter to ER, January 15 (RL-ER).
ER replies: letter, Jan. 26 (LL).
Heney to ER: Aug. 25 (RL).
ER to Hickok: Aug. 30 (RL-Hickok).
80 Cagney, et al.: *LA Times,* Aug. 19–20.
Buñuel: Marx, *A Gaudy Spree.*
Movie stars as dupes: *LA Times,* Aug. 30.
81 Thalberg on writers: Bob Thomas book.
Wilson investigation: Marx, *Mayer and Thalberg;* interview with Marx.

82 Hoover background: McElvaine book; Richard Norton Smith book; Carol Green Wilson book.
83 Hoover and Cleveland correspondent: letter to Michael Gallagher, Sept. 3 (HL).
83 Turns down $5,000: syndicated column by Maxwell Thayer, *Redwood Journal,* Sept. 7.
84 Whitaker background: McWilliams, *The Nation,* Apr. 14, 1951; Blumenthal book; Kelley book; Bloom book; interview with Clem Whitaker, Jr.
86 Republican party offer: interviews with Clem Whitaker, Jr., and Leone Baxter; Whitaker material in Hatfield papers (B).
Went into seclusion: Ross, *Harper's,* July 1959.
86 Nixon: Morris and Ambrose books.
87 Sinclair arrives at Algonquin: *NY Sun,* Sept. 4.
Gamblers "right," and "vision needed": *LA Examiner,* Sept. 4.

SEPTEMBER 4

88 Broun calls Sinclair: *EPIC News,* Sept. 17.
Broun's thoughts on *LA Times:* column, NY *World-Telegram,* Sept. 5.
Broun background: Kramer book; O'Connor book.
89 Broun on Sinclair: column, *NY World-Telegram,* Oct. 15, 1933.
Broun promise: *EPIC News,* Sept. 17.
90 Hanfstaengl's welcome: *NY Times,* Sept. 5.
Hanfstaengl sends "swine": *NY Times,* Aug. 30.
Hearst to Neylan: telegram, Sept. 4 (B-Neylan).
91 Textile strike: *NY Times,* Sept. 5.
92 Kennedy background: Koskoff book; Collier and Horowitz book; Schlesinger, *The Coming of the New Deal.*
Ickes: Ickes book.
93 Emerging from lunch: *NY Times,* Sept. 5.
La Guardia speech: *NY Times,* Sept. 4.
94 Loeb as driver: *EPIC News,* Sept. 17.
Loeb background: Veblen book; *Current Biography 1974; NY Times Magazine,* Dec. 12, 1971; Cash book.
95 Mencken on McAdoo: *The Vintage Mencken.*
Sinclair and FDR: *EPIC News,* Sept. 17; *I, Candidate;* Sinclair OH; Sinclair letter to wife, Sept. 10 (LL-MCS); *NY Times,* Sept. 5.
98 Cooke and Chaplin: Cooke letter to author; Cooke book.
Sinclair press conference: *I, Candidate; NY Times, LA Herald, Washington Post,* Sept. 5.
99 Rush back to New York: *EPIC News,* Sept. 17.
Sinclair and Farley: *Washington Post,* Sept. 5.

SEPTEMBER 5

101 Press conference: transcript, FDR press conference #141 (RL).
103 Press club speech: *Washington Post,* Sept. 6; *LA Herald,* Sept. 5–6; *EPIC News,* Sept. 17.
105 Fletcher: *LA Herald,* Sept. 7.
Writers: Gabler book; Rosten book; Schwartz book.
Mankiewicz to Hecht: Gabler book.
"A bloody fortune": Marx, *A Gaudy Spree.*
Parker background: Parker OH (Columbia); Frewin book; Kinney book; Meade book.
106 Parker returns: *LA Times,* Sept. 16.
107 Parker on Sinclair: review in *The New Yorker,* Dec. 10, 1927.
108 Sinclair hikes and meets Hopkins: *Washington Post,* Sept. 6; *EPIC News,* Sept. 17; *LA Herald,* Sept. 6.
109 Lindbergh case background: Kennedy book; Waller book.
Tugwell to FDR: Sept. 5, copy in Tugwell diary (RL).
110 FDR's trade: Ickes book.
Tugwell background: Moley, *The First New Deal;* Carter, *The New Dealers*; Schlesinger books.
Tugwell met Sinclair: Tugwell diary (RL).
Tugwell on Farley: Tugwell diary (RL).
111 Memo to President: Sept. 5 (RL).

SEPTEMBER 8

112 Luncheon: *NY Mirror,* Sept. 9.
Dinner party: *I, Candidate.*
113 Morgenthau: *I, Candidate.*
Ickes: *LA Herald,* Sept. 6; *I, Candidate.*
114 "So long as there are men": Mencken to Sinclair, Oct. 14, 1918 (quoted in Remley dissertation).
Jesus as dumb-bell: Sinclair to Louis Adamic, Aug. 5, 1926 (Remley article).
"To hell with Socialism": Mencken to Sinclair, Jan. 28, 1920 (LL, Remley).
Mencken on the "first-rate man": Introduction, *The Vintage Mencken.*
Sinclair admired Mencken: Sinclair to Adamic, July 31, 1926 (LL, Remley).
115 "I hear confidentially": Mencken to Sinclair, Feb. 7, 1933 (LL).
"Give the people time" and "blind envious fury": Manchester book.
Mencken article: *Baltimore Sun,* Sept. 10.
117 *Motion Picture Herald:* Sept. 8.
"Don't cut off the hand": recalled in *Script,* Sept. 15.
Schenck and Samish: Samish book.

118 Samish and billboards: Samish book.
Meeting of publishers: *EPIC News,* Sept. 10; Slome thesis (interview with Oliver Thornton).
Hearst on Mayer: telegram, Watson (for Hearst) to Coblentz, Sept. 8 (B-Coblentz).
119 Hoover on New Deal: *Washington Post,* Sept. 4; Hoover book.
Sinclair and Ickes on Hoover: *NY Times,* Sept. 5.
Wallace on Hoover: *NY Times,* Sept. 6.
120 Mooney: Gentry book.
Woodward: Woodward letter to Mary Craig Sinclair, Sept. 10 (LL).
121 FDR to reporters: transcript of press conference #142 (RL).

SEPTEMBER 9

125 Coughlin background: Brinkley book; Bennett book; Schlesinger, *The Politics of Upheaval.*
126 "Tugwell or Christ": *Des Moines Register,* May 4.
127 Sinclair and Coughlin: *I, Candidate; EPIC News,* Sept. 17.
128 Whitaker and excerpts: Ross, *Harper's,* July 1959; *I, Candidate.*
129 Whitaker and family: Ross, *Harper's,* July 1959; interview with Clem Whitaker, Jr.
Whitaker background: Ross, *Harper's,* July 1959; McWilliams, *The Nation,* Apr. 14, 1951.
130 Bogus circular: *EPIC News,* Sept. 10; *I, Candidate.*
131 Wagner's wife pressures: Wagner letter to Mary Craig Sinclair, Oct. 26 (LL-MCS)
Wagner background: Slide book; Sterling book.
132 Chaplin: Slide book.
Capra: *Script* anniversary issue, Jan. 1934.
Vanderbilt: Vanderbilt to Wagner, Jan. (UCLA-Wagner).
Wagner ed: *Script,* Mar. 17.
EPIC bee: *I, Governor.*
Wagner letter to Sinclair: Dec. 8, 1933 (UCLA-Wagner).
133 Wagner on Sinclair: *Script,* Sept. 8.

SEPTEMBER 10

134 Nuremberg: Burden book; *NY Times,* Sept. 5–11; Shirer.
135 AP reporter: *NY Times,* Sept. 11.

136 Pound to Sinclair: letter, Sept. 10 (Sinclair, *My Lifetime in Letters*).
Pound background: Carpenter book; Stock book; Paige book; *Current Biography 1942.*
"We are both firing": Pound letter to Sinclair (Harris).
"I believe": Pound to Sinclair, Dec. 5, 1930 (Harris).
Sandburg on Pound: *Current Biography 1942.*
Eliot: *Current Biography 1942.*
137 Pound on Italy: Stock book.
Hemingway, FDR, James Joyce: Stock book.
138 Bringing home bacon: *LA Herald,* Sept. 10.
Craig and assassination: Harris bio.
Einstein: letter to Sinclair, Dec. 27, 1930 (Sinclair, *My Lifetime in Letters*).
Sinclair and Craig: Harris; Sinclair OH.
139 "Love, Uppie": Sept. 10 (LL-MCS).
Teague background: Lillard article; Teague book; Magner White ms. (B-Teague).
140 Teague article: *LA Times,* Sept. 10.
Meeting: Teague letter to Joseph Knowland, Sept. 11 (B-Jos. Knowland).
141 Cagney background: McGilligan book; Cagney book; Freedland book.
142 Cagney in trouble: *LA Times,* Aug. 18–20.
143 Steffens and Cagney respond: Freedland book.
Steffens and Sinclair: Steffens letter to Hugh Jones, Sept. 6. (Steffens papers-Columbia).

SEPTEMBER 11

145 Long at hotel: *NY Times,* Sept. 12.
146 Textile strike: *NY Times,* Sept. 11–12.
Farley and FDR: Farley recounts, Sept. 11 (LC-Farley).
147 Farley's ambitions: Carter, *The New Dealers.*
Mayer in Paris: Marx, *Mayer and Thalberg;* Carey book; Crowther book.
148 Hearst on Hoover: Swanberg, *Citizen Hearst.*
Thomas to Dempster: letter, Sept. 11 (NYPL).
Leading California socialist: letter to Thomas, Sept. 7 (NYPL).
149 A few days ago: Dempster to Thomas, Sept. 4 (NYPL).
Thomas to Dempster: Sept. 11 (NYPL).
151 Long: *NY Times,* Sept. 12; Williams book; *Time,* Sept. 24.
Commonwealth Builders: *Time,* Sept. 24; Schlesinger, *The Politics of Upheaval.*
152 Dr. Hopkins: *NY Times,* Sept. 12.

SEPTEMBER 13

153 Sinclair returns: *LA Herald,* Sept. 12–13; *LA Daily News,* Sept. 14; *I, Candidate.*

154 Gordon: interview with author.

155 Chotiner: comments on C. C. Young speech of Aug. 23 (B-Young).
Merriam to Matt Sullivan: Sept. 3 (B-Merriam).
Cotton to McAdoo: Sept. 7 (LC-McAdoo)
McAdoo to Cotton: Sept. 8 (LC-McAdoo).
Hollywood Reporter: Sept. 13.

156 Pressure on Dempster: Leader article; author's interview with Dempster.
Thomas to Dempster: Sept. 13 (NYPL).

157 Hearst and Coblentz: Crocker (for Hearst) to Coblentz and Hearst to Coblentz, Sept. 13 (B-Coblentz)
Hearst and Brisbane: Hearst to Coblentz and Hearst to Brisbane, Sept. 10 (B-Coblentz).
Ickes and Hearst people: Ickes book.

158 Textile strike and FDR: *NY Times,* Sept. 14.

159 Gangsters: FDR to Hoover, Sept. 13 (RL).
Rutzebeck background: Rutzebeck book; *I, Candidate.*
Rutzebeck, Ferrari, Giannini: Rutzebeck letter to Sinclair, Sept. 15 (LL).

160 Giannini and O'Connor: O'Connor diary (B-O'Connor).

161 O'Connor to FDR: Sept. 13 (RL).

SEPTEMBER 14

162 Davies: Davies book; Guiles book.
Hanfstaengel background: Shirer book; Speer book; Lukacs book.

163 Smith: Shirer book.
Churchill: Lukacs book.
Dreiser to Gingrich: Sept. 13, from *Letters of Theodore Dreiser.*

164 Dreiser background: Lingeman book; Swanberg, *Dreiser;* Lehan book.
Masters: "Theodore Dreiser," *The Great Valley.*
Lewis and Dreiser: Swanberg book; Schorer book.

166 "I told them I was impotent": Swanberg, *Dreiser.*
Mencken: Swanberg, *Dreiser.*
Dreiser and Sinclair: Harris bio; Sinclair autobio.

167 Dreiser on brotherhood: letter to Sinclair, Dec. 18, 1924 (LL).
Pro-EPIC: Dreiser article in *Esquire,* Dec. 1934.

168 Thompson: *NY Times,* Sept. 15.
Lewis and Sinclair: Harris bio; Sinclair autobio.
Lewis on Sinclair: Schorer book.

169 Lewis and Tugwell: Schlesinger, *The Coming of the New Deal.*
Wardell episode: Sinclair, *The Lie Factory Starts.*
Fleishhacker background: Forbes book.
Vanderbilt: Vanderbilt, *Farewell to Fifth Avenue.*

170 Meeting: Rowell letters to Herbert Hoover, Sept. 12 and Sept. 15 (HL).
Johnson on Rowell: Ickes book.
Rowell disclaimer: letter to Cameron, Aug. 8 (B-Rowell).

171 Letters: all LL.
Fremont Older: Cora Older to Sinclair, Sept. 2 (LL).
Self-publishing: Sinclair, *The Lie Factory Starts.*

172 "The talk of rich men": Henderson letter to Sinclair, Sept. 11 (LL).

SEPTEMBER 16

173 Davies book; Guiles book.
Bierce: quoted in Hearst profile, *DLB 25.*
Hearst and Hitler: Coblentz book.

174 "Visiting Hitler": AP dispatch, Sept. 17.
Davies: Davies book; Guiles book.
Millikan on Sinclair: *Pasadena Post,* Sept. 15.
Einstein preface: Sinclair, *Mental Radio.*

175 Sinclair and Einstein: Sinclair autobio; Sinclair OH; Harris bio.
"Wicked tongue": Einstein letter to Sinclair, May 26, 1932 (LL).
Inscription: translated by John Ahouse.
Einstein background: Hoffmann book; French book; Einstein book.

176 "Never yet have I received": Einstein book.
Einstein to Sinclair: Jan. 29 (Sinclair, *My Lifetime in Letters*).
Einstein favored: Einstein book.
Millikan background: Kargon book; *Current Biography 1940.*

177 Millikan on Sinclair: *Pasadena Post,* Sept. 15.
Service and "It is so good": *Bridal Call Crusader,* Sept. 19.
Missionary: *LA Times,* Aug. 29.

178 Orlando: Orlando book; *LA Herald,* Feb. 9, 1935.
Halbert gets word: letter, Gerald Toll to Halbert, Sept. 13 (UCLA-Halbert).
"Professed reactionary": Halbert to Charles Busick, July 12 (UCLA-Halbert).
Assembly background: CRA Papers (UCLA).
Latest issue: *Assembly News,* Sept. 21.

179 *Cleopatra* and *Time* quote: *Time,* August 27.
DeMille background: Higham, *Cecil B. DeMille;* DeMille autobio.

180 DeMille to O'Connor: Dec. 18, 1933 (B-O'Connor).
DeMille on Sinclair: *LA Times,* Sept. 16.
Chaplin: *Script,* Sept. 15.

181 Creel background: Creel book; Creel profile in *DLB 25*.
Creel meeting: *I, Candidate.*
182 Sinclair letter to Farrar, Sept. 15 (LL).
Dempster: author's interview with Dempster; Dempster letter to Thomas, Sept. 17 (NYPL); *The New Leader,* Sept. 29.
Rogers on radio: transcript (Rogers Memorial).
183 Running for office: *NY Times,* Jan. 11.

SEPTEMBER 17

185 *Variety,* Sept. 18.
Belli and Merriam: interview with Belli.
Belli background: Belli book; Wallace book; *Current Biography 1979.*
187 Belli speaking: interview with Belli.
Teague background: Lillard article; Teague book.
"You aren't going to find": White ms. (B-Teague).
188 Verse: *LA Examiner,* Aug. 17, 1933.
Teague on "the people": speech, Dec. 17 (B-Teague).
189 Teague and Sinclair: letters to Joseph Knowland, Sept. 11 and 20 (B-Jos. Knowland).
Chandler: Johnson to McClatchy, June 3 (B-Johnson).
190 Blow against Sinclair: Johnson to Ickes, Sept. 17 (RL).
Winchell: Kennedy book.
192 EPIC background: EPIC OHs; author's interviews with Taylor, McCormick, et al.
Sinclair on blacks: *EPIC News,* Apr.; Hawkins, interview with author.
193 Twelve Apostles: interview with Frank Taylor; Borough OH (UCLA).
Estimate of 100,000 members: Singer quoting Rube Borough.
Donkey: *EPIC News,* May.
194 Campaign songs: LL.
195 Shrine rally and Scully: Scully letter to several friends, undated (but Sept. 1934) (LL).
Ryskind background: profile, *DLB 26.*
196 Sinclair remarks: Scully letter, undated (LL); *LA Daily News* and *LA Examiner,* Sept. 18; and Sinclair speech ms. (LL).
Ryskind threatens: Scully letter, undated (LL).
Scully article: *Esquire,* Nov. 1934.

SEPTEMBER 19

197 Hauptmann capture: Kennedy book; Waller book.
198 Mayer: *LA Examiner,* Sept. 20.
199 Cohn: *Pasadena Post,* Sept. 18.
Haight and Sinclair: *I, Candidate; EPIC News,* Sept. 24.
200 Teague meetings: Teague letter to Joseph Knowland, Sept. 20 (B-Jos. Knowland).
201 Sunkist and Lord & Thomas: Lillard article; Gunther book; Starr, *Inventing the Dream.*
202 Francisco: Gunther book; press release, Jan. 21, 1937 (Foote, Cone & Belding files, Chicago).
Teague and Francisco: Teague letter to Joseph Knowland, Sept. 20 (B-Jos. Knowland).
Admen: Fox book.
American Box: Rutzeback ("M") report to Sinclair, Sept. 20 (LL).
203 Lasker and Knox: Knox letter to Hoover, Sept. 20 (HL).
Lasker background: Gunther book; Meyers book; Cone book; Fox book; Lasker book; interview with Edward Lasker.
205 Knox to Hoover on meeting: Sept. 20 (HL).

SEPTEMBER 20

206 Textile strike: *NY Times,* Sept. 20–21.
207 Registrars at studios: *Variety,* Sept. 25.
208 Sinclair background: Harris bio; Sinclair autobio.
209 Cotton: *I, Candidate.*
Convention scene: *LA Herald,* Sept. 20; *LA Times,* Sept. 21; *I, Candidate.*
Creel: footage, Fox-Movietone newsreel (South Carolina).
210 Haight fight: *LA Examiner,* Sept. 21.
Samish on McAdoo: *Sausalito News,* Sept. 28.
211 GOP convention, platform, Merriam speech: *LA Times, LA Examiner, SF Chronicle,* Sept. 21.
Hatfield speech: Hatfield papers (B).
212 Screams knock down screen: *Sacramento Bee,* Sept. 21.
Downey reads: *I, Candidate.*
McAdoo calls him "governor": *Pasadena Post,* Sept. 21.
213 Creel: Fox-Movietone newsreel footage, Newsfilm Library (University of South Carolina).
Telegram: Sept. 20 (RL).
Lindbergh case: Kennedy book; Waller book; *NY Times,* Sept. 21–22.
214 Postconvention: *I, Candidate; LA Times,* Sept. 21–22.
Main Street: *SF News,* Sept. 20.

SEPTEMBER 21

215 Hearst on Hitler: cablegram to Crocker, Sept. 18 (B-Hearst).
Rogers: *NY Times,* Sept. 22.
Lecture: *LA Times,* Sept. 22.

216 Wilson on Shaw: Wilson book.
"Opium eater's dream": Longstreet book.
Interview: *LA Examiner,* Sept. 23.
Letter to Sinclair and "Pillory": Nov. 13, 1931, in Sinclair, *My Lifetime in Letters*.

217 Man with card file: Ainsworth, *Saturday Review,* Sept. 30, 1967.
Pacific Mutual background: Pacific Mutual archives.

218 Mailing leaflets and Forbes: letter, L. G. Campbell to George Hatfield, Sept. 24 (B-Hatfield).
Donating $7,500: minutes of Sept. 9 meetings, Pacific Mutual archives.
Breen to Wanger: MPPDA files (Academy).
"Gabriel" background: McConnell thesis; Swanberg book.

219 *Nation:* Apr. 26, 1933.
FDR to Hearst: Apr. 1, 1933 (RL).

220 *Christian Century:* May 10, 1933.
Sinclair on *Gabriel: LA Daily News,* Sept. 1933.
Wanger and Breen: memos in MPPDA files (Academy).
Film Weekly: Aug. 31, quoted in Leff book.

221 Hays Office background: Moley, *The Hays Office; The New Yorker,* June 10, 1933; French book; Hays book; Gardner book; Leff book.
Chaplin and Hays: FBI report, Aug. 15, 1922, cited in Leff book.

222 Breen and anti-Semitism: Vaughn, *Journal of American History,* June 1990, quoting Breen letter to Wilfrid Parson, Oct. 10, 1932 (Parsons Papers-Georgetown).
Eleanor Roosevelt: Leff book.
"Cuckoo": Telegram from Florence to Hays, Sept. 21 (Hays papers).

SEPTEMBER 22

223 Sullivan column: syndicated by *NY Tribune,* Sept. 22.

224 Textile strike: *NY Times,* Sept. 23.
Sevareid: Schlesinger, *The Coming of the New Deal.*

225 One tally: Slome thesis.
Behrens: Slome thesis.
Cameron: *Time,* Aug. 27.

226 Older letter to Steffens: Aug. 7.
Knowland: document, July 31 (B-Jos. Knowland).

227 Hoover to Knox: Sept. 22 (HL).
Wagner offer: *Script,* Sept. 22.
Billboard: Sept. 22.
228 Cohn: *Hollywood Reporter,* Sept. 22.
Laemmle: *EPIC News,* Sept. 24.
229 Rutzebeck reports: Signed "M," Sept. 14, Sept. 17, Sept. 17 again, Sept. 20 (LL).
230 *We Live Again* and Goldwyn background: Berg book; Gabler book; interview with Berg.
231 Wagner and Goldwyn: *Script,* Sept. 29.

SEPTEMBER 24

232 Rapf and Schulberg: author's interviews with Rapf and Schulberg; Gabler book; Schwartz book; Schulberg book.
233 Rapf and Warners: interview with Rapf.
234 Dreiser background: Swanberg book; Lingeman book.
Dreiser to coed: Sept. 24, *Letters of Theodore Dreiser.*
Dreiser's opinion of Sinclair: Dreiser article in *Esquire,* Dec.
235 Warden: Holohan letter, Sept. 20 (RL).
Woman in Hollywood: Ryan letter, Sept. 18 (RL).
Colpus letter: Sept. 22 (RL).
McAdoo to secretary: letter to Vera Ward, Sept. 24 (LC-McAdoo).
McAdoo to FDR: letter, Sept. 24 (LC-McAdoo).
236 Neblett: *LA Times,* Sept. 25.
Pat Brown background: *Current Biography 1960;* Brown OH (B); author's interview with Brown.
Elkington: Elkington OH (B).
237 Tobriner, Sinclair, Haight: interview with Brown.
Knowland to Teague: Sept. 24 (B-Jos. Knowland)
238 O'Donnell: *EPIC News,* Sept. 24.
Justus Craemer: Faries OH (B).
239 *EPIC News:* Sept. 24.
Newspaper details and Borough: Borough OH (UCLA); Borough article; *I, Candidate.*
"Borneo": Maxwell Thayer syndicated column, Sept. 7.

SEPTEMBER 26

242 FDR returns: *NY Times,* Sept. 27.
Ickes: Ickes book.

243 Catledge: *NY Times,* Sept. 23.
Van Dyke background: Cannom book; Skolsky column, Aug. 22; David O. Selznick OH (Columbia).
Speech to Crusaders: *LA Examiner,* Sept. 26.
244 Van Dyke to FDR: Sept. 26 (RL).
Pettijohn background: Hays book; Moley, *The Hays Office.*
245 Pettijohn to Hays: Sept. 26 (Hays papers).
Casey to Hays: Sept. 26 (Hays papers).
245 Meets the press: *I, Candidate; EPIC News,* Oct. 1; Slome thesis; *LA Times,* Sept. 27; *LA Herald,* Sept. 26.
247 "Almost collapsing grief": Sept. 16, 1933 (LL).
David and Upton background: Harris bio; Sinclair autobio; author's interview with David Sinclair.
248 *Herald-Tribune:* Sept. 22, 1933.
Letters, Nov. 8 and Nov. 13, 1933: LL.
Letter, Sept. 26: LL.

SEPTEMBER 27

250 Hearst: *NY Times,* Sept. 28.
Lindbergh: Kennedy book; Waller book.
252 Sinclair realized: *I, Candidate.*
Baby barter: *LA Times,* Sept. 27.
Vidor returns: *Variety,* Sept. 28.
EPIC News: May.
253 Vidor background and *Our Daily Bread:* Vidor book; McConnell thesis.
Reviews: *Hollywood Reporter,* June 30; *Film Daily,* Aug. 8; *Motion Picture Daily,* Aug. 18.
254 Mankiewicz: author's interview with Mankiewicz.
Kerr and McHenry: author's interviews with Kerr and McHenry; Kerr thesis.
255 Widest selection of this material found in Teggart scrapbook (B) and Nelson scrapbook (LL).
256 O'Melveny resumes activity: O'Melveny diary (Huntington).
O'Melveny background: Clary book; *California Law Business,* July 31, 1989.
257 O'Melveny followed closely: O'Melveny diary (Huntington).
O'Melveny and Cotton meet: Sept. 21, O'Melveny diary (Huntington).
"Working and dictating": Sept. 27, O'Melveny diary (Huntington).
258 Haight speech: ms. in Sinclair papers (LL).
Sinclair address: *LA Examiner,* Sept. 29.

SEPTEMBER 30

259 Perkins and FDR: Perkins book.
260 Moley background: Moley, *After Seven Years* and *The First New Deal; Current Biography 1945;* Carter book.
The New Republic: Sept. 12.
261 Moley's argument: *Today,* Oct. 6.
FDR to Moley: Moley, *After Seven Years.*
Mayer: *Pasadena Post,* Oct. 2.
"Provide the punch": *LA Herald,* Sept. 29.
262 Warren background: Warren book; Katcher book.
Presbytery: *LA Herald,* Sept. 26.
Pamphlets: in Teggart scrapbook (B).
263 Steffens message: in *The Letters of Lincoln Steffens.*
Steffens to Cantwell: Sept. 29, from Steffens, *Letters.*
Darcy background and Darcy and Sinclair: Darcy OH and Darcy autobio ms. (Darcy-NYU); Lyons book; Klehr book.
264 Sinclair on communism: Harris bio.
265 Steffens "liberal-bourgeois": letter to Darcy, April 28 (Darcy-NYU).
Pamphlet: in Darcy papers (NYU).
266 Rogers: radio show transcript (Rogers Memorial).
267 FDR: *NY Times,* Oct. 1–2.

OCTOBER 1

268 Lasker informed Hays: Lasker letter, Sept. 10 (Hays papers).
Lasker and czar: Lasker book.
All Hays letters: Hays papers.
269 Mayer and Merriam: telegram, Mayer to Merriam, Sept. 9, 1932 (B-Merriam).
White on Hoover: *NY Times,* Sept. 28.
"Smear": Hoover letter to Lewis Strauss, Oct. 1 (HL).
Hoover to Kent: Oct. 1 (HL)
270 *Saturday Review:* Oct. 6.
271 Dos Passos background: Carr book; Ludington book; profile of Dos Passos, *DLB 9.*
Letters: Dos Passos book. To Hemingway: July 27 and Aug. 20. To friend: Carr book.
272 Letters: Dos Passos book.
To Wilson: Dos Passos book, Sept. 24.
273 "Liberal" and "camp-follower": Dos Passos book.
To Sinclair: Oct. 1 (LL).
Disney: *EPIC News,* Oct. 1.

274 Chrysler: *LA Herald,* Sept. 29.
Flight of capital: *NY Times,* Oct. 3.
Nevada: *SF Chronicle,* Oct. 21.
275 *Wall Street Journal:* Sept. 26.
NY Times: Sept. 30.
Rutzebeck report to Sinclair: Oct. 2, signed "M" (LL).

OCTOBER 2

277 Rogers: column, *NY Times,* Oct. 3.
Ford and Sinclair: Harris bio; Sinclair autobio.
278 Ford quotes: Schlesinger, *The Coming of the New Deal.*
Moley article: *Today,* Oct. 6.
279 Rutzebeck: report of "M," Oct. 2 (LL).
Wilder and Sinclair: author's interview with Wilder.
280 Wilder background: Zolotow book; Taylor book; *Current Biography 1951;* interview with Wilder.
281 Wilder and Sinclair: interview with Wilder.
Rutzebeck: Oct. 2 memo (LL).
Mooney: letter to Sinclair, Sept. 27 (LL).
282 "Last Will": in Nelson scrapbook (LL).

OCTOBER 3

284 Mayer: *Pasadena Post,* Oct. 4.
O'Connor and FDR: O'Connor diary (B-O'Connor).
285 Farley to McAdoo: Oct. 3 (LC-McAdoo).
286 FDR, Kennedy, Hearst: letter to Hearst, Oct. 3 (RL).
Rogers column: *NY Times,* Oct. 4.
Trial: *NY Times,* Oct. 3–4.
287 Dreiser rebuked: *NY Times,* Oct. 4.
Voorhis and "boxes": interview with author.
288 Sinclair and boxes and "nationalizing women": *I, Candidate.*
289 Sinclair to Coughlin: Oct. 3 (LL).
Sinclair to son: Oct. 3 (LL).
Wilkerson background: Wilkerson book.
290 Wilkerson column: *Hollywood Reporter,* Oct. 3.
290 Wilson background: Marx books.
Off the payroll: MGM files for Wilson, Sept.–Oct. 1934.
291 United for California debuts: *LA Examiner,* Oct. 4.
Call took charge: Gottlieb and Wolt book.
292 Pacific Mutual: *EPIC News,* Oct. 8.

OCTOBER 4

293 Fairbanks and Schenck: *Miami Herald,* Oct. 5.

294 Schenck looks at sites: *LA Examiner,* Oct. 6.
Hays background: *The New Yorker,* June 10 and 17, 1933; *Current Biography 1943;* Moley, *The Hays Office* and *27 Masters of Politics;* Hays book; interview with Will Hays, Jr.
"Cleavage": Will Hays, Jr., speech, Nov. 5, 1988.

295 Hays in Chicago: interview with Will Hays, Jr.

296 Hays at head table: invitation in possession of Will Hays, Jr.
Phone bill: Interview with Will Hays, Jr.
Kennedy and Hays: Oct. 2 (Hays papers).

297 Hays to Hearst: Oct. 4 (Hays papers).
Realtors: *California Real Estate Magazine,* Oct. and Nov.

299 Willaman to Early: Oct. 4 (RL).

OCTOBER 5

301 Farley to McAdoo: Oct. 3 (LC-McAdoo).
Sinclair to FDR, McIntyre, Farley, Moley: all Oct. 5 (LL).

302 Wells and Sinclair: Sinclair autobio.
Wells and Stalin: *LA Daily News,* Oct. 9.
Sinclair and Stalin: Harris bio.

303 Marx and Sinclair: Marx books; interview with Marx.

304 Grauman's: Sinclair, *My Lifetime in Letters.*
Sinclair and Thalberg: Marx books; interview with Marx; MGM files; Harris bio.
Marx and Mayer: interview with Marx.
Thalberg ordered: Bob Thomas book.

305 Pacific Mutual: Minutes of meeting, Pacific Mutual archives.
Texas: Harris book; interview with Leon Harris.
Blyth, Harpo, money, Taylor and EPIC: interview with Taylor.

306 Warren: *LA Times,* Oct. 6.

307 Carr: *LA Times,* Sept. 28.
"California, Here We Come": in Teggart scrapbook (B).

308 Clerk's estimate: W. B. Manford letter to Bevans (B-Merriam).

OCTOBER 7

309 Marx Bros. background: Gehring book; Adamson book; Carey book; Bob Thomas book.

310 Mayer: *Variety,* Pasadena *Post,* Oct. 8.

311 Radek: *SF Chronicle,* Oct. 7.
Palmer: *LA Times* archives.
Called home: *EPIC News,* June 11.
312 *Script:* Oct. 6.
Hoover: *NY Times,* Oct. 8.
313 Thomas pamphlet: Teggart scrapbook (B).
Thomas on radio and Constitution Society: *I, Candidate.*
Norman Thomas: letter to Alan Clark, undated (NYPL).
314 Voorhis to Thomas: letter, Sept. 18, 1933 (NYPL).
Voorhis speech: Voorhis papers (Claremont).
Rogers at rally: *NY Times,* Oct. 8.
Rogers background: Alworth book; Wm. Brown book; Sterling book; Croy book; Betty Rogers book; *NY Times,* Aug. 17, 1935; interview with Will Rogers, Jr.
315 Runyon: Donald Day, *Will Rogers.*
317 FDR appoints Rogers: letter, FDR to Rogers, Oct. 8 (RL).
Radio show: transcript, Rogers Memorial.

OCTOBER 9

321 Pound to Sinclair: Oct. 9 (LL).
322 Davies and Hearst: Marx, *A Gaudy Spree;* interview with Marx.
Hearst on NRA: Hearst to Coblentz, July 18 (B-Coblentz).
Hearst in NY: *LA Examiner,* Oct. 10.
323 Howard: *NY Times,* Oct. 10.
FDR to Pittman: Oct. 9 (RL).
O'Connor, Coughlin, FDR: O'Connor diary (B).
Neblett to McAdoo: Oct. 8 (LC-McAdoo).
324 Storke, McAdoo, FDR: Storke book.
325 Dizzy to Rogers: *NY Times,* Oct. 10.
Sinclair and Crane-Gartz: Sinclair autobio.
Chaplin: Chaplin book.
326 Crane-Gartz's letters: Crane-Gartz book.
Woodward on Loeb: Oct. 2 (LL).
Sinclair to Broun and Coughlin: (LL).
327 "10 million lies": *LA Times,* Oct. 9.
Coldwell background: Levy book.
Money meeting: *SF News,* Oct. 10.
$10 million: Davis book and others.
328 Parker's material: Dickson scrapbook (UCLA).
Call: Gottlieb article; interview with Gottlieb.
329 Parker to Debevoise: Oct. 9 (Debevoise file).

OCTOBER 11

330 *Literary Digest: Pasadena Post,* Oct. 12.
Ballot: collection of author.
331 Mencken letter: *The New Mencken Letters.*
Riot: *LA Times,* Oct. 12.
332 Chaplin: Robinson book.
Mankiewicz: *Hollywood Reporter,* Oct. 11.
Mankiewicz and confiscating swimming pools: author's interview with Mankiewicz.
333 Murray and button: Scully letter to Sinclair, Oct. 15 (LL).
Wagner to Scully: Oct. 8 (LL).
Scully to Wagner: Oct. 10 (LL).
At luncheon: Scully letter to Sinclair, Oct. 20 (LL).
334 Medalie, Dewey: Debevoise letter to Parker, Oct. 10 (Debevoise file).
335 Coughlin: *LA Examiner,* Oct. 11, and *SF Chronicle,* Oct. 16.
Levit and CLAS army: memos and manuals (UCLA-Halbert).
Memo to employers: CLAS materials in Jos. Knowland papers (B).
336 *I, Menace:* Teggart scrapbook (B).
Garbutt: Garbutt letter, undated, Nelson scrapbook (LL).
Dentists: letter and materials in Warren papers.
Dentists respond: Dr. Wilfred Robinson letter to Warren, Oct. 18 (Warren).
337 Merriam and Call: Gottlieb and Wolt book.

OCTOBER 14

338 Shirley Temple background: Black book; Minott book; *LA Examiner,* Aug. 26; *Liberty,* Sept. 29.
339 Winchell: Sept. 21 column.
Shirley and Merriam: Black book.
340 Pettijohn attends meeting: minutes in Hays papers.
Trailers: *Variety,* Oct. 13.
Beverly Hills Bulletin: *EPIC News,* Oct. 15.
341 Sinclair claimed dirty tricks: *I, Candidate.*
Shooting Sinclair: interview with Leone Baxter.
Lewis attacked: *LA Examiner,* Oct. 16.
342 Faries: interview with author.
Belli: interview with author.
343 Garry: Garry book, *NY Times* obit, Aug. 19, 1991.
344 Lord & Thomas radio: *Variety,* Oct. 30.
Bennetts: Claire Sawdon letter to Norman Thomas, Oct. 26 (NYPL).
Farley: *NY Times,* Oct. 15.

345 Minor background: Klehr book; Gitlow book; *Current Biography 1941;* Minor papers (Columbia).

346 Minor and Sinclair: Harris bio; Sinclair autobio.
Arriving in SF: UP dispatch, Oct. 14.
Rogers: transcript of radio program (Rogers Memorial).

OCTOBER 15

348 Hauptmann: Kennedy book; Waller book.

349 Fox and Farley: Private file, Oct. 15 (LC-Farley).
Time: Oct. 15.
Fox background: Sinclair, *Upton Sinclair Presents William Fox;* Gabler book.

350 Fox and Sinclair: Harris bio; Sinclair autobio; Sinclair OH.
Mencken: letter to Sinclair, Apr. 4, 1933 (Remley).
Court decision: *Time,* Oct. 15.

351 Fox and Farley: Private file, Oct. 15 (LC-Farley).

352 McAdoo to Farley: Oct. 15 (LC-McAdoo).
Cotton: *EPIC News,* Oct. 15.
Vote fraud: *LA Times* and *LA Examiner,* Oct. 16.

353 All letters to Warren: Warren papers.
Warren had sent letter to office seekers: Oct. 8 (Warren).

354 Monroe to Warren: Oct. 5 (Warren).
Warren statement: GOP press release, Oct. 15 (Warren).

355 Whitaker and newspapers: interview with Clem Whitaker, Jr.; Ross, *Harper's,* July 1959; Behrens OH (B).
Editors demand contribution: Howe letter to Whitaker, Oct. 9 (B-Hatfield).
CLAS releases and cartoons: in Hatfield papers (B).

356 Hoover to Lasker: Oct. 15 (HL).

356 Hackett finds note: Hackett OH (Columbia)

OCTOBER 17

357 *Time:* Oct. 22.

358 Hackett: Hackett OH (Columbia); Schwartz book.
Cagney: Scully books.

359 Wilder: interview with author.

360 DeMille: *SF Chronicle,* Oct. 17.
Rogers: *NY Times,* Oct. 17.

361 Vote fraud case: *LA Times* and *LA Examiner,* Oct. 16–18.
Leaflets: in Teggart scrapbook (B) and Nelson scrapbook (LL).

363 Boy Scouts: *EPIC News,* Oct. 15.
United for California and White House: undated note (RL).
Visalia dairy: Oct. 24 notation, Halbert papers (UCLA).
Movie shorts: Hatfield letter to Cohn, Oct. 22 (B-Hatfield).
Downey to Whitaker: Oct. 16 (B-Hatfield).
Whitaker to Downey: Oct. 17 (B-Hatfield).
364 White: Smith book.
Long: McElvaine book.
Sinclair in Fresno: *LA Herald,* Oct. 17.
Sinclair to Dell: Oct. 17 (LL).
Makes prediction: letter to Don Politico, Oct. 17 (LL).
365 Sinclair to Gandhi and Wagner: Oct. 17 (LL).

OCTOBER 19

366 Cotton to McAdoo: Oct. 19 (LC-McAdoo).
EPIC charges on *Literary Digest: I, Candidate.*
367 Forbes background: Winans book; *Current Biography 1950;* Forbes, *Men Who Are Making the West;* Arthur Jones book.
368 Forbes on Sinclair: *LA Examiner,* Oct. 19.
369 Election short: at UCLA Film Archives.
371 1931 shorts: Ames article.
Carey Wilson: Hackett OH (Columbia); interview with Bright; interview with Rivkin.
372 Scully at dinner: Scully letter to Sinclair, Oct. 20 (LL).
374 All Sinclair letters and telegrams: LL.
Hauptmann: *NY Times,* Oct. 20.

OCTOBER 20

375 Hoover to Chandler: Oct. 20 (HL).
376 Forbes column: *LA Examiner,* Oct. 20.
Moody background: Engelman book.
377 With Young on radio: Aug. 16, transcript (B-Merriam).
378 Movie short protest: *EPIC News,* Oct. 22.
Feist in Colton: *Colton Courier,* Oct. 23.
Feist background: interviews with Sam Marx, Joe Cohn, Philip Dunne.
379 Vote fraud: *LA Times, Pasadena Post,* Oct. 21; *EPIC News,* Oct. 22 and Oct. 29.
Parker background: interviews with Kitty Parker, Ruth Cashman, Shelby Davis; *Who's Who;* Clary book; Starr, *Material Dreams.*

380 Parker arrested: *LA Examiner,* Jan. 18, 1929.
Raised million: letter to Debevoise, Oct. 20 (Debevoise file).
Letter to "Whitney": Parker to Debevoise, Oct. 20.
381 Hearst and Mayer: Swanberg book; Carey book; Marx, *Mayer and Thalberg.*
Sexual fixation: Marx, *A Gaudy Spree.*

OCTOBER 21

383 Mencken threat: letter to Sinclair, Oct. 16 (LL).
Mencken column: *LA Examiner,* Oct. 21.
385 Hall: *NY Times,* Oct. 21.
385 Steinbeck: Benson book.
386 Short aimed at "colored" audience: *NY Times,* Nov. 4.
Moley short: Max Stern syndicated Scripps-Howard column, Nov. 3.
387 Hoeppel and Troskey: *St. Louis Post-Dispatch,* Oct. 26.
Text of Farley letter: *EPIC News,* Oct. 22.
Sinclair to son: LL.
388 Rogers: transcript of radio program (Rogers Memorial).
Warren background: Katcher book; Warren book; Stone book.
389 Warren on radio: GOP press release, Oct. 21 (Warren).

OCTOBER 22

391 *EPIC News:* Oct. 22.
Cotton to Farley: LC-Farley.
Storke to Farley: Oct. 22 (LC-Farley).
Storke background: Storke book; *Current Biography 1963;* Storke papers (B).
392 Olson letter and FDR note: RL.
393 Levying tax: *Pasadena Post,* Oct. 22.
Columbia: Schwartz book.
Riskin, Capra, Lawson, Wexley: Schwartz book.
394 Lawson and Cohn: Brenman-Gibson book.
MGM and Marx: interview with Marx.
Rivkin: interview with author.
Mayer to writers, "Out of 47 books," and reporter from Eastern paper: *NY Times,* Nov. 4.
395 Bright, Sinclair, Wilson: interview with Bright.
Rogers: Day book.
396 Betting: *SF Call,* Oct. 17; *Pasadena Independent,* Oct. 22; UP dispatch, Oct. 23.
Townsend invites Sinclair: *LA Examiner,* Sept. 29.
Yorty: Bullens and Geyer book; author's interview with Yorty; Yorty OH.

397 Rogers: *SF Call,* Oct. 22.
Sinclair speech: *SF News,* Oct. 23; *I, Candidate;* Sinclair OH.
398 Pretty Boy: *NY Times,* Oct. 23.
399 Sinclair listens to FDR: *I, Candidate;* Sinclair OH.
FDR speech: *NY Times,* Oct. 23.
Fable: *I, Candidate.*

OCTOBER 23

400 Hopkins, Morgenthau, Moley: Schlesinger, *The Coming of the New Deal.*
FDR sees Creel, not Olson: *LA Herald,* Oct. 24.
401 Creel letter to Sinclair: Oct. 18 (RL).
Early to Eleanor Roosevelt: Oct. 23 (RL).
McAdoo to Storke: Oct. 23 (LC-McAdoo).
402 Hearst to Haight: published Oct. 24, *LA Examiner.*
403 Huey: *NY Times,* October 24.
Sinclair to Broun: Oct. 19 (LL).
Broun and son: Kramer book; O'Connor book.
404 Broun column: syndicated Scripps-Howard column, Oct. 24.
405 Brisbane and Broun: Kramer book.
Brisbane column: *LA Examiner,* Oct. 23.
Review: *NY Times,* Oct. 3.
Vidor to Hal Horne: USC.
406 McAdoo wedding: *LA Times, NY Times, Washington Post,* Oct. 24–25.
Sinclair to FDR: Oct. 23 (RL).
407 Troskey loses job: *NY Times,* Oct. 26.
Stealing Parker letter: *I, Candidate.*
Letter: Parker to Debevoise, Oct. 20 (Debevoise file).
408 Threats: *LA Examiner,* Oct. 25.
Pegler meets Sinclair: Pegler syndicated Scripps-Howard column, Oct. 25–26; *I, Candidate.*
409 Pegler background: Pilat book; Alexander article.

OCTOBER 24

412 FDR: transcript, press conference #152, Oct. 24.
413 Stein arrives: *NY Times,* Oct. 25.
Stein background: Sprigge book; Bridgman book; Greenfeld book.
414 American food: Sprigge book.
Vanderbilt: *NY Times,* Oct. 25.
Borah: *NY Times,* Oct. 13.
415 Movie short: at UCLA Film Archives.

417 Vidor to FDR: RL.
Sinclair to FDR: RL.
Meeting with Haight: *I, Candidate.*
418 Haight's financial backers: author's interview with Ray Haight, Jr.
Postcard poll: interview with Ray Haight, Jr.
Sinclair's response: *I, Candidate.*
Pegler calls: *I, Candidate.*
Rogers: *NY Times,* Oct. 24.
419 FDR softens: Schlesinger, *The Coming of the New Deal.*
Speech: *NY Times* and *Washington Post,* Oct. 25.
Sinclair and Haight: *I, Candidate.*
In Chico: *LA Examiner,* Oct. 25; UP dispatch, Oct. 24; *I, Candidate.*

OCTOBER 25

421 Pegler: Scripps-Howard column, Oct. 25.
422 Hopkins: *EPIC News,* Oct. 29.
Boss Tweed: Cleland book.
LA Times: Oct. 24.
423 *LA Examiner:* Oct. 25.
Hackett: Hackett OH (Columbia Univ.)
Wild Boys: Time, Nov. 12; *EPIC News,* Nov. 5; *I, Candidate.*
Huston: Huston book.
Warner Bros. as source: *NY Times,* Nov. 4.
424 Otto: *LA Daily News,* Oct. 26.
Sinclair to Farley and Hays: *LA Daily News,* Oct. 26.
EBIC Snooze: in Teggart scrapbook (B).
The Cat Parade: in Teggart Scrapbook (B).
425 *If I'm Governor:* Cornish to FDR, Oct. 16 (RL).
1934 Psalm, *Thunder*: in Teggart scrapbook (B).
Thunder background: *New Republic,* Nov. 14.
426 Letters to Louie: in Nelson scrapbook (LL).
Acting on tip: *LA Herald,* Oct. 25.
"I listened courteously" and Haight responds: *LA Daily News,* Oct. 26.
427 Haight goes to EPIC: *LA Examiner,* Oct. 26.
McAdoo wedding: *LA Times,* Oct. 25–26.
Registration case: *LA Times,* Oct. 26.
"A relatively small number": *LA Herald,* Oct. 24.
428 Positive developments: *LA Herald,* Oct. 25.
Debevoise to Parker: Oct. 22 (Debevoise file).
Catledge background: Halberstam book; *Current Biography 1975;* Talese book.
429 Catledge and Palmer: Halberstam book; interview with Halberstam.
McHenry, Sproul, debate: interview with McHenry; ms. of McHenry speech.

OCTOBER 26

431 Farley: *NY Times,* Oct. 26.
432 O'Connor and Giannini: O'Connor diary (B-O'Connor).
Giannini and Haight: undated O'Connor memo (LC-Farley).
O'Connor letter to Marvin McIntyre: Oct. 27 (RL).
O'Connor visits McIntyre: O'Connor diary.
Finds telegram: Giannini to O'Connor, Oct. 26 (RL).
433 Farley's explanation: *NY Times,* Oct. 27.
Literary Digest, Creel, EPIC response: *NY Times,* Oct. 27.
434 Merriam: *SF Chronicle,* Oct. 27.
Wilkerson: *Hollywood Reporter,* Oct. 27.
435 Murder: Sierra County Superior Court records (Downieville); *LA Examiner,* Oct. 28.
436 Standard Oil: Haynes book; Forbes book.
Kingsbury letter: Oct. 26 (B-Hatfield).
437 Hotchkiss: letter "T.W.G." to John Billings, Oct. 26.
Hailing Hearst: *LA Examiner,* Oct. 26.
Willicombe to Young, and Young responds: Oct. 26 (B-Hearst).
438 Gale cartoon: *LA Examiner,* Oct. 27.
Hays to Sinclair: *Motion Picture Herald,* Nov. 3; *Pasadena Post,* Oct. 29.
Sinclair to Creel: *LA Examiner,* Oct. 27.
Merriam: *NY Times,* Oct. 28.
439 Hatfield on shooting Sinclair: *Burlingame Advance-Star,* Oct. 27.

OCTOBER 27

440 Long: *NY Times,* Oct. 28.
441 "Not favored": Schlesinger, *The Politics of Upheaval.*
"Dumb stenographer": *NY Times,* Oct. 28.
Fish: *LA Examiner,* Oct. 29.
News-week: Nov. 3.
Herald-Tribune: Oct. 27.
442 Memo: O'Connor, Oct. 27 (RL).
McAdoo and football: O'Connor diary (B).
443 Tugwell and Dodd: Dodd book.
Putzi: *NY Times,* Oct. 28.
Dodd on Hearst: Dodd book.
Dodd and Tugwell: Dodd book.
444 Pegler on Merriam: Scripps-Howard column, Oct. 27.
445 Shirley: *Norfolk (Va.) Pilot,* Oct. 29.
McNitt quits: *LA Daily News,* Oct. 27.

446 Parker responds: *Pasadena Post,* Oct. 28.
Parker to Debevoise: Oct. 27 (Debevoise file).
Sproul and Crusaders: Sproul memos (B-Sproul).
447 Scheduled to appear: Zach Cobb to FDR, Oct. 20 (RL).
Bryan background: Wilson book; Bryan book; Koenig book.
Scopes trial: de Camp book.
448 Bryan to Farley: Oct. 16 (LC-Farley).
Bryan speech: *LA Examiner,* Oct. 28.

OCTOBER 28

449 Farley cartoons: *Washington Star* and *Post,* Oct. 28.
NY Times: Oct. 28.
450 O'Connor and Haight: O'Connor diary (B).
451 Letter to Sinclair: Oct. 28.
Anderson call: *I, Candidate.*
Anderson background: obituaries, *Variety* and *LA Examiner,* July 23, 1951; interviews with Robert Anderson and Elizabeth Young (longtime housekeeper).
452 Anderson to wife: Sept. 21 (LL-MCS).
Donated $150,000: Delmatier, et al. book.
Anderson suggests: *I, Candidate.*
Anderson's house: interview with Elizabeth Young.
453 Sinclair and Giannini: *I, Candidate.*
Giannini and O'Connor: O'Connor diary (B).
Forbes: Forbes book.
Giannini background: Forbes book; McWilliams, *California, The Great Exception; Current Biography 1947; San Jose Mercury-News,* Oct. 5, 1975.
455 Giannini and FDR and '34 campaign: Bank of America Archives; Antognini article; Posner article.
Giannini telegram: to John B. Elliott and others, July 18 (B-Storke).
Considered backing Merriam: telegram, Morrison to Giannini, and Giannini response, both June 25 (BOA).
Three days after primary: Morrison to Giannini, Sept. 1, and Giannini response, Sept. 11 (BOA).
Letters to Giannini: BOA.
Giannini on Southern Pacific and PG&E: Howe letter to Hatfield, Oct. 6 (B-Hatfield).
Giannini wires White House: Sept. 2 (RL).
456 Sinclair phones White House: *I, Candidate.*
Sinclair to Hays: Oct. 28 (LL).

To Walsh and Patman: LL.
Pettijohn picnic: *LA Examiner,* Oct. 29.
457 Coughlin: *NY Times,* Oct. 29.
Haight and Sinclair: Haight telegram to McIntyre, Oct. 29 (RL).

OCTOBER 29

458 Haight to McIntyre: Oct. 29 (RL).
459 From Berkeley: Women's Democratic group to FDR, Oct. 23; from Pasadena: Manning to FDR, undated; from L.A.: Alferi to FDR, Oct. 18 (all RL).
Telegram from "Pussie": Oct. 27 (RL).
Transcript of telephone conversation: RL.
461 O'Connor and Morgenthau: O'Connor diary (B).
Mencken: letter to Harry Wilson, Oct. 29, from *Letters.*
462 *County Chairman:* Sterling book.
Merriam and Rogers picture: *San Diego Tribune,* Nov. 1.
Murder case: Superior Court records, Sierra County.
McMahon to Warren: letter, Oct. 10 (Warren).
463 Baby Upton: Marshaw letter to Will Kindig (LL).
Hoover to Mahoney: HL.
464 Minor and Darcy: Darcy OH and autobio ms. (Darcy papers-NYU); Minor papers (Columbia).
Minor article ms. and radio address ms. in Minor papers.
465 Haight to Gianinni and Fox aide: BOA.
Sinclair on radio: printed in *EPIC News,* Oct. 29.

OCTOBER 30

467 Pegler: Scripps-Howard column, Oct. 30.
468 O'Connor statement: *LA Herald,* Oct. 30; *Pasadena Post,* Oct. 31.
Meets Anderson: O'Connor diary (B).
Variety, Oct. 30.
469 Chaplin: *Variety,* Oct. 30.
UCLA: *Daily Californian* Oct. 29–31.
470 Registration case: *LA Herald,* Oct. 30–31; *EPIC News,* Nov. 5.
471 O'Connor and Sinclair: O'Connor diary (B); O'Connor memo to Marvin McIntyre, Nov. 2 (RL); *I, Candidate.*
O'Connor and press: *LA Daily News,* Oct. 31.
O'Connor, Haight, Merriam: O'Connor diary (B); O'Connor to McIntyre, Nov. 2 (RL).

472 Cobb: *Eureka Standard,* Oct. 31. Background: Cobb book; McCallum book; *Current Biography 1951.*
Critical letter to Warren: Oct. 21 (Warren).
473 Warren on bums' rush: GOP press release, Oct. 30 (Warren).
Warren on vote-purge: GOP press release, Oct. 26 (Warren).
Warren to Fletcher: Oct. 29 (Warren).
Warren to Wilson: Oct. 30 (Warren).
474 Dempster statement: *LA Examiner* and *NY Times.*
Divine to Sinclair: Oct. 20 (SL).
475 Divine background: Weisbrot book.

OCTOBER 31

476 Court rules: *LA Herald,* Oct. 31; *LA Examiner,* Nov. 1; *EPIC News,* Nov. 5.
477 D.A. probe and Hepburn: *NY Times* and *Pasadena Post,* Nov. 1.
Hepburn background: Kobal book; Andersen book; Morley book.
478 "My mother is important": International News Service, May 1934.
479 Warner quoted in Louella Parsons: Oct. 31.
Hearst to Willicombe: B-Hearst.
480 Cotton to McIntyre: RL.
Farley to Cotton: LC-Farley.
Bergeron: *Washington Post,* Oct. 31.
Pegler: Scripps-Howard column, Oct. 31.
482 UCLA: *LA Times,* Nov. 2.
Merriam and O'Connor: O'Connor diary (B); O'Connor to McIntyre, Nov. 2 (RL).
483 *Bridal Call:* Oct. 31.
Sinclair and Aimee: *I, Candidate.*
484 Arnoll letter: UCLA (Dickson scrapbook).
Swink: statement in Warren papers.
Insurance men: Bogy letter, Oct. 6 (Keesling papers-Stanford). Also, Sawyer letter, Oct. 20 (Warren).
Hepburn: *NY Times,* Nov. 1.
485 All Sinclair letters: LL.
Douglas to Sinclair: Oct. 27 (LL).

NOVEMBER 2

486 FDR: press conference, Nov. 2 (RL).
Moses: Farley papers (LL).
487 FDR and Ickes: Ickes book.

Farley and O'Connor: O'Connor diary (B).
Farley and FDR: Nov. 2 (LC-Farley).
Dos Passos and letter to Wilson: Dos Passos book.

488 Debevoise to *EPIC News:* Nov. 2 (Debevoise file).

489 Stern reports anti-Sinclair activities: syndicated column, Nov. 2 (B-Stern).
Norris: *Oakland Post-Enquirer,* Nov. 3.

490 Catledge: *NY Times,* Oct. 30.
Hoyt booklet: reprinted in *Upton Sinclair Quarterly,* June 1981.
Warren: GOP press releases, Oct. 30–Nov. 2 (Warren).
Sinclair "cheerful": *LA Daily News,* Nov. 3.

491 Response to United Press: LL.
Dialogue with another reporter: *NY Times,* Nov. 3.

492 O'Connor with three Democrats: O'Connor diary (B).
Memo to McIntyre: Nov. 2 (RL).

493 Rogers: *NY Times,* Nov. 3.
UCLA: Criley OH (B-EPIC OHs).

494 Students shot at: *SF Chronicle,* Nov. 3.
Church rally: *LA Examiner* and *LA Daily News,* Nov. 3.
Aimee's pageant: *Bible Call Crusader,* Nov. 7.

495 Pasadena rally: *Pasadena Post,* Nov. 3.

NOVEMBER 3

497 FDR and Farley: *NY Times,* Nov. 4.
Farley memo: Nov. 3 (LC-Farley).

498 Cutting backs Sinclair: Cutting letter to Sinclair, Sept. 22 (LL).
Pegler: Scripps-Howard column, Nov. 3.

499 Movie short: in Newsfilm Library (University of South Carolina).

501 Parker and Debevoise: Parker telegram to Debevoise and letter, Nov. 3 (Debevoise file).

502 *Script:* Nov. 3.
Chaplin: in *Script,* Nov. 3.

503 Kerr: *LA Examiner,* Nov. 3.
Wilson: letter to Warren, Oct. 30 (Warren).

504 Samish: postcard, Nov. 1 (B-Knowland).
Raised $200,000 and "to hell with": Samish book.
Norton: *LA Herald,* Nov. 3.
EPIC rally: *I, Candidate;* Sinclair OH; Sinclair autbio; *EPIC News,* Nov. 5.
Barnsdall: Sinclair OH; *I, Candidate;* Dunlop book.
Chief Davis: *EPIC News,* Oct. 15.

505 Riots: *Variety,* Nov. 6.

NOVEMBER 4

506 *NY Times* and others: Nov. 4.
507 Flight: *NY Times,* Nov. 5.
Hearst: *LA Examiner,* Nov. 5.
508 Göring: *LA Examiner,* Nov. 4.
Boddy: *LA Daily News,* Oct. 25 and 31.
Giannini: *Pasadena Post,* Nov. 4.
509 McAdoo: *Sacramento Union,* Nov. 5.
Coughlin: *NY Times,* Nov. 5.
510 Farley: *NY Times,* Nov. 5.
Movie protests: *Variety,* Nov. 6.
Sacks: *EPIC News,* Nov. 5.
511 Thomas and gun: *Variety,* Nov. 5.
Aimee pageants: *Bridal Call Crusader,* Nov. 7 and 14.
512 Stars attend: *Bridal Call Crusader,* Nov. 7.
Belfrage: Belfrage book.
McWilliams visit: McWilliams, *The Education of Carey McWilliams;* McWilliams OH (UCLA).
513 *New Republic* articles: Aug. 22, Nov. 7.
Dummy: *LA Herald,* Nov. 5.
Rogers: transcript at Rogers Memorial.

NOVEMBER 5

515 Gamblers: *SF News,* Nov. 5; *LA Examiner,* Nov. 6.
516 Rowell: *Star-News,* Nov. 5.
Hollywood Reporter: Nov. 5.
Favorable coverage: Willicombe to George Young, Nov. 5 (B-Hearst).
517 Hearst: *LA Examiner,* Nov. 5.
Hoover to Charlotte Kellogg (HL).
Hyde Park prepares, Broun visits: *NY Times,* Nov. 6.
518 Farley changes speech: ms. (LC-Farley).
Wagner: Wagner letter to Neil Vanderbilt, Nov. 5 (UCLA-Wagner).
EPIC News, Nov. 5.
519 Chandler: *I, Candidate.*
Hichborn: Hichborn ms. (UCLA).
520 Stein: at Princeton, *NY Times,* Nov. 6. NY lecture: *NY Times,* Nov. 2.
Observations: Sprigge book; Greenfeld book.
Text of lectures: Stein book.
521 Dreiser: *Esquire,* Dec. 1934.

Merriam final speech: ms. (B-Merriam).
Rogers: *NY Times,* Nov. 6.
522 Sinclair last comment to reporters: *LA Daily News,* Nov. 8.

NOVEMBER 6

524 Man gropes: AP dispatch, Nov. 6.
FDR votes: *NY Times,* Nov. 7; newsreel footage, Newsfilm Library (University of South Carolina).
525 Long: *NY Times,* Nov. 7.
526 Sinclair votes: *Star-News,* Nov. 6; *Pasadena Post* and *LA Daily News,* Nov. 7; newsreel footage, Newsfilm Library.
Sinclair and newsreels: newsreel footage, Newsfilm Library.
Merriam votes: newsreel footage, Newsfilm Library.
527 Hoover votes: newsreel footage, Newsfilm Library.
O'Connor diary: B.
Hearst: Belfrage book.
528 Disputes at polls: *LA Herald,* Nov. 6; *SF Chronicle,* Nov. 6–8.
529 Sinclair and underworld: *I, Candidate.*
Sproul: *LA Times,* Nov. 7; Sproul memos (B-Sproul).
Farley statement: *NY Times,* Nov. 7.
FDR: *NY Times,* Nov. 7.
530 Rogers: *NY Times,* Nov. 7.
Hollywood: *Variety* and *Hollywood Reporter,* Nov. 7–8.
Francisco: *LA Examiner,* Nov. 6.
531 On the streets: *LA Herald,* Nov. 7.
Sinclair at home: *LA Daily News,* Nov. 7; *I, Candidate;* Sinclair autobio.
Knowland: Knowland letter to Glenn Willaman, Nov. 19 (B-Wm. Knowland).
EPIC studies fraud: *EPIC News,* Nov. 12.
532 Sinclair to Norris: LL.
Sinclair's thoughts, and Craig exclaims: *I, Candidate;* Sinclair autobio.
Wagner to Sinclair: *Script,* Nov. 17.
O'Melveny: his diary (Huntington).
533 Sinclair waits at studio: *LA Daily News,* Nov. 7.
Sinclair speaks: *LA Daily News, Pasadena Post, LA Examiner,* Nov. 7; *I, Candidate.*
534 Otto: *LA Daily News,* Nov. 7.
Merriam on Hearst: *LA Herald,* Nov. 7.
535 Mayer's party: *Hollywood Reporter,* Nov. 8.

Merriam wire: *Hollywood Reporter,* Nov. 7.
Mayer: *SF Chronicle,* Nov. 7.
Suicide: *LA Herald,* Nov. 7.

NOVEMBER 7

537 FDR: press conference #156 transcript (RL).
538 La Follettes and third party: *LA Examiner,* Nov. 9.
539 *Das Tageblatt:* Universal News Service dispatch, Nov. 7.
Hopkins: *NY Times,* Nov. 8; Sherwood book.
Farley and Fox: Farley papers (LC).
Hays to FDR: RL.
540 Rogers: *NY Times,* Nov. 8.
Final totals: Merriam 1,138,620 / Sinclair 879,537 / Haight 320,519; Hatfield 1,220,515 / Downey 1,002,832.
541 Giannini: *Wall Street Journal,* Nov. 9.
Jeffers: *SF Chronicle,* Nov. 8.
Write-ins: *Pasadena Post.*
542 Merriam, O'Connor, McAdoo: O'Connor diary (B).
O'Connor to FDR: telegram (RL).
Hoover to Merriam: Nov. 7 (HL).
Knowland to Merriam: B-Wm. Knowland.
543 Paramount rehiring: *Hollywood Reporter,* Nov. 8.
Colbert: *SF Chronicle,* Nov. 8.
Variety, Nov. 7.
Jacobs case: AP dispatch, Nov. 7; *LA Herald,* Jan. 24, 1935; court records, Superior Court, Santa Barbara.
544 Book: *I, Candidate.*
545 All letters: LL.
Downey: interview with Leone Baxter.
546 Olson: *LA Herald,* Nov. 7; *EPIC News,* Nov. 12.
Dills: *LA Times,* Nov. 26, 1989.
Voorhis, "with bowed head": press release and letter, Voorhis papers (Honnold).
547 Voorhis to Sinclair: LL.
Warren to Merriam: Nov. 7 (Warren).
Statement: GOP press release (Warren).
Hearst message: *LA Examiner,* Nov. 8.
548 Hearst to Brisbane: Nov. 7 (B-Hearst).
Hutton: *EPIC News,* Nov. 12.
Fraud reports: *EPIC News,* Nov. 12 and 19; *I, Candidate.*

Sinclair at headquarters: *LA Herald,* Nov. 7; *LA Times, LA Examiner, NY Times,* Nov. 8; *I, Candidate.*

549 Suicides: *I, Candidate.*
Escapes out window: *I, Candidate.*

550 Shooting: Sinclair OH; author's interview with David Sinclair.

EPILOGUE

551 Rowell: Hoover letter to Senator Vandenburg, Nov. 13 (HL).
Hoover "no part": Hoover letter to Bertran Snell, Nov. 9 (HL).

552 Pegler: letter to Sinclair, Jan. 18, 1935 (LL).
O'Connor: letter to McIntyre, Dec. 15 (RL).
McIntyre: letter to Farley, Jan. 16, 1935 (RL).
Farley: letter to Howe, Dec. 17 (RL).
Zeppo Marx and "Voice records well": *Pasadena Post,* Feb. 5, 1935.
Pound: letter to Sinclair, Dec. 19, 1934, and Jan. 30, 1935 (Sinclair, *My Lifetime in Letters*).

553 Einstein: letter to Sinclair, Nov. 23 (Sinclair, *My Lifetime in Letters*).
"Six months ago": *LA Daily News,* Nov. 12.
EPIC News: Nov. 12.
LA Times, SF Chronicle, NY Times: Nov. 8.

554 *Nation:* Nov. 14.
Literary Digest: Dec. 29.
Young: letter to Neylan, Nov. 22 (B-Neylan).
Neylan: letter to Hearst, Nov. 26 (B-Neylan).
Hearst: letter to Neylan, Nov. 27 (B-Neylan).

555 Hearst "secondhand Sinclair": telegram to Neylan, Jan. 23, 1935 (B-Neylan).
Merriam: election records in California secretary of state archives (Sacramento)
Walker: telegram to Farley, Nov. 9 (LC-Farley).
Farley and Moses: letter to Walker, Nov. 10 (LC-Farley).
O'Connor: O'Connor diary (B).
O'Connor: FDR letter to O'Connor, Nov. 11 (RL).

556 Giannini: O'Connor diary (B).
Hearst: Brisbane telegram to Hearst, Dec. 9 (B-Hearst).
Mencken remarks: Brayman book.
Mencken and FDR: Schlesinger, *The Politics of Upheaval.*
Brisbane: telegram to Hearst, Dec. 9 (B-Hearst).
FDR and cannibalism: Schlesinger, *The Politics of Upheaval.*
Mencken letter to Pound: Nov. 15, from *The New Mencken Letters.*

557 EPIC breakup, Otto and Olson: clips from *LA Daily News,* Nov. 24, and various L.A. newspapers, Dec. 13, 14; Sinclair, *I, Candidate.*

558 Sinclair and communism: Borough OH (UCLA); *LA Examiner,* May 18–19, 1935.

Lecture tour, Disney, and *Gnome-Mobile:* Sinclair autobio; Sinclair OH.

559 Goldwyn: Berg book.

Sinclair raves: *EPIC News,* Jan. 21, 1935.

Hearst to Hays: George Young to Joseph Willicombe, describing conversation with Fred Beetson of Hays Office, Nov. 30 (B-Hearst).

Vidor: Vidor papers, UCLA.

Sinclair speaks: Harris bio.

Wanger and Hays: MPPDA files (Academy).

Zukor: Hays ms. of his memoirs. (Hays).

560 Zeppo: *Pasadena Post,* Feb. 5, 1935.

Mayer and Sinclair: *LA Daily News,* Feb. 28, 1935.

Scully: *EPIC News,* Mar. 4, 1935.

Inventoried: Brownstein book.

Sinclair and Florida: *LA Herald,* Mar. 9, 1935.

Mayer speech: *The New Yorker,* Mar. 28, 1936.

561 Thalberg at party: Crichton book; Thomas, *Thalberg.*

Dunne: interview with author.

Anti-Merriam: Rosten book.

562 Knight: author interview with Mac Faries.

Palmer and Merriam: Halberstam book; Palmer OH (*LA Times* archives).

Time: May 20, 1935.

563 "Guess we started something": Rosten book.

564 Mencken article: *American Mercury,* May 1936.

Sinclair reply: letter, Apr. 28, 1936 (LL).

Mencken reply: May 2, 1936 (LL), and *American Mercury,* June–July 1936.

565 Sinclair to Mencken: Jan. 3, 1951 (LL).

565 "Few more dollars": Rogers radio broadcast, Nov. 11.

Sinclair-Long Debate: Rogers column, Nov. 16.

Sinclair reply: telegram to Rogers, Nov. 17 (LL).

Rogers and Hays: Will Hays, Jr., speech, Nov. 5, 1988.

Rogers's last words: *Will Rogers's Weekly Articles.*

Tributes to Rogers: Sterling book.

566 Chaplin voice test: Skolsky column, Nov. 11.

Modern Times: Maland book.

Wilder: interview with author.

Cagney and Steffens: Steffens papers.

Cagney and committee: *Current Biography 1942.*

567 Rapf: interview with author.
Schulberg "deported": interview with author.
Wilkerson: obit, *Hollywood Reporter,* Sept. 3, 1962.
Thalberg Jr.: Thalberg clip file (Academy).
Hepburn: Schwartz book.

568 Lippmann, Tugwell: Schlesinger, *The Politics of Upheaval.*

569 Sinclair sends message: July 5, 1935 (B-Olson).
Sinclair to FDR: telegram, Sept. 30, 1935 (RL).
Vanderbilt account: Vanderbilt book.
Vanderbilt advises FDR: Vanderbilt letter to Farley, Sept. 11, 1935; Farley to FDR, Sept. 12, 1935 (RL).
Marshaw: Carey McWilliams in *Westways,* Feb. 1936.

570 Whitaker and Baxter: McWilliams, *The Nation,* May 5, 1951; Kelley book; Ross, *Harper's,* July 1959; Baxter and Whitaker Jr. interviews.

571 Palmer: Palmer OH (*LA Times* archives); Halberstam book; Gottlieb and Wolt book.
Palmer retired: *LA Times,* Nov. 20, 1960.
Palmer and Upton: Palmer OH.

572 "Asa was the man": Faries OH (B).
Los Angeles magazine: Apr. 1986.
Samish: Samish book; Phillips book; McWilliams, *California: The Great Exception.*
Nixon: Morris book; Halberstam book.
Reagan: Morris book.

573 Farley: letter to Stanley Slome, Aug. 17, 1966, in Slome thesis.
Moley: letter to Stanley Slome, Aug. 11, 1966, in Slome thesis; Moley, *After Seven Years.*
Loeb: Veblen book.
Parker: interviews with Kitty Parker and Ruth Cashman.
Pelletier: Samish book.

574 Yorty and EPIC: *Current Biography 1967.*
Pegler on FDR: Pilat book.
Putzi: Speer book; Shirer book.
Belding: quotes from Harris bio and author's interview with Hans Zeisel.
Aimee: Lately Thomas book.

575 Sproul: Pettitt book.
Knowland: Dunlap book.
Behrens: letter to Slome, Feb. 22, 1968 (Slome thesis).
Haight: author's interview with Haight Jr.
Sinclair: Harris bio and Sinclair autobio.

576 ER, Koestler, Dos Passos, Sinclair to grad student: Harris bio.
Reads EPIC plan: Sinclair OH (Columbia).

577 Mosk: EPIC OHs (B).

McWilliams: Terkel, *Hard Times;* McWilliams, *Southern California Country.*
Hopkins: Sherwood book.

578 Schlesinger: *The Politics of Upheaval.*
Blumenthal: *The Permament Campaign.*
Landon campaign: Casey, *Public Opinion Quarterly,* Apr. 1937.
Catledge: Aug. 16, 1936.

579 *Variety:* Aug. 19, 1936.
Polls: Robinson, *Public Opinion Quarterly,* July 1937.
Specialists: Kaid book; Kelley; Blumenthal.
Diamond: Diamond, *The Spot.*
Reagan: Bloom book.

580 Sinclair: Harris bio and Sinclair autobio.
"Too many people": Hirschorn, *7 Days,* Nov. 2, 1988.
"This was a P.R. outfit": Notes and Comment, *The New Yorker,* Nov. 7, 1988.
White: White book.

581 *Newsweek:* Oct. 31, 1988.
Dukakis and sound bites: *NY Times,* Apr. 22, 1990.
Savings and Loan: *NY Times,* June 6, 1990.
Markle: *NY Times,* May 6, 1990.
Running more ads: *NY Times,* Oct. 21, 1990.
One year later: *NY Times,* Nov. 5, 1991. Analyst: John Phillips.

582 *Jeopardy!:* Andrea Rock.

BIBLIOGRAPHY

This is a list of books, magazine articles, and unpublished dissertations cited in the Notes. It omits many books and articles used for general reference and background only. It also leaves out all newspaper reports (since they are cited in the Notes day by day).

ADAMSON, JOE. *Groucho, Harpo, Chico and Sometimes Zeppo.* Touchstone, 1973.

ALBRECHT, ALFRED J. "A Rhetorical Study of Upton Sinclair's 1934 Campaign for Governor of California." Ph.D. dissertation, Indiana University, 1966.

ALEXANDER, JACK. "He's Against." *Saturday Evening Post,* Sept. 14, 1940.

ALWORTH, E. PAUL. *Will Rogers.* Twayne, 1974.

AMBROSE, STEPHEN E. *Nixon: The Education of a Politician.* Simon and Schuster, 1987.

AMES, RICHARD S. "The Screen Enters Politics." *Harper's,* March 1935.

ANDERSEN, CHRISTOPHER. *Young Kate.* Henry Holt, 1988.

ANTOGNINI, RICHARD. "The Role of A. P. Giannini in the 1934 California Gubernatorial Election." *Southern California Quarterly,* Spring 1975.

BADGER, ANTHONY J. *The New Deal.* Noonday Press, 1989.

BADGER, SHERWIN. "Uptonia: California's Millennium." *Barron's,* Oct. 1, 1934.

BAHR, ROBERT. *Least of All Saints.* Prentice Hall, 1979.

BALTER, MICHAEL. "The Way It Was," LA *Daily News Magazine,* July 15, 1984.

BARGER, BOB. "Raymond L. Haight and the Commonwealth Progressive Campaign of 1934." *California Historical Society Quarterly,* Sept. 1964.

BEAN, WALTON. *California: An Interpretive History.* McGraw-Hill, 1968.

BEHLMER, RUDY. *Inside Warner Brothers.* Viking, 1985.
BELLI, MELVIN. *My Life on Trial.* Morrow, 1976.
BENNETT, DAVID H. *Demagogues in the Depression.* Rutgers University Press, 1969.
BERG, A. SCOTT. *Goldwyn.* Knopf, 1989.
BLACK, SHIRLEY TEMPLE. *Child Star.* McGraw-Hill, 1988.
BLUMENTHAL, SIDNEY. *The Permanent Campaign.* Beacon Press, 1980.
BLOOM, MELVYN H. *Public Relations and Presidential Campaigns.* Crowell, 1973.
BOLLENS, JOHN C., and GEYER, GRANT. *Yorty: Politics of a Constant Campaigner.* Palisades Publishers, 1973.
BOLLENS, JOHN C., and WILLIAMS, G. ROBERT. *Jerry Brown.* Palisades Publishers, 1978.
BOROUGH, REUBEN. "Upton Sinclair's EPIC." *Occidental Review,* Summer 1965.
BRAYMAN, HAROLD. *The President Speaks Off the Record.* Dow Jones Books, 1976.
BRENMAN-GIBSON, MARGARET. *Clifford Odets.* Atheneum, 1981.
BRIDGMAN, RICHARD. *Gertrude Stein in Pieces.* Oxford University Press, 1970.
BRINKLEY, ALAN. *Huey Long, Father Coughlin, and the Great Depression.* Knopf, 1982.
BROUN, HEYWOOD HALE. *Collected Edition of Heywood Broun.* Books for Libraries Press, 1941.
BROWNSTEIN, RONALD. *The Power and the Glitter.* Pantheon, 1991.
BROWN, WILLIAM R. *Imagemaker: Will Rogers and the American Dream.* University of Missouri Press, 1970.
BRYAN, WILLIAM JENNINGS. *Memoirs.* John C. Winston, 1925.
BULLOCK, PAUL. *Jerry Voorhis: The Idealist as Politician.* Vantage Press, 1978.
BURDEN, HAMILTON T. *The Nuremberg Party Rallies.* Praeger, 1967.
BURKE, R. E. *Olson's New Deal for California.* University of California Press, 1953.
BURNS, JAMES MACGREGOR. *The Crosswinds of Freedom.* Knopf, 1989.
———. *Roosevelt: The Lion and the Fox.* Harcourt Brace Jovanovich, 1956.

CAGNEY, JAMES. *Cagney by Cagney.* Doubleday, 1977.
CANNOM, ROBERT C. *Van Dyke and the Mythical City.* Murray & Gee, 1948.
CAREY, GARY. *All the Stars in Heaven: Louis B. Mayer's M-G-M.* Dutton, 1981.
CARLISLE, RODNEY. *Hearst and the New Deal.* Garland Publishing, 1979.
CARLSON, OLIVER. *Brisbane.* Stackpole Sons, 1937.
———, and BATES, ERNEST S. *Hearst: Lord of San Simeon.* Viking, 1936.
CARR, VIRGINIA SPENCER. *Dos Passos: A Life.* Doubleday, 1984.
CARTER, JOHN FRANKLIN (THE UNOFFICIAL OBSERVER). *The New Dealers.* Simon and Schuster, 1934.

———. *American Messiahs.* Simon and Schuster, 1935.

CASEY, RALPH D. "Republican Propaganda in the 1936 Campaign." *Public Opinion Quarterly,* Apr. 1937.

CASH, KEVIN. *Who the Hell is William Loeb?* Amoskeag Press, 1975.

CATLEDGE, TURNER. *My Life and "The Times."* Harper & Row, 1971.

CEPLAIR, LARRY, and ENGLUND, STEVEN. *The Inquisition in Hollywood.* Anchor, 1980.

CHAPLIN, CHARLES. *My Autobiography.* Simon and Schuster, 1964.

CHRISTENSEN, TERRY. *Reel Politics.* Basil Blackwell, 1987.

CLARY, WILLIAM W. *History of the Law Firm of O'Melveny & Myers.* Privately printed, 1966.

CLELAND, ROBERT G. *California in Our Time.* Knopf, 1947.

COBB, TY. *My Life in Baseball.* Doubleday, 1961.

COBLENTZ, EDMUND. *William Randolph Hearst: A Portrait in His Own Words.* Simon and Schuster, 1952.

COLLIER, PETER, and HOROWITZ, DAVID. *The Kennedys.* Warner Books, 1984.

CONE, FAIRFAX. *With All Its Faults.* Little, Brown, 1969.

COOKE, ALISTAIR. *Six Men.* Knopf, 1977.

CRANE-GARTZ, KATE. *Prophetic Letters, Vol. IX.* Published by Mary Craig Sinclair, 1937.

CREEL, GEORGE. *Rebel at Large.* G. P. Putnam's Sons, 1947.

———. "Utopia Unlimited." *Saturday Evening Post,* Nov. 24, 1934.

CRICHTON, KYLE. *Total Recoil.* Doubleday, 1960.

CROUCH, WINSTON W., and MCHENRY, DEAN E. *California Government.* University of California Press, 1949.

CROWTHER, BOSLEY. *Hollywood Rajah.* Holt, Rinehart & Winston, 1960.

CROY, HOMER. *Our Will Rogers.* Little, Brown, 1953.

DAVENPORT, WALTER. "Sinclair Gets the Glory Vote." *Collier's,* Oct. 27, 1934.

DAVID, LESTER. *The Lonely Lady of San Clemente.* Crowell, 1978.

DAVIES, MARION. *The Times We Had.* Bobbs-Merrill, 1975.

DAVIS, KENNETH S. *FDR: The New Deal Years.* Random House, 1986.

DAY, DONALD. *Will Rogers.* McKay, 1962.

DECAMP, L. SPRAGUE. *The Great Monkey Trial.* Doubleday, 1968.

DEFORD, MIRIAM ALLEN. *They Were San Franciscans.* Books for Libraries Press, 1941.

DELMATIER, ROYCE D., MCINTOSH, CLARENCE F., and WATERS, EARL G. *The Rumble of California Politics.* John Wiley & Sons, 1970.

DEMARCO, GORDON. *October Heat.* Germinal Press, 1979.

DEMILLE, WILLIAM. *Hollywood Saga.* Dutton, 1939.

DIAMOND, EDWIN, and BATES, STEPHEN. *The Spot.* MIT Press, 1984.

DILLING, ELIZABETH. *The Red Network.* Published by the author, 1934.

DINKIN, ROBERT J. *Campaigning in America.* Greenwood Press, 1989.

DLB (*Dictionary of Literary Biography*), various volumes. Gale Research.
DODD, WILLIAM E., JR., and DODD, MARTHA. *Ambassador Dodd's Diary.* Harcourt, Brace, 1941.
DOS PASSOS, JOHN. *The Fourteenth Chronicle: Letters and Diaries.* Gambit, 1973.
DREISER, THEODORE. "The EPIC Sinclair." *Esquire,* Dec. 1934.
———. *Letters.* Robert H. Elias, ed. University of Pennsylvania Press, 1959.
———. "Upton Sinclair." *The Clipper,* Sept. 1940.
DUNLAP, CAROL. *California People.* Peregrine Smith, 1982.

EINSTEIN, ALBERT. *Ideas and Opinions.* Crown, 1954.
ENGELMANN, LARRY. *The Goddess and the American Girl.* Oxford University Press, 1988.

FABER, DORIS. *The Life of Lorena Hickok.* Morrow, 1980.
FARLEY, JAMES A. *Behind the Ballots.* Da Capo Press, 1973.
———. *Jim Farley's Story.* McGraw-Hill, 1948.
FEDERAL WRITERS PROJECT. *The WPA Guide to California,* (1939). Pantheon, 1984.
FIELDING, RAYMOND. *The American Newsreel.* University of Oklahoma Press, 1972.
FINCHER, JACK. "The Mogul, the Magnate, the Muckraker." *Los Angeles,* July 1985.
FORBES, B. C. *Men Who Are Making the West.* New World Book Co., 1923.
FOX, STEPHEN. *The Mirror Makers: A History of American Advertising and Its Creators.* Morrow, 1984.
FRANCKE, WARREN T. "George Creel," *DLB 25.* Gale Research.
FREEDLAND, MICHAEL. *Cagney.* Stein & Day, 1974.
FREWIN, LESLIE. *The Late Mrs. Dorothy Parker.* Macmillan, 1986.
FROST, RICHARD. *The Mooney Case.* Stanford University Press, 1968.

GABLER, NEAL. *An Empire of Their Own: How the Jews Invented Hollywood.* Crown, 1988.
GARDNER, GERALD. *The Censorship Papers.* Dodd, Mead, 1988.
GARRY, CHARLES. *Streetfighter in the Courtroom.* Dutton, 1977.
GEHRING, WES D. *The Marx Brothers.* Greenwood Press, 1987.
GENTRY, CURT. *Frame-Up.* Norton, 1967.
———. *The Last Days of the Late, Great State of California.* G. P. Putnam's Sons, 1968.
GITLOW, BENJAMIN. *The Whole of Their Lives.* Scribner's, 1948.
GOLDSTON, ROBERT. *The Great Depression.* Fawcett, 1968.
GOTTESMAN, RONALD. *Upton Sinclair: An Annotated Checklist.* Kent State University Press, 1973.

GOTTLIEB, ROBERT. "Memories of Asa Call, L.A.'s Back-Room Mr. Big." *Los Angeles,* Aug. 1978.

———, and WOLT, IRENE. *Thinking Big: The Story of the Los Angeles Times.* G. P. Putnam's Sons, 1977.

GREENFELD, HOWARD. *Gertrude Stein.* Crown, 1973.

GUILES, FRED LAWRENCE. *Marion Davies.* McGraw-Hill, 1972.

GUNTHER, JOHN. *Taken at the Flood.* Harper & Row, 1960.

HALBERSTAM, DAVID. *The Powers That Be.* Knopf, 1979.

HARRIS, LEON. *Upton Sinclair: American Rebel.* Crowell, 1975.

HART, JACK. "The Information Empire." Ph.D. dissertation, University of Wisconsin, 1975.

HAYNES, H. J. *Standard Oil Company of California.* Privately published, 1980.

HAYS, WILL. *Memoirs of Will Hays.* Doubleday, 1955.

HICHBORN, FRANKLIN. *California Politics, 1891–1939.* Unpublished ms. (UCLA).

HIGHAM, CHARLES. *Cecil B. DeMille,* Scribner's, 1973.

HILL, GLADWIN. *Dancing Bear.* World, 1968.

HOFFMANN, BANESH. *Albert Einstein.* Viking, 1972.

HOOVER, HERBERT. *The Challenge to Liberty.* Scribner's, 1934.

HUSTON, JOHN. *An Open Book.* Knopf, 1980.

ICKES, HAROLD L. *The Secret Diary of Harold L. Ickes.* Simon and Schuster, 1953.

JAMIESON, KATHLEEN HALL. *Packaging the Presidency.* Oxford University Press, 1984.

JOHNPOLL, BERNARD K. *Pacifist's Progress: Norman Thomas and the Decline of American Socialism.* Quadrangle, 1970.

JOHNSTON, ALVA. "Will Hays: Czar and Elder." *The New Yorker,* June 10 and 17, 1933.

JONES, ARTHUR. *Malcolm Forbes.* Harper & Row, 1977.

JUDAH, CHARLES, and SMITH, GEORGE WINSTON. *The Unchosen.* Coward-McCann, 1962.

KAID, NIMMO, SANDERS. *New Perspectives on Political Advertising.* Southern Illinois University Press, 1986.

KAPLAN, JUSTIN. *Lincoln Steffens.* Simon and Schuster, 1974.

KARGON, ROBERT H. *The Rise of Robert Millikan.* Cornell University Press, 1982.

KATCHER, LEO. *Earl Warren, a Political Biography.* McGraw-Hill, 1967.

KAWIN, BRUCE F. *Faulkner's MGM Screenplays.* University of Tennessee Press, 1982.

KELLEY, STANLEY, JR. *Professional Public Relations and Political Power.* Johns Hopkins University Press, 1956.

KENNEDY, LUDOVIC. *The Airman and the Carpenter.* Viking, 1985.

KERR, CLARK. "Self-Help: A Study of the Cooperative Barter Movement of the Unemployed in California 1931–1933." Master's thesis, Stanford University, 1933.

KETCHUM, RICHARD M. *Will Rogers: His Life and Times.* American Heritage, 1973.

KLEHR, HARVEY. *The Heyday of American Communism.* Basic Books, 1984.

KNAPP, JEANNE M. *Don Belding.* Texas Tech University Press, 1983.

KNOWLES, A. S., JR. "John Dos Passos." *DLB 9.* Gale Research.

KOBAL, JOHN. *People Will Talk.* Knopf, 1986.

KOSKOFF, DAVID E. *Joseph P. Kennedy: A Life and Times.* Prentice Hall, 1974.

KRAMER, DALE. *Heywood Broun.* Current Books, 1949.

KRESS, MELVILLE. "Sinclair's Friend Mencken." *Upton Sinclair Quarterly,* Winter 1983–84.

LARSEN, CHARLES E. "The EPIC Campaign of 1934." *Pacific Historical Review,* May 1958.

LASH, JOSEPH. *Eleanor and Franklin.* Norton, 1971.

LASKER, ALBERT. *The Lasker Story.* Advertising Publications, 1953.

LAWSON, ANITA. *Irvin S. Cobb.* Bowling Green State University Press, 1984.

LEADER, LEONARD. "Upton Sinclair's EPIC Switch: A Dilemma for American Socialists." *Upton Sinclair Centenary Journal,* Sept. 1978.

LEFF, LEONARD J., and SIMMONS, JEROLD L. *The Dame in the Kimono: Hollywood, Censorship and the Production Code from the 1920s to the 1980s.* Grove Weidenfeld, 1990.

LEHAN, RICHARD. *Theodore Dreiser.* Southern Illinois University Press, 1969.

LEUCHTENBERG, WILLIAM. *Franklin D. Roosevelt and the New Deal.* Harper & Row, 1958.

LEVY, JOANN L. *Behind the Western Skyline.* Published by Coldwell Banker, 1981.

LILLARD, RICHARD G. "Charles C. Teague: Agricultural Statesman." *California History,* Mar. 1986.

LINGEMAN, RICHARD. *Theodore Dreiser: An American Journey 1908–1945.* G. P. Putnam's Sons, 1986.

LONGSTREET, STEPHEN. *All-Star Cast: An Anecdotal History of Los Angeles.* Crowell, 1977.

LUDINGTON, TOWNSEND. *John Dos Passos.* Dutton, 1980.

LUNDBERG, FERDINAND. *Imperial Hearst.* Greenwood, 1936.

LUKACS, JOHN. *The Last European War.* Anchor, 1976.

LYONS, EUGENE. *The Red Decade.* Bobbs-Merrill, 1941.

MALAND, CHARLES J. *Chaplin and American Culture.* Princeton University Press, 1989.

MANCHESTER, WILLIAM. *The Sage of Baltimore.* Andrew Melrose, 1952.

MANKIEWICZ, FRANK. *Perfectly Clear.* Quadrangle, 1973.

MARCUS, SHELDON. *Father Coughlin.* Little, Brown, 1973.

MARX, SAM. *A Gaudy Spree: Literary Hollywood When the West Was Fun.* Franklin Watts, 1987.

———. *Mayer and Thalberg: The Make-Believe Saints.* Random House, 1980.

MARX, SAM, and VANDERVEEN, JOYCE. *Deadly Illusion: Jean Harlow and the Murder of Paul Bern.* Random House, 1990.

MCCALLUM, JOHN. *The Tiger Wore Spikes.* Barnes and Co., 1956.

MCCONNELL, ROBERT LEE. "Hollywood and Political Issues." Ph.D. dissertation, Iowa University, 1977.

MCELVAINE, ROBERT S. *The Great Depression.* Times Books, 1984.

MCGILLIGAN, PATRICK. *Cagney.* Barnes and Co., 1982.

MCHENRY, DEAN. "Working for EPIC." *Upton Sinclair Quarterly,* Fall 1984.

MCPHERSON, AIMEE SEMPLE. *Aimee.* Foursquare Publications, 1979.

MCWILLIAMS, CAREY. *California: The Great Exception.* Greenwood Press, 1949.

———. *The Education of Carey McWilliams.* Simon and Schuster, 1979.

MEADE, MARION. *Dorothy Parker: What Fresh Hell Is This?* Villard, 1987.

MELENDY, H. BRETT. *Governors of California.* Talisman Press, 1965.

MENCKEN, H. L. *The New Mencken Letters.* Dial Press, 1977.

———. *The Vintage Mencken.* Vintage, 1955.

MEYERS, WILLIAM. *The Image Makers.* Times Books, 1984.

MINOTT, RODNEY G. *The Sinking of the Lollipop.* Diablo Press, 1968.

MOLEY, RAYMOND. *After Seven Years.* Harper Brothers, 1939.

———. *The First New Deal.* Harcourt, Brace & World, 1966.

———. *The Hays Office.* Bobbs-Merrill, 1945.

———. *27 Masters of Politics.* Funk & Wagnall, 1949.

MORGAN, NEIL. *The California Syndrome.* Prentice Hall, 1969.

MORLEY, SHERIDAN. *Katharine Hepburn.* Little, Brown, 1984.

MORRIS, ROGER. *Richard Milhous Nixon: The Rise of an American Politician.* Henry Holt, 1990.

MOWBRY, GEORGE E. *The California Progressives.* Quadrangle, 1951.

NUNIS, DOYCE B. *Past Is Prologue: A Centennial Profile of Pacific Mutual Life Insurance Company.* Published by Pacific Mutual, 1968.

O'CONNOR, RICHARD. *Heywood Broun.* G. P. Putnam's Sons, 1975.

ORLANDO, GUIDO. *Confessions of a Scoundrel.* John C. Winston, 1954.

OULAHAN, RICHARD. *The Man Who: The Story of the 1932 Democratic National Convention.* Dial Press, 1971.

PACKARD, VANCE. *The Hidden Persuaders.* David McKay Co., 1957.
PERKINS, FRANCES. *The Roosevelt I Knew.* Viking, 1946.
PETTITT, GEORGE A. *Twenty-Eight Years in the Life of a University President.* University of California Press, 1966.
PHILLIPS, HERBERT L. *Big Wayward Girl.* Doubleday, 1968.
PILAT, OLIVER. *Pegler: Angry Man of the Press.* Beacon Press, 1963.
POLLOCK, DALE. "The Use of Media in a Political Campaign." Master's thesis, San Jose State University, 1976.
POSNER, RUSSELL M. "A. P. Giannini and the 1934 Campaign in California." *Historical Society of Southern California,* June 1957.
POUND, EZRA. *The Letters of Ezra Pound.* Harcourt, Brace, 1950.
PRINGLE, HENRY F. "Yes, Mr. Mayer." *The New Yorker,* Mar. 28, 1936.

REMLEY, DAVID A. "The Correspondence of H. L. Mencken and Upton Sinclair." Ph.D. dissertation, Indiana University, 1967.
———. "Upton Sinclair and H. L. Mencken in Correspondence." *The Historical Society of Southern California.* Winter, 1974.
ROBINSON, CLAUDE E. "Recent Developments in the Straw-Poll Field." *Public Opinion Quarterly,* July 1937.
ROBINSON, DAVID. *Chaplin.* Collins, 1985.
ROGERS, WILL. *Daily Telegrams, Vol. 4.* Oklahoma State University Press, 1979.
———. *Weekly Articles, Vol. 6.* Oklahoma State University Press, 1982.
ROGIN, MICHAEL, and SHORER, JOHN L. *Political Change in California.* Greenwood, 1970.
ROOSEVELT, FRANKLIN D. *The Public Papers and Addresses, Vol. 3.* Russell & Russell, 1969.
ROSENBLOOM, DAVID LEE. *The Election Men.* Quadrangle, 1973.
ROSENSTONE, ROBERT A. "Manchester Boddy and the L.A. Daily News." *California Historical Society Quarterly,* Dec. 1970.
ROSS, IRWIN. "Whitaker and Baxter." *Harper's,* July 1959.
ROSTEN, LEO. *Hollywood.* Harcourt, Brace, 1941.
RUTZEBECK, HJALMAR. *Alaska Man's Luck, and Other Works.* Capra Press, 1988.

SABATO, LARRY J. *The Rise of Political Consultants.* Basic Books, 1981.
SAMISH, ARTHUR, and THOMAS, BOB. *The Secret Boss of California,* Crown, 1971.
SCHLESINGER, ARTHUR M., JR. *The Coming of the New Deal.* Houghton Mifflin, 1959.
———. *The Politics of Upheaval.* Houghton Mifflin, 1960.
SCHORER, MARK. *Sinclair Lewis: An American Life.* McGraw-Hill, 1961.
SCHULBERG, BUDD. *Moving Pictures.* Stein & Day, 1981.
SCHWARTZ, NANCY LYNN. *The Hollywood Writers' Wars.* McGraw-Hill, 1983.

SCULLY, FRANK. *Rogues Gallery.* Murray & Gee, 1943.
———. *This Gay Knight.* Chilton, 1943.
SELDES, GEORGE. *Even the Gods Can't Change History.* Lyle Stuart, 1976.
SHERWOOD, ROBERT. *Roosevelt and Hopkins.* Harper, 1949.
SHIRER, WILLIAM L. *The Rise and Fall of the Third Reich.* Simon and Schuster, 1960.
SHULMAN, IRVING. *Harlow.* Bernard Geis, 1964.
SINCLAIR, MARY CRAIG. *Southern Belle.* Sinclair Press, 1962.
SINCLAIR, UPTON. *The Autobiography of Upton Sinclair.* Harcourt, Brace & World, 1962.
———. *The Brass Check.* Published by the author, 1919. Reprinted by Arno Press, 1970.
———. *EPIC Answers; The Lie Factory Starts; Immediate EPIC.* Published by the author, 1934.
———. *I, Candidate for Governor; and How I Got Licked.* Published by the author, 1935.
———. *I, Governor of California, and How I Ended Poverty: A True Story of the Future.* Published by the author, 1933.
———. *My Lifetime in Letters.* University of Missouri Press, 1960.
———. *The Profits of Religion.* Vanguard, 1918.
———. *Upton Sinclair Presents William Fox.* Published by the author, 1932.
SINGER, DONALD L. "Upton Sinclair and the California Gubernatorial Campaign." Master's thesis, University of Southern California, 1966.
SLIDE, ANTHONY, ed. *The Best of "Rob Wagner's Script."* Scarecrow Press, 1985.
SLOME, STANLEY MELVIN. "The Press Against Upton Sinclair." Master's thesis, UCLA, 1968.
SMITH, RICHARD NORTON. *An Uncommon Man: The Triumph of Herbert Hoover.* Simon & Schuster, 1984.
SODERBERGH, PETER A. "Upton Sinclair and Hollywood." *Midwest Quarterly,* Winter 1970.
SPEER, ALBERT. *Inside the Third Reich.* Macmillan, 1970.
SPRIGGE, ELIZABETH. *Gertrude Stein: Her Life and Work.* Harper, 1959.
STARR, KEVIN. *Inventing the Dream: California Through the Progressive Era.* Oxford University Press, 1985.
———. *Material Dreams: Southern California Through the 1920s.* Oxford University Press, 1990.
STEFFENS, LINCOLN. *The Letters of Lincoln Steffens.* Harcourt, Brace, 1938.
STERLING, BRYAN B., and STERLING, FRANCES N. *Will Rogers in Hollywood.* Crown, 1984.
STOCK, NOEL. *The Life of Ezra Pound.* Pantheon, 1976.
STONE, IRVING. *Earl Warren.* Prentice Hall, 1948.
STORKE, THOMAS M. *California Editor.* Westernlore Press, 1955.

SWANBERG, W. A. *Citizen Hearst.* Charles Scribner's Sons, 1961.
———. *Dreiser.* Charles Scribner's Sons, 1965.
———. *Norman Thomas: The Last Idealist.* Charles Scribner's Sons, 1976.
SWING, RAYMOND GRAM. "EPIC and the Ohio Plan." *The Nation,* Oct. 3, 1934.
SYMES, LILLIAN. "California, There She Stands." *Harper's,* Feb. 1935.

TEAGUE, CHARLES C. *Fifty Years a Rancher.* Privately printed, 1944.
TERKEL, STUDS. *Hard Times.* Pantheon, 1970.
THOMAS, BOB. *Thalberg.* Doubleday, 1969.
THOMAS, LATELY. *Storming Heaven.* Morrow, 1970.
TROHAN, WALTER. *Political Animals.* Doubleday, 1975.
TUGWELL, REXFORD G. *The Democratic Roosevelt.* Doubleday, 1957.

Upton Sinclair Quarterly. Numerous issues 1981–1986. Robert O. Hahn.

VANDERBILT, CORNELIUS, JR. *Farewell to Fifth Avenue.* Simon and Schuster, 1935.
———. *Man of the World.* Crown, 1959.
VAUGHN, STEPHEN. "Morality and Entertainment: The Origins of the Motion Picture Production Code." *Journal of American History,* June 1990.
———. "William Randolph Hearst." *DLB 25.* Gale Research.
VEBLEN, ERIC P. *The Manchester Union Leader in New Hampshire Elections.* University Press of New England, 1975.
VIDOR, KING. *A Tree Is a Tree,* Harcourt, Brace, 1952.

WALKER, STANLEY. "They Tell Me He's a Big Man." *Saturday Evening Post,* Feb. 28, 1942.
WALLACE, ROBERT. *Life and Limb.* Doubleday, 1955.
WALLER, GEORGE. *Kidnap.* Dial, 1961.
WARREN, EARL. *The Memoirs of Earl Warren.* Doubleday, 1977.
WARREN, FRANK A. *An Alternative Vision.* Indiana University Press, 1966.
WATKINS, T. H. *Righteous Pilgrim: The Life and Times of Harold L. Ickes.* Henry Holt, 1990.
WEINBERG, ARTHUR, and WEINBERG, LILA. *Passport to Utopia: Great Panaceas in American History.* Quadrangle, 1968.
WEISBROT, ROBERT. *Father Divine.* Beacon Press, 1983.
WHITE, THEODORE H. *America in Search of Itself.* Harper & Row, 1982.
WILK, MAX. *Wit and Wisdom in Hollywood.* Atheneum, 1971.
WILKERSON, TICHI, and BORIE, MARCIA. *The Hollywood Reporter.* Coward and McCann, 1984.
WILLIAMS, T. HARRY. *Huey Long.* Knopf, 1969.
WILSON, CAROL GREEN. *Herbert Hoover.* Evans Publishing Co., 1968.
WILSON, CHARLES MORROW. *The Commoner.* Doubleday, 1970.

WILSON, EDMUND. *The American Earthquake.* Farrar, Straus & Giroux, 1958.
———. *Letters on Literature and Politics.* Farrar, Straus & Giroux, 1977.
———. "Lincoln Steffens and Upton Sinclair." *The Nation,* Sept. 28, 1932.
WINANS, CHRISTOPHER. *Malcolm Forbes: The Man Who Had Everything.* St. Martin's Press, 1990.
WINKLER, JOHN K. *William Randolph Hearst: A New Appraisal.* Hastings House, 1955.

ZOLOTOW, MAURICE. *Billy Wilder in Hollywood.* Putnam, 1977.

SOURCES

INTERVIEWS

All personal interviews except where noted with "c" for correspondence.

Robert Alderman, Leone Baxter, Don Belding, Jr., Melvin Belli, A. Scott Berg, Fay Blake, John Bright, Heywood Hale Broun (c), Edmund G. "Pat" Brown, Ruth Cashman, Joe Cohn, Alistair Cooke (c), Milen Dempster, Philip Dunne, McIntyre Faries, Emerson Foote, Don Francisco (nephew), Richard Gavin, Stan Gordon, Ronald Gottesman, Robert Gottlieb, Ray Haight, Jr., David Halberstam, Leon Harris, Augustus F. Hawkins, Will Hays, Jr., Dorothy Healey, Eleanor Hittleman, Richard Jennings, George Johnson, Clark Kerr, Edward Lasker, Leonard Leader, Mary Ellen Leary, Bud Lesser, Richard Lingeman (c), Mrs. William Loeb, Joseph L. Mankiewicz, Sam Marx, Larue McCormick, Dean McHenry, Rolf McPherson, Roger Morris, James Mussatti, Mort Newman, Dorothy Otto, Shirley Otto, Kitty Parker, Aletha Pettijohn (c), Bob Philippi, George Plimpton, Maurice Rapf, Allen Rivkin, Will Rogers, Jr., Budd Schulberg, Verne Scoggins, George Shibley, David Sinclair, Jean Sinclair, Stuart Spencer, Frank Taylor, Kendall Thurston, Jerry Voorhis, Clem Whitaker, Jr., Billy Wilder, Elizabeth Young, Hans Zeisel.

ORAL HISTORIES

B = Bancroft Library, UC–Berkeley. C = Columbia University. See key on page 587 for details on locations.

Earl Behrens (B), Rube Borough (UCLA), Edmund G. Brown (B), James Cagney (C), Asa Call (B), Robert and Florence Clifton (B), Sam Darcy (NYU), Helen Gahagan Douglas (B), Norman Elkington (B), McIntyre Faries (B), James A. Farley (C), John Anson Ford (B), Walter Haas (B), Albert Hackett (C), Dorothy Healey (UCLA), Ben Hecht (C), Nunnally Johnson (UCLA), Robert Kenny (UCLA), Goodwin Knight (B), William F. Knowland (B), Albert Lasker (C), John Howard Lawson (UCLA), Mary Ellen Leary (B), Ernest K. Lindley (UCLA), Joseph L. Mankiewicz (C), Larue McCormick (B), Dean McHenry (B), Carey McWilliams (UCLA and B), John Francis Neylan (B), Kyle Palmer (*LA Times* archives), Dorothy Parker (C), Ellis Patterson (UCLA), Frances Perkins (C), Herbert Phillips (B), Robert G. Sproul (B), Donald Ogden Stewart (American Film Institute), Earl Warren (B), Carey Wilson (C), Sam Yorty (B).

EPIC ORAL HISTORY PROJECT: To mark the fiftieth anniversary of the '34 campaign, Fay Blake and Mort Newman of Berkeley, California, conducted interviews with more than two dozen former EPIC workers (or interested observers). Blake and Newman turned over the cassette tapes to the Bancroft Library and wrote an article for *California History* (Fall 1984) summarizing their findings. Participants included Archie Brown, James Burford, Richard Criley, Ray Haight, Jr., Louise Todd Lambert, Larue McCormick, Dean McHenry, Edward Mosk, Stanley Mosk, Ellis Patterson, Frank Taylor, and Jerry Voorhis.

ARCHIVAL RESEARCH

Academy of Motion Picture Arts and Sciences (Herrick Library). Clip files on celebrities and film-related subjects. Collections of Walter Winchell, Sidney Skolsky, and Louella Parsons columns. MPPDA ("Hays Office") files on individual films.

Bank of America Archives (San Francisco). A. P. Giannini papers.

Bancroft Library (UC-Berkeley). Papers: E. D. Coblentz, Sheridan Downey, George Hatfield, William Randolph Hearst, Hiram Johnson, Robert Kenny, Joseph Knowland, William Knowland, William Gibbs McAdoo, Frank F. Merriam, Tom Mooney, John Francis Neylan, J.F.T. O'Connor, Culbert Olson, Chester Rowell, Robert G. Sproul, Thomas M. Storke, Charles C. Teague, C. C. Young. Also: Richard Teggart scrapbook of anti-Sinclair campaign materials. EPIC oral histories. Earl Warren oral history project. Many other oral histories.

Note: Frank Merriam's papers are complete, except in regard to the 1934 campaign and his years as governor. Merriam withheld this material when he donated his papers to the Bancroft, promising to send it along later, but he never did.

California State Archives (Sacramento). Earl Warren papers.

Columbia University (Rare Book and Manuscript Library). Papers: Robert Minor, Lincoln Steffens. Extensive oral history collection: Upton Sinclair, James Farley, Norman Thomas, and dozens of screenwriters and directors.

Grinberg Film Library (New York City). Paramount newsreel footage.

Honnold Library (the Claremont Colleges). Jerry Voorhis papers.

Hoover Presidential Library (Ames, Iowa). Herbert Hoover papers. Westbrook Pegler papers.

Huntington Library. Papers: Ralph Arnold, Clara and Robert J. Burdette, John Anson Ford, Henry W. O'Melveny, Louise Watkins. Also: Fred Walker scrapbooks on 1934 campaign.

Indiana State Library. Will H. Hays papers.

Library of Congress (Manuscripts Division, Washington, D.C.). Papers: George Creel, James A. Farley, Harold L. Ickes, William G. McAdoo, Mark Sullivan.

Lilly Library (Indiana University). Upton Sinclair papers: includes a quarter of a million letters, Frederick W. and Lucille C. Nelson scrapbooks on EPIC, 1933–1935, and other EPIC materials. Mary Craig Sinclair papers.

Los Angeles Times Archives. Historical materials. Kyle Palmer oral history.

MGM Files. Mainly relating to contracts, payroll, and individual movies. Now held by Turner Entertainment in Atlanta.

New York Public Library (Rare Books and Manuscripts Division): Norman Thomas papers.

New York University (Taniment Institute). Sam Darcy papers. Socialist Party papers and Earl Browder papers (microfilm).

Occidental University. Belt Collection of Sinclair books and Sinclairiana includes several scrapbooks of clippings related to '34 campaign.

Pacific Mutual Archives. Minutes of meetings of executive committee and board, fall of 1934. Company history.

Rogers Memorial (Claremore, Oklahoma). Will Rogers papers, scrapbooks, books, transcripts of radio programs, and other materials.

Roosevelt Library (Hyde Park). Papers: Democratic National Committee, Stephen Early, Lorena Hickok, Harry Hopkins, Louis Howe, Emil Hurja, Henry Morgenthau, Eleanor Roosevelt, Franklin D. Roosevelt, Rexford G. Tugwell. *Note:* Nearly all of the material relating directly to the '34 campaign is found in two of FDR's "Official Files": #1165 ("Sinclair") and #300 ("California").

Stanford University. Hoover Institution (Raymond Moley papers). Green Library (Francis Keesling papers).

University of California, Los Angeles

- *Film, Television and Radio Archives*—"California Election News No. 1 and 2" (film shorts).
- *Research Library*—Papers: Rube Borough, California Republican Assembly,

Robert Craig, Edward Dickson, Theodore Gerson, Sherill Halbert, John Randolph Haynes, Franklin Hichborn, Carey McWilliams, King Vidor, Rob Wagner.

University of South Carolina Newsfilm Library. "California Election News No. 3" and Fox-Movietone newsreel footage.

University of Southern California

- *Cinema-Television Library*—King Vidor papers.
- *Regional Cultural History Collection*—*LA Examiner* and *Herald-Express* clip files and photographs.

INDEX

PERMISSIONS ACKNOWLEDGMENTS

Grateful acknowledgment is made to the following for permission to reprint both previously published and unpublished material:

ALBERT EINSTEIN ARCHIVES, THE HEBREW UNIVERSITY OF JERUSALEM: Excerpts from personal letters of Albert Einstein. Reprinted by permission of the Albert Einstein Archives, the Hebrew University of Jerusalem.

BANK OF AMERICA: Quotes authored by A. P. Giannini from the Bank of America Archives. Reprinted by permission.

CHEVRON CORPORATION: Excerpt from a letter by Kenneth R. Kingsbury to Mr. Malcolm McAuley. Reprinted by permission of Chevron Corporation.

COLUMBIA UNIVERSITY, RARE BOOK AND MANUSCRIPT LIBRARY: Excerpts from the Robert Minor Papers. The Robert Minor Papers are owned by the Rare Book and Manuscript Library, Columbia University, and these excerpts are reprinted by permission.

CROWN PUBLISHERS, INC.: Excerpts from and some close paraphrasing of *Secret Boss of California* by Robert Thomas and Arthur Samish (pages 56–61). Copyright © 1971 by Robert Thomas and Arthur Samish. Reprinted by permission of Crown Publishers, Inc.

ENOCH PRATT FREE LIBRARY, BALTIMORE: Excerpts from quotes by H. L. Mencken from letters, columns, and books. Reprinted by permission of the Enoch Pratt Free Library in accordance with the terms of the will of H. L. Mencken.

ESQUIRE: Excerpts from "Author! Author!" by Frank Scully and an article by Theodore Dreiser on Upton Sinclair. First published in *Esquire* in November 1934. Reprinted courtesy of the Hearst Corporation.

FORBES: Excerpts from three "Fact & Comment" columns by B. C. Forbes from the October 1, 1934; October 15, 1934; and November 1, 1934; issues of *Forbes* magazine; "Fact & Comment" by B. C. Forbes, copyright 1934 by FORBES Inc., copyright renewed by the Estate of B. C. Forbes. All rights reserved; excerpts from two syndicated columns by B. C. Forbes from October 19, 1934, and October 20, 1934; syndicated columns by B. C. Forbes copyright 1934 by FORBES Inc., copyright renewed by the Estate of B. C. Forbes. All rights reserved. All excerpts are reprinted by permission and courtesy of The FORBES Archives.

FRANKLIN WATTS, INC.: Excerpts from and some close paraphrasing of *A Gaudy Spree* by Samuel Marx (pages 68–72). Copyright © 1987 by Samuel Marx. Reprinted by permission of the publisher, Franklin Watts, Inc.

THE HEARST CORPORATION: Excerpts from articles from the *Los Angeles Examiner* August 17, 1933; September 23, 1934; October 24, 1934; November 5, 1934; and November 8, 1934. All excerpts reprinted by permission of the Hearst Corporation.

THE HONNOLD LIBRARY: Excerpts from the H. Jerry Voorhis Papers housed at the Honnold/Mudd Library, the Libraries of Claremont Colleges. Reprinted by permission of the Honnold Library.

HENRY HOLT AND COMPANY: Excerpt from "Two Tramps in Mud-Time" from *The Poetry of Robert Frost,* edited by Edward Connery Latham. Copyright 1936 by Robert Frost. Copyright © 1964 by Lesley Frost Ballantine. Copyright © 1969 by Holt, Rinehart and Winston. Reprinted by permission of Henry Holt and Company, Inc.

THE HUNTINGTON LIBRARY; Excerpts from the 1934 journal of Henry William O'Melveny from the O'Melveny Collection at the Huntington Library, San Marino, California. Reprinted by permission.

LOS ANGELES TIMES SYNDICATE: Excerpts from an editorial published August 30, 1934; an editorial published September 27, 1934; an editorial published October 5, 1934; and an article by Kyle Palmer published October 7, 1934, in the *Los Angeles Times.* Copyright 1934, Los Angeles Times. Reprinted by permission.

SCOTT MEREDITH LITERARY AGENCY, INC.: Excerpts from and close paraphrasing of *Billy Wilder in Hollywood* by Maurice Zolotow (pages 52–59). Reprinted by permission of the author and the author's agents, Scott Meredith Literary Agency, Inc., 845 Third Avenue, New York, New York 10022.

WILLIAM MORROW AND COMPANY AND MELVIN BELLI: Excerpts from and close paraphrasing of *My Life on Trial* by Melvin Belli (pages 61–69). Copyright © 1976 by Melvin Belli and Robert Blair Kaiser. Reprinted by permission of William Morrow and Company and Melvin Belli.

NEW DIRECTIONS PUBLISHING CORPORATION: Excerpts from personal letters by Ezra Pound from *Ezra Pound: The Personal Letters of Ezra Pound.*

Copyright © 1992 by the Ezra Pound Literary Property Trust. Reprinted by permission of New Directions Publishing Corporation.

THE NEW YORK PUBLIC LIBRARY: Excerpts from two letters from Norman Thomas to Upton Sinclair dated September 27, 1933, and May 1, 1934; excerpts from two letters from Norman Thomas to Milen Dempster dated September 11, 1934, and September 13, 1934; excerpt from one letter from Norman Thomas to Peterson dated April 3, 1934. All letters contained in the Norman Thomas Papers, Rare Books and Manuscripts Division, The New York Public Library, Astor, Lenox, and Tilden Foundations. Reprinted by permission.

THE SAN FRANCISCO CHRONICLE: Excerpt from memo written by Chester Rowell in 1934. Reprinted by permission of *The San Francisco Chronicle.*

SCRIPPS HOWARD NEWS SERVICE: Excerpts from one Heywood Broun and five Westbrook Pegler columns. Reprinted by permission of Scripps Howard News Service.

UNIVERSITY OF PENNSYLVANIA PRESS: Excerpts from *Letters of Theodore Dreiser, Volume 2* edited by Robert Elias. Copyright © 1959 by The Trustees of the University of Pennsylvania. Copyright renewed 1978 by Robert Elias. Reprinted by permission of University of Pennsylvania Press.

THE WASHINGTON POST: Excerpts from "Rooseveltian Soliloquy" by H. Phillips (September 5, 1934) and excerpts from "l'affair Sinclair" by Carlisle Bergeron (October 31, 1934). Copyright 1934 by The Washington Post. Reprinted by permission.

ABOUT THE AUTHOR

Greg Mitchell's previous books include *Truth and Consequences: Seven Who Would Not Be Silenced* and *Acceptable Risks* (with Pascal James Imperato). His articles on the 1934 campaign have appeared in *American Heritage* and *American Film.* He has also written for *The New York Times, The Washington Post, The Los Angeles Times, the San Francisco Chronicle,* and many other publications. Currently he is serving as consultant to an eight-part PBS series, *The Great Depression,* scheduled to be aired in 1993.